IRAN TO INDIA

IRAN TO INDIA

The Shansabanis of Afghanistan,
c. 1145–1190 CE

Alka Patel

EDINBURGH
University Press

Edinburgh University Press is one of the leading university presses in the UK. We publish academic books and journals in our selected subject areas across the humanities and social sciences, combining cutting-edge scholarship with high editorial and production values to produce academic works of lasting importance. For more information visit our website: edinburghuniversitypress.com

Edinburgh University Press Ltd
The Tun – Holyrood Road
12 (2f) Jackson's Entry
Edinburgh EH8 8PJ

Typeset in 11/13 Adobe Garamond by
Servis Filmsetting Ltd, Stockport, Cheshire,
and printed and bound in Malta by Melita Press

A CIP record for this book is available from the British Library

ISBN 978 1 4744 8222 6 (hardback)
ISBN 978 1 4744 8224 0 (webready PDF)
ISBN 978 1 4744 8225 7 (epub)

Published with the support of the University of Edinburgh Scholarly Publishing Initiatives Fund.

Contents

List of Figures   vi
Acknowledgments   xii
Note on Dates and Transliteration   xiv
Map of Imperial Ambitions   xv
Map of Historical Ghur and Contiguous Regions   xvi
Genealogy of the Shansabanis of Afghanistan   xvii

Introduction: The Elephant and its Parts   1

1. Kingly Trajectories   40

2. Beginnings   79

3. The Early Shansabanis: Firuzkuh, Bamiyan, and Tiginabad/
   Old Qandahar, c. 1140s–1170s   132

4. One and Several: Gharjistan, Chisht, and Imperial Firuzkuh   190

5. The "Ports of India": Ghazna and Bust-Lashkari Bazar   237

6. Encountering the Many "Indias"   277

Epilogue: Iran to India   338

Appendix: Shansabānī Religious and Historical Inscriptions in
   Afghanistan and Pakistan   342
Works Cited and Bibliography   357
Index   391

Figures

I.1   Remains of Shah-i Mashhad *madrasa*, Gharjistan   2
I.2   Minaret of Jam, general view from northeast   3
I.3   Tiginabad/Old Qandahar, grave with brick vault   4
I.4   Shahr-i Zuhhak (fifth–thirteenth centuries), general view   5
I.5   Sarkhushak, Bamiyan Province, Building A   6
I.6   Ghazni, palace of Mas'ud III (1099–1115), excavation site,
      courtyard   6
I.7   Bust, arch and city walls   7
I.8   Pictorial view of part of an early Sultanate palace
      complex   7
I.9   Wall fragments and piers excavated at Lalkot   8
I.10 Mosque known as "Arhai Din-ka Jhonpra," founded
      c. 1199 CE   9
I.11 Mosque of Kaman, Rajasthan, India, founded *c.* 1195   10
I.12 Congregational Mosque, Herat, Afghanistan, *c.* 1200 CE,
      exterior   11
I.13 Congregational Mosque, Herat, interior   12
I.14 Tomb of Ghiyath al-Din Muhammad ibn Sam, Herat, prior
      to destruction in 1944   13
I.15 Tomb of Ghiyath al-Din Muhammad ibn Sam, Herat,
      reconstructed *c.* 1940s   14
I.16 Tomb of Salar Khalil, a.k.a. *ziyarat* Baba Khatim, Juzjan
      Province, Afghanistan   24
I.17 Tomb of Salar Khalil, interior   25
I.18 Tomb of Shahzada Sheikh Husain, Helmand Province,
      Afghanistan, *c.* 1200 CE   26
I.19 Tomb of Shahzada Sheikh Husain, interior   27
I.20 "The fortress and citadel of Ghazni (Afghanistan)," James
      Atkinson, watercolor, 1839   28
I.21 "Ruins of Old Kandahar Citadel," albumen print, *c.* 1880–81,
      Benjamin Simpson   28
I.22 Shahr-i Gholghola, general view, citadel, eleventh–thirteenth
      century   29
I.23 Herat-Ghuriyan highway, Herat Province, Afghanistan   30

I.I   Congregational Mosque, Isfahan, Iran, tenth century CE; exterior, east   49

I.2   Congregational Mosque, Isfahan, 1086–1087 CE; exterior, north dome   49

I.3   Congregational Mosque, Isfahan, *c.* 1090 CE; interior, south dome chamber   50

I.4   *Minar* known as Chihil Dukhtaran, *c.* 1100 CE, Jubara quarter, Isfahan   50

I.5   Chihil Dukhtaran *minar*, historical inscription panel   51

I.6   Chihil Dukhtaran *minar*, topmost epigraphic bands   52

I.7   *Mihrab* of mosque at Sin, north of Isfahan, *c.* 1132 CE   53

I.8   *Minar* of mosque complex, Sin, *c.* 1134–1135 CE   53

I.9   *Sin minar*, topmost epigraphic bands   54

I.10   Robat Sharaf, near Sarakhs, Razavi Khurasan Province, Iran, 1114–1115, 1154–1155 CE   55

I.11   Robat Sharaf, second courtyard   56

I.12   Robat Sharaf, oratory   56

I.13   Robat Sharaf, intrados of arch with stucco decoration   57

I.14   Palace of Mas'ud III, 1099–1115, Ghazni (excavation site)   58

I.15   Ghazni: minaret of Mas'ud III, 1099–1115; and minaret of Bahram Shah, 1118–1152   58

I.16   The Buddhist site of Tapa Sardar, near Ghazni, Afghanistan, third–ninth century CE   59

I.17   Vaulted corridor (*Ilkhanid*) north of tomb of 'Ala' al-Din Muhammad of Bamiyan, d. at Ghazna 1206 CE   66

2.1   Ahangaran, Ghur Province, Afghanistan   81

2.2   Jam-Firuzkuh, *minar* and confluence of Hari Rud and Jam Rud   85

2.3   Ahangaran, surroundings and banks of Hari Rud   86

2.4   Detail of Herberg's fieldwork map of central and southern Ghur, *c.* 1970s   88

2.5   Yaman, Ghur Province, Afghanistan: ruins of a square tower and cruciform "military structure"   89

2.6   Ghor Province, Yahan, fortification line and ruins   89

2.7   Ghor Province, Male Alau: brick tower, ruin, distant view   91

2.8   Ghor Province, Alana Valley: fortification line, ruins, distant view   92

2.9   Taywara vicinity, Ghur Province: watch tower   93

2.10   Between Pasa Band and Dahane Nawrak: cruciform interior of a defensive structure   94

2.11   Taiwara-Farah Rud   95

2.12   Ahangaran   95

2.13   Ghor Province, Yahan: fortification tower, ruin   96

2.14   Southern Ghur, southeast façade of a structure   97

2.15 Qala'-yi Chahar Baradar, Ghur Province   98
2.16 Ghor Province, Male Alau: brick tower with stone base, ruin   99
2.17 The "lost" *minar* of Qala'-yi Zarmurgh, *c.* 75 km south of
       Jam-Firuzkuh   100
2.18 *Minar* of Qasimabad, Sistan   101
2.19 Balkh, minaret of Daulatabad (1108–1109); exterior, full view   102
2.20 Detail of Figure 2.16: Male Alau, Ghor Province, brick
       tower, lower decoration   102
2.21 Damghan, Semnan Province, Iran: stucco dado with
       palmettes   103
2.22 Nizamabad, Iran: wall fragment with stucco decoration   104
2.23 Detail of Figure 2.16: Male Alau, Ghor Province   104
2.24 Taq-i Bustan, central Iran: column capital   105
2.25 Minarets of Ghazni, distant view   110
2.26 Nad-i Ali, Zaranj, Sistan: remains of tower   111
2.27 Remains of baked-brick tower, Khwaja Siyah Push, Sistan   112
3.1   Jam-Firuzkuh, Ghur Province, Afghanistan: remains of
       paved floor of probable mosque   138
3.2   Jam-Firuzkuh: remains of Qasr-i Zarafshan   140
3.3   Jam-Firuzkuh: remains of defensive towers   141
3.4   Jam-Firuzkuh: baked brick, plaster-lined cistern at Kuh-i
       Khara   142
3.5   Jam-Firuzkuh: minaret of Jam, general view   144
3.6   Detail of Figure 3.4: *mihrab* relief on east face of
       Jam-Firuzkuh minaret   145
3.7   Bamiyan: north cliff, eastern end with 35-m Buddha   147
3.8   The Bamiyan basin   149
3.9   Shahr-i Zohak, Bamiyan region, fifth–thirteenth century:
       general view, triangular plateau with fortifications   151
3.10 Shahr-i Zohak: general view, crenellated tower and walls   152
3.11 Shahr-i Zohak: fortress ruins, interior   153
3.12 Shahr-i Gholghola, Bamiyan region, eleventh–thirteenth
       century: general view, citadel   156
3.13 Shahr-i Gholghola: recovered wooden door leaves   157
3.14 Yakaulang, Saighan, and Kahmard Districts, western
       Bamiyan Province, Afghanistan   158
3.15 Qala'-yi Gauhargin, western Yakaulang District, Bamiyan
       Province   158
3.16 Bamiyan vicinity, structural remains   159
3.17 Killigan, eastern Yakaulang District, Bamiyan Province   160
3.18 Chehel Burj, eastern Yakaulang District, Bamiyan Province   161
3.19 Barfak II, a.k.a. "Danestama," *c.* 80 km northeast of
       Bamiyan: plan   162
3.20 Barfak II/"Danestama:" east side of central courtyard   163

3.21 Barfak II/"Danestama:" *mihrab* from southeast 164
3.22 Barfak II/"Danestama:" detail of stucco revetment in *mihrab* 165
3.23 Sarkhushak, north of Bamiyan 166
3.24 Sarkhushak, Building A: plans and elevations 166
3.25 Sarkhushak, Building E: plan and elevation 167
3.26 Sarkhushak, Building A: vault 168
3.27 Qandahar, Afghanistan: Qaitul *stupa* and citadel of Old Qandahar 170
3.28 Old Qandahar cemetery, Burial Mound A 172
4.1 Remains of Shah-i Mashhad *madrasa*, *c.* 1165–1175 CE, Gharjistan, Afghanistan 196
4.2 Shah-i Mashhad *madrasa* and Murghab River 200
4.3 Shah-i Mashhad *madrasa* on Google Earth with superimposed plan 200
4.4 Shah-i Mashhad *madrasa*: south façade 202
4.5 Shah-i Mashhad *madrasa*: possible tomb at southeast corner 202
4.6 Shah-i Mashhad *madrasa*, *c.* 1165–1175 CE: south façade 203
4.7 Shah-i Mashhad *madrasa*: southern monumental entrance 204
4.8 Shah-i Mashhad *madrasa*: south façade 205
4.9 Shah-i Mashhad *madrasa*: north entrance 206
4.10 Ghazni, minaret of Mas'ud III (1099–1115), with citadel in background 208
4.11 Ghazni, minaret of Mas'ud III (1099–1115), middle section 209
4.12 Chisht, mausoleums or *madrasa*/mosque complex, Herat Province, Afghanistan: Mausoleum A, exterior 211
4.13 Chisht: Mausoleum A, interior 212
4.14 Chisht: Mausoleum A, interior, inscription 213
4.15 Chisht: Mausoleum A, interior, arch 215
4.16 Chisht on Google Earth 216
4.17 Chisht: Mausoleum B, interior, *mihrab* 216
4.18 Jam-Firuzkuh, Ghur Province, Afghanistan: minaret of Jam, general view 218
5.1 Ghazna, Ghazni Province, Afghanistan: plan from aerial photograph of western part of city 243
5.2 Ghazna, central palace: plan of excavated areas and hypothetical reconstructions 244
5.3 Ghazna, central palace: fragment of painted stucco decoration, detail 1 245
5.4 Ghazna, central palace: fragment of painted stucco decoration, detail 2 245
5.5 Ghazna, central palace: fragment of painted stucco decoration, detail 3 246

5.6   Ghazni, palace of Mas'ud III (1099–1115): dado remnants   246
5.7   Detail of Figure 5.6: juxtaposition of Ghaznavid- and
       Shansabani-period revetments   247
5.8   Bust, Helmand Province, Afghanistan; general plan   248
5.9   Bust, citadel and arch: general view from northeast   249
5.10   Bust, citadel: seven-story well, arches   250
5.11   Bust, citadel: seven-story well interior shaft   251
5.12   Bust, arch, south pillar, carved decoration   252
5.13   Bust, arch: front face and intrados, north   253
5.14   Lashkari Bazar, Helmand Province: South Palace, plan of
       excavations   255
5.15   Lashkari Bazar, South Palace, southern façade   256
5.16   Lashkari Bazar, Summer (or Grand) Palace, exterior   256
5.17   Lashkari Bazar, South Palace: south portal detail   257
5.18   Lashkari Bazar, South Palace: Mosque of the Forecourt   258
5.19   Lashkari Bazar, South Palace: courtyard   258
5.20   Laskhari Bazar, South Palace: Oratory F, north of central
       courtyard   259
5.21   Lashkari Bazar, South Palace: Oratory F, stucco decoration   260
5.22   Lashkari Bazar, South Palace: Oratory F, *mihrab*   261
5.23   Lashkari Bazar, Palais aux Raquettes, exterior   265
5.24   Lashkari Bazar, South Palace: Audience Hall I   266
5.25   Lashkari Bazar, South Palace: Audience Hall I, detail of
       stucco revetments   267
5.26   Lashkari Bazar, South Palace: Audience Hall I, detail of
       paintings   268
5.27   Lashkari Bazar, South palace, view looking south   269
5.28   Lashkari Bazar, general view   270
6.1   Buddhist monastic complex, Takht-i Bahi,
       Khyber-Pakhtunkhwa Province, Pakistan   284
6.2   Rajagira Mosque, Udegram, Khyber-Pakhtunkhwa Province,
       Pakistan   286
6.3   Rajagira Mosque: *mihrab*   287
6.4   Temple, Kalar, West Panjab, Pakistan; exterior façade   288
6.5   Temple, Mari Indus, West Panjab, Pakistan   289
6.6   Large temple, Ambh Sharif, West Panjab, Pakistan   290
6.7   Temple, Nandana, West Panjab, Pakistan; interior   291
6.8   Large temple, Ambh Sharif, exterior: detail of *shikhara*   291
6.9   Mosque remains, Dibul-Banbhore, Sindh, Pakistan   292
6.10   Tomb attributed to Muhammad ibn Harun, Lasbela,
       Baluchistan, Province Pakistan   293
6.11   Congregational Mosque and Thamban Wari Masjid, Jam
       Jaskars Goth, Sindh Province, Pakistan; plans, elevations,
       drawings   294

6.12 Chhoti *masjid*, Bhadreshvar, Kachch District, Gujarat, India;
      interior   295
6.13 Tomb known as Shrine of Ibrahim, Bhadreshvar; interior   296
6.14 Temple, Bhodesar, Nagarparkar District, Sindh Province;
      exterior base of *shikhara*   297
6.15 Multan, West Panjab, Pakistan; tomb of Sheikh Yusuf
      Gardizi   301
6.16 *Ribaṭ* of Ali ibn Karmakh, Kabirwala, near Multan, West
      Panjab, Pakistan; plan   304
6.17 *Ribaṭ* of Ali ibn Karmakh   305
6.18 *Ribaṭ* of Ali ibn Karmakh: interior, *mihrab*   306
6.19 *Ribaṭ* of Ali ibn Karmakh: framing bands of *mihrab, in situ*
      c. 1980s   307
6.20 *Ribaṭ* of Ali ibn Karmakh: detail of epigraphic bands framing
      mihrab   308
6.21 *Ribaṭ* of Ali ibn Karmakh: detail of reused fragment   309
6.22 *Ribaṭ* of Ali ibn Karmakh: detail of pilaster framing *mihrab* 310
6.23 *Ribaṭ* of Ali ibn Karmakh: detail of base moldings of *mihrab*
      hood   311
6.24 Tomb of Sadan Shahid, Muzaffargarh, near Multan, West
      Panjab, Pakistan; exterior, west façade   311
6.25 Tomb of Sadan Shahid; east façade   312
6.26 Tomb of Sheikh Sadan Shahid, interior   312
6.27 Tomb of Sadan Shahid: exterior, detail of decorative niche   313
6.28 Tomb of Sadan Shahid, north half of east façade   313
6.29 Tomb of Ahmad Kabir, Dunyapur, near Multan, West
      Panjab, Pakistan; east façade   314
6.30 Tomb of Ahmad Kabir, from northwest   314
6.31 Tomb of Ahmad Kabir, interior   315
6.32 Tomb of Ahmad Kabir: exterior, detail of decorative niche   316
6.33 Tomb of Duagan, Sukkur, Sindh Province, Pakistan   317
6.34 Tomb of Duagan; exterior, detail of pilasters   318
6.35 Chhoti Masjid, Bhadreshvar Kachh District, Gujarat, India;
      detail of pilaster capital   318
6.36 Shrine of Ibrahim, Bhadreshvar; foreporch   319
6.37 Lal Mara Sharif, near Dera Ismail Khan, West Panjab,
      Pakistan; tombs at necropolis   320
6.38 Lal Mara Sharif, Tomb IV, west façade   322
6.39 Lal Mara Sharif, Tomb III, west façade   325
6.40 Lal Mara Sharif, Tomb I, west façade   326
6.41 Lal Mara Sharif, Tomb IV, west façade   326

Acknowledgments

The completion of any project is possible only because of the belief, sup-portiveness, and generosity of many. And an uncommon one such as this – involving more than one book – will, I am afraid, require trespassing on the aforementioned qualities long after the acknowledgments for *this* book are penned and in print. It is no exaggeration to say that the whole endeavor would not have reached this *sar manzil* without the unstinting contributions of others. I humbly and gratefully acknowledge the entities that have eased the way thus far, and the individuals who have embarked on this journey with me.

The project received its first boost with an American Institute for Indian Studies Senior Fellowship for completion of in-depth architec-tural documentation in north India (first begun during doctoral fieldwork throughout India and Pakistan). Thereafter, fellowships from the American Philosophical Society and the UC Office of the President supported fieldwork in Iran and Afghanistan. Iranian warmth and hospitality are world-renowned for good reason; I am particularly grateful to Professor Javad Abbasi (Firdausi University) for sharing his time, knowledge, and conversation. In Afghanistan, neither work nor the trip itself would have been possible without the guidance and support of Praveen Kumar KG of the Indian Embassy in Kabul; Dr. Daud Shah Saba, then Governor of Herat Province; Mr. Tarachand, Consul General of India in Herat; and Phillipe Marquis of the Délégation Archéologique Française en Afghanistan.

After foraging for and gathering vast amounts of data, its collation and composition into a narrative necessarily calls for cloistering, pref-erably with responsive interlocutors who help one feel less alone (and less crazy). Fellowships at the Getty Research Institute (GRI; 2017–18) and at the National Humanities Center (NHC; 2019) both provided the perfect balance of solitude for writing and meaningful conversations with wonderfully smart people. I cannot thank the GRI and the NHC enough; these opportunities renewed my own faith in the project and were instru-mental in completing the book manuscript of this first "installment."

Most recently (April 2020), the Dean's Office of the School of Humanities at the University of California, Irvine (UCI) provided the unique opportunity of a workshop on the manuscript *prior* to its finalization and submission to a press for review. It is worth stating in no uncertain terms that, at this stage in the work, the feedback from respected senior colleagues in such diverse fields as Anthropology, Archeology, Art History, and History – and spanning virtually all of the second millennium CE across western, southern, and central Asia – made the final product that much stronger. Surely, such a practice would be welcomed by all authors, not only for the assured improvement of their books, but also for the enduring conversations that are generated in such well-defined but informal contexts.

Supportive entities are, of course, made up of individuals. The absolutely top-notch librarians and research assistants at my home campus of UCI, the GRI and the NHC have earned my enduring thanks. Additionally, I extend my heartfelt gratitude to the students in the 2018 Getty Consortium graduate seminar – you all remained steady throughout the whirlwind engagement with Iconoclasm – and to the colleagues who brought fresh perspectives to our sessions. Among the latter were fellow Getty Scholars who patiently witnessed a novice's forays into topics as varied as colonial-era photography and the anthropology of nomadism, and to whom I am deeply grateful for their gentle guidance: John Falconer, Tim Murray, and Norman Yoffee.

At UCI and its vicinity, several colleagues – many of them also friends – deserve thanks as stalwart allies in this continuing project: Maureen Burns, Matthew Canepa, Touraj Daryaee, Saied Jalalipour, Sara Mashayekh, Laura Mitchell, Kavita Philip, Khodadad Rezakhani, and Amanda Swain. I am especially grateful to Amanda and Saied for their flawless execution of the aforementioned manuscript workshop, which brought together a roster of scholars whose generosity in engaging with the work and the insights they offered were truly humbling: Mitchell Allen, Catherine Asher, Warwick Ball, Thomas Barfield, Will Chamberlain, Richard Eaton, Vivek Gupta, Beatrice Manz, Fatima Quraishi, and Layah Ziaii-Bigdeli.

Adding to this already lengthy list of all who have a stake in this project, I happily include the following colleagues and friends for their unfailing help and support: Viola Allegranzi, Warwick Ball (yes, twice!), Roberta Giunta, Michael O'Neal, Jawan Shir Rasikh, Franziska Seraphim, Sunil Sharma, and David Thomas. By reading and commenting on chapter drafts, providing otherwise unobtainable research materials, and overall staying the course through my own fluctuating assessments of the value of my work (thank you again, David!), you were instrumental in making this happen.

Last, yet *never* least, my family: Didier, Anika, Max (you are missed), Christine S., and the Tarboxes – by your very presence, you make me better as a person, friend, mother, partner, scholar.

With such good fortune in colleagues, friends and family, I emphasize that any shortcomings in this work are my own.

Note on Dates and Transliteration

For accessibility and ease of reading the main text of this book, every effort has been made to make dates and transliterations less cumbersome. Rulers' reigns and timespans of specific years are provided in both Hijra and Common Era dates; while less specific ranges are given only in the Common Era. Furthermore, transliteration has been utilized where strictly called for: the many Arabic, Persian and Indic-language words throughout the main text and footnotes have not been transliterated; only the *ayn* and *hamza* have been differentiated. However, to be consistent with the extensive Arabic and Persian texts of inscriptions reproduced in the Appendix, all non-English words have been transliterated there: the Arabic–Persian adhering to the *International Journal of Middle East Studies* recommendations, and the Indic-language words following the guidelines in John T. Platts's *A Dictionary of Urdu, Classical Hindi and English*.

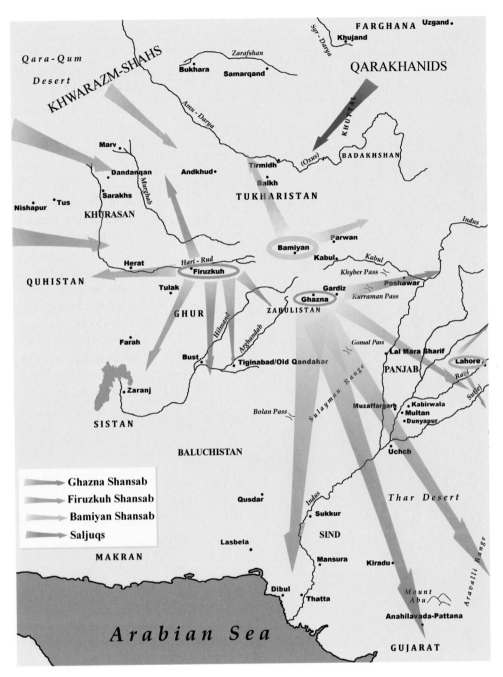

Map of Imperial Ambitions. © Didier Tais 2020.

Map of Historical Ghur and Contiguous Regions. © After Michael O'Neal 2015.

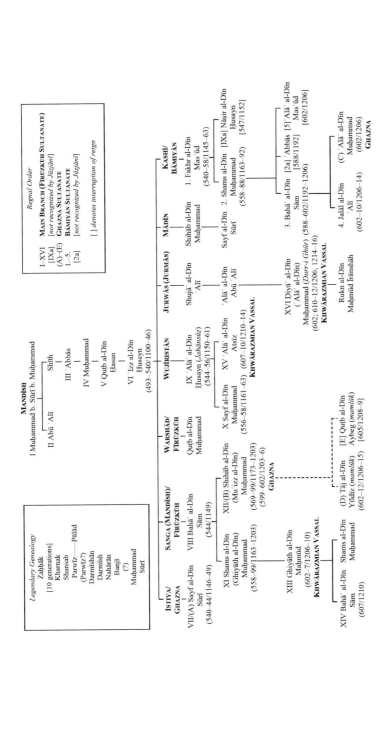

Genealogy of the Shansabanis of Afghanistan. © *By kind permission of Michael O'Neal 2013.*

Introduction:
The Elephant and its Parts

> There was a great city in the country of Ghur, in which all the
> people were blind. A certain king passed by that place, bringing
> his army and pitching his camp on the plain. He had a large and
> magnificent elephant to minister to his pomp and excite awe,
> and to attack in battle. A desire arose among the people to see
> this monstrous elephant, and a number of the blind, like fools,
> visited it, every one running in his haste to find out its shape and
> form. They came, and being without the sight of their eyes groped
> about it with their hands; each of them by touching one member
> obtained a notion of some one part; each one got a conception of
> an impossible object, and fully believed his fancy true.[1]

This version of the well-known parable of the blind men and the
elephant comes from the long *mathnavi* titled *Hadiqat al-Haqiqa*,
the ambitious last work of the poet Majdud ibn Adam Ghaznavi
(c. 1087–1130/1140 CE), best known by his *'urf*, Sana'i.[2] It is a fitting point
of departure for the ensuing project on the Shansabanis of Ghur, or the
"Ghurids" as they are commonly denoted in modern scholarship (but not
here, for reasons discussed below). Sana'i not only located the didactic
story in Ghur – whence unfolded the historical processes plotted in these
two volumes – the parable itself appears to have been transposed from
the Buddhist *Udana*, among the earliest compilations of the Enlightened
One's solemn utterances.[3]

In his intellectual inspirations for *Hadiqat*, Sana'i enacted the perennial continuity of sources and realities,[4] many defined as non-Islamic
and thus frequently understudied by modern "Islamicists" and others as
they investigate cultural productions emerging from the vast geography
of Islamic-Persianate Eurasia. Surely the poet would have been pleased to
know that, almost a millennium after his own lifetime, his selection[5] of
the elephant parable still provides a compelling homily: for our purposes,
Sana'i succinctly and humorously exposed our figurative blindness, born
of our temporal distance from the historical pasts we are trying to access –
a blindness that is arguably compounded by the increasingly narrow scholarly specializations mobilized to attempt such recoveries.

These volumes are about encountering a proverbial elephant – here symbolizing the seemingly sudden emergence in the mid-twelfth century of an obscure group from central Afghanistan into historical retrievability as the "Ghurids" – more accurately the Shansabanis (cf. below); and their even more amazing rise as they fashioned an empire extending from Herat in modern western Afghanistan to the Brahmaputra River in northeastern India–western Bangladesh. To date, the sequence of events leading to Shansabani ascendancy and the impetuses behind them are only partially known, however, the contemporaneous textual sources offering sometimes contradictory information or eliding them altogether (cf. Chapter 1). Furthermore, Shansabani architectural traces have been analyzed piecemeal, thus presenting a seemingly incomprehensible pastiche, not unlike Sana'i's elephant when perceived only through its individual parts. The present study essentially undertakes an *architectural biography* (see below): the two volumes bring together the corpus of Shansabani-patronized structures as among the primary historical sources with much to contribute toward our understanding of the Shansabanis, who were not only one of the "nomadic dynasties" emerging in Eurasia[6] as of the early second millennium CE, but an imperial formation impacting the subsequent trajectories of Central and South Asia.

Patronage of public or "civic" architecture such as *madrasa* complexes (Figure I.1) has been attributed to the Shansabanis, but their "capital" at

Figure I.1 *Remains of Shah-i Mashhad madrasa, Gharjistan (Badghis Province, Afghanistan). © Photograph Bernt Glatzer c. 1970.*

Figure I.2 *Jam, minaret of Jam (c. 1180) [sic], general view from northeast, with steep valley in background. © Photograph Josephine Powell c. 1960. Harvard Fine Arts Library, Special Collections.*

Jam-Firuzkuh in central Afghanistan (Figure I.2) long remained enigmatic due to its isolated location and lack of palatial remains; even more so was the Shansabanis' exclusively funerary presence in the strategically and commercially important region of Qandahar (Figure I.3). Their material footprint in the Bamiyan valleys (Figures I.4 and I.5; Figure I.22) – unexamined as a whole, until now (see Chapter 3) – is admittedly difficult to discern, given the mixture of reused and newly constructed traces, both on a significant scale. Even the momentous Shansabani conquest of Ghazna and Bust-Lashkari Bazar in *c.* AH 568–569/1173 CE resulted largely in renovations of existing palatial areas (Figure I.6), with only punctually

Figure I.3 *Tiginabad/Old Qandahar, grave with brick vault. From Whitehouse 1976: fig. IIa.*

built new monuments (Figure I.7). Notably, it appears to have been their entry into the north Indian *duab* in the later AH 580s/1190s CE that signaled new, monumental patronage in palatial (Figures I.8 and I.9) as well as religious ambits (Figures I.10 and I.11) – *both* replete with identifiably reused building materials. At the same time, in Herat the Shansabanis left distinct traces within the renowned, centuries-old congregational mosque complex (Figures I.12 and I.13), addorsing to its northeastern perimeter the tomb (no longer extant) of Sultan Ghiyath al-Din Muhammad ibn Sam (r. AH 558–599/1163–1203 CE; see Volume II) (Figures I.14 and I.15).

Although the imperial Shansabanis achieved and maintained their greatest territorial extent for only about two decades (c.1192–1210 CE), this was nonetheless a feat rarely seen for almost a millennium: in the first centuries of the Common Era, the Kushanas brought ancient Bactria,

Figure I.4 *Shahr-i Zuhhak (fifth–thirteenth centuries), general view, view along crenellated fortifications, with valley in background. © Photograph Josephine Powell c. 1960. Harvard Fine Arts Library, Special Collections.*

Gandhara, the Panjab, and the Ganga-Yamuna *duab* under their aegis. Thereafter, the Yamini-Ghaznavids (*c.* AH 365–582/975–1186 CE) conducted plundering raids into the *duab* but with minimal traces of an imperial presence there.[7] The Kushanas' imperial expansion had had important consequences for all of Eurasia throughout the first millennium CE.[8] Nearly a thousand years later, the Shansabanis created a similar confederate empire (see esp. Chapters 1, 3–5, this volume), extending from the western Hari Rud through the Kuh-i Baba range in modern Afghanistan, to the Sulaiman Mountains and the Indus valleys of modern Pakistan, and ultimately reaching the northern plains of modern India. In the footsteps of the Kushanas (rather than the Ghaznavids), then, the Shansabanis *re*-conjoined the Indic and Iranian cultural–geographical worlds and unleashed far-reaching consequences, this time throughout the second millennium CE into the present day.

As further examined in these volumes, two among these consequences

Figure I.5 *Sarkhushak, Bamiyan Province, Building A. From Baker and Allchin 1991: fig. 5.15.*

Figure I.6 *Ghazni, palace of Mas'ud III (1099–1115), excavation site, courtyard. Marble floor and dado remains. © Photograph Josephine Powell* c. *1960. Harvard Fine Arts Library, Special Collections.*

Figure I.7 *Bust, arch and city walls. © Photograph Josephine Powell* c. *1960. Harvard Fine Arts Library, Special Collections.*

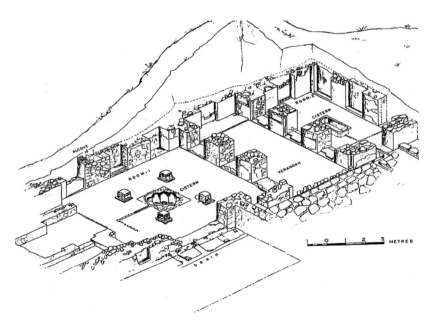

Figure I.8 *Pictorial view of part of an early Sultanate palace complex, exposed during the ASI excavations conducted 1992–1995. From Balasubramaniam 2005: 110, fig. 30.*

Figure I.9 *Wall fragments and piers excavated at Lalkot. © Courtesy of the Archaeological Survey of India, New Delhi.*

are particularly noteworthy. First, during the 1190s CE the Shansabanis' successful campaigns into the north Indian *duab* saw the establishment in the region of *their interpretation* of Perso-Islamic cultures of power[9] (cf. Chapter 1), to be contrasted to the Muslim mercantile presences along the subcontinent's coasts and some inland nodes dating from the eighth century onward.[10] Second, the Shansabani campaigns instigated a broad geo-historical momentum, which lasted through the early sixteenth century: successive waves of Islam-affiliated warlords entered the *duab* along the self-same northwestern corridors and ruled the region with varying longevities. This span of a bit more than three centuries – essentially from the 1190s until the arrival of the Timurid prince Babur (AH 888–936/1483–1530 CE) in 1525 – is generally bracketed in modern scholarship as the Sultanate period.[11]

But, despite four Persian-language monographs within the last fifty years on the Shansabanis, they are still deemed less than consequential in modern Western-language historiography, remaining in the shadows of their more famous contemporaries such as the Ghaznavids of Afghanistan and the Saljuqs of Iran, Central Asia, and Anatolia (*c.* AH 431–590/1040–1194 CE).[12] This striking divergence between Western and "indigenous *epistemological* values" – to modify Thomas de Bruijn's phrase for our immediate purposes[13] – certainly reiterates the fractured and contingent nature of regional "knowledges" at any given time. Indeed, this divergence leaves open the long and probably futile task of integrating "knowledges" into anything near a singular and shared Knowledge, even with the new

Figure 1.10 Mosque known as "Arhai Din-ka Jhonpra," founded, c. 1199 CE. Ajmer (Rajasthan, India), interior: prayer area, view of columns and ceilings. © Didier Taïs 2011.

Figure I.11 *Mosque of Kaman, Rajasthan, India, founded* c. *1195. Exterior: eastern façade with main entrance. © Photograph Alka Patel 2011.*

technologies and modes of communication constantly becoming available. On a more humble (and more optimistic) level, however, the present volumes' treatment of the Shansabanis at least mitigates their historiographical displacement. At the same time, I believe the subject presents important opportunities to craft much-needed methodological alternatives for approaching the historical pasts of South and Central Asia.

In their magisterial work titled *Empires in World History*, J. Burbank and F. Cooper proposed a capacious conceptualization of empires, *viz.* "large political units, expansionist or with a memory of power extended over space ... that maintain distinction and hierarchy as they incorporate new people." Such a working definition not only leaves room for a great variety of politico-economic hierarchical structures – that is, empires – through time, it also respects their staggering complexity. Burbank and Cooper's definition easily encompasses such dissimilar entities as the Roman and Mongol empires, bookending two soft ends of a spectrum of imperialisms: Rome, with its "notion of a single, superior imperial civilization open in principle to those who could learn its ways"; *versus* the Mongols, who "learned their statecraft from both Eurasian and Chinese sources ... sheltered Buddhism, Confucianism, Christianity, Daoism, and Islam; [and] where diversity was treated as both normal and useful."[14]

But a singular term for such a vast array of human organizations certainly belies the virtually infinite possibilities for their origins; their subsequent expansions and contractions; and their internal political, economic, social, and other operations. Empires were never instantaneous,

Figure I.12 *Congregational Mosque, Herat, Afghanistan, c. 1200 CE, exterior: southeastern portal (blocked).*
© *Photograph Alka Patel 2011.*

Figure I.13 *Congregational Mosque, Herat, interior: western* iwan, *vault.*
© *Photograph Alka Patel 2011.*

monolithic, or even unidirectional. Not only has empire-building always
occupied varying lengths of historical time, the regimes in question and
their elites were often perceived differently, depending on the time and
place within said empire – again evoking the poet Sana'i's homily of the

Figure I.14 *Tomb of Ghiyath al-Din Muhammad ibn Sam, Herat (addorsed to northern perimeter of Congregational Mosque), prior to destruction in 1944. From Glatzer 1980: fig. 12 (photograph R. Stuckert, 1942).*

elephant and the blind men of Ghur. Moreover, the methods for achieving empire were ad hoc and determined by specific circumstances, rather than prescribed beforehand.

Primarily – though *not* exclusively – relying on the Shansabanis' architectural patronage, the present work aims to reconstitute the proverbial elephant into a perceivable whole. It may appear contradictory, then, to pursue this aim in two volumes rather than one, but I believe this approach in itself presents an important opening. As the coming pages will show, the corpus of Shansabani foundations is datable by means of inscription, textual reference, and/or stylistic *comparanda* as falling within *c.* the early 1100s to *c.* 1215 CE – a corpus herein documented largely first-hand, analyzed, and also expanded. Such an architectural group permits a concentrated gaze on approximately eighty–ninety years of the mobilization of regional labor structures and the formation of new political hierarchies toward empire-building – an intimate entrée that is rare in the study of

Figure I.15 *Tomb of Ghiyath al-Din Muhammad ibn Sam, Herat, reconstructed c. 1940s.* © *Photograph Alka Patel 2011.*

any region or polity of nearly one thousand years before the present. But while Shansabani ascendancy was temporally brief, it was geographically and culturally vast, spanning the nomad–urban continuum of central Afghanistan (described below), along with the cosmopolitan emporia of Khurasan to the west; and to the east, the multi-confessional landscapes of the Indus's alluvia, and reaching beyond to the equally variegated north Indian *duab*.

With the Shansabanis' victories in northern India during the 1190s, a qualitative temporal and spatial divide seemed to crystallize between their western and eastern territorial presences, especially in light of the varyingly constituted histories and historiographies of these regions – and indeed those of the eastern Islamic world and South Asia overall. And yet, these regions were ultimately intertwined. The two-volume framework here allows for the analysis of their material and discursive archives separately, but necessarily in dialogue, each with the merited analytical focus. This volume (Volume I) concentrates on the areas now encompassed within modern Afghanistan and Pakistan, spanning the early twelfth century through *c.* 1190 CE. It thereby prepares the way for Volume II, which examines the Shansabanis' extremely consequential expansion into the Indo-Gangetic plains (*c.* 1192–1205 CE), and also traces the *westward* reverberations of the Shansabanis' politico-military successes. Volume II thus closes the cultural–geographical circle, creating a fuller picture of their short-lived but historically significant imperium, in other words an *architectural biography*.

Such a close examination of approximately eight–nine decades in the lifespan of the Shansabanis' confederate empire presents manifold additional avenues for inquiry. Among the foremost aims for the project at hand, however, is the untethering of scholarship on South and Central Asia's history of the second millennium CE from the apparently irresistible pull of a magnetic pole originating in pre-modern historiography, namely, the drive to write emphatically *Islamic* histories.

In the Arabic and Persian histories of the Islamic world dating roughly from the thirteenth through eighteenth centuries, we can justifiably observe that among their authors' pre-eminent drives was the adumbration of not only a "divinely ordained paradigm of the rise and fall of states," but specifically an *Islamically* ordained one.[15] Such a drive was plausibly even more pronounced on the perceived peripheries of this physical and moral world, as would have been the case in the environs of South and Central Asia. Arabic- and Persian-language authors writing about the region tended to treat the Shansabanis as one lock in the ever-lengthening, multi-stranded braid of *Muslim* dynasts. For some, the first lock of this braid would have been the Umayyad incursions of the eighth century, though the Ghaznavids might have shared this initiatory status particularly with regard to northern India.[16]

The continued presence of specifically *Islamic* dynastic lineages in South Asia was not lost on these historical authors (collectively): the above-mentioned braid of events continued its intricate and sinuous progress with the Shansabanis and then the so-called Delhi Sultanate (usually dated *c.* 1211–*c.* 1525 CE), which also engendered the creation of eventually independent states governed by confessionally Muslim elites throughout the Deccan. Ultimately, the advent of the Mughals and what were ostensibly the latter's successor states of the eighteenth century brought this Islamically ordained timeline into the very present of some of these authors.[17] In hindsight, then, even while the authors' presentation of the sequence of events was not strictly incorrect, their understanding of the Shansabanis' place in near-exclusively *Islamic* historical time arguably cleaved to the central purpose of writing an *Islamic* history. Furthermore, the composition of Islamic pasts was very much in keeping with the historical authors' moral universe(s), and the epistemological and literary conventions guiding their intellectual labors (see also Chapter 1, this volume).

Today, it is safe to say that the universes – moral and otherwise – providing the impetuses for scholarship are different, as are the epistemological and intellectual conventions guiding present-day authors. The seemingly inescapable urge to identify historical actors and processes within an Islamic, divinely ordained "history" does not *have* to be prevalent, and the need to legitimize a royal patron's rightful place in Islamic time and space is now obsolete. And yet – jarringly – the disciplinary specialties of "Islamic" history, art and architecture, archaeology, etc. have only grown in appeal and practitioners. And, as if echoing the aforementioned historical authors' collective urge to place their monarchs within Islamically ordained spacetime, scholarly works on South Asia's historical periods still elide various political formations – even with vastly different court cultures and socio-cultural geographies – into single monographs principally because of the Islamic confessionalism of these polities' elites.[18] In the face of these countervailing cross-currents, it is difficult – if not close to impossible – to "essay … non-sectarian histories of conquest and conflict," and also cultural transformation.[19]

The ensuing volumes *essay*[20] just such a non-sectarian retelling. They embrace the possibility for new understandings of South and Central Asia's history of the second millennium CE, offered by liberating the point of departure from an inherited urge to write an Islamic dynastic history. Certainly, the chapters that follow focus on the Shansabanis as a kinship-based elite, or *dynasty* (Figure I.3), and they trace their trajectory from unknown origins toward a confederacy of royal lineages exercising prerogatives broadly encompassed within notions of Perso-Islamic kingship – what could be termed a *history*. The work does *not*, however, take it for granted that this kinship-based group were *always* elites, nor that their relationship with Islamic confessionalism was a seamless one. The fissures thereby opened afford the opportunity – thus far too little utilized in the scholarship on Central and South Asia – to examine *which* "Islam" was favored by these *eventual* elites, and why (see esp. Chapters 2–4).

Of course, prior modern works have undertaken close analyses of historical dynasties of the Persianate world, perhaps most relevant being the monographs on the Ghaznavids, considered the predecessors of the Shansabanis in the regions now within modern Afghanistan through India (cf. Chapters 1 and 7). Prior to becoming prized *ghulam*s in the service of the Samanids (*c.* 820–1000 CE), the Ghaznavid dynasty's early founders Alptigin (d. AH 352/963 CE) and his own *ghulam* Sabuktigin (*c.* 940s–999 CE) – father of the famous Mahmud (r. AH 389–421/999–1030 CE) – both came from obscure origins in the vast steppe lands of Turkic and other populations, roughly spanning modern Uzbekistan and Kazakhstan through Mongolia.[21] The broad outlines of Sabuktigin's truly eventful life indicate that his integration into and eventual rise within the Samanid house were undeniably underpinned by a series of dialogical encounters with more than one aspect and type of "Islam."[22] Indeed, his rule on behalf of his Samanid overlords in Zabulistan-Zamindawar (southern Afghanistan; Figures I.1–I.2) and surrounding areas also included the deployment of selective "Islams" in the interests of statecraft (cf. Chapter 3, notes).

But the existing studies on the Ghaznavids, emerging from the last century of scholarship, treat them principally as Perso-Islamic kings who constructed an empire, once extending from Rayy in the center of the Iranian Plateau to Lahore in the Panjab, and possibly beyond (see esp.

Chapters 5 and 6). By contrast, rather than assuming largely *un*problematic transactions between a singular notion of kingship and a similar, broadly conceived Islam in Central–South Asia during the early second millennium CE, the present close study of the Shansabanis takes full advantage of the available evidence to examine the identifiable impetuses behind their actuations of kingship and *specific* processes of Islamization (see Chapters 1 and 2). We focus on a slice of time, *viz.* the long twelfth century, during which the Shansabanis emerged from unknown origins into historicity.

In Sana'i's homily, the role of the blind men of Ghur would be played by the scholars from several disciplines who have undertaken analyses touching upon the Shansabanis during a little more than the last half-century. These specialists have included historians, archaeologists and art-architectural historians – among the last of whom I would count myself. As specialists of "archives" encapsulating time periods and geographical areas, we understandably embrace our disciplinary locations. These allow us to stay abreast of the continually changing methodologies afforded by each of the aforementioned fields, and the sheer technological advances that also engender new approaches.[23] In fact, the present monographic project relies on the architectural patronage of the Shansabanis throughout modern Afghanistan, Pakistan, and India as a primary source to elucidate the *architectural cultures* in which they participated, and which they shaped in turn, as explicated below. But, I believe that in the case of the Shansabanis and the northwestern reaches of South Asia (modern Afghanistan, Pakistan, India) during the twelfth century, all too rigid and exclusive disciplinary *loci* have led to misperceptions of the "elephant" as a whole.[24]

Objects and texts dating to the early second millennium CE constitute important evidentiary *corpora*, elucidating what is generally a less accessible time and place of Eurasia's past. The textual sources on eleventh- and twelfth-century Afghanistan through India, which are the primary focus for historians, have been extensively analyzed and interpreted over the last century and more. Similarly, the Shansabanis' architectural and other material traces throughout their imperial expanse have attracted the expertise of art-architectural historians (cf. esp. Chapters 2–5 and Volume II). In fact, these bodies of evidence have been juxtaposed and even deployed in tandem, thereby combining the information from more than one part of the proverbial elephant. As a result, F. B. Flood summarized thus the modern perception of the Shansabanis, which has remained more or less unchanged over the last sixty years[25]:

Although ultimately ephemeral (and thus largely ignored by historians and art historians alike) ... [the Ghurid polity's] conjoining [of] northern India with large swaths of eastern Iran and Afghanistan for the first time [*sic*] ...

created the conditions for mobility between these contiguous realms on a previously unimaginable scale. The expansion of the Shansabanid lands to include
vast areas that had traditionally fallen outside the *dar al-Islam* presented the
parvenu Ghurids and their agents with a double imperative: to project their
authority and legitimize their position within the *dar al-Islam* and to provide
effective governance in the newly acquired Indian territories that had formerly
stood without it.

While this description of the Shansabanis is – again – not strictly
incorrect, it accrues principally from two parts of Sana'i's elephant, *viz.*
those elucidated by the rather rigidly circumscribed disciplinary *loci* of
history and art-architectural history. Fortunately, the Minaret of Jam
Archaeological Project (MJAP), directed by Dr. David Thomas, has
recently brought to light a third pachydermal part, making apprehension
of the whole "beast" that much more attainable: rigorous archaeological
surveys and excavations by MJAP specialists during the mid-2000s in
central Afghanistan's Ghur province, at the site of Jam-Firuzkuh (Figure
I.2) – now generally believed to be the *sard-sir* encampment or summer
"capital" of one branch of the Shansabani confederacy (cf. Chapters 2–4) –
provide us with invaluable data of the *material* conditions of the lives
of the Shansabani elites and at least some of their cohabitants at the
locality.[26]

Making sense of the whole range of seemingly unrelated or only
circumstantial data for the Shansabanis, as well as the existing *lacunae*
therein, is not unlike the sensation of following the elephant's trunk (for
example), only to discover an entirely new and seemingly dissimilar yet
ultimately connected part of an organic terrain. It has necessitated forays
into the additional discipline of anthropology, and therein the study of
nomadic pastoralists and other transhumant populations, often referred to
as "barbarians."[27] The principal hypothesis animating the present project
is that, during the first few decades of the twelfth century, the Shansabanis
experienced an ancestral shift from being *more* nomadic and/or seasonally
transhumant ("barbarians") to *more* sedentist power-brokers, not necessarily reaching either end of the nomad–urban continuum.[28] Recently,
Patricia Crossley further clarified that:

> [n]omads can be designated more concretely as pastoralists – people at some
> moment in time depending primarily upon the care and processing of animals
> for a living, but always living and trading within a broader context of agricul-
> tural, urban economies.[29]

Following Crossley, then, for convenience I use the less cumbersome
"nomadism" and "transhumance" and their adjectival derivatives to encompass the full range of nomadic pastoralism and seasonal transhumance.

As for the Shansabanis and the consequential changes to their lifeways, these undoubtedly took place in response to a variety of social, economic, political, and perhaps environmental factors (see Chapters 2 and 3). But as is the case with all historical processes, in the end the surviving evidence allows for the perception of only *some* of these factors.[30] Again, Burbank and Cooper have provided perhaps the most succinct description of the accidental convergence of circumstances that eventually coalesce as imperialism:

> In conditions of wide access to resources and simple technology, small advantages – larger family size, better access to irrigation or trade routes, good luck, ambitious and skillful rulers – can lead to domination of one group over another, setting in motion the creation of tribal dynasties and kingships.[31]

I have found such an apprehension of the Shansabanis' transformation to be invaluable for making fuller sense of many, previously opaque or misunderstood aspects of their trajectories, both within Afghanistan and beyond.

It is also worth noting that, unlike other nomadic/transhumant groups who attained transregional politico-economic power – most relevant would be the contemporaneous Sajluqs (cf. esp. Chapters 1 and 3) – the Shansabanis' shift from textually unrecorded nomadism and/or transhumance to the elite status celebrated in panegyrics, and ultimate imperial demise, are all documentable within approximately eighty to ninety years. Their nomadic/transhumant beginnings, then, would not have been a distant memory evoked in the nostalgia of elders; some form of these lifeways was conceivably still within the lived experience of the scions of the three principal Shansabani lineages at Firuzkuh, Bamiyan, and eventually Ghazna (Chapters 3–5). Thus, the Shansabanis' pre- and early imperial history – the focus of Volume I – is directly relevant to our investigation of their transformation into transregional builders of empire in Volume II.

Bennet Bronson's well-known and tantalizingly titled essay, "The Role of Barbarians in the Fall of States" (1988), is equally useful in examining the reverse, state-*building* process. Defining "barbarians" essentially as members of "a political unit … that is not itself a state," the author summarized thus their situation:

> If rich barbarians successfully resist both their state-organized and unorganized but poorer neighbors, it is probably because they have set up a state themselves. Barbarians who remain barbarians are therefore poor.[32]

Following Bronson's inimitable directness, many of the Ghuri "barbarians" remained poor, while the Shansabanis obviously did not. All the more reason to be cognizant of a distinction, pertinent especially as of the mid-twelfth century: the historical inhabitants of the region of Ghur were and are logically referred to with the toponymic adjective *Ghuri*; however, a specific kinship-based clan emerged from among them, identified by historical sources as "the house of Shansab" or the Shansabanis.[33] As discussed in Chapter 2 this distinction becomes even more significant over time, as the majority of the Shansabanis' fellow Ghuris most likely did *not* undergo a similar shift in lifeways and economies from varieties of nomadism or transhumance to some degree and type of sedentism (or to empire-building dominance).

To be sure, historical writers such as Minhaj al-Din Siraj Juzjani (AH 589–658/1193–1260 CE) – our principal interlocutor throughout this work (cf. Chapter 1) – referred to the Shansabanis also as "the *maliks* of Ghur," and the appellation has understandably continued in modern Persian- and European-language scholarship.[34] However, in addition to a question of historical discernibility and greater accuracy regarding their politico-military ascendancy as of the mid-twelfth century, using the clan name of "Shansabani" for the protagonists of our story is also historiographically meaningful: To refer to the Shansabanis as "Ghurids" might reify the misinterpretation of their historical impact as limited to their region of origin and – in Barry Flood's term – ephemeral (see above). But as Flood himself rather contradictorily stated, their activities reverberated on "a previously unimaginable scale," so that distinguishing the Shansabanis as such from their fellow Ghuris seems only fitting.[35]

The present Volume's examination of the Shansabanis also provides an entrée into central Afghanistan's nomad–urban continuum, the *more* nomadic aspects of which have historically received less than their merited attention in a wide range of disciplines from history to archaeology and beyond (see Chapter 1). Certainly, the relative paucity of surviving material culture from nomadic societies – or, an alternative characterization could be that methods adequate to recovering these material traces are still coming into focus – has led to fewer studies on the histories of these populations.[36]

The real significance of nomadic groups is increasingly evident, not least because they interacted with *more* sedentist and urban populations to varying degrees, often as "peripatetic traders" supplying desirable commodities and/or labor, and exchanging or purchasing goods within urban and village contexts. Indeed, the seasonal migrations of nomads occasioned regular interactions with the settlements, villages, and towns along their routes of transhumance.[37] Nomads are therefore extremely important in fully grasping the economic and cultural layers of historical towns and cities, which all together shaped the landscape often over centuries.[38] The ensuing analysis attempts to contribute to a recuperation of more of the socio-cultural history of central Afghanistan, relevant both to apprehending the region's historical periods and also to understanding it more fully in modern times.[39]

Nevertheless, as alluded to above, the nature of the material remains of past nomadic/transhumant societies is only one of a series of challenges surrounding their retrievability. Given that most of the textual sources emerged from urban and even courtly ambits (mentioned previously), it is unsurprising that non-sedentist populations appeared in these texts only in passing, the reports occasioned by their interactions with the hegemonic power in a particular region (cf. Chapter 1). Moreover, many texts' *raison d'être* was to chronicle a regional or transregional power and enable its longevity in collective memories, so that the official reports of this power's interactions with nomadic and transhumant groups rarely depicted them as anything but "barbarians" (cf. Chapter 1). The result, then, is a virtual *lacuna* of source materials on historical nomads that are contemporaneous and, if not sympathetic, then at least interested in the vast spectrum of nomadic existences.[40]

This historiographical blind spot can be somewhat ameliorated by studies of modern nomadic societies. While these studies by no means provide direct substitutes for the ideal source materials just described, they can offer documentation of phenomena in very specific contexts, providing interpretive *simulacra* that aid us in devising plausible interpretations of the surviving traces of past nomadic and transhumant groups. Bearing in mind Richard Tapper's[41] salutary cautions against the *a*historical use of studies on modern nomads to understand their historical antecedents, two broad parameters for their consultation are in order: first, relying on works treating modern Afghanistan and Iran for *comparanda* permits geographical consistency, underscored by an active awareness of the alterations in climate and natural resources within these regions' various landscapes over the last one thousand years.[42] Second, rather than a narrow, one-to-one application of modern data to past events, judicious *juxtaposition* tends to be less anachronistic, and more open-ended in the range of meanings that come into view. Within these parameters, the picture that emerges of the Shansabanis frames a shift from pre-imperial nomadism/transhumance among their fellow Ghuri countrymen, to a regional and then transregional dominance, albeit with continuation of some aspects of their earlier lifeways (see esp. Chapters 2 and 3).

This project's focus on an obscure, transhumant/nomadic group of the past, and the elites emerging from it, might appear to be an unlikely subject for an art-architectural historian. These populations certainly produced portable objects such as metalwork and textiles, made possible by their regular purchase or barter of raw materials in towns and settlements, where in turn they might sell or trade the fruits of their labors.[43] But they had no need to construct monumental architecture, generally not possessing the requisite skills themselves, nor patronizing specialized workers to build for them (cf. Chapter 2).

A premise of the current work is that Perso-Islamic kingship during the period of the Shansabanis' emergence as a regional power in the twelfth century *required* cultural patronage, including architecture, wherein so many of the religious, intellectual, and juridical supports of rule were housed (see esp. Chapter 1). But rather than viewing architecture as solely an instantaneous phenomenon, being the monumental result of elite patronage, a perception of the built form within its larger nexus of processes of facture, varying uses, and shifting receptions all together aid in accessing a wider cross-section of its historical significances. Indeed, precisely *because* command and mobilization of skilled labor was requisite in the creation of built works, these serve as diagnostic points of reference for the emergence of new politico-economic elites – that is, previously unknown groups who came to possess the political and material capital required to have buildings constructed for them. Akin to Sana'i's elephant, then, discrete aspects of the built work hold immense potential for differing yet complementary insights into its milieu, and the groups of people who interacted with it throughout its existence (see, e.g., Chapter 2).

But, as modern investigators attempting to access a past, how might we understand the architectural "product" that historical patrons were underwriting, either through command or compensation? What were the range of standards that circumscribed its outcome? I propose the concept of *architectural culture* as an accommodating heuristic device to apprehend the collective span of the built works analyzed herein.

The writings of J. Sourdel-Thomine (e.g., 1960, *inter alia*) and M. Meister (esp. 1993, 2011) regarding "style," "idiom," and "mode" have initiated the difficult but essential process of coming to grips with coalescing patterns in the history of material–cultural production. These scholars had – very responsibly – applied their observations to their respective regions of expertise, Sourdel-Thomine distilling her long experience in the eastern Islamic world (greater Khurasan), and Meister his equally profound engagement with the building traditions spanning the Indus's alluvia through the north Indian plains. Collectively, these authors' writings are not merely relevant to the regions encompassed within the emerging Shansabani elites' annexations, they have formed the bases for my conception of architectural culture as a complex of constitutive mechanisms shaping their respective built environments, in turn allowing us to address the nature of the Shansabanis' participation within them.

This Volume and the next argue that the Shansabanis' territories – eventually extending into north India – encompassed three distinct and equally significant architectural cultures: modern central through western Afghanistan, interconnected with historical Khurasan; the Indus' alluvia; and the Indo-Gangetic plains.[44] The building groups located in these regions did not simply look different from each other: They were in fact convergent indices of several factors, including indigenous natural resources; materials of construction; architectural traditions and their *praxes*; and established labor structures or hierarchies. All of these factors together flexibly constituted the architectural culture operative in a permeably delineated *locus*, which served as the principal resource for architectural patronage among elite and non-elite echelons alike.

It must be emphasized that an architectural culture at a moment in time was far from monolithic, and the concept should be capacious in its synchronous application. Here, I find Holly Edwards's[45] notion of "spectrum piety" applicable within an architectural context: the virtually infinite historical iterations of an architectural culture spanned a wide spectrum, encompassing elite patronage, which is typically thought to set far-reaching, cosmopolitan standards. But not all structures in a given time and space were commissioned by elites or built by the same artisans. Since non-elite patronage also manifested the architectural culture in question, all its iterations should be viewed with parity, as points on the spectrum spanning elite or royal, cosmopolitan patronage, through non-elite or vernacular commissions. Rather than one being of lesser or greater value, *all* instantiations of an identifiable architectural culture serve as valid and equally valuable historical informants.

As such, an architectural culture would rarely evince drastic and sudden changes with shifts in political régimes, for example, or even the introduction of new religious practices.[46] Really, new architectural cultures took root within a region only with the influx of skilled laborers *and* the availability of the required building materials, both in terms of natural resources (e.g., stone deposits, earth usable for bricks) and "industrial" infrastructure (quarries, kilns, and fuel, etc.). In fact, multiple architectural cultures could co-exist within a region,[47] as the mobility of skilled laborers is a known phenomenon,[48] with the demands for their skills depending on the vagaries of their patrons' preferences. But while a regional, politico-economic elite by definition commandeered material resources and labor toward their own requirements, political shifts did not abruptly or even necessarily interrupt the inertia of a region's architectural culture(s), or the ways in which buildings were constructed or decorated. At the same time, it is also true that all *un*mechanized human practices change, more or less perceptibly, over time. The relationship between architectural patronage and the built form, then, cannot always be characterized in general terms, but largely on an individual and ad hoc basis.

The tomb of Salar Khalil (also known as the *ziyarat* of Baba Khatim) (Figures I.16 and I.17) in Afghanistan's Juzjan Province, about 40 km west of Balkh, and the tomb locally attributed to Shahzada Shaikh Husain near Bust (Figures I.18 and I.19) both serve as discrete and informative exemplars of an architectural culture in general, and in particular as manifestations of greater Khurasan's architectural culture, which occupies the majority of this Volume.[49] Along with *minar*s, and mosque and *madrasa* complexes, the "domed cube" configuration of these tombs was

Figure I.16 *Tomb of Salar Khalil, a.k.a. ziyarat Baba Khatim (west of Balkh), Juzjan Province, Afghanistan. From Sourdel-Thomine 1971: fig. XI.*

a long-standing and ingrained building practice throughout Central Asia by the latter half of the twelfth century, utilized in both monumental commemorations of royalty and the nobility, and in smaller-scale structures, as is the case in these examples.[50] Salar Khalil's otherwise extensive epigraphic program recorded no date, while Shaikh Husain's exterior inscriptional frieze was too eroded to glean the content. Although the subject of some debate (cf. below), both tombs have been dated to the twelfth–thirteenth centuries.[51] These structures are amply useful for our purposes, as they illustrate the inclusive notion of an identifiable architectural culture and the variability within it, even at the non-royal ends of its expressive spectrum. They also demonstrate the heuristic value of identifying an architectural culture, which both shaped and *was* shaped by the patronage of elites and others alike.

While both tombs adhere to the overall format of a domed space, they diverge in their respective funerary chambers, one being quadrangular (Juzjan) and the other octagonal (Bust). Moreover, the Bust tomb was largely open to the elements, more akin to a pavilion sheltering a grave, while the Juzjan tomb was a closed "cube" with only the entrance aperture. The most noticeable difference between them, however, is the amount of decoration and the variation in the respective iconographies: the exteriors

Figure I.17 *Tomb of Salar Khalil, Juzjan Province, interior. From Sourdel-Thomine 1971: fig. XV.*

and interiors of the Bust structure (Figures I.18 and I.19) carried decorations primarily consisting of baked bricks placed in horizontal or vertical clusters, and terracotta plugs deployed in a remarkable variety of ornament, ranging from textured surfaces; geometric patterns, including a plethora of medallions; to the angular Kufic frieze running along the exterior of the dome's octagonal base. Meanwhile, the Juzjan tomb (Figures I.16 and I.17) seemed to act as the stage for an elaborate epigraphic program of variations on the Kufic script against equally diverse backgrounds. Both the differences and commonalities in these tomb structures – located at two ends of the early Shansabanis' core imperial regions in Afghanistan – are worthy of note, as together they personify two of the manifold iterations within a region's architectural culture.

Figure I.18 *Tomb of Shahzada Sheikh Husain, near Bust, Helmand Province, Afghanistan, c. 1200 CE. From Crane 1979: fig. 5.*

The debate alluded to above, specifically surrounding the tomb of Salar Khalil, is significant as it illustrates the heuristic value of an architectural culture. The debate has centered on whether the structure merits a Ghaznavid or "Ghurid" attribution, based largely on the form and, to a lesser extent, the content of its epigraphy.[52] Indeed, any purely dynastic attribution for the structure in the twelfth century would be further complicated by the extremely intricate history of the Balkh region overall, which was a point of contestation among the Khwarazm-shahs, the Firuzkuh and/or Bamiyan branches of the Shansabanis, and the western Qarakhanids as Qarakhitay vassals (see Chapter 1; Figure 1.1).[53]

Salar Khalil is in fact remarkable due to the predominance of doxologies, and Qur'anic verses and references throughout its inscriptions; the use of an unmistakably hard-edged Kufic script with geometric terminals in the baked-brick exterior frieze (Figure I.15); and on its interior walls (Figure I.16), the juxtaposition of meandering calligraphic bands with incised stucco surfaces.[54] Based on these considerations, I concur with Sourdel-Thomine (1971) that the structure was most likely built during the latter half of the twelfth century, during the waning of Ghaznavid power in Afghanistan and these sultans' effective retrenchment to their eastern holdings around Lahore. The question of a definitive *dynastic* affiliation for the structure is not only difficult to answer, it may in fact be largely irrelevant, as the fractious political circumstances in the Balkh region during the later twelfth century seemed to exercise no visible impact on its form and decoration.

A structure such as the tomb of Salar Khalil not only exquisitely personifies the many factors contributing to its own process of becoming – that is, its architectural culture – it also demonstrates the impediment that an overdetermined reliance on dynastic labeling can create[55]: rather than facilitating entry into historically germane processes, the quest for a top-down dynastic appellation obscures our apprehension of changes in architectural culture that were incrementally effected, at least to some degree by the dialogue between shifts in patronage and the artisans' responses to them. It was just such a dialogue that the newly ascendant Shansabanis had to master if they were to achieve dominance both within their lands of origin and beyond. And it is this fundamental process that buildings help us

Figure I.19 *Tomb of Shahzada Sheikh Husain, near Bust, interior. From Crane 1979: fig. 8.*

to understand, whether among well-heeled Persianized elites grasping for an empire, or politico-cultural novices emerging from the nomad–urban continuum, thrust forward by what were essentially historical accidents such as "better access to ... trade routes, good luck ... [and] ambitious and skillful rulers."

* * *

Before embarking in earnest on this Volume's examination of the emergence of the Shansabanis on the eastern fringes of Khurasan during the mid-twelfth century, and their eastward progress to the Indus's alluvia shortly thereafter, the difficulty of fieldwork in large swaths of Afghanistan – including the central region of Ghur itself – must be acknowledged. Given the inaccessibility of many of the early Shansabanis' core areas of activity, projects such as mine perforce rely on historical and other documentation, which has come from a wide variety of sources.

The Fortress and Citadel of Ghuznee and the two Minars.

Figure I.20 *"The fortress and citadel of Ghazni (Afghanistan) and the two Minars. Tribesmen with camels, horses and pack bullocks in foreground," James Atkinson (1780–1852), watercolor, 1839. © Courtesy of the British Library.*

Figure I.21 *"Ruins of Old Kandahar Citadel," albumen print, c. 1880–81, Benjamin Simpson. © Courtesy of the Getty Research Institute, Los Angeles.*

Being a photogenic land of truly magnificent landscapes, architecture, and colorful people, Afghanistan has arrested the picturesque imagination at least since the First Anglo-Afghan War (1839–1841) (Figure I.19), continuing to do so into the Second Anglo-Afghan War (1879–1881) (Figure I.20) with the great popularization of photographic technology as a tool to "visit" distant and exotic lands without the inconvenience and risk of actual travel. This fascination with Afghanistan seemed to persist during the first eight decades of the twentieth century, as archaeologists and other scholars undertook more systematic surveys and studies. These latter works included the invaluable archive of photographs left by the intrepid Josephine Powell (1919–2007) (Figure I.21).[56] Throughout more than a century of depiction, Afghanistan's lofty ruins and nomadic populations appear unchanging (compare Figures I.21 and I.22), always furnishing aesthetically evocative subjects begging to be Orientalized. I myself could not help but capture the wide-open plains edged by mountains outside the

Figure I.22 *Shahr-i Gholghola, general view, citadel (eleventh–thirteenth century), with women in foreground. © Photograph Josephine Powell c. 1960. Harvard Fine Arts Library, Special Collections.*

Figure I.23 *Herat-Ghuriyan highway, Herat Province, Afghanistan.* © *Photograph Alka Patel 2011.*

western city of Herat (Figure I.23), appearing as natural proscenia upon which great histories unfolded.

But such modern fetishism actually distracts from the long-standing reality of these eastern parts of the Islamic-Persianate world. The regions within modern Afghanistan were collectively a busy place, being *the* strategic areas for control of much of Eurasia, as realized by the Sasanians, various Hunnic groups such as the Hephthalites, and the Western Turks – to name only a few who built and consolidated empires starting and sometimes ending there. Moreover, the picturesque but artificially empty vistas occlude the multifarious iterations of the above-mentioned nomad–urban continuum prevailing throughout the vast majority of the Iranian cultural world, including Afghanistan, well into the nineteenth century. The protagonists in forging imperial formations were not solely the regions' magnificent landscapes; they combined with enterprising populations, which spanned the nomad–urban continuum, to link the Iranian and Indic cultural spheres. Overall, it is to a more complete apprehension of this dynamism that the ensuing project is dedicated.

Notes

1. Translated by J. Stephenson 1911: 13. On this British officer in the Indian Medical Service and his early study of Sana'i's extremely complex *Hadiqat* (including the work's codicological history), see de Bruijn 1983: 122; and Allegranzi 2019a, vol. I: 29–30.
2. According to Lewis (1995: 120), it was Sana'i who first introduced the Buddhist parable of the blind men and the elephant into the literature of the Persianate world, a parable thereafter incorporated into the works of al-Ghazali (AH 450–505/1058–1111 CE), Jalal al-Din Rumi (d. AH 671/1273 CE), and others. Cf. also de Bruijn, "Sana'i" *EIr* (2012); but cf. also note *infra*.
3. Although "*Udana*" characterized a variety of Buddhists texts, principally in Pali, here the reference is to the third book of the *Khuddakanikaya*, which contained eighty stories and utterances of the Buddha. The utterances were mostly in verse, accompanied by prose accounts of the circumstances prompting them. The Buddhist elephant parable was predictably situated within the sacred geography of early Buddhism, so that the king referred to in the text ruled at Shravasti (Pal. Savatthi), where he summoned "all the men born blind in Savatthi" to describe an elephant. During the historical Buddha's lifetime (mid-first millennium CE), Shravasti was the capital of the powerful Koshala kingdom, located in the foothills of the Himalayas of modern Nepal. Cf. Buswell and Lopez 2014: 42, 383, 435, 443, 932; see also the English translation of the Pali *Udana* by D. M. Strong (1902: 93–96).
4. Thomas de Bruijn, among the principal scholars of Sana'i, described *Hadiqat* as "one of the most problematic works of Persian literature" for Western scholars, though in the Persian ecumene it has enjoyed a favored status over the centuries, providing "a promising source for the study of indigenous

literary values" (de Bruijn 1983: 119). Given *Hadiqat*'s homiletic *genre* and overall structure – didactic poetry paired with illustrative prose anecdotes – further juxtaposition with the Pali Buddhist canon may aid in dispelling the current confusion around its complex form. Cf. de Bruijn 1983, 119–163; de Bruijn, "Sana'i" *EIr* (2012); and Lewis 1995, 112–120. Indeed, such an interdisciplinary juxtaposition could also be fruitful for questions regarding the specific Buddhist texts that circulated throughout historical Bactria, and these texts' audiences and receptions.

5. Twelfth-century inhabitants of the regions within modern Afghanistan were surrounded by remnants of Buddhist monasteries and other structures. According to Melikian-Chirvani (1974: esp. 34ff., 64–65), certain "stereotypes" with identifiably Buddhist literary origins had also filtered into Persian poetry. While Lewis (1995: 120) concluded that Sana'i was the first Persian poet to have introduced the elephant parable into Persian poetry and literature (see note *supra*), the specific mechanisms by which Sana'i accessed the contents of Buddhist literature – was he versed in Pali, and were manuscripts available in Ghazna or accessible in the region? – are still to be determined. Alternatively, the poet might have made use of an *already* translated Persian version, in which case he would not have been the first Persian poet to integrate the parable in his œuvre.

6. I borrow the phrasing from Peacock's (2010: 3) important study on the early Saljuqs.

7. Aside from Ghaznavid-issued coinage – including the well-known Kufic-Sharada *dirham*s and figural *jital*s, the latter continuing in the Panjab for several centuries – no surviving architectural remains farther east in the *duab* region are known. Cf. R. Tye and M. Tye 1995: 43 and nos. 86, 89, 91–94.

8. Cf., e.g., Rosenfield 1967/1993: 41–54; also Ball, Bordeaux et al. 2019: 345. The convergence of Greek, Iranian, and Indian "symbols of power and victory" in Kushana iconography underscored the regular traffic of people from all of Eurasia's major cultural regions within Kushana-affiliated territories. Additionally, among the legacies of the Kushana period would be the coalescence of the anthropomorphic iconographies of Buddhism, which was to have enduring effects on the religio-cultural lives of peoples across Eurasia for centuries to come. Cf. Pons, "Kushan Dynasty ix. Art of the Kushans," *EIr* (2016).

9. I have found the recent engagements by Green (2019) and Spooner (2019) with the "Persianate" – with some modifications (cf. Chapter 1) – as a heuristic useful for delineating the process of attaining kingship that the Shansabanis undertook.

10. See, e.g., Patel 2010 for an overview of textual sources indicating seventh–eighth-century presence of Muslim communities in South Asia; cf. also Asif 2016: 13. The Shansabanis' north Indian activity is the principal subject of Volume II.

11. The origins of this catch-all rubric have been attributed to early twentieth-century scholarship on India (cf. Patel 2018: esp. 60) and the singularity of the term "Sultanate" in the face of the multiplicity of these polities and their

cultural productions has also been interrogated (*ibid.*, 60–67; see also Patel 2006: 9–11). Additionally, see *infra* in main text and notes.

12. The Persian-language monographs – two published in Afghanistan and two in Iran – were recently analyzed against the backdrop of these areas' respective nationalisms, emerging over the twentieth century. While the "extra-intellectual" impetuses of these works' authors were brought to the fore, "the cognizance of [such] factors on scholarship ... in western-language works" must also be borne in mind (Patel 2017: 144 ff.). Further, see Thomas (2018: 9 and *passim*) for a discussion of "the Ghurid interlude," coined by Bosworth (1968b: 166).

13. See de Bruijn 1983, cited *supra* in notes (my emphasis).

14. Burbank and Cooper 2010: 4, 8, 12–13, 15, 17–18.

15. Meisami 1993: 268. See also Hardy 1960: 113–118; Sarkar 1977: 28; Nizami 1983: 48–49; Siddiqui 2010, esp. 2–8. See also Auer 2012: 3ff.

16. For the early eighth-century Umayyad incursions into Sindh and their usages in colonial and later historiography, see Inden 2000: esp. 17 and notes. Also, while Asif (2016: 2ff.) discussed *Chach-nama*'s (*c.* 1226 CE) description of these events as the dubiously grand "beginnings" of Islam in South Asia, the campaigns of Mahmud of Ghazna into northern India have also commanded attention as originary in public and intellectual cultures over the last millennium (cf. Anooshahr 2009: 1–3).

17. See, e.g., Sen (2017) for analysis of Muhammad Ghulam Husain Tabatabai's *Sair al-Mutakhirin* (1779–80). For the earlier period of the sixteenth century, Anooshahr (2009: 23–26) intriguingly posited that the future emperor Babur's motivations for (and his perception of) his own campaigns into India were deeply colored by his thorough familiarity with Mahmud Ghaznavi's raids into the north Indian *duab* as gleaned from the works of 'Utbi and Juzjani. These interpretations of events and processes form a striking contrast with Bronson's (1988: 208–209) contemporary historicist view of northern India as "... one of the world's great civilized traditions [that was] within raiding range of unusually effective *barbarians*" (my emphasis) – cf. *infra* in main text and notes.

18. For a relatively recent example, see Flood's *Objects of Translation* (2009), whose timespan encompassed the ninth through the early thirteenth centuries, and the historical geographies of western Afghanistan through the Panjab and the Himalayan foothills, as well as the north Indian plains. The author stated: "... the centuries covered by this book have occupied center stage in colonial and nationalist constructions of a past that has been cast as a perpetual confrontation between Muslim invaders and Hindu resisters, a Manichean dyad that has structured and constrained the history of the region for almost a millennium" (*ibid.*, 2) – essentially reiterating the tautological inertia the current work is attempting to interrupt.

19. Cf. Amin 2002: 30, again with slight modification in the form of adducing the historical process of cultural transformation, for the purposes of this Introduction and the broader aims of these volumes.

20. Applied much in the same sense as Amin (cited *supra*), i.e., "to attempt, to try to do, effect, accomplish, or make (anything difficult)," in use as of the seventeenth century. Cf. *OED*, "essay."

21. This approximate regional span is taken from Cahen et al., "Ghuzz", *EI²* (2012). These authors admittedly concentrated on the *western* Oghüz and other Turkic groups, as these were mentioned in Arabic- and Persian-language texts, often through first-hand accounts of the merchants and pros-elytizers encountering them (see Chapter 2). The Oghüz's eastern brethren, the Toküz–Oghüz, remained more remote and lesser known.

22. Nazim (1933: 610–614, trans. 622–628) first published Sabuktigin's putatively autobiographical *Pand-nama*, which was to be found only as copied in a fourteenth-century text. It briefly mentioned Sabuktigin's boyhood among the Turkic Barskhan clan, his abduction and sale at the slave market of Nakhshab (modern Qarshi in Uzbekistan), and ultimately the Samanid *ghulam* Alptigin's purchase of him in Bukhara. Sabuktigin described the worship of stone idols among some Turkic tribes and his own skepticism of the practice, indicating his pre-destined conversion to Islam. Sabuktigin's origins also included the historiographically requisite Sasanian connections, cf. Bosworth 1973: 61. See also Barthold 1968: 261–262. Such a biographical trajectory was common among the slaves who rose to the status of *ghulam*s, as also indicated by the parallel story of Qutb al-Din Aibek – cf. Juzjani, vol. I, 1963: 415–416 (trans. vol. I, 1881: 512–514).

23. See, e.g., Wilkinson 2016: 3. A caveat is required here: satellite data usually col-lected for US and other super-power intelligence agencies have concentrated on more populated areas, "river valleys and along roads, leaving blank spaces especially in mountain and desert areas" (cf. Hammer et al. 2017: 5). Thus, at times even this otherwise invaluable resource can inadvertently reinforce his-torical *lacunae* in knowledge rather than remedy them. Nevertheless, the areas whence satellite data have recently been analyzed include the northern arc of Balkh and the Balkhab River, as well as the historically less explored southern reaches of Afghanistan around the Helmand River and Sistan. Satellite images of the latter, for example, have revealed at least 119 caravanserais built approx-imately every 20 km. Dated to the late sixteenth–early seventeenth centuries and considered to be part of a "centrally sponsored effort," these way-stations connected the Safavid (1501–1732) and Mughal (1525–1858) realms in uninter-rupted trade and travel routes, altering the view that the Safavid empire had entered a politico-economic decline by this period. Cf. Lawler 2017: 1364; Franklin and Boak 2019. For a recent study on hydrological development and change in the Balkh oasis during the ninth–thirteenth centuries – based on satellite data, in large part – see Wordsworth 2018. Other satellite data have reconfirmed earlier archaeological work in regions such as the vicinity of Qandahar, where ceramic finds imported from Safavid Iran were the most sub-stantive corpus unearthed by excavations (Crowe 1996: 314, 320). Provided all dating is accurate, these rediscoveries underscore the centrality of Afghanistan for the Indic and Iranian cultural worlds during the early modern period. See esp. Chapter 4 for the use of Google Earth and other satellite imagery toward the apprehension of historical data not previously gleaned from architectural complexes and their surrounding landscapes.

24. A perfect case in point would be the mid-twentieth century's strict divi-sion of intellectual labor among disciplines, amply demonstrated in works

of the eminent historian C. E. Bosworth (1928–2015), and those of the equally renowned and coeval anthropologist Fredrik Barth (1928–2016): Despite shared research geographies, the purely textual approach of the historian remained singularly unaffected by the on-the-ground, albeit modern findings of the anthropologist (and vice versa). Cf. *infra* in main text and Chapters 2–4.

25. Flood 2009: 91. This recent overall assessment of the Shansabanis has remained largely consistent beginning with Bosworth's scholarship of the 1960s, and extending through that of H. Edwards in the 1990s–2010s.

26. One of the major results of MJAP's efforts is, of course, Dr. Thomas' 2018 monograph, resulting from the only twenty-first-century archaeological work at Jam-Firuzkuh, from which the present book has benefited immensely. For the archaeo-botanical and -zoological analyses undertaken by MJAP, see, e.g., Thomas et al. 2006; and for ceramics esp. Gascoigne 2010 (*inter alia*).

27. Cf. Vasjutin 2003: 52; Mahmud 2009: 251–252; Elliott 2013: 5; Peacock 2015: 3ff. and notes. The idea of "barbarian" has, of course, derived from the seemingly parasitic raids on caravans and settlements by unindustrialized nomads. Bronson (1988) pointed out that "barbarians" possessed varying degrees of literacy and technological sophistication, and were considered "barbarians" simply because they lay *outside* a state's apparatus in terms of mobility and modes of production (i.e., varied and small-scale agricultural practices, "cottage" industries, sporadic and less taxable trading). Cf. also *infra* in main text and Chapter 1.

28. Cf. Thomas and Gascoigne 2016: 171–172. This premise is at variance with most previous studies, which assumed that "the population of the region [of Ghur] was largely sedentary, and had apparently been so since ancient times" (Habib 1992: 2). See also Bosworth 1961: 118, 133 n. 53. For the updated general characterization of the Shansabanis and their fellow Ghuris here, I rely on Thomas' monograph (2018, esp. pp. 3–10ff.). Cf. also Chapter 2.

29. Crossley 2019: xviii. Cf. also the work of the Collaborative Research Centre, "Difference and Integration," a joint project at the universities of Halle-Wittenberg and Leipzig: Büssow et al. (2011: 3) summarized the group's overarching "assumption that [nomads] follow rational choices no less than their sedentary counterparts … [for] example … preoccupation with the securing of pasture rather than an innate (and therefore irrational) lust for plunder [urging] the Turkic 'tribes' who had come to Anatolia in the eleventh century [to] head for the Caucasus."

30. Tracing the emergence of empires from nomadic or otherwise transhumant origins can be as fraught with preconceptions and generalizations as any other inquiry into large and multi-faceted socio-historical processes, underscoring the need for ongoing work to finesse more specific explanations. While anthropologists and historians have tended to favor some theories of state formation and the impetuses behind it, it is understood that no singular factor can explain the phenomenon among sedentist, nomadic, or in-between populations. For other overviews of favored theories of nomadic imperial formation, see Kradin 2003; also Crossley 2019.

31. Burbank and Cooper 2010: 9.

32. Bronson 1988: 200. Cf. also Vasjutin 2003: 51.

33. The poet Niẓami ʿAruḍi (fl. twelfth century) used the nomenclature in his *Chahar Maqala* ([trans. Browne] 1921: 8). Juzjani's explication of the myth-ical progenitor Shansab (or Shanasb) was itself derived from a lost gene-alogical work by Fakhr al-Din Mubarak-shah al-Marwarruzi, a *nadim* of Sultan Ghiyath al-Din – not to be confused with Fakhr-i Mudabbir (cf. also Chapters 1 and 6). See Juzjani, vol. I, 1963: 318–319 (trans. vol. I, 1881: 302); also Siddiqui 2010: 18.

34. Juzjani, vol. I, 1963: e.g., 318 (trans. vol. I, 1881: 300). See esp. O'Neal (2013: 22–30) for an informative overview of the historiography, beginning with the European "discovery" of the Shansabanis as Persian historical texts under-went translation in the late seventeenth century, through studies dating to the early to mid-twentieth century. Cf. Patel 2017 for modern scholarship in Persian.

35. The seemingly paradoxical tendencies of the long-term *effects* of dynastic lineages and their ephemerality appears to have been endemic to nomadic empires, as observed of the transregional nomadic empire(s) *par excellence* (Burbank and Cooper 2010: 93 and *passim*): "The empires established by Mongols were not long-lived, at least when compared to Rome or Byzantium. What makes Mongols count in world history are the connections they made across Eurasia and the imperial technologies they adapted, transformed, and passed on to later polities."

36. Among the initial recalibrations of methodology for the archaeology of nomadic societies has been Cribb's work (1991), emphasizing the indices of mobile groups' encampments within areas of study. Thomas (2018: 17, 50) effectively deployed the resulting concept of an archipelagic landscape, coined by Adam T. Smith, in which "urban centers [are] small islands of data linked by ephemeral networks in a sea of general obscurity" [!]. See also Stark 2005; Stark 2006a, 2006b; and Thomas and Gascoigne 2016: 173–176.

37. Cf. *supra* in main text; also Barfield 1981: 102–103; and Crossley 2019: 15–16

38. Notwithstanding the outdated generalization of "Middle Eastern Tribalism," particularly apropos here are Ernest Gellner's (1983: 422; *ibid.*, 445) early observations summarizing the contributions to a volume principally on tribal–pastoralist groups in Iran and Afghanistan: "These tribal societies are accustomed to a level of technology, in their agricultural, pastoral, military and domestic equipment, which seems to pre-suppose centres of artisan pro-duction and trade, in other words towns …" Given the nuancing over time of nomad–sedentist interactions, however, Elliott (2013: 6) proposed modifying Gellner's (1983: 447) earlier characterization of "the [nomadic] tribe [as] the anti-state" as actually a relationship that is *both* symbiotic and oppositional, already implied by Bronson (1988).

39. Certainly, the Afghan Boundary Commission reports of the mid- to late nineteenth century make constant reference to nomadic communities, a characteristic also photographed by Donald Wilber around Herat in the 1930s, and by the indefatigable Josephine Powell throughout Ghur during the 1960s (cf. *infra* in main text). These images harmonize with A. Kohzad's "tour reports" (see esp. 1951a; 1952; 1954a; 1954b; also discussed in Chapter

2), as well as late-twentieth-century studies of nomadic groups in central Afghanistan, e.g., Glatzer and Casimir 1983 – the last study being especially pertinent as the same scholars documented and published the magnificent Shansabani *madrasa* of Shah-i Mashhad (Figure I.1) (Badghis province; discussed in Chapter 4) in the late 1960s while following the migration patterns of Pashtun nomads. Indeed, Najimi (2015: 147) noted the seasonal presence of the Achakzay nomads in the *madrasa*'s vicinity in recent years, continuing the migration patterns noted by Glatzer (1983). See also Thomas 2018: 26.

40. Comparable challenges exist for other nomadic elites, most notably the Saljuqs: cf., e.g., Durand-Guédy 2010: 70–71; and esp. Durand-Guédy 2013a for the interpretation of textual sources. Also Peacock 2010: 6–14; Peacock, 2015: 2–19; and Chapter 1.

41. Tapper 1997: 18ff.

42. See Paul 2018b: 316–318 for just such a juxtaposition of modern and historical nomadism in the vicinity of the Balkh oasis. Bosworth (1961: 118) noted, e.g., that: "After the Mongol invasions the pastoral element among the population [of Ghur] increased; whereas [earlier] the Tajik inhabitants … had been primarily agriculturalists"; but he provided no specific evidence for the statement, seeming to rely on the assumption that the nomadic Mongols would have introduced or strengthened ways of life akin to their own. But long- and short-term changes in climate have had obvious impacts on society as a whole, and should be one of the primary considerations in differentiating historical and contemporary realities. While comparative data from Europe on the "Medieval Warm Period" (*c.* 700–1300 CE) might provide points of departure, extrapolating larger global trends would be conjectural at best. Nonetheless, Thomas (2018: 28) summarized that: "[t]he decimation of Afghanistan's natural flora and fauna in recent decades … means that modern data cannot be viewed as representative of the Early Islamic period" (eighth–thirteenth centuries). A possible case of drastic change in the landscape – whether due to environmental factors, shifts in riverbeds or irrigation practices, or a combination of all three – is the region of Sistan: here Klaus Fischer, one of this region's most ardent and thorough investigators, noted an "unusual extent of ruins" compared with the sparseness of the modern population (Fischer 1969: 337). But a further observation, *viz.* "the majority of watch towers, fortresses, rural estates (*rustaq*), 'open towns' (cities without walls) situated in the plain and fortified cities existed from the beginning of the 12th to the end of the 15th cent. A.D.," was only scantily evidenced by surface findings, thus Sistan's architectural chronology has remained inconclusive. Cf. Fischer et al. vol. II, 1974: XII; Genito 2014; see also Chapters 1 and 2.

43. As highlighted by Mahmud (2009: 251–252), reiterating A. A. Kohzad's (e.g.,1951a, 1952, 1954a/b) observations during the course of his travels throughout Ghur in the 1950s. See also Thomas and Gascoigne 2016.

44. Sourdel-Thomine (1960: 280; my trans.) avowed that: "… [t]he art flourishing in Afghanistan during the sixth/twelfth century deserves above all the qualification of a post-Saljuqid Khurasani art developed from the traditions of the region …" For the northwestern Indo-Gangetic region, see esp.

Meister 1993; and for what he termed the Gandhara-Nagara style of West Panjab and Khyber-Pakhtunkhwa (modern Pakistan) see Meister 2010; 2011 (and Chapter 6). For a full description of the three architectural cultures within Shansabani domains, see esp. Patel 2007/2011.

45. Edwards 2015: 71ff.

46. Cf. Patel 2004.

47. Sourdel-Thomine (1960: 280) declared with surprising rigidity that "post-Saljuqid Khurasani art [in Afghanistan] developed without undergoing the least innovation worthy of interest, for example upon contact with India" – an ahistorical understanding of stylistic purity that will be addressed in Volume II.

48. See Volume II for the explication of just such a process: during the last decade of the twelfth century and the first two decades of the thirteenth, artisans specially skilled in the building materials, concepts, and iconographies of northwestern India – in modern times eastern Sindh, Gujarat, and Rajasthan – made their way westward, along the corridors of mobility newly invigorated by the Ghazna Shansabanis' eastward expansion.

49. For the Juzjan structure, see Melikien-Chirvani 1968; Sourdel-Thomine 1971. For Bust, see Crane 1979. For overall bibliography, cf. Ball 2019: Nos. 149, 439.

50. See Grabar 1966 for early Islamic funerary structures, and esp. Pugachenkova 1978 for commemorative architecture in the environs of Balkh, where she documented a long trajectory of the architectural configuration through at least the fifteenth century. See also Hillenbrand 2000: 138; and Chapters 2, 4 and 6.

51. While the Juzjan tomb provided the forms and content of its extensive epigraphic program – discussed *infra* in main text (cf. also Appendix, Afghanistan I) – the one at Bust required other analytical tools: Crane (1979: 245–246) based his dating of the tomb on comparisons with similar decorative techniques in Iran and Central Asia, as well as the independent *stelae* found within the structure, which had a date range from the twelfth to thirteenth centuries. See also Sourdel-Thomine 1956; and Volume II.

52. The first publication of the tomb by A. Melikien-Chirvani (1968) attributed it to Ghaznavid presence in the region, while Sourdel-Thomine (1971) argued for Shansabani patronage.

53. See Paul 2018b: 323ff. for Balkh's shifting political fortunes during the twelfth century; for the numismatic evidence, cf. Schwarz 2002: e.g. Nos. 811, 824, 834; and the more synthetic study by O'Neal (2020). A similar debate has surrounded the tomb of al-Hakim al-Tirmizi (northwest of modern Tirmiz, Uzbekistan), with an epigraphic program noting only an ambiguous patron but no date, so that its construction and/or renovation has been attributed either to the eleventh century, possibly by a local western Qarakhanid ruler, or (most recently) to the mid-twelfth century: see Allegranzi 2020: 112ff.

54. Chapters 4 and 5 discuss the distinguishing stylistic features of Shansabani-period epigraphy, as well as the preponderance of Arabic-language and Qur'anic content along with the possible reasons for the latter. Suffice it to say here that the Qur'anic verses and references gracing the structure

(Appendix, Afghanistan I: 3–5) were not unusual in the overall corpus of Islamic architectural inscriptions: e.g., *Qur'an* III: 18–19 (Al 'Imran) was also part of epigraphic programs at Chisht and Ghazna, and throughout the eastern Islamic lands since at least the eleventh century (cf. Blair 1992: 9, 52, 56, 137, 153); meanwhile, the famous Throne verse (II: 255–256) was also present since at least the early eleventh century at Tirmiz (Blair 1992: 101), and at Chisht and Lashkari Bazar. Cf. also Chapters 4 and 5, and Appendix, Afghanistan III: 5, VIII: 4.

55. Blair (1985: 84) took up the application of dynastic appellations to art-architectural styles in her analysis of the Zuzan *madrasa* (AH 615/1218 CE), patronized by the local *malik* in the service of the Khwarazm-shah 'Ala' al-Din Muhammad Takish (r. AH 596–617/1200–1220 CE).

56. Even during the 1970s prior to the Soviet invasion of 1979 (and for scholars based within Afghanistan itself – e.g., N. Dupree 1977), Powell's photographs were regularly utilized both in popular guidebooks and more scholarly works as among the most thorough and meticulously documented archives of the more remote areas of the country. Powell's work was incredibly prescient, making possible the continuing research on this global region into the present day.

CHAPTER 1

Kingly Trajectories

The chronological scope of this two-volume project, namely AH 490s–610s, overlapping with the twelfth century of the Common Era, has been determined by the Shansabanis' appearance in historical records, and their imperial rise, expansion and *dénouement* along these temporal lines. The current volume focuses on the Shansabanis' early history; their initial expansions beyond Ghur-Zamindawar (see maps, pp. xv and xvi); and their fracturing into separate, geographically distinct lineages (see Genealogy, p. xvii) – a confederate empire – all taking place during *c.* AH 510–580s/1120s–1180s CE (cf. Chapters 3–5). The emphasis of the present volume, then, is on relevant events dating to approximately seven decades of the twelfth century in what is modern Afghanistan. Such a specific temporal and spatial focus might imply that a historical overview of the early Shansabanis would be largely a question of recapitulating the information in textual sources and existing scholarship. In fact, this is far from the case, for reasons that are historical as much as they are historiographical.

Although obviously never devoid of "history" per se, nomadic and transhumant groups rarely encountered the need to record in written form the events constituting their past. The challenges of recuperating oral histories are well known, moreover, especially as orally transmitted narratives underwent "translation" upon becoming written.[1] Concomitantly, the court-centered nature of most imperial chronicles and other textual sources meant that nomads and other transhumant populations received only passing references, their appearances in texts occasioned primarily by interaction with the hegemonic "state" in a particular region.[2] Indeed, the elision – if not erasure – by contemporaneous textual sources of the nomadic past even of the great Saljuqs (tenth–twelfth centuries), and a parallel silence regarding the continuation of non-sedentist mores in their imperial phase,[3] are all amplified in the case of the geographically remote Shansabanis. But, in addition to being a question of general historical import, a view of the Shansabanis during the late eleventh–early twelfth centuries – even in broad strokes – furnishes important data to bear in mind as the later rulers' trajectory broadened into an imperial arc, encompassing the valleys of the Indus and ultimately the plains of northern India (cf. Chapter 6 and Volume II).

The absence of major trading centers within Ghur meant little to report for the early Arabic-language geographers,[4] or other authors such as the anonymous writer of the tenth-century *Hudud al-'Alam* (c. 982 CE) – which betrays the proclivities and aims of these authors (and their modern heirs) rather than the historical importance of the region. In a similar vein during the eleventh century, the Ghuris rarely arrested the attention of Ghaznavid-period chroniclers such as al-'Utbi (c. 961–1036/1040 CE) and Baihaqi (AH 385–469/995–1077 CE), and when they did, it was not in flattering terms: they were recipients of punitive action for their banditry along caravan routes. The three well-known Ghaznavid expeditions into Ghur – two by Sultan Mahmud (r. AH 389–421/999–1030) to the fortified settlement of Ahangaran on the Hari Rud (cf. Chapter 2) and Khwabin in southern Ghur, and a third by his son Mas'ud (eventually Sultan Mas'ud I, r. AH 421–432/1030–1041) to the fortress at Jurwas (map, p. xvi) – were motivated both by the cessation of previously stipulated tribute to the Ghaznavid treasury, and by the Ghuris' disruption of caravan traffic.[5]

Considering the practical impossibility of entire caravans traversing the difficult terrain of the region, the Ghuris' brigandage likely took place on the major routes radiating from Herat and essentially skirting Ghur itself, either proceeding northeast toward Balkh and eventually India through the Khyber and other Gandharan passes; or headed southeastward toward Tiginabad/Old Qandahar, Baluchistan, Sindh, and ultimately the Indo-Gangetic plains.[6] Although these reports provided few specific facts, such as exactly where the bandit raids took place or indeed the commodities the raiders sought in waylaying the caravans,[7] they did indicate in broad terms that at least segments of Ghur's inhabitants practiced some form of banditry, likely as a supplement to other modes of production.[8] Furthermore, the lack of sustained passage of outside populations through Ghur surely also impacted its linguistic culture, as the dialect of Persian spoken here – or perhaps another language altogether – required Prince Mas'ud to rely on translators during his campaign.[9] The prevailing understanding of the region up to the twelfth century has largely followed the eminent C. E. Bosworth's (1928–2015) characterization: it had "no towns of note, but only agricultural settlements and – [the] most typical feature of the landscape – fortified places and towers (*qasr, qala, hisar, kushk*)"[10] marked a politically fragmented region, whose largely pastoral and bellicose inhabitants "practis[ed] agriculture and banditry [and] specialized in the production of weapons and war equipment."[11]

While the overall picture of historical Ghur and Ghuris is further enriched throughout this volume (see esp. Chapter 2), the ongoing scholarly efforts to re-integrate nomadic and transhumant populations into fuller apprehensions of regional histories and economies should be noted here. For example, M. S. Mahmud's Persian-language monograph on the Shansabanis[12] has initiated a much-needed re-examination of the evidence pertinent to Ghur. Citing the plentiful natural resources and mines of the region, as well as its well-known commodity of slaves, this author proposed that Ghur must have been linked with transregional commercial networks despite the absence of such references in the historical texts.[13] After all, Ghur's oft-cited mountainous landscape surely presented more difficulty for outsiders seeking access *into* the region, than for those long familiar with the terrain as they transported their goods *out*.

Thereafter in the twelfth century, the macroscopic perspectives of universal histories such as Ya'qut's (AH 575–626/1179–1229 CE) *Mu'jam al-buldan* and Ibn al-Athir's (d. AH 630/1233 CE) often cited *al-Kamil fi al-Tarikh* both mentioned Ghur and its inhabitants only infrequently. Even though they were by now more properly the ruling Shansabanis – identified thus by writers such as Nizami 'Aruzi, and Juzjani (see below) – they nevertheless continued to play minor roles in the eyes of the universal historians. As was the case in texts of various genres from the previous centuries, the Shansabanis made appearances principally when they intersected with the larger imperial formations of the Saljuqs and the Khwarazm-shahs. The expanded historical gazes and *raisons d'être* of these universal histories, then, seemed to alienate further this corner of the eastern Persianate lands and its inhabitants from the flow of the larger Islamic world.[14]

But at the same time, by the mid-twelfth century and the Shansabanis' initial ascendancy as a regional politico-military presence, the influx of unknown or unfamiliar power-seekers – warlords becoming warrior kings, to adapt terms used by M. A. Asif and A. Anooshahr[15] – and indeed their resounding successes within the Persianate world, were all undeniable and even well-known phenomena. So much so, that the invention of royal genealogies for newcomers was an integral labor performed by the scholarly *literati* whom these new courts patronized (cf. below). These invented genealogies created "a teleology of Islamic monarchies, [adhering to the] logic of historiographic expectations," which obviously occluded the rising groups' *historical* origins.[16]

Such a set of impetuses and intentions inhered in *Tabaqat-i nasiri* (completed before 1260), a universal history within the eponymous *tabaqa* genre of Persian historical writing. The work's author was the jurist and accomplished courtier Minhaj al-Din Siraj Juzjani (AH 589–658/ 1193–1260 CE) who, moreover, had been brought up within the Shansabani royal household at Firuzkuh. Despite *Tabaqat*'s ostensibly universal and trans-temporal purview, the disproportionately long sections (Ar.-Pers. *tabaqa*) on the Shansabanis revealed Juzjani's true focus. Following in the established tradition of royal genealogies, the author bestowed upon the Shansabanis the expected lineage springing from pre-Islamic mythology, whose principal repository was the *Shah-nama* and the literary production it engendered.[17] Admittedly, the requisite *genealogical* "origin myth" created for the Shansabanis was unusual, descending through the figure of Azhd

Zahhak – a "repugnant figure in the Iranian lands farther to the west …
[but commanding] popularity in the region of Ghazna and Zabulistan."[18]

Indeed, Juzjani dutifully provided a surfeit of origin stories for the
obscure transhumant clan who would come to be recorded in his and
others' chronicles as the Shansabanis. Addressing an array of the historiographical registers of his time, the author also granted a seemingly
unassailable Islamic pedigree to his patrons, claiming their conversion to
Islam by none other than the *khalifa* 'Ali himself during the first century of
the Hijra.[19] Additionally, Chapter 2 posits that Juzjani couched a possible
reference to their rural and probably nomadic-transhumant origins and
the beginnings of their transformation to elite status: A story in *Tabaqat*
centered on the Shansabanis' mythical progenitor Amir Banji and the
friendly Jewish merchant who became his ally and advisor comes across as
the parable-like narrative of upward politico-economic mobility. As apoc-
ryphal as the story undoubtedly is, we are nonetheless tempted to credit
Juzjani with an uncanny prescience, as if he had laid the crumbs along the
evidentiary trail sought by the modern investigator.

Tabaqat ensued from Juzjani's own family history and recollections. The
author was close to and invested in the Shansabanis' activities in Khurasan
(modern Afghanistan and contiguous areas; map, p. xv), as a result produc-
ing a virtually unique account of the early dynastic history of his patrons.[20]
Additionally, *Tabaqat* drew from another, equally first-hand work that
is unfortunately no longer extant: a versified genealogy by Fakhr al-Din
Mubarak-shah al-Marwarruzi (d. AH 601/1205 CE).[21] This Persian-Arabic
poet and writer on astronomy had dedicated the work to Sultan 'Ala'
al-Din Husain *Jahan-suz* (r. AH 544–556/1150–1161 CE), and thereafter had
continued in royal service, being mentioned as a *nadim* in the retinue of
Sultan Ghiyath al-Din Muhammad ibn Sam (r. AH 558–599/1163–1203 CE).
Juzjani apparently consulted the genealogy in the possession of Mah Malik,
the daughter of Sultan Ghiyath al-Din residing at Firuzkuh.[22]

Ghur's main economies of nomadism–transhumance rather than
commerce, and the region's general difficulty of access meant that the
aforementioned universal histories, such as Ibn al-Athir's *Kamil*, often
gathered information that was second-hand – though it was not necessarily unreliable (cf. below). Moreover, rather than re-litigating the
factuality of reported events among historical sources – already undertaken by others[23] – Juzjani and his *Tabaqat* act as the primary textual
interlocutors throughout this volume. Not only is *Tabaqat* the sole
surviving work essentially devoted to the Shansabanis, it also furnishes
the most fleshed out account of their early trajectory prior to the eastward expansions of the Ghazna branch – albeit according to its author's
priorities (cf. below and Chapters 2–4). Juzjani's own professional and
geographical movements curiously recapitulated those of his Shansabani
patrons: he faithfully served them throughout much of his life, also

from Lahore with the addition of their eastern territories, until their demise in the second decade of the thirteenth century. The Mongol campaigns of the 1220s CE compelled Juzjani to take refuge in Delhi, where he completed *Tabaqat* sometime before his death in 1260 CE.[24] But beyond this ontogenetic resonance between author and subject, *Tabaqat* also presents rare insights: throughout the work, subtle but discernible indices emerge of Juzjani grappling with the tensions between the "historiographic expectations" of twelfth-century Persian historical writing, and his own vested interests in crafting his patrons' memorial power for posterity. What we learn from these tensions, and the fissures between expectations and "reality," will be discussed later in the chapter and throughout this volume.

Attaining Kingship: Perso-Islamic Cultures of Power

The historical overview of the early Shansabanis in the latter part of this chapter reveals the *lacunae* that persist in our knowledge of their activities, even after the marshalling of evidence from material–cultural sources such as numismatics and architectural patronage. But while the *minutiae* of the Shansabanis' rise to regional and then transregional ascendancy may not be fully perceivable, tracing even its broad contours presents the opportunity to reflect on the Persianate ecumene specifically during the twelfth century. This temporally focused analytical gaze on the admittedly *longue durée* historical phenomenon of the Persianate permits, I believe, an enrichment of its more punctual manifestations.

At variance with recent reconsiderations of the concept of the "Persianate" – introduced by M. Hodgson in the last quarter of the twentieth century – I propose that, for the place and time of our investigation, "Perso-Islamic" is a more apt descriptive term for the elite cultures discussed forthwith.[25] Furthermore, rather than conceiving of these cultures of power, or prestige cultures, as *in*accessible except to those already within their ambit – that is, elites begetting elites – we must concede that courts throughout central and western Eurasia were often established by newcomers to the Persianate cultural world. What made this possible?

In attempting to answer such a broad question, I do not aim to define per se Perso-Islamic cultures of power, as they differed in their details at each court according to myriad historical contingencies (see, e.g., Chapter 3). Instead, it is more productive to adopt an inverted approach: what aspects of these prestige cultures facilitated access to kingship for ambitious interlopers such as the Shansabanis? Taking a cross-section of the twelfth century, and particularly the intersecting imperial formations of the Ghaznavids, the Saljuqs, and, eventually, the Shansabanis in what is now Afghanistan (map, p. xv), we can propose some tentative answers to the question of *how* unknown and patently non-elite groups attained kingship during this historical moment.[26]

Perso-Islamic prestige cultures should be understood as lexicons for rule, or collective "playbooks," which, when mastered and enacted, were tantamount to actuations of kingship in central–western Eurasia. It was this vast complex of elite cultures that effectively allowed populations far-removed from cultural capitals both in distance and lifestyles – especially nomadic and/or transhumant groups – to become power-brokers and even rulers. A group of unknown Ghuris exemplified such a process, eventually emerging as politico-military elites styling themselves as Shansabanis. Their emergence and other, similar developments throughout the Persianate world underscore – counterintuitively – the essentially *egalitarian* nature of Perso-Islamic court culture: a recognizable language or code of behavior that could enable kingship for pretty much anyone with the acumen to master it, and the resources to implement it.

What, then, were the aspects of twelfth-century Perso-Islamic cultures of power, or lexicons for rule, that up-and-coming groups could command in order to actuate kingship? Rather than static constituent elements or "ingredients" comprising these lexicons, it is more fruitful to conceive of three, overlapping and even fungible spheres of activity, with appreciably wide ranges of possible expressions: one sphere was Islamic confessionalism; a second, the large-scale patronage of cultural production in both *intellectual* as well as *material* forms; and third – though by no means least important – was mobility. It might seem unnecessary to point out that the last two spheres of activity were not peculiar to Perso-Islamic kingship, but they deserve emphasis as they were reiterative of Islamic confessionalism, and were arguably fundamental to the ascendancy of the principal powers of the twelfth-century Persianate world. All three of these overlapping spheres of activity left historical traces in the landscapes the Shansabanis inherited, thus providing them with aspirational models for attaining kingship. The rising Shansabanis came to act within these three spheres – elucidated further below – in tandem with accruing regional and then transregional economic, political, and military primacy.

Further, rather than conceiving of Perso-Islamic kingship as unbounded and infinitely reproducible, positing its approximate *geographical* extent is useful as a counterpoint. The Qarakhitay (*c.* 1125–1218 CE), a nomadic power who occupied the Balasaghun region (modern Kyrgyzstan) as of the 1130s CE, seemed to personify the eastern borders of Perso-Islamic kingship's currency. Although being in intimate contact with their vassals the Qarakhanids (*c.* 998–1213 CE) and other subordinate powers such as the Khwarazm-shahs (*c.* 995–1231 CE) – who espoused Perso-Islamic kingly affiliations – these polities' Qarakhitay overlords emphatically did not. Rather than converting to Islam, the Khitay rulers retained Buddhist–animist and Christian affiliations, creating a composite kingly culture of

"Khitan tribal elements [and] assimilated Chinese features" even as they ruled over a majority Muslim population comprising vassals and citizenry. In the eyes of their subject populations in Transoxiana and those farther east, Qarakhitay legitimacy was associated with the "high civilization" of China. Even though the region comprising this civilization was a concept often devoid of geographical and demographic accuracy, it behooved the Qarakhitay to maintain their eastern *loci* of aspirations: their imperial domains lay at the intersection of Persianate and Sinicizing ecumenes, throughout which such a projection of kingly personas was legible, effective, and accepted.[27]

During the twelfth century, the Yamini-Ghaznavids' (*c.* 998–1186 CE) instability attracted politico-military rivals into the pivotal region now bounded by modern Afghanistan. For the Ghaznavids, their core holdings in Zabulistan, al-Rukkhaj, and Zamindawar (map, p. xv) had collectively served as a springboard both toward the west, deep into Khurasan, as well as the east, to the Indus valleys and the north Indian plains. Thus, these core holdings were both strategically and commercially desirable (cf. Chapter 5). They were also where the Shansabanis were emerging as a local power and carving out the beginnings of their own imperium, embroiled in a long and fractious relationship with the Ghaznavids (see below and Chapters 2 and 3). The Shansabanis' rise in the fourth through eighth decades of the twelfth century also instigated confrontations with the Saljuqs (tenth–mid-twelfth centuries) as the latter sought suzerainty over the smaller polities on their eastern frontiers (cf. below), and the Khwarazm-shahs (twelfth–thirteenth centuries) and Qarakhanids (tenth–early thirteenth centuries), who were also attempting territorial expansion.[28] Afghanistan, then, was the canvas upon which the trajectories of the Persianate ecumene's major empires – which eventually included the Shansabanis – intertwined throughout the twelfth century.[29]

Although on quite different geographical scales, the spectacular debut of Saljuq power in the Persianate world during the eleventh century, and the meteoric rise of the Shansabanis in the twelfth, evince fascinating historical and historiographical parallels. Most significantly, the Saljuqs and Shansabanis were interlopers, entering from "outside" the elite Perso-Islamic prestige cultures they subsequently deployed toward kingship. The Saljuqs' Turkic *ethnie* and earliest associations with the territories of the tenth-century Khazars (in modern west Kazakhstan) were not their only exogenous characteristics; the principles of socio-political organization and the many cultural traditions arising from their nomadic life-world also rendered them largely "other" to the Persianate regions they came to dominate.[30]

The Shansabanis' ethnic and geographical origins technically lay *within* this Persianate world: their *ethnie* is generally thought to have derived from Iranian–Tajik populations[31]; and one could conceive of Ghur's geography as a "forgiving" zone permeably overlapping both the westernmost reaches of the Indic sphere and the eastern peripheries of the Persianate. But this borderland location combined with their own life-world along the nomad–urban continuum, creating palpable socio-political, linguistic (cf. above), cultural, and even epistemological distances between them and – to adapt Ernest Gellner's term – the "Great Tradition" of Perso-Islamic elite lifeways.[32] Indeed, as further discussed in Chapter 2, the topographic and ecological realities of the region of Ghur apparently compounded these *conceptual* (rather than physical) distances from the Persianate ecumene, though in the end both the tangible and the *in*tangible spaces were surmountable.

As also described in detail in the Chapter 2, the Ghuris (and among them the pre-imperial Shansabanis) were probably exposed to localized practices of Islam – perhaps even observing some of its religious mores – by the later eleventh century, if not before. It will be further argued that, in tandem with their gradual but discernible rise to regional prominence or "incipient" kingship, the early Shansabanis *overtly* adopted the trappings of Islamic confessionalism – part of the "playbook" of kingship prevalent in their specific milieu – in the first three or four decades of the twelfth century. Perso-Islamic patterns of kingship were initiated and sustained throughout the region *via* the precedents set by the Ghaznavids and reinforced by the Saljuqs – between whose territorial ambitions fell the home regions of the emerging Shansabanis (map, p. xv). Due to this serendipitous location, the Shansabanis were cast in the role of inheritors and eventual contributors to these rich cultural landscapes. In keeping with the above-described, overlapping spheres of activity that permitted the entry of outsiders into the complex of Perso-Islamic kingship, the beginnings of the Shansabanis' Islamic confessionalism were perceptibly declared – and thus retrievable by later investigators – by means of their *patronage* of architectural as well as other types of cultural production (cf. esp. Chapters 2 and 3).

A century or so before the recordable emergence of the Shansabanis – just after the establishment of the Ghaznavids (see below) – the Saljuqs had entered Persianate frames of reference. Sources generally from outside the Arabic–Persian scholarly traditions candidly assessed the eponymous Saljuq ibn Duqaq's embrace of Islam as part of a "design of conquest in the Muslim world": the historical texts' prevarications regarding the reasons behind Saljuq's fateful choice might have served as historiographical synecdoche of the western Turkic populations' uneven Islamic conversions as they encountered Islamic socio-religious practices filtering eastward along the byways of commerce, and met with again *via* the Saljuqs' own westward migrations.[33] Although the specific details remain conjectural, Islamic confessionalism and its manifestations became incumbent upon the Saljuqs as they entered the Persianate realms. In AH 431/1040 CE, the defeat of the Ghaznavid Sultan Mas'ud I (r. 1030–1041 CE) at Dandanqan by Saljuq ibn Duqaq's grandsons Tughril (r. AH 431–455/1040–1063 CE) and Chagri (AH 432–452/1040–1060 CE) meant that various constellations of their descendants held sway across central–western Eurasia – initiating prosperity as well as abundant building that would help define the architectural cultures of Iran and Central Asia until the Mongol incursions.

To their great advantage, the Saljuqs also inherited a sophisticated politico-cultural landscape: it was replete with centuries of accreted administrative infrastructure thanks to the multiple pre-Islamic imperial formations that had spanned western–central Eurasia.[34] Only the most recent among these had been the Sasanians (third–seventh centuries CE), whose "professionalization of a literate administrative class and the culture of the court ... were elaborations of what had gone before,"[35] and in turn were developed further according to the changing requirements of ever-burgeoning elites during the eighth through eleventh centuries. To be sure, the Saljuq sultans were notable patrons of architecture, but their works were particularly aligned with proclaiming their Islamic confessionalism (cf. below), with palace architecture serving very punctual functions.[36] In addition to the sultans, the upper echelons of military, political, and scribal personnel throughout the empire – part of the Saljuqs' inherited administrative infrastructure – were also patrons to a significant degree.

The city of Isfahan had held geographical, strategic, and economic significance at least since Sasanian times, becoming a centrally administered city – akin to a regional capital – for the Saljuqs in AH 443/1051 CE. It boasted a major *masjid-i jami* (congregational mosque) as of the mid-ninth century, which would undergo expansion, renovation, and even reconfiguration through the Safavid period.[37] Given the city's local and transregional importance, Saljuq rulers and their courtiers continued to patronize architecture and institutions throughout the city to maintain its prosperity. Approaching our period of investigation, we should highlight the interventions in Isfahan's overall fabric during the late eleventh–twelfth centuries, when major architectural projects attested to the vast array of personages and impetuses underlying this patronage.

Sultan Malik Shah (r. AH 464–485/1072–1092 CE) directed his famous *vazir* Nizam al-Mulk (AH 409–485/1018–1092 CE) to construct the Isfahan *jami*'s south dome *c.* AH 479–480/1086–1087 CE (Figures 1.1 and 1.2), possibly in response to the new dome upon Damascus's Umayyad mosque, commissioned by the *vazir* Abu Nasir Ahmad ibn Fadl in AH 475/1082 CE after a fire. In turn, Nizam al-Mulk's much younger political rival Taj al-Mulk engaged in dangerous intrigue with the elder statesman to win favor with the sultan, in part by commissioning a smaller but "in many ways ... aesthetically more successful" northern dome within the already magnificent mosque (Figures 1.1 and 1.3). Not long after, the *isfah-salar* Abi [*sic*] al-Fath ibn Muhammad commissioned a soaring *minar*

Figure 1.1 *Congregational Mosque, Isfahan, Iran, founded tenth century* CE, *exterior: view from east.* © *Photograph Alka Patel 2011.*

Figure 1.2 *Congregational Mosque, Isfahan, 1086–1087* CE, *exterior: north dome.* © *Photograph Alka Patel 2011.*

(Figures 1.4–1.6), now known as *Chihil Dukhtaran* ("40 Daughters"), in the city's Jubara quarter (AH 501/1107–1108 CE).[38]

Other rungs of society emerged throughout Isfahan's prosperous surrounding areas. An "ascetic" (Pers. *zahid*) commissioned a sizeable *minar* and contiguous mosque at the village of Gar, with the date of AH 515/1121 CE and his name inscribed in simple Kufic on the *minar*'s octagonal plinth. And at the northern village of Sin, members of an important local family of *qadi*s patronized a mosque and *minar* (Figures 1.7–1.9) dated to AH 526/1132 CE and AH 529/1134–1135 CE, respectively – the *minar* bearing the earliest epigraphically dated exterior use of blue-glazed tiles for the Kufic *bismillah* at its current summit (Figure 1.9).[39]

Collectively, much of the enormous corpus of late eleventh–

Figure 1.3 *Congregational Mosque, Isfahan, c. 1090 CE, interior: south dome chamber.* © *Photograph Alka Patel 2011.*

Figure 1.4 Minar *known as Chihil Dukhtaran, c. 1100 CE, Jubara quarter, Isfahan.* © *Photograph Alka Patel 2011.*

twelfth-century structures of the Iranian Plateau constituted the cosmopolitan expressions of what has been termed "Saljuq-patronized" architectural culture.[40] Building upon "what had gone before," the array of public/"civic" and palatial buildings subscribing to it were individual and varied, sharing general but uniquely expressed characteristics. Nevertheless, the combination of salient features circumscribing this architectural culture is identifiable: baked brick as the primary building material, with an increasing use of blue-glazed tiles for decoration; lofty hemispherical domes; squat, pointed arches; emphatic portals (*pishtaq*); extensive and stylistically varied, usually painted, architectural epigraphy; brick and stucco decorations of repeated geometric and floral-arabesque iconographies (deriving from Abbasid-period stucco practices), also painted; and, where present, cylindrical and soaring, "pencil-thin" *minar*s.[41] For our purposes,

Figure 1.5 *Chihil Dukhtaran* minar, *historical inscription panel.* © *Photograph Alka Patel 2011.*

this architectural culture expanded eastward with the Saljuqs' imperial ambitions.

The expansion of Saljuq imperialism from the principal cities of Rayy and Isfahan predictably followed well-trodden routes of commerce, communication, and pilgrimage (map, p. xv). Toward the east, the magnificently arresting elite accommodation known as Robat Sharaf (Figure 1.10) attested not only to this eastward expansion, but to several other factors besides: it was an important indication of the continued mobility of Saljuq rule (cf. below) well into the twelfth century, and of the typological variety encompassed within the prevalent architectural culture. Located on the principal route connecting Marv and Nishapur, Robat Sharaf formed a waystation for Saljuq officials and probably also the sultan and his immediate entourage. Based on its epigraphic program, André Godard (1948) proposed that the Robat was initially constructed *c.* AH 508/1114–1115 CE, perhaps even by Sharaf al-Din Abu Tahir ibn Sa'd al-Din ibn 'Ali al-Qummi, who was governor of Marv and eventually Sultan Sanjar's (r. AH 511–552/1118–1157 CE) *vazir*. Other surviving epigraphic remains indicated extensive renovations in AH 549/1154–1155 CE, possibly in the wake of the destructive Oghüz rebellions against Saljuq authority, which resulted in Sanjar's capture and humiliating imprisonment between AH 548 and 551/1153 and 1156 CE.[42] The Robat's brick construction, courtyard–*ivan* configuration (Figure 1.11), and the decorative repertory of extensive epigraphy and floral–geometric motifs (Figures 1.12 and 1.13) altogether provide an exemplar of non-religious building within the so-called Saljuq-patronized

Figure 1.6 *Chihil Dukhtaran* minar, *topmost epigraphic bands.* © *Photograph Alka Patel 2011.*

architectural culture of Khurasan. Beyond such waystations, Saljuq political power culminated at the major urban areas along principal routes of travel, so that regional nodes such as Tus-Nishapur and Herat became centers of their own radii of political and architectural–cultural dissemination (cf. Chapter 4).

As discussed in greater detail in Chapter 2, with Saljuq inroads into the Balkh and Sistan regions as early as the mid-eleventh century,[43] the above-mentioned "Saljuq-patronized" architectural culture also found manifestations in Afghanistan. The *minar* of Daulatabad, south of Balkh (Figure 2.19), for example, subscribed to the cylindrical profile of western Saljuq-period *minar*s, but the Daulatabad proportions conveyed a drum-like impression, rather than a "pencil-thin" one. Moreover, the epigraphic program was monumentalized on the shaft, proclaiming its patronage by the Saljuq *vazir* Abu Ja'far Muhammad ibn 'Ali (d. AH 515/1118 CE), the date of construction (AH 502/1108–1109 CE), and even the stucco worker and carpenter.[44] The general observations regarding proportions and epigraphy are also applicable to the known – though no longer surviving – *minar* at Qasimabad, near Zahidan (before AH 559/1164 CE) (Figure 2.18), about 240 km southwest of Zaranj-Nad-i Ali (in modern Iran's Sistan and Baluchistan Province). Qasimabad's equally elaborate epigraphic program apparently did not refer to Saljuq authority, mentioning instead two of the rulers of the local Nasri *malik*s of Nimruz/Sistan,[45] though the *minar*'s overall format certainly derived from western architectural–cultural ideas.

In the sense of coming from the "outside," both the Saljuqs and the emerging Shansabanis formed a contrast to the hegemonic power of the Ghaznavids, already entrenched in the Ghazna region by the end of the tenth century. While the Shansabanis eventually emerged from the anonymity of central Afghanistan's nomad–urban continuum, the Ghaznavids' progenitors had been youths captured as slaves from Eurasia's eastern Turkic steppes. But thereafter, these youths were effectively incorporated into royal service farther west, absorbed into and reared within the influential Samanids' (ninth–tenth centuries) courtly ethos as *ghulam*s and important courtiers on the rise (cf. Introduction). They were Turks who had nonetheless become *in*siders of the tenth-century Samanid court: the elite environment *par excellence*, the crucible that forged courtly styles and tastes especially *via* Persian literary production (as well as Arabic), casting long shadows over the following centuries of cultural patronage and consumption – the "Persianate millennium."[46] Indeed, we recall the supplanting of a purely Turkic origin for Mahmud Ghaznavi's father Sabuktigin (d. AH 421/999 CE) with a mixed Sasanian genealogy (cf. Introduction, notes).[47] As the Samanids waned and their *ghulam*s increased their independence in the

Figure 1.7 Mihrab *of mosque at Sin, north of Isfahan, c. 1132 CE. © Photograph Alka Patel 2011.*

Figure 1.8 Minar *of mosque complex, Sin, c. 1134–1135 CE. © Photograph Alka Patel 2011.*

Figure 1.9 *Blue-glazed, topmost epigraphic bands of* minar, *Sin. © Photograph Alka Patel 2011.*

areas of Balkh, Bamiyan, and ultimately Ghazna, the new rulers largely followed their erstwhile overlords' royal protocols, administration, and patterns of patronage.[48]

The Yamini-Ghaznavids' kingly context included, however, ineluctable specificities such as the material remains of previous political powers and religio-cultural presences. Their co-optation of these pre-existing strata is perhaps best demonstrated in the architectural remains surviving at the royal sites of Ghazna and Bust-Lashkari Bazar. The grand palatial architecture there (Figure 1.14) – discussed in detail in Chapter 5 – did not diverge substantially from the non-religious buildings surviving throughout the Persianate world, in fact echoing the courtyard–*ivan* plan at (for example) Robat Sharaf, complete with intimate oratories tucked away within royal ceremonial and reception spaces (Figure 1.12; compared with Lashkari Bazar's South Palace [Chapter 5]). However, monumental *minar*s (Figure 1.15) – towering above the central areas of the capital (Figure 1.14) and frequently encountered in other Afghan regions (cf. above and Chapters 2–4) – were distinct at Ghazna. Rather than the unmistakable "pencil-thin" cylinders marking urban fabrics in the central Saljuq lands,

Figure 1.10 *Robat Sharaf, near Sarakhs, Razavi Khurasan Province, Iran, 1114–1115, 1154–1155* CE. © *Photograph Alka Patel 2011.*

Figure 1.11 *Robat Sharaf, second, inner courtyard. © Photograph Alka Patel 2011.*

Figure 1.12 *Robat Sharaf, oratory. © Photograph Alka Patel 2011.*

the Ghazna *minar*s were originally two-storied, with a bottom stellate shaft supporting a tapering cylinder on top (cf. Figure I.20). Given the rarity of stellate *minar*s in the region – *comparanda* known only in Sistan (cf. Chapter 2) – the Ghazna examples have incited debate as to their precedents and/or inspirations.

The Yamini precinct of Ghazna lies within distant but visible view of the composite Buddhist–Brahmanical Hindu site of Tepe Sardar (fl.

Figure 1.13 *Robat Sharaf, intrados of arch with stucco decoration.*
© *Photograph Alka Patel 2011.*

through *c.* ninth century CE),[49] 4 km to the southeast. Given the wide-spread presence of Buddhism (and to some extent also the Shaivite branch of Brahmanical Hinduism[50]) throughout Afghanistan into the ninth century, W. Ball recently proposed the stellate plans to be "continuation[s] of the Buddhist tradition."[51] Skilled workers crafted "stepped stellate"

Figure 1.14 *Palace of Mas'ud III, 1099–1115, Ghazni, excavation site, foundation walls of buildings and apartments surrounding courtyard.* © *Photograph Josephine Powell c. 1960. Harvard Fine Arts Library, Special Collections.*

Figure 1.15 *Minarets of Ghazni: minaret of Mas'ud III, 1099–1115, and minaret of Bahram Shah, 1118–1152, distant view.* © *Photograph Josephine Powell c. 1960. Harvard Fine Arts Library, Special Collections.*

votive *stupa*s (Figure 1.16) for pious donors seeking spiritual merit at the region's already wealthy and powerful Buddhist monastic institutions, the Tepe Sardar example (among the numerous other Buddhist monasteries throughout Afghanistan) being one site located very near to the time and

Figure 1.16 *The Buddhist site of Tapa Sardar, Ghazni, Afghanistan, third–ninth century* CE: *upper terrace, star-shaped stupa (eighth century). F. Bonardi, neg. 7410–9. © Italian Archaeological Mission in Afghanistan, 1968.*

place of Ghaznavid ascendancy. The rarity of Ghazna's stellate *minar*s, and yet their proximity to such a prominent monastic establishment, renders Buddhist precedents that much more plausible. The Yamini–Ghaznavids, then, adapted to and even capitalized upon the cultural landscape *they* inherited, to create distinct interpretations of the Persianate world's cosmopolitan architectural cultures.

Notwithstanding the differences in geographical scale mentioned before, a further resonance between the Saljuqs and the Shansabanis is worth highlighting: the Saljuqs' disconcertingly rapid and thorough permeation of the Persianate lands and Anatolia – and ultimately even the very heart of caliphal authority in Baghdad by the mid-eleventh century – forms an intriguing parallel to the profound and reverberating effects of the Shansabanis' eastward campaigns deep into the north Indian *duab* during the last decade of the twelfth century. As noted in the Introduction and argued in detail in Volume II, it was the Shansabanis' politico-military and

architectural footprint in this region – more than the Ghaznavids' plundering raids – that irreversibly ushered the entire Indian subcontinent into
the Persianate world, and as one of the principal *loci* wherein Persianate
cultural production not only thrived, its practitioners also engaged with
Indic linguistic–cultural ambits for the following millennium.

These astounding successes – perhaps especially noteworthy for "outsiders" like the Saljuqs and Shansabanis – all underscore mobility, the third
proposed sphere of activity of Perso-Islamic prestige cultures, which made
kingship accessible for ambitious newcomers to the Persianate ecumene. It
might appear evident that the Saljuqs' and the Shansabanis' origins within
nomadic and transhumant lifeways, respectively, and their consequent
seasonal movements predisposed them to regular traversal of large distances across contiguous yet diverse eco-cultural terrains. In turn, adaptation to differing climates and topographies was a perennial feature of their
lifeworlds. Furthermore, flexible and consultative community and military
decision-making, and lack of investment in provisions and infrastructure
might have made nomad armies less reliable (see below), but, on the other
hand, the net positives were their virtually nil "operating expenses," agility,
and quick recovery from defeats. Arguably, all of these lived experiences
coalesced into a form of "cultural capital," enabling the expansive imperial
formations they managed to create across diverse landscapes.[52]

As noted above, the Yamini–Ghaznavids also conducted annual campaigns for plunder deep into the north Indian *duab* throughout the first
half of the eleventh century, the later sultans reinitiating them for a time
during the century's last decades.[53] Although the Ghaznavids ostensibly
adhered to a sedentist and overall more traditional courtly model, their
India campaigns in particular could have nonetheless combined "military purposes and seasonal migrations."[54] However, the Ghaznavids
never achieved a north Indian footprint akin to that of the Shansabanis,
whose "cultural capital" at least in part allowed them to succeed where the
Ghaznavids had not. In light of the historical trajectories and territorial
expansions of both the Saljuqs and the Shansabanis within the Persianate
world, it would seem that true mobility – *without* the rigidity and expense
of reigning courtly cultures – acquired a new significance for Perso-Islamic
kingship during the twelfth century.

Integrating Sources: A History of the Early Shansabanis

With a cognizance of the spheres of activity making it possible for
newcomers to the Persianate world to access kingship – specifically
Perso-Islamic kingship – we might more credulously envision the rapid
rise to elite status of a previously unknown group of Ghuris from central
Afghanistan's nomad–urban continuum to become the Shansabanis of

the mid-twelfth century. As also noted above, however, the contemporary authors examined historical vicissitudes while adhering to "historiographical expectations." The unidirectional linearity of hindsight, for example, is a characteristic to be borne in mind for *all* court chronicles (and no less for modern scholarship), which at least partly explains the inclusions *and* exclusions of events from textual narratives. The historical authors' investments – to varying degrees – in highlighting their royal patrons in the greater flow of history (such as it was conceived), and in "bending" the constitutive events *a posteriori* into a concatenation, ultimately resulted in the fabrication of a historical arc with a beginning, an apogee, and a *dénouement*.

It comes as little surprise, then, that the known texts – including Juzjani's *Tabaqat* – leave many unknowns for the period of this volume's focus on the early Shansabanis in modern Afghanistan and Pakistan, that is, prior to their entry into the north Indian *duab*. Partly in response to this historiographical state of affairs, one of the fundamental premises of this two-volume project is that architecture and material culture – especially archaeological finds and numismatics – serve as indispensable *primary* sources supplying evidentiary data, both enriching and at times apparently contradicting their textual counterparts.

In the fifth and sixth decades of the twelfth century, the Shansabanis' star seemed to rise steadily: their sphere of influence had rapidly extended beyond their encampments and/or seasonal settlements in historical Ghur. It is unclear precisely what prompted 'Izz al-Din's (c.1100–1146 CE) third son Saif al-Din (c.1146–1149)[55] to divide the ancestral territories – likely definable by areas of transhumance and cultivation patterns (i.e., pastures, agricultural areas, and dwellings[56]) – among his six brothers and himself (Genealogy, p. xvii). But it would not be unfounded to suggest that a role was played therein by customary laws governing property inheritance in some nomadic societies, observable among modern groups.[57]

With the Ghaznavids and – especially after their defeat at Dandanqan in AH 432/1040 CE – the Saljuqs both being distant powers whose authority was manifest principally at important regional centers such as Zaranj (Sistan),[58] Herat, and Balkh, Ghur's internal developments progressed with only rare outside intervention.[59] The overall outcome was a rapid, multi-directional expansion of Shansabani dominion far beyond the parameters of their seasonal transhumance (map, p. xvi), with a nominal recognition of the larger powers' suzerainty expressed mainly through tribute and ceremonial acknowledgment, for example, in the *khutba* and on coinage. Concurrently, the Shansabanis fractured into a loose confederacy of independent lineages based at Firuzkuh, Bamiyan, and ultimately Ghazna (see Chapters 3–5).

Juzjani's consistent implication of the paramountcy of the Shansabanis at Firuzkuh was surely overlaid on familial–political contestations. Some hierarchy probably inhered in the designation of Qutb al-Din as *malik al-jibal* – a grandiose title implying the designee's importance.[60] But at the same time, Qutb al-Din was 'Izz al-Din's second son, not his first and eldest, and neither he nor the eldest, Fakhr al-Din Mas'ud, were born to "the mother of the other Sultans." Further, it is unclear whether Qutb al-Din appropriated the title *himself* or, if not, why and when exactly it was bestowed upon him. It is not impossible that the somewhat steadier, commercially derived prosperity of Jam-Firuzkuh (see Chapter 2) enriched and emboldened Qutb al-Din to adopt the title. Such an emphatic self-elevation could justifiably have resulted from his otherwise secondary status as the son of a mother from a lesser pedigree.[61]

The situation was similar with the Shansabani lineage of Bamiyan, whose scions had come into possession of a region probably even more prosperous than Firuzkuh, thanks to its centuries-long centrality within commercial and pilgrimage networks (cf. Chapter 3). Several decades before Juzjani recorded the Firuzkuh rulers' concession of the title of *sultan* to their Bamiyan cousins in AH 586/1190 CE, coins minted during the reign of Fakhr al-Din Mas'ud (AH 540–558/1145–63 CE) at the elusive site of Parwan/Farwan, somewhere north of Kabul, claimed the title of *al-sultan al-'azam* for him.[62] Furthermore, Juzjani reported that as the eldest, Fakhr al-Din was not satisfied with his appanage of Bamiyan and, toward the end of his reign, unsuccessfully attempted the usurpation of Jam-Firuzkuh from his nephews Shams al-Din and Shihab al-Din – later Sultan Ghiyath al-Din (d. AH 599/1203 CE) and Sultan Mu'izz al-Din (d. AH 602/1206 CE), respectively.[63] From this admittedly fragmentary evidence, it could nonetheless be ventured that Juzjani, in keeping with the "historiographic expectations" of his time, attempted to salvage for posterity a Firuzkuh-centered Shansabani dynasty from what was in reality a periodic confederacy of disparate lineages. Often bitterly contentious in their own time, the author elected instead to portray the Shansabanis in a generally unitary light.[64] Thus, the actual impetuses and contingencies behind the reported events, along with their protagonists, are often to be discerned in non-textual historical indices.

The unforeseen and successive deaths of the first three *malik*s of Jam-Firuzkuh thrust to the forefront the dynamism of 'Izz al-Din's fifth son, 'Ala' al-Din Husain (r. AH 544–556/1150–1161 CE). Motivated by his brother Qutb al-Din's death at the Ghazna court of Bahram Shah (r. AH 512–547/1118–1152 CE) – even though a quarrel between Qutb al-Din and his brothers drove him thence in the first place – Saif al-Din "brought an army to Ghazna and captured it … and the first person of this clan to take the title of Sultan was Sultan Suri." Bahram Shah returned to Ghazna, however, and executed Saif al-Din and his advisors in a most humiliating way. In turn, Baha' al-Din died of "excessive anxiety and grief for the death of his brothers" while he was en route to Ghazna to exact vengeance.[65]

This last death provided 'Ala' al-Din an excuse he could not refuse. Ostensibly a thirst for vengeance but also a defiant personality, and doubtless a growing appetite for power and dominion – all underwritten by the Jam-Firuzkuh treasury replenished by the locality's commercial machinery – converged to impel 'Ala' al-Din Husain to deal a decisive blow to the Ghaznavids. In AH 544/1150 CE, while his eldest half-brother Fakhr al-Din Mas'ud remained at Kashi (Bamiyan), 'Ala' al-Din set out against the Ghaznavid sultan Bahram Shah and his forces to avenge the deaths of his three older brothers, two directly and one indirectly at the hands of the increasingly villainous Yaminis.[66] According to Juzjani's description of the confrontation's beginnings – unfolding upon the plains of Zamindawar, where both forces had converged – Bahram Shah had calculated that the mere mention of Indian elephants would deter 'Ala' al-Din from direct military engagement.[67] But the defiant Shansabani one-upped the Yamini's apotropaic threat, promising to match the elephants with the *Kharmil*, which was in reality a human "weapon" in the form of two champion Ghuri warriors whom 'Ala' al-Din ordered to bring down an elephant each. After the Kharmils' fulfillment of their ordered tasks and other disheartening setbacks, the Ghaznavid forces were defeated and Bahram Shah temporarily fled to India. Not satisfied with this defeat and still seeking thorough vengeance, 'Ala' al-Din immediately marched to Ghazna. The destruction he and his warriors unleashed on the Ghaznavid capital was also the fate of the royal sites of Lashkari Bazar and Bust, which he plundered and burned on his way back to Ghur from Zamindawar (cf. below).

Perhaps it was to be expected that, intoxicated with the avenging victory over Ghazna and its rulers, 'Ala' al-Din Husain shortly afterward openly challenged Saljuq authority, withholding the stipulated tribute of the famous Ghuri war equipment (among other items). Although not mentioned in Juzjani's *Tabaqat* – but recorded in Ibn al-Athir's *Kamil* – during the course of protracted military engagements in the vicinity of Herat, 'Ala' al-Din occupied this major commercial and cultural center long enough to issue coins with the Herat mint stamp.[68] But in a twist of events worthy of dramatization, in AH 547/1152/3 CE the well-known battle at Nab – a location between Chisht and Herat – determined 'Ala' al-Din's foreseeable future: the large-scale defection of Oghüz, Khalaj, and Turk horsemen from the Shansabanis to the Saljuqs brought about 'Ala' al-Din's defeat and even imprisonment within Sanjar's camp; although, the Shansabani ruler's quick wit earned him favor with Sanjar, who made him one of his boon companions and eventually released him.[69]

The reign of 'Ala' al-Din Husain and its significance, particularly for the Shansabanis of Firuzkuh, is gradually becoming clearer.[70] Recently, M. O'Neal (2016) presented coinage issued in the name of 'Ala' al-Din Husain that was probably minted at Ghazna *c*. AH 556/1161 CE, perhaps throwing a different light on this sultan's intended ambitions for the capital: the minting of coins there in his "second reign" – that is, the years after his release from Saljuq captivity in AH 548/1153 CE until his death in AH 556/1161 CE – strongly indicates that the sultan again besieged and even occupied Ghazna toward the end of his rule. This may hint that his earlier victory against Bahram Shah in AH 544/1150 CE had also been intended as a conquest intended to integrate Ghazna within Shansabani territories, rather than an act of avenging destruction. All in all, even though 'Ala' al-Din's violent revenge earned him long-term infamy and the epithet *Jahan-suz* or "World Incendiary," Juzjani likely described the actual destruction at the sites with not a little hyperbole.[71]

Meanwhile, Bahram Shah eventually returned from India, and he and his sons presided at Ghazna for another decade. But 'Ala' al-Din Husain's rampage had been both a symptom and an exacerbation of their decline: the Ghaznavids' hold over their own capital could not withstand the violent Oghüz takeover in AH 557/1162 CE[72] – after 'Ala' al-Din had *again* briefly occupied the capital the year before (cf. above). The reign of the last Ghaznavid sultan Khusrau Shah (r. AH 452–479/1160–1186 CE) passed almost entirely in the Panjab. Thereafter, the Shansabanis effectively inherited both the Ghaznavids' opportunities and challenges, entering some erstwhile Ghaznavid territories with little effort, while also provoking and confronting the Saljuqs with mixed results (see Chapter 5).

'Ala' al-Din Husain's wildly unpredictable reign – marked by successes, failures, and dramatic recoveries – was of a piece with the unforeseen events that elevated him to the Firuzkuh throne in the first place. Although the untimely death of his older brother Sultan Baha' al-Din had benefited 'Ala' al-Din, his position was unsafe due to the existence of claimants to the Firuzkuh throne: Baha' al-Din's two young sons, Shams al-Din and Shihab al-Din. Although 'Ala' al-Din had the boys imprisoned in the fort of Wajiristan, fate restored their rightful prerogatives: upon 'Ala' al-Din's death, his son and successor Saif al-Din (r. AH 556–558/1161–1163 CE) ordered the release of his cousins from their ten-year imprisonment, but the latter's own unexpected death in AH 558/1163 CE meant that the older Shams al-Din was crowned Ghiyath al-Din, Sultan of Firuzkuh. Precisely what 'Ala' al-Din had tried to prevent had nonetheless come to pass.

Sultan Ghiyath al-Din's younger brother Shihab al-Din eventually went on to great successes of his own, including the establishment of a third Shansabani lineage (cf. map, p. xv; Genealogy, p. xvii; Chapters 4 and 5). Having captured Ghazna in AH 569/1173–1174 CE by means of a joint effort with his older brother Sultan Ghiyath al-Din, Shihab al-Din was eventually crowned Sultan Mu'izz al-Din,[73] and shortly thereafter went on to consolidate the ex-Ghaznavid holdings throughout Zamindawar. The younger Shansabani also "extracted Multan from the hands of the Qaramatis [Shi'a-affiliated Isma'ilis]" in AH 571/1175–1176 CE. This was a momentous period for the Firuzkuh Shansabanis as well.

According to Juzjani, in the same year "the armies of Ghur and Ghazna were prepared" for Herat: that is, possibly as reciprocation for support in the Ghazna victory, Ghiyath al-Din called upon his younger brother to join in the campaign. Their joint efforts were again successful, and the Shansabani forces took Herat from Baha' al-Tughril al-Sanjari, one of Sultan Sanjar's residual deputies. The occupation of this renowned city of eastern Khurasan also led to the submission of the *malik*s of Sistan, "who sent envoys and submitted themselves in unanimous service to the king [*padshah*, i.e., Ghiyath al-Din]."[74]

At this juncture, it is worthwhile considering the consequences of these victories upon the Shansabanis' changing military manpower. Nomadic contingents had been substantial within 'Ala' al-Din Husain's forces when he confronted Sanjar at Nab in AH 547/1152–1153 CE, and their defection was at least partially responsible for the Shansabanis' defeat. But with the victory at Ghazna, the Shansabanis surely gained access to Khurasan's *ghulam* economy, fueled by the large-scale demand for Turkic youths among all the ruling powers of the Persianate world; the old Yamini capital had been one of the principal regional markets for this specialized military labor.[75] Although the city's decade-long occupation by the Oghüz could have reduced the supply of *ghulam*s from the Eurasian steppe, circumstantial evidence would indicate that the flow was not altogether interrupted: after all, Mu'izz al-Din's eastward campaigns only grew in number and distance *after* the Ghazna victory (cf. below), ultimately resulting in the Shansabanis' foothold in the north Indian *duab* thanks in large part to the military skills and leadership of the well-known Mu'izzi *ghulam*s Qutb al-Din Aibeg,[76] Taj al-Din Yildiz, and Baha' al-Din Tughril (cf. Volume II).

The Herat victory – only about a year after that of Ghazna – would certainly have provided even greater access to the valuable military resource of *ghulam*s for westward campaigns, though these appear to have been less successful than their eastward counterparts. Although Shansabani coinage was minted at Marv (captured AH 597/1201 CE), and at Astarabad in Gurgan (possibly AH 600/1204 CE), it is curious that no issues are known from the pre-eminent Khurasani emporium of Nishapur, where a Shansabani victory over the Khwarazm-shahi forces in AH 597/1201 CE led to the city's occupation until AH 601/1205 CE. Moreover, with the possible exception of the tomb of the last Ghazna Shansabani ruler 'Ala' al-Din Muhammad (d. AH 602/1206 CE) west of Nishapur at Bistam (Figure 1.17),[77] there is no known Shansabani architectural patronage beyond Herat.

In the east, the last of the Yamini–Ghaznavids had essentially been relegated to Lahore as of the AH 570s/1170s CE, and Mu'izz al-Din seemed to be filling the politico-military vacuum left in their wake: in AH 574/1178 CE, he undertook his first – albeit unsuccessful – long-distance campaign, probably through Kurraman (west of Peshawar) and again *via* Multan-Uchh,

Figure 1.17 *Sheikh Bayazid complex, Bastam, Semnan Province, Iran: vaulted corridor (*Ilkhanid*) north of tomb of 'Ala' al-Din Muhammad of Bamiyan, d. at Ghazna 1206* CE. *© Photograph Alka Patel 2011.*

to Anahilavada-pattana in northern Gujarat (map, p. xv).[78] This was the capital of the mighty Chaulukyas, a ruling house that was paramount throughout northwestern India's coastal and inland regions – mapping onto the modern Indian states of Gujarat and southern Rajasthan – between the later tenth through early fourteenth centuries. According to Juzjani, the Chaulukya forces under either Mularaja II (r. 1176–1178) or his young successor Bhimadeva II (r. 1178–1242) repelled Mu'izz al-Din's attack, again in part with the use of war elephants.[79]

Evidently learning from this reverse, Mu'izz al-Din and his forces subsequently operated within shorter eastward *radii*. They conducted a successful campaign to Peshawar in AH 575/1179–1180 CE. But, after a show of force against the Ghaznavid sultan Khusrau Malik at Lahore in AH 577/1181 CE – the first of three such campaigns, as described below – Mu'izz al-Din again widened his circuit: in AH 578/1182 CE he marched to the Indus's *débouchement* at Dibul – now generally thought to be the archaeological site of Banbhore[80] – in southwestern Sindh, "captur[ing] the whole of that seaside country and, taking much wealth, he ordered return [to Ghazna]."[81] It is possible that, in lieu of possessing a maritime port in Gujarat, the Shansabani sultan aimed for neighboring Sindh: during the twelfth century, the famed Dibul was still a major riverine emporium on the Indus, serving as a crucial link between the Indian Ocean world and the overland routes upriver – important enough, in fact, to be preceded by at least one fortified bastion as the first line of defense from the Indus's sea access (see esp. Chapter 6).

Thereafter, it would appear that the status of the last Yamini–Ghaznavids required a final resolution. For all future incursions into the north Indian plains, unfettered possession of the important city of Lahore was necessary, given its pivotal location in the center of the Panjab and in practically a straight line between Ghazna and the heart of the Ganga–Yamuna *duab*.[82] This meant the eradication of any lingering Ghaznavid loyalties in the region. Thus, Mu'izz al-Din's second campaign to the Panjab in AH 581/1185 CE left destruction in its path around Lahore, and the posting of a loyal deputy at nearby Sialkot signaled the gradual cornering of the Ghaznavids within their last stronghold.[83]

It is unsurprising that, in response to this obvious aggression, Khusrau Malik mobilized his own forces to besiege Sialkot, forces that included contingents of Kukhar tribesmen.[84] Failure to capture the fort – and thus no reward for their trouble – led the Kukhars to desert Khusrau Malik. Largely defenseless, the last Ghaznavid ruler was finally captured by Mu'izz al-Din the following year (AH 582/1186 CE) and brought back to Ghazna. As if yet another trophy of the momentous Shansabani triumph over the Yamini–Ghaznavid house, Khusrau Malik was sent to Sultan Ghiyath al-Din at Firuzkuh, where the *minar* commemorating the capture of Ghazna already towered over the heart of the Firuzkuh

Shansabanis' *sard-sir* royal encampment (cf. Chapters 3–5). Thence, the last Ghaznavid sultan was dispatched to imprisonment and eventual death in Gharjistan.[85]

Notes

1. Cf., e.g., Tapper 1997: 32–33. Fredrik Barth's (1961) pioneering fieldwork among the Basseri of southern Iran during the mid-twentieth century actually revealed a polyglot milieu of Persian- and Turkish-speaking tribes, though his data collection relied on oral reports of remembered pasts. These reports were at times contradictory – e.g., regarding the tribe's hoary origins (Barth 1961: 52) – but surprisingly consistent about recent history and the formation of alliances and confederacies (Barth, 72ff., 86ff.). The Basseri's tendencies were to be contrasted to the Shahsevan, whose "different versions of origins … reflected … differing constructions of their identity" (Tapper 1997: 317). On the linguistic diversity *among* certain nomadic pastoralists in Iran and Afghanistan, cf. Tapper 1983: 11–12. See also Khazeni (2009) on the Bakhtyari of Iran, specifically the work known as *Tarikh-i Bakhtyari* (1910–1911), "a sweeping combination … [of] oral histories and geographical lore"; and Chapter 4.

2. See, e.g., Paul 2018b: 325–326 for the Oghüz nomads in Balkh and their intersections with the Saljuq presence there, and the historical authors' views of "Khurasani history of this period in terms of a sedentary–nomad dichotomy, a perspective that continues to inform modern scholarly literature." Admittedly, the data of textual sources – additionally narrowed by their focus on reigns, courts, and dynasties – can be supplemented with epigraphy and numismatics. Nevertheless, mobile populations remain largely unrecoverable even in this expanded catchment of information.

3. For the Saljuqs, see Peacock 2010: 53ff.; Peacock 2015: esp.13; Durand-Guédy 2013a, 2013b. Thomas (2018: 21–23ff.) also discussed the varying degrees of erasure from the historical record of nomadic populations, often dismissed as unruly and otherwise undesirable social elements – a theme running through the works of the early Arabic geographers and into modern historical studies. Cf. also Rao 1982 (mentioned *infra*); Thomas and Gascoigne 2016: 171ff.

4. Cf. Bosworth 1961.

5. See Baihaqi (trans. Bosworth) 2011, vol. I: 195, 198–207. Also Bosworth 1961: 126 and n. 22; Bosworth [1963] 2015: 118, 121, 227; Bosworth 1968a: 35; Bosworth 1973: 121; Bosworth [1977] 1992: 68–69; Mahmud 2009: 59–60; Inaba 2013: 78; O'Neal 2016a; Allegranzi 2019a, vol. I: 45; Rasikh 2019: ch. 2. Juzjani, vol. I, 1963: 329 (trans. 1881, vol. I: 319–320) briefly mentioned raids into Ghur also during the time of Sultan Mahmud's father, the trusted Samanid *ghulam* and military leader Sabuktigin (d. AH 389/999 CE), when the latter had received the region from Tukharistan to Zamindawar as a reward for his loyal service to his Samanid overlords. Cf. also Chapter 3 (notes).

6. Detailed in Deloche, vol. I 1980/1993: 29–32 and maps II and III; see also

Ruthven and Nanji 2004: 54–55. The position of Ahangaran in the northern reaches of historical Ghur – see Chapter 2 – strongly indicates that some Ghuris were intercepting caravans on the northern route from Herat toward Balkh and beyond. Sultan Mahmud's punitive campaigns there relatively soon after his succession were surely motivated by commercial *and* political factors. Ghaznavid control of Balkh and its surroundings was tenuous in the early years, if we give credence to the *Faḍaʾil al-Balkh*, which states that it was only as of the eleventh century that Ghaznavid-appointed *qadis* were posted in Balkh. This more codified legal structure usually superseded the local, public tribunal system that was customary in many parts of the Persianate world; the process was, expectedly, often not free of conflict. Cf. Azad 2013: 118–119. Not only did the northern Herat–Balkh caravan route comprise an important artery of mercantilism and communication, the zone was vital to Mahmud's control of Khurasan and his increasing independence from his Samanid overlords (Bosworth 1973: 44–46). See also Paul 2018b: 319–320; and de la Vassière 2018: 135–137 for the "gigantic [Kushan] military camp" with a citadel north of Balkh that was likely most used in the Ghaznavid period. The fortress of Jurwas, on the other hand, has not been conclusively located, though its association with the sub-region of Darmashan could indicate southern Ghur, toward Zamindawar (where Khʷabin likely lay). Here again, the above-mentioned caravan routes *via* Tiginabad/Old Qandahar might have been just too tempting to resist for some Ghuris, particularly during the over-wintering months of their seasonal migrations to the south. Cf. Whitehouse 1976: 474ff. for the southern routes *via* Tiginabad/Old Qandahar (see also Chapter 3). It should be remembered that the most direct route of access to Ghur from Ghazna lay *via* Zamindawar – where Mahmud left his three sons while on campaign in Ghur (Baihaqi [trans. Bosworth] 2011, vol. I: 195–196); clearly the Ghaznavid sultans felt compelled to secure *both* the northern and southern routes from the Ghuris' depredations.

7. If the French traveler J. P. Ferrier's reports of the Turkman and Baluchi tribes of Iran and Afghanistan in the mid-nineteenth century can serve as a remote parallel for such activities in the historical past, it is worth considering that the Ghuris also may have been after the *people* traveling with the caravans rather than their goods. The desire for human commodities (according to Ferrier, "man-stealing") may be borne out by the flourishing slave trade centered on historical Ghur, so often mentioned in pre-modern texts. See Ferrier (trans. Jesse) 1976: 83–86; cf. also Khazeni 2012a: 141–143; and Næss 2015 (I am grateful to Dr. Tim Murray for the reference).

8. The phenomenon of mobile groups raiding caravans or even settlements and cities is well known. There is an unfolding scholarly reconsideration of these seemingly parasitic acts, however, as inevitably the impetuses for raiding differed according to specific groups and their circumstances. See further Næss 2015.

9. Cf. Baihaqi (trans. Bosworth) 2011, vol. I: 195, 198–207; and Bosworth 1968a: 35. It is noteworthy that mid-twentieth century Afghan–Pashtun nationalism led the historian ʿAtiq Allah Pazhvak to propose a Pashto dialect as the historical language of Ghur (cf. Patel 2017: 151–152).

10. The image of a heavily fortified landscape and also Ghuris' specialization in special armaments (see below in main text) emerged already from Baihaqi's descriptions (trans. Bosworth), vol. I, 2011: 199–204, vol. III: 97–98 (note 446 to AH 421/1030 CE).

11. Cf. Bosworth (1961: 118, 124; Bosworth [1977] 1992: 68), who cited Ya'qut, and relied largely on Marquart's observations, in turn gleaned from al-Biruni.

12. Mahmud 2009: esp. 242ff.

13. Mahmud 2009: esp. 251–254; also Hunter 2010: 82. See Patel 2017 for the historiographical context and analysis of Mahmud's monograph. The historical texts' frequent mention of the Ghuris' arms manufacture further underscores their undoubtedly symbiotic relationship with settled society, echoing Gellner's observations above. See also Thomas and Gascoigne 2016: 174ff.; Thomas 2018.

14. See O'Neal 2015; O'Neal 2016a. Ghafur (1960: 1–12) also provided an overview of the contemporary and later textual sources with information on the Shansabanis, though adopting Barthold's (1968: 30) characterizations of "the second half of the 12th and the beginning of the 13th century [as] one of the darkest pages of Muslim history," and the text-based data as contradictory and requiring "very critical study" (borne out by Bosworth 1977/1992: 115ff.). Ghafur's useful survey of the contemporary works, including those unfortunately lost and known only through later authors' citations, encompassed both the chronicles patronized by other courts and containing some mention of the Shansabanis (e.g., al-Rawandi's *Rahat al-Sudur wa Ayat al-Surur*, c. 1205, principally focused on the Saljuqs), and those written within the Shansabani courts themselves, such as Fakhr al-Din Razi's *Risala-yi Bahaiyya* (see also Chapter 3), dedicated to the Bamiyan ruler Baha' al-Din Sam (r. 1192–1206) (cf. *infra* in main text). However, given the evident participation of the non-extant works and their authors in the Persianate literary world and its conventions of poetry and prose – an assumption bolstered by the *surviving* texts – it is practically certain that the overall corpus offered little more data, perhaps only allusions to the Shansabanis' pre-imperial nomadic ancestors and lifeways.

15. See Asif 2016: 51–55, 57–60; Anooshahr 2018b: 2–3.

16. I borrow the phrasing from Anooshahr (2018b: 2 and n. 3), whose work focused on the fifteenth- and sixteenth-century emergence of the great Eurasian empires of the Ottomans, Safavids, and Mughals. Anooshahr's incisive analyses of the crafting of their identities also informs parallel processes in the tenth–twelfth-century period of nomadic confederacies coming to rule large swaths of the Islamic world, most notably the Saljuqs. See also, *inter alia*, Bosworth 1968a: 40–41; Bosworth 1973: 61–62; Meisami 1993; and Chapter 3.

17. See Bosworth 1973: 55 and *passim*; esp. Meisami 1999: 20–21, 37–45; also Peacock 2018: 4ff.

18. Cf. Bosworth 1961: 125–126 and n. 32. The transformation of Zahhak from the tyrant and sinner of canonical texts – such as al-Ghazali's (d. AH 504/1111 CE) *Nasihat al-muluk* (cf. Lambton 1981/2006: 122–123) – to a desirable ancestral figure perhaps best demonstrated the great epistemological/conceptual

distances between mainstream Persianate trends and the largely isolated populations inhabiting the hinterlands of even renowned urban centers such as Ghazna – further exacerbated in the case of Ghur: Juzjani's erudition must have had to concede to his patrons' decidedly provincial perceptions.

19. See Juzjani, vol. I, 1963: 320 (trans. vol. I, 1881: 301ff.). Cf. also Meisami's (1993) study of the process by which pre-Islamic Iranian mythology and specifically Islamic sources together provided origins during the eleventh century.

20. See esp. Volume II for the texts patronized at the north Indian courts, which have little to offer on the early Shansabanis in Afghanistan. Kumar (2007: 21–22, 92, 297) addressed this issue, though more specifically regarding northern India's Persian literary culture during the early thirteenth century, which tended to be "Delhi-centered" and "wedded to the history of a unitary state formation." Even Uchh Sharif, the contemporaneous *locus* of political power and cultural capital, and the site of Nasir al-Din Qabacha's court in upper Sindh, patronized its own cohort of scholars and poets and witnessed the circulation of these *literati* – most notably Juzjani himself – between the two rival cities. See Alam 2003: 138–141.

21. Due to the confusion introduced by E. Denison Ross (1922), it bears reiteration that this personage must be distinguished from Fakhr al-Din Muhammad ibn Mansur Mubarak-shah al-Quraishi (*'urf* Fakhr-i Mudabbir), a Persian litterateur who began his career at Ghazna under the later Ghaznavids. The latter's decline and eastward retreat prompted the writer's own emigration to Lahore and eventually Delhi. No doubt in part due to overlapping professions, careers, and lifespans (and, no doubt, names), Fakhr-i Mudabbir was initially confused with the genealogy's author Fakhr al-Din Mubarak-shah. Cf. Juzjani vol. I, 1963: 318–319 (trans. vol. I, 1881: 301–302). Also Khan 1977; Siddiqui 2010: 17–18; Bosworth 2012a; Auer 2012: 22–23; Auer 2018: 96 and n. 5.

22. Juzjani, vol. I, 1963: 318–320ff. (trans. vol. I, 1881: 300–302ff.)

23. See esp. O'Neal 2016a; O'Neal 2015; O'Neal 2020; Cribb 2020. I am grateful to both authors for sharing advance copies of their forthcoming publications.

24. Cf. Rasikh 2019: ch. 3. The various genres of Persian prose and poetry in India largely derived from the broader Persianate world of the time (Kumar 2007: 366; Alam 2003). The political and cultural specificities of the Indian location nonetheless filtered into even the universal history or *tarikh* tradition, to which Juzjani's *Tabaqat* belonged. Despite *Tabaqat*'s multifaceted representation of events (cf. Siddiqui 2010: 93ff.), Kumar (2007: 367) distinguishes the work as an atypical *tarikh*, highlighting its grouping of people according to "social affinity" – in itself perhaps a subtle but firm erasure of the Shansabanis' "lowly" non-sedentist origins.

25. Cf. Hodgson (esp. vol. II, 1977: 293–94) for the coining and explication of the term. For a recent engagement with the concept, see esp. Green (2019: esp. 7), who undertook its transtemporal and spatial interrogation, proclaiming "the need to analytically denaturalize Persian's [as a language] civilizational ties to Islam and denationalize its primordialist ties to Iran."

26. As symptomatic of the current scholarly status quo, Spooner (2019: 305)

observed that "nomadic tribal communities have been an important factor in Islamic and Persianate history down to the present," but went on to retain the distinction between "Arab (tribal, Sunni) and Persian (urban, Shi'i)" (*ibid.*, 308). Rather, re-examining these broad and largely artificial divisions requires investigation of how nomadic groups in fact *transcended* them – a transcendence amply evidenced throughout the "the Persianate millennium."

27. Cf. Biran 2004; Biran 2005: 94ff., 196 and *passim*; Bosworth 2010; McClary 2020: 7ff.

28. Bosworth, 1961, 1965, 1973, 1992; Pazhvak 1968: 90, 94–95; O'Neal 2016a.

29. Thomas (2018: 29) rightly eschewed the otherwise perspicacious C. E. Bosworth's historically anachronistic term of "buffer state" to refer to the coalescing Shansabanis of the first half of the twelfth century: the phrase was first used only in the late nineteenth century to describe the status of the then Durrani–Pashtun kingdom of Afghanistan *vis-à-vis* Britain and Czarist Russia in the so-called Great Game; moreover, while the Shansabanis' homelands of seasonal transhumance were technically sandwiched in between the Saljuqs and the Ghaznavids, their early territorial presence was far from bounded and fixed, as the modern term would imply. Nevertheless, the term was used again to refer to the Balkh region in the seventh century: cf. de al Vassière 2020: 127.

30. Cf. Durand-Guédy 2013a, 2013b. Following the same author (2018), it is important to highlight the integration of the luxurious trellis tent (Pers. *khargah*) – initially associated with "Turanian" or Turkic contexts of the Eurasian steppe lands – as a part of the visual and textual description of power in western Eurasia's Perso-Islamic courts by the eleventh century. While this incorporation surely signaled mobility and agility as a part of royalty (cf. *infra* in main text and Chapter 3), "[i]n Iran the *khargah* remained exclusively a status symbol ... not imply[ing] a change of lifestyle: the urban location of the Iranian court" (*ibid.*, 835). See also *infra* in main text and notes.

31. Bosworth 1961: 118.

32. See Gellner 1983: 446; also Introduction and Chapter 4.

33. Peacock 2010: 122–23; Peacock 2015: 25ff. See also this author's discussion of the Christian author Bar Hebraeus – who drew upon the *Malik-nama* tradition, like his counterparts of the Perso-Arabic histories – and therein the motivations behind Saljuq conversion to Islam (*ibid.*, 246–247). A parallel Muslim-convert progenitor figure was Satuq Bughra Khan (mid-tenth century) of the Qarakhanids (cf. Bosworth 2010: 22).

34. Cf. Peacock 2015: e.g., 39, 48.

35. Spooner 2019: 301.

36. See Durand-Guédy 2013b for the Saljuq period's "clear break with the past" especially in terms of the spatial organization of power. Cf. also Chapter 3.

37. See esp. Blair 1992: 160–161; and Lambton and Sourdel-Thomine 2008: 167–170, 172–174.

38. For the Isfahan *jami'*, see Blair 1992: 160–167; Hillenbrand 2015. For the example of the *Chihil Dukhtaran minar*, cf. Smith 1936: 318–323; Y. Godard 1936: 361–363.

39. For Gar, see Smith 1936: 323–337; Y. Godard 1936: 363. For Sin: Smith 1936:

327–331; Smith 1939; Y. Godard 1936: 363–364; Miles 1939: 11–14; Bloom 1989: 160.

40. Cf. Introduction. Despite Sourdel-Thomine's own reservations, she generally leaned toward such dynastic appellations, both for the Saljuqs and the "Ghurids" (cf. Sourdel-Thomine 1953; Sourdel-Thomine 1960: esp. 277). However, the author did clarify early on that, for the Saljuqs "the term did not suppose a strictly dynastic remit, but designated … all the constructions erected at the time when Saljuq power played a primary role in the Islamic lands" (1953: 109 n. 3) – a useful clarification since, as we see in the main text, Saljuq-affiliated elites and other personnel were robust and visible patrons. See also Hillenbrand 1994: 152. The architectural culture under discussion has also been described as the "wider architectural koine" specifically in reference to Qarakhanid-patronized buildings (McClary 2020: 108).

41. Peacock 2015: 248.

42. See Godard 1949: 10–11, 31, 54 and *passim*; and Kalus, *TEI*: Nos. 34503, 34495, 34499, 34491, 34493, 34497, 37426, 40834, 34501; Peacock 2015: 107–109.

43. Cf. Bosworth 1994: 381–386; Peacock 2015: 35–36, 41–42; Paul 2018b; see also *infra* in this chapter.

44. Sourdel-Thomine 1953: esp. 122–129.

45. See Tate 1910/12: facing 22, 26–27; esp. O'Kane 1984: 89–97; Bosworth 1994: 395–396.

46. Meisami 1999: 20ff.; Green 2019: 12–13, 16; Spooner 2019: 310ff.

47. By contrast, the Saljuqs "vaunted their [Turk] origins through their alien Turkish names, and introduced new political symbols and practices that originated on the steppe" (Peacock 2015: 3). This difference might be explicated at least in part through the differing historical origins of the two ruling groups: The Ghaznavid progenitors' and early sultans' memories and knowledge of their natal world, the Eurasian steppe, would be at best faint, given their steeping in the Perso-Islamic prestige culture of the Samanid court; by contrast, the un-enslaved and free Saljuqs' active infiltration into the Persianate world allowed less compromised memory and cultural pride to travel westward with them.

48. See esp. Bosworth 1968a: 36ff.; Bosworth 1973: 61; Peacock 2015: 3. See also Chapter 3 (notes) for Sabuktigin's enduring loyalty to the Samanids.

49. For fascinating "hybrid" iconographies combining Buddhist and Brahmanical elements at Tapa Sardar near Ghazna, see Taddei 1968; Taddei and Verardi 1978; Verardi and Paparatti 2005. The proximity of the Buddhist–Brahmanical site to the east of the great capital of Ghazna led scholars to consider the potential interaction between the later residents of Ghazna and the abandoned pre-Islamic ruins: Tapa Sardar could have been the Shahbahar or Shahrabad of Ghaznavid sources, mentioned by Baihaqi and Gardizi, and in the poetry of Farrukhi and Ansari: located a *farsakh* from Ghazna in the plain, troops were reviewed here before their departure on *ghazwa* to India. Cf. also Bosworth [1977] 1992: 56. Linguistically, Shahbahar or "the king's temple" [?] makes reference to the Buddhist *vihara*, often incorporated into Arabic toponymic suffixes as *bahar*. Cf. Taddei 1968: 109–110; Melikian-Chirvani 1974: 8–10; Allegranzi 2014: 109–110; Errington 2017: 44. According to a more

recently proposed chronology, Tapa Sardar was probably abandoned in the eighth century; rather than a sudden destructive episode such as an Arab raid causing its abandonment, Verardi and Paparatti (2005: 441–442) described a more gradual process set off by the Chinese Tang rulers' divestment from the region and the consequently more impactful Arab campaigns there. Cf. also Rezakhani 2017: 183–184. The lapse of only two centuries between Tapa Sardar's disuse and the establishment of the Ghaznavid dynasty offers intriguing possibilities regarding the awareness and perhaps reuse of the Buddhist–Brahmanical site by the residents of nearby Ghazna.

50. As of at least the seventh century CE, various sects of Brahmanical Hinduism attracted growing numbers of adherents in eastern Afghanistan, becoming more evident in archaeological finds from Kabul and its vicinity, attributable at least in part due to the westward extension of the Sahis of Kashmir and Panjab. Cf. Rehman 1979: 33–34; Klimburg-Salter 1989: 55–56; Klimburg-Salter 2008: 132; Baker and Allchin 1991: 10ff.; Errington 2017: 43. Studies of Jaina metal sculptures found in the vicinity of Kabul and dating to the sixth and twelfth centuries have provided evidence of Jainism in eastern Afghanistan, likely in the form of traveling Jain merchants: stylistically the recovered sculptures seem to originate in northwestern India (Pal 2007/2012). It is possible that the singular find of a broken marble *jina* in the Bamiyan valley may have been locally carved, given the marble's similarity to that of the Ghazna tombs (see Volume II), though the stone also calls to mind the great marble deposits in the Gujarat–Rajasthan region. Cf. Fischer 1962.

51. Cf. esp. Ball 2020 (forthcoming); for Tepe Sardar, see Ball 2019: No. 1180 for the most up-to-date bibliography.

52. Cf. Irons 2003; Thomas 2018: 26; Malagaris 2020: 36–38, 51–52. See also *infra* in main text and Chapters 3, 5 and 6.

53. Cf. Bosworth [1963] 2015: 75–76 and *passim*; 235; Bosworth [1977] 1992: 61–67; Pinder-Wilson 2001: 165–166. See also Chapter 4.

54. Inaba 2013: 89ff.

55. The genealogy of the Shansabanis recently reconstructed by O'Neal (2016a) makes it possible to associate dates with reigns beginning at the dawn of the twelfth century CE (AH end fifth–sixth centuries). At least some of the reigns and sequences of events can be verified from parallel sources, most notably the ascendant Shansabanis' interactions with the Saljuqs, and the waning arc of the Ghaznavids in Zamindawar: in addition to Juzjani, twelfth- through fourteenth-century sources include Nizami 'Aruzi (fl. early twelfth century), Ibn al-Athir (1160–1233), Juvaini (1226–1283), and Rashid al-Din (1247–1318). Cf. Ghafur 1960.

56. This extrapolation is derived from studies of the imperial Saljuqs who, even after Tughril's adoption of the title *Sultan* (1038) and Malik Shah's (r. 1053–1092) move from Rayy to Isfahan as his seat of political power, "the dynasty pursued an itinerant lifestyle, not from town to town, but rather from pasture to pasture" (Durand-Guédy 2013a: 172).

57. Cf. Juzjani vol. I, 1963: 335–336 (trans. vol. I, 1881: 339–340) for Saif al-Din Suri's division and distribution of patrimony among his brothers. Barfield (1993: 100–102) observed that modern nomadic pastoralists in southwestern

Asia based succession on the agnatic line, and tended to regard the single household or tent as the basic socio-economic unit, rather than a "joint-family ideal" where males "pool their labor and animals under the direction of their father." Thus, property would be fractionally divided upon a patriarch's death, effectively constituting a system of "anticipatory inheritance" (Barth 1961: 19–20). It has additionally been observed that, while these groups might claim to adhere to Qur'anic stipulations of property division, the realities of agnatic inheritance generally excluded females; only in cases of agnate conflict would religious authorities be invoked, who tended to be more exacting about Qur'anic adherences while adjudicating disputes (cf. Barfield 1993: 101). Another prominent historical example of nomadic anticipatory inheritance was the division of existing *and* future conquests between Saljuq ibn Duqaq's grandsons Tughril and Chaghri in the early eleventh century CE (Peacock 2016: 6).

58. Although the exact political hierarchy of the Sistan Maliks *vis-à-vis* the Shansabanis is not clear, Bosworth's view of Sistan overall was that the region was caught up in the larger politico-military developments in Khurasan, being subject to the Ghaznavids and the Saljuqs throughout the eleventh and mid-twelfth centuries, eventually ending up as Shansabani vassals upon accession of Sultan Ghiyath al-Din to the throne of Firuzkuh (AH 558/1163 CE). They, like the Shansabanis, succumbed to the Khwarazm-shahs by *c.* AH 612/1215 CE. See Juzjani vol. I, 1963: 395–396 (trans. vol. I, 1881: 447–448); Bosworth 1994: 398–399; O'Neal 2013: 58–59.

59. The one documented example of this external interference resulted from Mahmud Ghaznavi's punitive campaign to Ahangaran in Ghur in AH 401/1011, to discipline the Ghuris' caravan raiding: according to Juzjani (vol. I, 1963: 329–330 (trans. vol. I, 1881: 320–329), the sultan removed Muhammad ibn Suri and his older son Shish in favor of the more pliant and younger son Abu 'Ali.

60. O'Neal 2016a.

61. Cf. Juzjani vol. I, 1963: 335, 385 (trans. vol. I, 1881: 338–339; *ibid.*, 422); Edwards 2015: 94. Saif al-Din Suri's designation as distributor of patrimony was itself indicative of the cultural preference for sons of lawful wives – presumably women of commensurate ancestry – as technically he was only 'Izz al-Din's third son. Among the seven male children (no mention being made of females in this generation), the eldest Fakhr al-Din was born to "a Turki servant," while the second Qutb al-Din also to "a woman … of no high name … the doorkeeper and servant of the mother of the other sultans …" Such hints seem to indicate that a melding of the Shahsabanis' (and likely other Ghuris') customary laws of inheritance with the more orthodox Islamic laws pertaining to dispensation of patrimony had not yet taken place. See also Chapter 3. The Shansabanis may never have come to follow strict Islamic orthodoxy in patrimonial inheritance: upon Ghiyath al-Din's death at Herat in AH 599/1203 CE, Mu'izz al-Din, now the eldest male, also proceeded to distribute appanages to his own *male* agnates, as his uncle Saif al-Din had done more than a half-century earlier. Cf. Juzjani, 1963 vol. I: 335, 385 (trans. vol. I, 1881: 471–472). Thus, even after the Shansabanis' public espousal and

patronage of Sunni orthodoxy (the Shafi'i *madhhab* at Firuzkuh and Herat, the Hanifi at Ghazna; cf. Chapter 4) age-old customary inheritance laws apparently remained in place.

62. Cf. Cribb 2020: 122, esp. for a discussion of the location of Parwan/Farwan; and O'Neal 2020: 202–204, 209–210.

63. Cf. Juzjani vol. I, 1963: 335 (trans. vol. I, 1881: 371–372 and *passim*, 424–425); also O'Neal 2020: 201, 207.

64. Cf. also O'Neal 2020: esp. 210.

65. Juzjani vol. I, 1963: 338 (trans. vol. I, 1881: 343).

66. Cf. Juzjani vol. I, 1963: 337, 338, 393–395 (trans. vol. I, 1881: 340–343, 439–445); Bosworth [1977] 1992: 113–115. See also *infra* in main text; and Chapter 4.

67. Cf. Juzjani vol. I, 1963: 341–342 (trans. vol. I, 1881: 350–351). Bahram Shah's expectation that his threat of elephants would suddenly make 'Ala' al-Din capitulate had appeared cryptic until recently: the elephant's diabolical associations within Islam had to be reconciled with their increasing numbers in the Ghaznavid arsenal, where they became invaluable destructive and tactical weapons. Mahmud had attempted to distract from his reliance on elephants by very propagandistically raiding and destroying India's "infidel" idol temples during the latter part of his reign. Cf. Anooshahr 2018b. However, it is possible that a century later, Bahram Shah still thought the threat of elephants would frighten his less worldly foe (prior to the Shansabanis' own campaigns to India; cf. Volume II), or perhaps he assumed the elephant's diabolic associations lingered among the Shansabanis in light of their more recent and thus *lesser* Islamization, accompanied by an incomplete literacy in Islamicate culture.

68. According to additional numismatic evidence, 'Ala' al-Din's son and successor Saif al-Din (r. AH 556–558/1161–1163 CE) also successfully occupied the city in AH 557/1162 CE, at least for a short period before his death (see Chapter 4). Cf. O'Neal 2016a; O'Neal 2020: 199–200.

69. Cf. Juzjani vol. I, 1963: 346–348 (trans. vol. I, 1881: 357–361); Leshnik 1968: 39; Bosworth [1977] 1992: 118–119; O'Neal 2016a. For the Saljuqs' nomadic military power, see Peacock 2015: 50, 143, 168, 224. See also *infra* in main text.

70. Another notable "conquest" during the reign of 'Ala' al-Din Husain was that of Gharjistan, which was apparently effected through a marital alliance: 'Ala' al-Din married Hurr Malika, the daughter of the reigning *shar* (not unlike the hereditary title of the Shah of Bamiyan; cf. Chapters 3 and 4), who was nonetheless only "one of the Maliks of Gharjistan." See Juzjani vol. I, 1963: 349 (trans. vol. I, 1881: 363). It was only during the reign of his famous nephew Shams al-Din ibn Sam (eventually Sultan Ghiyath al-Din, r. 1163–1203), however, that the magnificent *madrasa* of Shah-i Mashhad was constructed in Gharjistan (Chapter 4).

71. See Juzjani vol. I, 1963: 343–344 (trans. vol. I, 1881: 353–356); Bosworth [1977] 1992: 117–118; also O'Neal 2016a. Despite Juzjani's description of 'Ala' al-Din Husain's destruction of Ghazna and Bust-Lashkari Bazar as reaching legendary proportions, it has been archaeologically ascertained that these sites were still salvageable in the 1170s, even after the decade-long Oghüz encampments

at Ghazna in the 1160s. A little more than twenty years later the newly crowned Sultan Mu'izz al-Din went on to add his own mark to Ghazna and Lashkari Bazar, with architectural patronage consisting of palace renovations and other works. Cf. Chapter 5.

72. Cf. Bosworth [1977] 1992: 124–125; O'Neal 2016a.

73. O'Neal (2016a) has pointed out that the precise moment of the younger Shansabani's adoption of the regnal *laqab* is not clear: not only is there numismatic evidence for continued usage of "Shihab al-Din," but this *laqab* was frequently used to refer to the younger Shansabani in north Indian Sanskrit inscriptions (cf. Prasad 1990: 4, 8, 12, 28, 30). By contrast, "Mu'izz al-Din" was used in the Perso-Arabic inscriptions on the Qutb mosque – esp. the northern entrance – and on the first story of the Qutb *minar* (Horovitz 1911–1912: 14–18). See Volume II.

74. Cf. Juzjani vol. I, 1963: 357–358, 396 (trans. vol. I, 1881: 377–379, 449).

75. Cf. Barthold 1968: 237–238, 329–330, 338–339; Bosworth [1963] 2015: 98–102; Kumar 2007: 77–79; Peacock 2015: 217ff.

76. As described by Fakhr-i Mudabbir (in Ross 1922: 397ff.), a *qadi* named Fakhr al-Din Kufi purchased Aibeg at the market of Nishapur, where the flow of Turk slaves was even more active than in Ghazna's market. Aibeg thereafter passed into the Mu'izz al-Din's possession. It is all the more surprising, then, that there is no known Shansabani coinage minted at Nishapur (cf. *infra* in main text).

77. Cf. O'Neal 2016a; and O'Neal 2015; O'Neal 2020. Despite the last Shansabani ruler's burial at the Sheikh Bayazid complex at Bistam, at present it is unascertainable whether the tomb structure was actually constructed by or for him. Cf. also Adle 2015: 242–243; and Volume II.

78. See Juzjani vol. I, 1963: 397 (trans. vol. I, 1881: 451). Juzjani's mention of Multan-Uchh as midway points from Ghazna would point to eastward passage into the Indus regions *via* the Gomal Pass – cf. Deloche (trans. Walker) vol. I, 1993: 26–27. However, for at least a century since the Ghaznavids' eastward campaigns, and well into the thirteenth century, the favored route between Ghazna and the middle through upper Indus areas appears to have been *via* Kurraman – a major mint site for the Ghazna Shansabanis' *jital*s. Cf. Tye and Tye 1995: Nos. 138, 174–178; and esp. O'Neal 2015.

79. While Juzjani (vol. I, 1963: 397 (trans. vol. I, 1881: 451)) named Bhimadeva – i.e., Bhimadeva II, r. 1178–1241/2 – as the triumphant foe, the reign of his predecessor Mularaja II (r. 1176–1178) also overlapped with the date of the Shansabani campaign. In the corpus of Chaulukya copper-plate inscriptions, the imperial genealogies (Skt. *vamsavali*) of at least three major land grants credited Mularaja with the defeat of the *garjjanaka*s or *mleccha*s (among the many labels for the northwestern invaders in Indian inscriptions and other sources, as summarized for the eighth through early seventeenth centuries by Chattopadhyaya 1998: 92–97). See Patel 2004: 5–6 and notes; and Volume II. While it is quite possible, then, that Mularaja II in fact led the Chaulukya forces repelling this first Shansabani campaign far beyond the Indus, Juzjani's substitution of Mularaja's successor Bhimadeva (II) in his recounting of the episode was not only an easy confusion – one's reign ended and the other's

began apparently in the very year of Mu'izz al-Din's incursion – it also heightened a historical parallel: Mahmud's oft-cited Somnath campaign of AH 416/1025 CE confronted the Ghaznavid sultan with the Chaulukya *maharajadhiraja* Bhimadeva I (r. *c.* 1022–1064 CE). Cf. Bühler 1877: 186, 213; Trivedi 1994: 165. As further discussed in Volume II, during this defensive campaign against the Shansabanis the Chaulukya forces were militarily aided by their Nadol Chahamana feudatories. Cf. Kielhorn 1907–1908: 72; Bhandarkar 1911–1912: 71–72.

80. Although the archaeologists who initially excavated at Banbhore remained circumspect regarding its identification as Dibul (e.g., F. Khan 1963: 50), the site is now viewed to be that of the pre-eminent Indus port center (A. Khan 2003: 2). Cf. also O'Neal 2013: 64–65; and *infra* in this chapter.

81. Juzjani vol. I, 1963: 397 (trans. vol. I, 1881: 452).

82. Cf. esp. Deloche (trans. Walker) vol. I, 1993: 30–34.

83. The strategy of obtaining command of a fort near a targeted stronghold, and placing a loyal deputy there awaiting further orders – in this case, Husain ibn Kharmil – very much echoed the later Shansabani inroads into the heart of the Chahamana territories: In AH 588/1192–1193 CE, a garrison under the command of the *ghulam* Qutb al-Din Aibek was stationed at the fort of Kuhram, in the vicinity of Mirath and within striking distance of Delhi, and ultimately the Chahamana capital of Ajmer (Ajayameru). See Juzjani vol. I, 1963: 397–398, 401 (trans. vol. I, 1881: 453–454, 469–470); Edwards 2015: 96–97, 111; and Volume II.

84. There is continuing confusion between two ethnonyms, *viz.* Gakkhaṛ (گکهر) and Kukhar (کوکهر), possibly perpetuated by copyists' orthographical errors over the centuries. Juzjani's mention of the last Ghaznavid sultan's mercenary allies as the Kukhar may have actually referred to the Gakkhaṛ. A tribal group with the latter name has been documented in West Panjab and southern Kashmir, characterized as a "war-like Muslim tribe … of indigenous origin … [and] agriculturalists by profession." The retention of some non-Islamic practices – e.g., prohibition of widow remarriage – may indicate a gradual, perhaps selective conversion to Islam not unlike that of the Ghuri tribes of Afghanistan, among whom some non-Islamic practices likewise persisted (cf. Chapters 2 and 3). The Gakkhaṛ "homeland" fell within the areas of Ghaznavid control during the late twelfth century, though whether the tribe was consistently agriculturalist during the last millennium remains unknown. Cf. Juzjani vol. I, 1963: e.g., 398 (trans. vol. I, 1881: e.g., 455); Rahman 1979: 31–32; Ansari 2012; Hanifi 2012; O'Neal 2013: 65 and n. 40.

85. Juzjani vol. I, 1963: 398 (trans. vol. I, 1881: 456–457) See also Bosworth [1977] 1992: 129–131 for a more detailed account, supplemented with the reports of historical authors in addition to Juzjani.

CHAPTER 2

Beginnings

> Origins are a seductive necessity for historians.
>
> M. A. Asif

The epigraph above comes from M. A. Asif's recent book on the thirteenth-century text known as *Chach-nama*.[1] The text was the work of 'Ali Kufi, dated to AH 623/1226 CE and dedicated to Sultan Nasir al-Din Qabacha, ruler of Uchh and Multan in the southwestern Panjab AH 599–625/1203–1028 CE. *Chach-nama* and its patron have some bearing on our considerations here: they provide a preview of the historical arc of the Shansabanis, as they emerged from obscure beginnings in central Afghanistan and went on to create an extremely consequential imperial expanse. The select military entourage of the Shansabani sultan Mu'izz al-Din of Ghazna (r. AH 568–602/1173–1206 CE) included Qabacha, who had been a *ghulam* participating in the sultan's eastward campaigns to the Indus and ultimately to the north Indian plains during the late 1170s–1190s (cf. Chapters 1 and 5).[2] Mu'izz al-Din was assassinated near Lahore in AH 602/1206 CE; since he had no male progeny, his closest *ghulam*s were his heirs, and the "patrimony" of the sultan's conquests was divided among his favorites, including Qabacha.[3]

Asif's at times polemical position "against origins" or beginnings was, arguably, necessary to crack the proverbial nut that has been *Chach-nama* in the modern historiography on Islam in South Asia.[4] Certainly, Kufi's own avowal that his work was an early thirteenth-century Persian translation of a lost eighth-century Arabic original[5] already signaled the bifurcations between historical phenomena and their phenomenologies. Whether translation or new composition,[6] Kufi's *Chach-nama* was as much about the eighth-century integration of Islam into South Asia's cultural fabric, as it was about the historical consequences and intentional power of these events for its author and his audiences of the thirteenth century and beyond. And yet more than a millennium later, the obsessive scholarly and political pursuit of Islam's *beginnings* in South Asia – often amounting to nothing more than attestations of the Otherness of Islam and Muslims – has had dramatic and irreversible impacts on the lives of generations of people in this part of the world, and in South Asian diasporas elsewhere.[7]

Nevertheless, far from pinpointing an exact chronological or geographical point of origin per se for the Shansabanis – something that is not possible given the current state of knowledge – this chapter underscores the fact that the origins of many protagonists throughout history, particularly those with non-elite beginnings, remain undocumented and ultimately unrecoverable.[8] Their ethnogeneses, ensuing either from the protagonists' own invention or *a posteriori* piecing together by modern academics (as is the case here and, really, in all modern studies), are nothing more nor less than the synthesized results of the needs and conventions of the moment of writing inhabited by the court chronicler or modern investigator. The resulting narrative may withstand sustained scrutiny or it may not, depending on further recovery of information on the region and its inhabitants over time. An exploration of the Shansabanis' pre-imperial history essentially provides a case study of the intriguing process by which an obscure kinship-based group, practicing seasonal transhumance and/or some form of nomadism, underwent a seemingly sudden rise to regional and transregional prominence.

Indeed, unearthing a plausible, *non*-mythical early history of the Shansabanis, and the way of life of their forebears during the eleventh through the first half of the twelfth centuries is more than a "seductive necessity": it serves one of the fundamental aims of this project, namely, "essay[ing] non-sectarian histories of conquest ... conflict," and cultural transformation.[9] The search for Shansabani beginnings helps us to confront the complexities inherent in "Islam," its many cultural, political, *and* religious implications, as well as the impetuses for conversion and/or public confessionalism. Rather than a general explication of historical adoptions of Islam, the early Shansabanis provide one concrete iteration of what were multifarious and contingent processes across historical Eurasia, each deserving of close analysis in its own right.[10]

The general paucity of textual sources, and the literary conventions reigning in those that do exist,[11] urge the investigator to turn to other potential repositories of information, wherein there may be indications of the Shansabanis' pre-imperial beginnings. Among the notable alternative avenues for gleaning clues are the available numismatic data[12] and – the focus here – the architectural remains scattered throughout Ghur (e.g. Figures 2.1, 2.5–2.10, 2.13–2.16). With the exceptions of the Saghar *minar* (Figure 2.17) and probable summer "capital" of Jam-Firuzkuh (Figure 2.2) – discussed further in the current and following chapters – the vast majority of historical Ghur's built environment can be characterized as one of monumental decadence: the architectural landscape of central through southern Ghur consisted of pre-existing square or round multi-story towers, fortified enclosures of varying sizes on plains and promontories, and possibly interconnected lookout structures along the principal long-distance routes of travel (Figures 2.5–2.8).

Figure 2.1 *Ahangaran, Ghur Province, Afghanistan. © Photograph Warwick Ball, c. 1970s.*

This chapter argues that, during the later seventh–tenth centuries, the structures of central–southern Ghur (subsequently ruined) had surely been erected as monuments commanding the surrounding landscape, and served imperial purposes for the late Sasanian–Hephthalite or Western Turk elites.[13] By the eleventh–twelfth centuries, however, these same structures were no longer monuments projecting imperial presence; rather, they were repurposed as temporary shelters for people, their animals and goods, and likely also reused on occasion as fortifications against aggressors. These remains were decidedly *not* the later imperial Shansabanis' magnificent *madrasa*s, mosques, and tombs at Chisht, Jam-Firuzkuh, and Herat (see Chapters 3 and 4, and Volume II), which housed sacral institutions and represented a ruling presence. Nevertheless, the abandoned and decaying structures were eminently useful for the *pre*-imperial Shansabanis and other Ghuris.

Many of Ghur's architectural remains have been surveyed, documented, and interpreted before.[14] Given the dramatically diminished direct access to Afghanistan during the last four decades, previous studies continue to be indispensable, essentially enabling the work of subsequent generations of scholars from several disciplines.

I argue in a later section of this chapter that most of the previous architectural analyses of Ghur's architectural landscape put forward conclusions based on untested assumptions of chronology. Here, bringing to the fore the tried and true art-historical methods of rigorous visual analysis and comparative contextualization, I conduct more thorough stylistic and iconographic examinations of these significant physical traces, comparing them with more firmly dated examples. This fresh perspective does much to reveal the world of the pre-imperial Shansabanis and other Ghuris, and the effects of this early existence on the Shansabanis' later imperial identities.

For our purposes of attaining a glimpse of the geographical and cultural beginnings of the Shansabanis during the eleventh–mid-twelfth centuries – that is, prior to and around the time of their emergence into the "history" conveyed by the textual sources – it is important to focus on their principal geographic vectors of activity within present-day Afghanistan. These vectors were of course initially concentrated in the heartland of Ghur, geographically delimited and architecturally analyzed below. But, as described in Chapter 1, it is worth bearing in mind that by the 1150s, the Bamiyan valley to the east was the site of an established collateral Shansabani lineage, while the Firuzkuh Shansabanis had also pushed far southward to Tiginabad/Old Qandahar, beyond what were likely their ancestral over-wintering areas in southern Ghur-Zamindawar (see Chapter 3). Then, by the later 1160s, Shansabani presence was documentable northwest of historical Ghur in the region of Maimana (Badghis Province) and northeastward toward Balkh, firmly within the historical geography of greater Khurasan. By the 1180s, Shansabani control had extended westward from Ghur to include Herat and its vicinity. All of these expansions and their architectural footprints will be discussed in the following chapters.

Ghur

In current political maps, historical Ghur (map, p. xvi) is surrounded by the contiguous provinces of Farah, Herat, and Badghis on its western flank; Faryab and Sar-i Pul to the north; Bamiyan, Daykundi, and Uruzgan along the eastern flank; and Farah and Helmand provinces to the south. Ghur Province itself comprises ten districts named according to their more prominent towns. These districts appear to be much more spacious and less numerous than the tiny and multiplied divisions of the eastern provinces of Kabul, Logar, and Nangarhar, for example – no doubt reflecting the great differences in population density among these regions of the country in modern times.

This seemingly ordered landscape of the present varied greatly in the past. The deeply carved terrain in much of Ghur makes satellite data difficult to use without on-the-ground verification.[15] And the interventions in the built environment resulting from the Mongol campaigns of the second and third quarters of the thirteenth century may have erased many indices of populations inhabiting Ghur's mountainous lands, further obscuring the beginnings of the Shansabanis' coalescence as an imperial lineage.[16] Expectedly, then, an overall socio-cultural apprehension of historical Ghur, parallel with the eastern and western reaches of Afghanistan described elsewhere in this volume, still has not come into view. While the tracts from Kabul westward until Bamiyan and its valleys are better known thanks to the abundance of Buddhist monastic establishments and their attraction for pilgrims from afar who were prolific travel writers,[17] Ghur itself has resisted such knowledge economies, its mountainous terrain and the supposed insularity of its inhabitants making methodical exploration more perilous and reportage less frequent.[18]

Despite the challenges – and perhaps *because* of them – a piecing together of the region's historical, cultural, and religious traces should be attempted. The varying degrees of artificiality in determining the political boundaries of nation-states in the twentieth century have already been subjected to rigorous analysis. Such a perspective is equally necessary for the domestic parceling *within* nations of provinces and states, which are frequently delineated for ease of administration – including gathering of census data, taxation, and revenue collection – rather than strictly adhering to the historic extents of linguistic and cultural geographies. Static administrative boundaries of modern times call for deconstruction all the more when treating a landscape largely determined by the varying degrees and types of transhumance and/or nomadic pastoralism among its populations. In addition to sparse references in texts, information from archaeological surveys/excavations and also modern observations can be useful in better imagining the extent and geography of historical Ghur. Lastly, we must bear in mind that the conceptualization of Ghur during the tenth through mid-twelfth centuries not only differs from the political maps of today, it has varied through time as well, depending on the shifting bases of power of prominent chieftains in the region.

Ahmad Ali Kohzad,[19] among Ghur's most thorough explorers in the mid-twentieth century, described the region as "a fortress surrounded by yet other mountains ... which has no doors, or if there be any, are narrow valleys difficult of access." However, such a description should not render Ghur impenetrable, given the region's many (principally non-sedentist?) inhabitants, both in the past and in the present (Figures 2.11 and 2.12). The eminent Afghanistan scholar Louis Dupree's observations are also worth recalling: the mountains "never truly served as barriers to cultural, economic, or political penetration, but merely funneled peoples and ideas along certain routes."[20] The northern reaches of Ghur, then, were hemmed by mountains (primarily the foothills of the Hindu Kush), which, rather than preventing movement, diverted it to the seasonally passable routes of access to Ghur's valleys. The region's southern reaches bordered the dry and flat plains of Zamindawar and Sistan (map, p. xvi).[21]

A constant of Ghur's landscape would have been its major northern river, the west-flowing Hari Rud. Although being a source for water, the river was not easily navigated or forded, and thus did not facilitate travel and communication. Nevertheless, its banks hosted at least two significant locales between modern Chaghcharan and Chisht-i Sharif, associated with the Shansabanis and their ancestors: Ahangaran lay on the river's southern bank, while the settlement of Jam-Firuzkuh straddled both banks (Figure 2.2). Each site was mentioned in Ghaznavid and later textual sources, respectively. While Ahangaran (see below) served as the seat of power of one or more of the local chieftains thought to be the forebears of the Shansabani sultans, the latter is now generally accepted to have been the summer capital – more likely a *sard-sir* royal encampment, as discussed further below and in Chapter 3 – of the initial branch of the Shansabanis of Firuzkuh (*c.* 1145 CE). These settlements and their respective roles for the Shansabanis and their predecessors are treated in succession.

The early fort and settlement of Ahangaran (Figures 2.1 and 2.3) was the site of the encounter between the Ghaznavid sultan Mahmud and the Ghuri chief Muhammad ibn Suri (d. 1011), referenced in Chapter 1. This chief evidently held some sway over the sub-region of Mandesh, which extended from the Hari Rud's southern banks northward to the borders of Darmashan, identified as another sub-region of Ghur. Thus, even though Ahangaran appeared to be the northernmost fortress of Ghur in pre-modern times, the conceptual frontiers of the region lay farther northeast and northwest, encompassing, respectively, the Chaghcharan basin through the edges of Gharjistan.[22] Southward, Mandesh stretched to the very heartland of Ghur, which was anchored by the mountain peak of Chehel Abdal. Kohzad (1954a: 23) noted in the mid-twentieth century that the area around Chehel Abdal and the Mandesh region overall "ha[d] all the necessities for animal rearing and husbandry," implying that subsistence in the region was quite possible.[23]

Modern documentation at the historical site of Ahangaran (Figures 2.1 and 2.3), a fortification with two concentric walls atop a rocky promontory rising gently above the Hari Rud, shows cultivated fields below stretching to the river banks and relying on it for irrigation.[24] Notwithstanding changes in the region's geo-climatic features over the centuries, it is conceivable that historically also, Ahangaran and its vicinity were home to largely transhumant populations. These groups resided in constructed villages – such as Ahangaran itself – only in the colder winter months, and moved into tents on the banks of the Hari Rud during the warmer periods of the year.[25] In modern times, specifically the mid-twentieth century, the well-watered Ahangaran Valley's inhabitants were not only agriculturalists, some among them also wove rugs. The valley in fact witnessed the constant visits of nomadic populations, many traveling to the month-long Khirgai market near Chagcharan, which was "a yearly meeting of nomads from [Afghanistan's] remotest corners." There, brisk trade occurred in

Figure 2.2 *Jam–Firuzkuh, minar and confluence of Hari Rud and Jam Rud. © Courtesy of David Thomas.*

Figure 2.3 *Ahangaran, surroundings and banks of Hari Rud. © Photograph Jawan Shir Rasikh, c. 2010.*

livestock as well as hand-made objects and textiles.[26] The wide spectrum of lifestyles within the Ahangaran Valley, certainly in the present day and probably also in the past, reiterates the conceptual importance of the nomad–urban continuum for understanding not only the Shansabanis' forebears and their milieu of origin but also, as we shall see below, their later imperial history.

By the mid-twelfth century (*c.* AH 539/1145 CE), the Hari Rud boasted a second Shansabani-affiliated site at its confluence with the Jam Rud. The probable Shansabani summer "capital" of Jam-Firuzkuh (Figure 2.2) was established quite possibly in the vicinity of a primarily Jewish settlement already existing nearby as of the early eleventh century.[27] The site received notable architectural patronage probably upon its inception, which continued through AH 565–575/1170s CE and perhaps later (see esp. Chapters 3–5). Farther west of Jam-Firuzkuh lay Chisht and Awbeh, the last two being eastern satellites within the orbit of the great Khurasani emporium of Herat. Ghur's eastern flank beyond Chagcharan already touched upon the mountainous edges of Bamiyan and its many valleys. Thus, northern Mandesh and especially Darmashan – edging Badghis, Faryab, and Sar-i Pul provinces on modern maps – most likely formed the northern arc of historical Ghur as understood by the Shansabanis' eleventh- and twelfth-century forebears.

According to Juzjani, even after the Shansabanis' emergence as a prominent regional power in the mid-twelfth century, at least some of the elites and their entourages and other followers continued to undertake annual, seasonally determined migrations along a northeast–southwesterly axis. The

Shansabani elites spent only the summer months of the year at Firuzkuh, despite this "capital" being monumentally conceived, as noted above. It was approximately forty *farsangs* to the south in the region of Zamindawar, and probably at a specific location therein, that the Shansabanis spent the winter months.[28] Firuzkuh, then, was essentially the Shansabanis' *sard-sir* or summer encampment of their seasonally transhumant existence, complemented by the *garm-sir* or over-wintering area in the region of Zamindawar near the borders of Sistan.[29] For our present purposes, these predictable movements furnish the broad regional span of the pre-imperial Shansabanis during the eleventh–twelfth centuries.

Ahangaran and Jam-Firuzkuh (Figures 2.1 and 2.2) merit juxtaposition not only for their locations along the Hari Rud, but also for their varying suitability as the Shansabanis' eventual *sard-sir* royal encampment. Indeed, scholarly debate as to whether Jam-Firuzkuh was in fact the Shansabani summer "capital" endured through much of the twentieth century, centering precisely on the site's *un*suitability. Aside from the admittedly magnificent *minar* (Figure 2.2) and even with the archaeological recovery of its adjacent, monumental mosque (cf. Chapters 3 and 4), little else indicates the site's royal status. Furthermore, its location was remote, not easily accessible along the northern routes from Herat toward Balkh; and its fastness in a mountainous landscape provided limited space for pasturage, also being insufficient for seasonal agriculture along with the encampments of royal retainers and soldiery. By contrast, Ahangaran (Figures 2.1 and 2.3) met most of these requirements, with its location on a well-watered plain. This locality had the added advantages of being one of the crossing points of the Hari Rud, as well as having ancestral associations for the pre-imperial Shansabanis.[30] Nevertheless, little doubt now remains that the Shansabanis chose Jam-Firuzkuh over Ahangaran as the site for their summer residence.

Beyond the above-mentioned migration patterns, little precision is forthcoming in delineating the southern extent of Ghur. Zamindawar as a historical region has been identified, of course, but in the current state of scholarship a specific locality as the likely site of the Shansabanis' winter "capital" can be only tentatively suggested. Calculations of its possible location have been put forth, though inconclusively, based on Juzjani's mentions of distance from Firuzkuh and comparison with the numerous fortifications identified in the southern part of Ghur, particularly in the area of Taiwara and perhaps beyond[31] (then extending into modern Farah province), as discussed below. Southern Ghur was evidently well-watered by its three rivers: the long Farah Rud, the Rud-i Ghur, and the Khwash Rud. By the twelfth century, then, it was this *c.* 250-km expanse from northern Ghur to the borders of historical Zamindawar and Sistan that constituted the core home region of the eventual Shansabani elites and their seasonal transhumance.

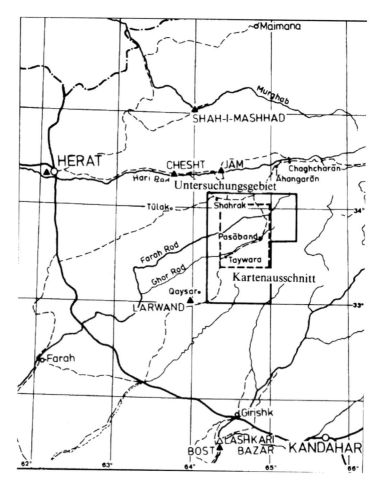

Figure 2.4 *Detail of Herberg's fieldwork in central and southern Ghur, c. 1970s.*
From Herberg 1982: II.

Aside from Ahangaran and Jam-Firuzkuh, many other architectural
remains dot historical Ghur's central–southern stretches (Figures 2.5–2.11),
being generally scattered with few discernible areas of concentration.
The photographic documentation in Ghur in the 1960s by the intrepid
traveler-photographer Josephine Powell (mentioned in this volume's
Introduction), and architectural surveys by the scholars Werner Herberg
and Warwick Ball in the 1960s and 1970s,[32] reveal a cultivable but rugged
landscape. In Herberg's (Figure 2.4) survey of the structures still standing
at various locations spanning from north of the Farah Rud through the
southern areas beyond the Rud-i Ghur, he observed that in general they
rarely stood atop peaks or inclines, but commonly at the bases of cliffs
and protectively flanking passages through valleys (Figure 2.5).[33] At times
multiple structures were also grouped together, so that they could have
enclosed (partly or completely) cultivable areas or pastures (Figure 2.6).

Figure 2.5 *Yaman, Ghur Province, Afghanistan, ruins of a square tower and cruciform "military structure" with remains of defensive wall. From Herberg 1982: fig. 3.*

Figure 2.6 *Ghor Province, Yahan, fortification line, ruins. © Photo by Josephine Powell c. 1960. Harvard Fine Arts Library, Special Collections.*

Since the vast majority of the surviving structures in the region appear
to have been intended for defense and surveillance, scholars have interpreted it as the stage for continual skirmishes and close-quarter battles.
Such a picture of historical Ghur was first painted by Bosworth (see also
Chapter 1), *viz.* an isolated and politically fragmented region of "fortified domesticity" whose internally squabbling inhabitants repelled outsiders throughout historical memory.[34] Furthermore, modern studies
have accepted at face value Juzjani's assertion that 'Abbas ibn Shish
(early–mid-eleventh century), a scion of the rival Shishani lineage (also
collateral to the pre-imperial Shansabanis), built the fortifications still
standing in central–southern Ghur, thereby dating them to a short period
probably sometime in the first half of the eleventh century.[35] Indeed,
this domino effect of accepted assumptions appears to have resulted in a
focus largely on defensive structures in southern Ghur. Ball, for example,
explained an apparent concentration of defense and surveillance structures in Ghur's southern reaches as the Shansabanis' principal line of
defense against the Ghaznavids, necessitated by the latter's vast empire and
particularly their presence in the contiguous area of Bust-Lashkari Bazar
during the eleventh century.[36]

However, a much-needed re-examination of central Ghur's built environment is undertaken here, encompassing the typologies, and decorative
styles and iconographies of the built remains themselves. It is equally
important to bring to bear upon the analysis what is known of the lifestyles and economies of the pre-imperial Shansabanis and their fellow
Ghuris. I point to the possibility of an alternative time span of construction for at least *some* of southern Ghur's standing structures: the late or
post-Sasanian through early Islamic (seventh–tenth centuries) periods,[37]
which would thereby pre-date the Shansabanis and their immediate
forebears. Additionally, the documented traces of decoration on some of
Ghur's architectural remains plausibly suggest non-defensive functions
for them as well. These new possibilities for understanding Ghur's architectural landscape are not only supported by the architectural evidence,
they also fit better into the *more* nomadic/transhumant lifestyles of the
Shansabanis' pre-imperial ancestors. But, as ever, it must be remembered
that the ensuing analyses and conclusions remain tentative, based on the
documentation of scholars working in the region through the late 1970s
when it was more accessible.

It was noted above that Ghur's built remains comprise either walled
enclosures with integrated square or semi-circular corner bastions, or
individual "dwelling towers,"[38] the latter being more common (Figures
2.6–2.8). The construction materials were locally sourced and consisted
primarily of sun-dried bricks, which formed walls atop stone footings
varying in height (Figure 2.9). Some variation in brick sizes was also
observed, ranging from 33 cm to 48 cm in length and 8 cm to 11 cm in

Figure 2.7 *Ghor Province, Male Alau, brick tower, ruin, distant view.*
© *Photograph Josephine Powell* c. *1960. Harvard Fine Arts Library,*
Special Collections.

height, but any regional correlations or chronological indicators have as yet to be established. Although baked bricks were present, they were never documented *in situ*, but rather scattered nearby, and may have been used sparingly for decoration or perhaps now collapsed parts of structures. Wood seemed to play virtually no role in the construction.[39]

All structures tended to be up to three stories tall (Figure 2.10); many of the towers as well as larger complexes, consisted of superimposed rooms within a tower, or a small number of spaces within an enclosure. They hinted at short- or long-term habitation, with some of the interiors of upper rooms bearing traces of possible painted decoration, indicating that they could have been the living quarters; however, the date range of these decorations remains unknown. These possibly residential rooms were raised above lower ones that could have been used for storage, or perhaps shelter for livestock.[40] Since excavations have not been carried out at any of these locations, and only surface surveys with photographic documentation and schematic drawings are available, the patterns of usage remain conjectural.

Figure 2.8 *Ghor Province, Alana Valley (junction of routes to Khissar, Parchaman, Nili, and Tiawara), fortification line, ruins, distant view. © Photograph Josephine Powell* c. *1960. Harvard Fine Arts Library, Special Collections.*

According to the drawings of the surviving structures made by Herberg and Ball, there is a remarkable variation in ground plans.[41] As noted above, the towers were circular or angular on plan, and either independent or addorsed to larger enclosures or buildings. The larger complexes exhibited the greatest variety of plans among themselves, ranging from rectangular enclosures to cruciform structures (e.g. Figure 2.10), with some combining these forms in more complex layouts. While a more systematic survey and certainly archaeological excavation could both aid in determining at least a relative chronology or developmental sequence among these plans, at present the documentation stands as it is, lacking the evidence for larger patterns of change over time.

Overall, southern–central Ghur's surviving structures seem recalcitrantly resistant to dating, both in terms of period of construction and longevity of use. No epigraphic data have been recovered, so there are no known foundation dates, patrons, or builders as points of departure

Figure 2.9 *Taywara vicinity, Ghur Province, watch tower. From Herberg 1982: fig. 1.*

for plausible spans of occupation/use, or clues regarding the functions of the sites and structures. Nor does the fabric of the remains themselves, comprising walls primarily of unbaked brick (rarely baked) atop tall stone footings – as described above – provide diagnostics of date, as this construction method was prevalent in pre-Islamic strata throughout Afghanistan.[42] In the face of these challenges, it is worth interrogating – insofar as this is feasible, with parallel or illustrative data supporting the little direct evidence – whether the pre-imperial Shansabanis and other Ghuris of the eleventh century were indeed the fashioners of this land-scape, as implied by Juzjani and generally accepted in modern scholarship. Would these groups' historical *habitus*, largely constituted of certain life-styles and economies, have allowed or even called for the construction of numerous "dwelling towers," fortified enclosures, and other structures for defense and surveillance?

Figure 2.10 *Between Pasa Band and Dahane Nawrak, cruciform interior of a defensive structure. From Herberg 1982: fig. 6.*

As described in the preceding chapters, the early Shansabanis and other Ghuris spanned the continuum between nomadism and sedentism, with many groups engaging in seasonal transhumance combined with spot agriculture. Modern Taimani and Firozkohi nomads inhabiting the areas immediately north and south of the Hari Rud (east of Herat) provide illustrative parallels in broad contours,[43] which can inform historical understandings of transhumant and nomadic–pastoralist groups such as the pre-imperial Shansabanis and their fellow Ghuris.

The southern Taimanis' summer shelters of rectangular black tents (Figure 2.11), made of willow poles and woven goat hair coverings (*palas*), required no specialized architectural skill per se. Although it is noteworthy that their tents tend to mimic winter village dwellings, and the tent coverings are traditionally woven by women. By contrast, the Firozkohis' yurts (Figure 2.12) were heavier and laborious to erect, resulting in a more expensive dwelling that also required camel or other large-scale transport. Given the yurt's characteristics as a dwelling type, it was used by groups with short migration circuits, and only in regions within the circulatory patterns of artisans skilled in crafting their specialized wood frames.[44]

All in all, the lifeways described above appear to preclude the need for coordinated projects of immovable architecture,[45] such as dwelling towers and fortifications interconnecting vast swaths of land. Transhumant and nomadic–pastoralist existences instead require principal concentrations of time, energy and resources upon moveable dwellings, animal hus-

Figure 2.11 *Taiwara-Farah Rud. © Photograph Warwick Ball, c. 1970s.*

Figure 2.12 *Ahangaran. © Photograph Warwick Ball, c. 1970s.*

bandry, small-scale farming, and the production of portable commodi-ties. Transhumant rather than nomadic segments of the population – for example, the inhabitants of Ahangaran in northern Ghur, of whom the above-mentioned Firozkohis might be descendants – could have estab-lished settlements for seasonal occupation during specific periods of the year (Figures 2.1 and 2.3). Moreover, the specialized expertise required in erecting relatively portable winter dwellings, such as yurts, appears not to be endemic to transhumant groups, but rather the latter *purchase* it from skilled crafters, and that only where these workers are available. In fact – and insofar as modern *praxes* reflect historical ones – even these artisans' specific expertise of fashioning construction elements in *wood* would have evidently had no place in the exclusively brick and plaster architecture of the region (see above). Southern–central Ghur's building programs, then, seem altogether dissonant with mainly transhumant and nomadic ways of life.[46] Rather than constructing entirely new and compex built environments, the region's historical inhabitants' varying degrees of movement would instead have called for repairing, repurposing, and reusing inherited architectural landscapes.

During A. A. Kohzad's tours of central–southern Ghur in the mid-twentieth century, his local informants among the region's inhabitants, particularly in the Yaman Valley southeast of Taiwara, assigned notably different builders to the towers/fortifications, attributing virtually all the local ruins to the pre-Islamic centuries.[47] There may be a basis for these oral histories: one of the most noteworthy features of many of the region's ruined structures, whether sole towers or larger complexes, is their surface decoration (Figures 2.13–2.16). Based on first-hand docu-

Figure 2.13 *Ghor Province, Yahan, fortification tower, ruin, with decoration typical of region. © Photo by Josephine Powell c. 1960. Harvard Fine Arts Library, Special Collections.*

Figure 2.14 *Southern Ghur, southeast façade of a structure. From Herberg 1982: fig. 9.*

mentation, Herberg described these structures as thickly plastered on the exterior, with many having decoration incised or molded on their surfaces while the plaster was still wet.[48]

The decorative motifs on central–southern Ghur's remains evince some

Figure 2.15 *Qala'-yi Chahar Baradar, Ghur Province. © Photograph*
Warwick Ball, c. 1970s.

consistency, being principally shallow patterned hollows creating trian-
gle and diamond shapes across much of the surface (Figures 2.13–2.16).
Motifs of arches in series were confined toward the tops of structures
(Figures 2.16 and 2.23). In some cases, such as the walls of Qala'-yi Chahar
Baradar and the stone-footed brick towers at Muna Ala (Figures 2.15 and
2.16) – both within a few kilometers of each other – square or rectangular panels framed tightly wound and molded circular patterns evoking
stylized flowers or floral motifs, interlaced with gently curving double
lines.[49] The hemispherical arch series toward the top of the Muna Ala
tower (Figures 2.16 and 2.23) has additional molded decorations within
the arches, possibly derived from a shell or floral design (see below). What
appear to be column capitals at the arches' springing were emphasized with
a triangular motif in relief. Above the arches more horizontal, frieze-like
panels containing thicker circles with smaller central holes, interlaced with
the diagonal lines are visible. Again, it may be tempting to consider these
decorative motifs as diagnostic of at least a relative chronology in which
to place their towers or structures, for example, one "progressing" from
simple to complex in order to explain the varying intricacy and variety
of decoration. However, any timelines must remain tentative, given the
absence of supporting archaeological and epigraphical data.

The method of fashioning the decoration found on many of central–
southern Ghur's ruins, as well as its iconography and style (Figures 2.13–
2.15), all stand in notable contrast to the known Saljuq and Ghaznavid
*minar*s that have been brought up as comparisons (late eleventh–twelfth
centuries; cf. also Chapter 1). More significant for our purposes, they diverge

Figure 2.16 *Ghor Province, Male Alau, brick tower with stone base, ruin, with scroll pattern decoration. © Photograph Josephine Powell* c. *1960. Harvard Fine Arts Library, Special Collections.*

from the Da Qadi *minar* (Figure 2.17): this recent rediscovery has been put forth as possibly the early Shansabani-patronized "lost" *minar* of Qalaʿ-yi Zarmurgh, located near Saghar, 75 km southwest of Jam-Firuzkuh.[50] Surface deterioration has been extensive on the Da Qadi tower, leaving behind no inscriptional traces and lacking the bottom bands of decoration and epigraphy horizontally framing the shafts of most twelfth-century Saljuq *minar*s. Nonetheless, its tapering cylindrical shaft, the remaining upper bands of geometric decoration, and the division of the *minar*'s shaft by means of these and likely additional bands, overall emulate the region's better-known *minar*s, such as the no longer extant one at Qasimabad in Sistan (*c.* 1125–1150 CE) (Figure 2.18) and the Daulatabad *minar* south of Balkh (early twelfth century) (Figure 2.19).[51]

Although the *minar* at Da Qadi will be analyzed in greater detail later in the chapter, it should be noted here that the ornamentation on central–southern Ghur's structures (Figures 2.13–2.16, 2.20, 2.23) differs markedly from the Da Qadi *minar* as well as the other *minar*s (Figures

Figure 2.17 *The "lost" minar of Qala'-yi Zarmurgh,*
c. 75 km south of Jam-Firuzkuh. From Thomas
2014: 26.

2.17–2.19) in material as well as form: the latter's decorative bands were fashioned with baked brick and some stucco so that, where brick was used, the decorative repertory was limited to geometric and minimally curving designs.[52] By contrast, the exclusive use of a malleable plaster on Ghur's central–southern remains accommodated curving and semi-floral patterns, even in deep relief. While the Da Qadi *minar* emulated the baked-brick Saljuq and Ghaznavid towers – aspiring to a "cosmopolitan" building tradition prevalent throughout the Persianate regions, as discussed below – central–southern Ghur's *qasr*, *qala'* and *kushk* emerged from a distinct architectural culture. Despite Juzjani's general attribution of the ruins to the tenth or early eleventh century, and modern scholars' general acceptance of the date, many of central–southern Ghur's ruins point toward an *earlier* span of time, namely the late or post-Sasanian–early Islamic periods of the late seventh–tenth centuries. (It is impossible to ascribe this timeframe to *all* of Ghur's remains, given the current inaccessibility of the region for first-hand documentation.)

The pre-Islamic affinities and chronology of the construction and decoration of many of central–southern Ghur's structures are borne out by juxtaposition with stucco architectural decoration dating to the later Sasanian centuries (Figures 2.21, 2.22, 2.24). Several sites in the vast empire's easternmost reaches – notably excluding western Afghanistan[53] – have undergone archaeological exploration/excavation and analyses of their stucco decoration, *viz.* Bandian (fifth century CE), Tepe Hissar near Damghan (fifth–sixth century), and Mele Hairam near Sarakhs (fifth–seventh centuries) (all in modern Iran). However, given the fragility of stucco as a material, and the consequent loss of much of the original Sasanian corpus, relevant examples from different periods and regions of Sasanian ascendancy must also be considered.[54]

Repetitive and abundant molded patterns suffused many of the plaster surfaces of central–southern Ghur's built remains (Figures 2.13–2.16, 2.20), demonstrating a palpable resonance with Sasanian parallels. The curved and

Figure 2.18 Minar *of Qasimabad, Sistan. From Tate 1912–1912: opp. p. 22.*

at times tightly wound double lines on Ghur's buildings (Figure 2.20) – often framing or meandering among flush, deeply carved or stamped floral motifs – echo the widespread framing technique of Sasanian stucco decoration: relevant examples come from both the Sasanian east at Tepe Hissar (Damghan, fifth–sixth century CE) (Figure 2.21), as well as the west at Nizamabad (south of Tabriz) (Figure 2.22).[55] Moreover, the stylized, high-relief rendition of floral elements characterizing the known Sasanian stucco corpus forms an intriguing continuum with the fleshily sculpted floral whorls on some of Ghur's structures (Figures 2.15, 2.16, 2.20, 2.23).

Figure 2.19 *Balkh, minaret of Daulatabad (1108–1109), exterior, full view: cylindrical, decorated in "light and dark" (Hazar Baf) style of brickwork; bands of Kufic and Naskhi script, both inscriptions and decoration; bricks, unglazed, and incised stucco. © Photograph Josephine Powell c. 1960. Harvard Fine Arts Library, Special Collections.*

Figure 2.20 *Detail of Figure 2.16, Male Alau, Ghor Province, brick tower, lower decoration. © After Josephine Powell c. 1960. Harvard Fine Arts Library, Special Collections.*

Figure 2.21 *Damghan, Semnan Province, Iran, stucco dado with palmettes, Sasanian. From Kröger 1982: tafel 89.*

Motifs of arches in series on the plastered surfaces of Ghur's remains – for example, toward the top of the Muna Ala tower (Figure 2.23), also discussed above – illustrate the capacious heuristic of architectural culture and the nature of the relationship between the Sasanian expanse's "cosmopolitan" stucco decoration, and the manifestation of these practices in the empire's eastern reaches in modern Afghanistan. These arcade motifs were also part of the iconography of Sasanian stucco decoration, as seen at sites such as Taq-i Bustan (*c.* fourth century CE) (Figure 2.24), where the finely worked stucco covering a column capital exhibited arches in series with exquisite, seashell-like striations in their semi-circular hoods. This common decorative motif was, as is evident, adapted into the local repertory of south–central Ghur as well, but here the fine, shell-inspired lines were interpreted as a broad three-lobed design – likely the outcome of the differing pliancy of the available plaster and the skill of the artisans working it.

Figure 2.22 *Nizamabad, Iran, wall fragment with stucco decoration, Sasanian/early Islamic? From Kröger 1982.*

Figure 2.23 *Detail of Figure 2.16: Male Alau, Ghor Province, brick tower, upper decoration. © After Josephine Powell c. 1960. Harvard Fine Arts Library, Special Collections.*

The proposal of a late seventh–tenth century span for the initial construction of central–southern Ghur's architectural remains – their renovation,
repurposing, and reuse possibly continuing well into the twelfth century
and beyond – also concords with the region's historical trajectory. Given
the significance of Sistan–Khurasan for both Sasanian imperial consolidation, and the later Sasanians' lingering rebellions against the onslaught
of Arab-Umayyad ascendancy (see below), the presence of pre-Islamic

Figure 2.24 *Taq-i Bustan, central Iran, column capital (Sasanian). Kröger 1982: tafel 40.*

remains in the adjacent parts of Ghur should not elicit surprise. Indeed, the Islamic-Umayyad and -Abbasid extensions into Sistan during the late seventh through eighth centuries did not progress unchecked, but rather were protracted over at least the next 150 years. Leaders with local power bases, such as the Saffarids (eighth–thirteenth centuries, with various suzerains), themselves arising from the earlier influx of Umayyad and Abbasid expeditionary forces, embarked on their own ongoing struggles for supremacy.[56]

The historical sources describe incessant confrontations between the Rutbils and – initially – the Umayyad- and Abbasid-deputed forces, and eventually Saffarid loyalists and others. "Rutbil" was likely a hereditary title for the rulers of Zabulistan, parts of al-Rukhkhaj, Zamindawar, and Sistan,[57] whose seasonal capitals were distributed between northern *sard-sir* or summering grounds in Zabul, and the southern *garm-sir* in Zamindawar in the winter months (map, p. xvi).[58] The military engagements between the enigmatic Rutbil's allied military contingents (including "Turks") and the equally varied, Islam-affiliated forces were frequent and ongoing at least up to the end of the ninth and likely into the tenth century. According to *Tarikh-i Sistan*, the bellicosity was prolonged as most confrontations between the military presences did not result in definitive eradication of either side: in cases of victory for the Islam-affiliated forces, the Rutbil paid high indemnities in lieu of being deposed outright, which in turn perpetuated general instability in the region.[59]

Equally significant for our purposes is a discernible pattern among strengthening or newly coalescing polities in the aftermath of the Sasanian empire's *dénouement*: their emulation of the Sasanians through architectural patronage and continuity in ceremonial and ritual cultures, essentially "assert[ing] their legitimacy by placing themselves firmly in the line of past Iranian kings".[60] The sandwiching of southern Ghur between Zamindawar and Sistan(-Khurasan) could have facilitated the extension there of a "Sasanianizing" architectural culture during the late centuries of the first millennium CE.

The working conclusion I offer, then, is that Ghur's *already existing* towers and fortified structures continued to play an important role for the Shansabanis' pre-imperial ancestors as well as other Ghuris, who formed part of the complex and ever-changing nomad–urban continuum of Ghur and its contiguous regions. The Ghuris – including among them the group who would eventually identify themselves as the Shansabanis – repurposed and/or reused this inherited landscape and its built environment, especially during their winter sojourns in the *garm-sir* of southern Ghur, touching on the borders of Zamindawar and Sistan. In light of the alternative dating proposed here for central–southern Ghur's towers and other structures, it seems worthwhile to reassess the dismissive characterization of Ghuris in general as an unruly and decidedly disruptive people. A more nuanced understanding of their political and cultural milieu prior to the twelfth century is now beginning to emerge, as we bear in mind both their degrees of transhumance/nomadism, and their inheritance of a built environment largely pre-determined by their Hephthalite, Sasanian, and/or Western Turk predecessors.

During the eleventh and twelfth centuries, Ghur's location as "the buffer-zone between [the] two empires" of the Ghaznavids and Saljuqs apparently ensnared the region within the imperial wrangling and skirmishes often taking place uncomfortably close to its permeable "borders."[61] While this point of contact was admittedly a politico-military bane for the Ghuris, *architecturally* speaking it could be seen as a boon: Sasanianizing trends had already entered the region, as noted above. Furthermore, the pre-eminent imperial formations of the eleventh–twelfth centuries vied for supremacy in its environs, enabling the influx of the brick-based architectural culture emerging from farther west in Saljuq Iran (cf. Chapter 1). This identifiable set of building practices incorporated some components from their Sasanian predecessors, but essentially were coalescing as the transregional and "cosmopolitan" imperial language of a new age, dawning as much on the larger Persianate world as on the emerging Shansabani clan.[62]

Emergence into "History"

The oft-quoted anecdote in Juzjani's *Ṭabaqat* of the inter-clan competition between the Shansabanis' mythical progenitor Amir Banji ibn Naharan and another important personage of Ghur called Shish ibn Bahram appears to be a legendary "origin myth" more than reportage of fact. The story's basic plot consists of the rivalrous Ghuri chieftains seeking mediation by the great 'Abbasid Caliph Harun al-Rashid (r. AH 169–193/786–809 CE) himself, based at his magnificent court in Baghdad. Juzjani's tale also described the intercession on behalf of Banji by a Jewish merchant: this figure's function as a synecdoche of the Jewish communities of Afghanistan has already been borne out by the epigraphical, architectural, and archaeological evidence gradually emerging from the region over the last century of surveys and documentation, illuminating its socio-economic history.[63] This "origin myth," then, may hold further historical kernels, akin to the noted confessional and professional affiliation of one of the protagonists, *viz.* the Jewish merchant.

In essence, Juzjani's story was a Pygmalion-like tale of the advantages of transformation from provincialism to urbanity. Both the mentioned Ghuri chiefs were rough and uncouth in dress and manner, given their origins in a remote area supposedly out of the reach of the refinements of Islamicate civilization – arguably at one of its apogees by the ninth century; both of them were therefore unfit to enter the caliph's court. But Banji was friendly with a Jewish merchant from Ghur, cosmopolitan and wise in the ways of the world due to his own far-reaching travels in pursuit of commerce. Heeding his advice on dress and behavior, Banji came into the caliph's presence much better prepared than his rival Shish. In Harun al-Rashid's arbitration, Shish ibn Bahram was awarded military command over Ghur, while Banji was awarded the region's governing authority and the title of *amir* – the latter clearly the superior position and presumably the greater reward for Banji's ability to adapt to the cultured ways of comportment and overall self-presentation prevailing at the caliph's glittering court.[64]

Juzjani's pithy anecdote certainly mythologized the age-old and continuing rivalry between the Shansabanis and their collateral relations the Shishanis, resurfacing periodically even after the two lines were allied by marriage (see esp. Chapter 4). More compellingly, it hinted at the Shansabanis' origins in central Afghanistan's nomad–urban continuum of the early second millennium CE (continuing into modern times). But ultimately, I propose that the story encapsulated the Shansabanis' – and perhaps also the Shishanis' – own larger process of transformation from transhumance and/or nomadic pastoralism into a *more* sedentist and courtly imperial lineage, commanding (at least for a few decades) an ostensibly Perso-Islamic empire *via* a seasonally transhumant elite. The logically following lines of investigation, then, would encompass at least an approximate timeframe in which this transformation occurred, and the possible impetuses behind it. Moreover, how thorough was the transformation – were pre-imperial mores relinquished completely, or maintained to a discernible degree even as the Shansabanis attained regional and then transregional prominence? Finally, what role did Islam play in the process? Again, the architectural remains within historical Ghur provide a unique point of departure for answering these questions.

Processes of socio-political transformation are virtually impossible to recuperate from textual sources alone: as we have seen, the Shansabanis' pre-imperial history is not thoroughly reported even by Juzjani (cf. Chapter 1), surely in part due to their less than favorable "barbarian" origins. At the same time, material culture primarily records these subtle and *longue durée* processes' outcomes, such as manifest alterations in the built environment, rather than the processes themselves (cf. Introduction and Chapter 1). However, consideration of the available traces in conjunction with each other, and with anthropological studies documenting shifts in lifeways and economies within modern transhumant and/or nomadic societies, may provide informative parallels for conceiving of the Shansabanis' historical transformation.

It was argued earlier in this chapter that the pre-imperial Shansabanis and other Ghuris of the eleventh and early twelfth centuries, still practitioners of varying degrees of transhumance/nomadism, repurposed or reused Ghur's extensive architectural remains. In the present attempt to recreate with some plausibility their process of transition toward regional politico-economic dominance, the recent rediscovery of a *minar*-like tower at the rural settlement of Da Qadi (Figure 2.17), 75 km southwest of Jam-Firuzkuh, may prove to be extremely fortuitous. The *minar* gives credence to Juzjani's mention of such a structure at the site of Qala'-yi Zarmurgh, which has been plausibly located in the vicinity of Da Qadi. Moreover, Zarmurgh was supposedly the place of origin of the above-described rube-become-cosmopolitan Amir Banji, the legendary progenitor of the Shansabanis during the eighth–ninth centuries.[65] This significant rediscovery may signal and even help to date the early phases of the Shansabanis' public avowal of Islam – rather than their conversion per se, as discussed below. Ultimately, it could help mark the beginning of the Shansabanis' ability to patronize skilled laborers with exposure to building practices that were *trans*regional, prevalent beyond Ghur's nomad–urban continuum, and which were increasingly pertinent as the Shansabanis began to emulate their imperial contemporaries the Saljuqs and the Ghaznavids.

Although first-hand documentation of the *minar* at Da Qadi must await the region's (and Afghanistan's) greater accessibility, David Thomas and his colleagues have analyzed the tower as far as possible through photographs, combining their observations with the requisite input of local villagers with knowledge of the structure, its surroundings, and other historical remains in the vicinity.[66] Understandably, the authors were reluctant to assign a definitive date to the tower, owing not only to the current impossibility of rigorous excavation or direct study at the site, but also due to the absence of epigraphic fragments on or around the remains that could stylistically hint at chronology. Generally speaking, Thomas and his collaborators related the *minar*'s surviving decorative iconography and style principally to Saljuq-patronized towers in the Persianate expanse dating to the first half of the twelfth century.[67]

As described earlier in this chapter, the Da Qadi *minar* shows stark differences with central–southern Ghur's reused and repurposed architectural remains, the two broad types of structures subscribing to distinct architectural cultures. Ghur's stone-footed, brick and plaster ruins hearkened to the late Sasanian–early Islamic presences in the region during the seventh–tenth centuries. Meanwhile, the Da Qadi *minar*, made of baked brick with some additions of wood and clay for structural integrity, ensued from very different building practices: this *minar* and related parallels formed an essential typology within an architectural culture initially fomented by Saljuq patronage,[68] which eventually became the transregional and cosmopolitan architectural language adopted by imperial formations of the eleventh–twelfth centuries throughout the Persianate world.

The dissemination of cosmopolitan Persianate building practices in southern Afghanistan appears to have occurred certainly by the beginning of the eleventh century, and possibly before. Saljuq *minars* surely served as aspirational impetuses for Ghaznavid towers, the surviving examples having been attributed to Mas'ud III (r. 1099–1114) and Bahram Shah (r. 1118–1152), now the most prominent remnants of Ghazna's once magnificent *urbs* (Figure 2.25). The Ghaznavid *minars*' stellate – rather than cylindrical – plans *formally* evoke the remnants of Buddhism in their vicinity, as well as two known towers from central Sistan: one at Zaranj-Nad-i Ali (Figure 2.26); the other, known as Khwaja Siyah Push (Figure 2.27), near Chakhansur (north and northeast of Qasimabad, respectively). These towers' plans combined pointed and semi-circular flanges, and have also been cited as precedents for Delhi's Quṭb Minar (founded *c.*1199 CE).[69] The early Shansabanis would not have had to look impossibly far, then, for workers specialized in brick construction, whose skills would have been required for building the *minar* at Da Qadi: several such towers were already standing in the contiguous regions of Sistan (Figure 2.18)[70] and Zabulistan (specifically Ghazna) (Figure 2.25), as well as farther afield at prominent emporia like Balkh (Figure 2.19).

Figure 2.25 *Minarets of Ghazni, distant view.* © *Photograph Josephine Powell c. 1960. Harvard Fine Arts Library, Special Collections.*

In the process of assigning the Da Qadi *minar* a definitive place within the twelfth-century phase of this cosmopolitan Persianate architectural culture, it is important to note the similarities as well as the significant differences between this tower and its relevant contemporaries, specifically those at Ghazna and in the Sistan and Balkh regions. For it is inescapable that the Da Qadi exemplar diverges from these others in scale, and in the variety and quality of its decorative program.

The Ghazna *minar*s (Figure 2.25) likely measured about 44 meters in height when both the stellate and cylindrical shafts were in place (prior to *c.* 1915; cf. Figure I.20); while the Balkh and Qasimabad towers (Figure 2.18 and 2.19) reached at least 30 meters.[71] Based on the average dimensions of the fired bricks used in such constructions, Thomas et al. proposed that Da Qadi's *minar* could have been between 7.2 and 10.4 meters in height.[72] Further, even though Da Qadi's tower followed its larger *comparanda* in tapering toward the top, perhaps also having balconies in wood or another material, it probably did not have an upper shaft (as

Figure 2.26 *Nad-i Ali, Zaranj, Sistan, remains of tower. From O'Kane 1984, fig.*
14c. Photograph T. Ward (early twentieth century) from the Royal Geographical
Society, London.

at Ghazna). In sum, at approximately one-third the height of the Balkh
and Qasimabad *minar*s – and probably only one-fourth the height of the
Ghazna towers – Da Qadi's *minar* would not have reached the impressive
proportions of the works commissioned by royal and elite patrons in the
broader region.

Coupled with its comparatively diminutive scale, the Da Qadi tower
also had a restricted decorative program. All of the other *minar*s mentioned above exhibit a variety of decorative iconography, ranging from
crisp geometry and Kufic epigraphy executed in brick, to dense floral
motifs and *naskh* inscriptions executed in stucco.[73] By contrast, Da Qadi's
minar shows only the geometric motifs resulting from the arrangement of
bricks at different angles in series. While the tower could have had a plaster
or other veneer with additional decoration, as it stands the structure shows
only the remains of brick-based decorative elements.

The not insubstantial differences in scale and decoration between Da
Qadi's *minar* and the royal- or elite-patronized parallels at Ghazna and
those in the Sistan and Balkh regions – not to mention the *minar* of
Jam-Firuzkuh itself (see Chapters 3 and 4) – could lead to the conclusion
that the Da Qadi example belonged to a different time period, or even to
a different tradition altogether. However, Thomas and his collaborators
pointed out that these differences may "indicate limited means and/or
technological knowledge."[74] As put forth in the Introduction, an architectural culture should be conceived as a spectrum spanning elite or royal,

Figure 2.27 *Remains of baked-brick tower, Khwaja Siyah Push, Sistan.*
From Fischer et al. 1974: ill. 253.

"cosmopolitan" patronage as well as non-elite, "vernacular" iterations:
Rather than one being of lesser or greater artistic merit, *all* instantiations of
an identifiable architectural culture serve as equally valuable and informative historical expressions. For now, we must be satisfied with the proviso
that more thorough access to Da Qadi and its surroundings will eventually
provide less equivocal answers to the questions still lingering around the
date and architectural–cultural belonging of its *minar*.

   Without epigraphical and other types of evidence, at present it is possible to put forth only hypotheses regarding the timeline and impetuses
for constructing the Da Qadi *minar*. But based on Juzjani's mention of
such a structure and its location, it is not unreasonable to propose that
the tower was the result of Shansabani patronage at the beginning of the
twelfth century. In turn, we must trace the consequential ramifications of
such a proposal. The tower itself was not only an "Islamic" gesture, it was
pronouncedly an act of architectural patronage. It could thereby signal not
only the Shansabanis' public declaration of an Islamicate identity, but also
the beginnings of an awareness of and transition toward the Persianate cultures of power prevalent among the elites of this geo-cultural expanse. As
discussed in Chapter 1, these cultures were iterated distinctly within each
polity, yet they can be conceived as founded upon three broad spheres
of activity, *viz.* Islamic confessionalism, patronage, and mobility. Quite
conceivably, in the first quarter of the twelfth century the Shansabanis

adopted an avowedly Islamicate public presence, as they were increasingly distinguishable from the many transhumant or/and nomadic groups of the region. Implicit within this change of status was their ability to command greater resources, some of which they dedicated to proclaiming their religious affiliation, albeit on a scale and in a context that was still far from the cosmopolitan currents of the Persianate world.

Such a seemingly momentous and certainly consequential change of lifeways and economies is by no means implausible. Among modern nomadic populations of the Iranian world, it is important to note that the variations between nomadism and sedentism can exist both *between* affiliated or related groups, as well as *within* a single one, so that some members are *more* sedentist than their transhumant and nomadic kinsmen or others. Increasing association with settled or urban localities and sedentarization can take place for diametrically opposed reasons, namely, the accumulation of surplus capital and purchase of land; or decline in fortune and ultimate impoverishment, requiring employment by villagers or other settled groups. Once undertaken, the process can be furthered by the already *more* sedentist co-members of a group, who would provide their transhumant or *more* nomadic comrades and kinsmen with ready village or urban connections for labor opportunities, and sale or purchase of supplementary or luxury goods.[75] Such a process could have unfolded at Qala'-yi Zarmurgh, as the Shansabanis' initiated their transition toward a lifestyle *less* of seasonal transhumance, and *more* of an imperial formation with seasonal "capitals."

A question requiring focused discussion with regard to the early coalescence of the Shansabanis is that of Islamization. Scholarly consensus on Ghur's Islamization has been that the region's inhabitants were largely hemmed in by a difficult, mountainous geography resisting both integration into wider commercial networks and the proselytism of Islam (or any other widely dispersed socio-religious system), probably until the eleventh-century Ghaznavid campaigns there.[76] Prior to this period, "the paganism of Ghur was of an indigenous variety and without outside connections."[77] But probably by the early decades of the twelfth century, the Shansabanis' seemingly sudden patronage of Da Qadi's *minar* – an architectural form distinctly evoking Perso-Islamicate culture (if not Islamic ritual) – requires a more nuanced explanation than the homogenizing and ultimately nondescript framework of "Islamization." If the Shansabanis required a transregional mercantile ethos and accompanying religious culture for furthering their political and economic ambitions, why not emulate the numerous Jewish mercantile communities throughout Afghanistan and convert to Judaism, as did the ninth-century Khazars north of the Caspian Sea? Islam was not the only choice.[78]

An important consideration must be brought to bear on the Shansabanis' apparently instantaneous espousal of Islam: perhaps it was not altogether instantaneous. Ghur itself surely did not remain immune to Islam and particularly Perso-Islamicate cultural forms given the continuous presence of both in neighboring Sistan and Zamindawar – presences beginning in the eighth century and continuing uninterrupted into the twelfth: on the heels of the Arab-Umayyad forays of the late seventh century, the entry of the Arab-Abbasids there engendered volatile Kharijite reactions in the eighth–ninth centuries, emerging particularly from Sistan.[79] Thereafter the Saljuqs and Ghaznavids continued the influx of Islam-affiliated ruling ideologies and imperial presences into these regions.

During the first two decades of the eleventh century, the infiltration of some form of Islamic religio-cultural presence in Ghur only increased. According to C. E. Bosworth, the Ghaznavids' own expediency in solidifying their hold over the important commercial emporium and intellectual center of Nishapur was instrumental in this process[80]: although Maḥmud Ghaznavi's father Sabuktigin had been a supporter of the Karramiyya, this populist sect's appeal to and rousing of the city's skilled labor groups – not to mention their increasing antipathy toward Nishapur's more orthodox *madhhabs* – required their removal to the hinterlands. Bosworth proposed that the sultan deputed the Karramiyya to the outlying areas of Ghur and perhaps elsewhere, where their notorious proselytizing zeal would find fertile ground among rural and transhumant/nomadic–pastoralist populations (cf. also Chapter 4). In the end, however, Mahmud Ghaznavi's dislodging of the Karramiyya from Nishapur and their entry into Ghur would have been only the most direct and documentable exposure to Islam for the Ghuris, who were in all likelihood already exposed to Islam's ideologies and religio-cultural mores from at least the preceding century or more.[81]

Within modern nomadic societies, anthropological studies have long noted a "poverty of ritual activities" – and specifically their traces, that is, ritual structures: nomadic life was structured around annual migrations and temporary settlements rather than the observation of feasts, fasts, and all-encompassing calendrical systems, especially if the latter were unsynchronized with seasonal transhumance.[82] In light of this overarching nomadic tendency, it is plausible that, given the pre-imperial Shansabanis' transhumance and/or nomadism, demonstrations of Islamic adherence would be difficult to recuperate, as would many other social and cultural aspects of their activities. Nevertheless, even if Islam co-existed with the region's "indigenous paganism," it is not implausible that some Ghuris, and particularly the Shansabanis' pre-imperial ancestors, had already been exposed to Islam for at least 200 years prior to the twelfth century, by which time a predisposition toward this religious and cultural ethos could have solidified.

By the beginning of the twelfth century and the construction of the Da Qadi *minar*, the advantages of some degree of adherence to Islam –

or at least recognizable demonstrations of this adherence – would have been increasingly evident to the ascendant Shansabanis. Although their pre-imperial forebears had doubtless participated in the mercantile networks within Afghanistan, the truly transregional connections needed for long-term commercial sustainability appear to have been plied largely by the region's Jewish communities, such as the one of Jam-Firuzkuh.[83] But in Afghanistan during the eleventh–twelfth centuries, empire-building – essentially another mode of benefiting from commerce, with the added advantage of being able to structure and direct it – lay in the hands of confessionally Muslim elites such as the Saljuqs and Ghaznavids. In order to become fitting competitors in an already crowded field of imperial contenders, and to fill the vacuum left by the declining Saljuq and Ghaznavid powers, appropriation and deployment of these fading predecessors' legibly *Islamic* – with a strong Persianate twist – imperial presences afforded the best outlet for the Shansabanis' own burgeoning political and economic momentum.

The adoption of Islam, however, was not sufficient for effective *kingship*, particularly in light of the extremely variegated nature of *both* by the beginning of the second millennium CE. Precisely because the Shansabanis' transformation from autonomous or nominally ruled nomads and/or practitioners of seasonal transhumance into expansionist rulers is not fully retrievable from the surviving textual and/or material sources, another look at the story related by Juzjani can provide at least the bases for further insights.

Aside from Amir Banji, the other protagonist of Juzjani's anecdote was the cosmopolitan Jewish merchant from Ghur, who surely served as narrative short-hand for the appreciable Jewish community of Jam-Firuzkuh. As noted above, Jews were settled in the area from at least the early eleventh century and remained possibly through the last quarter of the twelfth century,[84] based on the dates in the Judeo-Persian inscribed tombstones rediscovered at Kushkak, outside Jam. Taking into account the activities of the other important Jewish settlements in Afghanistan, it seems that the one at Jam-Firuzkuh would also have been prompted by mercantilism.[85]

But again, the location of Jam-Firuzkuh was less than propitious for commerce: although the site lay at the confluence of the Jam Rud and the Hari Rud, the rivers were volatile and seasonally difficult to cross.[86] Moreover, the site was within a mountain fastness not easily accessed from the well-plied routes connecting Herat, Balkh,[87] and beyond toward the northeast. Nevertheless, Jam-Firuzkuh's Judeo-Persian funerary inscriptions noted a variety of professions among the deceased, such as goldsmith and banker. This variety in turn would indicate that the area might have been equipped with at least some of the auxiliary "industries" and labor specialties of banking and manufacture necessary for the full development and exploitation of a mercantile economy. In the end, then, Juzjani's figure of the Jewish merchant likely personified a small but apparently thriving Jewish community at Jam-Firuzkuh, established there by the first half of the eleventh century and remaining active until the Mongol campaigns of the 1220s.

Juzjani also highlighted in his story the friendly and mutually beneficial interaction between Amir Banji and the Jewish merchant from Ghur, probably evoking the tenor of relations between the pre-imperial Shansabanis and Jam-Firuzkuh's Jewish inhabitants. In studies of modern transhumant and nomadic groups, large and small transactions have been documented as *de rigueur* between them and farmers, villagers, and townspeople along their seasonal migration routes. In fact, the necessary regularity of these routes even enabled the mutual extension of credit.[88] Thus, it is not implausible that, during the Shansabanis' perennial transhumance to and from their *sard-sir* "home," they developed trading partnerships with the Jewish mercantile community already settled there. In the end, Jam-Firuzkuh benefited the increasingly ambitious Shansabanis, displacing Qala'-yi Zarmurgh as a prominent *sard-sir* destination and eventual summer "capital" by the mid-twelfth century. Jam-Firuzkuh's commercial–economic potential may have been uneven, but any *access* to this potential required mediation, which was embodied in the locality's Jewish merchants and others with skills related to mercantilism.

Large nomadic confederacies from the Eurasian Steppes were undergoing various types and degrees of Islamization already by the tenth century CE, diversifying Islam itself as a political and religious ethos. Prominent among these neophytes were the Saljuqs of greater Iran and eventually Anatolia, who came to dominate the very centers of Islamic religio-political authority embodied in the Abbasid *khalifa* at Baghdad. With the nearly 150-year Saljuq presence spanning from Baghdad *via* Isfahan to Marv (mid-eleventh through twelfth centuries), nomadic lifeworlds combined with the Abbasids' Perso-Islamic imperial and administrative cultures to create palpable distinctions between the western and eastern Islamic lands.[89] Although less of a direct threat to Baghdad itself, the Ghaznavids represented another noteworthy group of empire-builders of the period, *viz.* ancestrally Turkic military slaves whose fantastic territorial gains earned them an enduring reputation over the centuries.[90]

Overlapping temporally and geographically with the Shansabanis, the Saljuqs and Ghaznavids were not only their formidable competitors in imperial expansion, they also served as aspirational models of prevalent courtly cultures (see Chapter One). Each of these three important pre-Mongol political formations of the eastern Islamic lands accommodated Perso-Islamic models of empire and imperial expansion on their own terms, responding to their respective pre-imperial histories, the demands of their political geographies, and the subjects constituting their respective political formations. For the rising Shansabanis, then, similarly contingent factors helped determine their adoption of some Perso-Islamic mores – such as a fabricated pre-Islamic genealogy emerging from mythical ancient Iran – alongside their continued adherence to indigenous and non-Islamic traditions ensuing from the cultural economies of transhumance/nomadism.

Notes

1. Asif 2016: 22 (see also below in main text).
2. For Qabacha see Juzjani vol. I, 1963: 418–421 (trans. vol. I, 1881: 531–544).
3. Juzjani related the anecdote of a courtier pointing out – rather audaciously – that the sultan's lack of sons meant his legacies had no heirs, to which the sultan replied, "[While] to other sultans are [born] one or two sons, several thousand are [born] to me, meaning the Turk slaves [*bandagan*], who will inherit my kingdoms, and [they] will read the *khutba* in my name." Cf. Juzjani vol. I, 1963: 410–411 (trans. vol. I, 1881: 497); and Allegranzi 2019a, vol. I: 46. See also Kumar (2007: 86ff.) for a description of the marital alliances among the Turk *ghulam*s presiding over the eastern territories (including Delhi), which were instituted by Mu'izz al-Din as the "patriarch" to mimic Islamic marital practices – i.e., paternal cousin marriage – and establish inter-generational allegiances. Cf. also Chapter 6.
4. Asif 2016: 22.
5. Kufi (trans. Fredunbeg) 1900: esp. 95–98, 154–157; Siddiqui 2010: 28–29, 34–35; Asif 2016: 14, 86–92.
6. Habib (2017: 108), in his review of Asif's book, adduced detailed evidence maintaining *Chach-nama* as a translation of an earlier Arabic text; he summarized as "a questionable thesis" the notion that it was Kufi's original composition.
7. Cf. esp. Asif 2016: 2–12 and *passim*.
8. The previously unknown geographical and historical origins of many communities in Afghanistan are gradually receiving attention. For example, the widespread Ghorbat of Afghanistan – found in pockets spanning Sistan through Qunduz, and Badghis to Jalalabad – were the subjects of a fascinating anthropological study by Aparna Rao (1982). The author explored the possibility of this and the Indian *jat* origins of five other tribal confederacies. Although the antiquity of the Ghorbat's self-created ethnogenesis is unknown, it is noteworthy that they also subscribed to descent from *Shah-nama* heroes (cf. Rao 1982: 41). One of the study's important contributions is its documentation of the negative connotations that *jat* origins have throughout Afghanistan, principally due to their nomadism (rather than their supposedly foreign origins). Indeed, Bosworth (2011: 17) highlighted the contradictory descriptions of Inner Asian Oghüz confederations in Arabic geographies, whose authors characterized them as "purely steppe dwellers in felt tents, with no towns," even though substantial settlements of Turks and (Muslim) Iranians were not uncommon in the same regions.
9. Cf. Amin 2002: 30; and Introduction.

10. See esp. Chapter 1, for a discussion of the Saljuqs' historical adoption of Islam during the tenth century CE and their later confessionalism.

11. In addition to the focus here on the twelfth century, Anooshahr (2018b: 2–3) outlines the process for the fifteenth- and sixteenth-century emergence of the global Islamic empires, but applicable here also: "… Persian historical narratives reified and attempted to construct stable categories such as 'kings' [and] 'dynasties' … out of chaotic military–political events … invent[ing] identities for the individuals involved (no longer as a band of armed men but as 'founders' or 'warrior-kings')."

12. Cf. esp. recent studies by Cribb 2020; Cribb 2020 (forthcoming); also O'Neal 2016; O'Neal 2020. See also Chapter 1.

13. See esp. Ball (2020), who convincingly argued that the various zones encompassed within modern Afghanistan are unique for their array of "vigorous pre-Islamic art and architecture," attributable to the incursions of various Hephthalite groups during the fourth century onward and the subsequent expansion of the Western Turk empire (late sixth century). Cf. also *infra* and Chapter 3.

14. Among the pioneering documentation of Ghur's architectural remains I include the photographs of Josephine Powell, available at: http://hcl.harvard.edu/libraries/finearts/collections/photographers_archives.cfm. While Powell's photographs were complemented by Herberg's documentation and preliminary analyses (1978, 1982), Powell's work continued to be useful for Ball's (2002) study of the region. See also Introduction and *infra* in main text.

15. Thomas 2018: 249 and *passim*.

16. While there is surely more information to be gathered, to date O'Neal's (2017) meticulous mapping of the Mongol campaigns in Afghanistan does much to identify the zones likely experiencing the greatest impact from their incursions. It is probable that there were at least three separate though simultaneous campaigns and nodes where more than one raiding party overlapped, specifically (from east to west) at Parwan, Ghazna, Ahangaran, Jam-Firuzkuh, Marv al-Rudh, and Herat. At least one raid probably reached Tiginabad/Old Qandahar. Curiously, among the three raids converging at Ahangaran, there was only one documentable offshoot southward into the heart of Ghur. This raiding party appears to have reached the Rud-i Ghur's headwaters in the Yakhan Valley, closely following the Ghuris' (including the Shansabanis' ancestors) north–south migration routes. While Juzjani's direct experience of the Mongol campaigns in Afghanistan renders his *Tabaqat* among the most important sources on the period, his patronage by Delhi's Nasir al-Din Mahmud (r. AH 644–664/1246–1266 CE) surely also played a role in the author's interpretations. Jackson (2017: 19) observed that Juzjani's exaggeration of Mongol destruction "enabled [him] to portray the Delhi Sultanate as the sole surviving bastion of Islam," with the book taking on "at times an apocalyptic tone." Nizami (1983: 90–92), however, thought Juzjani's firsthand account of the Mongols was valuable, in particular his balanced portrayal of Chingiz Khan. Cf. also Auer 2012: 19; Auer 2018: 101–102. But rather than a Mongol monopoly on destruction, several centuries later other actors also continued the erasure of Ghur's historical traces: internecine turmoil among

the Durranis at Herat in the early nineteenth century brought destructive repercussions to Ghur. Cf. Ferrier (trans. Jesse) 1976: 248ff.; and note below.

17. Bamiyan has always been on one of the principal routes joining the northern and southern regions of the Hindu Kush, and also served as an administrative center west of the mountains during both the pre-Islamic and Islamic periods (A. A. Kohzad 1951a: 13; Klimburg-Salter 1989: 21; Klimburg-Salter 2008: 132; and Chapter 3). Its internal significance as well as being a major *entrepôt* on the India–Central Asia artery off the trans-Asiatic silk routes rendered it desirable for all local powers (cf. Klimberg-Salter 1989: 24), including the early Shansabanis and their collateral lineage at Bamiyan (see below in main text). Despite the great Mongol massacre at Bamiyan, however, it was *not* among the nodes of convergence of the Mongol campaigns. Cf. O'Neal 2017; Jackson 2017: 80, 158.

18. See also Thomas 2018: 39–44. The Ghuris, rather than having an endemic antipathy to outsiders, were rightly affected by the far-reaching historical ripples of the Great Game. Ferrier (trans. Jesse, 1976: 248ff.) noted that the Ghuris he encountered were extremely suspicious of outsiders, Afghan and foreigner alike, given the recent and continuing devastations unleashed on the region from Herat: in the 1830s the city had been besieged by Qajar forces under Russian guidance, while the western khanate of Herat was nominally ruled by Kamran, son of Shah Mahmud (r. at Kabul 1800–1803, 1809–1818). But his *vazir* Yar Muhammad had effectively usurped rulership from the legitimate Durrani descendant and ordered the razing of all architectural remains in the vicinity of Ghur's famous citadel of Khissar (see below in main text), out of fear that rebels and other enemies could quarter there and eventually launch attacks against Herat from the east. Cf. Dupree [1997] 2012: 343–371.

19. A. A. Kohzad 1951a: 5.

20. Cited by Thomas 2018: 52. Juzjani vol. I, 1963: 328 (trans. vol. I, 1881: 318) of course first described "the natural impregnability of the strong mountains which are in Ghur."

21. In his tours of Ghur, Kohzad (1954: 64ff.) also noted that the region's southern areas boasted more abundant villages than its northern ones – understandable given that the Sistan plains were the over-wintering grounds for many nomadic populations. This is surely a long-standing socio-economic pattern, pertaining since at least the twelfth century when the Shansabanis also migrated southward for the winters. See further *infra* in main text.

22. See A. A. Kohzad (1953: 59–62); O'Neal 2016a. Certainly, in the tour reports of A. A. Kohzad (esp. 1953: 56) an intimate connection between historical Ghur and Gharjistan to its northwest seems to emerge, underscored by these regions' shared semi-sedentist populations of the Tajik Firozkohi summering there (also Jawan Shir Rasikh, pers. comm., December 2017). Indeed, modern Abdali Pashtun nomads have also migrated across the provincial boundaries between Ghur and Gharjistan (cf. Glatzer 1983: 215ff.). This strong inter-regional connection could have spanned several centuries, as hinted by the relatively early Shansabani presence in Gharjistan of the 1160s (noted *supra* in main text) and their architectural patronage of the monumental Shah-i

Mashhad *madrasa* (1165–1176 CE). These observations are meant to underscore what may be obvious, *viz.* that the historical frontiers of Ghur were porous and even seasonal, requiring an expansive and flexible understanding of it and its contiguous regions.

23. A. A. Kohzad 1954a: 23. See also O'Neal 2016a. As of the nineteenth century, historical Ghur could be conceived as encompassing the areas of transhumance and/or nomadic pastoralism of the Firozkohi and Taimani populations (see *infra* in main text and notes): the Firozkohis' ambit extended from Bala Murghab (modern Badghis Province) to the Hari Rud's northern banks; and the Taimanis' from the Hari Rud as far as Girishk, near Lashkari Bazar. Cf. esp. Maitland 1888: 605–608.

24. While A. A. Kohzad's (cf. esp. 1951a, 1954a, 1954b) extensive reports on the settlement of Ahangaran and the larger region are extremely valuable, I am deeply grateful to Jawan Shir Rasikh (pers. comm., December 2017) for sharing not only his photographs of the site and its vicinity, but also his enlightening observations. See also Ball 2019: No. 15.

25. See esp. A. A. Kohzad 1954b: 13: though the ensuing description is of populations farther south in the Yakhan Valley (discussed below), the author made the useful distinction between "migrant" (i.e., transhumant) and "nomadic" populations: the nomads traditionally traveled much farther in seeking seasonally hospitable climates, while their "migrant"/transhumant counterparts moved only from built dwellings to collapsible ones such as yurts, largely within the same area (e.g. Figure 2.12). Numerous parallels are also forthcoming from Turkic nomadic populations, such as the Khazars (tenth century), and the contemporaneous Oghüz (Golden 2013: 50–51, 54).

26. A. A. Kohzad 1953: 57ff.; also Barfield 1981: 97ff. for added data from northeastern pastoral nomads, who "are tied far more closely to the market economy than are many … farmers."

27. Gascoigne's (2010: 145) analysis of ceramic finds from Jam-Firuzkuh left open the possibility that, based on comparative material from Marv (Turkmenistan), some unglazed coarse wares from the site might be datable even prior to the eleventh century, thus before the earliest dates on Jam-Firuzkuh's Judeo-Persian tombstones. Cf. also *infra* in main text and notes.

28. Cf. Juzjani vol. I, 1963: 364 (trans. vol. I, 1881: 385–386); Thomas 2018: 149. Admittedly, the notion that the Shansabanis' summer rather than winter settlement evolved into a "capital"-like locale creates a contrast to the sedentizing tendencies of most other transhumant and nomadic pastoralist groups, whose winter encampments or settlements usually constituted their initial *foci* of consolidated political power and the formation of ruling elites. Cf. Golden 2013: 22, 30, 59.

29. This circuit of movement was possibly the residue of an *il-rah,* a collective term referring to the prescribed routes of seasonal transhumance traceable to the Shansabanis' *more* transhumant lifestyle prior to the mid-twelfth century. Taken from the fieldwork of Barth (1961: 4–5) among the Basseri confederacy of tribes in southern Iran, the term *il-rah* encapsulates the affective concept of "tribal road": The *il-rah* in fact varied among the major nomadic groupings of the region, each having their own traditional route of seasonal migration.

Some of the Basseri tribesmen who had gradually abandoned nomadism for greater sedentism – mostly due to land ownership and agriculture – nonetheless exhibited "a continuing emotional interest in and identification with nomad life and ways" (Barth 1961: 106). Cf. also Barfield 1993: 96–97. In the case of the imperial Shansabanis, the *il-rah* could have been more a convenience and haptic trace of their pre-imperial ancestors, rather than a subsistence necessity, perhaps even compelled by many nomadic societies' ambivalence if not out-right disdain toward sedentism (cf. Golden 2013: 22, 51).

30. Cf. Thomas 2018: 37. Tellingly, Thomas's monograph (2018: 1–2 and notes, 146–150, also 315–319) confronts Jam-Firuzkuh's lingering ambiguity in its opening pages and closes with plausible explanations of it. I am grateful to Warwick Ball (pers. comm., April 2020) for his observations on the two sites' suitability as the summer "capital."

31. Cf. Thomas 2018: 19, 40, esp. 149, for hypotheses regarding the Shansabanis' *garm-sir* destination. Recently, W. Ball (pers. comm., April 2020) proposed a few other sites as possible over-wintering "capitals" for the Shansabanis, including Qala'-yi Qaisar (Ball 2019: No. 875). Among the most promising of these could be Shahr-i Kuhna, about 100 km south of Taiwara: not only does it have the discernible *arg-shahristan* (round citadel–quadrangular settlement) plan – indicating pre-Islamic origins – it is also in the vicinity of Ziyarat-i Imam, a probable Ghaznavid-period shrine (*ziyarat*) of the late eleventh century. See Thomas 2018: 253; Ball 2019: Nos. 1047, 1130, 1267.

32. The above-mentioned documentary tours of Afghanistan were all principally carried out during the first three quarters of the twentieth century, as access to the country as a whole became more limited after the Soviet invasion of 1979. Wannell nonetheless pursued an impressive itinerary in 1989–1990 (cf. Wannell 2002). Constituting the bulk of documentation still available on Ghur and many other parts of the country, these archives have been inval-uable for me given the inaccessibility of large parts of Afghanistan during my 2011 fieldwork. Cf. Thomas (2018: 113ff.) for a thorough summary of the available data and interpretations of southern Ghur's built remains.

33. Herberg 1982: 80–81.

34. Bosworth 1961; Edwards 1991: 90.

35. Juzjani **vol.** I, 1963: 332 (trans. vol. I, 1881: 331–332); see also O'Neal 2013: 40 and *passim*; O'Neal 2016a. An exception would be Herberg's (1982: 83) dating: based on what he saw as the stylistic and technical consistency of dec-orative motifs on the surviving structures, he proposed that they were "part of a chronologically restricted building programme, probably that of Baha al-Din," no doubt also relying on Juzjani's report of this ruler's directions to building four fortresses on the borders of "Ghur, Garmsir, Gharjistan, and the mountain tract of Hirat." This dating would place southern Ghur's forti-fications in the mid-twelfth century, just after the ruler's "completion of … edifices and the royal palaces" of Firuzkuh. However, Herberg provided no further evidence for his assertions in the form of comparable examples, or any further reasons for a seemingly instantaneous fortification of the landscape in this period.

36. Ball 2002: 41–44; see also Edwards 2015: 98–99. Although focused around

Awbeh and Chisht-i Sharif and elsewhere in the eastern reaches of Herat Province, Franke and Urban's rigorous surveys in 2004–2006 are still useful. This work brought to light seventy-three previously undocumented structures, more than half of which lie in Chisht district. Nearer to Herat "large sacral buildings" (Franke and Urban 2006: 6) – e.g., the Gunbad-i Shohada and other *ziyarat*s, shrines, and mosques – are numerous, but they decrease steadily farther east: the east–west corridor along the Hari Rud, south of Chisht, is peppered with what appear to be fortifications and/or surveillance structures, including single towers (e.g., Kushk, Burj-i Qaria-yi Dehran, Dara-yi Takht) and small complexes (Qala'-yi Sarkari, Rabat-i Chawni), all in all not unlike the architectural landscape of southern Ghur (cf. also Chapter 4, below, and *infra* in main text). My own brief survey of areas west of Herat toward Ghuriyan (2011) also revealed single towers and small complexes. Altogether, these new findings demonstrate that areas other than central–southern Ghur also evinced clusters of similar structures, though the dating of *all* examples is still uncertain. See also Thomas 2018: 120–124. But given the prominence of nomadic populations throughout Afghanistan's history (cf., e.g., Dupree [1997] 2012: 57–65), the remains possibly evoke shared historical patterns where earlier fortification- or tower-strewn landscapes remained in enduring use by various populations over time (see also Chapter 3).

37. Intriguingly, Juzjani (vol. I, 1963: 328 (trans. vol. I, 1881: 317–318) provided a subtle hint that southern Ghur's terrain was well-fortified by the ninth century: evidently when the Saffarids emerged from Sistan onto a larger stage, for our purposes reaching the region of al-Rukhkhaj, "the tribes of the Ghuris fortified themselves on the summits of the rocks, and remained in safety; but they used to be at constant enmity with each other … keeping up a war from *kushk* to *kushk* …" Juzjani's only utilitarian regard of architectural remains, and complete *dis*regard of their chronology – typical of most textual sources – makes it difficult to know to which specific *kushk*s he referred, or their dates. Cf. Chapter 3, for a discussion of the term *kushk*, and more generally the pre-modern receptions of architecture in the Persianate-Islamic world. As a historiographical reflection, Juzjani's usage of material culture primarily as backdrop throws into even higher relief the present work's focus *precisely* on these elided historical indices, laying bare the very different methods of recapturing the past in modern times.

38. Although the "dwelling tower" was identified as characteristic of Sistan (Fischer 1970: 485), it serves to describe many of Ghur's individual towers, which also likely functioned as part-time residences (see main text). Overall the survey and documentation of Sistan by K. Fischer and his colleagues in the 1960s–1970s is relevant to our analysis of southern Ghur, not least because the non-sedentist lifestyles prevailing among the region's inhabitants effectively blurred strict lines of delineation: akin to southern Ghur, Fischer documented many ruined fortifications and individual towers throughout Sistan, though pointedly noting that there were certain building types he considered regionally specific to it, along with the technique – especially in towers – of combining the mud-brick structure with decoration in burnt or baked

brick. Cf. esp. Fischer 1971: 46, 50. Cf. also Ball and Fischer 2019: 487–505. The Helmand–Sistan Project (HSP), directed by William Trousdale, undertook further documentation in the region during the 1970s, which Mitchell Allen is currently preparing for publication with W. Trousdale (M. Allen, pers. comm., February 2020).

39. See esp. Herberg 1982: 75, 78; Thomas 2018: 114–116.

40. Cf. Herberg 1982: 73; Ball 2002.

41. See esp. Herberg (1982: 71) for a typological juxtaposition of the various rectangular and cruciform plans of the structures he documented; this is supplemented by Ball's (2002: 29, 39) additional drawings of more complex plans of single towers and small structures.

42. Cf. the analyses of Danestama (Le Berre 1970), a Buddhist site possibly repurposed during twelfth century (Shansabani?); Darra-i Killigan (Lee 2006); and especially the pre-Islamic fort of Shahr-i Zuhak, characterized in broad architectural terms as "fit[ting] into the sizeable group of pre-Mongol fortresses of central Afghanistan ... for example, Chehel Burj and Qaisar" (Baker and Allchin 1991: esp. 91 – these authors also had to rely on photographic documentation of Ghur's remains for comparative analysis). These complexes are discussed in Chapter 3. The extensive ramparts of Balkh (ancient Bactres) took full advantage of the site's rocky promontory as the base on top of which rammed-earth walls were erected (cf. Dagens, Le Berre and Schlumberger 1964). All of these sites' distance from Ghur – located as they were either within the ambit of the Bamiyan Valley and its offshoots, or far north in the plains of Balkh – indicate that there was a recognizable pan-regional architectural culture throughout most parts of Afghanistan.

43. I have relied on Szabo and Barfield's (1991: 48, 68) documentation of the areas of activity of the modern Taimanis and Firozkohis – both part of the Chahar Aymaq confederacy – indicating their possible informativeness for historical populations there. Additionally, P. A. Andrews' detailed study of tentage has posited historical data worthy of consideration, *viz.* the possible impacts of Mongol and later Timurid tent traditions on those of the Chahar Aymaq (cf. esp. King, vol. II, 1999: 155, 175, 363, 472, 682, figs. 6–8). Finally, the Afghan Boundary Commission's reports are extremely useful, providing a view on the populations at least one century in the past: e.g., on the Firozkohis and Taimanis as part of the Chahar Aymaq confederacy, see Maitland (1891: 107–141); Sing (1891: 161–204).

44. As intimated above, Szabo and Barfield's (1991) work on indigenous domestic architecture in Afghanistan has served as an invaluable resource here. See esp. Szabo and Barfield 1991: 29–31, 49–50, 59–61, 69–71. According to Captain R. E. Peacocke's (1887: 148) observations during the 1880s on behalf of the Afghan Boundary Commission, the Firozkohis considered their northern boundary to be at Piwar near Bala Murghab (modern Badghis Province). The Firozkohis' circuit of seasonal transhumance in the late nineteenth century was 130 miles east–west, and 45–80 miles in breadth, according to Maitland (1891: 112).

45. Cf. Barth (1961: 101–102) for a discussion of the comparable limitations of the nomadic–pastoralist Basseri of southern Iran.

46. It is worth noting that mid-twentieth-century archaeological surveys of Ahangaran and its vicinity yielded unglazed painted ceramics initially dated to "Kushano-Sasanian" occupation, which has usually meant *c.* 500 CE. Cf. Baker and Allchin 1991: 107–109 and fig. 4.29 (reproduced from Leshnik 1968); Ball 2019: No. 15; Ball, Bordeaux et al. 2019: 391. This would have impacted the significance of the site for our purposes, rendering it a pre-existing and thus *inherited* site for the pre-imperial Shansabanis. However, Franke's (2016d: 235–236) recent analysis of comparable unglazed painted pottery in the Herat Museum has resulted in assigning that entire collection to the tenth–thirteenth centuries, concurrent with the glazed and other types. The Herat examples that most closely parallel the Ahangaran finds include Cat. Nos. PP120–PP127.

47. Cf. A. A. Kohzad 1954a: 29, 31; Wannell 2002: 236–237.

48. Herberg 1982: 80; (cf. also Thomas 2018: 116).

49. Both sites are among the many significant but scantily documented locales throughout central and southern Ghur. Qala'-yi Chahar Baradar was also known as Pa'in Mazar, and Muna Ala as Mullah Ala and Mala Alau: cf. esp. Ball 2002: 33–35; Ball 2008: 151–152 for a general description of the Ana Valley, with Muna Ala in its western reaches; also Ball 2019: No. 742. For Qala'-yi Chahar Baradar, see Ball 2019: No. 787, and map 20.

50. Juzjani vol. I, 1963: 328, 331 (trans. vol. I, 1881: 318, 331). Mentioned in M. N. Kohzad 1959; and published with analysis by Thomas et al. 2014 (also listed in Ball 2019: No. 974). Thomas et al. (2014: 139) proposed that the "lost" *minar* of Qala'-yi Zarmurgh (discussed *infra* in main text) was most comparable "geographically, stylistically, and perhaps chronologically … [with] the mud-brick [*sic*] decoration on the Hephthalite and early Islamic fortresses of Ghur," indirectly suggesting a pre-Islamic date for the latter. As detailed below, however, the decorative programs of these two corpora of structures actually ensue from discrete architectural cultures.

51. For the Daulatabad *minar*, see Sourdel-Thomine 1953: 122–129; Ball and Fischer 2019: 484–487. For the Qasimabad *minar*, see Tate [1910] 1977: 22 and facing, 270 and facing; and esp. O'Kane (1984: 97), who provided a span of 1125–1150 CE for the *minar's* construction, based on stylistic and epigraphic comparison with more securely dated Saljuq towers, including the one at Daulatabad. The dissemination of *minars* across Afghanistan adds further weight to Najimi's (2015: n. 46; cf. also Chapter 1) observations regarding the mobility of specialized artisans, and their availability for patronage/employment at varying locales. See also *infra* in main text.

52. Many Saljuq *minars*, the two Ghaznavid examples, and, of course, the later *minar* of Jam-Firuzkuh (AH 570/1174–75 CE) combined baked brick and stucco in their epigraphic programs: while the Kufic or decorated (floriated) Kufic tended to be executed in brick, the letters seem at times to be placed against highly ornate, floral-arabesque backgrounds fashioned of stucco. The *naskh* and other more curvilinear calligraphic styles were also executed in the more pliant stucco. See Sourdel-Thomine 1953; Pinder-Wilson 2001; cf. also Appendix.

53. A locality close to our area of study would be the Zoroastrian pilgrimage site

and *irbidistan* (Zoroastrian priestly institution) near Kuh-i Khwaja, now in modern Iran's Sistan and Baluchistan Province. The construction method of stone foundations supporting sun-dried brick walls, widespread throughout pre-Islamic Afghanistan, was prevalent here as well (Ghanimati 2000: 144). Given the difficulty of pinpointing dates within the span of the Sasanian centuries – particularly in heavily trafficked landscapes such as the historically well-traversed Sistan – it is unfortunate that the site's sample collections were not more thoroughly published (fieldwork was conducted separately by A. Stein and E. Herzfeld in the early twentieth century; for the Herzfeld reproductions see Kröger 1982: pls. 23/6 [painting], 103/1–2, 104/4 [stucco]). Further sampling and ^{14}C analysis in the 1990s resulted in the discernment of two or three construction phases for the complex, ranging from the late Parthian through late Sasanian periods (second–seventh centuries). Cf. Ghanimati 2000; Canepa 2013. However, Kröger (2005) dated the site to the "early Sasanian period" or *c.* third–fourth centuries CE. For the other sites, see Schmidt 1937: 337–338; also Kimball 1937: 347–350, fig. 173, pls. LXXIV–LXXV; Kröger 1982: pls. 88, 1–7 and 89, 1–7; Kröger (2005); Boucharlat 2019: 362–363.

54. Even with important discoveries during the intervening decades, Kröger's 1982 monograph still serves as the main reference for Sasanian stucco finds from across the empire, representing a transregional study of the medium throughout the Sasanian lands. See also Kröger 2005; Boucharlat 2019: 351.

55. It should be noted that Kröger (2005) posited stylistic and iconographic echoes of late Sasanian stucco from sites such as Nizamabad and Tepe Mil in that of early Islamic palace complexes (e.g., Khirbat al-Mafjar, late seventh–early eighth centuries CE). Characterizing the process as one of "both a continuity and a change" initiated by the work of "northern Persian" artisans working in Palestine, it forms a possible parallel to the processes unfolding in the eastern reaches of the Sasanian realms during the seventh–tenth centuries as noted here.

56. Cf. Bosworth 1994: 9ff.

57. Marquart, relying on observations gleaned from al-Biruni (cited in Bosworth 1961: 124), considered the usual root of RTBL in Arabic sources as erroneous, arguing instead for "Zunbil" as a title (not a personal name) of a ruling lineage with lingering Hephthalite or Western Turk origins. The repeated occurrence of the term in *Tarikh-i Sistan* ((trans. Gold) 1976: esp. 74 n. 1, 170) hints at a localized nomenclature. But most scholars now favor the RTBL root over Marquart's reading, as the likely Arabicization of the Turkic title *iltäbär*: see Bosworth 1968a: 34–36; Bosworth 2008: 97–99, 106–109; Ball 1988: 134–135; Ball 1996: 399; Inaba 2010; Gardizi (trans. Bosworth) 2011: 128, n. 18; Rezakhani 2017: 165ff; N. Sims-Williams (cited by W. Ball, pers. comm., April 2020); Ball 2020. Notwithstanding the etymological arguments above, al-Biruni's characterization of Zamindawar's famed shrine of Zun/Zhun as dedicated to a minor sun deity can be circumstantially confirmed. Zamindawar lay on well-trodden commercial routes linking Panjab (and ultimately the subcontinent) with the greater Iranian world. Multan in southern Panjab was not only a significant commercial node but also home to the

famous Brahmanical temple dedicated to the solar deity Aditya, and directly communicated with Zamindawar; Brahmanical trends thus easily traveled westward and likely resulted in derivative cults. For Multan's regional and transregional overland connections, see Deloche [1980] 1993/94: 26–27 and fig. II; Dani 1982; Rehman 1979: 66; Edwards 2006: 22; and esp. Chapter 6. The mutually augmentative nexus between pilgrimage and trade has been extensively studied, e.g., Ray (1996: 5 and *passim*).

58. Inaba 2013: 90; Rezakhani 2017: 140–145, 165–168; and Chapter 3. The commerce along these routes, moreover, invited raids by Ghuri tribesmen along the southern reaches of their own annual migrations. Cf. also Bosworth 1961: 118; Mahmud 2009: 54; and Chapter 1.

59. Cf. Anon., *Tarikh-i Sistan* (trans. Gold) 1976: 74–75, 86–87, 101, 111, 114, 119, 167, 170–172, 216. Apparently, when central Umayyad demands became oppressive, there were even periodic alliances between local Arab forces and the Rutbil (see ibid., esp. 89–96, 163–164). See also Bosworth 1968a: 34–36, 121; Ball and Fischer 2019: 460; Ball 2020.

60. Michailidis 2015: 136. See also Ball 2020. Later patrons "could have indeed understood [the motifs] to reflect an earlier tradition" (M. Canepa, pers. comm., February 2018). Parallel to Michailidis' characterization of the architectural patronage of the Bawandids (mid-seventh–fourteenth centuries), a similar continuity with Sasanian architecture was discernible in Ṭahirid (821–873) palatial constructions (cf. Finster 1994). Subsequently, the well-known Buwayhid (932–1062) inscriptions at Persepolis demonstrated the importance of pre-Islamic Iranian kingship especially for dynasties with local origins, including the adoption of titles such as *shahanshah*. Cf. Blair 1992: 32–37. See also Canepa's (2015: 92–99) analysis of Sasanian dynastic sanctuaries and the dissemination of "Iranian kingship as a global idiom of power." Finally, Bosworth (1968a: 23) confirmed the proclivity toward Sasanian imperial practices specifically in Sistan, where "the local consciousness … had strong feelings of solidarity with the ancient culture and traditions of Iran." See also *ibid.*, 35 for the prestige and emulation of the Sasanian empire throughout Central Asia during the centuries after its demise; and Bosworth 2008: 97ff. It should also be mentioned that Sasanian coinage types continued to be emulated in the empire's eastern lands, possibly as late as the eighth century (Rezakhani 2020).

61. Cf. Bosworth [1977] 1992: 68; and Introduction (notes).

62. In terms of architectural patronage, regional variations among the far-flung Saljuq domains were discernible for a variety of reasons, perhaps especially due to the increasing politico-economic fragmentation of the empire through the *iqta'* system (Peacock 2016: 19–21). Nevertheless, the *iqta'* holders, some becoming more independent of the Saljuq sultans over time, "also sought to enhance their own prestige by creating regional courts modeled on the Seljuk precedent, which acted as centers for artistic and cultural patronage" (*ibid.*, 15).

63. While the figure of the Jewish merchant from Firuzkuh has had multiple historical resonances – discussed forthwith – recent re-examination of the name "Banji" has also borne fruit as to its possible origins: analysis of pre-Islamic

coinage bearing mint names ranging from Zabul through Balkh has led Rezakhani (2020) to propose that "Banji" might be an Arabicized corruption of "Pangul," one of the regional rulers named on the aforementioned coins. As for the Jewish merchant, Fischel (1965: 149–150) also relied on the figure as a point of departure for his analysis of the Judeo-Persian funerary inscriptions from Jam-Firuzkuh's Jewish cemetery, a small group of which were rediscovered in the 1960s, with more subsequently coming to light. Approximately seventy-four funerary markers – carrying a total of at least ninety-one Judeo-Persian inscriptions – were found over the course of several decades at a short distance from the famous *minar* of Jam-Firuzkuh, in the Jewish cemetery cut into the mountainside at Kushkak. They commemorated personages of different occupations, with dates of death starting in the early eleventh century and continuing through end of the twelfth. See also Habibi 1980: 42; Pinder-Wilson 2001: n. 37; Lintz 2008; Lintz 2009; Hunter 2010; Thomas 2018: 214ff. The tripartite mural inscription at Tang-i Azau, about 200 km east of Herat and also in the vicinity of Jam-Firuzkuh, is datable to the fourteenth century. Cf. Ball 2019: No. 1144. The implications of the existence of a Jewish community at Jam-Firuzkuh, *prior* to its designation as the Shansabanis' summer capital in the mid-twelfth century, are explored below.

64. Juzjani vol. I, 1963: 324–327 (trans. vol. I, 1881: 311–316); also Edwards 2015: 98.

65. Cf. Juzjani vol. I, 1963: 328, 331 (trans. vol. I, 1881: 318, 331); for a discussion of the relevant passages from Juzjani, see also Thomas et al. 2014: 139–140.

66. According to the local reports gathered by Thomas et al. (2014: 136, 139–140), the ruins of a mosque "over 100 years old" lie adjacent to the tower; its salvageable wooden elements – mainly pillar bases – have been incorporated in the new village mosque as a reminder of the no longer usable structure. (Incidentally, the mosque's dating to the nineteenth century is supported by the lines of poetry by the Turkish poet Hafiz Burhan (1897–1943) inscribed on the aforesaid wooden components.) The frequent association of *minar*s with mosques may hint at the replacement of an older structure in the nineteenth century. Moreover, the *minar* and mosque ruins are by no means the only probably historical remains in the vicinity: on an adjacent promontory lie the foundation stones of a ruined fortified palace, locally known as *qasr-i dukhtar-i malik* ("castle of the king's daughter").

67. Thomas et al. 2014: 138.

68. Cf. esp., e.g., Sourdel-Thomine 1960; Blair 1985.

69. Cf. Ball and Fischer 2019: 495–498; Ball 2020; and Volume II. The Sistan towers lack any remaining epigraphic data and so provide no indication of patron or date, but have been assigned stylistically to the eleventh (Pinder-Wilson 2001: 173) or twelfth century (O'Kane 1984: 100); the earlier date may be more credible based on the handling of the brick revetment, and the comparability of the towers' stellate plans to those of eleventh-century Saljuq tomb towers (e.g., Gunbad-i Qabus, dated by inscription to AH 399/1009 CE). Thus, there was more than one formal precedent within Afghanistan even for *minar*s. As with the Qasimabad *minar*, the Nad-i Ali tower did not figure in Fischer et al.'s documentation of Sistan's archaeological remains in

the 1960s–1970s, indicating that it too had collapsed by this time. A print of Tate's photograph of the Nad-i Ali tower remnant (1910–1912: 202 and facing) is also in the Royal Geographic Society's collection (London). Cf. also O'Kane 1984: pl. XIVc.

70. Sistan as a source for the skilled laborers required to build the *minar* at Da Qadi can be supported by its proximity. However, according to the extensive surveys and documentation by Fischer (and his larger team) throughout Sistan, the region was distinguishable from many other parts of Afghanistan in the local architecture's frequent combination of mud and burnt brick, particularly in the decorative elements. Cf. Fischer 1971: 50; Fischer et al. 1974: illus. 252–254; Tate [1910] 1977: 22, 270 and facing figures; O'Kane 1984: 90. Indeed, the possibly early date and peculiar form of the region's brick towers – cf. above in notes – only reinforce Fischer's observations regarding Sistan's architectural distinctiveness.

71. For Ghazna, see Pinder-Wilson 2000: 155. Tate ([1910] 1977: 271) estimated the Qasimabad *minar* to be "one hundred feet [*c.* 30 meters] … at the outside." Hillenbrand (1994: 148) confirmed that Saljuq *minar*s generally reached heights of about 30 meters. Cf. also Bloom 1989: 170–172.

72. Thomas et al. 2014: 137.

73. For Ghazna as a comparative example, see Appendix, Afghanistan VI.

74. Thomas et al. 2014: 138.

75. N. Yoffee, pers. comm., November 2017; also Barfield 1993: 106–107. Barth (1961: esp. 105–110) documented just such a process of "patchwork" sedentarization among the Basseri, i.e., affecting only parts of the self-identified group, rather than *en masse*. Sedentarization among nomadic groups is a known phenomenon (cf. also Golden 2013: 30), though the processes' *specifics* differed in each instance, depending at least in part on a region's unique circumstances, including economic bases and travel networks, both of which the nomads helped to shape or shift over time depending on their activities. These specifics and the economic factors prompting them, as well as the larger consequences for nomadism in general, continue to be debated: see Barfield 1981: 165–170 for a succinct differentiation of studies on nomadism in Iran (esp. Barth 1961), whose Basseri subjects have been considered the most comparable example here) and Afghanistan.

76. E.g., Mahmud 2009: 60.

77. Bosworth 1961:125.

78. Here, I take up Jackson's (2017: 333 and *passim*) meaningful chapter subheading "The Choice of Islam." The author has provided a significant (if brief) overview of the various contingent factors in religious conversion, demonstrating that adopting Islam – or indeed any other transregional socioreligious system – as the "state" religion was the result of many historical and regional contingencies. In the case of the several Mongol khanates, for example, shifting from adherence to and patronage of their small-scale ritual practices to larger religious systems varied widely, with the eastern khanates opting for Tantric Tibetan Buddhism precisely as a statement of contrast from their mainstream Chinese Buddhist subjects. Thus, "it was not necessarily the case … that the Chinggisid princes of Western Asia would succumb to

… the Muslim majority. Realpolitik could instead have dictated moving in a completely different direction" (*ibid.*, 334). In parallel fashion, Crossley (2019: 87–88) explored the array of religio-cultural choices and their consequences among the Bulgars. For the Khazars and Judaism, cf. Amitai 2008: 283–284 and notes; Kaplony 2008: 320–321; and esp. Golden (2013: 53–56), who noted that, parallel to the Shansabanis' "origin myth," the Judaicization of the Khazar ruling elites – encompassing both the *qaghan* or sacral king, and the subordinate governing king (Ar. *malik*) – had also begun during the reign of Harun al-Rashid.

79. See esp. Bosworth 1994: 67–69, 79–80; Siddiqui 2006: 19–20.

80. Bosworth 1961: 128–129.

81. See also Gardizi (trans. Bosworth) 2011: 57; Bosworth 2008: 100; Bosworth 2012c. For the Karramiyya in Nishapur and Ghur, cf. Bulliet 1972: 12–13, 68ff., 71ff.; Zysow 2012; and Chapter 4. Regarding the Karramiyya's proselytism in particular, Amitai (2008: 283–284) noted that, while they were "the best organized group of Sufi character … [with] *khanqah*s in Farghana, Khuttal and Samarqand," they actually were *not* very successful agents of Islamic conversion among the Turkic peoples of Transoxiana during the tenth–eleventh centuries. Much needed re-examination of the long-held notion of Sufis as the major force in the Steppe Turks' Islamization has led scholars to propose instead that traveling Muslim merchants, a few select political–military figures, and even mainstream but itinerant *fuqaha'* were the more likely purveyors of exposure – with only *eventual* conversion – to Islam among the Turkic peoples. See Flood 2005a: 272 and *passim*; cf. also Chapter 4.

82. See esp. Barth 1961: 135–136; Barfield 1981: 76–77; Amiri 2020: 151–152. Gellner (1983: 446) additionally advocated for "… a tribal Little Culture, which does not meet the standards of an old Great Tradition, [and] should not be denied for the past simply because it no longer satisfies the needs of a more urbanized, centralized, literate society which has replaced it."

83. During the first and second millennia CE in West through Central Asia (and beyond), identifiable religious communities – such as Manicheists, Buddhists, Nestorian Christians, and Muslims – had constituted major mercantile forces within larger polities. Their commercial power lay largely in the ability to partner with co-religionists, kinsmen, and others to create and utilize vast transregional networks for the circulation of goods and capital. The "corporate" integration of these mercantile networks made religious conversion advantageous, as in the case of the Uighur conversions to Manicheism, and the Bulgar conversions to Islam (see Jackson 2017: 333–334). It was perhaps due to the absence of such identifiable modes of "incorporation" (i.e., conversion) into "Hinduism" that the networks of Gujarati, Panjabi, and Marwari merchants in Central Asia did not achieve the prominence and longevity of other groups. Cf. esp. Dale 1994; Levi 2002.

84. While the presence of Jewish communities throughout Afghanistan – attested at Bamiyan and Ghazna (cf., e.g., Haim 2012; Haim 2019) and elsewhere – Jam-Firuzkuh's tenuous geographic connectivity and "the dearth of clearly stratified occupation" led D. Thomas (pers. comm., October 2018) to raise the

possibility that the tombstones might have been posthumous memorials to venerated ancestors, rather than collectively indicating a sizeable Jewish settlement in the area. Nevertheless, it should also be noted that the apparent eleventh-century *terminus post quem* of the Jam-Firuzkuh Jewish community is in line with the evidence of Jewish communities at other important commercial cities/emporia in Afghanistan, such as Bamiyan, whence a sizeable collection of letters between Jewish family members have begun to provide invaluable information regarding their mercantile interests, as well as religious, liturgical, legal, and even poetic activities. Cf. http://web.nli.org.il/sites/NLI/English/library/news/Pages/Afghan-Geniza.aspx. Documents within this collection also furnish information about Jewish groups settled at yet other Afghan cities such as Ghazna as of the eleventh century: see Haim 2012.

85. The anecdotal figure of the Ghuri Jewish merchant served as an important historical clue for Fischel's (1965) and others' initial analyses of the Jam-Firuzkuh tombstones. See also Moline 1973/74: 147–148. For other studies of the inscriptions and the Jewish communities of Afghanistan, cf. *inter alia*, Fischel 1965; Pinder-Wilson 2001: n. 37; Lintz 2008; Lintz 2009; Hunter 2010; Thomas 2018: 214ff.; and above in main text and notes.

86. See esp. Thomas 2018: 54, 174, 189. Indeed, the disastrous flood of the Hari Rud, probably *c.* AH 595/1199 CE, which caused the destruction of the mosque adjacent to the famous *minar* of Jam-Firuzkuh, was noted by Juzjani, vol. I 1963: 375 (trans. vol. I, 1881: 404).

87. Given the significance of Balkh (ancient Bactra) in northern Afghanistan as "the emporium of India" at least since the ninth–tenth centuries, it is little surprise that an established Jewish mercantile community resided within the *rabad* – just outside the *madina*, though all still within the fortified city – as indicated by the Bab al-Yahud. Similarly, the Bab al-Hinduwan signified an Indian merchant community also in residence at Balkh. Cf. Bosworth 1988.

88. Cf. Barth 1961: 9–10, 97–100, 102; Barfield 1981: 28, 97ff.; Barfield 1993: 94–95, 99–100; Mahmud 2009: 251ff. See also Barfield (1981: 102; 1993: 98) for the contentious – though still regular – relations between nomads and farmers with respect to the damage done to crops by the former's grazing animals.

89. Although providing parallels to the Shansabanis' nomadism and participation in Perso-Islamic forms of kingship, clearly the Saljuqs did not go from *ruled* to *rulers*, but rather "inundated the Iranian world en masse, in their tribal and clan units" (Vàsàry 2015: 16). Moreover, Abbasid expansion into Iran and beyond during the late eighth century had already brought "eastern" Sasano-Iranian courtly practices into the Islamic world (see Finster 1994: 17–18). It was Saljuq political and military control of the Abbasid caliph and his capital at Baghdad, however, which created a more palpable east–west conduit, instigating the arrival of intellectuals and others westward to Baghdad. But rather than absorbing Baghdad into a fulcrum of power effectively shifting eastward toward the Saljuqs' preferred base at Isfahan, these migrations actually reified the political, social, and cultural differences between Baghdad and the Saljuq "east." Cf. Durand-Guédy 2013b: 325–326, 332–334; Van Renterghem 2015; also Peacock 2015: 134ff., 163–164, 168–169.

90. The reputation of the Ghaznavids appears to have been founded largely on their India campaigns, which served multiple purposes such as gaining public admiration and the support of the Abbasid *khalifa* at Baghdad, in turn further spreading the dynasty's renown. Cf. Bosworth 1966: 87ff. Recent analyses of the textual sources reporting events during Ghaznavid ascendancy have underscored the multiple motivations behind the India campaigns, emphasizing that facticity was less the authors' goal than communicating the polyvalent meanings of these campaigns in their own time. Cf. Anooshahr 2006; Anooshahr 2018a.

CHAPTER 3

The Early Shansabanis: Firuzkuh, Bamiyan, and Tiginabad/ Old Qandahar, *c.* 1140s–1170s

In *c.* AH 539–540/1145–1146 CE, Qutb al-Din Muhammad (d. AH 543/1148 CE), 'Izz al-Din's second son (Genealogy, p. xvii), established his seat at Firuzkuh – now generally accepted to be near the village of Jam, at the confluence of the Hari Rud and Jam Rud (Figure 2.2).[1] In virtual simultaneity, the Shansabanis expanded eastward beyond Ghur to the great religious center and commercial entrepôt of Bamiyan, where Fakhr al-Din Mas'ud (r. AH 540–558/1145–1163 CE), 'Izz al-Din's eldest son, presided over an agnatic Shansabani lineage that ruled the region through the early thirteenth century. In the late 1150s, the infamous 'Ala' al-Din Husain *Jahan-suz* (r. AH 544–556/1149–1161 CE; further discussed below) departed from Firuzkuh southward and wrested Qandahar – quite possibly the medieval Tiginabad (see later in this chapter) – from his arch enemies the Yamini-Ghaznavids.[2] It was from here that, little more than a decade later in AH 568/1173 CE, the brothers Shams al-Din Muhammad and Shihab al-Din Muhammad – two of 'Izz al-Din's grandsons, and nephews of the notorious 'Ala' al-Din *Jahan-suz* – would set out to eradicate the Oghüz bands occupying Ghazna. Upon achieving this victory, Shihab al-Din was crowned Sultan Mu'izz al-Din there, thus creating a third Shansabani lineage at the once grand, erstwhile Yamini capital (cf. esp. Chapter 5).

The present chapter's focus on the late 1140s through early 1170s CE – prior to the definitive Shansabani conquest of Ghazna AH 569/1173–1174 CE – encompasses the initial phase of Jam-Firuzkuh and the early Shansabani campaigns to Bamiyan and Tiginabad/Old Qandahar. Against the background of this multi-directional expansion, the Shansabanis' architectural patronage in the successively acquired power bases is extremely varied, defying any expectations of a recognizably unified and singular imperial presence. In fact, this variety seems to belie centralized imperial expansion (cf. also Chapter 1, above).

Archaeological investigations at the site of Jam-Firuzkuh brought forth virtually no evidence of palatial architecture from the time of Shansabani occupation (1140s–*c.* 1215), despite Juzjani's mentions of large palaces and forts there. Instead, the early Firuzkuh Shansabanis seem to have concentrated on defensive and religious–civic structures (Figures 3.1–3.6; see below). As mentioned in Chapter 2, and argued more thoroughly in this chapter, more than a conventional capital city Firuzkuh was likely a royal *sard-sir* (summer) encampment – internally and externally well-defended, to be sure (Figures 3.2 and 3.3; see below): its imposing *minar* (Figures 3.5 and 3.6) was one of probably very few monuments per se marking the locality. At the same time, the Bamiyan region (Figures 3.7–3.13) boasts perhaps the broadest array of structures evincing Shansabani-period interventions. But rather than a singular mode of building, Bamiyan and its contiguous valleys encompass an appreciable architectural variety, ranging from reuse and repurposing of pre-existing complexes (Figures 3.9–3.13), to large-scale new constructions (Figures 3.24–3.27). Old Qandahar (Figures 3.28 and 3.29) rounds out the Shansabanis' arc of initial expansion and is even more enigmatic than the other sites: here only funerary mounds can be associated with Shansabani presence.

Although the Chisht, Gharjistan, and Ghazna-Bust region are discussed more thoroughly in Chapters 4 and 5, they merit brief mention here: the nomadic Oghüz had occupied Ghazna and its vicinity for over a decade by the time the Firuzkuh forces effected their momentous victory there in AH 568/1173–1174 CE (see below). But even after this long period of neglect at the old Yamini capital, and likely active deterioration during the nomadic bands' presence, Ghazna and Bust-Lashkari Bazar still presented usable architectural fabrics, which apparently minimized the need for new Shansabani-patronized constructions.[3] It is only in the western and northern directions from Jam-Firuzkuh at Chisht and Gharjistan that the Shansabani presence left behind newly commissioned monumental architecture.

Doubtless, some of the varying methods of making an imperial mark were inflected by the Shansabanis' *pre*-imperial transhumant and/or nomadic beginnings, which continued in modified form into later years (see Chapter 2). These lingering mores surely combined with the exigencies of the occupied territories' own pre-existing landscapes, resulting in a noticeable variety among the early Shansabani annexations. The analyses in Chapters 2–5 of the surviving built remains, then, are essential not only for obtaining a complete picture of the Shansabanis' early imperial expansion; they are equally so for a thorough understanding of the disparate cultural and historical geographies throughout Afghanistan during the twelfth century. Bamiyan, Tiginabad/Old Qandahar, and the outward routes from Jam-Firuzkuh to Chisht, Gharjistan, and Balkh – all integrated to varying degrees within the age-old Khurasani commercial networks radiating in multiple directions from Herat – had each undergone very different developments from the early centuries of the Common Era (and before). These inherited circumstances in turn impacted each of the respective areas' distinct later significances for local and transregional imperial interests well into the second millennium CE. It is worthy of remark (even in hindsight) that the co-existing differences among these Shansabani presences outside Ghur seem to serve as harbingers presaging the later, larger-scale and yet distinctly region-specific modes of "conquest" along the banks of the Indus and beyond (cf. Chapter 6, and Volume II).

As discussed in Chapter 1, the Shansabanis' quickly increasing sphere of influence was not necessarily the outcome of a strategy emanating from a "center." Rather, it seems frequently to have been the result of *ad hoc* and piecemeal campaigns from the newly invested appanages. Their architectural patronage would buoy this understanding. But, recreating the precise process of expansion is made all the more difficult by various aspects of the *textual* sources closest to the events. The prime among these sources would of course be Juzjani's *Tabaqat* of the mid-thirteenth century, along with surviving near-contemporaneous works belonging to various other genres.[4]

One challenging aspect of Juzjani's *Tabaqat* (as well as other texts) may seem merely mechanical, but it is far from immaterial. In addition to the still cautious identification of Firuzkuh,[5] the majority of places Juzjani named as the Shansabani brothers' appanages are as yet only conjecturally located. For example, the precise whereabouts and extent of the territory of Warshada, the appanage of 'Izz al-Din's second son Qutb al-Din Muhammad – the eventual "founder" of Firuzkuh – are unknown.[6] Although, Qutb al-Din's subsequent search "in [various] directions for a place to build a well-fortified stronghold and a wondrous city as a capital" could indicate that Warshada was in the vicinity of Jam-Firuzkuh. Ultimately, Qutb al-Din's selection of this locale as his seat attested to his acuity and foresight, given the more stable, commerce-based prosperity of the settlement and its vicinity.[7]

Aside from Warshada's hypothetical location, only Kashi and Wajiristan can be identified. Kashi was the appanage of Fakhr al-Din Mas'ud, 'Izz al-Din's eldest son, and can be surmised as a part of or near modern Chaghcharan (capital of present-day Ghur Province). Wajiristan, the appanage of 'Ala' al-Din Husain *Jahan-suz* (the "World Incendiary"; see below), was apparently located directly west of Ghazna. But the appanages of 'Izz al-Din's other sons – *viz.* Madin, given to Nasir al-Din Muhammad; Sanga to Baha' al-Din (d. AH 544/1149 CE); and even the Istiya of Saif al-Din himself – are only approximately locatable, if at all.[8]

Early Firuzkuh

By the time of 'Ala' al-Din Husain *Jahan-suz*'s vengeful and supposedly spectacular destruction of Ghazna and Bust-Lashkari Bazar in AH 544/1150 CE, his older half-brother Qutb al-Din had already initiated a Shansabani hold over Firuzkuh. As detailed previously, due to Qutb al-Din's pre-mature death, Firuzkuh was left to his agnatic successors and ultimately inherited by 'Ala' al-Din himself.

In contrast to the abundant information in Juzjani's *Tabaqat* regarding military confrontations and political alliances, the work offers little on Firuzkuh as a settlement or its architecture, such as the population or extent and general location of its buildings. In the seventeenth *tabaqa* on the Shansabani sultans and *malik*s of Ghur, the author mentioned Firuzkuh only infrequently, referring to it as "a fort and a city" without further detail. He does note that after Qutb al-Din's decampment to Ghazna, Baha' al-Din "edified the city and completed the royal buildings and the palace (*qasr*)."[9]

Only an intimation of the ruler's residence and central area of Firuzkuh can be gleaned from *Tabaqat*, and that also from multiple parts spanning several sultans' reigns over approximately sixty years. The majority of the information – meager as it is – comes from the later, imperial phase of the site (cf. also Chapter 4): in the entry on the penultimate Shansabani sultan Ghiyath al-Din Mahmud (r. AH 602–606/1206–1210 CE), Juzjani reported that, during the time of this ruler's more renowned father Sultan Ghiyath al-Din Muhammad (r. AH 558–599/1163–1203 CE), the *qasr* known as Baz Kushk-i Sultan ("the hilltop [called] 'the Sultan's Pavilion/Palace'") was located in the middle of the city. Furthermore,

> ... the *qasr* is a building whose equal is not found in any other kingdom or in any capital ... in height and area, and with columns (*arkan*), belvederes (*manzar-ha*), galleries (*riwaqat*), and towers/crenellations (*sharfat*) no engineer has created [before]. On top of the *qasr* are five golden turrets (*kungura*), each one three *gaz* and a little over in height, and two *gaz* in circumference; and also two golden *huma*, each the size of a large camel. After the conquest of Ajmer, Sultan-i Ghazi Mu'izz al-Din Muhammad had sent those golden pinnacles and *huma* to Sultan Ghiyath al-Din's capital as a token of his servitude, along with much else of rarity and value, such as a golden ring with a golden chain and two (golden) orbs (*kharbuza*, lit. "watermelon") that were five *gaz* by five *gaz*, and two golden kettle-drums (*kou*) that were brought by cart ... Sultan Ghiyath al-Din ordered the ring and chain, and those orbs (*kharbuza*) to be suspended in the monumental entrance portal (*pishtaq*) of the *masjid-i jami'* of Firuzkuh ...[10]

From this brief passage, it is apparent that Firuzkuh's *masjid-i jami'* was largely incidental for Juzjani, its entrance merely serving as the stage for display of part of the plunder from Ajmer, which probably reached Firuzkuh c. AH 590–591/1194–1195 CE (cf. Volume II). At the same time, even though Juzjani focused more on the Shansabanis' *qasr* or royal palace upon Baz Kushk-i Sultan than any other structure, the palace complex's precise dates of construction remain unclear, as it was already in place when the Ajmer plunder arrived. Despite – or perhaps because of – the considerable time that both Juzjani and his father Maulana Siraj-i Minhaj spent at Firuzkuh, the author provided no precise description of the site. In fact, his mentions of the city seem to "verge on the incredible" and "result in a conflated account of a capital …" when compared with the recent archaeological work at the site, as discussed further on.[11]

In light of the role played by architecture – particularly palatial architecture – throughout the Persianate ecumene until the late eighteenth century,[12] the dissonance between *Tabaqat*'s formulaic descriptions of the site and its archaeology are, in fact, not surprising. Chapter 1, argued that, for pre-modern power-seeking elites, architectural patronage was an important means of labor mobilization, and the resulting structures also served as monumental markers of territory and as effective tools for the establishment of bases of socio-cultural power. In short, architectural activity was instrumental in the creation of an empire, as further discussed in Chapter 4.

But for pre-modern Persian authors, their patrons, and their audiences, the palace complex was both a symbol of royalty as well as "a special place as a nexus of power which join[ed] the human and the cosmic … a symbol of something beyond the merely material." The palace had a "rhetorical function … through its affect, [which was] as essential as its residential, administrative, productive, and ceremonial functions."[13] Thus, like the poetic-literary, religious and other intellectual luminaries gracing royal courts, patronage of palaces also provided one of the many manifestations of royal prerogative and power. Indeed, Juzjani's descriptions of Firuzkuh's buildings contain many elements directly echoed in *qasidas* (panegyric Persian poems) of the late eleventh–twelfth centuries, whose metaphorical flourishes help us not so much to "see" palaces as perceive what they *meant*.[14]

As might be expected, then, Firuzkuh's archaeology does not corroborate Juzjani's descriptions. Instead of a grand *qasr* commanding the center of Firuzkuh, it is the preponderance of defensive, religious, and possibly commercial buildings that has been archaeologically attested. It was partially this textual–archaeological discrepancy, along with other historical preconceptions, that had resulted in grave doubts about Jam-Firuzkuh as the Shansabanis' summer "capital."[15] But the work of Dr. David Thomas and the Minaret of Jam Archaeological Project (MJAP) between 2003 and 2005 have further eroded lingering skepticism of Jam-Firuzkuh as the Shansabanis' *sard-sir* destination. Even with limited time and curtailed resources, Thomas and his colleagues conducted excavations, surveys, soundings and analyses – the last also encompassing the finds from the staggering number of robber holes marking the site's mountainous terrain. Indeed, MJAP's (ongoing) studies, together with continuing anthropological research on nomadic and transhumant populations, and the consequent rethinking of archaeological methods for recovering the latter's physical traces, have helped to bring into focus a plausible picture, *viz.* a mercantile settlement that was adopted by an increasingly powerful and persistently transhumant elite as one of their seasonal encampments.

As is the case with most of the cultural geography of Afghanistan (see also below), all discussions regarding Jam-Firuzkuh and its surroundings in the mid- to late twelfth century must bear in mind at least three provisos, two historical and one modern. The historical provisos emerge from textual and archaeological indications: Juzjani mentioned that a flood destroyed the Firuzkuh *jami'* during the reign of Sultan Ghiyath al-Din Muhammad, but after his brother Mu'izz al-Din's successful India campaigns in the 1190s[16] – thus only a little more than two decades before the Mongol campaigns into Afghanistan (1220s). This "major depositional event" was documentable in the most recent archaeological exploration of the area east of Firuzkuh's famous *minar* – as discussed below, a zone that yielded a probable mosque or prayer area (Figure 3.1).[17] This natural disaster apparently wrought extensive destruction on what was likely the politico-religious focal point of the settlement, where other structures of note could have existed – and noted by Juzjani – but were ultimately swept away by the flood.[18] And of course we cannot discount the Mongols: in AH 617/1222 CE Firuzkuh underwent extensive destruction and large-scale slaughter of its remaining inhabitants at the hands of the Mongol Ögedey and his armies, so that much (if not all) of the city's pre-Mongol architectural fabric is no longer visible.[19]

Coupled with this compromised archaeological context is the forced incompleteness of archaeological survey and excavation. Given the endlessly fluctuating security situation in central Afghanistan, and governmental delays in issuing permits, the admirable work of Dr. Thomas and the other MJAP members had to be left only partially finished as of 2005. While he and his specialist colleagues in the field continue their analyses and publication of the data already collected (including GIS studies, ceramics, epigraphy, etc.; see below), many aspects of the site's archaeological context remain unexplored. All the observations offered below, then, must remain hypothetical, subject to modification depending on the emergence of more archaeological and other data over time, which may add detail to what is proposed here or open alternative understandings of the site.

Nevertheless, MJAP's explorations of Jam-Firuzkuh have supplied critical information regarding the erstwhile summer "capital," which *Tabaqat* lacked. The team's survey of domestic architecture, concentrated on the sloping west bank of the Jam Rud facing the famous *minar*, documented structural remains of well-built walls of stone, together with combination walls of stone and mud brick, some with plastered surfaces. The data indicated a populous terraced settlement, though likely of relatively short

Figure 3.1 *Jam-Firuzkuh: remains of paved floor of probable mosque located east of* minar.
© *Courtesy of David Thomas.*

occupation. But the "concern for, and investment of resources in, the aesthetic qualities of the buildings" signaled that a settled, rather than transhumant or nomadic, population resided in these permanent dwellings during much of the year. Furthermore, remnants of a large, arcaded structure on the Hari Rud's north bank were not for defensive purposes, but rather "more reminiscent of the shop fronts in the traditional souqs of the Islamic world."[20] The archaeological evidence thus far, then, supports the idea that Firuzkuh was an already existing mercantile settlement – Juzjani's cosmopolitan Jewish merchant serving as its personification (cf. Chapter 2) – with which the early Shansabanis established a mutually profitable association, and which probably brought further growth in the area's settled and nomadic populations.

The one complex for which no specific archaeological evidence could be found was Juzjani's lofty and crenellated Kushk-i Sultan, supposedly located atop a natural elevation (Pers. *baz*) in the center of Firuzkuh and serving as the Shansabanis' *qasr*. Instead, indications of elite occupation were concentrated largely in defensive structures on surrounding promontories. The ruins known collectively as Qasr-i Zarafshan (Figures 3.2 and 3.3), for example, stretch along the north bank of the Hari Rud, the most substantial remnant being a conical tower of mud bricks on a stone footing. The tower is comparable with the defensive remains documented in the south of Ghur (Chapter 2) and west of Bamiyan (see below), though it lacks the plaster surfaces with molded or incised designs. However, the Qasr's local name of Arg-i Dukhtar-i Padshah – "Citadel of the Emperor's Daughter" – seems to carry a royal association.[21] Farther above the Qasr stands the "refuge" called Kuh-i Khara ("Black Mountain"?), which provided more certain signs of elite occupation: a large cistern lined on three sides with baked bricks (Figure 3.4); turquoise-glazed brick fragments; and a significant number of high-status ceramic sherds such as *mina'i* ware. Although, the disturbance caused by numerous robber holes makes it difficult to put forth definitive conclusions regarding the full range of occupation at these primarily defensive structures.[22]

The Jam-Firuzkuh remains are not altogether unusual in light of the Shansabanis' continued transhumance and/or nomadism throughout the twelfth century, consisting of seasonal movements between their summer encampment or "capital" of Firuzkuh and its winter counterpart in Zamindawar (cf. Chapter 2). Again, their contemporaries the Saljuqs offer a parallel *modus vivendi*. The Saljuqs of Iran (*c.* 1038–1194) largely preferred a textile palatial architecture in the form of luxurious royal tents, and at times cloth enclosures (*saraparda*) incorporating architecture with a limited footprint such as a *kushk*, a single- or two-story pavilion for viewing (or being viewed).[23] The name of Kushk-i Sultan for the Firuzkuh *qasr* could very well have referred to just such a structure – swept away by the flood of 1199 CE and/or the Mongols. Thus, Juzjani *metaphorically* – rather than

Figure 3.2 *Jam-Firuzkuh: tower remains of Qasr-i Zarafshan. © Courtesy of David Thomas.*

literally – attributed multiple towers, belvederes, and arcaded promenades to the complex, in line with the royal symbolism expected in textual (and largely poetic) descriptions.[24] In practical terms, the nomadic and/ or transhumant lifestyles of the Saljuqs and the Shansabanis would have

Figure 3.3 *Jam-Firuzkuh: remains of defensive towers.* © *Courtesy of David Thomas.*

required ample pasturage, which was not easily found within traditional urban or settled areas. (As discussed in Chapter 2, these requirements were difficult to meet also at Firuzkuh.[25]) Their extensive encampments likely included large textile enclosures (*saraparda*) for the elites, as well as

Figure 3.4 *Jam-Firuzkuh: baked brick, plaster-lined cistern at Kuh-i Khara, looking north. From Thomas 2018: fig. 5.24.*

individual tents, and would have been pitched outside established towns and cities.[26] Furthermore, given the Saljuqs' reliance on armies of allied nomadic groups – increasingly true also for the Shansabanis as of the 1150s, if not earlier – vast, open spaces beyond an *urbs* were a necessity as well.

In the end, even though the Shansabanis quite plausibly relied mainly on textile palatial architecture, Firuzkuh's defensive structures, where elite occupation is also in evidence, were still essential: it is possible that the Shansabanis provided the security necessary for the mercantile trade mainly carried out by the region's networks of Jewish communities, who in turn helped to replenish the Shansabanis' (eventually imperial) coffers, forming a politico-economic loop not only increasing the Shansabanis' power but also integrating them further into Firuzkuh's very existence.[27]

MJAP's exploration of the area immediately to the east of the famous *minar* (discussed further in Chapter 4) unearthed an evidently extensive flooring of baked bricks, with two shaft fragments of toppled columns of the same material lying on the southern edge (Figure 3.1). The flooring consisted of varying patterns, ranging from herringbone to large rectangular bricks laid as paving – the column fragments were found atop the latter – strongly hinting at the possibility of a large, columned mosque associated with the *minar*. But MJAP's exploration of the area in five soundings along its northern perimeter (edged by the Hari Rud's southern bank), rather than overall excavation, precluded the collection of many other valuable data – a *lacuna* hopefully to be remedied by future work. In the meanwhile, the paved floor's likely extent and dimensions cannot be determined, nor those of any associated structure. Further, while fragments of a baked-brick wall were found abutting the riverbank delineating the northern wall of the possible mosque, it remains unclear whether a *qibla* wall existed: if so, it would have abutted the *minar* on the latter's east.[28] Notwithstanding the missing information, MJAP's analyses of the baked-brick flooring and other findings concluded that the encompassing structure was in all likelihood a mosque, and one to which the Shansabanis were "unlikely to have devoted fewer resources" than to the magnificent *minar* adjacent to it.[29] However, it is unknown whether the unearthed structure was the first one in that location, perhaps having superseded an earlier (smaller?) mosque and even an accompanying (less imposing?) *minar*.

It is generally assumed that Jam-Firuzkuh's *minar* (Figure 3.5) and the newly found mosque abutting it were constructed in tandem in the early 1170s, prior to which the "capital's" Muslim population – including its persistently transhumant Shansabani elite – would have prayed and gathered in humbler, less monumental or even temporary structures.[30] However, the probable absence of a Shansabani palatial complex per se (as described above) would not preclude their patronage of other structures, which, for a relatively new elite of humble origins, would have fulfilled symbolically more potent functions than the archetypal palaces of established urban rulers. Juzjani's incidental mention of Firuzkuh's *jami* and its monumental portal (*pishtaq*), where some of the plundered spoils were displayed upon their arrival from Ajmer (cf. above), implied only that the grand structure was already in place by the mid-1190s; this did not necessarily preclude the existence of an earlier structure at the site, perhaps one that was subsequently expanded or even replaced.

The Shansabanis' continued transhumance would seem to demand that some more lasting sign of their presence at Firuzkuh – such as a markedly central place for Islamic worship – serving as a steady reminder of their commanding status, perhaps especially during the initial phases of their dominance over the settled and relatively prosperous mercantile population of Firuzkuh. Based on the Shansabanis' own activity during the earlier part of the twelfth century – discussed in Chapter 2 – it is worth considering that the place of prayer unearthed by MJAP was at least initiated in the late 1140s–1150s, shortly after Qutb al-Din established himself as *malik al-jibal* at Firuzkuh, and more than two decades before the construction of the famous *minar*, which had a very pointed epigraphic program and commemorative function (cf. Chapters 4 and 5). The Shansabanis had already patronized laborers with a localized, vernacular familiarity with Persianate architectural culture when they commissioned the construction of the Da Qadi *minar*. This structure might have been ensconced within a mosque complex, and the site has tentatively been identified as Qala'-yi Zarmurgh, their *sard-sir* "capital" prior to Firuzkuh (as argued in Chapter 2). But by the mid-twelfth century, the Shansabanis' prominence and resources had risen considerably, allowing them access to skilled laborers who were *au courant* of the broader, cosmopolitan Persianate architectural trends. These

Figure 3.5 *Jam: minaret of Jam (c. 1180) [sic], general view. © Photograph Josephine Powell c. 1960. Harvard Fine Arts Library, Special Collections.*

building conventions had been shaped throughout the previous two centuries by the robust patronage of the Saljuqs and the military aristocracy of the Ghaznavids. Thus, increased means and access to the necessary skilled workers meant that the Shansabanis could commission the whole range of architectural forms within the former's repertory, including mosques, *minar*s, *madrasa*s, *'idgah*s, and a variety of other buildings.

Indeed, the well-known Jam-Firuzkuh *minar* (Figure 3.5), discussed in further detail in Chapter 4, may provide an *iconographic* hint of the prior existence of an *'idgah* if not a mosque – neighboring the *minar*. In her re-examination of the *minar*, archaeologist and epigraphist Janine Sourdel-Thomine painstakingly analyzed its epigraphic and decorative program. While the significance and uniqueness of the entirety of Surat Maryam (Qur'an XIX) on the *minar*'s lower shaft is addressed in the following chapter, here it is useful to highlight the low-relief motif of a blind arch on its east–west axis (Figure 3.6): nestled among the complex web of Qur'anic and historical inscriptions, and geometrical and vegetal

Figure 3.6 *Detail of Figure 3.4: Jam, minaret, view of* mihrab *relief on east face.*

ornamentation, a towering pointed-arch blind niche distinguishes the eastern face of the *minar* from the other surfaces. In fact, the most important verses of Surat Maryam (Q. XIX: 35–41) were ingeniously placed at the apex of this niche motif, which, together with its *qibla* orientation, strongly points to its function as a *mihrab*.[31]

Sourdel-Thomine cautioned against considering the *minar*'s ornamented niche as "a secondary *mihrab*, but rather [as] adding an *Islamic* element to the symbolic, religious and sacred quality of a monument with marked cardinal orientations" (i.e., *via* the decorative programs of each of the eight faces).[32] Nevertheless, a *mihrab* on the *minar* would have been redundant *vis-à-vis* an adjacent mosque's *qibla* wall, and too close to the latter to allow for separate worship. Given the labor and resources invested in the *minar* – including the difficult spatial calculations required to integrate the *mihrab* motif and its meaningful verses seamlessly within the complex decorative program – it is safe to assume that one of the principal aims of the overall œuvre was to be visible, if not also *legible* (cf. Chapter 4). Thus, at the time of the *minar*'s construction, it is possible that an unroofed prayer area or *'idgah* might have already been in place, even marking the *qibla* by means of a low wall permitting visibility beyond.[33] The eventual construction of the *minar* in AH 570/1174–1175 CE obviously served multiple purposes, as discussed in the next chapter; a significant one, however, could have been the monumental marking of the direction of prayer.

One final point awaits explication. Juzjani's mention of the Firuzkuh *jami's pishtaq* (cf. above) hints at a monumental structure rather than an open space for prayer, probably in the same location to the east of the *minar*. This grand, most likely enclosed, building was evidently *in situ* by the mid-1190s, in time to display some of the Ajmer plunder. Such a mosque and its surely impressive *qibla* wall would have eventually blocked the view of the *mihrab* on the *minar*'s eastern face, seeming to replace it with the mosque's *qibla* wall. This blatant subordination of the *minar*'s *mihrab* could have resulted from the gradually fraying alliance between the Shansabani sultans and the Karramiyya, whose doctrinal sway over the region had led to the unusual choice of the entirety of Surat Maryam (Q. XIX) on the *minar*'s surface (cf. Chapter 4). But, by the 1170s and afterward, the Shansabanis' increasingly cosmopolitan ambitions required distance from the Karramiyya's admittedly reduced, localized appeal. It is worth considering, then, that a new *masjid-i jami'* was constructed sometime after the *minar*'s completion in 1174–1175 CE and before Juzjani's mention of the *jami' pishtaq* in the context of events occurring in 1194–1195 CE. This architectural gesture would have subtly but firmly sidelined the Karramiyya, while still maintaining the *minar*'s symbolism as the commemoration of the definitive Shansabani conquest of Ghazna (see esp. Chapter 4).

The Shansabanis' continued transhumance and their use of Jam-Firuzkuh as a *sard-sir* encampment helps to explain the absence of a permanent *qasr*, the role of palace amply fulfilled by "textile architecture" possibly in combination with small immoveable structures such as *kushk*s. Nevertheless, it might be expected that these ambitious elites made an early and enduring statement of their newfound dominance over Firuzkuh, an already existing settlement with established commercial networks. Prior to the famous *minar*, expending resources on the construction of a large place of prayer or *'idgah* would unequivocally declare their religio-political identity, concomitant with their commanding status, in the language of imperialism then current in the region: the strongly Persianate Islam of the Saljuqs and Ghaznavids. Prior to AH 570/1174–1175 CE and the erection of the famous *minar*, it is difficult to imagine how else the transhumant Shansabani elite would have made their presence felt at their *sard-sir* "capital" during their migratory absence for much of the year, if it were not for an enduring monument like a place of Islamic worship.

Ultimately, Jam-Firuzkuh makes a compelling case for an entirely different way of understanding the import of Persian textual sources in the study of something as seemingly indelible as architecture. Pre-modern Persian authors relied on a repertory of visual and poetic symbolism primarily derived from a sedentist royal court model, which did not concord

Figure 3.7 *Bamiyan: north cliff, eastern end, with 35-m Buddha (fourth–fifth century), distant view. © Photograph Josephine Powell c. 1960. Harvard Fine Arts Library, Special Collections.*

with the inner workings of a new elite continuing their seasonal transhumance. This urban court model, then, should be considered an even greater *abstraction* – rather than falsification – of the *locus* of power particularly in the case of elites from obscure, nomadic or transhumant origins.[34] With the increasingly refined archaeological work underway on empires emerging from nomadic confederacies, the juxtaposition of textual descriptions and archaeological finds is both increasingly imperative and, thankfully, possible.

Bamiyan

The UNESCO world heritage site of Bamiyan (Figure 3.7) looms large in the contemporary imagination. It is hard to think of Afghanistan or Buddhism without evoking Bamiyan – the mind's eye of the modern world arrested as much by its Buddhist monuments, as by the destruction of this magnificence in the name of a supposedly retrogressive Islamic iconoclasm.[35] In light of Bamiyan's modern notoriety and its cultural and political resonances, its true physical presence is commonly collapsed into the narrow area of UNESCO designation. Bamiyan's overall importance seems towering enough to be timeless, so that the basin's actual history and geographical extent fade into the hazy mists of memory and imagination.

The historical town of Bamiyan had in fact sprung up due to its command of a basin extending roughly 50 km east–west, with a maximum width of 15 km. It occupied the perfect position for travelers as they embarked on or concluded journeys through difficult mountain passes, which were and continue to be dangerous yet unavoidable challenges in traveling between Central Asia, Bactria, and northwestern India. The principal Bamiyan valley constituted "the great capital of a royal kingdom" according to the seventh-century Chinese pilgrim Hsuan Tsang (602–644 CE).[36] But a more accurate historical conception of the locale would encompass the basin as a whole, including the associated valleys of Funduqistan, Fuladi, Kakrak, and Nigar (Figure 3.8), and the traversable passages to its west extending ultimately into Ghur.[37] Furthermore, if the remarkable large-scale artistic and architectural patronage at the site of Bamiyan is any indication, its transregional significance came into being no earlier than the mid- to later sixth through tenth centuries CE (see below).

It is true that the location of Bamiyan northwest of Kabul, essentially on the India axis from Balkh and Qunduz (*via* Kabul and Gardiz), assured the area some traffic from the early centuries CE as the combined result of commerce and Buddhist proselytism. To wit, archaeological explorations of Bamiyan's valley floor have recovered the remains of freestanding structures, most likely Buddhist monasteries, whose occupation has been assigned to the third through fifth centuries CE. Then a century-long lapse intervened, though afterward the monasteries were reoccupied, and continuously so from the sixth through the late tenth centuries CE.

However, the dates of Bamiyan's two famous colossal Buddhas, once standing within painted niches in the principal valley's cliff face, do not span the entire period of the valley's domination by Buddhist monasticism; rather, they were made during a specific historical moment. Art historians have dated these monumental works to *c.*550–600 CE, based on stylistic comparisons of the Buddhas' sculpted forms with more securely dated works. Additionally, recent ^{14}C analyses of surviving organic materials from the Buddha sculptures verified these conclusions.[38] The remarkably abundant, consistently high-quality and large-scale artistic patronage throughout Bamiyan's valleys as of the later sixth century CE arguably signified a greater concentration of economic and political resources in the area as well.

The Bamiyan basin's increasing prominence in the mid-first millennium

CE was not tied to a growth in adherence to Buddhism per se, but rather to a pivotal recrafting of political alliances in the region. After the defeat of the Hephthalites at the battle of Gol-Zarriun (mid-sixth century) primarily at the hands of the "Chinese" or Western Turks, the ever-present Sasanian *shahanshah*s eventually allied with the latter in order to maintain some control of their eastern territories. Aside from this new regional power structure, however, it remains unclear whether the previously dominant Hephthalites were completely displaced, or still present in regional pockets. The interrelated dynasties of Kabul and Zabul – the latter being the Rutbils of the early Arabic sources (see Chapter 2, and below) – and the Shar of Bamiyan all pledged loyalty to the *Yabghu* presiding over the Western Turks' territories south of the Oxus. But it is debated whether the

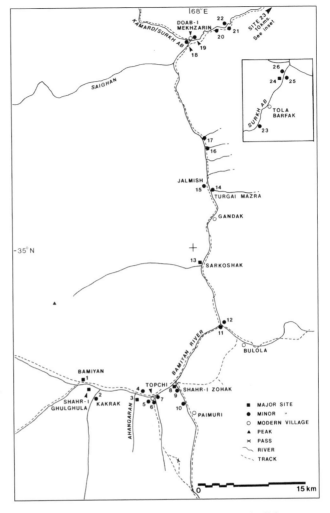

Figure 3.8 *The Bamiyan basin. From Baker and Allchin 1996: map 3.*

local rulers were themselves Western Turk or Hephthalite, and whether they relied for regional administration upon a newly created echelon of Turks, or a lingering Hephthalite "aristocracy."[39]

Notwithstanding the still unknown aspects of the region's political landscape during the mid-first millennium CE, it is evident that the rise in Bamiyan's fortunes coincided with the rise of the Western Turks in Tukharistan (Bamiyan and northward). We saw that, during the early centuries CE, Bamiyan had served as only a middling way station when small Buddhist monasteries facilitated and benefited from the trickle of commercial and other traffic. By *c.* 600 CE, however, Western Turk interventions had transformed the Bamiyan basin into a cosmopolitan but largely *Buddhist* commercial powerhouse, most vividly attested by its magnificent artistic production, wherein "artists ... continued to have access to the highest quality materials [and] worked with iconographic themes related to religious practices in contemporaneous Central Asia".[40]

The new rulers and their loyal vassals and/or kinsmen were all pragmatically ecumenical: in order to reconfigure commerce to their advantage, they emphasized the north–south routes through Bamiyan, largely displacing the east–west "trans-Gandhara" corridor as the primary access connecting India and Central Asia. Already an established Buddhist site, they might have further enforced passage through Bamiyan by adopting it as the *dynastic* center of the newly ascendant Khaganate, while its *political* center or regional capital was probably Qunduz.[41] A dynastic imprimatur would permit the Western Turks to profit greatly from Bamiyan's traffic of people (including merchants), goods, and ideas on the north–south trajectory through their territories.[42] Inadvertently or not, the Khaganate also encouraged – perhaps patronized – the institutions and practices of Buddhism already established in the area, even if these lay outside the Western Turks' ritual associations (cf. Chapter 2 and below).

The five contiguous valleys comprising the core area around Bamiyan (Figure 3.8) appear to have been primarily dedicated to Buddhist monasticism and dotted with artificial and natural grottoes, all domiciling Buddhist rituals and monastic residences.[43] However, political and administrative control of the area, necessarily monitoring access along the various routes in and out of the basin, was concentrated in hilltop complexes such as the well documented Shahr-i Zuhak (Figures 3.9–3.11) and the spectacular, recently re-surveyed Shahr-i Ghulghula (Figures I.22, 3.12, 3.13). Indeed, Bamiyan and its immediate areas to the north and west are replete with remains of rambling complexes large and small, usually atop high promontories, seeming to form a geographic, climatic, and even architectural continuum with the Shansabanis' home region of Ghur immediately to the west and south (cf. Chapter 2).[44] The mid-twentieth-century surveys by Marc Le Berre (published in the 1970s–1980s); subsequent surveys, documentation and analysis by Z. Tarzi (esp. 1977, 2007); and, finally, excavations by P. Baker and R. Allchin (1991) at Shahr-i Zuhak have been invaluable for obtaining a glimpse of the Bamiyan basin's non-religious architecture. This corpus, together with the Buddhist monasteries and other religious sites,[45] enables an overall apprehension of the region's pre-Islamic architectural culture, its continuation into later periods, and its commonality with building practices in other regions of Afghanistan.

Shahr-i Zuhak (Figures 3.9–3.11) as the better-studied hilltop site in the Bamiyan basin serves as an example of the area's architectural developments. Archaeologically, the initial foundation of Shahr-i Zuhak and nearby hilltop complexes has been attributed to the Sasanian–Hephthalite period, up to *c.* 500 CE, though phases of occupation at most Bamiyan sites continued for several centuries afterward. With the rise of the Western

Figure 3.9 *Shahr-i Zohak (fifth–thirteenth century), general view, triangular plateau with fortifications, from south.* © *Photograph Josephine Powell* c. *1960. Harvard Fine Arts Library, Special Collections.*

Turks in the sixth century and the consequent shifting of political alliances, a later phase of building apparently took place outside the core area of Bamiyan in the secondary valleys. Nevertheless, virtually all complexes datable to the pre-Islamic centuries shared broad characteristics.[46] It should also be emphasized that, while it is tempting to assign an *exclusively* military function to the complexes atop Bamiyan's rocky promontories – an interpretation seemingly justified by the ongoing politico-military power-plays in the region – close examination of the remains themselves indicates that their uses varied, and that they acquired defensive and other military functions only over time.[47]

Shahr-i Zuhak and other complexes consisted of brick walls atop footings of stone, or stone-rubble masonry (Figure 3.9) – a building method also encountered in central through southern Ghur. Most complexes had corner towers or bastions with circular or angular plans (Figures 3.9 and 3.10), their elevations exhibiting equally familiar geometric patterns. But

Figure 3.10 *Shahr-i Zohak (fifth–thirteenth century), general view, crenellated tower and walls. © Photograph Josephine Powell* c. 1960. *Harvard Fine Arts Library, Special Collections.*

in Ghur the decorations were pressed, incised into or molded from wet plaster, while in Bamiyan they were made out of the brickwork itself (Figure 3.10). As has been noted for the architectural remains in central through southern Ghur, in the Bamiyan region also, the degree and complexity of exterior surface decoration underscored the possibility of non-defensive functions, at least for some phases of the structures' existences.[48]

The Bamiyan structures' seemingly better state of preservation – or perhaps, simply more available documentation – than their Ghuri counterparts permits a clearer understanding of interior spaces as well: the non-intersecting vaults and elliptical domes (Figure 3.11) are indicative of pre-Islamic Central Asian building practices.[49] Finally, *in situ* interior mural paintings were documented particularly in the structures dotting the routes of access to the west of Bamiyan (Figure 3.18).[50] Altogether, these data help to identify an architectural culture with minor regional variations encompassing large swathes of Afghanistan during the pre-Islamic

Figure 3.11 *Shahr-i Zohak (fifth–thirteenth century), fortress ruins, interior.
corridor. © Photograph Josephine Powell* c. 1960. *Harvard Fine Arts Library,
Special Collections.*

periods of Sasanian, Hephthalite, and Western Turkic dominance – that
is, the sixth through tenth centuries CE – evidenced from Balkh through
Bamiyan and Ghur, and likely extending into Sistan as well.[51]

With the enduring shift in routes of travel and commerce to foster
Bamiyan's position as a regional entrepôt, the area continued to be something of a valuable territorial possession for local powers even after the
Sasanians' and Western Turks' respective and gradual disintegrations. To
be sure, the relentless 'Umayyad and 'Abbasid incursions into Afghanistan
had disrupted political stability from the end of the seventh through
eighth centuries, also causing a noticeable diminution in the volume of
traffic through Bamiyan. Eventually, the Sistani Saffarids' and ultimately
the Samanids' successes (i.e., further erosion of Turkic power) restored
some calm, though the locale was no longer the great cosmopolitan center
of the preceding two centuries. Nevertheless, Bamiyan and contiguous
areas passed into the hands of the Samanids' *ghulam* general Sabuktigin

(d. AH 389/999 CE), father of Sultan Mahmud of Ghazna (r. AH 389–421/ 999–1030 CE), and eventually served as a Ghaznavid mint city.[52] Bamiyan remained in Ghaznavid possession until the mid-twelfth-century rise of the Shansabanis.

According to Juzjani, shortly after Ala al-Din Husain *Jahan-suz*'s enraged destruction of Ghazna and Bust-Lashkari Bazar in AH 545/1150 CE, he "turned toward other conquests and captured the regions of Bamiyan and Tukharistan." Here, he installed his eldest brother Fakhr al-Din Mas'ud, whose descendants held the area until their rendition to the Khwarazm-shahs in the first decade of the thirteenth century. But 'Ala' al-Din's initial annexation was evidently not definitive, as he had to return *c.* AH 548/1153–1154 CE to "[bring] under his sway the districts of Bamiyan and Tukharistan," along with the southern areas around Bust (Zamindawar). This would have occurred upon his release after several months in Saljuq captivity, during which time "a group of amirs and dignitaries from the mountains of Ghur … and a group of seditious persons from Kashi" not only put Nasir al-Din from Madin ('Ala' al-Din's nephew) on the throne of Firuzkuh, they also "expropriated the royal treasury and property."[53] It is possible that in suppressing this rebellion, 'Ala' al-Din had to reinstate control over the eastern tracts, attempting to declare the paramountcy specifically of the *Firuzkuh* Shansabanis (cf. Chapter 1). Despite these political vagaries, however, by all appearances Bamiyan and its surrounding valleys continued to comprise a notable mercantile–agricultural complex in the twelfth century. In this respect, it was surely not unlike Jam-Firuzkuh; in fact, given Bamiyan's much longer commercial history and more advantageous location, the latter was at least as prosperous as its western Shansabani counterpart, and probably more so.

As set forth in Chapter 1, cultural patronage – encompassing poetic, literary, and architectural creations – was a fundamental protocol of courtly life throughout the Persianate world, emerging from the politico-economic importance of cultural production. The Bamiyan Shansabanis came to be notable cultural patrons, even rivaling their Firuzkuh cousins.[54] For example, the well-known *littérateur* Nizami 'Aruzi al-Samarqandi (fl. *c.* 1100–1150s CE) was in Saljuq service during the first half of the twelfth century, but later entered 'Ala' al-Din Husain's court, which was presumably at Firuzkuh. However, he ultimately dedicated his *Chahar Maqala* to Husam al-Din 'Ali Abu al-Hasan, a Shansabani prince of Bamiyan (Fakhr al-Din Mas'ud's youngest son), indicating that he was probably lured to the Bamiyan court by the greater benefits offered to him.[55] Fakhr al-Din Mas'ud's grandson, Sultan Baha' al-Din of Bamiyan (r. AH 588–602/1192– 1206 CE), was apparently an even more eminent patron of letters and architecture: this sultan patronized Fakhr al-Din ibn 'Umar al-Razi (*c.* AH 544–606/1149–1210 CE), one of the greatest philosophers and theologians after al-Ghazali (d. AH 504/1111 CE), occasioning al-Razi's dedication of *Risala-yi Baha'iyya* (no longer extant) to him.[56] Juzjani additionally recounted (at some length) that his own father Maulana Siraj-i Minhaj was subject to Baha' al-Din's repeated entreaties to leave Firuzkuh and join the Bamiyan court.[57] Maulana finally acquiesced – in fact, "*without* the permission of Sultan Ghiyath al-Din" – for which Baha' al-Din rewarded him with two *madrasa*s "[having] grants (of land) and plentiful benefactions."[58]

All the more surprising, then, is the apparent paucity in traces of newly constructed twelfth-century architecture in the Bamiyan region. Juzjani made note of amply endowed *madrasa*s during the reign of Sultan Baha' al-Din – though without the embellishments of his description of Firuzkuh's Baz Kushk-i Sultan. Moreover, parallel to what we saw at Firuzkuh, circumstantial evidence supports the assumption that the Bamiyan rulers – at the very least Baha' al-Din – would have patronized civic and religious architecture, and also palatial complexes (cf. below). But few remains can be dated *exclusively* to the late twelfth century. Of course, we must bear in mind that subsequent intervention in a landscape like Bamiyan – more heavily traversed than Ghur – would cause substantial changes in and erasures of historical traces over almost a millennium. The Mongol retribution visited upon Bamiyan (1221–1222 CE) alone could have done much of the job, given the Chinggisids' extraction of disproportionate penalties from locales simply resisting their onslaught, not to mention the extermination of entire populations in return for any deaths of Chinggis Khan's family members and associates in the course of the sieges.[59] Nevertheless, there are still surprisingly few indications of architecture newly built in the second half of the twelfth century.

By contrast, evidence of the re*occupation* and re*purposing* of various sites throughout the Bamiyan basin *has* survived the effects of time. Based on the study of ceramic assemblages from several of the latter sites, their reoccupation has been principally dated to the later twelfth-century Shansabani command of the region.[60] The excavations at Shahr-i Zuhak (Figures 3.9 and 3.10), along with surface surveys of the nearby hilltop complexes of Sarkhushak (Figure 3.23), and recent excavations at Shahr-i Ghulghula (Figure 3.12) and in the core Bamiyan valleys, can be considered together with the documentation of numerous historical remains on the routes of passage to the west of Bamiyan (Figures 3.14–3.18). As it stands, the available evidence seems to indicate a shifting Shansabani presence in the region, quite plausibly mapping onto their consolidation of control over the valley and its surroundings, and adapting to the defensive needs of these newly acquired territories (see below). As we know, Bamiyan ultimately served as the seat of a collateral and competing Shansabani lineage, achieving variable success *vis-à-vis* its Firuzkuhi cousins.

Archaeological explorations of the Hindu Kush brought to light at least ten advantageously perched complexes along Bamiyan's western access routes (Figures 3.14–3.18).[61] Further documentation and – ideally – excavation at least at some of these sites would be required for beginning

Figure 3.12 *Shahr-i Gholghola, general view, citadel (eleventh–thirteenth century).* © *Photograph Josephine Powell* c. *1960. Harvard Fine Arts Library, Special Collections.*

to attain chronological and functional understandings of the many ruins atop these western promontories. Nevertheless, for now it is plausible that initial construction in these areas came about sometime in the pre-Islamic centuries, possibly during the proposed expansion of architectural activity into the surrounding valleys as the Western Turks extended their reach southward throughout Tukharistan and consolidated their presence in Bamiyan (see above).

The surface decorations on many structural remains (Figure 3.15) have been described as "characteristic Ghurid geometrical pattern[s] composed of lines of incised triangles." But given the enduring use of similar architectural decorations even into the nineteenth and twentieth centuries, they are far from diagnostic of chronology. Indeed, the complexes' structural techniques (Figures 3.16 and 3.17) as well as the remnants of interior painted decorations (Figure 3.18) are instead indicative of initial construction in the pre-Islamic centuries of the mid-first millennium CE.[62] As was the case with most of the other hilltop complexes throughout the Bamiyan region, these western sites were in all likelihood also reused and possibly repurposed throughout the following centuries, making archaeological excavation and analysis all the more necessary for precise dating.[63]

Another complex indicating twelfth-century occupation is Barfak II, also known as Danestama, located to the northeast of Bamiyan on the right bank of the Surkhab River (Figures 3.19–3.22). While the overall site comprised approximately seventy-five grottoes and caves in the foothills surrounding a group of structures, a free-standing building among the latter interests us here. This brick structure with rubble footing was square on plan, having near-circular towers diagonally addorsed at the corners, and hemispherical towers centered in three of the four walls (Figures 3.19 and 3.20). Probably double-storied, it was configured around a courtyard with four *ivan*s, the one on the southeast also serving as a monumental entrance. Adjacent to this entrance on its north was a corner chamber with a *mihrab* in its western wall (Figure 3.21). Though missing the top, the remaining niche had a flat (rather than hemispherical) back wall, whose stucco revetment was replete with interlaced hexagons and six-pointed stars (Figure 3.22). Each of the shapes was filled in with stylized floral, vegetal, and circular motifs, in turn pierced with numerous holes to create a visual play of voids and solids, light and shadow. Although M. Le Berre expressed surprise at finding "in a monument of the Islamic period the half-wall of diaper-masonry so characteristic of the Buddhist mon-

Figure 3.13 *Shahr-i Gholghola, recovered wooden door leaves (whereabouts unknown). From Baker and Allchin 1996: 31.*

uments of Afghanistan and the pre-Islamic monuments of the central Hindu Kush," archaeologists have favored an eleventh- or twelfth-century date for the structure as a whole, based on the presence of this *mihrab* and its stucco decoration.[64]

Given its proximity to the major Buddhist and possibly Western Turk dynastic center of Bamiyan itself (cf. above), and in light of the abundance of surviving pre-Islamic structures throughout the area, it is not impossible that Danestama was originally a pre-Islamic site, repurposed during the twelfth century. We know, of course, that the continuation of building practices despite political changes was consistent with the nature of architectural cultures (see Introduction), so that brick walls upon rubble

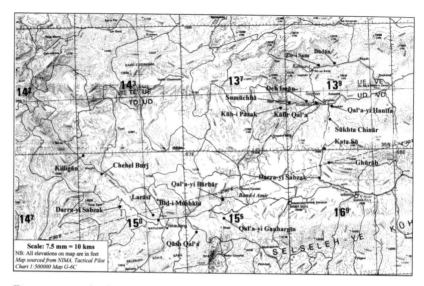

Figure 3.14 *Yakaulang, Saighan, and Kahmard Districts, western Bamiyan Province, Afghanistan. From Lee 2006: map 1.*

Figure 3.15 *Qala'-yi Gauhargin, western Yakaulang District, Bamiyan Province: south-east side. From Lee 2006: fig. 3.*

footings by themselves do not indicate pre-Islamic construction. But the presence of pre-Islamic pottery fragments, even in lesser quantities than Islamic sherds, signal possible occupation of the site prior to the proposed twelfth-century date of the *mihrab* and its stucco revetment.[65] Furthermore, the overall plan of the structure, *viz.* four *ivan*s around a central courtyard

Figure 3.16 *Bamiyan vicinity, structural remains. From Le Berre 1987: pl. 87d.*

and corner bastions, was commonplace among the free-standing Buddhist monastic complexes of Central Asia, particularly of the fifth–eighth centuries, and also eminently usable for Islamic-period institutions such as *madrasa*s, palatial structures, and even fortified military garrisons. Finally, it is worth recalling that the region's great commercial prosperity and royal presence resulted in lavish architectural (and artistic) patronage throughout the second half of the first millennium CE, much of which continued to be serviceable to newcomers establishing a politico-military presence in the region. Indeed, like their predecessors, the Shansabanis had taken

Figure 3.17 *Killigan, eastern Yakaulang District, Bamiyan Province: detail of ornamentation in room on south wall. From Lee 2006: fig. 32.*

advantage of other usable structures in Bamiyan, and Danestama could have been another such act of architectural pragmatism.[66]

But not all Shansabani intervention in the Bamiyan region involved pre-existing structures. At variance with Zuhak and possibly Danestama, and the numerous ruins to the west of Bamiyan, the fortified hilltop site of Sarkhushak (Figures 3.23–3.26) apparently had no pre-Islamic architectural fabric in its extensive remains. Located to Bamiyan's north and commanding a promontory at the confluence of the Bamiyan and Shibar rivers (Figures 3.8 and 3.23), the site's principal construction probably took place during the Shansabani ascendancy in Bamiyan, or the second half of the twelfth century, likely having later phases of occupation as well.[67] Documentation of the site identified the remains of two residential/palatial structures[68] – one with multiple interconnected stories sophisticatedly arranged on a gradient (Figure 3.24); one mosque, and a tomb with a *mihrab*[69] (Figure 3.25); a possible *hammam*; a quadrangular and apparently fortified structure with circular corner bastions[70]; and about forty artificial grottoes in a spur of the rocky promontory.

As with the other Bamiyan-area complexes, more systematic exploration is also needed here. But it is still apparent that Sarkhushak's mosque and tomb architecture utilized domical profiles, three-pointed arches,

Figure 3.18 *Chehel Burj, eastern Yakaulang District, Bamiyan Province:
unidentified ornamentation. From Lee 2006: fig. 24.*

and lofty interior spaces – all architectural devices associable with the
larger Persianate-Islamic world. By contrast, its residential/palatial structures consisted of elliptical corridors (Figure 3.26) directly evoking the
pre-Islamic fabric of Zuhak, and exhibiting "horizontal squinches" and
corbeled ceilings apparently akin to *Indic* methods of construction.[71] Thus,
Sarkhushak not only distinguished itself as one of the rare, newly commissioned constructions quite possibly of Shansabani patronage in the main
Bamiyan valleys, it intriguingly reconciled the continuity of the regional
architectural culture with discernibly Islamic ritual structures, while integrating Indic building practices as well.

The recent DAFA-led Franco-Afghan excavations at Shahr-i Ghulghula
(Figures I.22, 3.12 and 3.13) are germane at this juncture. These investigations have unearthed fascinating indications of more than one phase of

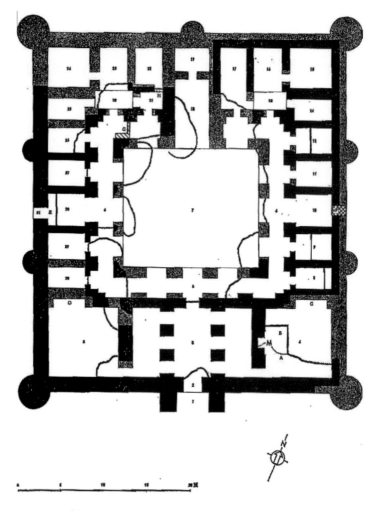

Figure 3.19 *Barfak II, a.k.a. "Danestama," c. 80 km northeast of Bamiyan: plan. From Le Berre 1970: 47.*

reuse and reoccupation at the site, although *no* apparent new construction can thus far be attributed specifically to Shansabani presence in the area during the later twelfth century.[72] Such a refinement of architectural chronology emerges from comparison of the Ghulghula remains with those of Sarkhushak.

Like Shahr-i Zuhak (see above), Ghulghula was also constructed during pre-Islamic centuries, but Zuhak exhibited comparatively little evidence of later reoccupation *vis-à-vis* Ghulghula: for example, extremely few Islamic-period glazed wares emerged from Zuhak, while Ghulghula's ceramic corpus was dominated by a truly impressive quantity and variety of Islamic-period painted glazed wares with vegetal, geometric, and calligraphic or pseudo-calligraphic decoration, as well as fine glazed wares

Figure 3.20 *Barfak II/"Danestama," east side of central courtyard.*
From Le Berre 1970: pl. IIa.

with molded decorative designs in shallow relief appliqué.[73] In addition
to Ghulghula's extensive ceramic finds, earlier documentation of the site
had already revealed two notable mosques: one with a *qibla ivan* overlooking a large courtyard; and the other, a larger one probably with four
*ivan*s around a courtyard.[74] Finally, the rediscovery of intricately carved,
double-leaf wooden doors (Figure 3.13) strongly suggested Shansabani
presence here: the arabesque motifs in relief, contained within incised
geometric shapes, create an overall effect not unlike a door leaf recovered
during Jam-Firuzkuh's surface explorations.[75] The pre-Islamic structural
cores at Ghulghula, then, quite possibly received additional architectural
details during Shansabani occupation in the second half of the twelfth
century.

   Franco-Afghan surveys and excavations on the western slopes of the
Ghulghula promontory in 2014–2015 revealed extensive historical remains
of palatial architecture, albeit deteriorated due to modern occupation and
modification. Nevertheless, elevations and plans of the older architectural
remnants – some extending up to 10 meters above ground – were identified and analyzed, resulting in close parallels to surviving Ghaznavid

Figure 3.21 *Barfak II/"Danestama," mihrab from southeast. From Le Berre 1970: pl. IIIc.*

palaces constructed and occupied throughout the eleventh–early twelfth centuries. The elevations of Ghulghula's building remains were also punctuated with blind arcades, not dissimilar to the large Southern Palace at Lashkari Bazar (see Chapter 5): in both cases, the walls most often showed a large, blind central arch flanked on each side by three smaller ones. Moreover, the traceable contours of historical walls highlighted a preference for cruciform configurations, that is, central courtyards with alcoves in the centers of the four sides (the four-*ivan* plan), creating intersecting perpendicular axes.[76] Such configurations were also in evidence at Lashkari Bazar and, most noticeably, at the royal palace of Ghazna, which was until recently attributed to the Ghaznavid sultan Mas'ud III (r. AH 492–508/ 1099–1115 CE), but is now thought to have had several prior phases of construction and occupation.[77]

In comparison with Sarkhushak's distinctively "hybrid" palatial architecture – combining Indic and Islamic-Persianate building forms and construction methods – Ghulghula's remains appear to be largely, if not exclusively, reminiscent of the Persianate palaces of Ghazna and Lashkari

Figure 3.22 *Barfak II/"Danestama," detail of stucco revetment in* mihrab.
From Le Berre 1970: pl. IV.

Bazar.[78] It could be proposed, then, that the site overall experienced at least two documentable phases of *re*occupation: Whatever pre-Islamic fabric remained at the site was certainly visited by later builders of palatial structures, probably during the Ghaznavid command of the Bamiyan region from the end of the tenth through early twelfth centuries. With the establishment of a Shansabani branch at Bamiyan *c.* 1150 CE, the Ghaznavid palatial remains could have been reoccupied, obviating the need for new construction (as we will see in Ghazna itself: cf. Chapter 4).

Figure 3.23 *Sarkhushak, north of Bamiyan. From Le Berre 1987: pl. 116a.*

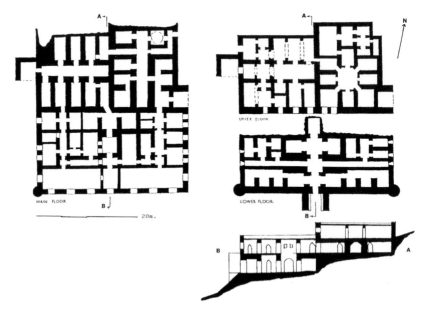

Figure 3.24 *Sarkhushak, Building A, plans and elevations. From Baker and Allchin 1996: fig. 5.13.*

The Shansabani occupation of sites throughout the Bamiyan region can be understood at least partially in relation to this branch of the Shansabanis' continued monitoring of access to the core valleys. Moreover, their probable reuse of westward hilltop sites can also be explained by the contiguity of Ghur to the west, and the traffic between the two regions.

But the geo-political mapping of power had shifted as the Shansabanis gained a foothold in the Bamiyan basin: rather than the area being an extension of power radiating southward throughout Tukharistan with late Hephthalite–Western Turkic control as in the sixth through ninth centuries (see above), by the later twelfth century the Bamiyan Shansabanis had to contend with disaffected Saljuq governors, the encroaching Oghūz, and the Qarakhitay, all poised to approach from the north. The Shansabani construction of Sarkhushak – boasting both palatial as well as possibly military structures, built by the architecturally skilled labor available in the region – surely aided in the vigilance against an entirely new gamut of enemies.[79] The possible reoccupation of Danestama also falls in line with these northern threats, lending further weight to a military or at least multi-faceted purpose for this complex.[80]

If indeed the palatial complexes at Sarkhushak are attributed to Shansabani patronage, they may present something of a surprise given the archaeologically attested *absence* of a permanent royal residence at Firuzkuh (cf. above). But the temptation to compare the two agnatic lineages, and to reduce them to a seemingly necessary but ultimately

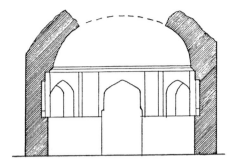

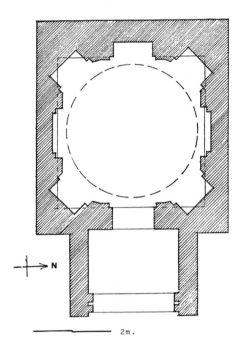

Figure 3.25 *Sarkhushak, Building E, plan and elevation. From Baker and Allchin 1996: fig. 5.18.*

artificial parity, can be avoided if we recall the great variety both *within* and *among* transhumant/nomadic groups. The acknowledged symbiosis among these multiple lifeways, effectively constituting the nomad–urban continuum, was one in which the Shansabanis had participated since pre-imperial times; in fact, it was arguably a factor in their very ascendancy as a regional elite still preserving some form of transhumance (see esp. Chapter 2).

Shansabani clansmen had already been exposed to a more sedentist lifestyle, and some may have taken it up at an earlier stage than is historically documentable. While Firuzkuh and the Hari Rud's banks continued to function as *sard-sir* for the Firuzkuh Shansabanis, the Bamiyan basin's cul-

Figure 3.26 *Sarkhushak, Building A, vault. From Baker and Allchin 1996: fig. 5.17.*

tural milieu – defined in part by its centuries of cosmopolitan Buddhism –
quite likely demanded a more sedentist court structure of the Bamiyan
branch of Shansabanis. In light of their earlier exposure to settled lifestyles
and economies, the Bamiyan lineage's transition to palace dwelling – also
in reoccupied contexts, such as Shahr-i Ghulghula – appears more credible. Thereafter, in the course of consolidating and maintaining power,
the Bamiyan Shansabanis appear to have reoccupied *and* commissioned
new palatial complexes, not unlike their Ghaznavid predecessors.[81] In any
case, the end result was that, despite their agnatic connections, the two

Shansabani lineages functioned variably as elites and performed royalty quite differently from each other, conforming to the demands of the localized politico-economic and cultural circumstances of the areas respectively constituting their disparate bases of power.

Tiginabad /Old Qandahar

Excavations to the south of the historical site generally referred to as Old Qandahar, located 4 km west of modern Qandahar,[82] were conducted between 1974 and 1978 – the last to have been carried out there. They unearthed a long and surprisingly fluctuating history at the site, a mystery exacerbated by the varying names applied to the locale and its vicinity from the Hellenistic period onward. Although "Tiginabad" and "Old Qandahar" may appear anachronistic given these vagaries of naming, they are used here to focus on the settlement and its surrounding area's relevance specifically for Shansabani expansion during the second half of the twelfth century.[83]

The transit routes radiating southeastward from Herat, passing through the regions of Zamindawar and al-Rukhkhaj and ultimately reaching India, were as important as their northern counterparts toward Balkh, or again to India *via* Bamiyan and Kabul. Thus, the plains of al-Rukhkhaj were punctuated with settlements testifying to uninterrupted long-distance trade from the pre-historic eras onward (see also Chapter 2). Old Qandahar was among the locales benefiting from this continuous flow of people and goods through the region. Moreover, the fates of the city and its nearby Buddhist monastery were discernibly intertwined.

Looking down upon Old Qandahar and its plains was the famous Qaitul Buddhist complex (Figure 3.27) comprising a *vihara* and tall *stupa*, which still seems to command the vista from its prominence atop the Qaitul ridge. The Buddhist complex was founded quite possibly as early as the third century CE during the Mauryan presence in the region, and akin to most other Buddhist sites closely associated with travel routes, it served as a commercial node for the regularly passing traffic of merchants, pilgrims, and others. The Qaitul monastic establishment was actively patronized through the seventh or early eighth centuries CE, a span of time when Old Qandahar down on the plains was also a major emporium. The prosperity of both the city and the Buddhist complex was surely augmented by their proximity to Zamindawar, the regional *garm-sir* destination for the Rutbils undertaking seasonal transhumance between Zabulistan and al-Rukhkhaj-Zamindawar (see Chapter 2).

By the eighth century, however, the increasing conflagrations between these rulers and the incoming 'Umayyad and 'Abbasid deputies disrupted commerce and travel *via* the southern routes emerging from Herat. The

Figure 3.27 *Qandahar, Afghanistan. Qaitul stupa and citadel of Old Qandahar.* © *Photo by Warwick Ball, c. 1970s.*

disturbances took their toll on the Qaitul Buddhist monastic complex, abandoned by the eighth century without any scope for revival.[84] During the same time frame, if not before, Old Qandahar had also contracted to a shadow of its former self. By the mid-twelfth century and the likely Shansabani presence there, the site's status was even more uncertain, having experienced a pronounced decline in settled mercantile and associated occupation over several centuries, though nomadic populations likely continued visitations to the area. Later eleventh- and twelfth-century Persian texts mentioned a certain Tiginabad in the same region, probably referring to Old Qandahar's later iteration as a settlement of greatly reduced size.[85] In fact, Juzjani implicitly confirmed the identification of Old Qandahar as at least in the vicinity of Tiginabad, if not the same settlement, in the context of the Shansabanis' sacking of Ghazna and Lashkari Bazar in AH 545/1150 CE.[86] But it should be noted that Tiginabad/Old Qandahar's diminution in both size and importance between the eighth and fifteenth centuries is remarkable given its location, which had rendered the entire area "at *all* times in its history … a major frontier stronghold of immense strategic value."[87]

Given Tiginabad/Old Qandahar's minor status by the mid-twelfth century (and earlier), the reasons behind a Shansabani campaign and/or presence there, along with the nature and duration of their stay during initial expansion outside their ancestral Ghur, may seem less than apparent.[88] However, the skirmishes over the site between the Ghazna Yaminis and the Shansabanis highlight not only its importance for the continuing power struggle in the region, the *Firuzkuh* Shansabanis' ultimate victory in capturing it further reveal the politico-economic differences between this branch and their Bamiyan cousins. Certainly, Tiginabad/Old Qandahar's location between Ghazna and Bust-Lashkari Bazar made it much more strategically relevant to the Shansabanis of Firuzkuh than to their cousins at Bamiyan. In AH 552/1158 CE,[89] 'Ala' al-Din Husain once again confronted Ghaznavid forces and wrested the locale, interrupting the Yamini transit corridor between Ghazna and al-Rukkhaj-Zamindawar.[90] Moreover, the discernible post-conquest "footprint" at Tiginabad/Old Qandahar seems to reflect a distinctly Firuzkuh Shansabani character, rather than one evoking their palace-dwelling Bamiyan relatives.

The above-mentioned excavations at Tiginabad/Old Qandahar during the 1970s unearthed an extensive cemetery – surprisingly vast, in fact, with an extent surpassing the settlement itself.[91] The cemetery contained burials largely following Islamic prescriptions, that is, north–south placement of unburned bodies with faces oriented toward Mecca – the *qibla* being in a westerly direction from South Asia – within graves devoid of any goods buried with the deceased. Among the burials, two large mounds, which the archaeologists referred to as Mound A and Mound B, were visible and even prominent features of the landscape calling for excavation.

Figure 3.28 *Old Qandahar cemetery, Burial Mound A, octagonal platform looking south. From Whitehouse 1976: pl. III.*

Mound A (Figure 3.28) contained two sequential burials, each of a small child, both oriented north–south with the faces turned west. The grave also exhibited features seemingly outside strict Islamic burial norms, however: the first body was placed within a small and vaulted, subterraneous mud-brick crypt, marked above ground by a rubble and mortar octagonal enclosure that was itself filled in to create a platform. Atop the first burial was that of another child, still within the octagonal enclosure and platform. The entirety of Mound A had been covered over with earth. The second nearby burial, Mound B, revealed itself to be less elaborate upon excavation, but still following similar protocols: the body of an adult and probably elderly woman facing west was placed in a north–south trench grave, surrounded by a rectangular enclosure, the whole contained within an earthen mound.[92]

Scholarly consensus has generally dated Mounds A and B to the mid-twelfth century, more specifically associating both with the Shansabani presence at Tiginabad/Old Qandahar. The strongest chronological indications for this dating have been the ceramic fragments, whose earliest sequences fell within the twelfth century based on comparable finds from Lashkari Bazar.[93] Moreover, the combination of discernibly Islamic and non-Islamic burial practices in the two graves – and others may yet come to light – could be interpreted as making a stronger case for Shansabani association rather than refuting it: We have noted in Chapter 2 that the Shansabanis' own cultural practices were rooted within the pre- or early Islamic temporal *strata* of west–central Afghanistan, with continuations or modifications over time. It is not impossible, then, that burial practices continuing those of their pre-imperial, and *more* nomadic and/or transhumant forebears were still in place during these early phases of their ascendancy outside historical Ghur.[94]

As for the impetuses behind the foray to Tiginabad/Old Qandahar in the first place, and the Shansabani presence documentable there: it is not unimaginable that, with Ghaznavid power gradually declining in the region – particularly after 'Ala' al-Din's much touted destruction of Ghazna itself and Bust-Lashkari Bazar – the Firuzkuh Shansabanis attempted to revive Tiginabad/Old Qandahar as a commercially and strategically pivotal emporium once again. After all, the eastward transit routes from Herat skirting Ghur to the south, passing through Tiginabad/Old Qandahar upon entering and exiting India, continued to be just as viable as their northern counterparts.

As with Bamiyan and the slate of new politico-military contenders and rivals appearing on the horizon by the twelfth century (see above), Tiginabad again proved itself a strategic point of military operations: the Oghüz occupation of Ghazna signified yet another (nomadic) enemy in the region certainly for the Firuzkuh Shansabanis, whom Shihab al-Din – though subordinate to his older brother Shams al-Din, titled Ghiyath al-Din as of AH 558/1163 CE – had nonetheless persistently tried to dislodge throughout the 1160s. But it was only through a joint effort of *both* brothers that the Oghüz were finally routed; as a result, the Firuzkuh-based Shansabanis could claim definitive occupation of the erstwhile Yamini capital in AH 569/1173–1174 CE (after prior brief stints there by 'Ala' al-Din Husain – cf. Chapter 1). This victory accrued to the younger Shihab al-Din, who was finally crowned sultan, receiving the surely long-awaited title of Sultan Mu'izz al-Din (cf. also Chapters 4 and 5). Tiginabad/Old Qandahar likely served a strategic purpose for the Firuzkuh Shansabanis, then, but barring rediscovery of additional evidence, it appears that Shansabani presence there left behind only burials of a very few, albeit seemingly important personages.[95] It is, of course, quite possible that the continuing lifestyle of transhumance of this branch of the Shansabani clan might have left other, less conventional archaeological traces in the material record, recovery of which would require surveying and even excavating afresh at the historical city and in its vicinity.[96]

Multiple Shansabani Imperial Architectures

Compared with the available documentation of Ghur's built remains (cf. Chapter 2), the more extensive archaeological explorations of the Bamiyan basin as well as Tiginabad/Old Qandahar permit several overarching observations. There are noteworthy material and historiographical parallels between the Shansabanis' appanages in Ghur, Bamiyan, and al-Rukkhaj-Zamindawar. The core areas of Bamiyan and Firuzkuh were in fact central nodes in the discernibly differing cultural and economic geographies of eastern and western Afghanistan, while the Ghazna–Tiginabad/

Old Qandahar region in the south was ensconced within networks linking the Indic and Iranian worlds since at least the early first millennium CE.[97] Not only did these regions serve as stages upon which an obscure clan, originating in the region's nomad–urban continuum, coalesced as imperial lineages; they also adumbrate the Shansabanis' ingenious reuse of inherited landscapes replete with the remains of rich and deep histories (see also Chapter 1).

Indeed, all three areas must also be recuperated from the elisions and silences of textual sources. Past authors' virtual erasure of the Shansabanis' origins in the transhumance/nomadism of Ghur – and everything else that was erased alongside – have already been discussed (see Chapters 1 and 2). But a similar silence surrounding the Shansabanis' reuse and repurposing of pre-Islamic sites and structures in the Bamiyan region is difficult to ignore. Indeed, without the analysis of the surviving architectural remains at Firuzkuh and Bamiyan, knowledge of Shansabani presences there would be limited to the perfunctory textual mentions of the cultural patronage incumbent upon Perso-Islamicate rulers, with no intimation of their remapping of the geo-political terrain as they contended with new adversaries. And without even the sparse archaeological data from Tiginabad/ Old Qandahar, insight into the impetuses behind the Shansabani campaigns into al-Rukkhaj-Zamindawar would be altogether unrecoverable.

It bears reiteration that the Bamiyan Shansabanis in particular might have conformed to their specific local requirements for maintaining power by constructing palaces. This architectural patronage, arguably quite new for a Shansabani clan, did not preclude reoccupation and repurposing of a built environment, making the reuse in Bamiyan really a continuation of the collective Shansabanis' pre-imperial transhumant/nomadic practices (see Chapter 2). The simultaneity of these seemingly divergent ways of shaping a landscape actually encapsulates the *real* complexity of the nomad–urban continuum, wherein populations adapted to their changing circumstances with surprising alacrity. In their respective continuities and adaptations, the Shansabani imprints at early Firuzkuh, Bamiyan, and Tiginabad/Old Qandahar prefigure the subsequent, place-specific empire-building that the lately established *third* branch – the Ghazna Shansabanis – undertook throughout farther-flung conquests eastward to the Indus and beyond (cf. esp. Chapter 6, and Volume II).

Furthermore, by the 1170s it could be said that there was no singular Shansabani elite, but rather separate and even competing agnatic lineages at Firuzkuh, Bamiyan, and eventually Ghazna (cf. Chapters 4 and 5). The fragmentation of inheritance, customary among modern nomadic groups (cf. Chapters 1 and 2), could in fact be suggestive of the increasing politico-economic independence of these various Shansabani lineages. Seniority, however, rested ostensibly with Ghiyath al-Din and the Firuzkuh Shansabanis: this branch was part of a *westward* geo-historical momentum reinforced by Firuzkuh's mercantile economy and connectivity with the cosmopolitan cultural geography of greater Khurasan *via* Herat, the age-old commercial emporium and politico-cultural center, whence the routes of communication branched out to the east and north (cf. Introduction and Chapter 2).[98] Firuzkuh's westward links had distinguished its eponymous appanage from that of Bamiyan since the days of 'Ala' al-Din *Jahan-suz*, for example, in the many important military campaigns that could be undertaken with a consistently replenished treasury, in addition to the marital alliances with neighboring regions (cf. Chapter 4). A third imperial lineage at Ghazna, initiated as of the mid-1170s with Shihab al-Din's crowning as Sultan Mu'izz al-Din there, garnered great notoriety with their spectacular victories in India (cf. Chapters 5 and 6, and Volume II).

All the principal and minor Shansabani lineages were interrelated and also intermarried; but, as underscored here, each was increasingly independent and adaptive to its respective base of power. Indeed, this very responsiveness to particularized circumstances was a *modus vivendi* arguably deriving from the Shansabanis' earlier transhumance, or physical and affective mobility between nomadic and sedentist lifeworlds. The respective Shansabani lineages established at Firuzkuh, Bamiyan, and eventually Ghazna responded to and helped to shape their regional specificities, constituting yet another glimpse of "the organization talent [*sic*], cosmopolitanism, pragmatism, adaptation, and integration ability of … nomadic societies".[99]

Notes

1. For a distillation of bibliographic references, see Ball 2019: 468.
2. Based on comparisons with firmly identified coinage and other factors (e.g., invocations of Baghdad *khalifa*s), O'Neal (2016b) has attributed several previously unexamined coins of 'Ala' al-Din Husain to the Ghazna mint *c.* AH 555/1160 CE. This attribution would indicate that Ala al-Din again successfully took the city and considered it a part of his domains before the Oghüz occupation of the 1160s. Cf. *infra* in main text.
3. Remarkably, it appears that the *re*occupation of Ghaznavid-patronized palatial and other structures at Ghazna and Bust-Lashkari Bazar by Shihab al-Din – properly called Mu'izz al-Din after his installation and crowning at Ghazna – and his *ghulam*s was not inconsequential: the palatial architecture attributable to the period of early Shansabani establishment in northern India *c.*1192–1200 has much in common especially with precedents at Lashkari Bazar, probably signaling the increasing habitation of built structures – rather than the "textile architecture" of before – at least by the Ghazna branch of the Shansabanis and their *ghulam*s. See esp. Chapter 5.
4. See *infra* (main text and notes) for a discussion of Nizami 'Aruzi's *Chahar Maqala* and its importance for contextual information regarding the Firuzkuh

and Bamiyan Shansabanis, and the significance of cultural production by means of elite patronage.

5. See esp. Thomas's (2018: 146–150) overview of the debates surrounding the identification of Firuzkuh as the enigmatic Shansabani "capital"; cf. also Chapter 2.

6. As discussed *infra* in the main text, doubts regarding precise locations persist despite – again – O'Neal's (2016a) excellent mapping of the known Shansabani-associated toponyms. Cf. also O'Neal 2013: 16.

7. See Chapter 2, for Jam-Firuzkuh's integration into regional commercial networks, thanks in large part to the mercantile Jewish community established there as of the eleventh century, prior to Shansabani presence. Cf. also Juzjani, vol. I, 1963: 336 (trans. vol. I, 1881: 339); O'Neal, 2016a; Thomas 2018: 216.

8. See O'Neal 2016b for Wajiristan's location; also Leshnik's (1968: 47–48) discussion of Warshada in relation to Firuzkuh, etc.; and Thomas 2018: 39–41. M. Ashtiany, the commentator on Baihaqi's surviving text (most recently translated by Bosworth), also confronted the puzzling mentions of place names, noting that "the accounts of the Ghaznavid campaigns into Ghur provide considerable onomastic and topographical information, whose significance is unfortunately now obscure" (cf. Baihaqi [trans. Bosworth] vol. III, 2011: 97–98). In his copious commentary on Juzjani's text, Raverty (1881: 339, n. 8) noted other historical writers' (though specifically citing only the seventeenth-century *Burhan-i Qati‘*) mentions of Istiya, which was "the name of one of the mountains … between Ghaznin and Hirat" – still too large a swath of the country to identify the locality, probably a mountain fortress. However, the apparent extension of the Istiya appanage to include Tiginabad during Shihab al-Din's (later Sultan Mu‘izz al-Din) possession of the latter would indicate its location somewhere in southern Ghur, near the *garm-sir* of Zamindawar and Tiginabad/Old Qandahar (cf. Bosworth [1977] 1992: 122; O'Neal 2016a; and *infra* in main text). Furthermore, the location of Madin could have been in either northeastern Ghur, within the ambit of Kashi, or in the northwest near Gharjistan: the unsuccessful rebellion *c.* AH 547/ 1152–1153 CE and attempted occupation of Firuzkuh during ‘Ala' al-Din's "imprisonment" by the Saljuq Sultan Sanjar (r. AH 512–552/1118–1157 CE) – when he actually served as the Sanjar's boon companion – apparently originated near Kashi, and the usurping claimant to the seat was "Malik Nasir al-Din Husain, son of Muhammad of Madin, who was the son of the brother of ‘Ala' al-Din." Cf. Juzjani vol. I, 1963: 348 (trans. vol. I, 1881: 361–362); see also below in main text. It may be more likely, however, that Madin abutted Gharjistan, as Saif al-Din Muhammad's (r. AH 556–558/1161–1163 CE) campaign against the Oghüz, who were encroaching from the northwest, took him to Gharjistan and Madin. See Juzjani vol. I, 1963: 352 (trans. vol. I, 1881: 367 and n. 5).

9. Juzjani vol. I, 1963: 336, 337 (trans. vol. I, 1881: 339, 341). See Ball 2019: No. 468, for a brief site description and map, as well as an invaluable bibliography.

10. Juzjani vol. I, 1963: 375–376 (trans. vol. I, 1881: 403–404, 405). Even a cursory comparison between Raverty's nineteenth-century translation of this passage and my own here makes apparent the need for a fresh examination and trans-

lation of Juzjani's *Tabaqat* overall. The comparison may not reveal egregious differences at first sight, but close scrutiny, particularly of the architectural terms and their optimal translations, demonstrates the importance of *Tabaqat* overall while also urging the text's juxtaposition with other literary *genres* to obtain its "hors-texte" significances.

11. Cf. Thomas 2018: 149, 151. It bears noting that scholars have similarly lamented the lack of exact details in prose and poetry produced also at the Saljuq court at Isfahan, which Durand-Guédy (2010: 79–80, 88–90) has posited as the Saljuq summer capital, at least as of the reign of Malik Shah when the need to "domesticate" the Turkmen nomads among Saljuq ranks came to the fore. Nevertheless, where there is incidental and largely metaphorical–ceremonial mention of architecture, it becomes apparent that "the Saljuq dynasty left its mark on spaces of two kinds … the military and the religious," rather than the palatial (cf. *ibid.*, 92–100).

12. It is noteworthy that the *textual* engagement with and utility of architecture, particularly across the various genres of Arabic and Persian historical writing, seemed to remain symbolic and metaphorical until the late early modern period. Descriptions of the physical reality and even materiality of the built environment apparently shifted only in late eighteenth–early nineteenth-century historical writing: see esp. Khazeni 2018.

13. Cf. Meisami 2001: 21; and *ibid.*, 42 (citation of Winter 1993: 39).

14. Meisami 2001: 22.

15. The debates surrounding the location of Firuzkuh and whether the *minar* at Jam was indeed part of the Shansabani "summer capital" originated during the later nineteenth-century Afghan Boundary Commission's information-gathering tours (esp. Holdich 1910: 223ff.). It is noteworthy that many of the variant opinions were engendered by historically anachronistic preconceptions regarding capitals (e.g., Leshnik 1968); processes and markers of Islamization (e.g., Maricq and Wiet 1959); and the transhumance/nomadic pastoralism of the Shansabanis (e.g., Wiet 1959; Herberg 1982). Vercellin (1976) did, nonetheless, address some of these issues.

16. Cf. Juzjani vol. I, 1963: 375 (trans. vol. I, 1881: 404).

17. Thomas 2018: 160ff.

18. Pinder-Wilson (2001: 166) lamented that Juzjani did not specify whether it was the Jam Rud or Hari Rud that flooded and overtook the mosque, but seemed to spare the *minar*; MJAP's invaluable archaeological work at the site all but definitively indicated that it was the Hari Rud that broke its banks, since "fluvial deposits overlying the courtyard paving in all the soundings [became] thinner to the west" (Thomas 2018: 173).

19. Cf. Thomas 2018: 152; also Juzjani vol. II, 1963: 127–128, 132–133 (trans. vol. II, 1881: 1047–1048, 1057). There is archaeological evidence that Firuzkuh's settled population witnessed at least some destruction of households and belongings, according to Thomas (2018: esp. 205). However, it should also be noted that the continued transhumance of the *Firuzkuh* Shansabanis and, quite possibly, the largely "textile architecture" of these elites would have presented difficulties in recovery from the archaeological record even without

Mongol destruction. Cf. Durand-Guédy (2013a) for comparative examples from Saljuq contexts throughout Iran; and also *infra* in main text.

20. Thomas 2018: 184, 190–191.

21. Noted by Herberg and Davary (1976: 61) and utilized by Thomas (2018: 174–176) in his analysis of the archaeological finds at Qasr-i Zarafshan.

22. Thomas 2018: 173–184.

23. For the Saljuq royal encampment at Isfahan, see esp. Durand-Guédy 2010: 93–101. Cf. also Durand-Guédy 2013a: 175–182 for a discussion of the *kushk* incorporated into Saljuq encampments. The author also brought to light intriguing discrepancies between various Persian textual passages referring to the same royal residential complex, most notably the periodic substitution of the term *kushk* with *qasr* (*ibid.*, 153). Evidently, some historical Persian authors deemed *qasr*, rather than *kushk*, to be more in keeping with the unique role played by palaces as embodiments of royal power.

24. It cannot escape our notice that Juzjani largely relied on what was by the eleventh century not only the "basic repertoire of typical components of palace descriptions," but also recognizable rhetorical devices. The former included *manzar* (belvedere), *riwaq* (gallery, columned promenade), and *shuruf* (towers or crenellations); while the latter were exemplified by descriptions of the unprecedentedness of the overall complex, symbolized in the inability of the engineer/geometrician (*muhandis*) to have imagined or created such a palace before. Cf. *supra* Juzjani's description of Baz Kushk-i Sultan; and esp. Meisami 2001: 24, 26, 28, 29.

25. According to D. Thomas (pers. comm., April 2018), it is difficult to identify where, exactly, in the vicinity of Jam-Firuzkuh the space would have been available to accommodate large encampments.

26. Recent scholarship on the Saljuqs and their building of empire rightly eschews any essentialist idea of an innate preference for nomadic pastoralism ensuing exclusively from their Turkic origins; rather, Durand-Guédy (2013a: 173) has suggested that "the distribution of power [in the medieval Persianate world] precluded them from living like urban Iranians." Cf. Chapter 1; also Durand-Guédy 2013b; Durand-Guédy 2018; Peacock 2015: 143ff., 172. For a discussion of small architectural elements incorporated into Saljuq tent "palaces," see esp. Durand-Guédy 2013a: 154ff. Not only the early Saljuqs but also the later Saljuq Sultan Malik Shah (r. AH 464–85/1072–92 E) – who "enjoyed unparalleled authority during his long reign" – maintained a studied distance from even their major urban conquests: Tüghril and Chaghrï remained in their camp after their momentous conquest of Marv (*c.* 1035); Tüghril also decided against settling in Baghdad after its occupation in AH 447/1055 CE; Malik Shah preferred the environs of Isfahan; and, of course, Sanjar was frequently encamped somewhere in the vast expanses surrounding Marv, Herat, Tus-Nishapur – near which the twelfth-century Robat Sharaf may have provided part of the royal encampment (Figures 1.10–1.13) – and Isfahan. Cf. Durand-Guédy 2013b: 328–335; Peacock 2015: 143, 166–172.

27. Not *all* of the surveillance or defensive structures documented at Firuzkuh proffered signs of elite occupation, nor were they all necessarily of the same date. In 2003 MJAP re-examined ruined towers first documented by Herbert

and Davary (1976), to the east of the probable mosque (see *infra* in main text) and *minar* on the north and south banks of the Hari Rud: with the exception of one ruin, they were of weak construction and likely not for defense but vigilance, seemingly designed for *inward* surveillance of the city and its inhabitants, rather than focused outward toward the valleys granting access to Jam-Firuzkuh from the east. Thus, Thomas (2018: 184) proposed that these eastern towers might have been constructed during the tumultuous pro-Karramiyya riots of 1199 (cf. Chapter 4), or after the Shansabanis' fall and Firuzkuh's occupation by the Khwarazm-shahs, *c.* 1215.

28. For the wall remnants, see Le Berre, in Sourdel-Thomine 2004: 54–61, and *ibid.*, 95; also Thomas 2018: 159–160. The placement of the Jam-Firuzkuh *minar* has been described as "idiosyncratic," given its location on the *qibla* side of the mosque (Flood 2005b: 538). Pinder-Wilson (2001: esp. n. 43) noted that Saljuq minarets were frequently located at or near the north corner of their mosques. Although, the Nayin *jami*'s (tenth century) southeastern minaret, and Barsiyan's (eleventh–twelfth century) on the northwest rather supports Hillenbrand's (1994: 154) observation that "there seems to have been no consistent practice governing the location of single minarets within the mosque." The location of Jam-Firuzkuh's *minar* at the northwest corner of the probable mosque/*'idgah-minar* complex (as described *infra* in main text), then, may actually indicate an overall adherence to Saljuq precedents, rather than a deviation from them.

29. Dr. David Thomas, pers. comm., May 2018; cf. also Thomas 2018: 160–173.

30. Dr. David Thomas, pers. comm., May 2018; see also Flood 2005b: 538; Flood 2009: 95–96.

31. See Sourdel-Thomine 2004: 93–95, 149, 154; Flood 2005a: 276, 279–281; Flood 2005b: 538, 541; Flood 2009: 99; Lintz 2013: 91, 95–96. By consulting his own dig books and calculating orientations *via* Google Earth, Dr. David Thomas (pers. comm., July 2018) verified that the *minar*'s niche motif was oriented to approximately 260°, thus plausibly functioning as a *mihrab* (from Jam, Makka is 245°). The Karrami concordance with some Hanafi tenets (Zysow 2012: pts. I, ii, v) would have made the preferred Hanafi *qibla* in Central Asia of due west (270°) acceptable also to the Karramiyya. For the customary *qibla*s of the Hanafis and Shafi'is in Central Asia, see D. King (1982, 1995); and esp. Chapter 4. Moreover, Dr. Thomas 2005 documentation of a modern "nomad mosque," roughly outlined with stones and oriented to the *minar*'s east face, indicated that the niche served as a *mihrab* in recent times as well.

32. Sourdel-Thomine 2004: 95 (emphasis added).

33. Shokoohy and Shokoohy (1987: 129–132) proposed that the *'idgah* they identified 1 km northwest of Bayana/Sultankot in eastern Rajasthan dated from the 1190s, or the period of the forays into northern India undertaken by the Ghazna Sultan Mu'izz al-Din and his military deputies (see Volume II). The authors further claimed that an architectural precedent for this type of prayer space could have existed at the eleventh-century South Palace at Lashkari Bazar, specifically the so-called Great Mosque of the Forecourt. However, notwithstanding the unusually elongated plan of this structure, it

is unlikely to have been an *'idgah*: remains of columns in *both* phases of the building indicate that it was roofed (cf. Schlumberger 1978: 67–79 and pls. 23, 93–96). Nevertheless, it is of course possible that the simple, open-air prayer area comprising an *'idgah* was a known architectural type in Khurasan, and that examples pre-dating the fourteenth century both in Iran and India have tended not to survive precisely due to their meager physical "footprints" – as would have been the case at Jam-Firuzkuh. For a no longer extant Tughluq-period (mid-fourteenth century) *'idgah* at Multan, cf. A. N. Khan 1983: 177.

34. In her analysis of architectural descriptions in the panegyric poetry (*qasida*) produced at the Ghaznavid and Saljuq courts, Meisami (2001: 30, 41–42) highlighted the growing abstraction in poetic references to palaces; over time the poetry contained fewer descriptive details, increasingly substituted with metaphors and rhetorical flourishes by the mid-twelfth century. By way of explanation, she proposed both a broadening base of patronage beyond royalty to the religious and military elites, and an attendant shift in the very function of the palace from a forum of artistic creativity to a display trophy. The less than illustrious origins of the Shansabanis not only called for all the royal symbolism and legitimation of power that could be mustered, their chronicler Juzjani was heir to the poetic-literary traditions of the literati patronized by the Ghaznavids and Saljuqs. Understandably, then, his architectural descriptions served largely symbolic rather than documentary purposes.

35. Cf. esp. Flood 2002 for the historical and modern meanings of the Bamiyan Buddhas' destruction; for Bamiyan's "posthumous" designation as a UNESCO site, see Manhart 2006. See Inaba 2019 for the changing receptions of Bamiyan's Buddhas from the tenth through nineteenth centuries.

36. Cited by Tarzi 2007: 98. See also Thomas 2018: 58–59; Ball 2019: No. 100, for a thorough bibliography.

37. Cf. de Planhol (1988); Klimburg-Salter 1989: 10–11; Ball 2008: 164–173; Lorain 2018. This conception of the Bamiyan basin also emerges from Baker and Allchin's (1991) excavations at Shahr-i Zuhak and related sites (see *infra* in main text), and from Lee's (2006) documentation of the historical fortifications in western Bamiyan Province. For Funduqistan, Fuladi, and Kakrak, see also Ball 2019: Nos. 330, 332, 508, respectively.

38. Manhart 2006: 49; Tarzi 2007: 97, 107, 118ff.; Klimburg-Salter 2008: 132, 135, 140. Ball, Bordeaux et al. (2019: 391 and notes) espouse a date of the mid-seventh century for the Buddhas, however.

39. Cf. Rezakhani 2017: 141–142, and *ibid.*, 164–165 for a brief discussion of these debates. See also Tarzi 2007: 121–122; Crossley 2019: 50–53.

40. Klimburg-Salter 2008: 151.

41. Ball (2020) reiterated Klimburg-Salter's (1989: 134–136) earlier assertion. For the major site of Qunduz (along with associated mounds in the vicinity), see Ball 2019: Nos. 194, 569, 930, 931, 1160. Such a politico-dynastic geography would be continuous with that of the Kushanas (first–fourth centuries CE), whose political base was at Bagram but lavish patronage was dedicated to their dynastic center of Surkh Khotal. Cf. also Ball 2019: Nos.

122, 1123, respectively; and Ball, Bordeaux et al. 2019: 350–351, 353–360, 376–379.

42. The tandem existence among these differing axes of communication between Central Asia and India – the north–south axis *via* Bamiyan also incorporating the more southerly reaches of Zabul and Zamindawar – nonetheless resurfaced during the Ghaznavid and later periods. Cf. Inaba 2013: 90.

43. Perhaps an exception to this overall emphasis on Buddhist monastic and religious architecture in the contiguous valleys was Kakrak, to the southeast of Bamiyan: here, to the north of the grottoes, a small walled structure (fort?) has been dated to the early phase of Shahr-i Zuhak, i.e., *c.* 500 CE. Cf. Le Berre 1987: 81; Baker and Allchin 1991: 157. For a brief description of Kakrak's Buddhist ritual and monastic remains, see Tarzi, vol. I, 1977: 78. A description of the extremely rich grottoes of Fuladi was provided by Dagens 1964: 43–48, figs. and pls.

44. Cf. Le Berre et al. 1985–1988: 776, 782, 783; Lorain 2018. While Le Berre and others have noted the topographical and architectural parallels between the Bamiyan basin and Ghur – the latter being less clearly defined given the lack of both historical and modern documentation there – they did *not* pursue these observations further, to conclude that in Ghur much of the architectural landscape was reused and repurposed by later populations. Cf. Chapter 2.

45. The Bamiyan valley and specifically the Funduqistan monastery – the valley's only free-standing mud-brick structure (other complexes principally being grottoes of various dimensions) – has offered evidence of Brahmanical–Hindu cultic presence, similar to the coexistence of Buddhist and Brahmanical cults at various sites in the vicinities of Kabul and Ghazna. Worthy of special mention was the exquisite Mahisha-mardini from Funduqistan, preserved only in Durga's multiple arms and zoomorphic demon in marble (now lost). Cf. Bernard and Grenet 1981; Klimburg-Salter 1989: 73–74; Ball 2008: 188–189; Ball 2019: No. 332; and Chapter 2.

46. See Le Berre 1970: 45ff.; Baker and Allchin 1991: 55ff., 99–100; Lee 2006: 243–244; Thomas 2018: 118–119 (brief discussion); Ball 2019: No. 1052; Ball, Bordeaux et al. 2019: 391. Fischer (1969: 344) and Baker and Allchin (1991: 99) proposed that in the Bamiyan structures larger bricks were generally older than smaller ones, the latter likely indicating Islamic-period renovations or consolidations of existing structures. However, brick sizes are notoriously inconsistent, and only serve as a general indication of pre-Islamic or Islamic period construction (W. Ball, pers. comm., April 2018).

47. See esp. Le Berre et al. 1985–1988: 780–781. Centuries-long occupation and repeated renovations were evident at Shahr-i Zuhak itself where, during the Timurid period (fifteenth century), apertures possibly for firearms were created on the perimeter walls. Cf. Baker and Allchin 1991: 99. The virtually uninterrupted use of ancient structures is not unique to the Bamiyan region, also having been noted in Gandhara (Fischer 1969: 359) and widely documented in Sistan. Cf. Fischer 1969: 354; Fischer 1970: 484–485; Fischer 1973: 138, 143.

48. Cf. Baker and Allchin 1991: 35ff., 99. For Ghur, see Chapter 2.

49. Baker and Allchin 1991: 61.

50. Lee (2006) documented the architectural remains to the west of Bamiyan proper; see also *infra* in main text, and Thomas 2018: app. 3.

51. For Sistan, cf. Fischer et al. 1974: illus. 36–38, 41, 43. Fischer (1971: 46, 50) also noted the regional developments within Sistan of certain building types and, above all, techniques of decoration, particularly the combination of mud-brick structures having a combination of stucco and *burnt*-brick decoration.

52. Bamiyan, together with the rest of Tukharistan, Balkh, Gharjistan, and Ghur, were given to Sabuktigin as a reward for his admirable victories in Khurasan on behalf of his Samanid overlords; cf. Bosworth 1973: 44; Baker and Allchin 1991: 22–24. According to al-Muqqadasi (*c.* 985 CE; cited in *ibid.*), by the time of Ghaznavid presence in the area in the tenth century, the town of Bamiyan was walled and had a congregational mosque, thriving market, several suburbs, and four city gates. Also noteworthy is the possibility that, both during and after Sultan Mahmud's reign and the Ghaznavids' firm hold over territories spanning from Ghazna through Balkh, wealthy non-Muslim merchants were still prominent in Bamiyan: Baihaqi praised the merchant Abaveyh, who rebuilt the bridge of Bamiyan "with a single arch, displaying great elegance and beauty" (Baihaqi [trans. Bosworth] vol. I, 2011: 367). The merchant's name appears to be a Persian transliteration of the Indic (perhaps Buddhist) *Abhaya*; although, Ashtiany offers the unlikely alternative that the name was a hypocoristic form of *'Abd Allah* (*ibid.*, vol. III, 2011: 167). Moreover, the Shars as the pre-Islamic dynasts of Bamiyan were kept in place during the Arab-'Umayyad and A'bbasid incursions, not being definitively eradicated even after the Saffarids' late ninth-century successes there (Le Berre et al. 1985–1988: 782–783).

53. Juzjani vol. I, 1963: 348, 384 (trans. vol. I, 1881: 344, 361–362). Evidently, Fakhr al-Din Mas'ud appeared innocent of any collusion with the Madin Shansabanis, thus retaining the Bamiyan region as his appanage, passed on to his descendants for another three generations. By Juzjani implied that, by the reign of Ghiyath al-Din Muhammad (AH 553–599/1163–1203 CE) at Firuzkuh, the paramountcy of the *Firuzkuh* Shansabanis was firmly established over the others, as indicated by Ghiyath al-Din's personal conferral of the title "sultan" upon his cousin Shams al-Din Muhammad (r. AH 553–588/1163–1192 CE), perhaps the first of the Bamiyan rulers to receive it. See Juzjani vol. I, 1963: 378 (trans. vol. I, 1881: 427); see also *infra* in main text and notes; and for the contentious relations among the Shansabani branches, see Chapter 1.

54. Cf. Juzjani vol. I, 1963: 388 (trans. vol. I, 1881: 428–430); and Chapter 2.

55. While in the service of the Saljuq sultans Muhammad I (r. AH 498–512/1105–1118 CE) and Sanjar (r. AH 512–552/1118–1157 CE), Nizami 'Aruzi likely moved with the court throughout Khurasan, as glimpsed in the autobiographical introduction of the *Chahar Maqala* (cf. also Peacock 2015: 167). The circumstances in which he joined the Firuzkuh Shansabani court remain unknown, though it would be intriguing indeed to have his eyewitness view of his erstwhile patron Sanjar's defeat and capture of 'Ala' al-Din Husain near Herat in 1152/3 CE, and the reasons for Nizami 'Aruzi's own stay in hiding

in the city afterward. See Gholam-Hosayni 1990; also Nizami 'Aruzi (trans. Browne 1921) 1978: 7–11.

56. Cf. Ghafur 1960: 2, 150–151; Anawati 2012.

57. Juzjani's dedication of an entirely separate section (XVIII) of *Tabaqat* to the "Shansabaniyya of Tukharistan and Bamiyan" contains the lengthy passage on his father Maulana Siraj-i Minhaj's move to Bamiyan from Firuzkuh. Historiographically, such an organizational device in *Tabaqat* places the Bamiyan branch of the family on a par with the one at Jam-Firuzkuh. It could also be that, given his encomium of Maulana, Juzjani separated and highlighted the Bamiyan branch as much to attest to its status, as to pay homage to his father's erudition and piety. Cf. Juzjani vol. I, 1963: 389 (trans. vol. I, 1881: 430); also Nizami 1983: 76–77. Edwards (2015: 112) cited another example of Juzjani's subordination of historical events to individual narrative in his all too brief report on the Ghazna Shansabani expansion into the Indus Valley (Chapter 6). Rasikh (2020: 113) described the emphasis of ties to well-known personages as "a literary trope for medieval Muslim historians with which they document consciously their personal, familial, and professional biographies."

58. Cf. Juzjani vol. I, 1963: 389 (trans. vol. I, 1881: 429–431) with emphasis added.

59. It is well known that many areas lying in the Mongols' eastward progress suffered destruction, e.g., the Marv oasis where Mongol forces ransacked Sultan Sanjar's mausoleum while seeking precious objects as loot. See Hillenbrand 2011: 280; Jackson 2017: 175. Bamiyan was especially unfortunate, however, to have been the place where Chinggis Khan's favorite grandson Möe'tügen was killed, for which the entire population was massacred and the town and its surrounding valleys gutted – a level of ruination apparently still visible through the fourteenth century. Cf. Gardin 1957: 228; and esp. Jackson 2017: 158. Indeed, Inaba (2019: n. 35) noted the absence of Bamiyan-minted coinage after the thirteenth century – a possible indication that Mongol destruction had enduring politico-economic effects on the region. In contrast to Bamiyan, it appears that only one Mongol incursion entered into the heart of Ghur, heading southward from Kashi or Ahangaran and reaching the headwaters of the Rud-i Ghur; while it is possible that the party pushed through to Tiginabad/Old Qandahar, the regions of al-Rukhkhaj and Zamindawar had always been more readily accessible *via* Ghazna from the east. Cf. O'Neal 2017; see also Chapter 2.

60. Gardin's (1957) study of ceramics from the Bamiyan basin focused almost exclusively on the finds from Shahr-i Ghulghula (see *infra* in main text), which he contextualized within the ceramic production of the wider Islamic-Persianate cultural sphere of Iran and Central Asia. It is only the cursory but still very valuable study of 250 ceramic shards collected by Marc Le Berre during his 1974–1975 surveys of parts of the Hindu Kush – principally Bamiyan's secondary valleys – that provides an overview of developments and tentative ceramic as well as architectural chronologies of the region. Cf. Le Berre et al. 1987; Le Berre et al. 1985–1988.

61. The work of Le Berre and his contemporaries of the Délégation Archéologique Française en Afghanistan (DAFA) (1987; 1985–1988), and that of Lee (2006)

has already been cited for the Hindu Kush fortifications; for additional bibliography see also Ball 2019: Nos. 189, 239, 286, 398, 489, 845, 862, 1021, 1039, 2045, 2046, 2141.

62. See Lee (2006: 229 and *passim*) for a "Ghurid" dating of the ruins, and Baker and Allchin (1991: esp. 99) for the centuries-long use of decorative iconographies. The mural paintings from the western Bamiyan area were not unique of course, but conceivably an extension of the lavish painted programs in numerous grottoes and structures in Bamiyan and throughout the region's other principal valleys, particularly abundant in Funduqistan, Foladi, and Kakrak. Indeed, the common curved striations in these paintings (Figure 3.18) immediately evoke the nimbuses frequently seen behind the Buddha's head: e.g., Klimburg-Salter 2008: pl. V, det. 3. Cf. also Klimburg-Salter 1989: e.g., pls. XVIII, XXIII, XXIV fig. 26, LXXX fig. 103, and LXXXIV–LXXXVI. The eighth–ninth-century caves in Jaghuri (west of Ghazna) likely also had some paintings, though their unfinished (at Tapa Zaytun) or extremely eroded states make it difficult to identify traces. Cf. Verardi and Paparatti 2004: 104 and pl. XLVIIa–c. See Chapter 2 for Herberg's (e.g., 1982) documentation of traces of interior mural painting within Ghur's architectural remains. Pre-Islamic architectural cultures throughout the vast central span of Afghanistan, then, included painted programs.

63. Lee (2006: 238–241) also mentioned painted scenes from *Shah-nama* documented in 2002 at Chehel Burj (one of the farther western complexes, also visited by Maricq and Wiet [1959]); unfortunately, the paintings disappeared shortly afterward, probably looted and offered for sale at clandestine markets in Pakistan or Iran. See also Thomas 2018: app. 3; Ball 2019: No. 189; Ball, Bordeaux et al. 2019: 399.

64. Le Berre 1970: 45 (my trans.); also Fischer 1978: 351–352; W. Ball, pers. comm., April 2018; Ball 2019: No. 109; Ball 2020; Ball, however, considers Danestama's "interpretation as a *madrasa* [i.e., newly built] … a convincing one." The mosque known as Darra-i-Sheikh at Gorzivan (Faryab Province) presents a parallel to Danestama: also quadrangular in plan with circular corner towers, and a more complete *mihrab* with stucco revetment and remains of painted decoration. The additional surviving fragments of a floriated Kufic inscription of Darra-i-Sheikh led to its tentative dating in the later twelfth century, based on comparisons with inscriptions from Sar-i Pul (historical Anbir) and the *minar* of Jam-Firuzkuh. Cf. Bivar 1966; esp. Pinder-Wilson 1980: 97–98; Ball and Fischer 2019: 487; Ball 2019: No. 248; and Chapter 2. However, it is conceivable that Darra-i-Sheikh's *mihrab* was also a later addition to the structure, as proposed here for Danestama (see following in main text).

65. Le Berre (1970: 50) himself confessed to the collection of "only those ceramic fragments that appeared most interesting to us and unpainted pottery was not retained" (my trans.). Baker and Allchin's (1991: 195–196) subsequent exploration of Danestama resulted in the identification of pottery fragments and the extant vaulting as comparable to those from Shahr-i Zuhak, *c.* 500 CE. A prime example of the four-*ivan* Central Asian Buddhist monastery would be Ajina Tepe (cf. Litvinsky [1984] 2011), and within Afghanistan the recently excavated

Mes Aynak provides a *comparandum*. See *infra* in main text for possible military uses of the four-*iwan* structure with corner bastions, e.g., at Sarkhushak.

66. It is noteworthy that, as early as the eleventh century, Persian poets of the eastern Islamic world such as Gurgani (fl. *c.* 1050 CE) were familiar with Buddhist monasteries, whose square plans, central courtyards flanked by *ivan*-like alcoves, and even interior paintings inspired metaphorical references, or may have served as devices of *mis-en-scène* (cf. Melikian-Chirvani 1982: 6–7; and Introduction). This apparent first-hand familiarity with Buddhist monastic interiors could have come from remnants of these structures in the landscape, and/or the result of their not infrequent repurposing as *madrasa*s or other identifiably Islamic purposes.

67. Cf. Le Berre 1987: 88–93; Baker and Allchin 1991: 161–179; Thomas 2018: 118–119; Ball 2019: No. 1004. Baker and Allchin confirmed the dating with analysis of surface ceramic finds, consisting mostly of sgraffiato wares and one sherd of lusterware from Rayy, all datable to the late twelfth–early thirteenth centuries.

68. It is indeed unfortunate that Juzjani did not describe Sarkhushak's supposed palatial structures in his section on the Bamiyan Shansabanis; they would have surely lent themselves with ease to the metaphorical apprehension of the palace as a symbol of royal greatness, common in eastern Persianate literary culture during the twelfth century (cf. *supra* the section on Firuzkuh).

69. Quite possibly, Baker and Allchin's Building E (Figure 3.25), occupying the promontory's highest point (to the north of the multi-level, graded residential/palatial structure), was a commemorative structure with a *mihrab*. While the other mosque (Building F) exhibited an east–west rectangular plan axially oriented along the *qibla*, Building E's compact footprint and profile essentially comprised a domed cube with addorsed entrance on the east – on axis with the western wall's *mihrab* – making it directly comparable to the eleventh- or early twelfth-century *ziyarat* of Imam-i Khurd near Sar-i Pul (ancient Anbir). Cf. Bivar 1966: esp. 57–62; Blair 1992: 201; Ball and Fischer 2019: 487.

70. The basic plan of the quadrangular structure (Building D), with its four circular bastions at the corners, is clearly evocative of the possibly repurposed Buddhist monastery of Danestama and other Central Asian Buddhist monastic structures (see *supra* in main text). It should also be mentioned that dyed and folded textiles were recovered from Building D, which of course does not necessarily preclude its simultaneous function as a military garrison. Cf. Baker and Allchin 1991: 163.

71. For the Indic elements cf. esp. Le Berre 1987: 92; Baker and Allchin 1991: 63, 65, 163. The introduction of Indic construction methods urges consideration of a late twelfth-century date for at least some Sarkhushak structures, as the Shansabanis' Indian campaigns arguably brought more skilled laborers westward from India, as proposed in Volume II.

72. The résumé here of the findings from Shahr-i Ghulghula emerged from the invaluable archaeological fieldwork in 2014–2015 around the Bamiyan region conducted by Thomas Lorain (Scientific Secretary, DAFA); while areas of Shahr-i Ghulghula's western slope were surveyed and some also excavated,

the topmost "citadel" still awaits exploration in upcoming seasons. In the 2014–2015 tours, Lorain and his team also encompassed the site of Chehel Dukhtaran to the south of Shahr-i Ghulghula. Cf. Lorain 2018; also Ball 2019: No. 1042.

73. See esp. Gardin 1957; cf. also Gascoigne 2010 for discussion of parallels and divergences between ceramic finds at Shahr-i Ghulghula and Jam-Firuzkuh. Now that the ceramic collections of the Herat Museum have undergone analysis, further parallels will surely emerge and better contextualize the Bamiyan–Ghulghula assemblages: cf. Franke 2016b, 2016c; Müller-Wiener 2016; Franke and Müller-Wiener 2016. Ultimately, *all* of these considerations must be framed against the glaring need to revisit the entirety of Gardin's collected ceramic corpus and his conclusions, not least given the fact that the materials were largely gathered through purchases at local markets rather than from documented archaeological contexts; and the sheer quantity of remains that would have probably exceeded the very short period of production proposed by Gardin (T. Lorain, pers. comm., September 2018).

74. Cf. Godard 1951: 5, figs. 1 and 4; Ball 2019: No. 1042.

75. See Baker and Allchin 1991: 28–30; Rugiadi 2006; Ball 2008: 166, 171; Thomas 2018: 217, 220. Lorain (pers. comm., September 2018) noted that the wooden doors' whereabouts now are unknown. While Warwick Ball (pers. comm., April 2018) confirmed Shahr-i Ghulghula's pre-Islamic construction – citing a Buddhist *stupa* and a hoard of T'ang Chinese bronzes recently documented there – he also noted a fundamental difference between Zuhak and Ghulghula: while Ghulghula was "the more urban site for Bamiyan (albeit fortified) … in use down to the Mongol conquest, [Zuhak was] solely a fortification." Ghulghula's high-quality ceramics, the intricately carved wooden doors, and the recent documentation of probably Ghaznavid-period palatial remains (cf. below in main text) would suggest multiple functions for the complex, including a royal residence/palace. Cf. Godard 1951; Gardin 1957; Baker and Allchin 1991: 28–30.

76. Cf. also Godard 1951.

77. R. Giunta, pers. comm., July 2018; Giunta 2020; cf. also Chapter 5.

78. Lorain 2018.

79. Cf. Bosworth 1988; Baker and Allchin 1991: esp. 163; and see Chapter 4. See also O'Neal (2020: 205–207) for numismatic evidence elucidating the nature of the Shansabanis' periodic occupations of Balkh as they confronted their various adversaries, including the Khwarazm-shahs in the 1190s CE.

80. Danestama is comparable with another, somewhat mysterious and probably multi-purpose structure northeast of Multan (Pakistan), just east of the Indus River's current flow. It was newly constructed in the third or fourth quarter of the twelfth century, though documentation by the present author in 1998 took note of older fragments used as building material in the walls; moreover, the Indus structure's plan very much echoes Danestama (Figures 6.16 and 6.17). Cf. Dani 1982: 183; Mumtaz 1985: 39–42; Edwards 1991; and Chapter 5.

81. See esp. Inaba (2013), and the discussion of the many Ghaznavid palaces (e.g., Balkh, Ghazna, Bust-Lashkari Bazar, Nishapur), palace–garden complexes (e.g., also Nishapur, Herat, Bust), as well as royal tent complexes used by the

Yamini sultans, frequently characterized as "Iranized Turks" (*ibid.*, 75) due to their extensive movements across far-flung tracts and occasional residence within "textile architecture." The sultans' movements also combined seasonal transhumance with military expeditions (*ibid.*, 89).

82. The modern city (Shahr-i Nau) swallowed within it the quadrangular, walled city laid out by Ahmad Shah Durrani *c.*1755, itself replacing Nadirabad, the garrison established by the warlord Nadir Shah Afshar (d. 1747) in the 1730s as he was on his way to plunder the Mughal treasury in Shahjahanabad (Old Delhi). Cf. N. Dupree 1977: 279ff.; Matthee and Mashita [2010] 2012); and *infra* in notes.

83. Symptomatic of the multiple and changing names of Old Qandahar is its sobriquet "Shahr-i Kuhna," which is also applied to a locality outside the city of Farah (Farah Province), and to another site in the region of Zamindawar (Helmand Province): cf. Ball 2008: 228–233; Ball 2019: Nos. 522, 1047; and Chapter 2. For the time frame of the present study, Ball's (1988) observations are important to bear in mind: the Old Persian Harahuvatish for the entire region was Hellenized as Arachosia, and in turn Arabicized as al-Rukhkhaj in early geographies (ninth–tenth centuries). Likely due to the Turkic Ghaznavids' presence in the area, the locality came to be called Tiginabad as of the eleventh century. It was not until the thirteenth century that the name "Qandahar" was applied to the city. Cf. Ball 1996: 400–401; Ball, pers. comm., February 2018; Bosworth 2012b.

84. For the presence of an eighth-century 'Umayyad coin hoard in the Qaitul *vihara*, see Helms (1982: 14), who further noted the possible "spiritual coexistence" of the local Zun/Zhun cult plausibly dedicated to a solar deity, Buddhism and Islam. See also Helms 1983; Ball 1996: 399; Errington 2017: 43; and Chapter 2 notes. The extensive documentation and analysis of the Qaitul Buddhist complex unfortunately still awaits publication, even though the British Institute for Afghan Studies conducted surveys and excavations throughout the *entire* area – encompassing both the Old Qandahar citadel and the *stupa* overlooking it – in their 1974–1978 seasons (Ball, pers. comm., February 2018).

85. Ball (1988: 135–137) proposed that, given the appearance of the locale's name as "Qandahar" only in sources dating from the thirteenth century and later, the Shansabanis could have initiated the name change: the association of "Tiginabad" with the recognizably Turkic presence of their enemies the Ghaznavids surely spurred the Shansabanis to appropriate the site by means of naming it with a term rooted in discernibly local Persianate traditions, both as a sign of victory and of their own induction into a prominence outside their ancestral Ghur. But the fact that Juzjani referred to the location *only* as Tiginabad, making no mention whatsoever of Qandahar, would indicate that the name change did *not* originate with the Shansabanis, but probably later than the sparse traces of their presence there (see *infra* in main text).

86. Cf. Juzjani vol. I, 1963: 243 (trans. vol. I, 1881: 111). Nevertheless, the debate surrounding whether Qandahar and Tiginabad are one and the same needs "considerable ... work ... before [it] can be put to bed": Ball (pers. comm.,

April 2020) has put forth the additional possibility of Kushk-i Nakhud, a.k.a. Sabz Qala' (66 km west of Qandahar) as Tiginabad, as the site might have been larger than Qandahar itself, and ceramic finds there have been dated from the first through fifteenth centuries CE.

87. Ball 1988: 138 (original emphasis), and Ball 2008: 230; see also Helms 1982: 15; Helms 1997: 3–4. The city reclaimed real imperial significance only when the Timurid ruler Husain Bayqara (r. AH 874–912/1470–1506 CE) established a mint there in the late fifteenth century. Cf. Inaba 2010.

88. The depredations of Nadir Shah Afshar (1688–1747) and his forces during his India campaign – where the aim was plunder of the Mughal treasury and libraries – resulted in considerable destruction in the vicinity of Old Qandahar in the mid-1730s. This in turn has rendered a full *re*construction of earlier phases of the city quite difficult. Cf. Whitehouse 1976: 473; Ball 1996: 402. The Afsharid soldier-adventurer's initial choice of the southern route *via* Qandahar in 1736 was clearly strategic, rather than commercial or practical, however: after their brief sojourn in the Qandahar region, the Afsharid forces ultimately turned northeast toward Kabul and Jalalabad. They entered India *via* the Khyber Pass in 1738–1739, visiting intimidation and destruction upon all in their path, whenever necessary. See Dupree 2012: 330–331.

89. Ball (1988: 135) suggested that the Shansabani presence in Tiginabad/Old Qandahar commenced in AH 521/1127 CE, which would fall within the reign of 'Izz al-Din Husain (r. 1100–1146 CE). The nature of the archaeological evidence (see *infra* in main text) nonetheless points to the later date of *c.* AH 552/1158 CE, when the Shansabanis were a more important politico-military and economic presence in the region. Moreover, the confusion between 'Izz al-Din and 'Ala' al-Din *Jahan-suz* in Khwafi's fourteenth-century *Majmu'al-i Fasihi* – the source noting AH 521/1127 CE for the Ghaznavid–Shansabani confrontation – was actually cited by Raverty in his copious footnotes to Juzjani's text (cf. trans. vol. I, 1881: 110, n. 5). Again, the later date as noted by Juzjani himself seems the more probable. The at best indirect references to these events in two contemporaneous sources – *viz.* Juzjani and Fakhr-i Mudabbir – have added to the tentativeness of dating. Cf. also Bosworth [1977] 1992: 121–122.

90. See also Chapters 1 and 5. Sultan Ghiyath al-Din granted the fort of Istiya to his as yet untitled but ambitious younger brother Shihab al-Din, likely in the mid-1160s (cf. Chapters 4–5). During the previous generation of Shansabanis, the region had been the appanage of Saif al-Din (d. AH 544/1149 CE) who, among 'Izz al-Din's seven sons was the third born, but the first by his *lawful* wife and thus took precedent over his two older half-brothers. The locality of Istiya can be tentatively placed within the Shansabanis' *garm-sir*. Cf. Juzjani vol. I, 1963: 335–336 (trans. vol. I, 1881: 339–340).

91. See Whitehouse 1976: 484; Whitehouse 1996: 4–5; Ball 1996: 400; Ball pers. comm., February 2018.

92. Two excavation reports by Whitehouse (1976 and 1996) reflect different stages of the archaeological work. For example, the earlier report (1976) was published prior to the rediscovery of the second burial in Mound A.

93. Cf. Whitehouse 1976: 483; Whitehouse 1996: 4; Crowe 1996: 314; Ball, Bordeaux et al. 2019: 433–434. Whitehouse in particular proposed parallels

with Lashkari Bazar Group IX (see Gardin 1963: 135). Additionally, Taddei (1979: 910ff.) suggested that the similarity between the octagonal enclosure-platform of Mound A and the tomb known as Sultan Ghari in Delhi, dated to the 1230s CE, lend formal and circumstantial evidence for Shansabani dating and patronage of Tiginabad/Old Qandahar's Mound A (and possibly Mound B). The parallel with the later Sultan Ghari is also mentioned by Edwards (2015: 102).

94. Hephthalite burials in Afghanistan certainly provide comparable parallels to the excavated Tiginabad/Old Qandahar mounds, and with good reason, given the Rutbil command of the area well into the ninth century. It is also noteworthy that mound burials, or *kurghan*s, were quite different from urban burial practices and have been "associated with the nomadic nations of Central Asia"; some scholars have used the dissemination of *kurghan*s to trace movements of nomadic groups. Cf. Ball 1996: 400–401. But, cf. Hüttel and Erdenebat (2010: 4–5) on the study of Eurasian nomadic horsemen since the seventeenth century as essentially a one-sided "archaeology of graves … a cultural history … limited to the history of burial rituals …" desperately needing to be balanced with the archaeology of nomadic settlements for a "more authentic picture of the cultural scope and diversity of nomadic empires of the steppe …" See Chapter 5; and Volume II for the more orthodox Islamic burial and tomb of the later patriarch Sultan Ghiyath al-Din Muhammad (d. AH 599/1203 CE) in Herat.

95. In the context of the events unfolding in the 1160s–1170s, Juzjani vol. I, 1963: 396 (trans. vol. I, 1881: 448–449) had described Tiginabad as the largest city in *garm-sir*, as well as the pivot of the Ghaznavids' downfall when the Shansabanis captured it. Quite possibly, the Oghüz bands fleeing Saljuq reprisals in Khurasan only accelerated the gradual depopulation of the region (see *supra* in main text). Cf. also Bosworth [1977] 1992: 124–125. Thus, even Tiginabad might have appeared to be a large city in a region largely emptied of its inhabitants. Tiginabad could also be seen as the origin of the Yaminis' irreversible defeat, since it was from there that the Shansabanis launched successful operations against Ghazna itself.

96. Cf. Thomas 2018: 135–136; see also *supra* in main text and notes.

97. Cf. de Planhol [2000] 2012.

98. The family hierarchy was not without contestation, as is evident in the Bamiyan Shansabanis' adoption of royal titles on their coinage several decades prior to their official conferral – see Chapter 1.

99. Hüttel and Erdenebat 2010: 5.

CHAPTER 4

One and Several: Gharjistan, Chisht, and Imperial Firuzkuh

The architectural corpus analyzed here spans approximately the late 1160s–1170s, encompassing the Firuzkuh Shansabanis' *sard-sir* "capital" and other sites radiating westward toward Herat, and northwest to Gharjistan. The buildings and complexes consist of the following examples, discussed in the proposed chronological order, which is, admittedly, at some variance with previous scholarship: The *madrasa* known as Shah-i Mashhad near Jawand in Gharjistan (Figure 4.1), which was founded in AH 561/1164–1165 CE and likely completed a decade later, probably also included a tomb (Figure 4.5).[1] Chisht's two domed structures, one with a *mihrab* (Figures 4.12 and 4.17), evidently belonged to a larger complex that was possibly a *madrasa*, located east of Herat and dated by inscription to AH 562/1167 CE (construction and renovation probably extending before and after this date). Finally, the famous *minar* of Jam-Firuzkuh (Figure 4.18), also discussed in Chapter 3, has an inscription that was re-read as dating to AH 569/1174 CE, superseding the previous reading of AH 590/1193–1194 CE (cf. below). All of these buildings and sites are important surviving examples of monumental architectural initiatives within the purview of the Firuzkuh Shansabanis.

Although the Bamiyan Shansabanis – discussed in Chapter 3 – doubtless undertook architectural projects in their territories, the absence of firmly datable evidence makes further examination of their patronage quite difficult, with the possible exception of forays into the Balkh oasis.[2] It should also be noted that, by this period, the Firuzkuh and Ghazna Shansabanis' building activities included, respectively, monumental architecture and extensive interventions in pre-existing complexes, the latter phenomenon also calling for a concentrated analysis in its own right in Chapter 5. As will be subsequently discussed in detail, the documentable architectural footprints specifically of the Ghazna Shansabanis in Afghanistan – and by extension those of the architectural culture of the eastern Persianate world – were particularly impactful throughout their campaigns farther east, first to the Indus's alluvia and ultimately to India (see also Volume II).

A significant difference between the preceding chapter's earlier architectural group and the one analyzed here is the extensive architectural epigraphy on the latter, at times warranting discussion at some length (cf.

later in this chapter and Appendix). As we shall see below, the epigraphic programs of these later foundations frequently reveal theological debates, shifts in legal thought, and far-reaching changes in the nexus of religion and politics, all occurring within the expanding realms of the increasingly divergent Shansabani lineages of Firuzkuh and Ghazna – one oriented westward toward Khurasan, the other eastward toward India (see Chapters 5 and 6). Altogether, prior studies of the Gharjistan and Chisht *madrasas*, the previous and recent analyses of the *minar* of Jam-Firuzkuh, as well as excavations at the site, provide invaluable points of departure for better understanding the impetuses and processes behind the making of these buildings and complexes, especially as they became sacral institutions.[3]

Architectural patronage certainly evidenced the Shansabanis' active presence in an area, perhaps indicated earliest at Da Qadi/Qala'-yi Zarmurgh and the site's *minar*, likely dating to the first two or three decades of the twelfth century (see Chapter 2). But as of the 1170s onward, Shansabani patronage unequivocally demonstrated the mobilization of a different caliber of skilled labor: with Shansabani foundations reflecting the cosmopolitan building trends prevalent in elite circles across the Persianate world, it is evident that their resources were rapidly burgeoning beyond those of a few decades before. Finally, it would appear that, while the Firuzkuh Shansabanis retained a lifestyle of seasonal transhumance, the Bamiyan and Ghazna branches constituting the rest of the confederacy might have been largely shifting toward a sedentism marked by palace dwelling, at least for part of the year (see Chapters 2, 3, and 5).

Shansabani Imperial Architectures

Existing studies on Shansabani-patronized buildings and complexes in Afghanistan have approached them collectively, characterizing them overall as "a remarkable range of civil, religious and commemorative architecture … [that was] part of a coordinated campaign to champion Islam".[4] But we saw in Chapter 3 that, in fact, inescapable differences emerged among the indices of Shansabani presences at early Firuzkuh, Bamiyan, and Tiginabad/Old Qandahar, at least according to the surviving evidence. The early Shansabanis at Firuzkuh appear to have eschewed patronage of palatial architecture, despite its being *de rigueur* for Perso-Islamic kings according to their chroniclers and panegyrists. Instead, they concentrated on more "civic" foundations such as places of prayer, and probably defensive structures. Tiginabad/Old Qandahar was a site likely occupied by the Firuzkuh Shansabanis, a territory morphing into an expansionist political entity; but excavations and surveys there unearthed fewer architectural traces of Shansabani presence, the more nomadic traces not being easily recoverable. On the other hand, the Bamiyan Shansabanis' architectural patronage seemed to be focused largely on repurposing pre-existing structures and complexes. This was evidently the case at the numerous fortifications and citadels to the west of Bamiyan, including Shahr-i Zuhak. Furthermore, at Shahr-i Ghulghula Ghaznavid-period structures were apparently put to Shansabani use. Although new construction in the Bamiyan region occurred less frequently, the newly built palatial complex at Sarkhushak nonetheless indicated a court life and ceremonial gradually diverging from that of their Firuzkuh cousins.

The differences between the earlier commissions discussed in Chapter 3, and the monumental foundations at later Firuzkuh and its ambit, as well as the interventions at Ghazna and Bust-Lashkari Bazar (Chapter 5), are even more significant. Thus, the juxtaposition of *all* of these architectural corpora – such as they are known from their surviving traces – makes it clear that any singular, overarching characterization such as "Shansabani/Ghurid architecture" would be untenable.

Here, it is important to note that what might appear to be a largely silent, background process must in fact be foregrounded in the study of an empire emerging from transhumance and/or nomadism and consisting of various lineages: given the particularly complex and often piecemeal process of Islamization among nomadic and many other non-elite groups (cf. Chapter 2), it is necessary to re-examine the scholarly assumption that, in general, patrons determined the ultimate outcomes of their projects. Actually, how much interest did the historically and even persistently transhumant Shansabani elites of Firuzkuh and Ghazna – though the latter increasingly engaged with already existing palace architecture (see Chapter 5) – have in determining the architectural forms and epigraphic programs of the buildings they commissioned? What did it fundamentally *mean* for nomadic, seasonally transhumant, or gradually sedentizing elites to patronize monumental architecture? Addressing these questions helps to shed light on the nature, inner workings, accumulation, and exercise of power by the Firuzkuh Shansabanis. In the context of historically transhumant/nomadic elites crafting a loosely intertwined imperium – and one spanning multiple cultural geographies – we must revisit the role and input of the patron in the design of buildings and their inscriptions, as well as the reception of the structures and their epigraphic programs by the many groups using and maintaining them.

By means of close examination, the Firuzkuh Shansabanis' large-scale architectural projects elucidate the encounter between *more* nomadic and sedentizing elites and the Perso-Islamic cultural complex. The latter encompassed – but was not limited to – Persianate literary and other cultural productions as well as what might be termed for convenience the "Great Tradition" of Islamic orthodoxies (cf. Chapter 1). The internal divisions of these orthodoxies and the resulting, periodically violent contests for intellectual, juridical, and politico-economic sway, were especially legible in the epigraphic programs on monumental architecture: specific Qur'anic inscriptions and Hadiths came to be appropriated by some *madhhab*s to express their distinctive theologies.[5] As a result, some architectural foundations also proclaimed their sectarian affiliations through their epigraphic programs, as was the case for the Jam-Firuzkuh *minar*.[6] The ensuing examination traces the dialogue between the architecture of the Firuzkuh Shansabanis and the *specific* cultural geography they inhabited, which was one among several cultural–geographical zones in the region now bounded by the nation-state of Afghanistan (cf. Chapter 1). Ultimately, an apprehension of the role of architectural patronage in constructing an empire – literally and figuratively – is important not only for elites emerging from transhumance/nomadism, but for *all* historical state-builders.

The ensuing chapter encompasses Shansabani architectural patronage up to the definitive conquest of Ghazna in AH 568–569/1173–1174 CE, to which date the famous *minar* of Jam-Firuzkuh has been convincingly reassigned (see below). The aggregation of the corresponding architectural corpora is justifiable not only due to this significant historical event, but also by the locations and characteristics of the surviving buildings: the Chisht and Gharjistan complexes and the Jam-Firuzkuh *minar* were new, monumental foundations located within the broader architectural culture of Khurasan – at the eastern edges of the Persianate world – with substantial and extremely meaningful epigraphic programs evincing their localities' palpable participation in the theological and political developments throughout the eastern Islamic lands. Meanwhile, the Shansabani vestiges at Ghazna and Bust-Lashkari Bazar, in the Zabul–Zamindawar corridor (map, p. xvi), were altogether of a different order, being primarily interventions in the architectural fabric of Ghaznavid-period palace complexes, rather than new constructions per se (see Chapter 5). The distinguishable and localized historical geographies of these contiguous areas, and their overall significance for the Shansabanis as a confederacy, are best understood by means of clustering and juxtaposing these architectural groups.

Gharjistan, Chisht, and Imperial Firuzkuh

As is to be expected after our previous searches for even brief, contemporary textual descriptions of Shansabani-patronized architecture (cf. Chapters 2 and 3), little information is forthcoming in written sources. The lengthy section XVII of Juzjani's *Tabaqat*, with many chapters on the reigns and activities of the Shansabani *malik*s and sultans of Ghur and

presumably one of the principal *foci* of this particular work more broadly
(see Chapter 1), nevertheless mentioned very few specifics regarding the
locales where the Firuzkuh Shansabanis resided or brought under their
sway. To wit, the continuing search for the winter "capital" of Zamindawar
was discussed in Chapter 2, while the descriptive vagaries pertaining to
Firuzkuh itself, and the resulting debates surrounding its identification as
the Shansabani summer "capital," have been addressed in Chapter 3 and
elsewhere.

Juzjani also made no mention of Chisht, about 150 km east of Herat,
where two domed structures are what remain of probably another important complex, which originally had an extensive program of cursive and
Kufic inscriptions, three of which referred to Shansabani rule (Figures
4.12–4.15, 4.17).[7] Remnants of the cursive inscription on the interior of the
better preserved southern structure (Figure 4.12 [left structure], 4.13, and
4.14), ringing the base of its dome, named Shams al-Dunya wa al-Din,
presumably a reference to Sultan Ghiyath al-Din, "in [whose] days the
renovation (*tajdid*) of this building was ordered" (Figure 4.14); the Kufic
inscription ending on the east interior wall (Figure 4.15) lists the date of
10 Jumada al-Awwal 562 AH, or 7 March 1167 CE, which, it should be
noted, would render anachronistic the use of the sultan's non-regnal *laqab*
(discussed below).[8]

One partial exception to *Tabaqat*'s overall laxity regarding locations
and their descriptions (cf. Chapter 2) was the region of Gharjistan, northwest of historical Ghur, which entered Juzjani's narrative multiple times:
according to the author, shortly after Qutb al-Din's departure for Ghazna,
his brother Baha' al-Din (d. 1149) struck an alliance with the Shars of
Gharjistan during the early days of Shansabani ascendancy at Firuzkuh,
allowing the reinforcement of Ghur's defenses *via* the construction of new
fortifications there and elsewhere. After Baha' al-Din's death, 'Ala' al-Din
Husain *Jahan-suz* called up forces from Gharjistan in AH 545/1150 CE as he
prepared for his momentous confrontation with Bahram Shah of Ghazna
on the plains of Zamindawar (cf. Chapter 1). 'Ala' al-Din Husain further
cemented the Firuzkuh–Gharjistan alliance by marrying Hurr Malika, the
daughter of Shar Ibrahim ibn Ardashir.[9] It would appear that Shansabani
presence in Gharjistan – and quite possibly the alliance between the two
ruling houses – continued through the 1160s–1170s. At this time, there was
a *madrasa* at Afshin – an unmapped locality, which Juzjani incidentally
noted as the capital of the Gharjistan Shars.[10] The *madrasa*'s importance
lay in its presiding head being the prominent Karrami Imam Sadr al-Din
Ali Haisam of Nishapur.[11]

Also dating to this period is the foundation inscription of Shah-i
Mashhad, which unequivocally indicates that a female patron – presumably
Taj al-Harir Jauhar Malik, wife of Sultan Ghiyath al-Din – commissioned
the magnificent complex (Figures 4.1 and 4.7).[12] While Shah-i Mashhad's

function as a *madrasa* has long been accepted, recent re-examination of its remains and the elaborate inscriptional program led A. W. Najimi[13] to propose that the complex's southeast corner contained the tomb of Saif al-Din (r. 1161–1163) (Figure 4.5), 'Ala' al-Din *Jahan-suz*'s son. Saif al-Din was betrayed and treacherously assassinated in AH 558/1163 CE by his *sipahsalar* 'Abbas ibn Shish, who belonged to the long-time rival Shishani clan,[14] while the two were engaged in a military campaign preventing the Oghüz from traversing Gharjistan and threatening Ghur. Notably, Shah-i Mashhad's patron Jauhar Malik was not only the wife of Sultan Ghiyath al-Din, she was also the sister of Saif al-Din, so that brother and sister were Ghiyath al-Din's paternal cousins.[15]

Given the altered routes of communication throughout central Afghanistan in the modern day, both the Chisht and Gharjistan complexes – not to mention the seemingly enigmatic but pivotal site of Jam-Firuzkuh (cf. also Chapter 3) – have all received much less scholarly attention than they deserve. Moreover, the majority of recent and ongoing studies – including this one – have had to rely largely on archaeological and photographic documentation conducted decades earlier. Nevertheless, re-examination of the structures' architectural fabric, decorative iconography, and inscriptional programs provides invaluable insight into the coalescence of the Firuzkuh branch of the Shansabani confederacy, and the alacrity of this newly coalescing elite – despite their origins in the nomad–urban continuum – in joining the fray of architectural patronage to achieve political ends.

Until recently, both the Chisht and Gharjistan complexes appeared to have existed in splendid isolation, as monumental and heavily inscribed behemoths suddenly rising above expansive swaths of cultivated fields or mountainous landscapes, which were crossed here and there by through-ways plied principally by nomads (Figure 4.4).[16] Such apparent isolation would undermine the substantial investment of labor and resources required in building what were originally large and rambling complexes; they appear to have been intended for habitation, just as their painstakingly planned and executed inscriptions were intended for reading, at least by the learned among their residents and passers-by.

In the early 2000s, the mapping and documentation of structural remains from Herat toward Chisht, extending eastward and flanking the Hari Rud, turned up residual traces of a very different historical landscape. To be sure, many remnants of fortified towers continue to be difficult to date, presenting problems not dissimilar to those in dating the structural remains in southern Ghur and west of Bamiyan (cf. Chapters 2 and 3). However, the formal characteristics and modes of construction of several other ruins along the Herat–Chisht routes indicate that these were either built – or perhaps already in use – during the period of Ghaznavid, Saljuq (late tenth–mid-twelfth centuries) and later political presences in

Figure 4.1 Remains of Shah-i Mashhad madrasa, c. 1165–1175 CE, Gharjistan, Badghis Province, Afghanistan. © Photograph Bernt Glatzer c. 1970.

the area.[17] These newly mapped architectural remains essentially outline a network of large and small structures marking passages along the Hari Rud, seemingly punctuated by nodes of culmination, quite possibly like the originally sizeable complex at Chisht (discussed further below). While similar exploration, mapping, and documentation are still to be conducted for Shah-i Mashhad and its vicinity of the lower Murghab River (Figures 4.2 and 4.3), re-conceptualizing both of these magnificent monuments as integral nodes in networks facilitating travel and communication appears to be historically more accurate; moreover, such a contextualization helps to explain the complexes' lavishness and – above all – their prominent epigraphic programs.

Shah-i Mashhad (Gharjistan)

In his seminal work of 2009, F. B. Flood agreed with and adduced further evidence toward the scholarly consensus that Shansabani adherence to and patronage of the Karramiyya continued unfaltering through AH 595/1199 CE, "when the sultans of Ghur abruptly terminated their association with [them], embracing the orthodox *madhhabs* ... of Islam instead."[18] He cited four additional points in support, including the possibility that the tomb–*madrasa* complex of Shah-i Mashhad – dated to AH 561–570/1165–1175 CE, as noted above – was a Karrami institution (Figure 4.1). Another point was the erection of the *minar* of Jam-Firuzkuh in *c.* AH 569/1174 CE (Figure 4.18), whose epigraphic program of all of Qur'an XIX (Surat Maryam) has been convincingly interpreted as a Karrami proclamation (cf. Appendix, Afghanistan VII: 5).[19] Flood's third evidentiary *datum* was a luxurious, four-volume illuminated Qur'an, dated by colophon to AH 584–585/1189 CE: the extensive commentary (*tafsir*) copied at the end of each Sura was originally composed by the leading Karrami of eleventh-century Nishapur, Abu Bakr 'Atiq ibn Muhammad al-Surabadi (d. *c.* AH 494/1101 CE). According to Flood, the commentary indicated that this Qur'an "was among the manuscripts commissioned by the Ghurids for a Karrami madrasa," perhaps even Shah-i Mashhad. Finally, Juzjani described Ghiyath al-Din's "conversion" to the Shafi'i *madhhab* as being effected through a dream or vision that came upon the sultan sometime in AH 595/1199 CE.[20]

However, there is equally compelling evidence, both material as well as circumstantial, that the Firuzkuh Shansabanis patronized sects beyond the Karramiyya long before AH 595/1199 CE, much earlier than Flood and others have proposed. The Ghaznavids and Saljuqs – the Shansabanis' predecessors and contemporaries (respectively) in the region – had benefited from fomenting competition among the various schools of legal–theological thought while attempting to establish and maintain control over various parts of Khurasan. The juridico-intellectual rivalry was the by-product of cultural patronage, one of the spheres of activity identified as integral to the actuation of Perso-Islamic kingship during the twelfth century (cf. Chapter 1). Stoking inter-*madhhab* competition most often resulted in the amassing of greater and more centralized power precisely in the hands of rulers and their agents.[21] In light of these established precedents of state-craft, it seems only natural that the Shansabanis – an emerging elite with a transregional presence in Gharjistan as early as the 1150s, followed by an even more consequential entrée into Ghazna by the 1170s – would also extend their patronage to other *madhhab*s precisely at the time of creating and consolidating their bases of power. Ghiyath al-Din's *official* shift from Karrami to Shafi'i affiliation in AH 595/1199 CE did not necessarily preclude patronage of other *madhhab*s beforehand, particularly by members of the sultan's family.

While Shafi'i and Hanafi theologians, jurists, and their followers tended to dominate politico-intellectual culture in the urban centers of eastern Iran, their influence did not extend with equal impact into more remote areas.[22] Since the time of Ibn Karram (d. AH 255/869 CE), the Karramiyya were much more adept than their urban colleagues at travers-ing the distance between intellectual–cultural centers and their hinter-lands. According to Bosworth, Ibn Karram had proselytized in "Ghur, Gharchistan, and the countryside of Khurasan, denouncing both Sunnis and Shi'is alike, appealing especially to the peasants of those regions."[23] He eventually entered Nishapur with Gharjistani adherents already in tow.[24] In the early eleventh century, Sultan Mahmud Ghaznavi evidently first urged the Karramiyya (back) toward Ghur as he attempted to rid Nishapur of at least one of the contentious *madhhab*s that had made control of the city a constant balancing act among its prominent intelli-gentsia.[25] The Karramiyya's famed austerity underpinned their successful penetration of a difficult terrain like that of Ghur, relieved only by vil-lages and mountainous strongholds rather than large commercial centers. Although many among the Sunni *madhhab*s considered the Karramiyya to be anthropomorphists – and thus outright heretical – the sect continued to hold some sway in the less trafficked reaches of Khurasan and elsewhere well into the late twelfth century.[26]

Among the agriculturalists, nomadic pastoralists, and other non-urban populations in regions such as Ghur, the Karramiyya simplified Islamic orthodoxy and preached direct and unschooled access to Islam. For example, the Karramiyya were known among Khurasan's more mainstream jurists for considering verbal utterance of *Shahada* as tantamount to full conversion. While the city-centered *madhhab*s vigorously criticized them for these practices, the latter actually garnered the Karramiyya enduring and loyal followers. Notwithstanding the orthodox *madhhab*s' objections to such simplifications,[27] such an easy distillation of Islam was conceivably more efficacious than rigidly complex teachings for the conversion of

relatively isolated groups far from well-traveled routes and in the hinterlands of Khurasani centers.[28]

Given the frugality, if not asceticism, for which the Karramiyya were
known, it seems unlikely that a monumental and lavishly decorated
madrasa complex such as Shah-i Mashhad would conform to their ideo-
logical and practical standards.[29] Karrami proselytism was indeed carried
out through group activity, and was closely associated with residence in
and operation from communal lodgings or *khanaqah*s, which also served
as sites of instruction and other charitable work (e.g., feeding and sheltering the poor). But historical authors often used *khanaqah*, *ribat*, and
madrasa interchangeably: by the twelfth century, these structures were all
multi-functional, communal spaces intended principally for instruction,
at times including a tomb and/or a mosque or other place for prayer.[30]
Moreover, the term *madrasa* did not necessarily imply large-scale construction: the increasing monumentality of *madrasa*s throughout the
mid- to late eleventh century has in fact been seen as a development at
least partially attributable to the Saljuq push to control Khurasan through
patronage of select *madhhab*s.[31] Thus, while textual sources referred to
Karrami institutions as *madrasa*s in cities such as Nishapur, it is improbable that these were the towering edifices associated with the orthodox
*madhhab*s favored both by the ruling elites and the economically prominent mercantile groups.[32] Ultimately, an exquisitely illuminated Qur'an
could command ascetic spiritual fervor *qua* ritual object; its architectural
equivalent, however, would surely be perceived as alien to the austerity
that characterized Karrami preceptors and their principles, an austerity
that continued as one of the few constants over time, distinguishing their
modus vivendi from that of the other *madhhab*s.[33]

But eliminating a Karrami affiliation for Shah-i Mashhad brings us
little closer to definitively ascertaining the *madhhab* – or possibly more
than one[34] – housed at the *madrasa*. The complex was designed and built
on a monumental scale and, even after much deterioration, retains traces
of an exquisite decorative program encompassing admirably executed
monumental inscriptions (discussed further below). These characteristics
emphatically point to the complex's affiliation with the established legal–
theological schools favored in Khurasan, quite possibly the Hanafi and/
or the Shafi'i *madhhab*s – the latter proposed by S. Blair.[35] Nevertheless,
the orientation of Shah-i Mashhad, along with its extensive and unusual
epigraphic program, both lead to more questions than answers, and point
to multiple possibilities for the complex's sectarian affiliation.

Shah-i Mashhad has a nearly north–south orientation (Figures 4.2 and
4.3), so that the whole complex deviates counterclockwise from the cardinal directions of true south and west (180° and 270°, respectively) by only
a few degrees, possibly due to accommodation of the terrain – though
this is unverifiable without on-site study. Since 243.69° would be Shah-i

Figure 4.2 *Shah-i Mashhad* madrasa *and Murghab River.* © *Google Earth 2018.*

Figure 4.3 *Shah-i Mashhad* madrasa *on Google Earth, detail with superimposed plan (from Najimi 2015: 153).* © *David Thomas 2018.*

Mashhad's precise *qibla* – achieved by hypothetically rotating the complex several degrees further counterclockwise – M. Casimir and B. Glatzer declared this "distinct deviation … a problem which … has not been sufficiently examined."[36] Thankfully, during the intervening years since Casimir and Glatzer's initial rediscovery of and publications on the site, scholars such as David King have examined this "problem" extensively, providing invaluable insight into why not only Shah-i Mashhad but many contemporaneous mosques and other religious structures, ranging from the Maghrib through Central Asia, were not always precisely oriented toward Mecca.

It is well known that, by the second millennium CE, the mathematical specialties of trigonometry, astronomy, and stellar calculation were sophisticated fields of study throughout the Islamic world.[37] But, pre-modern *qibla* determination had never been a purely "scientific" matter. Architectural *qibla* orientations in particular frequently resulted from "folk astronomy": this was, in brief, a varying combination of the regional or local prevalence of a given *madhhab*; any local awareness of the Ka'aba's own complex cosmography, as well as its orientations according to pre-Islamic wind theory; and topography and/or pre-existing urban development. The preferred *qibla*s of all the *madhhab*s and associated or independent smaller sects are not known – much less the fascinating, socio-historical reasoning behind them.[38] For present purposes, however, it is fortunate that the preferred *qibla*s of the Hanafis and the Shafi'is, the two most prevalent *madhhab*s in Khurasan, *are* known: while the Shafi'is subscribed to a *qibla* due south (180°), the Hanafis subscribed to a *qibla* due west (270°).[39] Nevertheless, in the absence of an exhaustive catalog of architectural orientations across the Islamic world through the thirteenth century, it is still unclear how closely or consistently these prescribed *qibla* orientations were actually followed,[40] even though they were favored by two of the most prominent Sunni *madhhab*s.

The orientation of Shah-i Mashhad along a near exact north–south axis could accommodate either or both of the prevalent Khurasani *madhhab*s' preferred *qibla*s. But the complex's already deteriorated – and worsening – state of preservation (Figures 4.1 and 4.4) impedes more detailed observations. Based on an extant but previously unread *naskh* inscriptional fragment on the monumental southern entrance, A. W. Najimi proposed that the surviving domed chamber at the quadrangular compound's southeastern corner (Figure 4.5) contained the tomb of a deceased male personage, quite possibly the slain Shansabani sultan Saif al-Din (d. AH 558/1163 CE). Although the surviving fragment does not name Saif al-Din specifically, the association is tenable based on the sultan's death having occurred in the general vicinity of the *madrasa*, shortly before its foundation.[41] Furthermore, we recall that Saif al-Din was the brother of Shah-i Mashhad's patron, Queen Jauhar Malik (see above). The poor state of preservation, however, makes it impossible to determine whether there was a *mihrab* in the chamber. And the outright disappearance of the rest of the large compound precludes knowing if one or more prayer areas were housed elsewhere within it, much less their *qibla* orientations. Nevertheless, it is noteworthy that Shah-i Mashhad's overall north–south orientation accommodates the *qibla*s prescribed by both the orthodox *madhhab*s dominant in Khurasan.

Figure 4.4 *Shah-i Mashhad* madrasa, *south façade.* © *Photograph Bernt Glatzer* c. *1990?*

Figure 4.5 *Shah-i Mashhad* madrasa, *possible tomb of southeast corner.* © *Photograph Bernt Glatzer* c. *1970.*

Ever since the rediscovery of Shah-i Mashhad in 1970, its epigraphy and extensive ornament have commanded as much attention as its structural features. The inscriptions' calligraphic styles range from knotted and interlocking Kufic, to elongated *naskh* and *thuluth* against lush floral backgrounds (see Appendix, Afghanistan IV). Indeed, scholars have come to consider the complex's ornamental–structural wholeness to be an overarching characteristic of Shansabani foundations, so that "[i]n Ghurid buildings, architecture *was* the structure and decoration; and decoration and structure were the architecture." The content, calligraphic styles, and variety in materials and techniques of the *madrasa*'s epigraphic program have long been the subjects of discussion and debate, with there being scholarly consensus only on the difficulty of discerning the program's presumably multiple and complex meanings.[42]

Casimir and Glatzer deciphered the first four verses of Surat al-Fath (Q. XLVIII) in Kufic script on the surviving eastern end of Shah-i Mashhad's monumental south façade, whose imposing central portal

Figure 4.6 *Shah-i Mashhad* madrasa: *south façade, detail of inscription.* © *Photograph Bernt Glatzer* c. *1970. Courtesy of IsMEO, Rome.*

carried the Arabic foundation inscription in an even more ornate, plaited Kufic (Figures 4.1 and 4.6).[43] The original symmetry of the façade makes it plausible that the western flank continued with at least three more of the Sura's following verses (Q. XLVIII: 5–7).[44] Much more recently, Najimi deciphered or reinterpreted five previously unread or differently interpreted inscriptions on Shah-i Mashhad's southern and northern façades, in addition to the cursive inscription referring to a deceased male's tomb (cf. above).[45] The other five include the *takbir* of *tashriq*[46] in *thuluth* script on the inner eastern face of the main southern portal (Figure 4.7), below an Arabic Kufic inscription naming, presumably, the master builder, or the one who "completed this building, the servant Ahmad ibn Mahmud" (Figure 4.8). On the extant pier of the northern portal of the complex, Najimi deciphered verses 22–24 of Surat al-Hashr (Q. LIX) in Kufic script, as well as a

Figure 4.7 *Shah-i Mashhad* madrasa, *southern monumental entrance, interior with inscription.* © *Photograph Bernt Glatzer* c. *1970.*

naskh inscription of a Hadith apparently of Shiʻi association (Figure 4.9).[47] The presence of verses from Surat al-Fath is unusual in the eastern Islamic lands,[48] and Najimi's new readings and reinterpretations make all the more poignant the lingering questions about the *madrasa*'s sectarian affiliation(s), the patron's role in the complex's conception, as well as the intended audience(s) of the inscriptions. The import of juxtaposing all of these inscriptions in an admittedly complicated epigraphic program is discussed below.

But first, it should be noted that many factors rendered difficult both reading and also fully comprehending epigraphic programs, not only at Shah-i Mashhad but also at the other architectural sites attributed to this first phase of elite patronage within the territories of the Firuzkuh Shansabanis (cf. Volume II for late twelfth-century architectural patronage). Even though Shansabani-patronized inscriptional programs were almost exclusively in Arabic,[49] their varying and ornate scripts often hindered rather than facilitated reading. Furthermore, the inscriptions varied greatly in content, ranging from Qur'anic verses, historical and funerary inscriptions, Hadith, and possibly even didactic texts – the last exemplified in Shah-i Mashhad's *takbir* of *tashriq*. All of these challenges were probably as pronounced or perhaps even more so when the buildings' programs were complete. Thus, all considerations of the overall design, composition, and readership of the inscriptions on monuments throughout the Firuzkuh Shansabanis' realms must necessarily proceed from the premise that readers of the inscriptions were extremely few.[50]

Figure 4.8 *Shah-i Mashhad* madrasa, *south façade, detail of inscription.*
© *Photograph Bernt Glatzer* c. *1970.*

In fact, it is not unreasonable to propose that the Shansabani elites themselves were unable to read inscriptions in their entirety, much less determine the *minutiae* of their content or the overall compositions of the epigraphic programs. Two broader historical realities bolster the idea that literary documentation and literacy in general – as understood in the modern sense – were not common throughout Afghanistan during our period of focus. First, the historical trajectory of the Shansabani elites and their emergence from – and likely some maintenance of – pre-imperial transhumance and/or nomadism made for a selective knowledge of the "Great Traditions" of Islamic juridical and theological doctrines, and perhaps even Islamic religious practices.[51] Among the Shansabanis' forebears – spanning an array of lifestyles across the nomad–urban continuum (cf. Introduction and Chapter 2) – literacy was not always a requisite, nor was it necessarily widespread: the past and present of many self-identifying groups, for example, were frequently recorded and preserved in collective memory and transmitted orally across generations, captured in written form only a considerable time afterward, if at all.[52]

We have seen that the vast differences between urban center and hinterland were instrumental in the version of "Islam" that was propagated: while some Karrami legal and theological scholars were known to have been the erudite interlocutors of other *madhhab*s in Khurasan's great emporia,[53] their comrades' proselytism of a thoroughly simplified version of Islam among non-urban inhabitants – embodied in the Karrami tenet that mere

recitation of *Shahada* was tantamount to full Islamic conversion (see above) – likely bypassed even the limited, mnemonic literacy of other pre-modern Islamic populations.[54] Such a loophole would have been all the more necessary among people of rural, nomadic, and/or transhumant lifestyles, largely living beyond the urban settlements of what is now Afghanistan. Thus, royal Shansabani involvement in the sophisticated epigraphic and decorative programs of their monumental commissions was conceivably secondary to that of the literate, even well-read advisors and eventual users of the buildings. Execution of the designs by generationally trained artisans, specialized in various aspects of building and decoration, surely contributed a formative element as well.[55]

Figure 4.9 *Shah-i Mashhad* madrasa: *north entrance, detail of inscription.* © *Photograph Bernt Glatzer* c. *1970.*

This is not to say that, as patrons of "civic" architecture, the Shansabani sultans and their families and associates made absolutely no mark on their foundations or the latter's complex epigraphic programs. But it must be borne in mind that at least the Shansabani family members – if not also their nobles and other associates – certainly differed from their most proximate contemporaries. The Ghaznavids, for example, whose scions had been thoroughly educated in Sunni Islam and steeped in Persianate culture, were surely discerning patrons probably even intervening in architectural and epigraphic details.[56] The Shansabanis, though also preoccupied with consolidating and expanding an imperial presence (like the Ghaznavids), nonetheless had come to an *overt* embrace of Islamic socio-religious mores and Persianate ceremonial

forms in relatively recent times; and it was argued in Chapter 2, that they
did so in large part for the purposes of projecting an imperial image. In
light of their historical circumstances, the Shansabani elites were surely
little interested in the subtleties of epigraphic messaging. Beyond aspiring
to monumental precedents – as proposed below – the details of Shah-i
Mashhad's complicated inscriptional program were surely left to the more
learned, future inhabitants and frequenters of their monumental foundations, *viz.* theologians, jurists, their students, visiting intelligentsia, and
literate passers-by.

In the specific case of Shah-i Mashhad, the great variety in content
of the *madrasa*'s surviving inscriptions points to expert and intentional
epigraphic choices, probably made by its well-read dwellers rather than
its royal patron(s). Although no definitive conclusions are forthcoming
due to the disappearance of the majority of the complex and its inscriptional program, what remains seems to encompass contradictory trends:
while a few of the inscriptions follow epigraphic developments in the
eastern Islamic lands and beyond, others notably diverge from them. The
northern entrance's verses from Surat al-Hashr (Q. LIX) (Figure 4.7),
for example, were not uncommon, particularly in funerary contexts in
the Levant, Egypt and the Maghreb from the first two centuries of the
Hijira, and in greater Iran as of the eleventh century.[57] The presence of
these verses further supports the probability of a tomb within the *madrasa*,
perhaps even that of the Shansabani sultan Saif al-Din (discussed above).

By contrast, the presence of a possibly Shiʻi Hadith on the northern
entrance (Figure 4.9), and the *takbir* of *tashriq* on the southern entrance
(Figure 4.7), are both unusual. Quotations from Hadith were rare in the
eastern Islamic lands, there being but one documented instance from the
early eleventh century,[58] and no known quotations of the *takbir* at all. Shiʻi
groups had not often suffered persecution since Ghaznavid ascendancy in
greater Khurasan, particularly if their activities did not interfere with the
political elites.[59] But, even though a Hadith from the Shiʻi canon on the
madrasa would not necessarily be remarkable, it seems improbable that
Shiʻi instruction would take place there given the Shansabanis' Sunni
affiliation. It should also be noted that, in general purport, the quoted
Hadith is not dissimilar to Hadith 425 in *Sahih* of al-Bukhari (AH 194/810
CE–AH 256/870 CE), thus generally accepted by the Sunni *madhhab*s.[60] The
takbir on the southern entrance's interior is currently inexplicable, except
possibly as a didactic inscription. Ultimately, the *madrasa*'s surviving
epigraphic program not only intimates a sectarian ecumenicalism, it may
also point to localized developments that will become clearer after analysis
by specialists in Islamic theology and/or further archaeological work.

While much of Shah-i Mashhad's inscriptional program doubtless
emerged from the input of the ʻulamaʼ and other learned individuals who
would be its future residents, one prominent part of the epigraphy could

Figure 4.10 *Ghazni, minaret of Mas'ud III (1099–1115), with citadel in background. © Photograph Josephine Powell c. 1960. Harvard Fine Arts Library, Special Collections.*

have been the expression of the royal patrons' preference: the initial verses of Surat al-Fath (Q. XLVIII) as the principal inscriptions on the *madrasa*'s main façade along the complex's southern perimeter (Figure 4.1). Verses from this Sura were extremely rare in monumental epigraphy anywhere in the Islamic world, with their first documented occurrence in the eastern Islamic lands on the *minar* of Mas'ud III (r. AH 492–509/1099–1115 CE) at Ghazna (Figures 4.10 and 4.11).[61] This memorable and towering architectural work had been among the structures that escaped Sultan 'Ala' al-Din Husain's sacking of the city after his defeat of Bahram Shah in AH 544–45/1150 CE – the occasion that earned him the sobriquet *Jahan-suz* (cf. esp. Chapter 1) – only about fifteen years before the foundation of Shah-i Mashhad.[62]

Pinder-Wilson convincingly proposed that the Ghazna *minar*'s inscriptional program had been inspired by the resumption of successful campaigns to northern India during the reign of Mas'ud III in the early twelfth century, after a lapse of about a half-century during which the Ghaznavid

Figure 4.11 *Ghazni, minarets of Ghazni: minaret of Mas'ud III (1099–1115), middle section, detail. © Photograph Josephine Powell c. 1960. Harvard Fine Arts Library, Special Collections.*

house had seen turbulent internal strife.[63] Mas'ud III's re-initiation of the profitable and propagandistically important Indian raids reclaimed some of the Ghaznavids' lost imperial glory, and also provided the sultan with the occasion to erect a towering structure commemorating what were essentially *his* victories.[64] The inscription of Surat al-Fath – unprecedented in its entirety of twenty-nine verses[65] – was in fluid cursive against a floral background, contained within a band meandering around quadrangular panels occupying the *minar*'s remaining surface areas (Figure 4.11). But equally notable was the royal appropriation of a visual device traditionally reserved for religious epigraphic content. Interlocking (*ma'aqali*) Kufic, ingeniously forming a grid of words, was not uncommon on funerary *stelae* and architectural surfaces (eleventh–twelfth centuries); but the content of these inscriptions had virtually always been religious in nature, such as the names of the first four *khalifa*s, or doxologies. However, the horizontal band of square panels near the base of the *minar* – its lower positioning making it more legible – was filled with the sultan's *kunya* and some of his regnal titles.[66] Thus, the monumental *minar* was a victory tower in form as well as decoration.

Although the full circumstances of Shah-i Mashhad's construction are not known, it is safe to say that this complex was much more than – or at least quite different from – a victory tower. Surat al-Fath was likely *not* inscribed in its entirety here nor were the quoted verses in cursive, as at Ghazna, where they formed a contrast to the less legible, ornate, or interlocking Kufic of the regnal titles. At Shah-i Mashhad, however, the selected Qur'anic verses from Surat al-Fath and Surat al-Hashr survive in the generally less legible Kufic.[67] In fact, the verses from Surat al-Fath on the south façade actually appear subordinate to the much more ornate and larger, plaited Kufic of the foundation inscription of the central arch, as if building up to the façade's epigraphic apex (Figures 4.1 and 4.6).

Given the Firuzkuh Shansabanis' imperial aspirations – and, arguably, their furthering of these aspirations by patronizing Khurasan's more prominent Sunni *madhhab*s – the inclusion at Shah-i Mashhad of verses from Surat al-Fath appears to be an indexical citation of their reputed predecessors the Ghaznavids. Rather than an *exclusive* "desire to convert the heathen" or to commemorate the recent military victory against the Oghüz,[68] it was conceivably the emulation of an iconic monument and its dynastic context that also led the Shansabani queen Jauhar Malik, Shah-i Mashhad's patron, and/or her spouse Sultan Ghiyath al-Din to choose verses from Surat al-Fath as part of the *madrasa*'s epigraphic program. Ultimately, Shah-i Mashhad accomplished multiple aims for the Firuzkuh Shansabanis: the patronage provided them with an architectural "debut" as patrons of *madhhab*s that were prominent across Khurasan. At the same time, such an epigraphic proclamation also invoked the imperial echelon of the Ghaznavids, who were once illustrious but now were on the wane, superseded by the Shansabanis.

Chisht

Given the proximity of the two surviving domed structures at Chisht (Figures 4.12), it is probable that they originally formed part of a larger complex.[69] This foundation adduces even more evidence in favor of the activity of *madhhab*s other than the Karramiyya in Shansabani-ruled lands prior to the end of the twelfth century.

On the interior surface of the western structure, the cursive inscriptional frieze at the base of the dome (Figure 4.12 [left structure]; Figures 4.13 and 4.14) records in Arabic the renovation (*tajdid*) of the building "in the days of Shams al-Dunya wa al-Din" (see also above). There is little doubt that this personage was the Shansabani sultan Ghiyath al-Din, since the surviving remainder of the inscription continues with his *kunya* Abu al-Fath, his *ism* Muhammad, and *nasab* of ibn Sam.[70] The accompanying

Figure 4.12 *Chisht, mausoleums (or* madrasa/*mosque complex), ruins: Mausoleum A, exterior, southern façade. © Photograph Josephine Powell* c. *1960. Harvard Fine Arts Library, Special Collections.*

Kufic inscription (Figure 4.15) furnishes the date of AH 562/1167 CE in Persian.[71] Chisht's less preserved, northeastern structure (Figure 4.12 [right structure]) also has an Arabic inscription with Ghiyath al-Din's correct titles, but in foliated Kufic and, notably, as they eventually appeared at the imposing *jami* of Herat at the end of the twelfth century.[72]

By considering the southwestern domed structure's *naskh* and Kufic inscriptions together, the seemingly egregious anachronism of the sultan's pre-regnal *laqab* of Shams al-Dunya wa al-Din – applicable only prior to AH 558/1163 CE – in the cursive text may present us with a chronological clue, not only for the structure but also the overall complex. It is worth considering that the southwestern structure was completed before the northeastern one, and *prior* to AH 558/1163 CE, or at least before wide circulation of the sultan's regnal *laqab* of Ghiyath al-Din.[73] The contents of the southwestern structure's *naskh* inscription, then, would also have been composed at this earlier date, thus still using the sultan's earlier name. The separate Kufic inscription in the same structure, however, lists the date of AH 10 Jumada I 562/4 March 1167 CE, but only after a long series of Qur'anic verses rather than the description of an event. Given that the cursive and Kufic inscriptions are separate, it is possible that the latter does not refer to the above-mentioned renovation (*tajdid*), but rather to some other, as yet not fully known, intervention in the structure or complex as a whole.

Figure 4.13 *Chisht, mausoleums (or* madrasa/mosque complex*), ruins: Mausoleum A, interior, corner pillars and two adjoining walls with inset arches, with bands of inscriptions following outline of upper arches and running horizontally across midpoint of arches. © Photograph Josephine Powell c. 1960. Harvard Fine Arts Library, Special Collections.*

Like Shah-i Mashhad, the Chisht structures are also oriented along a north–south axis with a slight deviation, but here clockwise, with the buildings' western walls again facing just perceptibly off true west (Figure 4.16).[74] While the nature of the original complex is difficult to discern with certainty, parts of the epigraphic program and other features of both domed structures provide clues as to what was likely a site with multiple functions. Tellingly, the more deteriorated northeastern building (Figure 4.12 [right structure], Figure 4.16) still preserves a *mihrab* on its western wall (Figure 4.17); in its original state the *mihrab* was probably plastered and covered with lavish molded stucco decoration, remnants of which are still *in situ* above the arch. The large pointed-arch motifs diagonally above and on either side of the *mihrab* not only echo the latter's form, but the curves of the arches contain bands framing the above-discussed foliated Kufic inscription with Ghiyath al-Din's titles. Smaller medallions

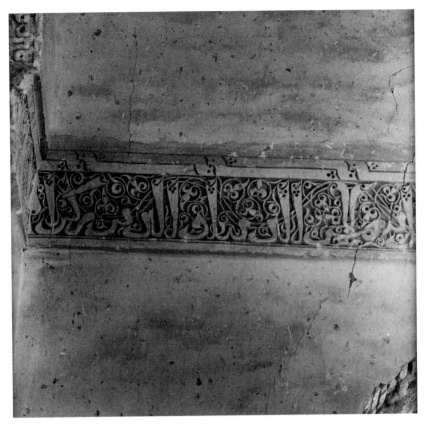

Figure 4.14 *Chisht, mausoleums (or madrasa/mosque complex), ruins: Mausoleum A, interior, inscription, detail. Powell: "Detail of [inscription] which has been read to me, 'In the days of the kingdom of Al Mozafar Almansour ...'"**
*Cf. Appendix II, Afghanistan III:4, below, for an updated reading of this inscription.

within the large corner arches contain the names of the first four *khalifas*, the Prophets, *Shahada*, and doxologies. The smaller, paired-arch motifs in between contain doxologies.[75]

Although only a small portion of the Chisht complex's epigraphic program survives – not dissimilar to Shah-i Mashhad – it is noteworthy that the available inscriptions as well as the complex's formal characteristics point toward a funerary function for the site, probably serving other purposes as well. The domed chamber layout of the northeastern structure, discussed above, strongly suggests that it was a tomb with a *mihrab* – a not uncommon architectural typology in the eastern Islamic lands by the later twelfth century.[76] Additionally, the western domed structure, while apparently not having a *mihrab*, provides ample epigraphic indications of a funerary association through its interior inscriptions. The cursive inscription beginning in the southeastern corner with the anachronistic mention of Shams al-Dunya wa al-Din (Figures 4.13 and 4.14), continues with parts of verses 23–24 of Surat al-Hashr (Q. LIX), which was also part of the epigraphy on Shah-i Mashhad's northern entrance, and whose frequent presence on epitaphs, and funerary *stelae* and architecture has already been noted (cf. notes above).

The western structure's Kufic inscription (Figure 4.15) contains the common verses 255–257 from Surat al-Baqara (Q. II), among which is the famous Throne verse (Q. II: 256). The text continues with verses 18–19 from Surat Al ʿImran (Q. III), "the most popular Koranic text on monuments from early Islamic Iran."[77] As if by deliberate contrast, the Kufic inscription progresses with verses 1–3 from Surat al-Ikhlas (Q. CXII), which were undocumented in Blair's inscriptional corpus of the eastern Islamic lands from the ninth through early twelfth centuries, but common particularly in funerary contexts (mainly epitaphs) from the ninth century onward in Egypt, and also in Iran and the Red Sea coast of northeast Africa.[78]

Furthermore, a consideration of the directional orientation of the Chisht complex (Figure 4.16) and an examination of the site's broader historical context, together provide a fascinating if complicated picture of multiple *madhhabs* active in the region, probably through indirect means. First, the orientation of the *mihrab* within Chisht's northeastern structure could hint at a Hanafi affiliation for the complex, or at least a portion of it. As discussed in relation to Shah-i Mashhad (cf. above), pre-modern *qibla* orientations were calculated largely by means of "folk astronomy," in which the preferred *qiblas* of regionally dominant *madhhabs* were among the determining factors. While the Shafiʿis were known to use a south-oriented *qibla*, Hanafi *qiblas* tended to be oriented west. The Chisht complex's nearly north–south axis could have accommodated either or both orientations, similar to the layout of Shah-i Mashhad. But at Chisht, the surviving *mihrab* in the northeast structure has a westerly orientation, thereby seeming to dispel any ambiguity in favor of a Hanafi affiliation.

Finally, it is possible that, particularly *if* there was a Hanafi-affiliated presence at the Chisht complex, other *madhhabs* were also active in the vicinity, if not directly then through a type of surrogate representation. Chisht was certainly within the ambit of the Khurasani commercial center of Herat, only 150 km to the west, which in turn was well connected with Nishapur and other such great emporia beyond. But as noted earlier in this chapter, the direct influence of the city-based *madhhabs* was considerably diluted in the hinterlands, precisely where the more intrepid activists among the Karramiyya had identified proselytizing opportunities.

The Karramiyya were not alone, however, in their unorthodox proselytizing methods in both urban and hinterland milieus (cf. above in this chapter). Charismatic spiritual masters or Sufis (also *pir, murshid*) – identifiable by a characteristic woolen cloak (*suf*) or other mark of poverty – were also gathering followers devoted to their teachings, in cities such as

Figure 4.15 *Chisht, mausoleums (or* madrasa/mosque *complex), ruins: Mausoleum A, interior, arch, with inscription, detail. © Photograph Josephine Powell c. 1960. Harvard Fine Arts Library, Special Collections.*

Nishapur and Herat, and in less traveled reaches.[79] Although the followers of Sufi masters originated in various rungs of society – ranging from lay devotees of prosperous mercantile backgrounds through artisans and craftspeople, as well as the indigent poor – true renunciants (*murid*) would eventually coalesce as orders (*tariqa*) around their *pir*s, coming to be associated with specific *khanaqah*s. There was great variation among Sufi *tariqa*s in both geographical reach and longevity, with some attaining hereditary followings (*silsila*) able to spread the *pir*'s teachings far and wide through a process of associative fragmentation: new *silsila*s could be established, particularly in areas at a distance from their spiritual order's origin, yet remain affiliated, even loosely, with the memory of the initial *pir* and the spiritual teachings attributed to him.[80] The eponymous Chishtiyya was just such a Sufi order, having associations with the locality of Chisht as early as the ninth century, but attaining its

Figure 4.16 *Chisht on Google Earth, October 2018.*

Figure 4.17 *Chisht, mausoleums (or* madrasa/mosque complex), ruins: Mausoleum B, interior, mihrab, with decorative stucco work. © Photograph Josephine Powell c. 1960. Harvard Fine Arts Library, Special Collections.*

greatest followings and long historical presence throughout the Indian subcontinent.[81]

Given the migration of the order's *pir*, Mu'in al-Din Sijzi Chishti (AH 536–633/1142–1236 CE), to northern India probably by the 1180s, when the Ghazna Shansabanis took Lahore (see Chapter 5), it is unlikely that the monumental remains of the Chisht complex housed the Sufi order; their *khanaqah* would have been housed by another, probably more humble structure.[82] Moreover, the complex's at least partial Hanafi affiliation – as argued above – would further make a link with the Chishtiyya or other Sufis precarious. Although spiritual teachings definable as mystical or "Sufi" encompassed enormous variety, in general it can be said that they were of a very different order than theological–juridical doctrines. Being much more personal, performative, and "ascetic–mystical"[83] as spiritual paths, Sufi teachings could not uniformly be associated with any of the orthodox *madhhab*s, and in fact could have gravitated toward Shi'ism and particularly its Isma'ili expression.[84]

The decidedly independent or *un*orthodox expressions of Islam associated with Sufism overall made it all the more likely to appeal to non-urban populations (not unlike Karrami teachings). Nevertheless, Bulliet noted that, certainly in eastern Khurasan, "mysticism was almost non-existent among the Hanafis … and most directly associated with the Shafi'i party" at least through the early twelfth century.[85] While the evidentiary *lacunae* make all observations conjectural, this brief digression on the Sufism burgeoning in Afghanistan during the twelfth–thirteenth centuries supports the idea that at Chisht also, where the Shansabanis were epigraphically acknowledged, *madhhab*s and spiritual movements other than the Karramiyya could have benefited – probably *via* indirect avenues – from the Shansabanis' political presence and perhaps even patronage.

The Minar of Jam-Firuzkuh

The preceding observations regarding the multiplicity of *madhhab*s in areas ostensibly within the Firuzkuh Shansabanis' purview in no way refute the Karrami affiliation of the *minar* at Jam-Firuzkuh (Figure 4.18). If anything, the foregoing scenario lends additional support for the *minar*'s interpretation as a monumental vehicle for Karrami expression, at the very heart of the Firuzkuh Shansabanis' *sard-sir* "capital." However, the *minar*'s epigraphic program was arguably the Karramiya's swan song, serving as an indication of their curtailed sphere of influence – increasingly focused on the Shansabanis' royal summer encampment and the local population – and their last response to these straitened circumstances before the Firuzkuh Shansabanis *officially* espoused the Shafi'iyya in AH 595/1199 CE.

Sourdel-Thomine's[86] definitive re-dating of the Jam-Firuzkuh *minar* from AH 590/1193–1194 CE to AH 570/1174–1175 CE certainly divests it of

Figure 4.18 *Jam, minaret of Jam (c. 1180), distant view along valley floor.* © *Photograph Josephine Powell c. 1960. Harvard Fine Arts Library, Special Collections.*

any association with the Shansabanis' campaigns into the north Indian plains: two unsuccessful forays took place in AH 573/1178 CE and AH 587/1191–1192 CE, and it was not until AH 589/1192–1193 CE that the Shansabanis gained a foothold in the north Indian *duab* (cf. also Chapter 1 and 6, and Volume II). Nevertheless, the *minar*'s architectural form and typology undeniably connect it to the *minars* still standing in the Persianate world, in the territories affiliated both with the Saljuqs and the Ghaznavids – the latter particularly at the erstwhile Yamini capital. The Shansabanis' known emulation of their Ghaznavid predecessors – discussed above – strongly suggests that the Jam-Firuzkuh *minar* also served to commemorate an important military triumph. Furthermore, the presence of all of verse 13 and the beginning of verse 14 from Surat al-Saf (Q. LXI), promising imminent victory (Ar. *fath*) to those who believe in Allah, also supports the proposal that commemorating a victory was a significant – if not the principal – impetus behind the *minar*'s construction.[87] Although placed toward the pinnacle, the verses' rendition in square Kufic allowed for some legibility, at least of certain words, permitting even the less literate among its beholders to recognize the verses.

Indeed, the ideal occasion for commissioning such a monument had presented itself only the year before: in AH 568/1173 CE, a joint push by *both* of Baha' al-Din's sons finally routed the Oghüz encamped at Ghazna, resulting in the Shansabanis' definitive occupation of the city, the crowning of Shihab al-Din as Sultan Mu'izz al-Din, and the establishment of a third Shansabani lineage there – discussed in detail in Chapter 5. Such a significant victory would clearly warrant a monumental commemoration like the splendid *minar*.[88] Moreover, the location of the *minar* at Jam-Firuzkuh, rather than at Ghazna, distinguished it from its architectural predecessors and signified a Shansabani appropriation of the form and its signification. Ultimately, the *minar* plausibly played the role of a victory "trophy": although Shihab al-Din was crowned Sultan Mu'izz al-Din at Ghazna, the *minar*'s location at Jam-Firuzkuh – and its concomitant absence at Ghazna – would serve as a constant (if dyadic) reminder of the familial hierarchy wherein the Firuzkuh Shansabanis sought to be the senior-most lineage of a territorially expanding confederacy.

The analysis of Shah-i Mashhad's extant inscriptions earlier in this chapter revealed not only the significance of the epigraphic programs on Shansabani-patronized architecture, it also underscored these patrons' circumscribed role in determining their content. The distinctive (but complementary) purviews of the Shansabanis as architectural patrons, *vis-à vis* the theological, legal, and literary intelligentsia they also supported, does much to explain the most prominent component of the Jam-Firuzkuh *minar*'s epigraphic program: all of Surat Maryam's (Q. XIX) ninety-nine verses, meandering vertically and delimiting decorative panels all around the *minar*'s lowermost cylindrical shaft (see Appendix, Afghanistan VII: 5).

J. Sourdel-Thomine and F. B. Flood convincingly argued that the Karramiyya still installed at Firuzkuh likely chose this Sura as the *minar*'s epigraphic centerpiece, aiming it at their theological rivals rather than their Shansabani patrons. The Shansabani elites' increasing connections with the more prominent *madhhab*s of Khurasan – as argued throughout this chapter – would have warranted just such a gesture. The Shansabani conquest of *Hanafi* Ghazna, and the towering commemoration of the victory at Firuzkuh, served as the Karramiyya's monumental refutation of the charges of anthropomorphism that the more prominent Sunni *madhhab*s had leveled against them, beginning as early as the eleventh century.[89] The Shansabanis' lack of engagement with the finer points of theology would have made one Sura as acceptable as any other. But for the Karramiyya, such a riposte to their detractors was a matter of political and economic survival, as they attempted to hold on to the dwindling support of their sole remaining royal patrons.

The preceding treatment of early buildings in the ambit of the Firuzkuh Shansabanis has aimed to highlight the manifold significances of architectural patronage in building empire, as much for elites emerging from nomadism and/or seasonal transhumance as for all other power-brokers. Indeed, the Shansabani elites' limited conversance with literary cultures beyond recognizable Qur'anic phrases or verses, and other common Arabic doxologies, also resulted in an epigraphic corpus devoid of the types of poetic, political, and other inscriptions in Persian that graced (for example) Ghaznavid complexes.[90] Nevertheless, by commissioning a monumental public structure such as the Shah-i Mashhad complex, leaving at least an acknowledged presence at Chisht, and erecting the Jam-Firuzkuh *minar*, the Firuzkuh Shansabanis were simultaneously extending patronage to the various *madhhab*s and spiritual movements vying for greater politico-economic prominence throughout Khurasan. Perhaps most importantly, in the process of patronizing "civic" or otherwise landmark architectural sites – emphatically *not* palaces – the ambitious Firuzkuh Shansabanis were literally and figuratively building their own bases of power. During the second half of the twelfth century, their projects daringly began to encroach on the well-plied networks of trade and communication radiating from the cosmopolitan emporia of Herat and Nishapur (cf. esp. Volume II).

Patrons and Patronage

The foregoing analysis of the more firmly attributable built traces of the Firuzkuh Shansabanis began with some seminal questions regarding architectural patronage. We interrogated what monumental building ultimately *meant*, what it accomplished especially for elites emerging from transhumant/nomadic lifestyles and economies and going on to create an empire. It is equally important to examine the overall relationship between patron and outcome, that is, historically, the degree to which the preferences of, and input by, the one(s) "paying the bills" impacted the architectural result. There is surely no unitary answer to the last question; investigators across disciplines would be hard-pressed to craft a convincing, universally applicable characterization of the relationship between *all* patrons and their projects, even within a specific region and timespan.

These considerations are all the more relevant for the Shansabanis, for at least two reasons. First, we have seen throughout Chapter 3, and this one that the plural "Shansabanis" actually encompassed essentially independent lineages, each responding to and shaping disparate cultural geographies that ranged from Bamiyan through Ghur, and eventually

Zabulistan–Zamindawar (cf. Chapter 5). Second, given the Shansabanis' origins in the nomad–urban continuum of seasonally transhumant and/ or nomadic lifeways, the fissure between patron and patronage becomes a particularly informative space to explore.

Blair rightly noted that, "[i]n both form and intent, Ghurid architecture continues that of the Ghaznavids."[91] However, much needs to be differentiated in the processes of *how* these two architectural corpora came to be. We have established elsewhere in this volume that the Shansabanis can and should be distinguished from their immediate predecessors the Yamini–Ghaznavids in many respects (see esp. Chapter 1), perhaps in none more than architectural patronage. Beginning with the high-ranking Samanid *ghulam* Alptigin (d. AH 366/977 CE) and his successor Sabuktigin (d. AH 389/999 CE) – both considered progenitors of the Yamini–Ghaznavid dynasty – *all* of this royal house's scions had been reared in cosmopolitan and courtly Perso-Islamic surroundings. Although of Turkic ethnic and linguistic origins, these *ghulam*s had been incorporated into the Samanid court, witnessing its active encouragement of Arabic- and Persian-language writing in both secular and religious fields.[92] Characterizable at least initially as a Samanid "successor-state," the Ghaznavid dynasty continued to feel the benefits of maintaining Arabic-language bureaucracy, while the rulers themselves were knowledgeable in and patronized literary production in Persian (and also Arabic).[93] This overall investment in a cultural "footprint" further intertwined Zabulistan within the commercial, intellectual, and religious networks of greater Eurasia (see also Chapters 2 and 3).

The Ghaznavids' immersively courtly background could not form a more glaring contrast to the Shansabanis' obscure origins in seasonal transhumance and/or nomadism. Nevertheless, the Firuzkuh Shansabanis quickly learned the mechanisms of attaining and exercising contextually appropriate kingship, including the commissioning of magnificent architectural complexes such as Shah-i Mashhad, Chisht, and the Firuzkuh *jami'* complex and its renowned *minar* (the specific subjects of the present chapter). Based on the significant differences between these sets of imperial patrons, however, I suggest that the Shansabanis' imposing buildings were as much – if not more – the results of input from courtly intelligentsia and the actual craftspeople who fabricated them, as from their royal masters.

For the Shansabanis, their transhumant/nomadic pre-imperial milieu could have perhaps offered some opportunity to experience built forms. This would have occurred as they encountered settled environments along their seasonal routes of transhumance, which spanned the length of historical Ghur. Although again a modern parallel, it is nonetheless useful to note the visitations of migrating nomadic pastoralists to Sufi *khanaqah*s, particularly when these are located along their paths of movement and/or near their seasonal market areas.[94] Regular contact with such establishments, and indeed the nomadic visitors' participation to varying degrees in the *khanaqah*'s activities – for example, *dhikr*, *urs*, or other gatherings – historically would have represented one of the principal avenues of exposure to an array of Islamicate socio-religious practices, and perhaps even the totality of some of these groups' actual knowledge of "Islam" and its associated architecture.[95] It is thus conceivable that, through their interactions with even minor architectural complexes, nomadic/transhumant visitors would gain at least a cursory apprehension of current styles, some among them also perceiving the buildings' more immediate functions and even their larger political implications.

Such regular seasonal, architectural, and urban interactions would have contributed little, however, toward deepening knowledge of the Qur'an and its exegetical traditions among groups such as the Shansabanis, or giving them comprehensive training in Persian literary history and composition.[96] In fact, taking into account their limited familiarity with Persianate courtly cosmopolitanism, it is understandable – rather than remarkable – that virtually no Persian inscriptions appeared on the imperial Shansabanis' buildings; their predilections naturally tended toward a select and effectively reduced group of Qur'anic verses and simple doxologies, which were by default in Arabic.[97] The differences between the rulers and at least some of their courtiers with regard to Qur'anic and exegetical conversancy would have to be bridged, then, in the course of selecting verses, Hadiths or other theologically significant material as part of devising architectural epigraphy. The religious and intellectual experts in the Firuzkuh Shansabanis' retinues and court would have conceivably made the initial selections from appropriate sources, even if these were pending the approval of their patron(s).

In the end, both in the historical moment and in hindsight, it accrues to the Shansabanis' credit that they understood and enacted, with great responsiveness, the urgency of building monumentally for an emerging transregional elite such as themselves: commissioning and endowing "civic" institutions was an effective way of commanding and mobilizing labor in their areas of control, even without erecting palaces. The actual fruits of this expenditure of resources, namely, the prominent architectural complexes centering and sustaining their environs, were not only attestations of economic wherewithal, they were also the most efficacious means of monitoring and eventually controlling legal thought and practice, which are among the very mechanics of empire along with military might and commercial prosperity. In the case of the Firuzkuh Shansabanis, the age-old Khurasani commercial networks and prosperous urban centers remained part of their architectural–cultural *habitus*; it is all the more noteworthy, then, that they apparently persisted in their preference of tent over palace, continuing their seasonal migrations between their summer and winter encampments or "capitals."

Notes

1. The dating of Shah-i Mashhad is not definitive due to the erosion of its inscriptional program, particularly the plaited Kufic on the principal southern portal (Figures 4.1 and 4.4) (inscription Nos. 1 and 2 in Casimir and Glatzer 1971). The initial reading of the date was AH 561/1165–1166 CE, modified later to AH 571/1176 CE, which continues to be accepted. Cf. Casimir and Glatzer 1971: 56; Glatzer 1973: 50; Blair 1985: 81. Najimi (2015: 148 n. 33, 151 n. 54), while not attempting to re-read the date itself in the inscription, does reconcile *both* proposed years by stating that a decade-long construction of the complex was realistic, "based on his experiences working on restoration projects in Afghanistan."

2. Cf. Introduction esp. for the Salar Khalil, west of Balkh (Juzjan Province), possibly falling within the ambit of the Bamiyan Shansabanis. These architectural remnants are datable to the later twelfth century, likely of non-royal but still elite patronage. See also Introduction and Chapter 1.

3. The Appendix gathers together the monumental historical and religious epigraphy from these structures, serving as a complementary reference to the discussion in this chapter and the following one of the import of this inscriptional corpus.

4. Blair 1985: 83.

5. Nishapur's sectarian riots are well known, thanks to the work of R. Bulliet and others: here, prior to the city's demise in the wake of the Oghüz raids of the 1150s, the two predominant and rival *madhhabs* of the Shafi'is and Hanafis were prone to violent confrontations. Among other Sunni orthodox sects, the Hanbalis and Malikis were relatively few in number, mustering less violence-inciting fervor. The Karramiyya also, even if marginalized as heterodox (discussed *infra* in main text), periodically amassed enough clout especially among the poor in the northwest of the city, to instigate violent eruptions against the dominant religious sects. Cf. Bulliet 1972: 12, 30, 74, 76; Zysow 2011/2012: pt ii; and Chapter 2.

6. For the association of Qur'anic inscriptions and Hadith with certain *madhhabs*, see Blair 1992: esp. 9–10, 52–53, 78. For the *minar* of Jam-Firuzkuh, see Sourdel-Thomine 2004: 153ff.; Flood 2005a: 270–273; and *infra* in main text.

7. While Blair (1985) first deciphered and published several of the Chisht inscriptions principally in the more intact southern Structure A, Dr. Viola Allegranzi is in the process of re-examining, transliterating, and translating the inscriptions in *both* the structures surviving at the site (see below). Her work is based on Josephine Powell's photographs from the mid-twentieth century, as well as a comparison with Ludvik Kalus' readings of the inscriptions, published on the digital database *Thesaurus d'Epigraphie Islamique* (*TEI*): cf. fiche 37804. I am deeply grateful to Dr. Allegranzi for sharing her work in progress, which henceforth is cited as Allegranzi 2019b (forthcoming). See also Ball 2008: 179–181; Ball 2019: No. 212 for a description of the site, plans and sections.

8. A possibly similar anachronism occurred on an undated *jital* minted at Kurraman (modern Parachinar), between Peshawar and Gardiz, naming one Shams al-Din as the sovereign. The coin has been attributed to the

Bamiyan ruler Shams al-Din Muhammad (r. AH 558–588/1163–1192 CE), since the ruler of Firuzkuh had relinquished this *laqab* in favor of Ghiyath al-Din by AH 588/1163 CE. Hence, the dilemma: the 1160s would be too early for the Shansabanis to have a territorial presence this far east; and yet, it is equally unlikely that the Bamiyan Shansabanis ever reached Gandhara, even at the height of their power in the 1190s CE. Cf. Tye and Tye 1995: 53 and No. 138; also O'Neal 2015. For a parallel instance in the case of Shihab al-Din/Sultan Mu'izz al-Din, see Chapter 1 (notes).

9. Cf. Juzjani vol. I, 1963: 354 (trans. vol. I, 1881: 369). An examination of Shansabani marital alliances could offer additional insight into the differing politico-economic wherewithal and consequent hierarchy among the various lineages. Over time and with Firuzkuh's growing coffers – refilled *via* a trade economy – the Firuzkuhi Shansabanis were able to enter marriage alliances outside Ghur (see main text), which were also more useful than marriage among kin. Meanwhile, the Bamiyan Shansabanis' marriages appear to have been largely among their Shansabani agnates, e.g., the marriage of Sultan Shams al-Din Muhammad (r. 1163–1192), Fakhr al-Din Mas'ud's successor, to Hurra-yi Jalali, the elder sister of the Firuzkuh and Ghazna sultans Ghiyath al-Din and Mu'izz al-Din (respectively), and the mother of the great cultural patron Baha' al-Din of Bamiyan (r. 1192–1206; see main text). Additionally, Malika-yi Jalali, Sultan Ghiyath al-Din's daughter, was betrothed to Baha' al-Din's son and heir Malik 'Ala' al-Din Muhammad. Cf. Juzjani vol. I, 1963: 379, 388 (trans. vol. I, 1881: 412, 428). Barfield (1981: 78) noted that modern nomads in northeastern Afghanistan rarely arranged matches among patrilineal cousins, instead preferring outside alliances and the larger affine networks afforded by such exogamous marriages. By contrast, paternal cousin marriage continues in force among the Arabian Bedouin (Barfield 1993: 77), an old practice that could have been the source of the orthodox Islamic prescriptions for such arrangements.

10. Juzjani vol. I, 1963: 337, 341, 349 (trans. vol. I, 1881: 341). Sourdel-Thomine (1976: 168) proposed that this site was the same as Shah-i Mashhad, citing both Juzjani and Le Strange (1930: 416). However, the location does *not* coincide with Shah-i Mashhad: cf. Glatzer 1973: 67, whose comments on the location are particularly weighty given his rediscovery of the complex, together with M. Casimir, in 1970 (Casimir and Glatzer 1971). See also Najimi 2015: 147; Wannell 2002: 242–243; and *infra* in main text. W. Ball (pers. comm., April 2020) has suggested that Shahr-i Arman could be the historical Afshin – cf. Ball 2019: No. 1033.

11. Juzjani vol. I, 1963: 362–363 (trans. vol. I, 1881: 385). The prominent mention of this individual may indicate that he was actually Muhammad ibn Haisam, the founder of the eponymous Haisamiyya of the later twelfth century. Ibn Haisam put forth significant revisions of Karrami theology and thus established this important "sub-sect" among the Karramiyya, with whom Fakhr al-Din Razi also engaged in his writings. The Haisamiyya were one of three such sub-sects representing later developments in Karrami thought. Cf. Zysow 2011/2012: pt vi.

12. For Taj al-Harir Jauhar Malik, see Juzjani vol. I, 1963: 357 (trans. vol. I, 1881:

376); also Casimir and Glatzer 1971: 56ff., Blair 1985: 81ff.; Najimi 2015: 149. For all sources on the complex and site, see Ball 2019: No. 1023.

13. Najimi 2015; see also below.

14. Juzjani vol. I, 1963: 354 (trans. vol. I, 1881: 367). As mentioned in Chapter 1, it might have been during these military actions that Saif al-Din briefly occupied Herat, where coins were issued with his *laqab* and the Herat mint stamp (see also O'Neal 2016a; O'Neal 2020: 200–201).

15. In this case, the apparent deviation from the generally exogamous marriages of the Firuzkuh sultans (note above) was in fact an extremely convenient use of the patrilineal cousin marriage prescribed within Islam. The marriage of Jauhar Malik and Shams al-Din presumably took place between AH 556–558/1161–1163 CE: it must be remembered that 'Ala' al-Din Husain *Jahan-suz*, upon acceding to the throne of Firuzkuh in AH 544/1149 CE, had imprisoned both the sons of his brother Baha' al-Din, likely when the boys were quite young. After 'Ala' al-Din's death in AH 556/1161 CE and the accession of his son Saif al-Din, the latter released his cousins and, perhaps by way of healing the familial breach, married his sister to his elder cousin Shams al-Din. Shortly after the nuptials, the unforeseen death of Saif al-Din occasioned yet another transferal of the Firuzkuh throne to a collateral Shansabani lineage (cf. Chapter 1). In hindsight, then, this *fourth* transferal was surely that much smoother and more acceptable by virtue of the marriage of Saif al-Din's sister to the eventual Sultan Ghiyath al-Din. Cf. Juzjani vol. I, 1963: 346, 395 (trans. vol. I, 1881: 357, 446–447).

16. Although documented in the 1970s and again in the 1990s, the modern interactions of nomadic populations with sites such as Shah-i Mashhad – precisely what led to the site's "discovery" by Casimir and Glatzer (1971) – may provide a useful parallel to the historical contacts between these groups and the monumental complexes dotting their migration routes. The notable deterioration in the complex within twenty years (Figures 4.1 and 4.4), however, is not necessarily attributable to this interaction, but rather to the agriculturalists of the region, who had greater need for the building materials readily available at abandoned monumental sites.

17. Franke and Urban and their archaeological team documented structures like Gunbad-i Shohada and Qala-yi Sarkari, both between Awbeh and Chisht, and Rabat-i Chauni, south of Chisht. Gunbad-i Shohada could have been a commemorative structure of the recognizable "domed cube" typology, quite plausibly attributable to late Saljuq/Shansabani presence (or later); the Qala and Rabat are square-walled compounds with corner circular towers, which, as we have seen in the case of Danestama (cf. Chapter 3), could have been pre-Islamic structures that were reused or repurposed during later periods, to be determined only with further study. Cf. Franke and Urban 2006: 7–15, 18–20, 22–23; and *infra* in main text.

18. Flood 2009a: 101; see also Chapter 2.

19. Sourdel-Thomine (2004: esp. 156ff.) first proposed the reinterpretation of the *minar*'s inscriptional program. See also Flood 2005a: 269–273; and Flood 2009a: 96–97. The Jam-Firuzkuh *minar* was also discussed in Chapter 3 – see also *infra* in main text.

20. Juzjani vol. I, 1963: 362 (trans. vol. I, 1881: 384). For the Karrami Qur'an, see Flood 2009a: 96; Flood 2009b. Thomas (2018: 122) briefly discussed the overall complex; as always, Ball (2019: No. 1023) has provided the most thorough bibliography of the site.

21. For the Ghaznavids, see, e.g., Bulliet 1972: 63–64, 68–70; Malamud 1994: 45–46. For Saljuq-period negotiations of sectarian rivalries, see Bulliet 1972: 72–74; Peacock 2010: 104ff.; Peacock 2015: 268–272.

22. See below in main text for possibly *indirect* infiltrations of the orthodox *madhhab*s into more remote areas, possibly *via* Sufi networks. Given the founder Muhammad ibn Karram's proselytizing origins in Sistan – though he might have been born in Mecca – it is possible that he made his way from Sistan to Khurasan *via* Ghur and Gharjistan, reportedly entering the great Khurasani emporium of Nishapur with a following of "weavers and others from depressed classes." See esp. Bosworth 1973: 165, 185–186; Melchert 2001; also Zysow 2011/2012: pt i.

23. Bosworth 1973: 185–186.

24. See also Bosworth [1960] 1977 (reprint): 1–2.

25. Bosworth (1961: 128ff.) initially put forward the idea that Mahmud dispatched Karrami preceptors into Ghur, but see also Malamud 1994: 47; Zysow 2011/2012: pt ii; and Chapter 3. These later Karrami "missionaries," then, quite possibly entered the region with such information as might have been preserved ever since a century before or more.

26. Cf. Bosworth 1973: 188–189; Malamud 1994: 39–43 and notes.

27. See Bosworth [1960] 1977: 8; also Zysow (2011/2012: pt iv) for a discussion of early concordances among Karramis, Shafi'is and Hanafis, as well as eventual divergences between the Karramiyya and other *madhhab*s. It is also important to bear in mind that, prior to the thirteenth century, as many as several hundred lesser known or lost theological sects were active throughout the central Islamic lands, and that the four *madhhab*s now accepted as "orthodox" crystallized and came to be considered as such only by the later 1200s. Cf. Makdisi 1971: 77; Makdisi 1981: 2ff.

28. Cf. Bosworth 1973: 183. According to Nizami (1998: 370–371), Ghur and Gharjistan were already crowded fields for proselytizers by the early twelfth century: in addition to the Karramiyya, disciples of the mystic 'Abd al-Qadir Gilani (d. AH 561/1166 CE) were also active in these same areas.

29. Recently, the *minar* of Jam-Firuzkuh has not only been re-dated from AH 590/1193–1194 CE to AH 570/1174–1175 CE, it has also been compellingly identified as a Karramiyya-inspired monument, particularly its unique epigraphic program (Sourdel-Thomine 2004: 156; cf. further citations below in main text and notes). The architectural typology of the *minar* versus the *madrasa*, however, sets the structures apart, as discussed *infra* (main text).

30. See esp. Tritton 1957: 98–100, 102–108; Sourdel-Thomine 1976; Pedersen, pt i and Hillenbrand pt iii in Pedersen et al. 2012; Zysow 2011/2012: pt ii. Melchert (2001: 237) in fact cited al-Maqdisi's (fl. 985) characterization of the Karramiyya as *al-khanaqa'iyyun*. It is noteworthy that, well into the twelfth century, textual sources also included *ribat*s as sites of instruction, not only in smaller towns but also in larger cities such as Baghdad; at times a communal

structure previously at the edge of a shifting frontier – the very definition of *ribat* – would be essentially repurposed as a place "for those devoted to the contemplative life … [and] for the spreading of learning." Cf. Tritton 1957: 106–108 and notes; Makdisi 1981: 9–34; Böwering and Melvin-Koushki [2010] 2012: pts i and ii; Edwards 2015: 120–121.

31. One of the methods of implementing imperial Saljuq control was *via* the patronage of various Sunni *madhhab*s in major urban centers – patronage that included the construction and endowment of lavish *madrasa*s. See Böwering and Melvin-Koushki [2010] 2012: pt ii. Bombaci (1966, cited in Allegranzi 2019a, vol. I: 161 n. 148) proposed that a possible precedent for the imposing Saljuq *madrasa*s, promulgated particularly by the famous *vizir* Nizam al-Mulk (AH 409–485/1018–1092 CE), might have been one of Ghaznavid patronage in Nishapur, dating to *c.* 1000 CE. See also Bulliet 1972: 250–251. For an accelerated proliferation of *madrasa*s due to Saljuq patronage, see Makdisi 1971: 81–82; Makdisi 1981: 31ff.; Bulliet 1994: 146–147 and *passim*; Peacock 2015: 211–215.

32. The classic studies by Bulliet (1972, 1994) on sources for Nishapur during the eleventh–early twelfth centuries demonstrate the intimate intertwining of economic, political, and intellectual interests among the "patricians" of the city. Nonetheless, there were rifts and reconciliations among them, and also with the rulers, depending on the situation – cf. also Bosworth 1973: 192–193.

33. Well into the eleventh century, while the Karramiyya were still in Ghaznavid favor in Nishapur and had attained high positions even in non-religious administration of the city, asceticism continued to be associated with them. Cf. Bulliet 1972: 42, 64ff.; esp. Bosworth 1973: 187–188; Bosworth [1960] 1977: 6–7. Whether this asceticism was "hypocritical" (Bosworth [1960] 1977: 11) or not, the rapid decline in the Karramiyya's fortunes shortly thereafter, and the consequent shift of their proselytism into the hinterlands, would have required even more that the adherents maintain frugal if not ascetic lifestyles.

34. By the tenth century, there were *madrasa*s in Egypt that were occupied by at least two *madhhab*s, wherein instruction according to each one took place at different locales throughout the complex, or if space was lacking, timings would be split. The multi-*madhhab* institution was not uncommon through the fourteenth century, and included such prominent foundations as Baghdad's Mustansiriyya, founded in AH 631/1234 CE to contain "four schools for the four rites …," effectively eclipsing the Shafi'i Nizamiyya (founded AH 459/1067 CE). Cf. Tritton 1957: 100–101, 104–105; and esp. Makdisi 1981: 34.

35. Blair 1985: 81.

36. I am grateful to Gwendolyn Kristy and David Thomas for helping determine Shah-i Mashhad's orientation: Gwendolyn Kristy located ArcGIS imagery of the site, and David Thomas superimposed on it the complex's plan as reconstructed by Najimi (2015: 153), whose own plan ensued from the studies by Casimir and Glatzer (1971: 55; cf. also *ibid.*, 58) and his own documentation of the *madrasa*'s standing remains in the early 1990s. The accurate *qibla* orientation is also from Najimi (2015: 148).

37. Cf. Akhmedov 2000: 195–199. Berggren (2000: 189–190) noted that "[the] mathematical sciences acquired Islamic dimensions as its practitioners became aware that their disciplines could be used to provide exact solutions to

problems unique to Islamic societies … Trigonometry found several areas of application, one of these being the determination of the direction of prayer, i.e. the determination of the direction of Mecca (the *qibla*), for a given locality." But, cf. *infra* in main text.

38. The astronomical thinking of Hanafis and Shafi'is in Samarqand during the eleventh century is known thanks to a text by al-Bazdawi (d. AH 482/1089 CE, of which a seventeenth-century manuscript survives in Cairo): the Shafi'is simply followed the precedent of the Prophet's *qibla* in Medina, which faced south – coincidentally also an auspicious direction in pre-Islamic wind theory, whence the south wind *qabul* (sharing the Arabic root q-b-l with *qibla*) brought rain to the Hijaz. The Hanafis, by contrast, relied on their immediate surroundings as determinants, basing their western *qibla* on the direction of the road from Samarqand to Mecca. See King 1982; King 1995; King 1993.

39. It should be observed that, given Karrami leanings toward Hanafi legal tenets (cf. Zysow 2011/2012: pt v), it is likely that the Karramiyya also adhered to a *qibla* due west (270°). The likelihood is bolstered by the *minar* of Jam, a monument in all probability of Karrami affiliation, which has a *mihrab* on its east face oriented 260°, very close to the Hanafis' western *qibla* ("true" *qibla* at Jam would be 245°). D. Thomas, pers. comm., May 2018; see also *infra* in main text and Chapter 3.

40. King 1992: 254.

41. See Najimi 2015: 154. It is lamentable that the author did not include a photograph of the previously unpublished inscription to aid in seeing its exact location within the epigraphic program of the southern façade, its scale, and its relationship with the façade's other inscriptions. Cf. also Appendix, Afghanistan IV:2.

42. Najimi 2015: 158 (emphasis added); and *ibid.*, 167–168 for a table listing the varying readings of some of the inscriptions. See also Casimir and Glatzer 1971: 56ff.; Glatzer 1972: 50ff.; Blair 1985: 83–86.

43. Casimir and Glatzer 1971.

44. Sourdel-Thomine (2004: 153–154) described in some detail the complexity involved in planning the monumental epigraphic program on the *minar* of Jam (cf. Chapter 3 and *infra* in main text), but also applicable to other sites. The challenges to overcome included the varying lengths of verses, and their placement such that size and script modifications according to space would be virtually unnoticeable. These factors were relevant also in the opening verses of Surat al-Fath: significant differences in length among verses 5–8 make it difficult to surmise how many would have continued on the no longer extant southwestern flank of the façade. Cf. also Ettinghausen 1974: 307–309.

45. Najimi 2015.

46. *Tashriq* refers to the eleventh through the thirteenth days of the month of Dhu al-Hijja, three days after 'Id al-Adha and also the three-day period of the end of the Hajj. It is the time of animal sacrifice, which in essence haptically recalls Abraham's (Ibrahim) willingness to sacrifice his son upon divine command. However, there was apparently no specific *takbir* to be recited during this period, at least according to al-Bukhari's *Sahih*. Cf. at: https://

sunnah.com/bukhari/25 (*Sahih* Book 25, "Kitab al-Hajj") and https://sunnah.com/bukhari/30: (*Sahih* Book 25, "Kitab al-Saum"). See also Appendix, Afghanistan IV: 3.

47. According to Najimi 2015: 163 (Appendix, Afghanistan IV: 9); but see *infra* in main text.

48. Blair (1998: 69) claimed that verses from Surat al-Fath were common on mosques, though evidently this assessment applied *outside* the eastern Islamic lands: Blair (1992) did not document a single occurrence on *any* building type through AH 500/1106 CE. However, at Barsiyan within the Isfahan oasis, Q. XLVIII: 1–5 appeared at the base of the dome of the complex's mosque – a complex including a *minar* and possibly a caravanserai; the mosque was dated by inscription to AH 528/1134 CE (about thirty-six years *after* the *minar*'s inscribed date of AH 491/1097–1098 CE) (cf. Godard and Smith 1937: 40–41). Finally, late eleventh- and twelfth-century quotations of the Sura's verses (Q. XLVIII: 1–5) come from Cairo, namely, at Mashhad al-Juyushi dating to AH 477/1085 CE; and a century later at the adjacent, "magnificent Citadel" (Ar. *qal'a*) of Cairo (Q. XLVIII: 1–3), initiated by the renowned Salah al-Din in AH 578/1183–1184 CE. Cf. *RCEA*, vol. 9 (1937) No. 3380; and Rabbat 1995: 68–73. Upon this first citation of the *RCEA*, we should bear in mind early critiques of this monumental project even by one of its editors, J. Sourdel-Thomine (1976: 265), who questioned "the role to be played … of a tool [whose] conception was already old [i.e., obsolete]." Hillenbrand (2012: 19) specified the *RCEA*'s in-built obsolescence and its consequences: "Strange as it may seem, Quranic inscriptions are recorded in this vast opus only when, as part of the same inscription, historical matter is included." Such is the case with the aforementioned Barsiyan complex, whose dome and *mihrab* inscriptions were not noted in *RCEA* – despite the latter's mention of a date (cf. also Kalus, *TEI* fiche No. 37215; Godard and Smith cited *supra*). It is possible, then, that important instances of Qur'anic citation may not factor into scholarly analyses simply because they do not appear in the *RCEA*. Cf. also Appendix.

49. All identified Shansabani-patronized epigraphy is in Arabic, with the exception of the Persian date of Chisht's southwestern structure (discussed *infra* in main text; Appendix, Afghanistan III: 5d). This overall trend is at variance with Ghaznavid and Qarakhanid epigraphic *corpora*, wherein Persian was increasingly used particularly as a language of architectural inscriptions, beginning in the early eleventh century and onward. Cf. Hillenbrand 2012: 21ff.; esp. Allegranzi 2015: 34 and *passim*; Allegranzi 2019a, vol. I: 47ff.

50. The actual readability of monumental epigraphy in pre-modern times has long been discussed in scholarship, beginning with Ettinghausen (1974). Scholarly consensus has stressed that "Islamic inscriptions were not expected to be read in this literal sense but rather functioned in an imagistic or symbolic manner, affirming the belief of the patron as well as that of the viewer" (Edwards 1991: 65). See also Thomas 2012: 145–146, 156–158.

51. It is more than likely that, well into the mid-twelfth century, the Firuzkuh Shansabanis also maintained some aspects of non-Islamic religious practices. Cf. Chapter 3 for Tiginabad/Old Qandahar in the plains of al-Rukkhaj,

where their forays in AH 552/1158 CE – only fifteen years before the conquest of Ghazna – seem to have left sparse but distinctive traces, e.g., in burial mounds: "hybrid" burial practices combining a *qibla* orientation of the deceased with unusual underground vaults and octagonal platforms above ground. Indeed, the south- and eastward campaigning armies of Mu'izz al-Din would have continued to encounter varieties not only in tomb structures, but also in burial practices, e.g., in Baluchistan and coastal Makran, where they campaigned in the 1180s (cf. Chapter 6). For these contiguous areas, cf., e.g., Hassan 1991: 79ff.

52. Khazeni's (2009: 13 and *passim*) work on central Iran's Bakhtyari tribes within Qajar realms (late nineteenth–early twentieth centuries) described its most useful source, *Tarikh-i Bakhtyari*, as "a tribal history and perhaps the first ethnography in the Persian language," compiled between 1909 and 1911; it was a sweeping combination of relevant passages from official Persian chronicles and "original material ... devoted to the oral histories and geographical lore of the tribes, including ... organization, administration, and customs." Historical empires originating in nomadic pastoralism, such as the Qara- or Ilak-khanids (mid-tenth–early thirteenth centuries) and the Qarakhitai (1087–1143; cf. Chapter 1), evince divergent literary developments strongly impacted by contact with the Islamic-Persianate *ecumene*: the Qara- or Ilak-khanid Satoq Bughra Khan Abd al-Karim's (d. *c.* 955 CE) embrace of Islam led not only to a wave of conversion among other Turks, arguably it also led to the creation of a *Turkic* – rather than Persian – literary tradition beginning in the 1070s. Cf. Biran 2012; Vàsàry 2015: 17ff. By contrast, modern scholars of the unconverted Qarakhitai still come across great difficulties when searching for primary sources, not least because of "the irregular record keeping of the nomadic Khitans and the unusually long time that passed from ... 1125 to the compilation of the [Chinese *Liao shi*] in 1344–45" (Biran 2005: 4).

53. For the larger juridical and even theological debates in which the Karramiyya engaged with other *madhhab*s, see Zysow 1988: 585 and *passim*; Zysow 2011/2012: pts iv and v.

54. Cf. Edwards 1991: 69.

55. Cf. Najimi 2015: 158–163 for a detailed description of the manufacture of inscriptions in brick and stucco; see also Chapters 2 and 3, for a discussion of the availability of local practitioners of the architectural culture prevalent throughout Khurasan. In the context of the Jam-Firuzkuh *minar* – cf. *infra* in main text – Lintz (2013: 96–97) also discussed collaboration among builders, artisans, theologians, and patrons.

56. For the typical career of a purchased Turk slave, see Barthold (1968: 227–228), who derived the trajectory from the Saljuq *vizir* Nizam al-Mulk's *Siyasat-nama*. For the Ghaznavids in particular, Allegranzi (2014: 113–114) summarized Baihaqi's praise of Mas'ud I's skills as architect/engineer (*muhandis*) (also Bosworth 1973: 139–141). Although this could have been rhetorical flourish in praise of his patron, it nonetheless appears that Sultan Mahmud had been diligent about the education of his sons in Persian and Arabic *adab*, and the early Ghaznavid sultans' courts "[u]ndoubtedly ... became brilliant

cultural centers" (*ibid.*, 131ff.). Cf. also Allegranzi 2015: 24–27. For a summary of the extensive patronage of poetry throughout the length of the Ghaznavid dynasty, see Allegranzi 2019a, vol. I: 23–31. See also Appendix, Afghanistan V and VI.

57. For Egypt and the Mediterranean, see, e.g., *RCEA*, vol. 5 (1934) Nos. 1838, 1879, 1917, 1931, 1938, 1950. In the eastern Islamic lands, two tomb towers at Kharraqan dating to the late eleventh century CE carry Q. LIX: 21–24 (Blair 1992: 9, 134, 172). According to Dodd and Khairallah (1981: II:130–131), whose work concentrated on architecture rather than smaller elements (e.g., epitaphs), parts of this verse series was first documented in Córdoba's *jami* dating to AH 354/965 CE, and thereafter principally in India, beginning with Delhi's Qutb mosque in AH 587/1191–1192 CE and continuing through the fifteenth century (see Volume II).

58. In Blair's (1992) compilation of inscriptions from greater Iran and Transoxiana of the ninth through early twelfth centuries, no *takbir* was documented, and only one Hadith – on a *mihrab* from Iskodar, dated to AH 400/1010 CE. Cf. Blair 1992: 10, 78; also Blair 1998: 69. At variance with Blair, Hillenbrand (2012: 19) claimed that Hadiths "often appear[ed] in building inscriptions." In fact, Hadith may have gone unrecorded in the *RCEA* because, unlike Qur'anic inscriptions, Hadith were not as often accompanied by historical data (date of foundation, patron, etc.) – the collection of which was the true aim of the monumental *RCEA*. See also *supra* in notes.

59. For Shi'a presence in Khurasan, cf. Bulliet 1972: 14–15; Bosworth 1973: 194–200; Bosworth 2012c. It is also noteworthy that 'Ali's name was repeated (in Kufic) on the eastern pier of the *madrasa*'s northern entrance, adjacent to the Hadith under discussion (cf. Casimir and Glatzer 1971: fig.12; Najimi 2015: 167). Moreover, in the epigraphic programs of the known Shansabani-patronized structures throughout modern Afghanistan and Pakistan, 'Ali was included in invocations of the Rightly Guided Caliphs of early Islam, e.g., in the stucco medallions decorating the *mihrab* of Chisht's northeastern structure, and in similar brick medallions on the *mihrab* of the *ribat* of 'Ali ibn Karmakh near Multan. For Chisht, see Allegranzi 2019b (forthcoming); for the Multan *ribat*, see Edwards 1991: 92; Edwards 2015: 110–133, 201–210; and Chapter 6. See also Appendix, Afghanistan III: 7b; and Pakistan I: 7.

60. Cf. at: https://sunnah.com/bukhari/81, or *Sahih al-Bukhari* 6416, Book 81 (print Vol. 8, Book 76, Hadith 425). See also Melchert 2012; and Appendix, Afghanistan IV: 9.

61. Pinder-Wilson 2001: 164ff.; cf. also Appendix, Afghanistan VI. Prior occurrences of Surat al-Fath's opening verses occurred at Qasr Kharana, Jordan (Q. XLVIII: 2) in AH 92/710 CE, and in the cupola of Cairo's al-Juyushi Mosque (Q. XLVIII: 1–5) in AH 478(?)/1085(?) CE. Farther east in the Iranian world, the verses (Q. XLVIII: 1–5) appeared in the Isfahan oasis' Barsiyan mosque. Cf. Godard and Smith 1937: 40–41; Dodd and Khairallah 1981: II: 118–120; and *supra* in notes.

62. The *minar* also survived the destruction left in the path of the Mongol contingent in pursuit of the Khwarazm-shah Jalal al-Din Mingburnu in the 1220s,

and the succeeding several centuries when the descendants of the Mongols – e.g., the Negüderi, or Qaraunas – held sway from Ghazna eastward. Cf. Bernardini 2020: 251–252; and *infra* in this chapter.

63. Pinder-Wilson 2001: 165. See esp. Bosworth [1977] 1992: 6ff. This "sequel" to the same author's earlier publication on the Ghaznavids (1973) essentially began with the Saljuq defeat of the Ghaznavid forces at Dandanqan, which arguably brought to an end the expansionist momentum set by Mahmud and continued by Mas'ud I. During the following eighteen years, thanks to heavy-handed Saljuq meddling in Ghaznavid succession, six Ghaznavid princes vied for the title of sultan either as claimants or actual rulers. Thereafter, the combined reigns of Ibrahim (r. AH 451–492/1059–1099 CE) and his son Mas'ud III (r. AH 492–509/1099–1115 CE) – ostensibly a long and seemingly stable period of more than a half-century – again resulted in short and con-tested successions (see also de Bruijn 1983: 34, 59). As noted above in the main text, the Shansabanis sacked Ghazna in AH 545/1150 CE. It is probable that the Oghüz occupation of Ghazna began as early as 1160, since Khusrau Malik (r. AH 555–582/1160–1186 CE) was apparently crowned sultan at Lahore. Cf. Bosworth [1977] 1992: 82ff., 123–131.

64. See Pinder-Wilson 2001: 166; Ball and Fischer 2019: 477–478. Mas'ud III's *minar* was most likely associated with an adjoining mosque, and also threw its shadow on the large Ghaznavid palace (R. Giunta, pers. comm., July 2018), discussed in Chapter 5. The precedent of commemorating a military victory with the erection of a *minar* – in association with a mosque – appears to have been firmly set already by Mahmud of Ghazna, who, according to Iltutmish's (r. AH 618–633/1221–1236 CE at Delhi) court poet Fakhr-i Mudabbir Mubarakshah (d. AH 625/1228 CE), commemorated what was likely his Kanauj victory of AH 409/1018–1019 CE by building a *minar* in Lahore (see Flood 2002: 103–107, also for the poet's mistake in the date of the campaign). Due to Lahore's millennium-long urban development, neither the *minar* nor its surrounding context is traceable. Based on surviving towers – e.g., at Ghazna, Jam-Firuzkuh, and Delhi – it is probable that the Lahore *minar* was associated with a mosque at some point, though the latter may not have been constructed simultaneously, as was the case at Jam-Firuzkuh and Delhi (cf. also A. N. Khan 1988: 304; Chapters 3 and 5; and Volume II for Delhi).

65. Evidently the Sura in its entirety appeared again in Isfahan, around the court-yard of the Imami *madrasa*, in AH 741(?)/1340(?) CE. See Dodd and Khairallah 1981: II:118; and *supra* in notes.

66. Cf. Y. Godard 1936: 367–369; Godard and Smith 1937: 351; Pinder-Wilson 2001: 158.

67. Cf. Edwards 1991: 64.

68. Blair 1985: 83. The *madrasa*'s funerary aspect – probably memorializing Sultan Saif al-Din (r. AH 556–558/1161–1163 CE, as noted *supra* in main text – would have very aptly combined with commemorating the fateful military victory on the heels of which he was assassinated.

69. Again, Thomas (2018: 122–123) briefly addressed the complex, but inaccurately states that it was "sponsored by Ghiyath al-Din" (cf. *infra* in main text). Ball (2019: No. 212) considered the two structures together, the western one being

a *madrasa* and the eastern one a mosque (cf. Figure 4.16). T. Lorain (Director of the Mission Archéologique Franco-Afghane – Bamiyan; MAFAB) has documented another example of two proximate domed structures indicating a larger original complex – possibly a *madrasa* – in the Bamiyan basin's Fuladi Valley. The site is now known as Khwaja Sabz Posh and has been attributed to the period of Ghaznavid or Shansabani dominance of the region. T. Lorain cited in Allegranzi 2020, n. xvii.

70. Cf. Blair 1985: 81–82; Allegranzi 2019b (forthcoming); Appendix, Afghanistan III: 4.

71. Cf. Appendix, Afghanistan III: 5d. Blair's (1985: 82) reading of the date was slightly corrected by Giunta (2010b: 177). The combination of Arabic and Persian in the same inscription was not uncommon in the epigraphy of the eastern Islamic lands during the eleventh through thirteenth centuries. Chisht's inscriptional program continued within the regional tendency of inscribing funerary and construction texts (and of course Quranic verses) in Arabic, while poetry and at times also dates were in Persian. Cf. Allegranzi 2015: 35; Allegranzi 2020, forthcoming.

72. Cf. Allegranzi 2019b (forthcoming); and Volume II.

73. I am grateful to Dr. Viola Allegranzi (pers. comm., September 2019) for sharing her ideas, to be published in a forthcoming work. See also Appendix, Afghanistan III: 4–5. Juzjani (vol. I, 1963: 354; trans. vol. I, 1881: 370) simply noted that Shams al-Din adopted the new *laqab* of Ghiyath al-Din, right after Saif al-Din's death and his own elevation to sultan and head of the Shansabani confederacy (i.e., eldest male descendant of 'Izz al-Din and his legal wife, rather than the Turkic maid – cf. Chapter 3). This would have occurred, then, in about AH 558/1163 CE. No doubt due to customary reverential respect toward overlords and patrons, Juzjani himself anachronistically referred to the Shansabanis with their regnal names even when narrating events that occurred prior to official entitlement, e.g., at the births of both Ghiyath al-Din and his younger brother Mu'izz al-Din (vol. I, 1963: 353ff.; trans. vol. I, 1881: 368ff.). However, the reverse anachronism at Chisht – of using an outdated *laqab* years after a regnal one was adopted – is unusual (Allegranzi, pers. comm., March and September 2019).

74. I am again grateful to Gwendolyn Kristy for obtaining satellite imagery of the structures at Chisht and sharing it with David Thomas and myself; this generated extremely informative discussions among us, which to me demonstrated the true intellectual generosity of these scholars.

75. Cf. Allegranzi 2019b (forthcoming); Appendix, Afghanistan III: 6–10.

76. While the "domed cube" form for tombs was in use by the tenth century in Transoxiana (cf., e.g., Grabar 1966: 17), apparently not all tombs had *mihrab*s. Tombs with *mihrab*s began to appear in the same period in the eastern Islamic lands: cf. *ibid.*, 21–22, 24, 32, 40; Patel 2015; and, of course, the discussion of Baba Khatim in the Introduction. See also Chapter 6.

77. See Blair 1992: 9, who also noted that the verses appeared frequently in writings of theologians with Mu'tazalite leanings, "as an allusion [to] and even declaration of their dogma." Cf. also Giunta (2010b: 124), who observed that these verses were "since the age of Mahmud [of Ghazna], the most frequently

attested verses in funerary inscriptions (all on marble) of [Ghazna] during the Ghaznavid and Ghurid eras."

78. Cf. *RCEA*, vol. 5 (1934) Nos. 1652, 1824, 1831, 1837, 1881, 1896; *RCEA*, vol. 6 (1935) Nos. 2052, 2058, 2061, 2094, 2119, 2135, 2143,2145, 2183, 2190, 2194, 2196, 2200, 2205, 2206, 2211, 2218, 2315, 2327, 2332, 2343, 2350, 2351, 2354, 2361, 2363, 2371, 2372, 2383, 2399. See also Appendix, Afghanistan III: 5d. It is noteworthy that verses falling within this range of Surat al-Iklhas (Q. CXII) were prominently quoted both on the renovations I have assigned to Mu'izz al-Din at Lashkari Bazar, and on the tomb attributed to Ahmad Kabir in the lower Indus region – cf. Appendix, Afghanistan VIII: 4; Pakistan III: 6, 20, 22; see also Chapters 5 and 6.

79. For a possible interaction between the Karramiyya and emergent Sufi orders during the eleventh century – specifically the commonality in *khan-qah*s between the two broad groups – see Trimingham 1971: 6–7; and esp. Böwering and Melvin-Koushki [2010] 2012: phase I. Modern and contemporary documentations of transhumant and nomadic communities have taken note of their interactions with spiritual centers or *khanaqah*s in the course of their migrations: e.g., Khazeni (2012: 137, 147–148) noted the eighteenth- and nineteenth-century visitations of shrines by Türkman nomads; Utas 1980: 64; Amiri 2020: 152–155. See also *infra* in main text.

80. Cf. Nizami 1998: 369. Precisely because of the described variety of origins and practices among Sufi masters as well as devotees (see *supra* in main text), a vast vocabulary accreted over time to refer to them: see esp. Ernst 1992: 5, 11; Green 2012: 8. Although removed in time from the twelfth century, Anooshahr's (2017) study of the Sufi Sheikh Muhammad Gauth Gwaliyari (fl. sixteenth century) of the Shattari order provides a fascinating example of the dissemination of a Sufi *tariqa*, in this case from early Safavid Iran to Mughal India, the shift in political engagement of the order over time and space, and some of the truly idiosyncratic rituals prescribed for gaining political power. For the Shattari *silsila*, see also Nizami 1998: 378–379.

81. See, *inter alia*, esp. Nizami 1961: 182–184; Nizami 1998: 377–378; Böwering [1991] 2011; Ernst and Lawrence 2002: 19ff; Auer, *EI³* (2016).

82. The lack of association between the monumental Chisht remains and the Chishtiyya would be further underscored by their purported adherence to poverty and eschewal of political connections, which presented a stark contrast to the Suhrawardiyya, for example. Cf. Nizami 1961: 177–180, 240–243; Trimingham 1971: 65–66; and Chapter 6. After Diez in 1924, Maricq and Wiet (1959: 69–70) were the second European scholars to analyze (however briefly) Chisht's architectural ruins and their inscriptions, but connecting the Chishtiyya only to the town rather than the remains of the monumental complex. Sourdel-Thomine (2004: 155) apparently drew the first direct association between the coalescing Sufi order and the ruined complex. See also Flood 2009a: 96–102. Nevertheless, this circumstantially derived and, in the end, most likely inaccurate association was already operative as of the later 1970s, e.g., in Utas' semi-anthropological fieldwork on Sufi orders in Afghanistan (Utas 1980: 65). Although circumspect, Blair (1985: 81–84) also implied an association of the Chishtiyya with the two surviving structures at

Chisht, describing it as the site "where the founder of the Chistiyya [*sic*] order of Sufis, Khwaja Abu Ishaq of Syria, had settled."

83. See esp. A. Knysh's (2017: 10ff.) insistence on this hyphenated usage in his dense and engaged recent history of Sufism.

84. As recently argued, particularly for the Suhrawardiyya, by Khan (2016: 3 and *passim*), who considered "the Shi'a milieu [as] probably the single most important factor that facilitated the rise of *tariqa* Sufism." Khan adhered to Trimingham's (1971: ch. I) tripartite developmental trajectory for Sufism generally throughout the Islamic world, with *tariqa* Sufism falling within 1100–1600 CE. See also Chapter 5.

85. Bulliet 1972: 41–43. The Shafi'is were not the sole *madhhab* to command affiliation, however distant, from spiritual masters perceived by some as Sufis. Indeed, texts by the famed Khwaja 'Abd Allah Ansari (AH 396–481/1006–1089 CE) of Herat, "one of the outstanding figures in Khurasan in the 5th/11th century," not only emerged from a Hanbali background, Khwaja's life overall demonstrates the true complexity of Sufism. The term "Sufi" was fluid, applied not only to renunciant masters – whose *khanqah*s were sometimes infiltrated by truly antinomian *qalandar*s (cf. Karamustafa 1994: 3–4) – but also to Hadith scholars and polemicists, at times varying over one lifetime. Cf. de Laugier de Beaureceuil [1982] 2011. See also Knysh (2017: 71–72ff.) for the "early Muslims ... subsequently co-opted into Sufism by its later proponents ..."

86. Sourdel-Thomine 2004.

87. Appendix, Afghanistan VII: 2, below. Cf. Ball 2008: 214–216 esp. for images and diagrams of the *minar*. Upon first analyzing the *minar*'s epigraphy, G. Wiet (1959: 27, nn. 1–2) has already noted that the recognizable phrase "help from Allah and imminent victory" ("... *nasr min Allah wa fath qarib*") had been common as of the later tenth century in Fatimid Ifriqiya (cf. also Sourdel-Thomine 2004: 128–129). Extricated from the remainder of the verse, the phrase seemed to take on a doxological function, appearing particularly on elite objects such as *tiraz* and ivory caskets – see, e.g., *RCEA*, vol. V (1934) Nos. 1622, 1811, 1841, 1846, 1847, 1848, 1849. It also appeared in architectural contexts, such as a stone construction text from Nablus, AH 410/1020 CE (*RCEA*, vol. VI (1935) No. 2310); and a marble restoration text at Cairo's Ibn Tulun mosque, dating to AH 469/1077 CE (*RCEA*, vol. VII (1936) No. 2716). Thereafter in the last decade of the twelfth century, Dodd and Khairallah (1981: II:132) listed its appearance at Delhi's Qutb Mosque in AH 587/1191 CE; see also Husain 1936: 109; and Volume II.

88. Juzjani vol. I, 1963: 357–358, 396 (trans. vol. I, 1881: 376, 449); see esp. Sourdel-Thomine 2004: 138ff.; Flood 2009a: 98; Flood 2009b: 93–94.

89. See Bulliet 1972: 203; Bosworth 1977; Malamud 1994: 39.

90. Cf. Bombaci 1966: 5ff.; Allegranzi 2015: 25ff.; Allegranzi 2019b (forthcoming); Allegranzi 2020; Appendix, Afghanistan V: esp. 3–4; and *infra* in main text.

91. Blair 1985: 84. Further and more specific parallels were drawn between the two architectural corpora by Pinder-Wilson 2001: 169–170. See also (*inter alia*) Ball 2020 (forthcoming).

92. Cf. Meisami 1999: 16–17. Although referring to the Mu'izzi *ghulam*s active

in the north Indian plains in the 1190s, Siddiqui's (2006: 14–15) observations are applicable to the higher rungs of the Turk slave market: "[T]hey were Persianized generals having nothing in common with the freeborn Saljuq or Ghuzz Turks … They were brought up as Muslims and trained in Muslim cultures and manners; the education of a slave was a good investment because an educated and cultured slave fetched a higher price."

93. Mahmud Ghaznavi was surely acting upon the imperative of transplanting strong Arabo-Persianate imperial foundations into Zabulistan and contiguous regions as he employed the "strong-arm methods" of virtually coercing scholars and literati to bejewel his court (cf. Bosworth [1963] 2015: 34, 129–130; Bosworth 1968a: 36, 38 and *passim*). See also Meisami 1999: 50ff. for a discussion of the possible reasons behind Mahmud's ambivalence toward Persian literature.

94. The areas of nomadism and seasonal transhumance were discussed in Chapter 2. For the Ghuris (and among them the future Shansabanis), their *garm-sir* areas in particular – in southern Ghur and Zamindawar, perhaps touching upon Sistan – would likely have offered a number of shrines or *ziyarat* dating from at least the eleventh century and likely earlier, though each of them surely fluctuated over the centuries in terms of their ability to attract pilgrims, depending on climate and shifts in river courses, among other unforeseeable factors. Cf. Ball 2019: e.g., Nos. 597/1114, 1264/2182, 1267.

95. For twentieth-century nomadic interactions with the shrines around Chisht, see esp. Utas 1980: 64. According to Khazeni (2012: 147–148), in the eighteenth–nineteenth centuries Central Asian Türkman nomads integrated Naqshbandi Sufi tombs in their migrations, particularly during their seasonal contacts with towns or market centers for commercial purposes. See also *supra* in this chapter. The reverse process of *murshid*s traveling to see their disciples in pastoralist communities – usually in the autumn, the traditional period of socializing when the harvest was in – was documented among the Helmand Baluch: cf. Amiri 2020: 153.

96. This was the case notwithstanding Green's (2019: 17) observation that "the gradually increasing numbers of [Saljuq- and Ghaznavid-patronized] madrasas and *khanaqah*s spread the use of written Persian across new *geographical* frontiers" (my emphasis): such proliferation of institutions of learning did not necessarily create greater Persian or Arabic literacy across lifeway frontiers, i.e., the nomadic/transhumant populations.

97. The absence of Persian on Shansabani-patronized architecture was noted by O'Kane (2009: 30) and Allegranzi (2019b [forthcoming], 2020), both of whom compared the Shansabani inscriptional corpus with that of the sophisticated and courtly Ghaznavids. By the time of the Ghaznavids' ascendancy in the eleventh century, Persian – both in verse as well as prose – had undergone a centuries-long rise alongside Arabic, particularly in courts of the eastern Islamic *ecumene*. By the dawn of the new millennium, specifically modern or "new" Persian had made inroads into the monopoly Arabic once had as *the* language of religious and literary textual production (cf. also Allegranzi 2015: 26–30, 32–35; Allegranzi 2019a, vol. I: 19–23; Green 2019: 9–10; and *supra* in main text).

CHAPTER 5

The "Ports of India": Ghazna and Bust-Lashkari Bazar

We witness in this chapter the coalescence of the third Shansabani lineage at Ghazna, and the architectural manifestations of this process at the erstwhile Yamini capital and its contiguous areas. Stylistic developments evidenced in the architectural fabrics of the principal palace at Ghazna (Figures 5.1–5.7), and of many of the built remains at Bust (Figures 5.9–5.13) and Lashkari Bazar (Figures 5.14–5.28), serve as plausible evidence of extensive Shansabani-period renovations there, most probably commissioned by Mu'izz al- Din himself. There is very little evidence, however, of new construction. From the surviving remains, we might surmise that, at least among some segments of the Ghazna Shansabani elites, the large-scale interventions at all of these sites were indications of a shift toward greater sedentism – perhaps better described as an emerging tendency toward residence in permanent rather than textile structures. These indices of change appear to have been carried even further upon the Shansabanis' entry into the north Indian *duab*, and will be treated in detail in Volume II.

Juzjani cursorily noted Mu'izz al-Din's summer and winter capitals (*dar al-mulk-i tabistan* and *dar al-mulk-i zamistan*) as Ghazna *and* Khurasan, and eventually Lahore *and* Hind (respectively). Thus, the sultan's residence was not limited to a principal city, but rather also encompassed its vicinity, not unlike the Saljuqs' royal encampments around Isfahan and other major urban centers.[1] Such an arrangement could have accommodated the requirements of both imperial expansion *and* the echoes of a transhumant lifestyle, facilitating campaigns in the respective areas where climate and resources were amenable. It is worth re-emphasizing that the Yamini–Ghaznavids also changed locations according to summer and winter: they had tended to avoid the cold and snowy winters of Ghazna, instead undertaking campaigns to the north Indian plains when the oppressive heat of summer was absent there.[2] It might appear that the Ghazna Shansabanis' movements followed in the seasonal footsteps of their predecessors. But in fact, these two dynastic elites converged upon these *modi operandi* through vastly different historical trajectories – the Shansabanis emerging from nomadism/transhumance within their scions' lifetimes, and the Ghaznavids adapting an inherited Perso-Islamic courtly culture to their specific circumstances (cf. Chapter 1).

It also bears reiteration that, throughout this book's analyses of architectural groups, prior scholarship has been invaluable as a starting point. Similarly here, the Italian, French, and other surveys and excavations at Ghazna and Bust-Laskhari Bazar obviate the need for exhaustive descriptions; they provide the solid bases for tracing the transformations of Ghazna and Bust-Lashkari Bazar into "new" imperial spaces.

Eastern Impulses

The long "house arrest" inflicted on the sons of Baha' al-Din by the infamous 'Ala' al-Din Husain *Jahan-suz*, their paternal uncle, ended only after the latter's death: perhaps helping to heal the familial breach, 'Ala' al-Din's son and successor Saif al-Din freed his cousins, even inviting the elder Shams al-Din into his retinue, while Shihab al-Din went to yet another paternal uncle, Fakhr al-Din Mas'ud, the patriarch of the Bamiyan lineage.[3] Fatefully, Shams al-Din participated in the campaign against the Oghüz in Gharjistan in AH 558/1163 CE, when Saif al-Din met his tragic death at the hands of the treacherous 'Abbas ibn Shish. It was this unforeseen event that led to Shams al-Din's crowning as Sultan Ghiyath al-Din at Firuzkuh in the same year (cf. Chapter 1).

Shihab al-Din's trajectory toward rulership was more protracted and uncertain. Juzjani implied to his readers that a stinging rebuke by Fakhr al-Din Mas'ud of his nephew's complacency finally stirred the young man's ambition. Upon sensing Fakhr al-Din Mas'ud's deep displeasure, Shihab al-Din apparently left Bamiyan for his newly crowned brother's court at Firuzkuh, where he surely had hopes of attaining independence and even distinction. When these hopes were not immediately fulfilled, Shihab al-Din withdrew to Sistan, taking refuge for about a year in Zaranj at the court of Malik Shams al-Din Nasri (r. AH 559–564/1164–1169 CE) – apparently a cruel tyrant to his own people, but eager to preserve good relations with his overlords the Firuzkuh Shansabanis.[4] Sultan Ghiyath al-Din coaxed his younger brother back to Ghur and bestowed on him the Istiya area, which lay in the vicinity of Tiginabad/Old Qandahar (cf. Chapter 3): it had been the appanage of the late patriarch Saif al-Din Suri (d. AH 543/1149 CE) during the early days of the Shansabanis' regional dominance. Eventually, Shihab al-Din was given the bigger prize of Tiginabad/ Old Qandahar itself. But this territory came with challenges due to its proximity to the Oghüz encampments in Ghazna and its environs.

With historical hindsight, it becomes clear that avuncular rebuke *alone* was not responsible for Shihab al-Din broadening his horizons, just as appeasing sibling tensions in itself was insufficient for Sultan Ghiyath al-Din to mobilize Firuzkuh's forces toward the conquest of Ghazna. In addition to these intimate impetuses, a sequence of specific events had to converge for the Shansabanis' long-awaited triumph over the erstwhile Yamini capital. In what could be termed a historical irony, it was the Oghüz who provided a pivotal catalyst for this victory: they had not only occupied Ghazna by *c.* AH 556/1161–1162 CE, their further encampments and disruptive movements ranged beyond Zabulistan into Zamindawar (map, p. xvi).[5] Thence, these disruptions touched Shihab al-Din's new territories of Tiginabad and its vicinity. His repeated confrontations with the Oghüz in turn brought him in contact with the once great capital: as the apparent core of the Oghüz's regional presence, the city necessarily had to have their encampments eradicated for a final solution to the "Oghüz problem."[6] In AH 568–569/1173 CE, the definitive routing of the Oghüz from Ghazna – the "Port of India" – established a third Shansabani lineage with the crowning of Shihab al-Din as Sultan Mu'izz al-Din.[7]

Past scholarship has tended to absorb the Ghazna Shansabanis into an overarching "Ghurid" dispensation. But considering them as a deputation acting on the orders of (or otherwise subordinate to) the Firuzkuh Shansabanis leads to a historical misperception: based on this assumption, the renown of the successful India campaigns usually accrues to the Firuzkuh branch as the senior lineage.[8] In Chapters 1 and 3, we already took note of the multiple geo-cultural, socio-economic, and indeed unforeseen historical factors – along with the possibility of intimate emotional interventions – that collectively presented alternatives to the textual interpretations (such as Juzjani's) of Shansabani expansion as a process centrally orchestrated from Firuzkuh. In addition, throughout the preceding chapters we have also seen the powerful *physical* indices of centrifugal tendencies among the Shansabani lineages, as they crafted imperial infrastructures in keeping with the differing cultural geographies they each inhabited.

Although a small market town in the mid-first millennium CE, Ghazna had grown to a sizeable commercial center by the tenth century. The settlement was the principal waystation on the Kabul–Qandahar route, with access to the Kurraman and Gomal passes (cf. Chapter 1) and the middle Indus's alluvia (map, p. xv). Moreover, with the Rutbils' dominance of Zabulistan and the contiguous region of Zamindawar possibly as late as the tenth century, Ghazna also became a major Buddhist monastic center. As was the case with Bamiyan, the site's command of an important node within a political geography combined with its Buddhist aspects, making it a busy commercial and pilgrimage center "securing the Central Asian and Iranian relations with India."[9]

It would not be unreasonable to propose, then, that the Shansabanis of Ghazna underwent a further differentiation as an increasingly independent lineage, akin to the Shansabanis of Bamiyan. Similar to their agnates, the Ghazna Shansabanis inhabited a distinct historical–cultural geography within Afghanistan: rather than the links of Firuzkuh with

greater Khurasan and its commercial emporia to the west, or the centrality
of Bamiyan as the nodal convergence of east–west and north–south communication routes, the commercial and cultural networks encompassing
Ghazna and the region of Zabulistan in general had long been oriented
toward the east and India (see Chapters 2 and 3). For Muʿizz al-Din
and his loyalists and dependents, then, the conquest of Ghazna in itself
was not enough; as had been the case for the Yamini–Ghaznavids before
them, the imperial machinery established here could be sustained only if
the location was used as a springboard for expanding eastward (see also
Chapter 6).

All in all, once again we see that the Shansabani lineages of the 1170s
CE would be better understood as a *confederacy* rather than a singular unit,
with the three agnatic branches having disparately expanding ambitions
(map, p. xv), but nominally subject to overlordship. Although anthropological analysis of modern tribal organizations in Afghanistan is plentiful –
perhaps most notably by the "accidental" architectural historians Glatzer
and Casimir – the question of confederation has been directly addressed
among the Basseri tribe and its larger Khamseh confederacy, their periodic
rivals the Qashqai confederacy, and the Bakhtyari tribes – all nomadic
pastoralists in south-central Iran. [10] While these studies have highlighted
differing circumstances and equally varied processes of confederation, they
also underscore confederation as *inherent* to the nomad–urban continuum: kinship-based and other groups tended to come together, that is,
confederate, as a response to shifting circumstances, often at the instiga-
tion of a leader and his lineage.[11] The Bakhtyari example may provide the
most useful parallel to the Shansabanis, as even in regions where imperial
presence was not constant or strongly perceptible – certainly the case in
Ghur – "confederations form[ed] ... in response to an external stimulus –
typically, a need for common defense or an opportunity for expansion or
conquest".[12]

There are some indications that Muʿizz al-Din only grudgingly acknowledged the seniority of the Firuzkuh branch of Shansabanis.[13] Moreover,
Ghiyath al-Din's ambitions of expansion into Khurasan apparently precluded any independent share therein for the Shansabanis at Bamiyan,
or for the lately established Ghazna lineage embodied in Muʿizz al-Din,
his dependents and military followers. The Ghazna Shansabanis had little
choice but to direct their energies toward India. Muʿizz al-Din and his
*ghulam*s were now oriented eastward, at least in part swept up in the
geo-historical momentum of their predecessors, the Yamini–Ghaznavids.
Collectively, Muʿizz al-Din's military successes – and arguably, also his
reverses – were to have more palpable, local, and transregional ramifications over the ensuing millennium.

Ghazna and Bust–Lashkari Bazar[14]

The multi-faceted significances of the Shansabani conquest of Ghazna cannot be sufficiently emphasized. This event was pivotal in the Shansabanis' overarching historical trajectory: the taking of the city certainly resulted in the irretrievable (if painfully gradual) demise of the Yamini–Ghaznavids, and the eradication of the Oghüz nomads from Zabulistan and Zamindawar introduced new horizons for Shansabani territorial expansion. And as already noted, the establishment of the collateral Shansabani lineage at the old Yamini capital not only expanded the Shansabani confederacy, it opened the way to India.

This chapter argues that the conquest of Ghazna could have had additional, meaningful consequences on a more intimate plane: the architectural remains at Ghazna and its attendant regions evince signs of a shift in lifeways for the new Shansabani lineage *vis-à-vis* their Firuzkuh cousins – a shift toward greater sedentism, which would also echo in the architectural remnants of their campaigns beyond the Indus into the north Indian plains (see this Volume's Introduction, and Volume II).

However, akin to the archaeological remains at Jam-Firuzkuh (cf. Chapters 3 and 4), any analysis of the documented architectural fabric as well as the still to be studied material remains of Ghazna and Bust-Lashkari Bazar also requires important caveats. It bears reiterating that the Mongol campaigns along the Zabulistan–Zamindawar corridor (map, p. xvi) and their various aftermaths, unfolding during the third through eighth decades of the thirteenth century, certainly disturbed what had survived of these urban and palatial sites' historical remnants.[15] In addition, given their multiple occupational layers, the Ghaznavid sites of southern Afghanistan comprised vast archaeological complexes requiring collaboration among a range of specialists from the pre-Islamic centuries onward. The sheer scale of these sites has meant that, despite many seasons of survey and excavation – cumulatively spanning the 1920s through 1970s[16] – they were worked upon only partially before political and military insecurity in Afghanistan made work there extremely difficult, if not impossible. Thus, like Jam-Firuzkuh, what is presented here must be viewed as provisional, until exploration in these areas can be reinitiated.

There are nonetheless important observations that *can* be made. Archaeological and art-historical analyses of the remains of Ghazna and Bust–Lashkari Bazar certainly revealed distinguishable phases of architectural intervention at these localities. As discussed in detail below, the generally accepted sequence of events is that the existing Ghaznavid-period buildings and complexes at Ghazna and Lashkari Bazar – Bust having been less studied – suffered partial destruction by fire. At Lashkari Bazar the destruction was evidenced on two occasions, the first attributable to 'Ala' al-Din *Jahan-suz*'s sacking in AH 544/1150 CE, and the second perhaps to the Mongol incursions of the early to mid-thirteenth century, after which apparently neither of these sites fully revived.[17]

The series of events recorded in Juzjani's *textual* narrative seem to concord with the evidence presented by *material* culture – further discussed below. The author's account of the destructive visitations of 'Ala' al-Din Husain *Jahan-suz* upon Ghazna and Lashkari Bazar in AH 544/1150 CE, could have resulted in the first signs of destruction by fire at both sites.[18] The partial date of AH 55x/1156–1165 CE in Lashkari Bazar's South Palace inscription (Figure 5.17) (cf. below) would then indicate intervention(s) at least at *this* site after the destruction. As outlined in Chapter 3, in AH 553/1158 CE 'Ala' al-Din Husain had demanded and eventually wrested Tiginabad/Old Qandahar from the recently defeated Ghaznavid sultan Bahram-shah. This Shansabani territorial gain effectively disrupted the Ghazna–Zamindawar route, preventing the later Ghaznavid sultans from easily traveling to Bust and Lashkari Bazar. The fragmentary date of Lashkari Bazar's South Palace inscription, then, could refer to work undertaken sometime *after* AH 553/1158 CE, when 'Ala' al-Din prevailed yet again over the Ghaznavid forces; this date falls within the decade-long span of the incomplete inscription.[19] But, as argued below, the substantial and large-scale renovations at Lashkari Bazar should be re-dated to a period after the final Shansabani takeover of Ghaznavid territories as of *c.* AH 569/1173 CE and onward.

Ghazna

Recent analyses focused on the marble, terracotta, and stucco architectural fragments ensuing from the Italian excavations at Ghazna – conducted more than a half-century ago (1950s–1960s) – are finally creating a fuller picture of Shansabani interventions here. Prior to these new studies, Shansabani traces at Ghazna appeared to have been extremely meager, limited to a reoccupation of an elite residence in the Rauza hills, overlooking the city's central area (Figure 5.1): here, among the many rediscovered objects was a store of remarkably well-preserved lusterware, which ultimately gave their name to the site as the House of Lusterware. The objects were collectively interpreted as dating to the late twelfth or early thirteenth century, definitely after the first Shansabani sack of Ghazna in AH 544/1150 CE, and likely also after the final victory of AH 569/1173 CE.[20] However, ongoing studies of terracotta architectural decoration, recovered from Ghazna's central palace, profoundly alter the perception of an ephemeral Shansabani presence in the city. It seems that the Shansabani interventions at the palace were more commensurate with their momentous occupation of the capital, and especially the crowning of Shihab al-Din as Sultan Mu'izz al-Din, who effectively appropriated – though with some needed territorial consolidation – the central Ghaznavid holdings encompassing

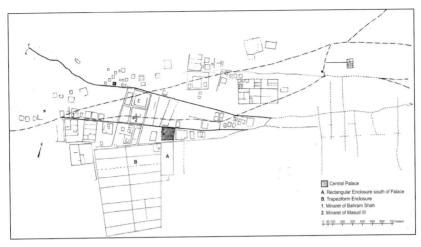

Figure 5.1 *Ghazna, plan from aerial photograph of western part of city.*
From Scerrato 1959: fig. 17.

Zabulistan and Zamindawar, through the easternmost borders of Sistan
(maps, pp. xv and xvi).

The central palace of Ghazna (Figures 5.1 and 5.2), to the east of the
minar of Mas'ud III – and surely falling in the shadow of the originally
much taller tower (Figure I.20) – was previously attributed to this sultan
through a web of tangential associations. But recent re-examination of
the archaeological data from this vast complex has led to a new understanding of the palace, encompassing a considerably more complicated
architectural development likely beginning at least a half-century before
the reign of Mas'ud III (r. AH 492–509/1099–1115 CE), and unfolding *via*
several identifiable phases.[21] Ongoing studies of the palace's terracotta and
stucco architectural decoration strongly suggest that a visible and perhaps
substantial mark was left there in the wake of the Shansabani victory of
AH 569/1173 CE as well.

More than three thousand terracotta and nearly seven hundred stucco
elements from the palace's decoration – many with epigraphy – are undergoing detailed study and recontextualization within the palace's various
building phases (Figures 5.3–5.5). These decorative components still carry
traces of paint, indicating their original polychromy.[22] Among the terracotta remains, several broken pieces retrieved from the northeastern
and southern zones of the palace's large central courtyard carried decipherable epigraphic fragments. Some inscriptions were simple doxologies
(e.g., *al-mulk li-llah*), echoing the simplicity of the inscriptional frieze
likely running along the walls of the palace's principal northern entrance.[23]
However, other fragments have been read as being part of a longer frieze
containing the *kunya* and *laqab*s of Sultan Mu'izz al-Din.[24]

These fragments bear an undeniable resemblance to the partial epigraphic

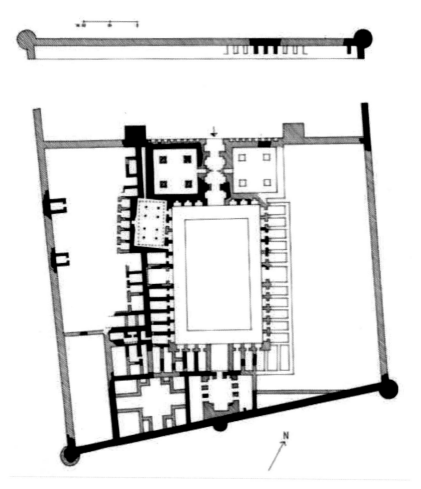

Figure 5.2 *Ghazna, central palace, plan of excavated areas and hypothetical reconstructions. After Giunta 2020: fig. 2.*

bands still *in situ* during the Italian excavations of the 1960s (Figure 5.6): the chunky, bold letters with decorative stem terminals standing out against a background of small, triangular solids and voids – emphasized further by being painted. Moreover, these terracotta epigraphic bands formed a stark, formal contrast to the refined marble dado below (Figures 5.6 and 5.7), which had consisted of rectangular panels carrying arabesques and floral motifs bordered by a continuous horizontal band of elegant floriated Kufic or *naskh*[25] (cf. below). Thus far, then, analyses of the painted terracotta epigraphic fragments from Ghazna's central palace point to very marked renovations of at least parts of the main courtyard's façade, probably executed during the reign of Mu'izz al-Din (r. at Ghazna AH 568–602/1173–1206 CE) and perhaps even shortly after the Shansabani conquest of the city.

Indeed, Mu'izz al-Din's notable renovations of the Ghazna palace

Figure 5.3 *Ghazna, central palace, fragment of painted stucco decoration. From Allegranzi 2021: fig. 3, detail 1 (repr. of IsMEO inv. no. C5612).*

Figure 5.4 *Ghazna, central palace, fragment of painted stucco decoration. From Allegranzi 2021: fig. 3, detail 2 (repr. of IsMEO inv. no. C2719).*

Figure 5.5 *Ghazna, central palace, fragment of painted stucco decoration. From Allegranzi 2021: fig. 3, detail 3 (repr. of IsMEO inv. no. C5784). Ghazna, central palace, fragment of painted stucco decoration.*

Figure 5.6 *Ghazni, palace of Mas'ud III (1099–1115), excavation site, dado remnants. © Photograph Josephine Powell c. 1960. Harvard Fine Arts Library, Special Collections.*

Figure 5.7 *Detail of Figure 5.6, Ghazni, palace of Mas'ud III, juxtaposition of Ghaznavid- and Shansabani-period revetments.*

were not limited to the additions of large, bold terracotta epigraphy towering above their predecessors' more refined marble dadoes. The 1950s Italian excavations at the site also unearthed approximately 160 glazed tiles, square or polygonal in shape, with molded decorative motifs. The glazes on the tiles were varied, their colors including green, yellow, brown, red, blue, and turquoise of various hues. The molded decoration encompassed a wide array of geometric, floral-arabesque, zoomorphic, and pseudo-epigraphic motifs. The relatively small number of these glazed tiles led the archaeologists to suggest they were used as punctual decoration, inspired by grid patterns on woven textiles of the time, which framed various floral, geometric, and animal motifs. Given the tiles' retrieval from the uppermost layers of the Ghazna palace, as well as a few at the House of Lusterware, Scerrato[26] opined that the tiles were manufactured most probably in the late twelfth and early thirteenth centuries, thanks to a local tile industry that had apparently survived 'Ala' al-Din's onslaught, the Oghüz occupation, until the definitive Shansabani conquest of the city. Thus, the new Shansabani sultan of Ghazna, seeing personified before him the value of monumental and distinctive imperial patronage, was reviving the glory of his newly acquired "capital" in his own way (cf. below and Chapter 6).

Bust

The expansive stretch southwestward from Ghazna to the citadel and settlement of Bust had long marked a busy thoroughfare. At least from Parthian times or the early centuries of the Common Era, the town of Bust and its imposing citadel had functioned as an important waystation, from whence branched a northward route into Zamindawar, touching upon southern Ghur; and another one eastward toward Tiginabad/Old Qandahar, and ultimately back to Ghazna again. Possibly since the time of the Samanids (tenth century), and almost certainly since that of Mahmud Ghaznavi's father Sabuktigin (d. AH 389/999 CE), a series of large residential complexes – and likely a few commercial buildings – had appeared on the Helmand's left bank several kilometers north of Bust, essentially creating an identifiable area *ex urbis*. This exurb's historical name of al-'Askar – now Lashkari Bazar, discussed below – could indicate that, during various moments prior to the eleventh century, the vast plain had been used for military encampments, which were dependent on nearby Bust.[27]

Given the Shansabani presence at Tiginabad/Old Qandahar as of the later 1150s (cf. above and Chapters 1 and 3), control of the entire corridor from Ghazna through Bust would have been advantageous, and was probably accomplished sometime shortly after the Shansabanis' fateful victory at Ghazna in AH 569/1173 CE.[28] Ensuring this region's integration firmly within the Shansabani ambit was not only impelled by its previous Ghaznavid connections; securing the Zabulistan–Zamindawar corridor was surely necessary for the newly titled Sultan Mu'izz al-Din's further kingly aspirations and territorial ambitions.

Bust itself was a significant fortified town, following the regionally widespread layout of a royal enclave (Pers. *arg*) ensconced within a larger walled settlement (Pers. *shahristan*) (Figure 5.8). Within these type of plans, the more secure enclaves were frequently at the outer edge of the citadel,

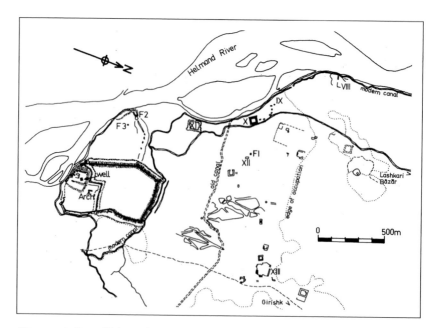

Figure 5.8 *Bust, Helmand Province, Afghanistan, general plan. From Ball 2019: No. 149.*

Figure 5.9 *Bust, citadel and arch, general view from northeast. © Photograph Josephine Powell c. 1960. Harvard Fine Arts Library, Special Collections.*

and perhaps even naturally protected on one flank by a river or cliff.[29] In the case of Bust, the layout followed the rising topography: two concentric enclaves were placed at the walled settlement's northwest corner, with the innermost enclave at a high promontory overlooking the town and plains below (Figures 5.8 and 5.9).[30] The enclosed enclaves decreased in accessibility, with the royal palace and other imperial machinery probably located within the highest and best protected area (Figure 5.9).

Understandably, both Bust and Lashkari Bazar had received lavish architectural attention from at least two of the great Ghaznavid sultans, Mahmud (r. AH 389–421/999–1030 CE) and his son Mas'ud I (r. AH 421–432/1030–1041 CE) during that dynasty's period of apogee. As these areas continued to play a significant role in the governance and control of Zamindawar and contiguous areas and byways, Mu'izz al-Din would have likely embarked on significant interventions there after the conquest of Ghazna in AH 569/1173 CE. But the nature of these interventions can only be tentatively understood with the currently available archaeological and other data. Further, based on the Shansabani patronage at Ghazna discussed previously – and on what we will see at Lashkari Bazar below – it is reasonable to propose that at Bust also, there was extensive reuse of the pre-existing Ghaznavid-era structures. New constructions were less frequent, however, as detailed forthwith.

The location of the mysterious "galleried" well within the upper enclave of the Bust citadel underscores this structure's importance (Figures 5.8, 5.10 and 5.11). Several of the well's seven stories were underground and led to a water catchment area.[31] However, no epigraphic finds or other chronological indicators have been associated with the structure, so that we can only conjecture as to its foundation date and period of use. While

Figure 5.10 *Bust, citadel, ruins, interior, seven-story well: man stands among upper floor arches. © Photograph Josephine Powell c. 1960. Harvard Fine Arts Library, Special Collections.*

predictably constructed of mud and baked brick, the well's extremely rare if not unique configuration appears to have no precedents in western Eurasia, but its form and function are comparable to the numerous stone stepwells throughout the Indian subcontinent.

The stepwell tradition extended from the seventh through at least the sixteenth centuries throughout the subcontinental region – and evidently also included Muslim patrons of what were essentially "civic" works for community benefit.[32] Numerous stepwells dating to the eleventh–twelfth centuries still survive throughout the north Indian *duab*, and would have surely been encountered during both the Ghaznavids' (*c.*1000–1040 CE) campaigns into northern India, as well as the Shansabanis' own forays as of the late 1170s, and more consistently in the 1190s – either or both of which could have served to transport the general concept from Hindustan to Zamindawar. Given the Bust structure's overall proportions and *structural* affinity with Ghaznavid- and Shansabani-patronized architecture, the well could be tentatively dated to the eleventh–twelfth centuries.[33]

Figure 5.11 Bust, citadel, ruins, interior, seven-story well: man stands among upper floor arches. © Photograph Josephine Powell c. 1960. Harvard Fine Arts Library, Special Collections.

The oft-illustrated, distinctive monumental arch inside the lower enclave of Bust (Figures 5.9, 5.12 and 5.13] would appear to be one of the few, new Shansabani foundations at Bust, perhaps along with the galleried well just discussed. The arch would certainly qualify as a project of imperial proportions, though its context and ultimately the impetus behind it both remain mysterious.[34] The arch's interpretation as a monumental entrance addorsed to a large mosque or other complex was refuted early on by the fact that elaborate stucco decoration graced its eastern and western surfaces, indicating its viewability from both sides (Figures 5.12 and 5.13).[35] Its more elaborately decorated eastern face carried Q. II: 127,[36] and, depending on the calligraphic spacing, possibly other verses as well. This part of Surat al-Baqara describes Abraham

> … raising the foundations of the House and Ismael [saying], "Our Lord, accept this from us. Indeed You are the Hearing, the Knowing."

Figure 5.12 *Bust, arch, south pillar, carved decoration. © Photograph Josephine Powell c. 1960. Harvard Fine Arts Library, Special Collections.*

Figure 5.13 *Bust, arch, front face and intrados, north, carved geometric decoration and inscription, detail. © Photograph Josephine Powell c. 1960. Harvard Fine Arts Library, Special Collections.*

On stylistic analysis particularly of the arch's epigraphy and geometric decoration, Sourdel-Thomine dated it to the third quarter of the twelfth century, basing the date range on comparisons with the epigraphy of Shah-i Mashhad.[37] As we saw in Chapter 4, the period of construction for that *madrasa* complex likely spanned a decade, from AH 561 to 571 (1165–1176 CE). Thus, a date for the arch at the end of this range (*c.* AH 570/1175 CE) would not be implausible.

Several aspects of the Bust arch suggest that it served as a triumphal monument commemorating an event falling within Shansabani ascendancy in the region. In his re-surveying of the Bust citadel, T. Allen proposed that the arch was part of a reconfiguration of the principal, ceremonial entrance into the lower enclave, which in itself served as a gateway to the upper more insulated area.[38] The arch was thus a public – even "civic" – structure, and also evinced an association with royalty and its ceremonial expression. With the proposed date of *c.* AH 570/1175 CE for the arch as a basis, it is conceivable that this monument was erected in virtual simultaneity with the Jam-Firuzkuh *minar*, acting as the other half of the dyadic declaration of the Shansabanis' final triumph over the Ghaznavids and the Oghūz, and the possession of the former's imperial centers (see Chapter 4). But rather than memorializing a Shansabani triumph that essentially acknowledged Ghiyath al-Din's seniority as at Firuzkuh, the Bust arch appeared to focus on the newly crowned Sultan Muʿizz al-Din. Given the far-reaching ramifications of this fateful victory, it is more than likely that some type of memorialization of it was also erected at their enemies' old capital of Ghazna but has since been lost.

Furthermore, as was the case with the Jam-Firuzkuh *minar* – discussed in Chapters 3 and 4 – the Bust arch's surviving epigraphy also stands out for the uncommonness of its content: according to Blair's authoritative study of the monumental inscriptions of the eastern Islamic lands, Q. II: 127 and its proximate verses were not documented in these regions, at least through the early twelfth century, and they appeared but rarely elsewhere.[39] But the ʿulamaʾ and other intellectuals within Muʿizz al-Din's ambit could easily find Qurʾanic verses appropriate to any occasion. Given the rarity of these particular verses, it seems that they were selected with specific intent. The actual message of the verse(s) is an invocation of divine blessing on a new "house," even a royal house – especially apropos here. The monument overall, then, could conceivably be proclaiming the establishment of the third Shansabani lineage and the new rule of Sultan Muʿizz al-Din throughout the Ghaznavids' erstwhile territories.

Lashkari Bazar

Very few firmly dated architectural elements – which were *not* portable, unlike coins, ceramics, and other objects – have been recovered at any of the three sites forming the subject of this chapter. One significant find was the inscriptional panel affixed to the southern façade of Lashkari Bazar's great South Palace (Château du Sud), *in situ* during the French-led excavations there in the 1960s (Figures 5.14, 5.15, 5.17): it bore the partial date of AH 55x, corresponding to the decade of 1156–1165 CE. Based on this dating, the renovations at Lashkari Bazar have been attributed primarily to the decade after 1150 CE, an attribution I propose to modify in the rest of this chapter.

Sourdel-Thomine's rigorous analyses of the architectural epigraphy and decoration at Bust and Lashkari Bazar resulted in compelling – if at times debated – conclusions.[40] Her deep knowledge of epigraphic styles and decorative iconographies, spanning virtually the entire Persianate world of the eleventh through fourteenth centuries, permitted convincing comparisons between the inscriptional and ornamental programs of Lashkari Bazar's South Palace and relevant Saljuq, Ghaznavid, and Shansabani parallels. Also taking into account the South Palace inscription's partial date of AH 55x/1156–1165 CE

(Figure 5.17), she attributed the renovations at the Palace to the years following 'Ala' al-Din Husain *Jahan-suz*'s destructive path through the region of Ghazna and Zamindawar.[41]

Sourdel-Thomine systematically identified the following mid-twelfth-century changes there (Figures 5.14 and 5.15): additions of epigraphic and other decorative elements to the Palace's principal southern façade, which Schlumberger contrasted to the "nudity" of the other façades (Figure 5.16)[42]; a *mihrab* in the Mosque of the Forecourt (Figure 5.18), part of the long esplanade approaching the Palace from the south; renovations of all four façades of the Palace's large central court (Figures 5.14, 5.19); the stucco revetment, epigraphic program, and *mihrab* of the oratory of Hall I (Figures 5.20–5.22), north of the central court; the stucco

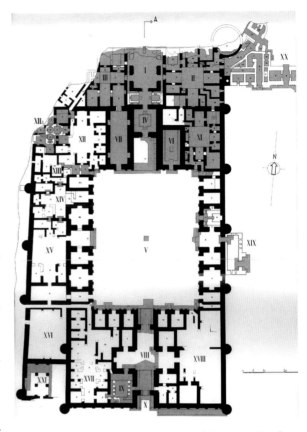

Figure 5.14 *Lashkari Bazar, Helmand Province, South Palace, plan of excavations. From Schlumberger 1978: pl. 4.*

imitating cut brickwork in Apartment II, northeast of the central court; and the molded stucco and incised geometric decoration in Building XX, a northeastern annex to the Palace. Sourdel-Thomine also attributed to Shansabani patronage a new decorative program in Residence XIII (Figure 5.23), the so-called "Palace of Racquets," close to Bust on its northeastern flank. Since very little other definitively datable evidence has been recovered elsewhere in this vicinity, ceramic and epigraphic finds – together with archaeological stratigraphy and references in historical texts – have been the principal clues for the aforementioned chronological sequence.[43]

With much less information at her disposal than we have now, Sourdel-Thomine applied the South Palace inscription's partial date of AH 55x/1156–1165 CE (Figure 5.17) to *all* later interventions within the complex. According to this chronology, the works would have taken place within the period immediately after 'Ala' al-Din Husain *Jahan-suz*'s mpaign of destruction at the site and throughout the Zabulistan–Zamindawar corridor in AH 545/1150 CE. To be sure, the partially surviving inscription could have referred to *some* work undertaken at the complex during this decade.

Figure 5.15 *Lashkari Bazar, South Palace, southern façade. From Sourdel-Thomine 1978: pl. 52b.*

Figure 5.16 *Lashkari Bazar, Summer (or Grand) Palace, ruins, exterior, southern wall, detail. © Photograph Josephine Powell* c. *1960. Harvard Fine Arts Library, Special Collections.*

Figure 5.17 *Lashkari Bazar, South Palace, south portal detail.*
From Sourdel-Thomine 1978: pl. 54d.

But given the long list of renovations, and particularly the nature of some of them, it is improbable that all the projects listed above were executed in the late 1150s. Major renovations would have been unlikely just a few years after 'Ala' al-Din *Jahan-suz*'s willful destructiveness there and in its environs, even though he might have ultimately planned to occupy the area – along with Ghazna itself – but ultimately left this to his next campaign in the region (cf. Chapters 1 and 3).

Angular Kufic doxologies, such as *al-mulk li-llah*, were added to the palace's main southern façade (Figures 5.15 and 5.16), as well as the interior court façades (Figures 5.14, 5.19). Such simple epigraphy was a far cry from the sophisticated verses on the dadoes of the Ghazna palace's central court, composed in various meters of the Persian poetic tradition and possibly glorifying the Ghaznavids' dynastic lineage and expounding legal and theological tenets. But at least in content – the rarity of *in situ* remains at Lashkari Bazar prevents stylistic comparison – the simple sayings *were*

Figure 5.18 *Lashkari Bazar, South Palace, Mosque of the Forecourt (photograph c. 1950s).* © *Courtesy of Musée des Arts Asiatiques-Guimet, Paris.*

Figure 5.19 *Lashkari Bazar, South (or Grand) Palace, ruins, courtyard.* © *Photograph Josephine Powell c. 1960. Harvard Fine Arts Library, Special Collections.*

Figure 5.20 *Laskhari Bazar, South Palace, Oratory F, north of central courtyard. From Schlumberger 1952: pl. XXXII, 3.*

in keeping with the later renovations of the same Ghazna palace (Figures 5.6 and 5.7), credited to Muʿizz al-Din (see above).[44] It would not be unreasonable to suggest, then, that the addition of these new decorative programs on the various surfaces of the palace were undertaken within the last quarter of the twelfth century (*c.* AH 570/1175 CE), after the definitive Shansabani conquest of the region, while Muʿizz al-Din was casting himself as successor to the Ghaznavids.

A half-century of new studies has added further nuance to Sourdel-Thomine's conclusions. Specifically, a distinctive South Palace renovation can now be more definitively pinpointed to the last quarter of the twelfth century. The *ivan*-like yet quite intimate prayer space directly abutting the magnificent Audience Hall I to its southwest (Figures 5.14, 5.20), known as Oratory F, surely boasted an exquisite decorative program in its day.[45] On its north and south walls were stucco dadoes with intertwining geometric lozenges framing arabesque-floral motifs, horizontally topped by a running frieze beginning with *Bismillah* on the north wall. The frieze continued with Q. XLVIII:1–6 (al-Fath) extending onto the

Figure 5.21 *Lashkari Bazar, South Palace, Oratory F, stucco decoration (photograph* c. *1950s). © Courtesy of Musée des Arts Asiatiques-Guimet, Paris.*

south wall, with possibly more verses from the same Sura (Figure 5.21). Oratory F's focal point was of course the west-oriented *mihrab* (Figure 5.22), flanked by several vertical bands of undulating floral arabesques and epigraphy: the band rectangularly framing the *mihrab* contained Q. II:256 (al-Baqara); in the niche's hood was Q. CXII:1–4 (al-Ikhlas) in repetition; and simple doxologies such as *al-mulk li-llah* were repeated in the niche's lower part. The overall decorative program of the Oratory can be aptly characterized as one evincing a *horror vacui*, "the compulsion to cover – almost to swamp – every available space of wall surface with decoration."[46]

We saw in Chapter 4 that several Qur'anic verses in Shansabani-patronized architectural decoration were otherwise rare or undocumented, both in the eastern Persianate regions and in the wider Islamicate lands. To be sure, Q. II:256 – the verse following the practically ubiquitous and revered Ayat al-Kursi (Q. II:255) – also appeared with some frequency in architectural epigraphy, extending from Palermo to Delhi and spanning the tenth through sixteenth centuries CE.[47] However, verses from Q. XLVIII had evidently first appeared in the eastern Islamicate world on the *minar* of Mas'ud III at Ghazna (*c.* AH 503/1110 CE), and within the mosque at Barsiyan in the Isfahan oasis, dated by inscription to AH 528/1134 CE. I subsequently proposed that, in the 1160s–1170s, the Ghazna decorative program had been the underlying inspiration for Shah-i Mashhad's epigraphy, particularly the inscriptional program gracing the complex's imposing south façade. Intriguingly, we shall see in Chapter 6 that the Sura's beginning verses appeared on yet another Shansabani-associated

Figure 5.22 *Lashkari Bazar, South Palace, Oratory F, mihrab.*
From Sourdel-Thomine 1978: pl. 147b.

building: the Tomb of Sadan Shahid (late twelfth century) near the city of
Multan in the middle-Indus region.[48]

Equally noteworthy are all four verses of Q. CXII, which were common
primarily in epitaphs from around the western Indian Ocean; however,
as discussed in Chapter 4, the Sura tended to be absent in the eastern
Islamicate world or the Persianate lands through at least the early twelfth
century. It was as of the 1160s that the verses appeared at Chisht, inside
the western domed structure associated with the Firuzkuh Shansabanis –
perhaps appropriately, as the complex likely had funerary associations.
Finally, the abundant use of doxologies, which helped to create the decorative *horror vacui* of Shansabani-patronized structures, had been well
attested from the mid-twelfth century onward.

Thus, it would appear that Q. XLVIII's first several verses, along with
the four verses of Q. CXII (often repeated) had become familiar to the
Firuzkuh Shansabanis, and were also employed thereafter in the Lashkari
Bazar renovations, which were within the purview of Sultan Mu'izz al-Din

and the Shansabani lineage newly established at Ghazna. In fact, both sets of verses came to be integral parts of the architectural decorations of buildings along the Indus's banks during the later 1170s–1180s, buildings constructed in the wake of the eastward campaigns of Mu'izz al-Din and the Ghazna Shansabanis.[49]

The use of these verses within the epigraphic program of the South Palace's Oratory F is significant for at least two reasons: since they came into limited circulation in the eastern Persianate regions – especially Afghanistan – with the architectural patronage of the Firuzkuh Shansabanis as of the 1160s CE, their presence at Lashkari Bazar renders unlikely the earlier date that Sourdel-Thomine suggested, *viz.* following 'Ala' al-Din Husain's violent passing through the region more than twenty years before. Instead, the verses' appearance points to a date *as of* the late 1170s certainly for this part of the South Palace, which would coincide with Mu'izz al-Din's interventions there. But these inscriptions hold additional importance for our purposes: adopting what could have been a group of Qur'anic verses coalescing in the architectural patronage of his older brother, it appears that the newly crowned Shansabani Sultan Mu'izz al-Din also left an intentional architectural mark upon his own hard-won imperial prizes. Indeed, this particular epigraphic association continued into Shansabani-associated architecture throughout the Indus's alluvia, as we shall see in Chapter 6.

A New Imperialism

This chapter's examinations of architectural remains attributable to the Shansabanis at Ghazna, Bust, and Lashkari Bazar enable several observations regarding the emergence of a third Shansabani lineage. Perhaps most tantalizingly, they reveal the new imperial *modus operandi* of the recently crowned Sultan Mu'izz al-Din and the Ghazna Shansabanis. These observations will be extremely important as we examine their expansionist activities farther eastward, initially throughout the plains and valleys intimately associated with the Indus River (Chapter 6), and ultimately in the north Indian *duab* (cf. Volume II).

Upon "zooming out" to a bird's-eye view of Sultan Mu'izz al-Din's establishment of Shansabani rulership over the Yamini–Ghaznavids' core imperial regions, we cannot help but note that, architecturally speaking, Shansabani authority was expressed primarily *via* a marked renovation and reuse of the existing built environment rather than the creation of it *ex novo*: palatial and other complexes were not razed and then erected anew; instead, distinguishable interventions in already present architectural fabrics declared the latter's new Shansabani affiliations. Thus, the commanding courtyard of Ghazna's principal palace received new revetments *above* (Figures 5.3–5.7) – rather than replacing or atop – its Ghaznavid-period marble dadoes, creating a discernible contrast between what was already there and what was added in the course of Mu'izz al-Din's renovations. At Lashkari Bazar, the mosque of the South Palace's forecourt quite possibly received a new *mihrab* (Figure 5.18), in this case covering its Ghaznavid-era predecessor, but the mosque itself was not entirely built anew. Additionally, this palace's southern exterior façade (Figures 5.15 and 5.16) and enormous central courtyard (Figures 5.14, 5.19) also acquired new decorations and revetments, and the intimate oratory abutting Audience Hall I (Figures 5.20–5.22) displayed Shansabani renewal in its decoration, perhaps especially in its epigraphic program (cf. above and below). It was only at Bust that we detected new construction datable to the late twelfth-century conquest of the region by Mu'izz al-Din (Figures 5.8–5.11), but this also occurred amidst what appeared to be pre-existing built remains that continued in use (e.g., Figures 5.12 and 5.13). Thus, Ghazna, Bust, and Lashkari Bazar all entered Shansabani possession largely through appropriation, rather than erasure and new construction.

We might term this specific mode of building empire *re-inscription* – a process that we will encounter in the Ghazna Shansabanis' forays ever farther eastward (see Chapter 6). Re-inscription encompassed the reuse and at times repurposing of societal assets such as the built environment, usually through new endowments (Ar.-Pers. *waqf*) toward architectural and infrastructural maintenance made by the newcomers in perpetuity. Another fundamental component of re-inscription would have been the imperial prerogative of minting coinage in the name of the victorious ruler. While continuity with the standards and iconographic fields of existing coinage preserved stability, the stamping of the incoming ruler's titles and name declared the ascendancy of a new imperial authority. 'Ala' al-Din Husain *Jahan-suz* had done just this upon his second conquest of Ghazna, continuing the typology of the late Ghaznavid ruler Khusrau Shah's (r. AH 552–555?/1157–1160? CE) coins but substituting his own titles and name. His nephew Mu'izz al-Din followed suit: he maintained the standards and fields of late Ghaznavid coinage, replacing the titles and names with his own – perhaps even airing the family's "dirty laundry" by revealing to the world his resentment against submission to his older brother, Sultan Ghiyath al-Din of Firuzkuh.[50]

Collectively, the architectural interventions at Ghazna and other imperial Ghaznavid sites indicate not only that enough had survived in recuperable condition despite 'Ala' al-Din Husain's depredations a quarter-century before, as well as the decade-long nomadic encampments of the Oghüz; they underscore a subtle process occurring in plain sight: re-inscription, rather than erasure and re-building, appears to have been Mu'izz al-Din's preferred method of claiming his conquests and building empire. To be sure, reoccupation of perfectly usable spaces was economical and expeditious, but it is still significant how *little* the Shansabanis actually built anew in the ex-Ghaznavid domains. I argue in Chapter 6 that, as the Ghazna Shansabanis successfully campaigned eastward, they implemented this preferred mode of building empire through re-inscription on an exponentially larger scale. Along the valleys and plains intimately linked with the Indus River, Mu'izz al-Din's followers commissioned small, usually funerary structures, but their conquests of the region at large were substantiated principally through the re-inscription of entire urban environments and landscapes, and the minting of coins – all of which had previously been *in*scribed with a Yamini–Ghaznavid presence for nearly two centuries.

Whether through annexation of previously unclaimed (or at least unmarked) territories, or the above-described process of re-inscription, a fundamental resource for the implementation of the Shansabanis' imperial expansion was the repository of religious, theological, and legal knowledge possessed by the 'ulama' and other scholars in their retinues. Arguably, among the more palpable indices of these intellectual elites' participation in empire-building were the epigraphic programs gracing Shansabani-patronized architectural projects. Chapter 4, proposed that, in addition to the skilled manual labor required in monumental building, equally skilled *intellectual* labor was instrumental in crafting the overall imperial affiliations and specific religio-theological messages these monuments proclaimed.

The architectural complexes associated with the Firuzkuh Shansabanis exhibited these intellectual laborers' contributions in the meaningful religious/theological content, which could have been selected only by scholars knowledgeable in the Qur'an, Hadith compilations, and exegetical literature. Thereafter, Mu'izz al-Din apparently carried forward the inscriptional corpus – albeit small, as it can only be gleaned from the Firuzkuh Shansabanis' building projects that still survive – into Zabulistan and Zamindawar as he laid claim to the Yamini–Ghaznavids' imperial centers. Moreover, the nusualness of the epigraphic content on the magnificent arch at Bust could indicate the intellectual elites' continued contributions to a growing corpus of favored epigraphy. Mu'izz al-Din and/or the intelligentsia in his service evidently implemented the small epigraphic corpus associable with the Shansabanis in these annexed territories – and also farther eastward throughout the Indus's alluvia. Here, with re-inscription being the Ghazna Shansabanis' principal mode of imperial consolidation, the architecture they *did* patronize, as well as these buildings' epigraphic programs, both become that much more significant (see Chapter 6).

A closer, more granular perspective on the architectural interventions discussed throughout this chapter yields additional, valuable observations. Overall, the Ghazna Shansabanis' re-inscriptions took place in royal and palatial contexts: these encompassed the probable renovation of the "Palace

Figure 5.23 *Lashkari Bazar, Palais aux Raquettes, ruins, exterior, north entrance. © Photograph Josephine Powell c. 1960. Harvard Fine Arts Library, Special Collections.*

of Racquets" close to Bust (Figure 5.23); and the distinctive interventions at the Ghazna palace (Figures 5.2–5.7), as well as at Lashkari Bazar's South Palace (Figures 5.14–5.22). All of these projects most likely would have been motivated by the intended utilization of these complexes – at the very least as "stages" for state ceremonial, if not also as residences.

Although there was no specific intervention attributable to the Shansabanis within the South Palace's Audience Hall I at Lashkari Bazar (Figures 5.24–5.28), we recall that abutting it immediately to the south was the exquisite Oratory F (Figure 5.20), which bore nearly unequivocal marks of Shansabani-period renovation. Hall I as the architecturally dominant part of the overall complex would have been extremely important for Mu'izz al-Din, the new ruler following in the footsteps of the Yamini–Ghaznavids. Considered by D. Schlumberger to be "without any possible doubt, the principal place of pageantry, the great audience chamber of the royal residence [i.e. the South Palace]," the Hall also initiated the kilometer-long, north–south central axis of the complex as a

Figure 5.24 *Lashkari Bazar, South Palace, Audience Hall I (north end of palace). From Schlumberger 1952: pl. XXX.*

Figure 5.25 *Lashkari Bazar, South Palace, Audience Hall I, detail of stucco revetments (photograph c. 1950s). © Courtesy of Musée des Arts Asiatiques-Guimet, Paris.*

whole (Figure 5.14).[51] It thereby exemplified and made real the ceremonial power that the Ghaznavid sultans had wielded as part of Perso-Islamic kingly comportment, which helped them to retain command of an empire with both westward *and* eastward ambitions. The Hall's gateway location over the vast complex of the South Palace (Figure 5.14); its lavish decoration (Figures 5.25 and 5.26), including a noteworthy epigraphic program and the famous frescoes of courtly figures in procession; and its commanding vistas over the Helmand (Figures 5.27 and 5.28) all surely instantiated an even grander and encompassing notion of kingship than thus far experienced by Mu'izz al-Din at the court of his uncle at Bamiyan, and that of his older brother at Firuzkuh – and we recall that he had spent a year in Sistan at the court of Malik Shams al-Din Nasri (see above in this chapter).[52] Mu'izz al-Din's conquests of Ghazna and Lashkari Bazar, then, personified the proverbial shoes he would have to fill if he also had aspirations of extensive dominions radiating in various directions from Zabul–Zamindawar (maps, pp. xv and xvi).

All of these indications of a transition toward a court-based and possibly more sedentist lifestyle for the newly titled Shansabani sultan of Ghazna collectively create a stark contrast to the absence of palatial architecture at Firuzkuh. Such a divergence is not unprecedented, however: at

Figure 5.26 *Lashkari Bazar, South Palace, Audience Hall I, detail of paintings. From Sourdel-Thomine 1978: pl. 9a.*

Bamiyan, the Shansabani lineage headed by Fakhr al-Din Mas'ud (r. AH 540–558/1145–63 CE) seemed to be cleaving toward palatial living, signaling an adaptive accommodation of the localized cultural and political economy of their immediate environment (cf. Chapter 3). At Ghazna also, then, the newly established Shansabani lineage appeared to be adopting the prevalent modes of kingship and the most effective modes of its actuation, which they *de facto* had inherited from their Yamini–Ghaznavid predecessors.[53]

The processes that appear to be evidenced in the architectural traces of the Shansabani conquest of the Ghaznavids' erstwhile territories should *not*, however, be considered instantaneous or unidirectional. While Shansabani renovations and modifications of the Yaminis' palatial

Figure 5.27 *Lashkari Bazar, South (or Grand) palace, ruins, looking south along Helmand River. © Photograph Josephine Powell c. 1960. Harvard Fine Arts Library, Special Collections.*

complexes – some undertaken on a grand scale – could be telling indications of the newcomers' occupation of these complexes, we would do well to bear in mind that any shift toward palatial habitation could have been sporadic, and ultimately would have been gradual: after all, ten years can be a momentous period of change in the life of an individual, even as it is virtually invisible in historical time. Perhaps most importantly, any shift from "tent to palace" did not have to be wholesale or irreversible. As captured in the concept of the nomad–urban continuum, nomadic–pastoralist and otherwise transhumant groups became *more* or *less* sedentist depending on prevalent circumstances and other contingencies (cf. Introduction and Chapter 2).

In the face of a discernibly growing tendency toward palace dwelling among the Ghazna Shansabanis and the possible waning of seasonal migrations in distance and/or frequency, the advantageous "cultural capital" of nomadism was surely not forgotten. For example, the greater

Figure 5.28 *Lashkari Bazar, ruins, general view: Central Palace, Pigeon House, and North Palace, seen from South Palace site looking north along Helmand River. © Photograph Josephine Powell c. 1960. Harvard Fine Arts Library, Special Collections.*

ease with which nomadic and transhumant groups conceptually and physically understood large swaths of contiguous cultural geographies, changing topographies, and varying climates; and their ability to traverse these expanses efficiently and *en masse*, were all acquired skills that were extremely valuable in following the geo-historical momentum of their empire-building Yamini predecessors.[54] And these conceptual skills would be not only useful but fundamental for the sustenance of the Shansabanis of Ghazna, as explored further in the next chapter.

Notes

1. Cf. Durand-Guédy 2013b: 328–335; Peacock 2015: 143, 166–172; see also Chapter 3.

2. See Juzjani vol. I, 1963: 405 (trans. vol. I, 1881: 489); Inaba 2013: 77–78 and *passim*; Allegranzi 2014: 100–101. See also Volume II.

3. Juzjani vol. I, 1963: 346, 353 (trans. vol. I, 1881: 357, 369–371).

4. Cf. Bosworth 1994: 398–399; O'Neal 2013: 58–59; Chapter 1, above.

5. Cf. Bosworth [1977] 1992: 124–126; Biran 2005: 48–52. The last author noted that the years of the Oghüz in Khurasan is "the middle period of Qara Khitai history (1144–77) … [and] certainly the least documented one," so that more is known of the conflicts between the Oghüz and the Saljuqs, whose unraveling permitted the nomads to roam unhindered in some areas, including Ghazna, until their routing by the Shansabanis.

6. Juzjani vol. I, 1963: 396 (trans. vol. I, 1881: 448–449).

7. As noted by Bosworth ([1977] 1992: 111–114), the eastern reaches of the Perso-Islamic world during the twelfth–thirteenth centuries, particularly the regions of Afghanistan and parts of Central Asia, received comparatively little attention in the surviving works of Arabic- and even Persian-language authors, the latter being "more concerned with such pressing questions as the break-up of the Great Seljuq empire … and the menaces from Central Asia of the Qara Khitai and the Khwarazm-shahs." Thus, Ibn al-Athir and Juzjani provide a rather skeletal chronology for the events leading to the Shansabani capture of Ghazna (AH 569/1173–1174 CE) and Gardiz (AH 570/1174–1175 CE), and the crowning of Shihab al-Din as Sultan Mu'izz al-Din at Ghazna. Cf. Juzjani vol. I, 1963: 357–358, 396 (trans. Vol. I, 1881: 376–377, 449); Bosworth [1977] 1992: 125; Edwards 2015: 96; O'Neal 2016a; Chapter 1.

8. The earlier scholarly summation of Mu'izz al-Din's status at Ghazna as one of "gilded vassalage" (Scerrato 1962: 265) has gradually shifted, so that Flood (2009a: 89ff.) defined "the apogee of Ghurid power" as an unusual arrangement of "the brothers rul[ing] in a condominium" (but cf. H. A. Khan [2016: 24] describing Mu'izz al-Din as "the second in command of the empire, who ruled in the name of his elder brother and regent"). As we have seen throughout this book, however, the centrifugal fragmentation of patrimony was a common and even usual tendency among many nomadic–pastoralist societies. Cf. also Introduction & *infra* in this chapter's concluding section.

9. See Bosworth [1963] 2015: 36; Planhol [2000] 2012. Ball (2020) noted that the Rutbils politically co-existed with the Kabul-based Turk-shahis, but their relationship is still to be clarified. See also Bombaci 1957: 248–250; Bombaci 1966: 4ff.; Lewis 1995: esp. 115ff.; Chapter 3.

10. E.g. Glatzer 1983; Glatzer and Casimir 1983; Barth 1961; Beck 1983; Garthwaite 1983.

11. Such was the case with the Basseri within the Khamseh confederacy, brought together by a charismatic and enterprising merchant ensuring safe caravan passage by allying five (Ar. *khamsa*) tribes under his aegis (cf. Barth 1961: 72, 86–90); and the late eighteenth-century Afsharid mobilization of various Turkic groups and their eventual confederation as the Qashqai to confront and negotiate later Qajar domination (Beck 1983: 287–289).

12. Cf. Garthwaite 1983: 314–321.

13. Cf. esp. O'Neal's (2020: 210–211) analysis of Mu'izz al-Din's silver coinage issued at Ghazna between AH 569 and 581 (1173–1185 CE), where he is named

السلطان الاعظم – effectively appropriating his older brother's title while referring to him with none. See also Chapters 3 and 4.

14. For brief descriptions see Ball 2008: 190–193, 240–246 (including Bust); for additional maps, plans, and bibliography cf. Ball 2019: Nos. 149, 358, 685; and for a summation of the extant evidence, see Thomas 2018: 59–60, 125–127, 132–135.

15. Upon being pursued by Chinggiz Khan in *c.*1220, the Khwarazm-shah Jalal al-Din's (r. AH 617–628/1220–1231 CE) recourse to Ghazna – his appanage, where he rallied troops – drew the Mongols there, where he defeated advance Mongol forces. There was destruction at Ghazna due to the confrontation, including the killing of its inhabitants and destruction of its *jami'*; but ultimately the Khwarazm-shah fled toward the Indus and the Mongols annihilated his forces on its banks in late 1221 (Jackson 2017: 80, 159, 165). Thus, it is unclear whether Ghazna would have received "more savage treatment than the vengeful Ghurid ruler 'Ala' al-Din Husayn *Jahan-suz*" had visited upon the city in *c.* AH 544/1150 CE (*ibid.*, 180). But even after Chinggiz Khan looked to new conquests beyond Afghanistan, the remaining bands of Negüderi or Qara'unas – former contingents of Mongol forces – held the entire territorial swath from Zabulistan (including Ghazna) eastward into the upper Indus valleys in their apparently lawless grasp until the early fourteenth century, making it a "no man's land." Cf. *ibid.*, 148, 183, 195, 197; also Bernardini 2020.

16. Prior to the 1950s and the beginning of Italian surveys and excavations in the Ghazna region, and the French archaeological activity in the vicinity of Bust-Lashkari Bazar, A. Godard had done initial photographic documentation at Ghazna in the 1920s, as seen in DAFA archives at the Musée Guimet, Paris (access kindly granted by M. J. Ghèsquiere, July 2018). J-C. Hackin's archive of the 1930s–1940s provided photographs of Bust and its environs: cf. *Lashkari Bazar* (1978): planches 42, 46. See also Ball, Bordeaux et al. 2019: 403.

17. For the two episodes of fiery destruction at Lashkari Bazar, see Schlumberger 1978: esp. 31, 37, 41; Sourdel-Thomine 1978: 21, 29, 36, 39, 54; Ball and Fischer 2019: 473; cf. also *infra* in main text. For the post-Mongol abandonment of Bust, see Allen 1988: 55, 56.

18. See *supra* in notes for Lashkari Bazar. For signs of destruction at Ghazna, see *supra* in notes for Mongol and post-Mongol impacts; also Bombaci 1966: 5ff.; Scerrato 1959: 52; Scerrato 1962: 265–266; Giunta 2005: 474ff.

19. See above in main text, and Chapters 1 and 3 for southward expansion by the Shansabanis of Firuzkuh, after the burning and destruction of Ghazna and Lashkari Bazar by 'Ala' al-Din *Jahan-suz* (AH 544/1150 CE).

20. Scerrato 1959: 49–52; also Thomas 2018: 126–127.

21. The initial association of the palace and Mas'ud III began with Bombaci's study of a marble fragment found in the modern *ziyarat* on the western perimeter of the palace mound: the fragment consisted of the top portion of a pointed arch with semi-circular lobes within, carrying an inscription of Q. II: 256 (the Throne Verse) along with the *kunya* and *laqab* of the sultan (cf. Bombaci 1966: 33ff., 9–20). Bombaci already questioned whether "the palace was really built by Mas'ud III, or was only readjusted by him." Recent re-examinations of the excavation records indicate that the palace's

irregular quadrangle itself may have been a repurposed caravanserai or other structure; thereafter, it underwent at least five phases of modification, the penultimate one being the addition of a large royal oratory on the western perimeter (approximately where the modern shrine stood): Giunta 2010b: 123–125; Giunta 2020: 164ff.; Allegranzi 2014: 111–112; Allegranzi 2019a, vol. I: 54–56; Allegranzi 2020a; Ball and Fischer 2019: 475–477; Laviola 2020: 28–29; and Appendix, Afghanistan V: 2.

22. Some of these finds had already been inventoried in the 1950s Italian Archaeological Missions to Ghazna, e.g., Scerrato 1959: fig.18. See also Giunta 2005: 479–480 and fig. 5; Artusi 2009: 121–122 (quoting Scerrato), 128; Laviola 2018. See also Appendix, Afghanistan V: 4.

23. The marble dado panels recovered from the palace's main entrance area have been interpreted as part of a decorative and epigraphic program specific to this part of the complex; cf. Appendix, Afghanistan V: 1. They are stylistically related to the dadoes from the central court, and generally dated to the same period (Appendix, Afghanistan V: 3–4). See Flury 1925: 74; Giunta 2010b: 125.

24. See esp. Giunta 2010b: 126–127; Allegranzi 2020a.

25. Cf. esp. Bombaci 1966: 19–29; also Giunta 2005: 478ff.; Giunta 2010b: 126–127. O'Kane (2009: 22–23 and n. 72) followed Bombaci's initial study of the dado slabs and characterized them as a (fabricated) genealogy of the Ghaznavid sultans beginning in pre-Islamic Iran, referencing *Shah-nama*. Recent re-examination of the slabs, and the recovery of others that had been repurposed as tomb markers, reveal other possibilities: there was likely more than one poetic composition comprising the inscriptional bands, and the genres of both the lengthy *mathnavi* and the panegyric *qasida* were likely represented. Notably, references to Islamic juridical and theological ideas indicate that at least some of the subject matter was religious and/or political in nature. Cf. Allegranzi 2015: 26ff; Allegranzi 2019a, vol. I:145–167; Allegranzi 2020a.

26. Scerrato 1962: 265–267.

27. See esp. Allen 1988: 55–58; Allen 1990: 26; Ball and Fischer 2019: 469–471.

28. Juzjani simply noted that "Mu'izz al-Din subdued the environs of Ghazna," and that the following year (AH 570/1175 CE) he conquered Gardiz. Cf. Juzjani vol. I, 1963: 396 (trans. vol. I, 1881: 449).

29. Although hesitant to consider this urban configuration as a "peculiarity" of Khurasan, Rante (2015: 17–20) brought attention to this overall layout in the development of several settlements throughout the vast region, ranging from Marv through Nishapur and dating from the Achaemenid through late Sasanian periods (first–seventh centuries; cf. also Collinet 2015: 127–128 and fig. 3; Laleh et al., 2015: 118; Ball, Glenn et al., 2019: 272–283). With the Arab conquests of Central Asia during the eighth century, further quarters (Ar. *rabad*) emerged to distribute the settled and incoming populations, with the Arabs usually within the enclaves. For early Islamic Afghanistan, see Franke 2015: esp. 81–84 and figs. 5, 27; Ball 2019: e.g., Nos. 99, 522, 874, 1006.

30. See Sourdel-Thomine 1978: 63ff.; Allen 1988: 58–60; Ball and Fischer 2019: 474, 544; Ball 2019: No. 149.

31. See esp. Ball 2019: No. 149 for elevations of the partly underground structure. As we have seen in Chapters 2–4, pre-modern textual sources were less than specific about the structures encountered on military campaigns – and in the case of the Ghaznavid campaigns, formulaic mentions of "idol-breaking" occluded rather than laid bare the details of engagement with the built environment.

32. Cf. Patel 2004: 54 and n. 24, 108–109, pls. 44–45.

33. For early stepwells in Gujarat – an area that had been pivotal for both Mahmud Ghaznavi in AH 416/1025 CE, and Mu'izz al-Din about 150 years later (cf. Chapter 6), see, *inter alia*, Jain-Neubauer 1981: 19–21 (and figs.). A parallel *numismatic* example of cultural practices moving west from the Indian subcontinent are *jitals*, one minted with the stamp of Nimruz: the location of the mint remains ambiguous, however, as the term denoted a region rather than a specific place as of the eleventh century; meanwhile, the city name of Zaranj was replaced by *shahr-i Sijistān* by the tenth century, even as *Nimruz* continued to be a region. By the thirteenth–fourteenth centuries, *Nimruz* had come to replace *shahr-i Sijistan* as a mint name. Thus, the question remains whether *Nimruz* and *shahr-i Sijistan* were effectively the names for Zaranj, changing over time (Bosworth 1994: 37, 367, 426, 441). Although Nimruz/Sistan was considered "the most westerly mint to adopt the jital" (R. and M. Tye 1995: 50 and Nos. 123, 124), O'Neal (pers. comm., July 2020) concluded that another example with the mint name of Marv would indicate the slightly farther western and also northern reach of the *jital* type. Cf. Nicol 2005: 176; and Volume II.

34. The ambiguity of the structure's *raison d'être* cannot be clarified by the remnant of the construction text, which followed the Qur'anic inscription(s) on the left side of the arch's east face (cf. *infra* in main text, and notes). Although this fragmentary text contained the expected phrase "… (he who) brought to completion this … in the year …," the referent for the definite article was unclear, except possibly a final *ta marbuta*. Sourdel-Thomine's (1978: 65) suggestion of *qubba* would certainly imply a memorial function for this arch, but she proposed this reading as tenuous. See Appendix, Afghanistan II.

35. Sourdel-Thomine (1978: 63) had assumed that the arch formed the entrance to a large building. After re-surveying the site, however, Allen (1988: 59–60, fig. 2) proposed that the arch could not have been a building entrance: not only were both faces of the arch decorated; additionally, insufficient space around the extant monument made it impossible for a mosque of commensurate proportions to have been constructed there. See also Ball and Fischer 2019: 474.

36. The publication (Sourdel-Thomine 1978: 64–65) notes Q. II: 121 as the cited verse; upon verifying the epigraphy and the author's translation, however, the correct citation would be Q. II: 127 – surely a simple typographical error.

37. Sourdel-Thomine 1978: 66.

38. Allen 1988: 59–60.

39. Blair 1992. The verses have been recorded at Qasr Kharana, Jordan and dated AH 92/710 CE; and on the minaret of Aleppo's *jami'* in floriated Kufic, datable to AH 483/1090 CE (the verses' *naskh* rendition on Delhi's 'Ala'-i Darwaza is

dated AH 711/1311 CE). See esp. Dodd and Khairallah 1981: 2:5. Also Appendix, Afghanistan II.

40. Schlumberger disagreed with dating portions of the South Palace to Shansabani presence, e.g., Hall I's oratory (see below in main text), which he placed during Khwarazm-shahi occupation *c.*1215 (noted by Sourdel-Thomine 1978: 39). In his review of the three-volume publication *Lashkari Bazar* (appearing at last in 1978, after Schlumberger's death), A. D. H. Bivar (1980) also disagreed with Sourdel-Thomine's attribution of Shansabani dates to many parts of the sprawling site. Notably, "in a treatment to be published elsewhere" the reviewer planned to "query ... the ascription of the [Bust] Arch to Ghurid times" (Bivar 1980: 386); to my knowledge his proposed re-dating of the monument to the reign of Mahmud Ghaznavi has not yet been published. Dani (2000: 559) also dated the "magnificently decorated arch" to the eleventh century without further argumentation. Due to the current lack of access to the site, and Sourdel-Thomine's analysis being the most thorough to date, her argumentation is broadly followed here (cf. *infra* in main text).

41. Cf. Sourdel-Thomine 1978: 42–45, 63–68. We have already discussed (cf. *supra* in main text) the monumental arch inside Bust's lower enclave (Figures 5.9, 5.12 and 5.13), a newly built rather than renovated structure to which she assigned a later twelfth-century date.

42. Schlumberger 1978: 20.

43. For the dating of the Lashkari Bazar renovations principally to AH 55x/1156–1165 CE, cf. Sourdel-Thomine 1978: 10, 21, 29, 39, 54, 57; also Appendix, Afghanistan VIII: 2. For Ghazna, see esp. Scerrato 1959: 42–52; Scerrato 1962: 267.

44. At Ghazna, some marble fragments datable to the Ghaznavid occupation of the site also carried simple Arabic sayings. See Giunta 2010b: 125; Allegranzi 2015: 27–28. These have to be contextualized, however, within the much longer, sophisticated Persian poetic verses probably gracing the entire interior surface of the palace's large central court. Cf. Appendix, Afghanistan V: 3–5; VIII: 1.

45. Compare the similar configuration of a small oratory ensconced within a large public space at the Saljuq waystation of Robat Sharaf (near Sarakhs, eastern Iran) – cf. Chapter 1.

46. Ball (2020) applied this description to both Ghaznavid and Shansabani architectural decoration, distinguishing it from the more restrained decoration on Saljuq-patronized buildings. Cf. Sourdel-Thomine 1978: 42, 44–45; Appendix, Afghanistan VIII: 4.

47. See Dodd and Khairallah 1981: 2:9–15.

48. As also noted in Chapter 4 (cf. notes), verses 1–3 of the Sura survive only in Cairo: at Mashhad al-Juyushi (AH 477/1085 CE); and the citadel of Salah al-Din (AH 578/1183–1184 CE), and nowhere else in the Islamicate regions. Cf. also Chapter 6; and Appendix, Pakistan II: 1.

49. See Appendix II, Pakistan III; and Chapter 6.

50. See esp. O'Neal 2016b; O'Neal 2020; Chapter 1. It is noteworthy that, despite the Ghaznavid minting of *jitals* at Ghazna and Bust from the reign of

Sabuktigin through that of Khusrau Malik, there are no known *jitals* attributable to Mu'izz al-Din from these mints (the farthest western ones being from Taliqan and Kurraman) (map, p. xv). Although, there were rare copper issues, which however diverged considerably from the *jital* type: cf. R. and M. Tye 1995: 41–49, 54 and, e.g., Nos. 83, 85, 87, 88, 89eI, 90, 95, 98, 101, 104, 105eI, 106, 107eI, 108, 112, 115, 190, 191.

51. Cf. Schlumberger 1952: 258–267; Schlumberger 1978: 38–41, 61–64 (my trans.); Appendix II, Afghanistan VIII: 3.

52. It is noteworthy that at Zaranj, Mu'izz al-Din would have witnessed the special status accorded to intellectual dignitaries, who were in fact courted to lengthen their stays by the Maliks of Sistan, in part to expound on points of religio-juridical import before an assembly. Such was the case with Juzjani's own grandfather Minhaj al-Din 'Uthman, as well as Ahwad al-Din Bukhari. See Juzjani vol. I, 1963: 277–278, 396 (trans. vol. I, 1881: 189–191, 447); Bosworth 1994: 398–399.

53. Among Mu'izz al-Din's other possible adoptions from his Ghaznavid precursors might have been his "collecti[on of] a corps of expensively trained slaves to make his writ run and his treasures and territories safe from clannish co-sharers" (Habib 1992: 7). From among the thousands of *bandagan-i Turk* Mu'izz al-Din likely purchased, he had select favorites – e.g., Taj al-Din Yildiz, Nasir al-Din Qabacha, Qutb al-Din Aibek, Baha' al-Din Tughril – all of whom he came to regard as his own children. Cf. also Chapter 2, and Volume II.

54. In his analysis of the military advantages possessed by nomadic groups, Irons (2003) employed the concept of "cultural capital" to encapsulate the modes of organization and skills that developed as a result of specific activities (e.g., livestock raiding). In describing the Mongols, Burbank and Cooper (2010: 4) observed their possession of "the technological advantages of nomadic societies – above all, a mobile, largely self-sufficient, and hardy military – [and] capacious notions of an imperial society ..." (cf. also Chapters 1, and 6). These studies are also extremely useful in pointing to the possible *conceptual* advantages emerging even from varying degrees of nomadic pastoralism. See also Barfield 1993: 144; Thomas 2018: 25–26.

CHAPTER 6

Encountering the Many "Indias"

In addition to the architectural traces already attributed to the Ghazna Shansabanis and analyzed in Chapter 5, several more survive along the Indus's shores and in its contiguous hinterlands, in what are the western reaches of the Indic sphere. I place five architectural sites within the period of their active presence there, *viz. c.* AH 575–600/1180–1205 CE – years that also witnessed their transformative and enduring successes farther east in the north Indian plains, analyzed in detail in Volume II. As was the case in the foregoing chapters of the present volume, previous scholars' work in the region under examination provides a solid foundation for analysis, and it is supplemented here with my own architectural documentation. Admittedly, the survival of historical data is always partial and random, and it is possible that even among the surviving remains not all have been correctly identified; new "discoveries" still expand the evidentiary corpus (as seen below). By gathering the available data and positing new identifications, plausible observations can be made based on what has managed to reach the moment of analysis. At the very least, I propose overarching characteristics and patterns that serve as points of departure for further study.

The first group, already attributed to the patronage of members of the Shansabani forces, consists of three funerary structures around the economically, politically, and spiritually important city of Multan (ancient Mulasthana) (map, p. xv). A funerary *ribat* near the village of Kabirwala (*c.* AH 576/1180 CE) (Figures 6.16–6.23) lies about 35 km northeast of the city; based on its foundation inscription, it has been identified as commissioned by the Shansabani-affiliated *sipahsalar* ʿAli ibn Karmakh, who was the *wali* of Multan at the time.[1] The structure locally identified as the tomb of Sadan Shahid (Figures 6.24–6.28), located southwest of Multan near Muzaffargarh, had been documented and also dated to the late twelfth century, based on comparative stylistic analysis. In 2011, Abdul Rehman and Talib Hussain published a tomb in the southeastern vicinity of Multan attributed to a certain Ahmad Kabir (Figures 6.29–6.32); the tomb's inscribed (in Arabic) date of AH 600/1203–1204 CE, as well as its overall form and decorative iconography, have both conclusively associated it with the Shansabani presence in the middle Indus region.

The rediscovery of this dated structure and its formal and iconographic parallels with the tomb of Sadan Shahid have bolstered the latter's dating to the late twelfth century.

At the necropolis of Lal Mara Sharif (Figure 6.37), located 250 km northwest of Multan toward Dera Ismail Khan but still along the Indus's alluvia, four domical structures made of brick clearly distinguish themselves from their surroundings due to their glistening, glazed-tile exterior and interior decorative programs. To date, they have been studied most intensively by Taj Ali and Holly Edwards, who attributed them either to the early eleventh-century Ghaznavid activities in the region, or to the second quarter of the thirteenth century, following the Mongol incursions.[2] However, based on our preceding analyses of the Shansabanis' pre-imperial and imperial architectural traces in Afghanistan and the revised dating of some of these structures (cf. Chapters 2–4), I consider the four tombs as part of the Shansabani affiliates' architectural patronage in the area.

Finally, two more tombs are located 450 km southwest of Multan and in the vicinity of modern Sukkur (Figures 6.33 and 6.34) – itself at the crossroads linking Panjab, Baluchistan, and Sindh (see below). They had been documented and briefly discussed by A. N. Khan (1988), and more extensively by M. Kevran (1996b), who each offered varying dates ranging from the tenth through early thirteenth centuries, again based on stylistic analysis and comparison with earlier structures.[3] But I propose that these tombs also be dated to the last two decades of the twelfth century, and thus considered part of the corpus of Shansabani-period funerary structures in the middle Indus region (see full discussion below). Collectively, then, all three of these architectural groups are invaluable sources for the nature of empire-building undertaken by Mu'izz al-Din and his dependents as they followed the geo-political momentum radiating eastward from Ghazna.

As will be discussed throughout this chapter, the structures attributable to Shansabani patronage in the Indus region evince an astounding variety in formal styles and also materials of construction. The one uniting factor among them, however, is the overall westward *qibla* orientation of the buildings with *mihrabs* (only the tombs of Sadan Shahid and Ahmad Kabir lacked *mihrabs* altogether). Precise coordinates are not available for these complexes but, based on the observations in Chapter 4 regarding pre-modern *qibla* orientations, it is fair to say that the *qibla*s of Shansabani-patronized buildings at the western edges of the Indic world – that is, Sindh and along the upper Indus's shores – were probably neither accurate nor consistent.

The general westerly direction of the surviving *mihrab*s, however, would indicate the *qibla* preferred by the Hanafis. This *madhhab* had remained dominant among the later Ghaznavid sultans despite Sultan Mahmud's leaning toward the Shafi'iyya.[4] Although, it should be noted that no unequivocal indication of Hanafi affiliation has been recovered from the extensive epigraphic program of the Ghazna palace. Nevertheless, Juzjani claimed that upon being crowned sultan of Ghazna, Mu'izz al-Din, "in conformity with the people of the city of Ghazna and its environs, accepted the *madhhab* of the exalted Imam [Abu Hanifa]." The westerly *qibla* orientations of the Ghazna Shansabanis' architectural traces along the Indus, then, would have been consistent with their new avowal of Hanafi juridico-legal affiliation.[5]

Indus Bound

Nothing like the disappointment of an elder, the inertia of historical momentum, and a little good luck to act as impetuses for ambitious actions with reverberations well beyond one's own lifetime! This convergence of factors could partially serve to explain – as plausibly as any other – the tireless campaigns of territorial expansion and consolidation that the recently crowned Sultan Mu'izz al-Din undertook within four to five years after taking possession of Ghazna and the erstwhile Yamini territories of southern Afghanistan. Mu'izz al-Din's eastward campaigns increasingly differentiated his new Shansabani lineage based at Ghazna from his agnates at Firuzkuh and Bamiyan. Furthermore – and, of course, unbeknownst to Mu'izz al-Din at the time – the spectacular victories of his military forces, extending ever deeper into the Indian subcontinent, were to have irreversible *longue durée* ramifications for the flow of people, ideas, and things between the larger Indic and Iranian cultural worlds.

I argued in Chapter 5 that the Ghazna Shansabanis' expansionist ambitions, and the underlying motivations behind the numerous and ambitious campaigns early on in Mu'izz al-Din's reign, did not appear out of nowhere. Rather, they came as the inextricable inheritance of conquering Ghazna, which was integrated into networks of commerce and communication that were strongly oriented toward India, and geo-politically poised for eastward imperialism. In important recent works, Waleed Ziad and Ali Anooshahr have both compellingly proposed that, ever since the first decade of Mahmud Ghaznavi's reign (AH 389–421/999–1030 CE), "the relationship of the Ghaznavid court with Hindu India was not simply one of predatory violence, but imperial over-lordship".[6] While the majority of historical authors patronized by the Ghaznavid rulers emphasized the near annual campaigns into northern India by Mahmud and Mas'ud I (r. AH 421–432/1030–1041 CE) as raids for plunder and destruction of "idol-houses" or temples, other important evidentiary sources indicate that the Ghaznavids' aims were more encompassing, their victories aimed at gaining rights of sovereignty in India (see the following sections of this chapter).

At least a few of the reported incidents of temple destruction were formulaic or exaggerated, and may be only the most legible result of larger intentions.[7] It has been argued, for example, that Mahmud's infamous Somnath campaign of AH 415/1025 CE was much more than a raid to strip a temple of its riches: in reality, it was likely a failed attempt at coastal access for an otherwise land-locked empire; gaining entry into the Indian Ocean networks *via* the coast of Gujarat – the hinge linking the western and eastern halves of the Indian Ocean world – would have been a most profitable maritime debut.[8] Upon occupying Ghazna, then, Sultan Mu'izz al-Din came into a capital whose sovereigns had purported to be both Perso-Islamic as well as Indian kings (cf. Volume II).

Inheriting the geo-political momentum of Ghazna goes far in explaining the newly crowned Shansabani sultan's military sorties and campaigns, undertaken almost immediately upon conquering the Ghaznavid capital and its dependent areas. The greater facility in commanding large swaths of geography and climate – part of the "cultural capital" resulting from nomadic pastoralism and/or transhumance in lifestyle and ancestry (cf. Chapters 1, 2, and 5, above) – surely served as a continuing advantage for the sultan. Indeed, we saw in Chapter 1 that Mu'izz al-Din's very first campaign was to the physically and culturally remote region of Gujarat in AH 574/1178 CE, only four or five years after occupying Ghazna. This initial campaign becomes all the more remarkable when we recall that Mahmud himself had campaigned but once in Gujarat, and that only toward the end of his reign, with no other Ghaznavid sultan campaigning there again.[9] In this particular instance, the new Shansabani sultan of Ghazna might have overestimated the advantages afforded by his experience in nomadism and/or transhumance and its "cultural capital," and the concomitant apprehension of contiguous geographies and climates. But he was quick to recover and plot strategies that ultimately led to remarkable successes in India, which were extremely consequential for centuries to come (see Volume II).

Inherited Landscapes, Re-inscribed

The Ghaznavids, particularly the sultans Mahmud and Mas'ud I, had certainly crafted an imperial Perso-Islamic presence westward in Khurasan, but they had also blazed pathways eastward from the plains of Ghazna, leaving traces in the architectural–cultural zones of the western Indic world as they proceeded to the *duab* of northern India. The inertia of this economic and geo-political momentum, which Mu'izz al-Din maintained after his conquest of Ghazna, presented him with yet more inherited landscapes (cf. Chapters 1 and 2): a Perso-Islamic imperial "infrastructure" – consisting of royal or elite-patronized mosques and other public institutions – that had been laid by his Ghaznavid precursors.[10] Much of the Shansabani activity in the same areas, along with their own imperial marks, are fruitfully conceived, then, as *re-inscriptions* of already existing socio-political assets within their own jurisdiction, for example, by means of substantial endowments (Ar.-Pers. *waqf*) to pre-existing architectural complexes and the institutions they housed. The larger territorial acquisitions were delegated to allied military leaders and their dependents.[11]

Chapter 2 explored the pre-imperial Shansabanis' extensive adaptation and reuse of the landscapes they inherited throughout historical Ghur. Given the early Shansabanis' greater transhumance and/or nomadism during the eleventh and early twelfth centuries, new construction of purpose-built, monumental architecture was neither needed nor possible – the latter due to the lack of sufficient surplus means to patronize laborers skilled in building traditions beyond the nomad–urban continuum. Things did, of course, shift considerably during the intervening three-quarters of a century or so, both in lifestyle as well as economy: by the early decades of the 1100s, it is probable that the Shansabanis were politico-economically surpassing other Ghuris, and their upward trajectory necessitated increasingly monumental architectural patronage. If the *minar* of Da Qadi has been correctly identified as that of Qal'a-yi Zarmurgh and accurately dated to the first quarter of the twelfth century (Chapter 2), we could surmise that, by this time, the Shansabanis had access to builders with some familiarity with Persianate traditions, and their ability to implement these on a localized level. Indeed, by the 1170s, large-scale construction had been undertaken by the Shansabani lineages at Firuzkuh and Bamiyan, and to a somewhat lesser extent by the newly crowned Sultan Mu'izz al-Din at ex-Ghaznavid sites, all of which surpassed the scale and quality of their own earlier efforts and placed them firmly within the courtly trends of the larger cosmopolitan Persianate world (cf. Chapters 3–5).

It is in fact Mu'izz al-Din and the Ghazna Shansabanis who stand out as we explore farther eastward. Not only were they the protagonists of these successful campaigns ever deeper into the Indic cultural world, they had also distinguished their particular mode of building empire as one primarily based on the re-inscription of pre-existing environments rather than the creation of new ones, as amply evidenced at Ghazna and Lashkari Bazar, and probably also Bust (see Chapter 5). As further demonstrated by the Shansabanis of Bamiyan also, those pre-imperial tendencies toward adaptation of inherited built forms and landscapes were not entirely superseded by the patronage of new buildings. But in the Indus-dependent areas and beyond, rather than only *physical* reuse or repurposing of inherited structures, *all* remnants of past empires and their attendant societal assets – particularly those of the Yamini–Ghaznavids – were meaningfully re-inscribed, layered with a Shansabani mark in addition to that of their immediate predecessors.

The cities of Lahore and Multan serve as plausible examples of the Ghazna Shansabanis' practices of re-inscription, as they entered the western corridors of the Indic sphere. Sultan Mahmud Ghaznavi had annexed Lahore probably quite early in his reign, near the beginning of his regular campaigns into the north Indian *duab*. The poet Fakhr-i Mudabbir (d. 1228; cf. Chapter 1), patronized by Iltutmish (r. AH 606–633/1210–1236 CE) at Delhi and writing during the early thirteenth century, made mention of Mahmud's commemoration of an Indian victory in AH 411/1019–1020 CE with the construction of a towering *minar* at Lahore.[12] Like its later parallels at Ghazna and Jam-Firuzkuh, the Lahore *minar* was probably associated with a nearby, contemporaneous mosque, possibly even the one identified in the lower *strata* of excavations within Lahore Fort.[13] Given the city's immense importance as the point of entry into and retreat from the north Indian plains, it was directly administered by deputies with military and legal authority, specially appointed by the Ghaznavid court throughout the reigns of Mahmud and Mas'ud I.[14] And we have already seen that Lahore was the refuge of the last two Ghaznavid rulers after the Shansabanis wrested Ghazna in AH 569/1173–1174 CE. Thus, this city was certainly well marked with an imperial Ghaznavid presence, and its continued strategic importance would make it equally valuable for Mu'izz al-Din's ambitions. Despite the absence of identifiable Shansabani-patronized architectural traces, the city could nonetheless have been appropriated and re-inscribed with Shansabani presence, for example, by means of continuing endowments to already existing mosques, *madrasas*, and other "civic" institutions.

This was precisely the Shansabani method of appropriating the long prosperous city of Multan, at the nodal crossroads linking Panjab with Sindh and Zamindawar, and destinations beyond in virtually all directions. Since at least the seventh century and probably earlier, this city had also been renowned for its temple to Aditya, a Brahmanical–Hindu solar deity, serving as an exemplar of the historical nexus intertwining commerce and pilgrimage.[15] In the late tenth century, Multan's Isma'ili *da'i* Halam ibn Shaiban finally destroyed the temple on the orders of the Fatimid *khalifa* al-Mu'izz li-Din Allah (r. AH 341–364/952–975 CE) and replaced it with a mosque. This new foundation was apparently in close proximity to another mosque, probably the *masjid-i jami'* founded upon Muhammad ibn Qasim's conquest of the city *c.* AH 95/714 CE (with later renovations and enlargements, of course).[16] The Shi'a-affiliated Isma'ili presence in Sindh, whose missionary activity in the region had begun perhaps half a century before,[17] had cultivated strong trading networks between the Mediterranean and the western coasts of the subcontinent *via* the Indus, far beyond the regional overland routes that had converged on the Aditya Temple. It was surely the profitable Isma'ili-directed commerce that prevented Mahmud from definitively eradicating them on his campaign there in AH 395/1005–1006 CE, despite their heretical status within Sunni Islam. According to Juzjani, Isma'ili communities remained in Multan until Mu'izz al-Din's campaign there in AH 571/1175–1176 CE, when their presence finally came to an end (see also above).

After taking Multan and its vicinity from the last of the Isma'ilis, Mu'izz al-Din evidently re-inscribed the area within the domains of the Ghazna Shansabanis: he made substantial endowments to various institutions, including the incomes of two villages for defraying the overall operating costs of the city's *masjid-i jami'*, as well as further provisions for the mosque and its *mu'adhin*, and five salaried instructors for *madrasas*. While it is possible that Mu'izz al-Din constructed a mosque and/or *madrasas* to which he made these additional endowments, it seems more likely that such institutions – particularly the *masjid-i jami'* – would have already existed in a prosperous and important city like Multan, which also had a long Islamic affiliation. Mu'izz al-Din's endowments, moreover, remained in place at least for the following two centuries, being recorded in the surviving correspondence of the mid-fourteenth century by the Tughluq-deputed governor of the city.[18]

Thus, the Shansabani sultan of Ghazna made a substantial mark on Multan and possibly also Lahore, even without patronizing new and monumental architecture but rather by appropriating their important institutions *via* endowments intended to exist in perpetuity, re-inscribing the cities as having entered within Shansabani domains. It is precisely the "blended-in" quality of Shansabani architectural traces that provides strong continuity with their discretely adaptive, region-specific modes of gaining control of the physical and cultural environments that they encountered during the early decades of their ascendancy, both in their homeland of Ghur and beyond.[19]

The clustering of surviving Shansabani-period sites along the middle Indus – traversed by the northeast–southwest corridors spanning the historically significant cities of Multan and Lahore and reaching beyond into Baluchistan (discussed subsequently in this chapter) – is certainly convenient for scholarly analysis. But an *exclusive* focus on these architectural traces would not elucidate the architectural and cultural geographies the Ghazna Shansabanis encountered on their other campaigns, for example, the northeastward foray to Peshawar and historical Gandhara and Swat in AH 575/1179–1180 CE, or the southeasterly push into Sindh in AH 578/1182 CE (cf. further below). Built remains of Shansabani presence in these regions may yet come to light; but even without securely identified traces of their successful campaigns there, we can reasonably suppose that the Shansabanis marked or otherwise re-inscribed their conquered tracts, which were most often commercially and strategically important urban centers and their associated environs. Preceding a concentrated treatment of the Shansabani-period tombs within the Indus-dependent areas, a brief excursion into Gandhara–Swat and Sindh–Baluchistan–Makran helps us to understand the varied cultural geographies, or the "many Indias," which the Shansabanis encountered, further bearing out their adaptive and region-specific approach to building and consolidating a confederate empire.

Gandhara and Swat

Even the westernmost reaches of the Indic cultural world – now within modern Pakistan and eastern Afghanistan – were far from an unvarying or uniform cultural geography. Rather, I propose that the region comprised at least two discernible architectural–cultural areas: the first, in the north interconnecting upper Panjab through historical Gandhara and Swat; the second, in the south encompassing Sindh, the Makran coast, and eastern Baluchistan. The differing – though *not* divergent, but rather complementary – historical trajectories of these respective areas from the early historic period onward, and their distinct cultural productions, necessitate their separate treatment. Albeit brief, this examination allows us to trace the varied landscapes the Ghazna Shansabanis came upon during their first forays eastward.

Mu'izz al-Din's campaign to Peshawar (AH 575/1179–1180 CE) – and most likely beyond into the surrounding valleys – brought him and the Ghazna Shansabanis face to face with a region that was home to various flourishing communities, whose identities crisscrossed confessional and occupational axes of belonging. Major Buddhist monasteries (Figure 6.1)

Figure 6.1 *Buddhist monastic complex, Takht-i Bahi, Khyber-Pakhtunkhwa Province, Pakistan. © Photograph Alka Patel 1997.*

and other religio-economic establishments such as temples (see below) had come up along important overland routes of communication during the first millennium CE, helping travelers to traverse the difficult terrain connecting Eurasia and the Indian subcontinent.[20] It was precisely the economic vibrancy of the region that had attracted Muslim military adventurers of the eighth–ninth centuries, who staked claims of control over pockets within the region. Similarly, the emergence of the Hindu-shahi rulers (*c.* 843–1026 CE) of Udabhandapura (near modern Attock on the Indus) – followers mainly of the Shaivite sects of Brahmanical Hinduism (cf. Chapter 1) – also relied on the economic networks of commerce and pilgrimage throughout ancient Gandhara and Swat to build their empire.[21]

The ascendancy of the Ghaznavids in Zabulistan by the end of the tenth century, and their eastward expansion shortly thereafter, brought the Gandhara–Swat region within the sights of Sultan Mahmud not only for its economic offerings, but also due to its function as one of the principal conduits into the north Indian plains. The region's midway position between the Khyber Pass and northern India ultimately rendered it an important waystation for the Ghaznavids, where there was little resistance to their entry, especially after the final defeat of the Hindu-shahi Anandapala in AH 400/1010 CE: certainly, this is the impression gleaned from the Ghaznavid sources' scanty mention of campaigns into Swat, and equally so from their architectural traces. Udegram's terraced Rajagira mosque and its small surrounding settlement (Figure 6.2) are among the few known Ghaznavid-period remnants in the region. Commanding a spectacular view of the valley below, the mosque of "Gandharan" masonry (Figure 6.3) – slabs of local schist in mortar – formed a continuation with the building methods employed in the region's Buddhist monasteries since the early centuries of the common era.[22]

Toward the southwest leading to the Panjab, at the southern limits of historical Gandhara, Ghaznavid-period authors enumerated several military confrontations specifically between Sultan Mahmud and Hindu-shahi rulers. Although no Ghaznavid-period architectural traces have definitively been identified in the area,[23] a distinct and enduring style of temple architecture – spanning the sixth–seventh through eleventh centuries and largely developed *via* Hindu-shahi patronage – was clearly in evidence. The Ghazna Shansabanis' campaign to Peshawar and beyond, then, brought Mu'izz al-Din and his forces into the erstwhile Hindu-shahi territories and surely included encounters with their architectural remains.

The scholarship of Michael Meister[24] has been seminal in understanding the architectural developments in the Salt and Hissar mountain ranges, spanning the modern Pakistani provinces of eastern Khyber-Pakhtunkhwa and West Panjab – the latter's historical extent reaching southward to the middle Indus around Multan. Meister convincingly posited the distinctiveness of this regional school of temple architecture, which he called

Figure 6.2 Rajagira Mosque, Udegram, Khyber-Pakhtunkhwa Province, Pakistan. © Photograph Alka Patel 1997.

Gandhara–Nagara, differentiating it from parallel eastern developments in northern and southern India.[25]

In arguing for the distinction of the Gandhara–Nagara school of temple architecture, Meister identified its three fundamental sources, which were a convergence of indigenous and imported conventions. Straddling both categories was the Buddhist architecture and iconography (*c.* 100 BCE–500 CE) of historical Gandhara, which encompassed localized interpretations and applications of Greco-Roman forms and iconographies. These Buddhist remains spanned northwest Pakistan through eastern Afghanistan, largely the area where Gandhara–Nagara temples are found. The influx of north Indian Nagara forms (fifth–seventh centuries CE) was equally evident, though locally interpreted based on the available building materials and also distinctive rituals (see below). Finally, elements from the temple architecture of Kashmir were also traceable in the regional temples'

Figure 6.3 *Rajagira Mosque, Udegram,* mihrab. © *Photograph Alka Patel 1997.*

architectural fabric.[26] Although no architectural treatises codifying the Gandhara–Nagara school have yet been found, Meister's comprehensive analyses of the surviving buildings have elucidated the developments in the regional style's forms and iconographies over time: decorative elements deriving from the Hellenistic past of the area, for example, continued to play important iconographic roles in Gandhara–Nagara decoration (Figure 6.4). Additionally, the distinctive and ubiquitous trefoil arch, possibly deriving from Kashmiri architectural forms, was also a characteristic feature of Gandhara–Nagara temples (Figures 6.4–6.6).[27]

The surviving temple complexes provide invaluable insights, including possibly new functions and rituals that distinguished them from their eastern counterparts. Unlike the north Indian examples, Gandhara–Nagara temples were constructed of the local volcanic stone (*kanjur*) hewn into blocks, permitting multi-storied interiors (Figure 6.6). The upper stories were usually single chambers, roofed with domes resting on stepped squinches (Figure 6.7). Access to the upper floors was provided by dark, narrow inclined corridors that were dimly illuminated and ventilated by

Figure 6.4 Temple, Kalar, West Panjab, Pakistan, exterior façade. © Photo by Alka Patel 1997.

apertures disguised in the temples' exterior surface decoration (Figure 6.8). Given these temples' notable formal (and structural) divergences from their north Indian cousins, they surely served different uses – some possibly defensive, as suggested by Meister.[28] They certainly housed localized rituals that seemed to distinguish Shaivite and other Brahmanical–Hindu religious practices in the region from those of the north Indian plains and elsewhere. Only further archaeological excavations and studies will clarify the contours of these important local developments. Indeed, the abilities of architectural traditions to meet localized ritual and other needs over time was further borne out into the twelfth century: as argued later in this chapter, the identifiable Shansabani architectural traces in the vicinity of the great city of Multan were in themselves further developments of the Gandhara–Nagara architectural canon.

Figure 6.5 *Temple, Mari Indus, West Panjab, Pakistan. © Photograph Alka Patel 1997.*

Sindh, Baluchistan, and the Makran Coast

In AH 578/1182 CE, the Ghazna Shansabani campaign to the renowned port of Dibul – now accepted to be the modern archaeological site of Banbhore[29] (Figure 6.9) – brought Mu'izz al-Din and his forces face to face with the commerce-driven, extremely prosperous, cosmopolitan region of coastal Sindh, which also extended to meet Gujarat toward the east, and to the west the Makran coast and its hinterlands in southern Baluchistan.[30] Merchandise and riches poured into and out of the area with equal vigor *via* the Indus, the mighty yet capricious river that served as an artery of the vast Indian Ocean world as it linked global maritime and overland routes.

Juzjani's description of Mu'izz al-Din's campaign as one "captur[ing] the whole of that seaside country" swept into broad strokes the many small and large entrepôts dedicated to the bustling flow of commerce, as well as the substantial urban centers that rose and fell depending on the Indus's

Figure 6.6 *Large temple, Ambh Sharif, West Panjab, Pakistan. © Photograph Alka Patel 1997.*

ever-changing course. In fact, just a century after the Shansabani campaign (and of course unanticipated by Mu'izz al-Din at the time), Banbhore–Dibul itself would experience a dramatic contraction of trade traffic as the Indus shifted several kilometers to the east, displacing Banbhore–Dibul in favor of Lahori Bandar as the principal riverine port.[31] Nevertheless, at the time of the Ghazna Shansabanis' entry into this world, Banbhore–Dibul and nearby commercial centers and ports still served as proverbial lynchpins along the Indus, connecting worldwide Indian Ocean littorals with the overland travel routes spanning the Eurasian landmass.

In large part thanks to the sustained commercial and cultural connections of the continuous coastline of Gujarat, Sindh, and Makran, the settlement of West Asian populations here and farther inland is documentable since the early historic era.[32] Rather than disrupting this flow of people and ideas, the emergence of Islam as an identifiable set of socio-religious affiliations and practices easily fit within the networks interconnecting essentially the entire "Old World." The immigration and integration of Muslim communities into the polities of the western coasts of the Indian subcontinent, then, was far from a novelty by the late twelfth century. Polities ruled by Muslim elites in this region – or with substantial presences of Muslims – were the result not only of the earlier 'Umayyad through Ghaznavid incursions (cf. Chapters 2 and 3), they were also sustained by local peoples with long histories of conversion to Islam and Islamization.[33]

To date, scholarly works on coastal northwestern India have – perhaps understandably –focused on the prosperous mercantile and other elites inhabiting the cosmopolitan urban centers dotting the region (cf. above and Bibliography). However, surviving material indices remind us of the participation of other, understudied populations in creating the regional dynamic of an *inclusive* cosmopolitanism, wherein multiple socio-religious mores and cultural forms coexisted. The late tenth-century influx of the Saljuq confederacies into the Iranian world, and their gradual extension

Figure 6.7 *Temple, Nandana, West Panjab, Pakistan, interior, top story.*
© *Photograph Alka Patel 1997.*

Figure 6.8 *Large temple, Ambh Sharif, exterior, detail of shikhara*
(curvilinear superstructure) surface decoration. © *Photograph Alka Patel 1997.*

Figure 6.9 *Mosque remains, Dibul-Banbhore, Sindh, Pakistan. © Photograph Alka Patel 1997.*

as far west as Anatolia by the twelfth century, also had reverberations into coastal India: Throughout the tenth through twelfth centuries, various nomadic–pastoralist groups identified as Baluch were displaced from their encampments, pastures, and fields within the ambit of the Caspian Sea, thereby undertaking long-distance overland migrations into the eventually eponymous region of Baluchistan.[34] Thus, a historically more accurate idea of cosmopolitanism – at least as gleaned from this well-trafficked region of South Asia during the twelfth century – should encompass and ensue from the cultural expressions of *both* urban-centered elites as well as other groups along the nomad–urban continuum.

Architectural traces of the wide range of peoples, their economies and lifeways in Sindh and its contiguous areas reinforce the need for this inclusive notion of cosmopolitanism, to which Mu'izz al-Din and the Ghazna Shansabanis would have contributed as they forayed into the region. Modest single-room, brick-constructed but elegantly decorated funerary structures such as the tomb attributed to Muhammad ibn Harun at Lasbela (historical Armabil), generally dated to the eleventh century (Figure 6.10),[35] evince clear typological and formal dialogues with the virtually unstudied, probably earlier or contemporaneous funerary structures scattered throughout Baluchistan – for example, around Lasbela itself, Kharan, Kalat, Panjgur, and Jalawar. Abundant terracotta plaques with geometric and floral motifs, as well as figural scenes of agriculture and herding, clad almost the entirety of these structures' exterior surfaces.[36] Small-scale cultivation and animal husbandry were not only life-sustaining

Figure 6.10 *Tomb attributed to Muhammad ibn Harun, Lasbela, Baluchistan, Pakistan. From Edwards 2006, fig. 3.*

and predominant among the various Baluch and other groups and confederacies settled or transhumant in the region, supporting the attribution of these mortuary structures to them. Indeed, the selective adaptations and reinterpretations of Islamic orthodoxy among nomadic pastoralists and other transhumant groups permitted the continuation of non-Islamic customs, which could be the basis for figuration on these nominally "Islamic" structures.[37]

Notably, the lavish decoration of the above-described commemorations was reduced to a series of "textile-like band[s] of carved brickwork" on the tomb of Muhammad ibn Harun – predictably without figuration – and relegated to the upper parts of its elevation. The tomb's interior was also plain except for a pointed-arch *mihrab* within a rectangular frame of zigzag bricks.[38] Taken altogether, it appears that the practice of cladding built surfaces with decorated terracotta plaques was a wide-ranging indigenous practice throughout Makran–Baluchistan and Sindh, documentable at least since the mid-first millennium CE on pre-Islamic remains,[39] and adapted to the architectural needs – quite possibly of a funerary nature – of settling or transitory populations such as the Baluch nomadic pastoralists and others. Ultimately, terracotta cladding was also integrated into the Islamic tombs of the region, but without the "non-Islamic" iconographies. Indeed, it is difficult to sustain a strict division between figural/ pre- or non-Islamic, and non-figural/Islamic decoration, so that figural and non-figural plaques may have been made concurrently for different patrons.

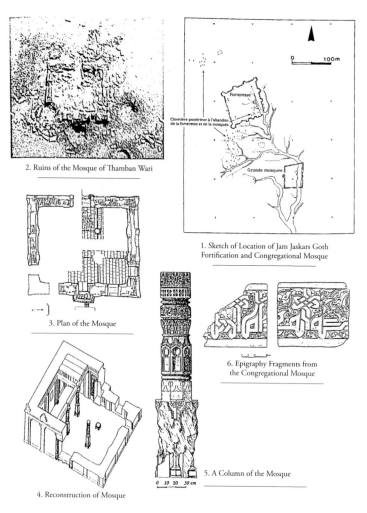

2. Ruins of the Mosque of Thamban Wari

Forteresse

Cimetière postérieur à l'abandon
de la forteresse et de la mosquée.

Grande mosquée

1. Sketch of Location of Jam Jaskars Goth
Fortification and Congregational Mosque

3. Plan of the Mosque

6. Epigraphy Fragments from
the Congregational Mosque

5. A Column of the Mosque

4. Reconstruction of Mosque

Figure 6.11 *Congregational Mosque and Thamban Wari Masjid, Jam Jaskars
Goth, Sindh, Pakistan, plans, elevations, drawings. After Kevran 1996: figs. 9–14.*

These buildings in the localized traditions – some attributable to the
Baluch and/or other nomadic pastoralists, and some to local saints and
heroes – were not the only built forms marking the landscape. The larger
projects patronized by elites in the region subscribed to distinct building
practices. For example, only 7 km southwest of Banbhore–Dibul – and
well within the circuit of the Ghazna Shansabani campaign of AH 578/1182
CE – lay Jam Jaskars Goth, one of the many large and small commercial
centers, fortified warehouses, and waystations punctuating the shores of the
Indus over time as it changed course toward the east.[40] This site's extensive
remains included a quadrangular fort (7,900 m²), a large congregational
mosque (3,000 m²), and a smaller but more complete mosque (about 1,300
m²); altogether "these monuments [were] not those of a village, but rather

those of an important agglomeration."[41] The exquisitely decorated smaller mosque here, locally known as the Thamban Wari *masjid* ("the mosque of columns") (Figure 6.11), exemplifies the style and material of construction favored by the elite strata of the polities spanning Gujarat, Sindh, Makran, and southern Baluchistan; it was a mode of building that co-existed with the above-described localized traditions.

Jam Jaskars Goth's Thamban Wari *masjid* was paved with brick, though the rest of its structural fabric – including the eponymous columns – were hewn from locally available stone. More intact and roughly contemporaneous structures at the site of Bhadreshvar, along the Kachh coast of Gujarat, provide comparable examples of flat-roofed mosques (Figure 6.12) and tombs, some with corbeled "domes" (Figure 6.13). Thamban Wari *masjid* has received only

Figure 6.12 *Chhoti* masjid, *Bhadreshvar, Kachch District, Gujarat, India, interior, column. © Photograph Alka Patel 2001.*

scanty publication thus far, but it is apparent that its structural components were carved with a confident expertise, the multi-shafted columns consisting of square, circular, and eight- or sixteen-sided sections. Their decorative programs seemed to draw from an established iconography, including motifs of diamonds in series; crisply rendered but still lush foliage; keyhole niches; and most notably the stylized but recognizable overflowing pot motif (Skt. *purnaghata*) well known from the decorative iconographies of the region's temple and other architectures (Figure 6.14). Given the *masjid*'s stylistic continuity with the surviving stone temples of the area, the colonial-era archaeologist Henry Cousens assumed that it "had been constructed from the materials of a Hindu temple ... [and] the Muhammadans chiseled out the images from the niches on the pillars."[42]

In more recent scholarship, the mosque has been summarily compared with "the stone temples of the region and the ... mosques and tombs constructed for maritime communities of Muslims".[43] But rather than

Figure 6.13 *Tomb known as Shrine of Ibrahim, Bhadreshvar, interior facing west.*
© *Photograph Alka Patel 2001.*

resulting from a process of local artisans meeting the ritual requirements of
settling Muslim communities on an ad hoc basis, it is important to understand the structure as part of an established set of architectural practices
prevalent in the lower Indus region, to be distinguished from those elsewhere in the western reaches of the Indic world (as discussed earlier in this
chapter). Discerning the *specific* set of traditions and practices from which
the building emerged provides not only a more complete understanding
of the Indic sphere's extremely variegated western areas, but also a material
glimpse into the Ghazna Shansabanis' encounter with yet another landscape of elite "orthodoxies" (cf. Chapter 4), which was quite distinct from
their expanded homelands in what is modern Afghanistan.

It would be accurate to state that, by the late twelfth century, South
Asia's Islamic ritual structures in the broadest terms constituted architectural typologies that had been seamlessly added to the repertories of
identifiable, regionally based building traditions and practices.[44] The stylistic and structural features of Jam Jaskars Goth's Thamban Wari *masjid*
are consistent with what the great scholar of temple architecture M. A.
Dhaky (1927–2016) called the Maru–Gurjara style.[45] This architectural
canon originated in the contiguous region of Gujarat–Rajasthan to the
east, now in modern India, and extended westward into Sindh, develop-
ing in tandem with Chaulukya supremacy in the overall area during the
mid-tenth through late thirteenth centuries.[46] The Maru–Gurjara architectural canon consisted of a prescribed set of building practices with
micro-regional developments over time. Arguably, practitioners of the

Figure 6.14 Temple, Bhodesar, Nagarparkar District, Sindh Province, Pakistan, exterior base of shikhara. © Courtesy of Fatima Quraishi.

Maru–Gurjara style were equipped to erect a great variety of buildings, ranging from mosques, tomb structures, elaborate sarcophagi, towering cenotaphs, and likely non-religious architecture.[47] Active patronage of the Maru–Gurjara style can be discerned well into the eighteenth century, spanning the areas from eastern Rajasthan through westernmost Makran, along with the contiguous inland areas in southern Baluchistan.[48]

At least one Maru–Gurjara architectural treatise, the *Jayaprrcha* of the early twelfth century, prescribed methods for identifying suitable terrain for building mosques (Skt. *rahmana-prasada*), and detailed the configurations of their plans, elevations, and decorative programs.[49] The relationship between formulated architectural knowledge and its application was a complex and reciprocal one across time and space, comprising experience through building innovation; accumulation and codification of prescribed principles; and eventual modification of these prescriptions with more building experience.[50] The survival of very few treatises into modern times, moreover, makes tracing this dialogical process tenuous at best. Rather, a much more complete understanding of architectural innovations over time – including the creation of new building types and decorative iconographies – has been provided by the surviving buildings themselves. The Jam Jaskars Goth Thamban Wari *masjid* and other Islamic ritual structures in contiguous areas are effectively the visible "records" of these intertwined processes: The structural and iconographic innovations, realized as Muslim patrons commissioned locally trained artisans to meet their architectural requirements, were then incorporated within the larger Maru–Gurjara canon. This canon was a responsive rather than an ossified point of reference, which enabled craftspeople to innovate *within* it, as they rose to the twin challenges of expanding architectural typologies as well as meeting the individual preferences of old and new patrons alike.

Thamban Wari *masjid* has been tentatively dated to the eleventh– twelfth centuries.[51] But without a date-bearing inscription or enough surviving epigraphy for paleographic analysis,[52] the structure's more definitive dating will depend on thorough stylistic and iconographic comparison with the region's more securely dated architectural remains. In the meantime, however, it is worthwhile noting that this building of the Maru– Gurjara style – and/or others throughout the many urban settlements scattered in the alluvia of the lower Indus – could have been commissioned by Mu'izz al-Din or his affiliates among the Ghazna Shansabanis. Since their pre-imperial days in inherited architectural–cultural landscapes, the Shansabanis' wont had been to adapt existing resources toward immediate ends (see esp. Chapter 2). Now on the brink of a transregional politico-economic ascendancy, their *modus* of building empire was emerging: rather than imposing an architectural ideal on their newly conquered territories, they patronized and effectively helped to develop the local building practices already prevalent in their regions of imperial activity.

Tombs along the Indus

Among the innumerable architectural remains from South Asia's past – and generally in large swaths of the world's architectural heritage – defensive and sacral structures have survived in greater numbers than their residential (particularly non-palatial) and other non-religious counterparts. Over time, buildings with religious and defensive functions have tended to be made of more durable materials such as baked brick, stone, or a combination thereof (cf. esp. Chapter 2). Moreover, these structures' continuing usefulness as sites of devotion or military importance – and in fact a combination of these functions in the *ribaṭ*, as discussed below – has earned them some form of investment in their well-being by the various communities surrounding them through the centuries. Certainly, these broad observations go some way in explaining the apparent preponderance of Shansabani-period tombs as traces of their forays eastward into the western reaches of the Indic world.

We have seen that, though Muʿizz al-Din maintained the eastward momentum of his Yamini–Ghaznavid predecessors, his actual mode of building empire deviated considerably from theirs in several respects; at least two of these deserve mention here. First, since the Ghaznavids had already laid – both proverbially and literally – the foundations of imperial control, Muʿizz al-Din and his followers frequently re-inscribed existing structures and even large landscapes upon annexation of the Ghaznavids' territories, as discussed above. Further, the Shansabani architectural traces that do survive – some already identified, others newly proposed here – were all of a funerary nature. An examination of possible reasons for this proclivity toward funerary architecture among the Ghazna Shansabanis indicates the continuation of some pre-imperial practices, as well as changes wrought in these practices as their Shansabani-affiliated patrons encountered the funerary traditions along the Indus' shores.

Quite independently of the Shansabanis, the burgeoning of Sufi networks linking South and Central Asia at least since the eleventh century, and likely earlier, led to the proliferation of – and increasing focus on – funerary architecture in the Indus region. But it is worth considering that an earlier Shansabani tendency toward expending resources on funerary sites and structures, discussed in Chapter 3, was also a factor in the preponderance of Shansabani tombs (discussed below). These structures were primarily of non-imperial patronage, likely commissioned by the trusted military leaders who – in addition to Muʿizz al-Din himself – actually constituted the Shansabani advance eastward from Ghazna. The structures' smaller scale, and their emergence largely from local rather than imported architectural practices, have contributed to the inherent difficulties in attributing them to Shansabani presence in the region.

The nexus between commerce and pilgrimage, so prevalent along the

Indus' alluvia, only grew more powerful after the Isma'ili destruction of Multan's Aditya Temple during the later tenth century. Although this act might have disrupted the overland pilgrimage traffic to the city – quite possibly from as far afield as Zamindawar (cf. above and Chapter 3) – commercial benefits overall actually increased: the active strengthening of maritime and transcontinental ties thanks to the Isma'ili *da'wa*, established in the region since the mid-ninth century, did serve Fatimid political ends and also provided a platform for Isma'ili proselytism in India. But the Isma'ili combination of religious zeal and commercial acuity – supported by the Fatimid *khalifa* – only increased the prosperity, renown, and reach of the area's commercial networks far beyond the overland routes of before.

It could be said that a significant architectural–cultural consequence of the commercial prosperity all along the Indus' dependent cities and hinterlands – driven in substantial part by Shi'a-affiliated Isma'ilis – was an increasing sacralization of the region's landscape. The supposedly heterodox status of Shi'ism within broader Islam – and even more so of Isma'ilism – perhaps acted as a natural magnet for the Sufi *silsila*s proliferating in western through central Eurasia, and making their way toward new horizons.[53] The ongoing contests among political powers to command the middle Indus region during the late eleventh through twelfth centuries did not alter Multan's pivotal position in the commerce–pilgrimage nexus encompassing the Indus's shores.

In fact, this city in particular was emerging as a "city of tombs": it had come to be the perfect place of convergence for prominent and obscure Sufi orders, each collectively founding their *khanaqah*s and immortalizing their deceased *pir*s with shrines large and small, some of which commanded wide devotion for centuries to come (Figure 6.15).[54] Thus, Multan and other Indus cities, along with their hinterlands, came to be sacralized landscapes punctuated by commemorations to deceased spiritual masters. The charisma these spiritual men often possessed meant that they were not always able or indeed willing to eschew the very worldly ambit of political intrigue.[55] By the late twelfth century, the accumulation of funerary sites throughout the middle Indus region could well have subtly urged a Shansabani emphasis on tombs or other types of funerary structures as well.

It should also be noted that the proclivity toward investing resources in commemorative sites had already been visible among the Shansabanis themselves during their early expansions beyond historical Ghur in the later 1150s. In Chapter 3 we analyzed the material traces of Shansabani presence in the area of al-Rukhkhaj–Zamindawar, specifically at Tiginabad/Old Qandahar (map, p. xvi). In *c.* AH 553/1158 CE, 'Ala' al-Din Husain *Jahan-suz* had again disrupted the Ghaznavids' corridors of movement between Ghazna and Zamindawar (and ultimately Sistan and Herat): following on the heels of his humiliating defeat of Bahram Shah

Figure 6.15 *Multan, West Panjab, Pakistan, tomb of Sheikh Yusuf Gardizi.*
© *Photograph Alka Patel 1998.*

in AH 544/1150 CE and his vengeful destruction of Ghazna and Lashkari Bazar, he wrested Tiginabad/Old Qandahar and its hinterlands from the Ghaznavids. Excavated Shansabani-attributed traces at the site appear to be funereal, in the form of two large tombs that simultaneously adhered to and also deviated from orthodox Islamic burial practices. It is well known that the many alterations of the region's landscape over the centuries render it extremely difficult to obtain a full view of Shansabani activity there. Additionally, the caution of archaeologists that assessments of nomadic societies should not be reduced to "an archaeology of graves" is a valuable one.[56] And yet, the preponderance of funerary buildings among the Ghazna Shansabanis' architectural patronage in the middle Indus region appears to support the idea that commemoration of the dead had commanded a significant portion of their material and cultural resources from earlier days. The perception of a predominantly funerary nature of architectural traces as they made their momentous entrée into the western reaches of the Indic world, then, may not be entirely the result of historical accident.

Remarkably, even the relatively few buildings or complexes datable to the period of Shansabani entry into the Indus region are themselves further distinguishable in three groups: the funerary *ribat* of 'Ali ibn Karmakh (Figures 6.16) and the other two, smaller single-room tombs, respectively attributed to Sadan Shahid (Figure 6.24) (near Muzaffargarh, southwest of Multan) and Ahmad Kabir (near Dunyapur, south of Multan) (Figure 6.29), share architectural features directly traceable to the above-described, distinctive and regionally dominant Gandhara–Nagara style of temple architecture, as discussed in greater detail below. By contrast, the two "twin" tombs at Sukkur (Figure 6.33) – about 450 km southwest of Multan on the northern borders of historical Sindh – possess the "domed-cube" profile that was extremely common for funerary structures throughout the Islamic world by this time (see Chapter 4, and below). Important elements in their decorative programs, however, link them to pre-Islamic traditions; but, rather than affinities with Gandhara–Nagara temple architecture as in the Multan *ribaṭ* and tombs, I suggest that the Sukkur structures were much more likely to have relied on the iconographies emerging from the Maru–Gurjara architectural ambit, patronized from the Gujarat–Rajasthan region in the east and reaching far westward into Sindh, Baluchistan, and Makran (see above in this chapter). Finally, the standing tombs at Lal Mara Sharif (Figure 6.37), approximately 250 km northwest of Multan (40 km south of Dera Ismail Khan) differ notably from both of the preceding architectural groups: even though all four buildings here exhibit variations of the "domed cube," their profiles are much less attenuated than at Sukuar, and they have extensive glazed-tile decorations on their exteriors and interiors.

Examining each of these groups in turn serves multiple purposes: such a focused exploration certainly demonstrates the great architectural "ecumenicalism" in the Shansabani-affiliated military leaders' patronage of buildings along the Indus' riverbanks. This reliance on the *locally* available skilled labor and material is a palpable continuation of the tendencies that had been characteristic of all three Shansabani lineages as they expanded within Afghanistan (cf. Chapters 2–5). Furthermore, the groups of buildings themselves furnish a unique glimpse of the coexistence of several architectural cultures along the westernmost borders of the Indic cultural sphere, along with the mobility of architectural and iconographic ideas *via* the people who communicated them.

The Multan Region

To date, scholarly analyses of the Shansabani-patronized structures surviving in the vicinity of Multan – *viz.* the *ribaṭ* of Ali ibn Karmakh and the two single-room tombs of Sadan Shahid and Ahmad Kabir – have "dissected" them into their respective "Indus Valley" and "Ghurid" or "Central Asian" components, with the admirable goal of apprehending how these buildings came to look and function in the way they did historically. Invariably, these structures' fascinating epigraphic programs have been ascribed to the latter categories, seemingly balancing out their "non-Islamic" decorative components by underscoring the consummately "Islamic" practice of citing Qur'anic verses within architectural iconographies.[57] By parsing the various contributing elements, however, we may be missing the specific and even unique factors that converged to create these buildings' forms, and which endowed them with ritual and other functions – albeit still only partially understood.

I propose that the Indus structures ensued from a combination of modes of manufacture: first, it should be borne in mind that buildings dedicated to Islamic ritual had probably been incorporated into regionally produced architectural treatises during the previous one to two centuries, and perhaps longer. This process of architectural codification, described above in relation to the prevalence of the Maru–Gurjara style along the Gujarat–Sindh–Makran coasts and their hinterlands (also further discussed below), was the result of an *already* assimilated combination of various "ingredients." Forms, iconographies, and configurations, recognizable across the surviving buildings, had been naturalized as part of an entirely accepted method of making ritual architecture for Muslim patrons within this particular architectural culture (cf. also Volume II). By continuing to dissect the buildings and list their constituent proportions and decorative details individually, we as scholars not only perform unnecessary work, we may actually misunderstand the processes by which these buildings came to look and function in the way they did at the historical moment being examined, namely, the Shansabani encounter with the western frontiers of the Indic world.

Second, the overall decoration and especially the epigraphic programs – the focus here – of these buildings are significant: the specific Qur'anic verses appearing on the Indus structures evince direct connections to the Shansabanis' architectural projects in central Afghanistan, initiated during the mid-twelfth century. The Qur'anic content of the decorative programs of the Afghan buildings was apparently being repeated, thus coalescing as an identifiable corpus on the Indus-area structures built in the wake of the Ghazna Shansabanis' successful campaigns eastward. In fact, much of this content was carried farther into the Shansabani architectural patronage in the north Indian *duab* (cf. below in notes and Volume II). Admittedly, none of the three structures in the Multan vicinity is preserved in its original state – either due to unchecked deterioration or, in the case of Ahmad Kabir, renovation. But, despite having a less than complete idea of their epigraphic programs, it is nonetheless worth observing that the Indus buildings' epigraphy had meaningful connections particularly with the Shansabani-patronized structures farther west.

The Shansabani-affiliated structures near Multan fall within the southern reaches of the Gandhara–Nagara style – discussed previously in this chapter – manifesting many of its recognizable decorative iconographies, such as the distinctive trefoil arch (Figures 6.17, 6.27, 6.32). Although few in number, these Shansabani-period buildings evince a consistency in both form and iconography to indicate the artisans' reliance on received architectural knowledge, rather than ad hoc experimentation. The tombs of

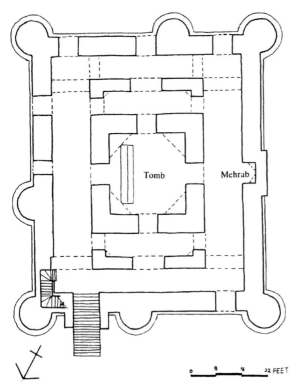

Figure 6.16 Ribaṭ *of Ali ibn Karmakh, Kabirwala, near Multan, West Panjab, Pakistan, plan. From Edwards 1991: fig. 1 (after Mumtaz 1985: fig. 3.3).*

Sadan Shahid and Ahmad Kabir were square, single-room structures originally capped by domes atop ogival squinches (Figures 6.26, 6.31). All four of their exterior façades have complementary decorative programs, underpinned by trefoil-arch niches framing the familiar Islamic doxologies (at Sadan Shahid [Figure 6.27]), or Qur'anic verses (at Ahmad Kabir [Figure 6.32]; discussed below). The lowermost moldings (Figures 6.28, 6.30) of their exterior elevations carried floral-arabesque and zoomorphic elements clearly emerging from the long-standing pan-Indic, Buddhist, and Brahmanical Hindu iconographic repertoires, and in the case of Sadan Shahid also the geometric knot recognizable from plaited Kufic epigraphic programs.[58] Both of these tombs additionally have horizontal and vertical running bands of Qur'anic inscriptions in *naskh* (Figures 6.28, 6.30) and historical inscriptions in Kufic (discussed below). Notably, the tomb of Ahmad Kabir also carried a Sanskrit donatory inscription in Sharada script on its southern façade. Although dual-language historical inscriptions were known particularly throughout northern South Asia,[59] the presence of Sharada script calls for further research, as it was apparently limited to the region of Kashmir as of the early eleventh-century demise of the Hindu-shahis.[60]

The much larger *ribaṭ* of 'Ali ibn Karmakh (Figures 6.16 and 6.17) followed a well-known architectural typology of the fortified monastic establishment common in Gandharan and Bactrian Buddhism (see also Chapter 3). The immense practicality of this architectural typology likely rendered it a popular building type into later centuries.[61] But rather than a central courtyard bound by rows of cells or rooms on most if not all four sides, this *ribaṭ*'s plan (Figure 6.16) consisted of multiple, perpendicular corridors surrounding what was likely a domed central tomb chamber. Significantly, the *ribaṭ*'s well-studied semi-circular *mihrab* (Figure 6.18) – whose lavish epigraphic program and other decorative iconography was centered around the (by now) familiar trefoil arch (Figures 6.19 and

Figure 6.17 Ribaṭ *of ʿAli ibn Karmakh, near Multan.* © *Photograph Alka Patel 1998.*

6.20)[62] – was part of the western north–south corridor, rather than being ensconced within a defined prayer area. Only more thorough examination of the *ribaṭ*'s architectural fabric and ideally its excavation will reveal whether the built space was reconfigured over time. But the occasional presence in the walls of carved brick fragments reused as building materials (Figure 6.21) indicates modifications, which could have altered the space surrounding the striking *mihrab*.

Despite its now seemingly auxiliary status within the *ribaṭ*, the *mihrab* serves as a quintessential synopsis of what had surely coalesced into a well-heeled set of iconographic (and architectural) conventions within the Gandhara–Nagara school. The ease with which not only pan-Indic but also locally interpreted iconographic elements have been deployed in the overall program strongly indicates expertise earned through practice: for example, the two different but equally successful renditions of the *purnaghata* (overflowing pot motif) – schematic on the innermost vertical epigraphic band (Figure 6.20), but more sculptural and fully rendered as capitals on the pilasters supporting the springing of the trefoil arch (Figure 6.22); as well as the molding sequence of concave and convex dentils, fleshy lotus leaves (Skt. *padmapatra*) and the angular fillet forming the base of the niche's hood (Figure 6.23), all indicate a deep familiarity with iconography and its placement that was appropriate in an Islamic context. Moreover, the impressive baked-brick renditions of Qur'anic verses in continuous friezes around the *mihrab* (Figures 6.24 and 6.25) – not unlike the larger friezes on the exteriors of the other two Multan-area tombs – were clearly an addition to the Gandhara–Nagara iconographic repertoire,

Figure 6.18 Ribaṭ *of Ali ibn Karmakh: interior,* mihrab. © *Photograph Alka Patel 1998.*

added as Islamic ritual buildings were constructed in the region over the centuries. Akin to Maru–Gurjara treatises codifying the prescriptions for making the *rahmana-prasada* (see above in this chapter), then, it is more than likely that the Gandhara–Nagara school had also developed just such a set of accepted conventions for local Islamic buildings, contained in treatises now lost or yet to be recovered.

The new Shansabani-affiliated patrons of Islamic ritual architecture in this region marked their territorial conquests not only with their buildings, but also by mobilizing locally based skilled laborers for construction of these projects. It is further probable that, given the distinctive characteristics that had emerged in the Shansabanis' earlier buildings in

Figure 6.19 Ribaṭ *of Ali ibn Karmakh: interior, framing bands of* mihrab, *in situ c. 1980s. From Edwards 1991, pl. IXb.*

Afghanistan – explored in previous chapters – their architectural preferences made some impact on the Gandhara–Nagara region. Although there are no surviving Ghaznavid-period architectural traces in the middle Indus area[63] with which to compare subsequent constructions – as was the case in Afghanistan – even by themselves the standing Shansabani-patronized buildings may provide plausible clues regarding their architectural contributions to the region.

As discussed in Chapters 4 and 5, the epigraphic programs on surviving Shansabani-patronized complexes in Afghanistan had consisted almost exclusively of Arabic and partially Persian historical inscriptions, Qur'anic verses, and doxologies. The Shansabani elites as erstwhile nomads and/or pastoralists had minimal exposure to the vast and extremely refined literary cultures of the Persianate world, and possessed a limited conversance with the Qur'an itself – a limitation that was surely even more pronounced in Qur'anic interpretation and exegesis. Therefore, with very few exceptions, the vast majority of Shansabani-patronized architectural inscriptions were likely selected by the 'ulama' and other members of the courtly intelligentsia, who either moved with them into the annexed areas or were already based there.[64] One exception to this overall tendency could have been a portion of the epigraphy on the main southern façade of Shah-i Mashhad (*c.* 1165–1175 CE) (Figure 4.1): here, along with the date and name of the founder, the original inscription might have included up to the first eight verses of Surat al-Fath (Q. XLVIII). Given the rarity of these verses' occurrences on monuments throughout the Islamic world, I argue

Figure 6.20 Ribaṭ *of Ali ibn Karmakh: interior, detail of epigraphic bands framing* mihrab. *From Edwards 1991, pl. IXa.*

that royal preference could have played a decisive role at Shah-i Mashhad as the Shansabani patron(s) emulated the imperial Ghaznavids through epigraphy (Figures 4.10 and 4.11).[65]

Thereafter, the beginning verses of Q. XLVIII again appeared within the Shansabani-associated renovations at Lashkari Bazar (Figures 5.20–5.22), which led us to observe that an epigraphic corpus could have been forming

Figure 6.21 Ribaṭ *of Ali ibn Karmakh: interior, detail of reused fragment.*
© *Photograph Alka Patel 1998.*

within Shansabani architectural patronage.[66] The Indus-area buildings lend
support to this observation: The Sura's first three verses (at least) were again
quoted on the Tomb of Sadan Shahid's eastern façade (Figures 6.25, 6.28),
forming a frieze that began as a vertical band on the northeast and continued
horizontally, terminating on the southeast of the façade.[67] The frame-like
arrangement of Qur'anic text – though different verses – was also prevalent
at the *ribaṭ* of 'Ali ibn Karmakh (Figures 6.21 and 6.22), and interpreted as an
iconographic configuration that likely came to form part of the prescribed decoration of Islamic ritual buildings specifically within the Gandhara–Nagara
architectural ambit (cf. above). Further evidence for this coalescing group
of Qur'anic quotations comes from the other small shrine near Multan, the
tomb of Ahmad Kabir (Figures 6.29 and 6.30), where all four verses of Q.
CXII (al-Ikhlaṣ) appeared on the east and north façades. We recall that this
Sura had made its debut in the Persianate regions of the eastern Islamic world
at Chisht (1160s), reappearing at Lashkari Bazar's exquisite Oratory F (Figure
5.21), and yet again here along the banks of the Indus.[68]

Indeed, the architectural projects undertaken by the Ghazna Shansabanis
along the banks of the middle Indus further expanded the epigraphic
corpus of Qur'anic verses that we had seen on Shansabani-patronized
monuments in Afghanistan. The "new" verses appearing along this eastern
frontier of their expansionist campaigns were the following (cf. also
Appendix, Pakistan I–III): on the *mihrab* of the *ribaṭ* of 'Ali ibn Karmakh
are Q. IX: 18–19 and 129 (al-Tauba); on the tomb of Ahmad Kabir's north
and west façade is Q. I: 1 (al-Fatiha), additionally, on the west façade are

Figure 6.22 Ribaṭ *of Ali ibn Karmakh: interior, detail of pilaster framing* mihrab
niche. © *Photograph Alka Patel 1998.*

Q. LV: 1–2 (al-Rahman) and Q. CVIII: 1–3 (al-Kauthar), and finally, on
the tomb's east façade is Q. XLII: 20 (al-Shu'ura).[69]

Many of these verses were not wholly unusual, also being attested
on buildings in Iran and Transoxiana.[70] One exception to this overall
tendency, however, was Q. XLII: 20 (al-Shu'ura) on the southeastern
end of the tomb of Ahmad Kabir's façade. This Sura was not among the
inscriptions documented by Blair on architecture in Iran and Central
Asia dating from the ninth through the early twelfth century.[71] But
intriguingly, Q. XLII: 19–20 were present on the late fifteenth-century
Bara Gumbad mosque in Delhi. Meanwhile, later verses such as 26–27
of Q. LV graced the arched portal of the tomb of Mir Sayyid Bahram at
Kirminiyya (Uzbekistan), which Blair dated *c.* AH 500/1106 CE.[72] But the

Figure 6.23 Ribaṭ *of Ali ibn Karmakh: interior, detail of base moldings of* mihrab hood. © *Photograph Alka Patel 1998.*

Figure 6.24 *Tomb of Sadan Shahid, Muzaffargarh, near Multan, West Panjab, Pakistan: exterior, west façade.* © *Photograph Alka Patel 1998.*

Sura's earlier verses were instead documented at Delhi's Qutb Mosque (Q. LV: 1–14), founded by the Mu'izzi *ghulam* Qutb al-Din Aibek *c.* AH 588/1192 CE after the momentous victory at the second battle of Tara'in. Verses 1–12 appeared also on the outer southern entry to the tomb of Iltutmish (*c.* AH 630/1233 CE) in the same complex. This tomb also carries

Figure 6.25 *Tomb of Sadan Shahid: exterior, east façade. © Photograph Alka Patel 1998.*

Figure 6.26 *Tomb of Sheikh Sadan Shahid, interior. © Photograph Alka Patel 1998.*

Q. CVIII: 1–3 (al-Kauthar) on the same entry. Finally, even though Q. CXII: 1–3 (al-Ikhlas) were present at Chisht (cf. Chapter 4), it is also worth remarking that Q. CXII: 1–4 were carved in relief at Delhi on the north entry to the tomb of Iltutmish (cf. Volume II).[73]

This is precisely where we might underscore an added significance of the Shansabanis' middle Indus Qur'anic quotations: like the verses from Surat al-Fath (Q. XLVIII) traveling with the Shansabani conquests from Shah-i Mashhad in central Afghanistan to the tomb of Sadan Shahid along the banks of the Indus, they may provide a glimpse of the larger body of preferred Qur'anic content originally appearing on no longer extant or partially preserved buildings in Afghanistan. Equally important to note is that many of these verses continued to appear on structures patronized specifically by the Ghazna Shansabanis in north India, reinforcing the idea that there was indeed an identifiable, enduring corpus of Qur'anic verses throughout the vast expanse of Shansabani conquests.

Figure 6.27 Tomb of Sadan Shahid: exterior, detail of decorative niche. © Photograph Alka Patel 1998.

The other two groups of tombs datable to the Shansabani presence at the opposite ends of the Indus's flows, namely those at Sukkur in Sindh and Lal Mara Sharif in Panjab, appear to have been decorated with pseudo-epigraphic designs containing no decipherable messages (Sukkur), or simple linear elements (Lal Mara Sharif). Moreover, these two groups derive from distinct architectural traditions – perhaps understandably, given the approximately 800 km separating them on the Indus's southern and northern extremes, respectively. Therefore, they receive separate treatment below.

Figure 6.28 Tomb of Sadan Shahid: north half of east façade. © Photograph Alka Patel 1998.

The Lower Indus

On stylistic grounds, A. N. Khan dated the two tombs at Sukkur to the late twelfth–early thirteenth centuries, falling within the timeframe of Mu'izz al-Din's campaign to Banbhore-Dibul (AH 578/1182 CE) and the probable posting of deputies in Sindh.[74] In support of this dating, it should also be noted that the type of script mimicked in the tombs' pseudo-epigraphy is stylistically resonant with the epigraphy on the Firuzkuh Shansabanis' monumental projects farther west: the angular treatment of *hastae* is combined with equally angular knots, evoking the rendering of the script within the exquisite epigraphic program at Shah-i Mashhad (cf. Chapter 4). In local tradition the tombs are attributed to saintly figures, one to a certain Sheikh Shakarganj and the other to one Khattal al-Din Shah, but neither of these

Figure 6.29 *Tomb of Ahmad Kabir, Dunyapur, near Multan, West Panjab, Pakistan, east façade. From Rehman and Hussain 2011, fig. 21.*
© *Color photograph courtesy of A. Rehman.*

Figure 6.30 *Tomb of Ahmad Kabir: exterior from northwest.* © *Courtesy of A. Rehman.*

personages appears in other historical sources. In the 1980s when H.
Edwards conducted her fieldwork
and documentation, she noted that
the local inhabitants also referred
to the tombs as commemorating
Suhagan ("the bride") and Duagan
("the pious woman").[75] The latter
structure was much better preserved
in the 1990s, and serves here as the
focus of analysis relevant to both
(Figures 6.33 and 6.34).

The structures are located only
about 200 meters from each other
and were clearly conceived according to the same overall concept:
their profiles were determined
by a cube with a high-drummed
dome, the latter appearing more
prominent atop the cubes' relatively small volumes below (Figure
6.33). The interiors are devoid of
decoration, with the exception
of double squinches, pyramids of
dentils punctuating the transition

Figure 6.31 *Tomb of Ahmad Kabir: interior.*
From Rehman and Hussain 2011, fig. 20. © Color
photograph courtesy of A. Rehman.

corners, and a row of diagonally placed bricks at the springing of the
domes in both tombs. Their exteriors, however, are visually striking. In
both cases, the cubical body is divided into three horizontal registers:
the bottom-most sequence of moldings has a practiced and familiar feel,
pierced on four sides by entries and collectively providing the base for
the tall middle section. Here, each of the four sides of the cube is divided
into tall, rectangular blind niches by means of pilasters with *purnaghata*
capitals – recognizable despite their schematic renditions – upholding
scrolled brackets (Figure 6.34). The resulting rectangular niches serve as
the ground for cut-brick geometric and pseudo-epigraphic decoration.
The cubical body's corners were conceptually "reinforced" by more
pilasters with the same capitals. This principal portion of the elevation
is balanced by horizontal bands of cut-brick, pseudo-epigraphic decoration, and further geometric bands culminating in a cornice.

Although tombs of saintly figures varied widely, and some grew into
imposing structures with centuries of devotional visitations and dona-
tions,[76] the Sukkur structures' tall presences hearken to a different purpose.
The buildings' overall proportions and rather lavish exterior decorative
programs – including tall pseudo-epigraphic bands – point to a "worldly"

Figure 6.32 *Tomb of Ahmad Kabir: exterior detail of decorative niche with Quranic inscription. © Courtesy of A. Rehman.*

character more befitting tombs of politico-military actors. Further, the Shansabanis' ambivalent engagement with the minutiae of epigraphy did not preclude the desire for the presence of script; but surely saintly and perhaps even erudite personages would have preferred that the script convey an actual message, rather than using it for mere decoration. During the last decades of the twelfth century, the need to consolidate territories already traversed by the Ghaznavids furnished the circumstances for architectural commemorations of the military deputies who were in Mu'izz al-Din's service as he pursued imperial ambitions eastward toward the Indus (and beyond).

But the Sukkur tombs are both geographically and formally quite distant from the tombs of Sadan Shahid and Ahmad Kabir, the latter located about 450 km northeast in the vicinity of Multan. Given the development of the distinctive Gandhara–Nagara school of architecture throughout the Panjab into modern Khyber-Pakhtunkhwa Province, it may be tempting to attribute all of the recognizable iconographic elements of the Sakkhar tombs – such as the *purnaghata* capitals – to this style as the only repository in the region from which to draw such decoration. But close stylistic analysis – not to mention an awareness of geographical location – strongly suggest other sources for the decorative programs of the Sindh structures.

As discussed above, the region of Sindh had long been incorporated into the ambit of the Maru–Gurjara architectural tradition, radiating eastward from the areas of Rajasthan–Gujarat in north India. While many exemplars of this style evince a highly sculptural approach to architecture, replete with a notable plasticity in both structure and decoration, more planar and architectonic strains also survived. I have argued elsewhere that it was precisely this strain that was seminal to

Figure 6.33 *Tomb of Duagan, Sukkur, Sindh, Pakistan.* © *Photograph Holly Edwards.*

creating an architectural language for *Islamic* ritual buildings in the region.[77]

The rendition of the *purnaghata* capitals can be meaningfully diagnostic of architectural tradition as well as timespan. By the later tenth century and onward, the pot overflowing with lush foliage, the *purnaghata*, had already reached varying degrees of stylization and even abstraction within the more architectonic branch of the Maru–Gurjara style. Both temples as well as the Islamic ritual buildings of Gujarat and Sindh showed progressively more motif-like renditions of the *purnaghata* (Figures 6.14, 6.35), reducing the iconographic concept to its constituent parts and at times embellishing each of them. At Sukkur (Figure 6.34), this process of abstraction reached a culmination, probably due to reasons of stylistic interpretation as much

Figure 6.34 *Tomb of Duagan, Sukkur, exterior, detail of pilasters.*
© *Photograph Holly Edwards.*

Figure 6.35 *Chhoti Masjid, Bhadreshvar: interior, detail of pilaster capital.*
© *Photograph Alka Patel 2001.*

as the medium of baked brick, which precluded truly plastic treatments
of three-dimensional forms. Furthermore, while pseudo-epigraphic decoration is not known within the Maru–Gurjara ambit, Kufic epigraphy
(Figure 6.36) – the visual source for the angular pseudo-epigraphy at
Sukkur – had become part of the iconography of Islamic ritual buildings
constructed within this tradition. Thus, rather than reflexively attributing
all of the Shansabani-period structures along the Indus' shores to the

Figure 6.36 *Shrine of Ibrahim, Bhadreshvar: foreporch, detail of Kufic inscription at base of ceiling. © Photograph Alka Patel 2001.*

Gandhara–Nagara style as a generic source for their forms and iconographies, detailed analysis suggests that Shansabani-affiliated patrons of structures adhered to the architectural conventions that were prevalent in the respective sites' larger landscapes. Once again, this adaptive command of their newly consolidated territories echoed the earliest indications of their activities throughout the varied cultural geographies of Afghanistan.

The Upper Indus

So far, the compelling architectural evidence for the Ghazna Shansabanis' continuation of their adaptive command of new territories – an inclusive *modus operandi* that relied on local building practices – creates an unusually varied vista of "conquest": rather than imposing an architectural signature of pre-designed forms and iconographies, we have seen that Shansabani-affiliated patrons embraced ways of building that were already in place, facilitating the further development of these local practices. There was apparently no "imperial style" that was consistently evoked by the Ghazna Shansabanis. The absence of such a model, or set of features, with which scholars might identify architectural remains certainly renders much more difficult the already challenging process of tracing the transition to elite status of seasonally transhumant and other obscure, non-elite groups. But the absence of such restrictions can also permit reconsideration of architectural remains previously attributed to different dates or patrons.

Indeed, in light of recent scholarship and emerging evidence, it is

Figure 6.37 *Lal Mara Sharif, near Dera Ismail Khan, West Panjab, Pakistan, tombs at necropolis.*
© *Photograph Alka Patel 1997.*

worth reconsidering the dates of the four tombs with *mihrab*s at Lal
Mara Sharif (Figure 6.37), located about 250 km northwest of Multan
(and about 750–800 km north of Sukkur). As noted by H. Edwards,[78]
the four tombs can be conceived in two groups, wherein Tombs I and
II have circular, bastion-like towers addorsed on all four corners, while
Tombs III and IV are simple domed cubes; Tomb IV additionally has
an octagonal drum supporting its dome. These formal variations do not,
however, seem to indicate any great difference in dating, as the glazed-tile
decorations and other details largely unify the structures. Collectively,
the Lal Mara buildings appear to be a clustered addition to an emerging
necropolis of the eleventh century and onward, expanding upon the vast
graveyard of Chira that stretched 2 km to the south.[79] Here, at least
two single-room, originally domed, tomb-like structures contrast to the
smaller graves blending into once cultivated fields, indicating that this
landscape had begun to be memorialized since the eleventh century,
extending northward with the addition of the four Lal Mara tombs.
Beyond stylistic considerations, none of these structures – either at Chira
or at Lal Mara – have inscriptional or other elements that can help in
dating them more definitively.

   However, the extensive presence of blue and white glazed tiles in the
decoration of all four of the Lal Mara tombs has been the focal point of

chronological considerations. There is scholarly consensus that the greatly varied and experimental nature of the molded and incised motifs on the tiles, and the unevenness of their glazing – resulting in gradations especially in hues of blue – are hints that the Lal Mara tombs were among the earliest instances of buildings with glazed-tile decoration along the Indus's alluvial areas.[80] Although it is more certain that this decorative technology reached its apogee in the monumental tombs erected in the city of Multan throughout the fourteenth century, when precisely this technology was introduced – and consequently the date of the Lal Mara tombs – still remains a debated question. Some scholars have argued for an eleventh-century introduction of the tile technology, citing the numerous visitations to the region by the Ghaznavid sultans, either directly to Indus cities such as Multan or *en route* to India, during which construction and tile application could have taken place. Others have proposed a mid-thirteenth-century date instead, as "the transfer of this craft from Afghanistan and Khorasan likely occurred in the wake of the Mongol depredations," which brought many skilled craftspeople into Indus-contiguous regions as they sought new patronage.[81]

There is the third, intermediate possibility of dating the Lal Mara tombs to the last two decades of the twelfth century, as the Ghazna Shansabanis were consolidating the entire region. This possibility is raised by the recent scholarly re-dating of the Shansabanis' key architectural activities in Afghanistan, namely, the magnificent *minar* towering over the Firuzkuh Shansabanis' *sard-sir* encampment or summer "capital," and the Ghazna Shansabanis' renovations and modifications at Ghazna and Lashkari Bazar (cf. Chapters 3–5). Additionally, our own examination earlier in this chapter of the Ghazna Shansabanis' other architectural traces in the middle Indus area, and at Sukkur in Sindh, lends contextual support to this proposed re-dating of the Lal Mara tombs.

The origins of a propensity toward commemorative structures among the Ghazna Shansabanis and their kin-based and other dependents was discussed above, as a possible continuation of tendencies embedded in what was actually a quite recent, *more* transhumant and/or pastoralist history. Given the probable non-royal but still elite status of the patrons, single-room tombs rather than more imposing mausolea were the preferred scale of construction. Moreover, it was equally discernible that, rather than importing pre-designed architectural ideas for their needs, these patrons had relied on locally based building traditions, cumulatively creating an unprecedented variety among structures dating to the same two decades. This primary reliance on localized architectural conventions was consistent with an overall *modus operandi* of adaptive consolidation and re-inscription of their new territories, rather than the imposition of imperial command on them. This perspective, then, allows for the inclusion of the Lal Mara tombs as part of the Ghazna Shansabanis' activities

Figure 6.38 *Lal Mara Sharif, Tomb IV: exterior, west façade, detail of glazed-tile decoration.* © *Photograph Alka Patel 1997.*

in the region, fitting within the architectural diversity they had already demonstrated in their patronage.

The introduction of glazed-tile technology into the area of the northern Indus's alluvial plains is, admittedly, difficult to date with precision. Preliminary studies of the glazed tiles recovered at Ghazna by Italian archaeologists in the 1950s concluded that the production of this decorative material likely began during the eleventh-century highpoint of the Ghaznavid empire, ceasing temporarily as of *c.* 1150 CE and 'Ala' al-Din Husain *Jahan-suz*'s destruction of the capital. Shortly thereafter, Ghazna was occupied by bands of Oghüz nomads, whose peripatetic presence and irregular use of the site did not call for glazed-tile production. But since the tiles were found in the upper and thus later occupational *strata* of the Ghazna palace, Scerrato proposed that the Shansabanis re-initiated glazed-tile-making there after their definitive occupation of the city in the mid-1170s (cf. also Chapter 5).[82] Furthermore, the re-dating of the Jam-Firuzkuh *minar* to AH 568/1174–1175 CE (previously AH 588/1193 CE) – likely serving as a commemoration of the Shansabanis' victory at Ghazna – also has consequences for our understanding of the dissemination of glazed-tile usage: the presence of bright blue tiles on the *minar*, emphasizing the inscriptional band of the Firuzkuh sultan Ghiyath al-Din's royal titles, indicates that the technology had made its way eastward from Saljuq Iran (cf. Figure 1.9) at least a half-century prior to the Mongol campaigns of the 1220s. The conveyance of glazed-tile technology to the upper Indus's shores, then, could have occurred sometime during the eleventh through twelfth centuries.

A final, important point for consideration is the decorative iconography of the glazed tiles on the four Lal Mara structures, and its distinctiveness from the decorations of the other Shansabani-period structures along the Indus. Akin to the Sukkur tombs (see above), at Lal Mara also there is no epigraphic program. But in contrast to the former, the Lal Mara tombs carry no pseudo-epigraphy, either.[83] Instead, the glazed blue tiles, forming horizontal bands on the tombs' exterior façades, carry varieties of rustically rendered geometric and curvilinear motifs (Figure 6.38). The tiles were complemented by glazed and unglazed ceramic plugs in a range of geometric shapes, framing doorways and appearing extensively on the interior surfaces of the tombs; but the tiles themselves appear to be uniformly square.

These characteristics differ greatly from the glazed tiles recovered from the central palace at Ghazna, which came in a plethora of shapes and were decorated with a wide variety of floral, arabesque, and zoomorphic motifs. Also, the Ghazna decorative iconographies were rendered in a uniformly polished manner, and could be termed cosmopolitan in that they formally echoed visual–organizational practices that were transregionally recognizable across the Persianate regions (cf. Chapter 5). Such cosmopolitanism, then, formed a stark contrast to the localized, or "vernacular," shapes on the Lal Mara tiles, which hearkened to very different iconographic traditions and stylistic practices.

R. Azeem had already noticed the uniqueness of the Lal Mara tiles when he suggested that their inspirations lay outside the decorative traditions documented along the Indus's alluvia, and certainly beyond the more cosmopolitan traces surviving in Khurasan during the eleventh through thirteenth centuries. He further observed that "there was clear evidence of [the Lal Mara tombs'] strong relationship with the pre Muslim [*sic*] tombs of … Baluchistan." But Azeem did not pursue the concrete possibilities of this smaller-scale but still transregional connection, claiming the absence of direct routes of communication between Makran–Baluchistan and the areas around the upper Indus. [84]

The Baluchistan link must be revisited for both historical–geographical *and* formal reasons. The cultural and physical geographies of Baluchistan and the upper Indus, and routes of travel between them, may in fact be more difficult to traverse now, than they were a millennium ago. The centers of Kalat, Kharan and Panjgur in Baluchistan, and even the Makran coast were all communicable along the entire course of the Indus.[85] Moreover, as we saw above, the influx and expansion of the Saljuqs and their dependent clans into the Iranian Plateau during the tenth through twelfth centuries instigated in turn the large-scale migrations of Baluch tribal confederacies from Kirman eastward to the Makran coast and its hinterland, ultimately giving their name to the region. But many – if not the majority – of Baluch tribes continued to be nomadic pastoralists, pursuing further migratory pathways connecting Makran and the eponymous region of Baluchistan with inland areas in seasonally and commercially driven transhumances.[86]

Moreover, the typological, iconographic, and stylistic resonances between the Lal Mara and Baluchistan tombs should also be re-examined. As discussed earlier in this chapter, the pre- and early Islamic tombs in Baluchistan consisted of the familiar domed cube with no outwardly visible transition zone – thus creating formal parallels between, for example, the Lasbela tomb attributed to Muhammad ibn Harun (Figure 6.10) and Lal Mara's Tomb III (Figure 6.39). Also mentioned above were the unidentified, possibly earlier terracotta-clad tombs near Baluchistan's settlements and towns, such as Kalat, and scattered in less trafficked landscapes: these domed-cubed burial structures also had no exterior transition zone and were virtually covered with square, unglazed terracotta plaques, placed in horizontal registers separated by decorative friezes. Indeed, the Lal Mara tombs' patterned placement of blue glazed tiles over much of their exterior surfaces echoes the unidentified Baluch tombs more closely than the "textile-like bands" of the Lasbela tomb attributed to Muhammad ibn Harun. This juxtaposition of the surviving structures' variations on the domed-cube architectural typology, and especially the surface decoration among all of them, only reinforces the Baluchistan–Panjab "relationship": the Lal Mara tombs both maintained the resonances with their Baluch parallels (Tombs I and II [Figure 6.40]), while also complicating the plans to hide the dome-cube contact behind octagonal facing (Tomb IV [Figures 6.38, 6.41]).

In the end, surely it would be unsurprising that the Shansabani-affiliated military leaders campaigning along the upper Indus would commission funerary structures adhering to the basic domed-cube typology with the rustic decoration described above. The active demographic connections between Baluchistan and western Panjab, maintained by Baluch and perhaps other nomadic pastoralists *via* their seasonal migrations, would have communicated the localized, "vernacular" aesthetics of such rustic motifs and styles across the two regions. Moreover, the incipient technology of blue-glazing was evidently available and favored along the upper Indus. There is no reason that the Shansabanis' by now well-evidenced tendency to patronize the prevalent building traditions *within* an architectural–cultural region – rather than importing traditions from without – would not have been followed here. The Shansabani patrons of these funerary structures called upon the locally available architectural and decorative practices for commemoration as they campaigned in the western Panjab.

Figure 6.39 *Lal Mara Sharif, Tomb III: exterior, west façade.* © *Photograph Alka Patel 1997.*

Spanning Imperial and Architectural Spectra

This chapter's examination of the Ghazna Shansabanis' architectural traces in the Indus-dependent areas affords unique insights regarding their methods of building and consolidating their imperial presence throughout the region. These insights will be key considerations as we accompany them farther eastward on their forays into the north Indian *duab* in Volume II. Indeed, the Indus-dependent areas remained seminal well beyond the period of Shansabani presence there, serving as connective pathways between the eastern Iranian and western Indic cultural worlds, particularly for subsequent seekers of empire in the Indian subcontinent, during nearly a half-millennium into the sixteenth century (cf. Introduction).

The marshalling of evidence in this chapter has allowed us to observe that re-inscription continued to be Muʻizz al-Din's preferred *modus* of establishing his imperial writ in these newly occupied areas. Chapter 5 argued that the Shansabanis re-inscribed the imperial centers of the Yamini–Ghaznavids throughout Zabulistan and Zamindawar. Vast architectural complexes, with still salvageable architectural fabrics, were renovated and perhaps even reoccupied as residences. These evidentiary data signaled not only the Shansabanis' regional ascendancy, but also provide us with hints at shifts from tent to palace among some of the elites.

In the plains and valleys contiguous to and dependent upon the

Figure 6.40 *Lal Mara Sharif, Tomb I, exterior, west façade. © Photograph Alka Patel 1997.*

Figure 6.41 *Lal Mara Sharif, Tomb IV, exterior, west façade. © Photograph Alka Patel 1997.*

Indus, however, Muʿizz al-Din and his military commanders implemented re-inscription on a scale unseen in the Yamini–Ghaznavids' erstwhile imperial centers. Here, the Shansabanis encompassed entire urban areas and their hinterlands by means of re-inscription, so that important regional centers such as Multan and Lahore came under the Shansabani aegis without extensive *new* architectural projects. These cities and their surrounding landscapes had received a Perso-Islamic imperial "infrastructure" during the preceding nearly two centuries, as the Ghaznavids had counted the territories through the western Panjab as part of their empire until their final defeat at the hands of the Shansabanis in AH 581/1185 CE. Muʿizz al-Din astutely perceived the speed, economy, and efficacy of re-inscribing existing buildings, institutions, and cities by means of his own endowments, rather than having to build spaces and populate them anew (cf. above in this chapter). While re-inscription furnished enormous advantages for the Ghazna Shansabanis, it problematizes the modern investigator's task: Muʿizz al-Din's interventions, even on a scale aggrandized beyond architectural complex to *urbs*-hinterland, are that much more difficult to glean and thus understand.

Nevertheless, this chapter analyzed the structures that *are* epigraphically attributed to Shansabani presence in the Indus region, or can be associated with it otherwise. As already noted, none of the surviving Indus buildings apparently resulted from royal patronage – though clearly ensuing from patrons with the means to access skilled laborers. The *ribaṭ* outside Multan might come closest to royalty, given its commissioning by the Muʿizzi *sipahsalar* ʿAli ibn Karmakh. The other two tombs in Multan's vicinity were also quite possibly patronized by nobility (cf. below). Although not conclusive, it is reasonable to propose that, in the case of Multan, the sights of royal patronage had been focused on re-inscription of the city's major architectural complexes as Shansabani institutions. Thus, the hinterland was relegated to Muʿizz al-Din's nobles to make their own marks – though collectively, these would still accrue to an overall *Shansabani* authority in the region.

The Indus structures' respective locations and discernible features united them into three distinguishable groups. The Multan-area tombs included decorative elements traceable to the Gandhara–Nagara architectural culture, combined with prominent epigraphic programs. The latter frequently included Qurʾanic verses and doxologies known from Shansabani buildings farther west in their home regions, and among their conquests in Zabulistan and Zamindawar (Chapters 4 and 5). Meanwhile, Kufic-style pseudo-epigraphy graced the Sukkur buildings, along with other decorative elements that placed them within the Maru–Gurjara ambit. Finally, in overall form and decorative practices, the Lal Mara tombs evinced connections with funerary architecture in the contiguous, southwestern region of Baluchistan. Paradoxically, the immense variety in these surviving structures' modes of manufacture attests to what might be termed the Shansabanis' architectural *modus operandi*: the three groups each adhered to their respective architectural–cultural environments, demonstrating the Shansabani-affiliated patrons' consistent reliance on localized skilled laborers. Furthermore, the remarkable variety among these structures underscores the variegation in style and materials imbuing the western frontiers of the Indic sphere, providing a salutary caution against circumscribing this region within any artificial homogeneity.

Based on these discernible features, it is tempting to cleave the Shansabani-attributed architecture throughout the Indus regions into iterations of "cosmopolitan" and "vernacular" building traditions. Certainly, the Multan-vicinity structures seem to espouse a recognizable (if incipient) imperial aesthetic, thereby fitting within the "cosmopolitan" category, just as the Sukkur and perhaps especially the Lal Mara tombs deviate from it. However, the above caution regarding artificial homogeneity is equally relevant here: the exigencies of varying cultural geographies in this overall region provided a plethora of building traditions that were robustly area-specific, mitigating against sudden impositions of new architectural ideas. This reality must be placed alongside the imperial culture of the Ghazna Shansabanis – wherein, for example, re-inscription superseded imposition. Rather than being monolithic and rigid, such an imperialism evinced a notion of authority that was contingent and spontaneous. These two factors together contributed to the continued variety in built forms, even as the Shansabanis crafted an empire that was ultimately more ambitious and encompassing than that of their renowned Yamini predecessors.

Notes

1. 'Ali ibn Karmakh was probably appointed *wali* of Multan sometime after the Shansabani campaign to the Multan region in AH 571/1175–1176 CE (see also main text). However, the *sipahsalar* was appointed to Lahore as of AH 582/1186 CE, the year of the third and final Shansabani campaign in the Panjab, which definitively signaled the end of the Ghaznavid house. Cf. Juzjani vol. I, 1963: 398 (trans. vol. I, 1881: 456).

2. Taj Ali's doctoral dissertation (Bonn, 1987) is the only known, focused and thorough treatment of the site, later published as a monograph in the series Memoirs of the Department of Archaeology, University of Peshawar (Ali 1988). See also Edwards 1990: 231–254, 412–428; Edwards 2006: 27–28; Edwards 2015: 145ff., 211–229 (in the last work, the author's reconsideration of the site resulted in her attributing it firmly to the thirteenth century). A brief description of the four Lal Mara tombs appears also in Dani 2000: 560.

3. See A. N. Khan 1988: 306–307, 311–316, 322; M. Kevran 1996b: 136–143. Upon comparing the Sukkur tombs with the so-called tomb of Muhammad ibn

Harun near Lasbela (ancient Armabil) in Baluchistan, Khan dated the Lasbela structure earlier, the original possibly erected upon the death of Muhammad ibn Harun, who had been in the entourage of Muhammad ibn Qasim during the early eighth-century 'Umayyad entry into Sindh. However, he attributed the cut-brick decoration on the structure's exterior to a later date when the tomb was repurposed, *viz.* "used for [a] second burial which might belong to the Ghaznavid period of the eleventh century." Kevran expanded the date span of these structures to the tenth–twelfth centuries, based on comparisons with surviving Central Asian tomb structures and their decorations, which were nonetheless supplemented by "certain exotic characteristics that lead one to think that Central Asian influence was not alone in determining their ornamentation."

4. Bosworth 1966: 87.

5. For the Ghazna palace, see esp. Allegranzi 2019a, vol. I: 146ff.; also Juzjani vol. I, 1963: 362 (trans. vol. I, 1881: 384). Cf. also Chapters 4 and 5; Appendix, Afghanistan V.

6. Ziad 2016; Anooshahr 2018b: 12.

7. Cf., e.g., A. N. Khan 2003: 14; Anooshahr 2006: 278, 286ff.; and esp. Anooshahr 2009: 62–73, where the precedents for *ghazw* and Mahmud's own role in utilizing them in constructing his image for posterity are explored. Ziad (2016: 651) also questioned "the political motives behind iconoclastic narratives in primary and secondary sources." Notably, Anooshahr (2018b: 26–27) has proposed that Mahmud's use of war elephants, particularly in westward Ghaznavid campaigns into Khurasan and beyond, created an identity problem of sorts for the Ghaznavid rulers: the elephant's diabolical associations in the Islamic *ecumene*, paired with its formidable and even undefeatable value as a "weapon," presented a dilemma that could be resolved only with emphatic *ghazi* credentials, *viz.* the destruction of temples, or idol worship in its most tangible form. Thus, "the reports of temple desecrations in India enter the various accounts [of Ghaznavid campaigns] *only after* elephants appear on the scene" (original emphasis).

8. Cf. esp. Patel [2004] 2007 for an overview of the pivotal role the coast of Gujarat played in the Indian Ocean world during the eleventh through fifteenth centuries; also Thapar 2004: 18–37. For a reinterpretation of the Ghaznavids' Somanatha campaign as one of longer-term "conquest" rather than plunder, cf. Patel 2005. For a parallel re-examination of the Ghaznavids' forays into Gandhara-Swat as more than temple raids, *viz.* as "pursu[ing] long-term objectives", see Ziad 2016: 652 and *passim*; and *infra* in main text.

9. For the India campaigns of Mahmud and Mas'ud I, see Bosworth 1973: 75–76, 235; Inaba 2013: 78–79. For the re-initiation of campaigns into the north Indian *duab* during the reign of Mas'ud III (1099–1112), see esp. Bosworth [1977] 1992: 85–87; and Chapter 4.

10. E.g., Mahmud Ghaznavi's firm control of the Gandhara–Swat region by means of mosques, *madrasa*s, and rest-houses; the site of Manikyala, e.g., was described by Gardizi ([trans. Bosworth] 2011: 111–112) as in continual use through the reign of Mas'ud I. See also Siddiqui 2010: 11–12.

11. A case in point would be of course the aforementioned 'Ali ibn Karmakh,

deputed to Multan and its vicinity, and eventually Lahore. Cf. *infra* in main text.

12. A century earlier during the late eleventh century, Lahore was already known as "little Ghazna," due to its political and cultural significance for the Ghaznavids: the important Ghaznavid poet Mas'ud Sa'd Salman (*c.* 1046/1049–1121 CE) was not only born there, he was "a courtier and a poet and an established member of the early Iranian aristocracy base in India" (Sharma 2000: 15–16, 19–20). For continued Ghaznavid focus on Lahore, see also Allegranzi 2019a, vol. I: 43–46.

13. Cf. esp. G. M. Khan 1991: 129; A. N.2003: 14, 17; Flood 2002: 104–105; Jackson and Andrews 2012. For greater detail regarding the transformation of Lahore from a garrison town to a provincial Ghaznavid capital of culture, see Edwards 2015: 41–43, 46–52. See also Chapter 4, above.

14. Bosworth (1973: 75–77) described Ghaznavid attempts at a "dual administration" as early as the closing years of Mahmud's reign, more closely linking at least the Panjab with the central Ghaznavid lands. The sultan posted Ghaznavid military and legal authorities there to administer the area directly, and the arrangement seems to have endured through some part of the reign of his son Mas'ud I. Meanwhile, the north Indian *duab* was too distant from Ghazna to be administered as an annexed territory, and tribute from the region to the Ghazna treasury came principally in the form of plunder from the near annual campaigns, which were prevented in some instances by means of a hefty advance payment, as had been the case with the city of Multan during Mahmud's campaign there in AH 395/1005–1006 CE (cf. also *infra* in main text).

15. Cf. esp. Deloche (trans. Walker) vol. I, 1993: 24–27; Edwards 2006: 22; Asif 2016: 41, 49–50; and Chapter 2.

16. See esp. A. N. Khan 1983: 177; Friedmann and Andrews 2012; Edwards 2015: 28–31. However, al-Biruni recorded that Halam ibn Shaiban had replaced the 'Umayyad mosque with his own residence; the mosque was rebuilt by Sultan Mahmud Ghaznavi after his entry into the city in AH 395/1005–1006 CE (quoted in Asif 2016: 112).

17. Isma'ili missionary activity in Sindh began as early as the later ninth century, likely even before the establishment of the Fatimid capital at Mahdiyya in Tunisia in AH 297/909 CE. Cf. Flood 2009: 50ff.; Friedmann and Andrews 2012; H. A. Khan 2016: 7–8; Asif 2016: 45.

18. Cf. A. N. Khan 1983: 177, 317.

19. Edwards (2015: 103) summarized the proposed re-inscription of inherited landscapes and built assets by the Shansabanis as "a certain courtly continuum." Cf. also Chapters 2, 3, and 5.

20. While Deloche (vol. I, 1993: esp. 26 [trans. Walker]) marshalled historical evidence toward delineating major routes, recent work by Neelis (e.g., 2011: 230 and *passim*) has explored complementary sources such as historical "graffiti" to trace the seasonal and shifting capillary routes in the mountains beyond the upper Indus.

21. See esp. Rahman 1979: 33, 52, 228 and *passim*. Even during the rise of the Hindu-shahi rulers in the mid-ninth century, Arab-Muslim contingents

– splintered from the southern 'Umayyad–'Abbasid forces in Sistan and its environs – were resident in the northwest, as evidenced by at least four known bilingual inscriptions from Swat – cf. notes *infra*; also Chapters 2 and 3.

22. The Italian excavations of the site have done much to clarify its chronology and some cultural activity. The mosque itself underwent two phases of construction, the latter likely in the mid-eleventh century, according to an Arabic inscription on a reused decorated marble slab. The cemetery west of the mosque – behind the *mihrab* in fact – unearthed a conspicuous shrine of a revered personage, and an overall sequence spanning the twelfth and thirteenth centuries; curiously, some graves contained *both* human and animal bones – an unusual and unorthodox Islamic practice, "probably the result of … some local beliefs" (Bagnera 2006: 225). See also Rahman 1979: 275–276; G. M. Khan 1985; Manna 2006; Giunta 2006.

23. Scant remains of Ghaznavid-period intervention at Giri, near Taxila (ancient Takshashila) consisted of an enclosure with rooms along the perimeters – possibly a caravanserai or *ribāṭ* – and a small mosque in the large central courtyard-like space. It is possible the mosque alone was of Ghaznavid construction, as the remaining structure's extremely practical layout was a staple among the region's civic–public complexes since at least the mid-first millennium CE. Interestingly, the complex's architectural fabric consisted of *kanjur* and lime mortar, the distinct local building materials that were standard in the Gandhara–Nagara ambit. Cf. Rehman 1991: 38–40; A. N. Khan 2003: 14–15, 17; and see *infra* in main text.

24. E.g., Meister 2010.

25. Cf. Meister 2010: esp. 12–13.

26. See esp. Meister 1996; Meister 1997/98: 45ff.; Meister et al. 2000; Meister 2010: 58–59.

27. See also Meister 1997/98: 45; Meister et al. 2000: 41.

28. Meister 2010: 33.

29. Earlier skepticism regarding the identification of Banbhore as Dibul, the eminent Indus port city, ensued in part from the seemingly late foundation of the large "Arab-style" congregational mosque at the site (Figure 6.9), in which the earliest of the thirteen plaited Kufic inscriptions bore the date of AH 109/727 CE (cf. F. A. Khan 1963: 16ff; A. N. Khan 2003: 2–4). For an overview of the textual sources (ninth through eighteenth centuries) regarding historical Dibul, see esp. Kevran 1999b: 81–89, who clarifies that the modern debate surrounding the identification of Banbhore as Dibul has been stoked by the oft-shifting course of the Indus itself; see also Patel 2011. Indeed, the identification of Banbhore–Dibul is supported by surrounding sites, e.g., Ratto Kot, preceding Banbhore–Dibul on the west and serving as "a first line of defense and communication for the rich commercial centre …": Kevran 1993: 17 and *passim*; cf. also Kevran 1992: 148–172.

30. See esp. Patel [2004] 2007: 36–40; Flood 2009: 15ff. See also Asif 2016: 115–116.

31. Cf. Kevran 1993: 26–37 for the accumulation of forts and "fortified warehouses" that served various functions over time in relation to Dibul, particularly as

the Indus's course shifted farther east and created new configurations of its complex *débouchement* into the sea; cf. also Kervan 1999a: 150–152; Kervan 1999b: 116–118 for a proposed sequence of the gradual displacement of Dibul as the pre-eminent Indus river port city, and its dwindling importance and de-emphasis in historical sources through the seventeenth century.

32. Much important work has been done on the pre-Islamic networks linking the western through eastern Indian Ocean littorals (see Bibliography); works such as Daryaee 2003 and Bopearachchi 2006 provide concentrated *foci* on maritime communication between West and South Asia; see also Patel 2011 for an overview of the available evidence and its implications. As recently reiterated by Asif (2016: 26ff.), the very vastness of the "Indian Ocean world" – from the Mediterranean through Southeast Asia – impedes any treatment encompassing all of its shores and dependent societies across the centuries, not least since smaller and larger networks and their nodes of contact shifted over time. Thus, even though the *entirety* of the subcontinent's coastlines were imbricated within the transoceanic routes of the Indian Ocean world, it is most fruitful to conceive of and concentrate on tighter networks, e.g., Sindh "as an Indian Ocean region ... long connected with Arabia ... contain[ing] settlements, trading connections, and ports that predated the birth of Islam ... and continued after the rise of Muslim political power in the region" (*ibid.*, 32, 44–46). It was observed *supra* in the main text that the oceanic interconnections did not operate in isolation on a macro level, being in essence the maritime complements to intricate overland and riverine networks: a granular view of these regional connections can be gleaned from a variety of cultural artifacts, including poetic works such as the late twelfth-century *Samdesharasaka*, composed in Prakrit probably at Jaisalmer (modern Rajasthan, India), which "reveals mercantile geography along the path anchored by Uch and the long string of Cholistani forts [to Khambhat, historically on the Gujarat coast]" (*ibid.*, 71–73).

33. Cf. Patel [2004] 2007: 55; Asif 2016: 49–50.

34. See esp. Pehrson 1966: 2; Baloch 1991: 247–248; Spooner [1988] 2010: pts 3 and 4; Edwards 2015: 180–181.

35. Muhammad ibn Harun, the personage putatively commemorated here, was a military leader of the 'Umayyad forces in Sindh–Makran during the early eighth century; but it is improbable that the structure was contemporaneous with this historical figure, since monumental funerary commemoration was not characteristic during the Umayyad caliphate, nor would an active military frontier have been a propitious site for such a building project. See esp. A. N. Khan 1988: 305–307; A. N. Khan 2003: 38–39; Dani 2000: 561; Edwards 1990: esp. 366–371; Edwards 2006: 21–25; Edwards 2015: 175–183.

36. See esp. Hassan 1991: 78–85, and figs. 2–9 – among the only published images of these fascinating mortuary structures. Without argumentation, A. N. Khan (2003: 50–51) has considered other domed structures in Baluchistan, abundantly clad with decorated terracotta plaques but eschewing figuration, as datable to the fourteenth century as the tombs of the so-called Nikodari – perhaps referring to the trailing Mongol contingents of Negüdaris (cf. Chapter 4 notes). These tombs' decorative plaques contrast with above-

mentioned, smaller ones in the Panjgur vicinity (northwestern Baluchistan) carrying simplified equestrian and other scenes with rudimentary figures.

37. For the Baluch groups and their occupations, see esp. Pehrson 1966: 4, 10–11, 16; also Amiri 2020: 157 for the Helmand Baluch, within whose ambit above-ground vaulted rooms for entombment were also documented. Cf. Chapter 2, for a comparable picture of the pre-imperial Shansabanis and other Ghuris.

38. See Edwards 1990: 366–369; Edwards 2015: 178–179.

39. Explorations of Tor-Dherai, northeastern Baluchistan, revealed more loose terracotta plaques with pre-Islamic Buddhist–Brahmanical motifs such as *swastikas*, and plastically rendered floral elements also evoking *stupa* or temple iconographies; these are comparable with the terracotta plaques from the great *stupa* of Mirpur-Khas (eastern Sindh). Apart from the Tor-Dherai and Mirpur-Khas finds, it is difficult to posit even a relative dating for the remaining plaques. See Cousens 1929: 82–97 and esp. pl. XXIV; Stein and Konow 1929: figs. 25–28; Stein and Konow 1931: 38 and fig. 5.

40. See esp. Kevran 1993; Kevran 1999b.

41. Cf. Ibrahim and Lashari 1993: 19–24; Kevran 1993: 22–24; Kevran 1996a: 46–47; Kevran 1999a: 148–150; Kevran 1999b: 72–73.

42. Cf. Cousens 1929: 126. For eleventh- and twelfth-century temple remains in the vicinity of Bhodesar (Tharparkar district, Sindh), see also Raikes 1859: 10–12, 83–84. I am grateful to Dr. Fatima Qureshi for providing photographs of Tharparkar's architectural remains; her monograph on the architecture at the vast Makli necropolis and its sources is eagerly awaited.

43. Flood 2009: 46.

44. See esp. Dhaky 1968: 68, 71ff.; Patel [2004] 2007: 79, 93; Patel 2015: 88–90. The Maru–Gurjara style (cf. *infra* in main text) is still most often associated with temple architecture; its dissemination within India, alongside the movement of Jaina communities during the twelfth through sixteenth centuries and into the present day, has most recently been studied by Hegewald (2015).

45. M. A. Dhaky (1967) first used the term "Maru–Gurjara" in discussing the magnificent temples at Kiradu (Barmer district, southwestern Rajasthan cf. Volume II). In a later work (Dhaky 1975), he charted the combination of temple-building practices in central–southern Rajasthan (ancient Maru-desha), and mainland Gujarat and adjacent Saurashtra (ancient Gurjara-desha) during the later tenth–eleventh centuries to form what he called the Maru–Gurjara style. It should be noted that, consistent with the emphasis on visual analysis and the identification of distinct styles that were prevalent in 1960s–1970s art-historical scholarship – particularly on historical South Asia – very little investigative energy was spent in identifying the historical mechanisms for such stylistic developments (e.g., changes in taxation or other factors leading to migrations of artisan groups etc.). Such work has been undertaken through a study of inscriptions surviving from earlier periods in the region (cf., e.g., Ray [2004] 2007), demonstrating a possible approach for later centuries as well. Despite scholarly attention being focused on the Maru–Gurjara canon and its treatises, the work of A. Hardy (e.g., 2015) has initiated what will hopefully develop into equally detailed scholarship on the region of Malwa in

north–central India, where the architectural treatise *Samaranganasutradhara* was composed during the eleventh-century reign of the legendary Paramara ruler Bhojadeva (r. *c.* 1010–1055). Cf. also *infra* in notes.

46. See Patel [2004] 2007: 5ff.

47. Although beyond the purview of the current book focused on the Shansabanis and their "slice of time" – which they admittedly superseded in terms of their brief ascendancy's long-term impact (cf. Introduction, and esp. Volume II) – it is worthwhile noting here that a distinct and abundant body of stone architectural remains, surviving from Sindh to western Makran–Baluchistan, urgently call for analysis. Dani (2000: 571) referred to the remnants at Makli as "the Thatta school of architecture in Sind." But I would argue that, collectively, these remains provide a unique and fascinating opportunity to trace the remarkable innovations within the Maru–Gurjara style (cf. *infra* in main text), as its practitioners applied it to the ritual and architectural developments within South Asian Islam. While temples and mosques ensuing from the Maru–Gurjara tradition still stand at several sites in Sindh's Tharparkar district, extensive funerary remains, ranging from imposing mausolea to small-scale stone sarcophagi and cenotaphs, at sites such as Makli (near Thatta), Chaukhandi, and continuing farther west at Taung, Jerruk, and eventually Lasbela (Baluchistan), are arguably significant developments of the building practices prescribed by the Maru–Gurjara canon. For Kalat and its environs in central Baluchistan, see the albeit brief descriptions of Charles Masson 1843: 389–390. Documentation and initial analysis of many related remains in Sindh have been conducted by Zajadacz-Hastenrath 1978; Baloch 1991; Bokhari 1992. Indeed, all of these gradually differentiating yet somehow relatable architectural developments beg the question of the validity of a singular "style," and the concept's ability to encompass socio-religious communities, regions, and centuries.

48. For some extremely important but neglected stone remains of *chhatri* tombs at Gwadar (western Makran), see Stein and Konow 1931: 72–73 and figs. 19 and 20 (Masson for central Baluchistan, mentioned *supra* in notes). These remnants' evidently distinct stone treatment, both as a building material and medium of decorative expression, calls for comparison with similar tombs at, e.g., Bhadreshvar and Makli, and strongly suggest that their construction was carried out by Maru–Gurjara trained artisans. These remains would mark the farthest western reach of the Maru–Gurjara canon. Cf. also elsewhere in notes for coastal and overland connections linking Gujarat, Sindh, and ultimately the continuing coastline westward. Certainly, the Baluch nomads would have encountered and contributed to the juxtaposition of clearly distinguishable vernacular and elite architectural activity within the same landscape (cf. *supra* in main text and notes) – a tendency quite possibly continued by the incoming Shansabanis.

49. See esp. Dhaky 1968: 67–68, 72ff.; Patel [2004] 2007: 83ff.; Patel 2015: 89. The contiguity of the regions of Rajasthan–Gujarat and Malwa may have been attested in their respective treatises: Dhaky (1968: 68) noted that another manuscript titled *Jayaprrcha*, surviving in fragmentary form, had been produced in Malwa, also in the twelfth century and perhaps earlier. While noting

this work's origins, Dhaky did not, however, address the question of whether the text actually contained the same content as its Maru–Gurjara namesake, or simply bore the same name even though its content differed (not uncommon in pre-modern textual practices). This would be an important point, since if the former was the case, then like the Maru–Gurjara *Jayaprrcha*, the Malwa *Jayaprrcha* would have also contained prescriptions for constructing mosques, albeit conforming to the conventions localized within its regional purview.

50. See esp. Patel [2004] 2007: 79ff.; Patel 2015: 88; Desai 2012: 472ff.

51. Kevran 1999a: 149.

52. The inscriptional fragments from the site consist of a small fragment *in situ* to the left of the *mihrab* of Thamban Wari *masjid* and other loose fragments retrieved from the larger congregational mosque. However, they provide too little information regarding calligraphic style or content to warrant secure dating: although Ibrahim and Lashari (1993: 15–21) compared the fragments with Ghaznavid and later architectural epigraphy in Afghanistan, Allegranzi (pers. comm., April 2019) found them comparable to earlier architectural inscriptions of the eleventh century.

53. For the early development of Sufism, of course the "classic" reference has tended to be Trimingham 1971: esp. 5–18; see also Karamustafa 1994: 3–5 for the more antinomian of the renunciant orders. H. A. Khan (2016) has concentrated on the Indian developments of Sufi orders and their until now little-known connections with Shi'ism and particularly Isma'ilism.

54. A prime example of devotional longevity is the tomb of Sheikh Yusuf Gardizi (d. AH 546/1152 CE) (Figure 6.15), whose shrine was tile-clad and much expanded by the sixteenth century and has continued to have hereditary caretakers into the twentieth century (see Mumtaz 1985: 43–44; Edwards 2015). The sheikh arrived in Multan about seven decades after Mahmud Ghaznavi's persecution of the city's Isma'ilis and its collateral destruction. His arrival seems to have coincided with and fomented the revival of Multan, providing "renewed vigor around another non-Sunni [i.e., Sufi] focus." See esp. Edwards 1990: 74–75, 246.

55. Such was the case with another one of Multan's early Sufi sheikhs, Baha' al-Din Zakariya (AH 578–661/1182/3–1262 CE), the founder of the Suhrawardiyya in India whose *khanaqah* in the city was "a place of great political and strategic significance" (Nizami [1961] 1978: 221ff., 240). Thus, the stark contrast between the Chishtiyya and the Suhrawardiyya regarding contact with figures of political authority was established from the entry of the latter into the region. See also Sobieroj 2012; F. A. Khan 2016: 31–35.

56. Cf. Hüttel and Erdenebat's (2010: 4–5) reflections on past archaeological studies of the Uighurs at Karabalgasun, as they reported on their own findings. See also Azeem (1991: 89–90), who touched upon the small early tombs (tenth–eleventh century?) in Baluchistan, attributing these to Muslim Baluch tribes whose nomadism "was not likely to have developed … monumental buildings." Cf. also *infra* in main text and notes.

57. See esp. Edwards 1991: 89ff.; Kevran 1996: 154ff.; Flood 2002: 132ff.

58. For cogent scholarship on floral and zoomorphic iconographies and

symbolism, see, e.g., Falk 2006: 145–146; also Dallapiccola 2018; Smith 2018. These studies update but also still complement the vast data contained in earlier works, such as those of James Fergusson (1808–1886); Vincent A. Smith (1848–1920); Heinrich Zimmer (1890–1943); and the extensive bibliography of A. K. Coomaraswamy (1877–1947).

59. Several bilingual Sharada–Persian or Sharada–Arabic inscriptions have been documented, though generally dating earlier: e.g., a foundation text from the Tochi Valley (Khyber-Pakhtunkhwa Province, Pakistan), whose Kufic Arabic portion provided the date of AH 243/847 CE, and the partially surviving Sanskrit portion's letters were "neither pure Nagari nor pure Sharada" (cf. Dani et al., 1964: 128ff.); another bilingual Persian–Sharada inscription – the Persian text in Kufic letters – was recovered near Zalamkot (Swat) and dated to AH 401/1011 CE (see Rahman 1998).

60. Cf. Rehman and Hussain 2011: 69–70. I am also grateful to Dr. Jason Neelis (pers. comm., April 2019) for sharing his insights on the Sharada script and its regional histories. The relegation of this script to Kashmir may call for reconsideration: the inscription on this structure along with the recent rediscoveries of Qarlugh coins with Sharada legends (second half of the thirteenth century), minted at Ghazna and Kurraman, are collectively providing evidence of the longer-lived and wider-spread of Sharada at least into the thirteenth century. Cf. Bhandare 2020: 231–233.

61. See the discussion of this architectural configuration's longevity in Ball 2020; and Chapters 4 and 5.

62. With the systematic looting of historical sites, either for local building materials or for illicit trafficking of antiquities, structures change rapidly. Thus, as Edwards conducted her documentation of the site during doctoral fieldwork in the 1980s, she found more of the *mihrab*'s epigraphic program *in situ* than I did more than ten years later in 1999.

63. Cf. *supra* in this chapter for a discussion of the textual references to possible Ghaznavid architectural patronage in Lahore and Multan; and the documentation of Ghaznavid traces in Swat.

64. Given the long presence of Muslim polities in the region – whether as elite rulers or mercantile groups – there is little doubt that scholars of Islamic theology and law were resident here and available for consultation. Cf. *supra* in main text.

65. Cf. Chapter 4; Appendix, Afghanistan IV: 4, VI: 3.

66. See Chapter 5; Appendix, Afghanistan VIII: 4.

67. Cf. A. N. Khan 1988: 320–321; Ali 1993: 135; Flood 2001: 139–141.

68. See Appendix, Afghanistan III: 5, VIII: 4 and Pakistan III: 6, 20, 22.

69. For the *ribaṭ*, see esp. Edwards 1990: 182–193, where connections are posited between the choice of Qur'anic verses and the patron's Karrami affinities; also Edwards 1991: 92. Khan (1988: esp. 310–311) focused principally on the foundation text, simply noting that the *mihrab* carried Qur'anic inscriptions including the Throne verse (Q. II: 256), but this could not be verified by later scholars (looting of fragments from the *mihrab* has been continuous). For Ahmad Kabir, see Rehman and Hussain 2011: esp. 63–65.

70. E.g., Q. IX: 18 had previously appeared throughout the Isfahan oasis: around

the *mihrab* cupola of the Nayin *jami' masjid* (tenth century); on the Barsiyan *mihrab* (AH 528/1134 CE); at the Muhammadiyya Mosque (AH 500/1106 CE); and the *jami's* of Zavareh (AH 530/1136 CE) and Ardistan (AH 555/1160 CE). Q. IX: 129 was also documented again at the Nayin *jami'*. Cf. Dodd and Khairallah 1981: II:43, 60; Blair 1992: 38, 177–178, 194.

71. Blair 1992.

72. Blair 1992: 206.

73. Cf. Husain 1936: 112, 113; Dodd and Khairallah 1981: II:113, 126, 149, 152; and Cf. Rehman and Hussain 2011: 63.

74. A. N. Khan 1988: 311–316.

75. Edwards (2015: 190–200) considered the association of the saints with the structures to be a later attempt at linking the site with better-known spiritual figures (Shakar Ganj Shah is actually buried at Pakpattan), based on the first appearance of the association being in J. W. Smyth's *Gazetteer of the Province of Sind* (1919). She referred to the structures primarily with their current names, as also followed here.

76. See esp. the tomb of Yusuf Gardizi in Multan (Figure 6.15), which had been established during the later eleventh century, but due to its maintenance as a shrine and pilgrimage site over the subsequent centuries, the original, more humble structure has developed into a tile-clad complex. Cf. Edwards 1990: 73–75; Rehman 1991: 43.

77. See esp. Patel 2004; Patel 2015.

78. Edwards 1990: 236ff.

79. See esp. Ali 1988: 51–56; Edwards 1990: 412ff.; Edwards 2006: 27–28.

80. Edwards (2015: 150) observed the presence of "glassy, colouristic effects" on some Buddhist remains in the Indus valleys. But without excavated finds of kilns in the vicinity of these pre-Islamic structures, it seems dubitable that the decorations were of local production, possibly having been imported *via* the numerous *entrepôt*s of Sindh and Panjab.

81. See esp. Edwards 1990: 253.

82. Scerrato 1962.

83. Ali (1988: 44–45, pls. 31–34) assumed that some of the tile designs – particularly those placed at doorframes – were undeciphered inscriptions, but his own consultation of epigraphists seemed to disappoint this hope (cf. *ibid.*, 96).

84. Azeem 1991: 90ff.

85. Deloche (trans. Walker) vol. I, 1993: 24–27. In contrast to the present-day conditions – albeit among the Helmand Baluch, farther west in Afghan Sistan – see Amiri's (2020) description of "the dominance of the tribal system and the lack of capital and trade routes."

86. See esp. Pehrson 1966: 2; Spooner [1988] 2010: pt. 5.

Epilogue: Iran to India

This volume has focused on an initially unknown and nomadic/transhumant clan among the inhabitants of the region of Ghur, in what is now central Afghanistan – their story beginning for our purposes in the early twelfth century. During the course of this same century, roughly by the 1150s CE, this group of Ghuri kinsmen emerged as a confederate empire of multiple lineages. They adopted the trappings of Perso-Islamic kingship (Chapter 1) and called themselves Shansabanis. By the 1170s CE, the three principal lineages of this confederacy were based at Jam-Firuzkuh, Bamiyan, and the latest at the erstwhile Yamini capital of Ghazna. The separate and at times contentious branches attained elite status and regional dominance throughout what is modern Afghanistan, and temporarily in eastern Iran and Turkmenistan. By the mid-1170s, the Ghazna Shansabanis in particular seized upon that region's geo-historical momentum to expand into the Indus-dependent valleys, and ultimately into the plains of the north Indian *duab* (Volume II).

This story of a meteoric rise from anonymity among central Afghanistan's nomad–urban continuum to the pinnacle of an empire encompassing a variety of cultural landscapes was not as unlikely as it might first appear. Indeed, by the twelfth century the Persianate world had experienced the influx of several waves of "outsider" groups, particularly from the eastern steppe lands of Turkic Eurasia. Chapter 1 traced how many of these newcomers had been able not only to establish even more expansive empires than the Shansabanis – the Saljuqs, for example – but also helped transform the Persianate *ecumene* into one that was *inclusive* of lifeways distinctly "other" to prior, conventional courtly models. The Persianate world's more aptly termed Perso-Islamic cultures of power mediated access to kingship within this world by means of Islamic confessionalism, patronage, and mobility. Rather than being exclusive and closed circuits of prestige, then, Perso-Islamic kingly cultures were in fact attainable for those groups and individuals with the perspicacity to decode them and the means to implement their acquired knowledge.

Chapter 2 attempted to piece together specifically the Shansabanis' beginnings among the nomads and other practitioners of transhumance in central Afghanistan – an effort that remains incomplete given the general paucity of textual and material traces of these populations through time. The available data indicate nonetheless that their coalescence as an economically and then politically dominant regional presence was largely based on increasing interactions with the mercantile communities throughout their circuits of transhumance. Surely underpinning their ascendancy was the generation of surplus resources, even while engaging in seasonal migrations and pastoralism. During the eleventh and twelfth centuries – and likely before – the ancestors of the Shansabanis had been exposed to Islamic proselytism by variably heterodox groups such as the Karramiyya, and quite likely Sufis and other spiritualists as well. But by the mid-twelfth century, it was arguably the public acknowledgment and practice of an overtly orthodox Islam that ultimately resulted in their emergence as a regional and then transregional power, as well as the historical retrievability of this process. The patronage of skilled labor to construct the recently rediscovered Da Qadi *minar* encapsulated the Shansabanis' twofold transformation: regional politico-economic dominance and the concomitant proclamation of an Islam-affiliated identity.

Subsequently, Chapter 3 traced the growing bifurcation in lifestyles of the nominally senior or principal Shansabanis based at Firuzkuh, and their agnates at Bamiyan, further highlighting the rapid – even alacritous – adaptation of these two increasingly independent branches to their respective contexts. Despite Firuzkuh's albeit tangential location within the commercial networks radiating throughout Khurasan – networks that also interwove Khurasan's urban–intellectual centers – the Firuzkuh Shansabanis appear to have remained tent-dwelling and continued their seasonal migrations, essentially utilizing Firuzkuh as their *sard-sir* encampment or summer "capital." The most recent archaeological work at the site (2003–2005) revealed patronage of public structures, such as the more famous *minar* and its adjacent mosque(s), rather than palaces. It was the Shansabani branch at Bamiyan who exhibited palace-building and dwelling, and perhaps increasing sedentism over time, as evidenced by archaeological surveys at Shahr-i Zuhak and Shahr-i Ghulghula in the Bamiyan valley. This change of lifeways surely occurred in response to localized requirements for the exercise and performance of kingship, entrenched in the Bamiyan region's cultural history.

As seen in Chapter 4, well before their declared espousal of the Shafiʿiyya in AH 595/1199 CE, the Firuzkuh Shansabani elites had already outgrown their exclusive loyalty to the Karramiyya: they extended their contacts with the more orthodox – and politically and economically more powerful – Khurasani *madhhab*s. The magnificent Shah-i Mashhad *madrasa* (AH 560s/1165–1175 CE) demonstrated not only the Shansabanis' emulation of their Ghaznavid predecessors in its epigraphic program, the large and lavishly inscribed complex also hinted at their acuity in diversifying patronage among the prominent legal–theological schools of

Khurasan. The Shansabanis had come a long way from their obscure and humble beginnings among the nomads and transhumant groups of Ghur; they were now imperial contenders, on the brink of establishing a trans-regional empire.

Arguably, among the most pivotal moments in the Shansabanis' imperial arc was the conquest of Ghazna in AH 569/1173–1174 CE. But rather than a centrally directed expansion of territorial presence, this conquest brought about the establishment of a third Shansabani branch at the once magnificent Yamini imperial capital. With the crowning of Shihab al-Din as Sultan Mu'izz al-Din of Ghazna, the Shansabani empire took on a confederate yet centrifugal identity of hierarchically allied agnatic lineages, which were always vying for greater independence. Indeed, the Ghazna Shansabanis likely had the greatest momentum toward this independence, given their access to new territorial conquests and economic resources to the east in India. In any case, Chapter 5 explored the Shansabanis' initial architectural traces at Ghazna, which evinced a shift toward residence in the previous rulers' palaces: these were grandly renovated befitting the new imperial occupants. Quite plausibly, the Ghazna Shansabanis' incorporation of palace residency – alongside tent-dwelling – was both an emulation of their defeated and displaced predecessors, and also a response to politico-economic mores, this time pertaining in the region of Zabulistan and incumbent on this new lineage if they were to exercise effective imperial control. Overall, the mode of building empire that the Ghazna Shansabanis evinced throughout Zabulistan and Zamindawar could be termed *re-inscription*, wherein architectural complexes and their surrounding areas were adopted under the aegis of a new rulership.

Following the eastward geo-political connections of Ghazna and Zabulistan – forming a momentum impelling the Ghaznavids all the way to the north Indian *duab* during the eleventh century – the Shansabanis also looked toward the Indus and beyond for viable imperial expansion. Chapter 6 examined the Shansabanis' forays into the Indus-dependent regions during the later 1170s and 1180s CE, which confronted them with pre-existing imperial infrastructures established by the Ghaznavids in the previous century. Re-inscription, their mode of imposing and exercising imperial control amply evidenced in their initial conquests of the Ghaznavids' core territories throughout Zabul–Zamindawar (Chapter 5), was applied on exponentially larger scales: in the case of the Indus cities and their con-tiguous cultural and economic landscapes, overlaying or re-inscribing the Ghaznavids' already existing imperial frameworks – for example, endowed religious/"civic" institutions, coinage, circuits of mobility – with patronage proclaiming Shansabani ascendancy was the most effective in capitalizing on what was already there. Thus, the Ghazna Shansabanis were poised to attempt an imperial formation not seen in the region for a thousand years: the Ghaznavids could claim a largely peripatetic relationship with the north

Indian *duab*, but it had really been the Kushanas of the early centuries CE who had last *re*-conjoined the Iranian and Indic cultural worlds for the millennium to come. Despite a short imperial life of only about seven decades, the Shansabanis – specifically the Ghazna lineage – can be credited ultimately with leaving a substantial footprint in northern India. We are prepared, then, for examination of the separate and yet intertwined historical processes unleashed by the Ghazna Shansabanis in northern India, and their westward reverberations (Volume II).

Serving as a pivot between Volume I and Volume II is the question aptly phrased by T. Barfield: "at what point should we stop treating [the Shansabanis] as an example ... of pastoral nomads and begin thinking of them as elites with a nomadic pastoral heritage and history?"[1] This query is particularly germane, as the Shansabanis' entire imperial activity took place within a little more than half a century, and was thus within the lifetimes of clansmen who, based on the localized circumstances of their bases of power, effected transitions from *more* nomadic/transhumant to *more* sedentist lifeways (cf. Chapters 3 and 4).

The fundamental question posed by Barfield may have multiple answers as well as a singular, overarching one. The region-specific responses of the three Shansabani lineages – shifting lifeways and economies as circumstances required – demonstrated the complex flexibility of the nomad–urban continuum. It could also be said that non-elite empire-builders became "elites with a nomadic pastoral heritage and history" when it behooved them to think of *themselves* as such, desiring their court historians to project courtly images of them. And yet, the textual episteme of the Persianate world afforded little conceptualization of *non*-courtly kingship, historical reality being frequently sublimated *via* Persian historiographical conventions (cf. Chapter 1). Ultimately, the ineluctable historical trace is the Ghazna Shansabanis' expansion into the Indus valleys and the north Indian *duab*: for them, like their millennial predecessors the Kushanas (cf. Introduction), nomadism and/or transhumance appeared to be inextricable from their particular mode of empire-building, as it was their specifically derived "cultural capital"[2] (discussed in Chapters 1 and 5) that made such a vast, transregional and transcultural imperialism possible. It could be the case that the Shansabanis *never* fully transformed from nomadic or transhumant pastoralists to "elites with a nomadic pastoral heritage and history."

Notes

1. Barfield 2003.
2. Cf. Irons 2003.

Appendix: Shansabānī Religious and Historical Inscriptions in Afghanistan and Pakistan[1]

Introduction

This Appendix gathers the known Shansabānī-related epigraphy from modern Afghanistan and Pakistan. Religious inscriptions refer to Ḥadīth, Qur'anic verses, and doxologies; historical inscriptions contain names, titles, dates, and other historical data. Overall, the inscriptions gathered here date to the period of the Shansabānīs' initial emergence as politico-military elites in Afghanistan, specifically the three principal agnatic lineages based at Jam-Fīrūzkūh, Bamiyan, and eventually Ghazna spanning the third and fourth quarters of the twelfth century. The Ghazna Shansabānīs' rapid expansion into the lower Indus region – almost immediately after the conquest of the erstwhile Yamīnī capital in AH 569/1173 CE (see Chapter 5) – renders the inclusion of the more easterly epigraphic data extremely informative. The published sources for the inscriptions are listed in footnotes on each site, while their detailed discussion is to be found in the relevant chapters of this volume.

Virtually since the beginning of European compilations of Islamic epigraphy for scholarly purposes – for example, the *Répertoire Chronologique d'Épigraphie Arabe* (*RCEA*), initiated in 1931 at Cairo's Institut Français d'Archéologie Orientale – both religious and historical inscriptions have been published together. This approach has implied parity in the practices of documentation that are followed by the compilations, and has at least theoretically underscored the scholarly significance of both epigraphic genres.

However, this was in fact far from the case: as R. Hillenbrand[2] has pointed out specifically for the *RCEA*, historical inscriptions actually *determined* which religious inscriptions would be recorded, *viz.* only the religious texts preceding (very rarely following) historical ones were collected (cf. also Chapter 4 notes). Without direct access to the sites of study, investigators today would be largely working with only those inscriptions that the editors of the *RCEA* and other compilations deemed worthy of documentation. Fortunately, several scholarly works (books and articles) on epigraphy in various media – on architecture as well as portable objects – have emerged, particularly in the latter half of the twentieth century, to supersede such inherently biased methodologies.[3]

The present Appendix aims to contribute to this ongoing effort, particularly for the twelfth century in Afghanistan and Pakistan: here are *all* the known, deciphered, and discernible architectural inscriptions, conveying religious and/or historical content (e.g., Afghanistan IV: 2, 5–9). Moreover, discussions of these findings in the relevant chapters of this volume hopefully demonstrate the immense value of "purely" religious inscriptions, even when they did not accompany historical epigraphic content (cf. esp. Chapters 4 and 5).

It should be noted that, where inscriptions from periods other than that of Shansabānī ascendancy are relevant, they are generally cited and discussed in the notes (see, e.g., Pakistan III: 9). The one exception to this practice is the inclusion of some Ghaznavid-period epigraphy from Ghazna itself (cf. Afghanistan V and VI): the rationale guiding this decision has been that Shansabānī architectural patronage, both at this site and elsewhere in their territories, was undertaken in direct dialogue with the *in situ* monuments of their Ghaznavid predecessors. Since Shansabānī-patronized monuments were to some degree responding to those earlier architectural projects, the latter's epigraphic programs are provided here for reference.[4]

Finally, the inscriptions for each site and building have been arranged according to the anticipated movement around and through the built environment – essentially, a visitor's experience of it – and the hypothetical sequence of reading. Not only is it assumed that the Arabic–Persian inscriptions would be read from right to left, they also follow consecutively from exterior to interior spaces, and from the heights of elevations to their bases (top down). In some examples, such as the small tombs in the vicinity of Multan in the lower Indus region (Pakistan II and III), probable circumambulation would have directed a specific encounter of the epigraphy, so that the order of inscriptions follows what was likely clockwise progress around these structures.

Afghanistan

Balkh's Western Vicinity, Juzjan Province

I. Tomb of Sālār Khalīl[5]

Exterior, main entrance

1. Surrounding entrance frame, Kufic, Arabic: *Bismillah*, identification of structure as the tomb (مشهد) of Sālār Khalīl.
2. Horizontal inset above entrance, foliated and knotted Kufic: *shahāda*.

Interior

   3. Band around drum, bordered Kufic:
      a. *Bismillah*; phrase from Qur'ān IV:170–172 (al-Nisa'); phrase from Qur'ān XXVII: 19 (al-Naml); artisan Muḥammad ibn Aḥmad ibn Maḥmūd ([6]...عمل محمد ابن احمد ابن محمود).
   4. Continuous band following the trilobed arches, Kufic: الملك لله (periodically الملك repeated).
   5. Around the niche arches, floriated Kufic:
      a. east niche arch: partial Qur'ān II:255 (al-Baqara);
      b. north niche arch: Qur'ān II:163; Qur'ān X: 58 (Yūnus);
      c. west niche arch: Qur'ān III:18–19 (Āl 'Imrān).

Bust[7]

II. Arch[8]

   1. Eastern face, Kufic:
      a. right pier: Qur'ān II:127 (al-Baqara);
      b. left pier incomplete historical inscription (Arabic): من اتمام هذه [القبة؟] في سنة...[9]

Chisht

III. Funerary *Madrasa* complex(?)[10]

Southwestern structure, exterior:

   1. right of entrance, band framing entrance arch, *naskh*: indecipherable;
   2. right of entrance, panel beneath arch, *naskh*: indecipherable;
   3. left of entrance, panel beneath arch, *naskh*: Qur'ān XX:8 (Ṭaha).

Southwestern structure, interior:

   4. Continuous horizontal band at springing of arches, *naskh*:
      a. beginning in southeast corner, Arabic: *bismillah*; renovation (تجديد) of the building dated to the reign of Shams al-Dunya wa al-Dīn[11]; titles including الملك المعظم المؤيد المظفر...
      b. beginning in northeast corner, Arabic: royal titles, *kunya* (أبو الفتح), *ism* (محمد), and *nasab* (ابن سام);
      c. beginning in northwest corner: Qur'ān LIX:23–24 (al-Ḥashr);
      d. beginning in southwest corner: names of Allah.
   5. Continuous band around arches, floriated Kufic:

a. beginning in northeast corner: Qur'ān III:18–19 (Āl 'Imrān);
b. beginning in northwest corner: Qur'ān II:255 (al-Baqara);
c. beginning in southwest corner: Qur'ān II:255–257 (al-Baqara);
d. beginning in southeast corner: Qur'ān II:257; Qur'ān CXII:1–4 (al-Ikhlāṣ); Persian, AH 10 Jumādā I 562/4 March 1167 CE.[12]

Northeastern structure, exterior:

6. Band framing portal, bordered Kufic, Arabic–Persian:
   a. right remnant: السلطان المعظ[م]
   b. left remnant: بي تاريخ ربع الاخر سنة ...
   c. springing of entrance arch:
      i. north: المعظم
      ii. south: السلطان

Northeastern structure, interior, west wall:

7. Large blind niche above right of *miḥrāb*:
   a. band delineating arch, floriated Kufic, Arabic: royal titles including [ا]لاعظم الملك [؟] رقاب الأمم مو[لى ملوك العرب و العجم ؟]
   b. three (originally four?) medallions inside arch, *naskh*: ...أبو بكر ، عمر، علي
   c. horizontal band below 7b, cursive: و الحمد لله [سبحان الله]
8. Large blind niche above left of *miḥrāb*:
   a. band delineating arch, floriated Kufic, Arabic: ... [امير المؤمنين] (termination of 7a);
   b. four medallions inside arch, two legible, *naskh*: إسماعيل [؟] إبراهيم...
   c. horizontal band below 8b, termination of 7c, *naskh*: و لا اله الا الله و الله [ا]كبر
   d. within medallion below 8c, floriated Kufic: الله
9. Smaller blind niches centered above *miḥrāb*, floriated Kufic:
   a. right, horizontal band below arch: الله اكبر
   b. left, horizontal band below arch: الله اكبر
10. Small blind niche to left of 8:
    a. upper band, Kufic: الله اكبر
    b. inside panel, *naskh*: عمل محمد ابن ابي بكر \ المعروف [؟]

Gharjistan

IV. Shah-i Mashhad *madrasa* remains[13]

South (principal) façade, central arch:

1. Knotted Kufic, Arabic: *Bismillah*; female patron; AH Ramadan 561 or 571/July 1166 or March 1176 CE.

South façade, central arch:

2. Lower edge of arch, *nashkī*, Arabic: reference to a male personage's grave:[14] نور الله مرقده و يبسطه لحده
3. Inside central arch, *thuluth*: *Takbīr* of *Tashrīq*.[15]

South façade, right four arches:

4. Kufic, Qur'ān XLVIII:1–6 (al-Fath);
5. Kufic, Arabic: Maḥmūd, craftsman [?]: ...عمل محمود...; Aḥmad ibn Maḥmūd, builder [?]تم هذه البنا العبد احمد ابن محمود...

North façade, extant west wall of entrance *īwān*:

6. Kufic, *Bismillah*;
7. Kufic, Qur'ān LIX:22–24 (al-Ḥashr);
8. Kufic: علي، علي، علي (repetition);
9. *Naskh*, Ḥadīth enjoining Muslims "to be in the world like a guest";[16]
10. *Naskh* and *thuluth*, Arabic: ...رحل رسول الله صلى الله عليه و سلم

Ghazna[17]

V. Palace[18]

1. Top frieze running along approximately 148 marble dado slabs from the Ghazna palace's monumental north entrance; n.d., probably eleventh–twelfth centuries (Ghaznavid); *naskh*, Arabic:
   a. various benedictory texts in sequence.[19]
2. Three marble elements:[20]
   a. upper half of small arch, *naskh*:
      i. Qur'ān II: 256 (al-Baqara);
      ii. *laqab*, *kunya*, and *ism* of Mas'ūd III
         (السلطان العظم ابو سعد مسعود).
   b. Transenna I, five bands around geometric grill, *naskh*:
      i. عمل محمد ابن حسين ابن مبارك
      ii. ...و فرغ من اشدته...
      iii. في اول شهر...المبارك رمضان عظم الله
      iv. قدره سنه خمسين خمسمائه
      v. خمس مائه (AH 1 Ramaḍān 505/1–2 March 1112 CE].[21]
   c. Transenna II, five bands around geometric grill, *naskh*:

i. عمل عثمان ابن...ابن

ii. ...و فرغ من اشدته...

iii. في اول شهر الله

iv. المبارک رمضان [عظم] الله [قدرته؟] سنه

v. خمس و خمس مایه [AH 505/1112–1113 CE].[22]

3. Top frieze of marble dado slabs on walls of central court (partly *in situ*), floriated Kufic, Persian: *mathnavī* (*mutaqārib* meter), approximately 85–95 distiches, progressing counterclockwise from northwest through south and east sides; n.d., possibly early twelfth century (r. Masʿūd III, 1099–1115 CE):[23]

    a. west side:

        i. شاه محمود...(i.e., Maḥmūd ibn Sabuktigīn, r. AH 389–421/999–1030 CE);[24]

        ii. أبو سعید... (i.e., Masʿūd I, r. AH 421–432/1030–41 CE).[25]

4. Top frieze of marble dado slabs on walls of central court (partly *in situ*), floriated Kufic, Persian: *qaṣīda* [?] (*mujtathth* meter, rhyme -an), progressing from northeast corner to northwest corner (possibly extending further on both ends), likely two or more compositions.[26]

5. Baked brick and stucco fragments of monumental epigraphic bands, recovered in west and northeast of courtyard (above marble dado slabs V:1, 3):[27]

    a. Kufic, Arabic: benedictory texts, e.g. الملک لله، الملک (alone and/ or repeated);

    b. Kufic: *Bismillah*; Qurʾān III:18–19 (Āl ʿImrān) (stucco);[28]

    c. three different fragments, *naskh*, Arabic: royal titles, including: السلطان المعظم الم... (baked brick).[29]

VI. *Minār* of Masʿūd III[30]

1. Kufic: *Bismillah*; titles, *laqab* (السلطان العظم) *kunya* (ابو سعد), and *ism* (مسعود) of Sultan Masʿūd III.

2. Interlocking Kufic (in square panels): titles, *kunya* and *ism* of Masʿūd III.

3. *Naskh*: Qurʾān XLVIII:1–29? (al-Fatḥ).

Ghūr

VII. Jam-Fīrūzkūh *minār*[31]

First (topmost) band:

1. Kufic: *Shahāda*.

Second band:

2. Kufic: Qurʾān LXI:13 and first three words of 14 (al-Ṣaf).

Third band:

3. Kufic, references to Ghīyath al-Dīn:

السلطان المعظم سلطان غياث الدنيا و الدين أبو الفتح محمد ابن سام...

Fourth band:

4. Kufic, turquoise-blue tile letters: titles of Sulṭān Ghīyath al-Dīn.

Bottom-most section, above base (tallest horizontal division with several interspersed elements):

5. Undulating band forming circles and hexagons, Kufic: Qur'ān XIX:1–98 (Maryām); on east face Qur'ān XIX:34 in stellate knot at apex of large niche motif, probably serving as a *miḥrāb*.[32]
6. Panel on north face:
   a. craftsman's signature, *naskh* (Arabic): علي ابن ابراهيم النيشابوري
   b. Kufic: AH 570/1174–1175 CE.
7. Octagonal socle, Kufic: titles of Sulṭān Ghīyath al-Dīn (eroded).

Lashkari Bazar[33]

VIII. South or Great Palace ("Château du sud")

Exterior of palace:

1. Great Mosque of Forecourt, around *miḥrāb*:[34]
   a. on flanking wall to north, Kufic: الملك لله (repeated; tentative);
   b. on round pillars flanking north and south, Kufic, Arabic: individual words, e.g., دولة، امة، على, etc.;
   c. among debris, originally on wall surfaces or pillars, Kufic: doxologies, e.g., السلطان لله العظمة لله ، الملك لله
2. South façade, *Īvān* X, Kufic, Arabic: probable renovation text dated to AH 55x/1156–1165 CE.

Interior of palace:

3. Audience Hall I (northernmost *īvān* of palace, abutting and looking out on Helmand):[35]
   a. frieze around south entrance (partially *in situ*), Kufic:
      i. *Bismillah*;
      ii. Qur'ān XXVII:40–41 (al-Naml).
   b. Brick and terracotta "ring-like" fragments of pillarets forming part of overall decorative program, Kufic: الملك لله
4. Oratory F (southwest of Audience Hall I):
   a. continuous frieze beginning on north wall and continuing

on south wall, Kufic: *Bismillah*; Qur'ān XLVIII:1–6 or more (al-Fatḥ);

b. frieze framing *miḥrāb*, Kufic: *Bismillah*; Qur'ān II:256 (al-Baqara);

c. upper part of *miḥrāb*, Kufic: Qur'ān CXII:1–4 (al-Ikhlāṣ) repeated;

d. lower part of *miḥrāb*, Kufic: doxologies, e.g. القدر لله ، السلطان لله ، الملك لله

Pakistan

Lower Indus Region (near Multan)

I. *Ribāṭ* of 'Alī ibn Karmākh[36]

Miḥrāb

1. First (outermost) vertical band, floriated Kufic: Qur'ān IX:18–19 (al-Tauba).
2. Second vertical band, floriated Kufic, founder/patron: ...علي ابن كرماخ...
3. Flanking vertical pilasters, floriated Kufic: Qur'ān LXI:13 (al-Ṣaf).
4. Hood, top three horizontal bands, Kufic: الملك لله (repeated).
5. Hood, bottom horizontal band, floriated Kufic: Qur'ān IX:129 (al-Ṭauba).
6. Squinches, Kufic: الملك (right) لله (left).
7. *Miḥrāb* back wall medallions: محمد ، عثمان ، عمر، أبو بكر، علي

II. Tomb of "Sadan Shahid"[37]

Exterior, east façade:

1. Continuous vertical–horizontal–vertical band, from east–north to east–south corner, *naskh*: Qur'ān XLVIII:1–3? (al-Fatḥ).
2. Continuous vertical–horizontal–vertical band framing east–north niche, Kufic: الملک لله (repeated).
3. Square projections above 2, *naskh*: الله (repeated).
4. East–north niche, *gavākṣa*, *naskh*: الله
5. Continuous band framing entrance, *naskh*: الله (horizontally repeated, alternating with floral insets).
6. Bases of pilasters flanking entrance, *naskh*: الله
7. Continuous vertical–horizontal–vertical band framing east-south niche, Kufic: الملک لله (repeated).
8. Square projections above 7, *naskh*: الله (repeated).

9. East–south niche, *gavākṣa*, *naskh*: الله

10. Continuous horizontal band (above base moldings), *naskh*: يا الله (repeated).

Exterior, south façade:

11. Continuous vertical–horizontal–vertical band framing southeast niche: Kufic-style pseudo-epigraphy resembling الملك لله (repeated).

12. Ditto for southwest niche.

Exterior, north façade:

13. Continuous vertical–horizontal–vertical band framing northwest niche, Kufic: الملك لله (repeated).

14. Square projections above 1, *naskh*: الله (repeated).

15. Northwest niche, *gavākṣa*, *naskh*: الله

16. Continuous band framing entrance: الله (horizontally repeated, alternating with floral insets).

17. Continuous band framing northeast niche, Kufic: الله (repeated).

18. Square projections above 5, *naskh*: الله (repeated).

19. Northeast niche, *gavākṣa*, *naskh*: الله

20. Continuous horizontal band (above base moldings), *naskh*: يا الله (repeated).

West façade:

21. Continuous vertical–horizontal–vertical band framing west–north niche, Kufic: الملك لله (repeated).

22. Square projections above 9, *naskh*: الله (repeated).

23. West–south niche, *gavākṣa*, *naskh*: الله

24. Continuous band framing entrance, *naskh*: الله (horizontally repeated, alternating with floral insets).

25. Bases of pilasters flanking entrance, *naskh*: الله

26. Continuous vertical–horizontal–vertical band framing west–south niche, Kufic: الملك لله (repeated).

27. Square projections above 14, *naskh*: الله (repeated).

28. West–north niche, *gavākṣa*, *naskh*: الله

29. Continuous horizontal band (above base moldings), *naskh*: يا الله (repeated).

Interior, west upper wall:

30. *Naskh*, Arabic: beginning of two-line foundation inscription (... امر بي بنا).

III. Tomb of "Ahmad Kabir"[38]

East façade:

1. Socle medallions (two of four extant, right of stair [northeast]): swans.
2. East–north corner vertical band, *thuluth*: Qur'ān I:1 (al-Fātiḥa).
3. Continuous band framing east–north niche, floriated Kufic: الملك لله (repeated).
4. East–north niche panel, *naskh*: Qur'ān CVIII:1–3 (al-Kauthar).
5. Continuous band framing east–south niche, floriated Kufic: الملك لله (repeated).
6. East–south niche panel, *naskh*: Qur'ān CXII:1–4 (al-Ikhlāṣ).
7. East–south corner vertical band, *thuluth*: Qur'ān XLII:20 (al-Shū'rā).

South façade:

8. Socle medallions: swans (two).
9. Southeast niche panel: Śāradā (12 lines): … *kalyāṇa putrena* …; *Śaka* year 35; … *Sitā* …[39]
10. Southwest niche panel, "Western Kufic,"[40] Arabic:
    a. titles including شهاب الدين...السلطان المعظم
    b. AH 600/1203–1204 CE.

West façade:

11. Socle medallions (right to left): boar; horse; lion; elephant.
12. Vertical band, west–north corner: *thuluth*, Qur'ān I:1 (al-Fātiḥa).
13. Parallel vertical band: *thuluth* (?), Qur'ān LV:2 (al-Raḥmān).
14. West–south niche panel: *naskh*, Qur'ān CVIII:2–3? (al-Kauthar).
15. Vertical band, west–south corner: *thuluth*, Qur'ān LV:1 (al-Raḥmān).
16. West–north niche panel: *naskh*, Qur'ān CVIII:1–2? (al-Kauthar).[41]

North façade:

17. Socle medallion (northeast extant): swan.
18. Northwest corner vertical band: *thuluth*, Qur'ān I:1 (al-Fātiḥa).
19. Continuous band framing northwest niche: floriated Kufic, الملك لله (repeated).
20. Northwest niche panel: *naskh*, Qur'ān CXII:1–2? (al-Ikhlāṣ).
21. Continuous band framing northeast niche: floriated Kufic, الملك لله (repeated).
22. Northeast niche panel: *naskh*, Qur'ān CXII:3–4? (al-Ikhlāṣ).

Notes

1. Arranged alphabetically and chronologically.
2. Hillenbrand 2012: 19ff.
3. Among the most relevant works for Iran and Central Asia is of course Blair's (1992) comprehensive collection of inscriptions from these regions. Additionally, R. Giunta's masterly work on the funerary inscriptions found at Ghazna (2003), along with the follow-up article of 2017, serve as important sources for the inscriptions in Volume II (cf. also Afghanistan V–VI *infra*).
4. See esp. Chapters 4 and 5. A particularly noteworthy example of Ghaznavid–Shansabānī imperial dialogue – or rather, the latter's emulation of their famous predecessors – comes from the Shansabānīs of Fīrūzkūh: their court poet Fakhr al-Dīn Mubārakshāh al-Marvarrūzī (d. AH 602/1206 CE) – to be distinguished from the India-based poet known as Fakhr-i Mudābbir, a.k.a Mubārakshāh (fl. mid-thirteenth century) – apparently composed one of only two known pre-Mongol "dynastic *mathnavīs*," quite possibly using as his model the contents of the lengthy epigraphic program of the Ghazna palace's central court, which might have been the other surviving example of this poetic *genre* (see Afghanistan V). Fakhr al-Dīn's full composition is no longer extant, known only through subsequent quotations from it, e.g., in Jūzjānī's *Ṭabaqāt* (vol. I, 1963: 318–319; trans. vol. I, 1873: 300–302). Cf. Khan 1977: 127; and esp. Allegranzi 2019a, vol. I: 143–144 and n. 82.
5. Also known as "Bābā Khaṭīm *ziyārat*." Cf. Melikian-Chirvani 1968; Sourdel-Thomine 1971; Schneider 1984; and Introduction, above.
6. Sourdel-Thomine (1971: 315) characterized the Qur'anic references in this inscription as "*formules pieuses*," finding its remainder illegible. As later deciphered by Schneider (1984: 165), in fact the Qur'anic phrases appeared to form part of a prayer for the compassion of Allah upon the named calligrapher/decorator or builder.
7. The present volume's focus on the initial Shansabānī occupation of Bust–Lashkari Bazar (see Chapter 5) has necessitated the separate treatment of archaeological finds from sites: the well-known *stelae* recovered near Bust, from the tomb locally attributed to a certain Shāhzāda Shaikh Ḥusain ibn Shaikh Ibrāhīm, will be treated in Volume II. Nonetheless, see Sourdel-Thomine 1956; Crane 1979; and Introduction, for a discussion of the Shāhzāda Shaikh Ḥusain tomb.
8. See Sourdel-Thomine 1978: IB:65ff.; and especially Chapter 4.
9. Cf. Chapter 5 (including notes) for a discussion of the inscription's variable readings.
10. Cf. Blair 1985: 81–82; Kalus 2017: Fiche No. 37804; Ball 2019: No. 212. I reiterate my gratitude to Dr. Viola Allegranzi (2019b [forthcoming]) for sharing her work in progress on Chisht's epigraphy.
11. See Chapter 4 (esp. notes) for a discussion of the seemingly anachronistic presence of this *laqab*: As of AH 558/1163 CE Bahā' al-Dīn Sām's elder son had adopted Ghiyāth al-Dīn for his regnal title as sulṭān. See also Giunta and Bresc 2004: 227.

12. For a contextualization of the mixture of Arabic and Persian in the date, cf. Giunta 2010: 177.

13. After Casimir and Glatzer 1971; Glatzer 1973; Blair 1985: 81; Najimi 2015. See also Ball 2019: No. 1023.

14. Recorded only by Najimi (2015: 154); unfortunately, the author did not include a photograph of this previously unread inscription.

15. Najimi (2015: 157, 167) proposed the identification of this *takbīr*; but see Chapter 4.

16. Described as a specifically Shiʿī Ḥadīth by Najimi (2015: 162–163), though varying versions of it are to be found in Sunnī Ḥadīth collections as well – cf. Chapter 4.

17. As was the case with Bust (cf. *supra*), this volume's focus on the initial expansion of the Shansabānīs beyond Ghūr has required that treatment of the abundant funerary markers (principally tombstones) be undertaken in Volume II (cf. also Giunta 2003a; Giunta 2003b; Giunta 2017).

18. Only forty-four slabs were excavated *in situ*, principally on the west but also on the east and north dadoes of the courtyard; another 344 slabs were not *in situ*. According to Bombaci's (1966: 6) calculations based on the average width, a total of about 510 slabs could have comprised the dado revetment of the palace's interior courtyard. The marble dado was placed below the baked brick and stucco epigraphy above it (V: 5), probably datable to the Shansabānī occupation of the palace. Cf. also Bombaci 1966: 33–36; Artusi 2009; Rugiadi 2009: 108ff.; Giunta 2010a: 164–166; Allegranzi 2019 (2 vols.); Allegranzi 2020a; Ball 2019: No. 358; Laviola 2020: 28–29.

19. These marble dado elements are to be distinguished from V:3–4, being associated primarily with the northern entrance to the palace, or Hall XVII in the excavated palace's plan (see, e.g., Allegranzi 2019a, vol. I:71). Already in the early seasons of excavations at the site, Scerrato (1959b, cited in Giunta 2010b) had suggested they formed an independent epigraphic program, contained within the north entrance alcove and separate from the larger compositions of the central court. Cf. Rugiadi 2010: 2 (also cited in Allegranzi 2020a). Giunta (2010b: 125) intriguingly observed that benedictory phrases – albeit with some modifications – commonly occurred also on metalwork from eastern Iran during the eleventh–thirteenth centuries. Cf. Laviola 2020: 456–457.

20. See esp. Bombaci 1966: 3, 19–20, figs. 131 and 133–136; Giunta and Bresc 2004: 171–172, 213–214; Giunta 2010a: 123–125; Kalus 2017: Fiche Nos. 36936, 36938, 43574, 43578, 43580, 43594, 43602, 43654. The rediscovery of these fragments and their reconstitution as one element was paramount, as they likely date the addition of the western oratory (XIII on the excavated palace's plan [Allegranzi 2019a, vol. I:71]) to the reign of Masʿūd III (r. AH 492–509/ 1099–1115 CE).

21. The reading of Kalus (2017: Fiche No. 36936) is followed here; Giunta (2010b: 124) transliterated the date as corresponding to خمس و خمس مايه.

22. This inscription does not figure among Kalus's (2017; cf. note *supra*) re-readings of the published texts, so that Giunta's (2010b: 123) transliteration is followed here.

23. Bombaci's (1966: 13–15) initial epigraphic analysis of these extremely

important finds led him to observe that the meter(s) of the compositions on the *ex situ* slabs was "not clear, but it seems not to contradict the *mutaqārib* or the *mujtathth* of the text preserved *in situ*." Allegranzi's recent and extremely meticulous study of the dado slabs provided a modified understanding of the composition and contents of their inscriptions, as well as a period of composition probably post-mid-eleventh century, both of which are followed here. Cf. also Allegranzi 2020a; and *infra*. For the slabs carrying the *mutaqārib* meter, see Allegranzi 2019a, vol. I:70–84, 105–112, 120 and II:19–48, 64–76, 167–170, 173, 175–176, 183–192, 195–196, 204–207, 210–211, 213–216, 219. Cited here (and in note *infra*) are all the dado fragments bearing a discernible meter, whether found *in situ* or recovered *ex situ* – including at locales outside the Ghazna palace but in the city's environs, some having also been repurposed in other, usually funerary contexts (see, e.g., Laviola 2015).

24. Allegranzi's (2019a, vol. I:119–120; II:29) analysis of several dado slabs *in situ* along the central court's west perimeter noted elegiac content, with reminiscences of the poet Farrūkhī's (d. 1037–8?) compositions on the occasion of Sulṭān Maḥmūd's death. It is noteworthy, perhaps, that the simple and direct title of *shāh* is nowhere else associated with Sulṭān Maḥmūd, absent among other known numismatic and historical data; by contrast, it *was* associated with the Shansabānī Sultan Muʿizz al-Dīn on an undated coin minted at Ghazna (cf. Giunta and Bresc 2004: 166–168, 178, 206–208, 226).

25. Although very few certainties as to personages and dates emerge from the epigraphy of the Ghazna palace dadoes, the mention of Abū Saʿīd (Sulṭān Masʿūd I) and his posthumous title of *Amīr-i Shahīd* in the following distich is among the few "incontestable" data, interpreted by Allegranzi (2019a, vol. I:120, 126 and II:36–37) as a definitive *terminus post quem* for the epigraphic project, *viz.* 1041 CE or the death of Masʿūd I. See also Giunta and Bresc 2004: 168, 177, 208.

26. Cf. esp. Allegranzi 2019a, vol. I:114–115 and II:19–51, 61–63, 80–81, 83–84, 88–90, 92–96, 117, 123–124, 132–134, 159–160, 171–172, 193–195, 200–203, 217–218, 227–228, 233–235. The reader is referred to Allegranzi's study for the contents of the epigraphic fragments; again, only those lengthy enough to convey meter are cited here (also noted *supra*).

27. A few of these fragments were photographed *in situ* during the Italian excavations of the site in the 1950s–1960s. See Figures 5.6 and 5.7.

28. Not only were these Qur'anic verses extremely common in funerary inscriptions), they are the only attested Qur'anic epigraphy in baked brick, which has been dated to the Shansabānī occupation of the Ghazna palace in the last quarter of the twelfth century. Cf. Giunta 2010a: 126; and Chapters 5 and 6.

29. While the *laqab* was primarily associated with Sulṭān Muʿizz al-Dīn after his Ghazna victory (AH 568/1173–1174 CE) in numismatic, epigraphic, and textual sources, it was also to be seen on several coins of Maḥmūd ibn Ghiyāth al-Dīn (r. AH 602–607/1206–1210 CE [Khwārazm-shāh vassal AH 604/1207–1208 CE]); and on coins of three of the Shansabānī sultans of Bamiyan. Cf. Giunta and Bresc 2004: 225.

30. See Y. Godard 1936: I:367–369 and II:351; Pinder-Wilson 2001: 162–166; Giunta and Bresc 2004: 177, 187, 193, 194, 198, 201.

31. After Sourdel-Thomine 2004; Giunta and Bresc 2004: 218, 225; Lintz 2013. See also Ball 2019: No. 468.

32. See full discussion of the *minār*'s probable *miḥrāb* and orientation (*qibla*) in Chapter 4.

33. See esp. Sourdel-Thomine 1978: IB:11–15, 29–36, 42–50, 54–57 and planches; also Allegranzi 2020a. The specific locations referred to within this site are derived from *Lashkari Bazar* (1978) planches 2, 3, 4, 13, 23. Cf. also Ball 2019: No. 685. The sequence of inscriptions listed here has taken into account the probable dual principal axes of ingress into the palace: one from the south (*via* the eponymous bazaar preceding the palace itself), which would first bring the visitor to the forecourt's mosque (VIII:1), and then onto the main façade of the palace structure (VIII:2); and another, more ceremonial entrance on the palace's north perimeter from the Helmand's banks (VIII:3). The vastness of this site is well known, and to date its many structures (in varying states of preservation) have been only partially explored and documented. The focus here is on decipherable epigraphic remains dated either by content or style to Shansabānī presence; but several smaller architectural ruins besides those deemed palaces were also attributed to this period, based on anepigraphic motifs and their execution: e.g., Building Annex XX (northeast of South Palace), and the so-called House of Racquets (Residence XIII) about 1 km northeast of Bust. See Sourdel-Thomine, *op. cit.*, 54–55, 60–61.

34. Although undated, Sourdel-Thomine (1978: IB:57) attributed the *miḥrāb*'s epigraphic program to a second phase of intervention here, namely, Shansabānī renovations at the site overall (see also VIII:2–4), based on the "refinement of certain forms of letters … that would be difficult to imagine before the epigraphic development of the second half of the twelfth century in Afghanistan" (my trans.).

35. Sourdel-Thomine (1978: IB:35–36) was in favor of a late Ghaznavid date for parts of Audience Hall I's epigraphic program, likening the execution to works such as the *minār*s of Mas'ūd III and Bahrām Shāh (cf. Afghanistan VI). Even without Shansabānī renovations here, however, the ceremonial and architectural predominance of this audience hall would have surely required Mu'izz al-Dīn's engagement with it after his victorious occupation of Lashkari Bazar and its environs. See also Chapter 5.

36. Cf. Khan 1988: 307–377; Edwards 1990: 182–193; Edwards 1991: 92; Edwards 2015: 111–127, 201–210. The exterior of this structure is strikingly devoid of ornament or epigraphy, at least partially due to renovations over the centuries. Cf. Chapter 6.

37. See Khan 1988: 316–322; Ali 1993: 134–136; Flood 2001.

38. From Rehman and Hussain 2011.

39. Reproduced side-by-side with a line reading of the text in Rehman and Hussain (2011: 69–70). Further examples of bilingual Śāradā–Persian or – Arabic inscriptions have been published: cf. Dani et al., 1964; Rahman 1998; and Chapter 6 notes.

40. This style of script was denoted by the authors (Rehman and Hussain 2011: 66, fig. 12), though without further explication.

41. It is possible that the epigraphic bands were rearranged in the course of the intervening centuries: it is distinctly notable on this façade that the sequence of verses from Qur'ān CVIII is reversed according to the process of circumambulation. This reversal is to be contrasted to the north façade (Pakistan III: 20 and 22), on which the verses of Qur'ān CXII do appear according to the progress of a circumambulating worshiper.

Works Cited and Bibliography

Historical Works

Anon. *Tārīkh-i Sīstān*, trans. M. Gold, Literary and Historical Texts from Iran, 2. Roma: Istituto italiano per il Medio ed Estremo Oriente, 1976.

Bayhaqī, Abū al-Faẓl. *The History of Beyhaqi (The History of Sultan Masʿud of Ghazna, 1030–1041)*, trans. C. E. Bosworth, 3 vols. Boston, MA: Ilex Foundation, 2011.

Gardīzī, ʿAbd al-Ḥayy. *The Ornament of Histories: A History of the Eastern Islamic Lands, AD 650–1041*, ed. and trans. Clifford Edmund Bosworth, BIPS Persian Studies Series. London: British Institute of Persian Studies and I. B. Tauris, 2011.

Jūzjānī, Abū ʿAmr Minhāj al-Dīn ʿUthmān ibn Sirāj al-Dīn Muḥammad. *A General History of the Muhammadan Dynasties of India*, trans. Major H. Raverty, Elibron Classics Replica, 2 vols. London: Gilbert & Rivington, 1881.

Jūzjānī, Abū ʿAmr Minhāj al-Dīn ʿUthmān ibn Sirāj al-Dīn Muḥammad. *Ṭabaqāt-i Nāṣiri*, ed. Abdul Hai Habibi, 2nd edn. Kabul: Historical Society of Afghanistan, 1963.

Samarqandī, Niẓāmī al-ʿArūẓī. *Chahār Maqāla (The Four Discourses) of Nizami al-Aruzi al-Samarqandi*, trans. Edward G. Browne. 1978th edn. London: EJW Gibb Memorial Trust, 1921.

Sanāʾi, Ḥakīm Abū al-Majd Majdūd. *The First Book of the Hadiqatuʾl-Haqiqat, or the Enclosed Garden of the Truth*, trans. J. Stephenson. Calcutta: Baptist Mission Press, 1910.

The Udana or the Solemn Utterances of the Buddha, trans. D. M. Strong. London: Luzac, 1902, available at: https://archive.org/details/in.gov.ignca.9263.

Modern Persian Works

Abbārī, Asghar Farughī. *Tārīkh-e Ghūrīyān* (تاریخ غوریان). Tehran: Sāzmān-e Muṭālʿa wa Tadwīn-e Kutub-e ʿUlūm-e Insānī-ye Dāneshgāhā (SAMT), 2003.

Maḥmūd, Maḥmūd Shāh. *Tārīkh-e impirāṭūrī-e Ghūrīyān* (تاریخ امپراطوری غوریان). Kabul: Muʾassasa-ye Intishārāt-e Khāvar, 2009.

Pazkvāk, ʿAṭīq Allah. *Ghūrīyān* (غوریان). Kabul: Anjumān-i Tārīkh-i Afghānistān, 1968.

Roshanzamir, Mahdī. *Tārīkh-e Sīyāsī wa Niẓāmī-yi Dūdmān-i Ghūrī* (تاریخ سیاسی و نظامی دودمان غوری). Tehran: Dāneshgāh-e Millī-e Irān, 1978.

Works on Afghanistan

Adamec, Ludwig W .(ed.). *Historical and Political Gazetteer of Afghanistan*, 6 vols. Graz: Akademische Druck- u. Verlagsanstalt, 1972.

Adle, Chahryar. "Trois mosquées du début de l'ère islamique au Grand Khorassan: Bastam, Noh-Gonbadan/Haji-Piyadeh de Balkh et Zuzan d'après des investigations archéologiques," in *Greater Khorasan: History, Geography, Archaeology and Material Culture* (ed. Rocco Rante), 89–114. Berlin: De Gruyter, 2015.

Allegranzi, Viola. "Royal Architecture Portrayed in Bayhaqī's Tārīḫ-i Masʿūdī and Archaeological Evidence from Ghazni (Afghanistan, 10th–12th c.)." *Annali dell'Istituto Orientale di Napoli* 74 (2014): 95–120.

Allegranzi, Viola. "The Use of Persian in Monumental Epigraphy from Ghazni (Eleventh–Twelfth Centuries)." *Eurasian Studies* 13 (2015): 23–41.

Allegranzi, Viola. *Aux sources de la poésie ghaznavide. Les inscriptions persanes de Ghazni (Afghanistan, XI–XII siècles)*, 2 vols. Paris: Presses Sorbonne Nouvelle, 2019a.

Allegranzi, Viola. "New Epigraphic Data from a Ghurid Monument in Chisht-i Sharif: Expressing Power and Piety in 12th-century Afghanistan," paper presented at *Inscriptions from the Islamic World*, Cairo, 6–8 September 2019b, forthcoming.

Allen, Terry. "Notes on Bust." *Journal of the British Institute of Persian Studies, Iran* 26 (1988): 55–68.

Allen, Terry. "Notes on Bust (Continued)." *Journal of the British Institute of Persian Studies, Iran* 28 (1990): 23–30.

Artusi, S. "Architectural Decoration from the Palace of Masʿud III in Ghazni: The Italian Contribution (1957–2007)," in *The IsIAO Italian Archaeological Mission in Afghanistan 1957–2007: Fifty Years of Research in the Heart of Eurasia (Proceedings of the Symposium Held in the Istituto Italiano per l'Africa e l'Oriente, Rome, 8 January 2008), vol. 21: Conferenze* (eds. Anna Filigenzi and Roberta Giunta), 117–130. Rome: Istituto Italiano per l'Africa e l'Oriente, 2009.

Azad, Arezou. *Sacred Landscape in Medieval Afghanistan: Revisiting the Faḍāʾil-i Balkh*. Oxford: Oxford University Press, 2013.

Baker, P. H. B. and F. Raymond Allchin. *Shahr-i Zohak and the History of the Bamiyan Valley, Afghanistan*, Ancient India and Iran Trust Series, No. 1. Oxford: Tempvs Reparatvm, 1991.

Ball, Warwick. "The Seven Qandahars: The Name Q.ND.HAR. in the Islamic Sources." *South Asian Studies* 4 (1988): 115–142.

Ball, Warwick. "Chapter 12: General Conclusions: Historical Overview of the Kandahar Sequence," in *Excavations at Kandahar 1974 and 1975* (eds. Anthony McNicoll and Warwick Ball), 391–402. Oxford: Tempus Reparatum, 1996.

Ball, Warwick. "The Towers of Ghur: A Ghurid 'Maginot Line'?" in *Cairo to Kabul* (eds. Warwick Ball and Leonard Harrow), 21–45. London: Melisende, 2002.

Ball, Warwick. *The Monuments of Afghanistan: History, Archaeology and Architecture*. London: I. B. Tauris, 2008.

Ball, Warwick. "Afghanistan, Art and Architecture." In *Encyclopedia of Islam*,

3rd edn (eds. Gudrun Krämer, Denis Matringe, John Nawas, and Everett Rowson). Leiden: Brill Online, 2013.

Ball, Warwick. *Archaeological Gazetteer of Afghanistan*, revised edn. Oxford: Oxford University Press, 2019.

Ball, Warwick. "Buddhist Elements in the Architecture of Afghanistan, 1000–1250," in *The Architecture of the Greater Iranian World, 1000–1250* (ed. Robert Hillenbrand). Edinburgh: Edinburgh University Press, 2020.

Ball, Warwick, Olivier Bordeaux, David W. MacDowall, Nicholas Sims-Williams, and Maurizio Taddei. "Chapter 6. From the Kushans to the Shahis," in *The Archaeology of Afghanistan from Earliest Times to the Timurid Period* (eds. F. R. Allchin, Norman Hammond, and Warwick Ball), 344–459. Edinburgh: Edinburgh University Press, 2019.

Ball, Warwick and Yolanda Crowe. "General Conclusions: Historical Overview of the Kandahar Sequence," in *Excavations at Kandahar 1974 and 1975* (eds. Anthony McNicoll and Warwick Ball), 391–402. Oxford: Tempus Reparatum, 1996.

Ball, Warwick and Klaus Fischer. "Chapter 7. From the Rise of Islam to the Mongol Invasion," in *The Archaeology of Afghanistan from Earliest Times to the Timurid Period* (eds. F. R. Allchin, Norman Hammond, and Warwick Ball), 460–545. Edinburgh: Edinburgh University Press, 2019.

Ball, Warwick, Simon Glenn, Bertille Lyonnet, David W. MacDowall, and Maurizio Taddei. "Chapter 5. The Iron Age, Achaemenids, and Hellenistic Periods," in *The Archaeology of Afghanistan from Earliest Times to the Timurid Period* (eds. F. R. Allchin, Norman Hammond, and Warwick Ball), 260–343. Edinburgh: Edinburgh University Press, 2019.

Bernard, Paul and Frantz Grenet. "Découverte d'une statue du dieu solaire Surya dans la région de Caboul." *Studia Iranica* 10(1) (1981): 127–146.

Bernardini, Michele. "Les Qaraunas à Ghazni, XIIIe–XIVe siècles," in *Texts and Contexts: Ongoing Researches on the Eastern Iranian World (Ninth–Fifteenth C.)* (eds. Viola Allegranzi and Valentina Laviola), 249–268. Rome: Istituto per l'Oriente C. A. Nallino, 2020.

Bivar, A. D. H. "Seljuqid Ziayarats of Sar-i Pul (Afghanistan)." *Bulletin of the School of Oriental and African Studies* 29(1) (1966): 57–63.

Bivar, A. D. H. "Review of *Lashkari Bazar: une résidence royale ghaznévide et ghoride.*" *Bulletin of the School of Oriental and African Studies* 43(2) (1980): 385–386.

Bombaci, Alessio. "Ghazni." *East and West* 8(3) (1957): 247–260.

Bombaci, Alessio. *The Kūfic Inscription in Persian Verses in the Court of the Royal Palace of Mas'ūd III at Ghazni*, Reports and Memoirs, 5. Rome: IsMEO, 1966.

Bosworth, C. E. "Ghaznevid Military Organisation." *Der Islam* 36(1/2) ([1960] 1977): 37–77.

Bosworth, C. E. "The Early Islamic History of Ghur." *Central Asiatic Journal* 6(2) (1961): 116–133.

Bosworth, C. E. *The Ghaznavids, Their Empire in Afghanistan and Eastern Iran (994–1040)*. Beirut: Librarie du Liban, [1963] 2015.

Bosworth, C. E. "Notes on the Pre-Ghaznavid History of Eastern Afghanistan." *The Islamic Quarterly: A Review of Islamic Culture* 9 (1965): 12–24.

Bosworth, C. E. "Mahmud of Ghazna in Contemporary Eyes and in Later Persian Literature." *Iran* IV (1966): 85–92.

Bosworth, C. E. *Sistan under the Arabs, from the Islamic Conquest to the Rise of the Saffarids (30–250/651–864).* Rome: Istituto Italiano per il Medio ed Estremo Oriente, 1968a.

Bosworth, C. E. "The Coming of Islam to Afghanistan," in *Islam in Asia* (ed. Yohanan Friedmann), 1:1–22. Boulder, CO: Westview Press, 1984.

Bosworth, C. E. "Balkh ii. History from the Arab Conquest to the Mongols," in *Encyclopaedia Iranica*, online edition, 1988.

Bosworth, C. E. *The Later Ghaznavids: Splendour and Decay*, 1st Indian edn. New Delhi: Munshiram Manoharlal Publishers, [1977] 1992.

Bosworth, C. E. *The History of the Saffarids of Sistan and the Maliks of Nimruz.* Costa Mesa, CA: Mazda, 1994.

Bosworth, C. E. "Firuzkuh," in *Encyclopaedia Iranica*, December 15, 1999.

Bosworth, C. E. "The Appearance and Establishment of Islam in Afghanistan," in *Islamisation de l'Asia Centrale* (ed. Étienne de la Vassière), 97–114. Paris: Association pour l'avancement des études iraniennes, 2008.

Bosworth, C. E. "Additions to the New Islamic Dynasties," in *Living Islamic History: Studies in Honour of Carole Hillenbrand* (ed. Y. Suleiman), 14–31. Edinburgh: Edinburgh University Press, 2010.

Bosworth, C. E. "Fakhr-i Mudabbir," in *Encyclopaedia of Islam*, 2nd edn (eds. Th. Bianquis, C. E. Bosworth, E. van Donzel, W. P. Heinrichs, and P. Bearman). Leiden: Brill online, 2012a.

Bosworth, C. E. "Karramiyya," in *Encyclopedia of Islam*, 2nd edn (eds. P. Bearman, Th. Bianquis, C. E. Bosworth, E. van Donzel, and W. P. Heinrichs). Leiden: Brill online, 2012b.

Bosworth, C. E. "Ghurids," in *Encyclopaedia Iranica*, online edition, 2012c.

Bosworth, C. E. "Ghurids," in *Encyclopaedia of Islam*, 2nd edn (eds. P. Bearman, Th. Bianquis, C. E. Bosworth, E. van Donzel, and W. P. Heinrichs). Leiden : Brill online, 2014.

Casimir, Michael and Bernt Glatzer. "Shah-i Mashhad, a Recently Discovered Madrasah of the Ghurid Period in Gargistan." *East and West* 21(1/2) (1971): 53–68.

Crane, Howard. "Helmand–Sistan Project: An Anonymous Tomb at Bust." *East and West* 29 (1979): 241–246.

Cribb, Joe. "Chapter Four: The Monetary History of Begram," in *Charles Masson: Collections from Begram and Kabul Bazaar, Afghanistan, 1833–1838* (ed. Elizabeth Errington), 79–206. London: The British Museum, 2020.

Crowe, Yolanda. "Chapter 10: Glazed Ceramics," in *Excavations at Kandahar 1974 and 1975* (eds. Anthony McNicoll and Warwick Ball), 313–364. Oxford: Tempus Reparatum, 1996.

Dagens, Bruno, Marc Le Berre, and Daniel Schlumberger. *Monuments préislamiques d'Afghanistan*, Mémoires de la Délégation Archéologique Française en Afghanistan, vol. 19. Paris: Librairie G. Klincksieck, 1964.

de la Vassière, Étienne. "Inherited Landscapes in Muslim Bactra." *Eurasian Studies* 16 (2018): 124–141.

de Planhol, X. "Bamian i. The Bamian Basin," in *Encyclopaedia Iranica*, online edition, 1988.

de Planhol, X. "Gazni i. Historical Geography," in *Encyclopaedia Iranica*, online edition, [2000] 2012.

Dupree, Louis. *Afghanistan*, 8th edn. Karachi: Oxford University Press, [1997 3rd edn.] 2012.

Dupree, Nancy Hatch. *An Historical Guide to Afghanistan*, 2nd edn. Kabul: Afghan Tourist Organization, 1977.

Errington, Elizabeth. *Charles Masson and the Buddhist Sites of Afghanistan: Explorations, Excavations, Collections 1832–1835*, Research Publication, No. 215. London: The British Museum Press, 2017.

Fischel, Walter J. "The Rediscovery of the Medieval Jewish Community at Fīrūzkūh in Central Afghanistān." *Journal of the American Oriental Society* 85(2) (1965): 148–153.

Fischer, Klaus. "Archaeological Remains of Jainism in West Pakistan and Afghanistan." *Voice of Ahimsa* 121 (1962).

Fischer, Klaus. "Preliminary Remarks on Archaeological Survey in Afghanistan." *Zentralasiatische Studien* 3 (1969): 327–408.

Fischer, Klaus. "Projects of Archaeological Maps from Afghan-Seistan between 3120′ to 3050′N and 6200′ to 6210′E (with Three Maps in Folder)." *Zentralasiatische Studien* 4 (1970): 483–534.

Fischer, Klaus. "Historical, Geographical and Philological Studies on Seistan by Bosworth, Daffinà and Gnoli in the Light of Recent Archaeological Field Surveys." *East and West* 21 (1971): 45–51.

Fischer, Klaus. "Chapter 6: From the Rise of Islam to the Mongol Invasion," in *The Archaeology of Afghanistan from Earliest Times to the Timurid Period* (eds. F. R. Allchin and Norman Hammond), 301–355. New York: Academic Press, 1978.

Fischer, Klaus, Dietrich Morgenstern, and Volker Thewalt. *Geländebegehungen in Sistan 1955–1973 Und Die Aufnahme von Dewal-i Khodaydad 1970, vol. 2: Plates, Maps, Plans*, 2 vols. Bonn: Rudolf Habelt Verlag, 1974.

Flood, Finbarr B. "Between Cult and Culture: Bamiyan, Islamic Iconoclasm, and the Museum." *The Art Bulletin* 84(4) (2002): 641–659.

Flood, Finbarr B. "Ghurid Monuments and Muslim Identities: Epigraphy and Exegesis in Twelfth-Century Afghanistan." *Indian Economic and Social History Review* 42(3) (2005a): 263–294.

Flood, Finbarr B. "Review of *Le minaret ghouride de Jam: un chef d'oeuvre du XIIe siècle* by J. Sourdel-Thomine." *Art Bulletin* 87(3) (2005b): 536–543.

Flood, Finbarr B. "Islamic Identities and Islamic Art: Inscribing the Qur'an in Twelfth-Century Afghanistan." *Studies in the History of Art* 74 (2009b): 91–117.

Flury, S. "Le décor épigraphique des monuments de Ghazna." *Syria (Revue d'Art Oriental et d'Archéologie)* 6 (1925): 61–90.

Franke, Ute. "Ancient Herat Revisited. New Data from Recent Archaeological Fieldwork," in *Greater Khorasan: History, Geography, Archaeology and Material Culture* (ed. Rocco Rante), 63–88, Studies in the History and Culture of the Middle East. Berlin: De Gruyter, 2015.

Franke, Ute. "Glazed Earthenware from the 10th to the 13th Century," in *Herat through Time, vol. 3: Ancient Herat* (eds. Ute Franke and Martina Müller-Wiener), 138–183. Berlin: Staatliche Museen zu Berlin, 2016a.

Franke, Ute. "Herat from the 10th to the 14th Century," in *Herat through Time, vol. 3: Ancient Herat* (eds. Ute Franke and Martina Müller-Wiener), 75–86. Berlin: Staatliche Museen zu Berlin, 2016b.

Franke, Ute. "Monochrome Fritware from the 12th and Early 13th Century," in *Herat through Time, vol. 3: Ancient Herat*, 359–371. Berlin: Staatliche Museen zu Berlin, 2016c.

Franke, Ute. "Monochrome Glazed Earthenware," in *Herat through Time, vol. 3: Ancient Herat* (eds. Ute Franke and Martina Müller-Wiener), 319–357. Berlin: Staatliche Museen zu Berlin, 2016d.

Franke, Ute. "Unglazed Pottery from the 10th to the 13th Century: Magic Motifs," in *Herat through Time, vol. 3: Ancient Herat*, 231–317. Berlin: Staatliche Museen zu Berlin, 2016d.

Franke, Ute. "Archaeological Research in Qal'a-e Ekhtyaruddin: Excavations in the Upper Citadel – Trenches 1a and 1b," in *Excavations and Explorations in Herat City, vol. 2: Ancient Herat* (eds. Ute Franke and Thomas Urban), 93–319. Berlin: Staatliche Museen zu Berlin, 2017.

Franke, Ute. "Résumé: New Perspectives on Ancient Herat," in *Excavations and Explorations in Herat City, vol. 2: Ancient Herat* (eds. Ute Franke and Thomas Urban), 743–751. Berlin: Staatliche Museen zu Berlin, 2017.

Franke, Ute, Benjamin Mutin, and Cécile Buquet-Marcon. "Excavations in Kuhandaz," in *Excavations and Explorations in Herat City, vol. 2: Ancient Herat* (eds. Ute Franke and Thomas Urban), 689–731. Berlin: Staatliche Museen zu Berlin, 2017.

Franke, Ute and Thomas Urban. "Areia Antica – Ancient Herat: Summary of the Work Carried out by the DAI-Mission in Collaboration with the Institute of Archaeology, Ministry of Information and Culture, Kabul, August–September 2006." Berlin: German Foreign Office; German Archaeological Institute (DAI), 2006.

Franklin, Kathryn and Emily Boak. "The Road From Above: Remotely Sensed Discovery of Early Modern Travel Infrastructure in Afghanistan." *Archaeological Research in Asia* 19 (2019): 40–54.

Frye, Richard N. and Clifford Edmund Bosworth. "Herat," in *Historic Cities of the Islamic World* (ed. C. E. Bosworth), 153–155. Leiden: Brill, 2007.

Gardin, J-C. "Poteries de Bamiyan." *Ars Orientalis* 2 (1957): 227–245.

Gardin, J-C. *Lashkari Bazar: une résidence royale ghaznévide et ghoride, vol. 2: Les trouvailles; céramiques et monnais de Lashkari Bazar et de Bust*, 2 vols. Paris: Klincksieck, 1963.

Gascoigne, Alison. "Pottery from Jam: A Medieval Ceramic Corpus from Afghanistan." *Iran* 48 (2010): 107–151.

Ghafur, Muhammad Abdul. "The Gorids: History, Culture and Administration," University of Hamburg, 1960.

Giunta, Roberta. "Some Brief Remarks on a Funerary Stele Located in the Gazni Area (Afghanistan)." *East and West* 51(1/2) (2001): 159–165.

Giunta, Roberta. *Les inscriptions funeraires de Ġaznī: (IVe–IXe/Xe–XVe Siècles),*

Series Maior, 8. Napoli: Università degli studi Napoli "L'orientale", Dipartimento di studi asiatici, 2003a.

Giunta, Roberta. "Un texte de construction d'époque guride à Gazni," in *Studi in Onore de Umberto Scerrato per Il Suo Settantacinquesimo Compleanno*, 439–455. Rome, 2003b.

Giunta, Roberta. "Islamic Ghazni An IsIAO Archaeological Project in Afghanistan: A Preliminary Report (July 2004–June 2005)." *East and West* 55(1/4) (2005): 473–484.

Giunta, Roberta. "A Selection of Islamic Coins from the Excavations of Udegram, Swat." *East and West* 56(1/3) (2006): 237–262.

Giunta, Roberta. "Les inscriptions persanes dans l'épigraphie monumentale de la ville de Ghazni (Afghanistan) aux 6e–7e/12e–13e siècle," in *Iranian Identity in the Course of History. Proceedings of the Conference held in Rome, 21–24 September 2005* (ed. Carlo G. Cereti), 163–180, Serie Orientale Roma CV. Rome: Istituto Italiano per l'Africa e l'Oriente, 2010a.

Giunta, Roberta. "New Epigraphic Data from the Excavations of the Ghaznavid Palace of Mas'ud III at Ghazni (Afghanistan)," in *South Asian Archaeology 2007: Proceedings of the 19th Meeting of the European Association of /South Asian Archaeology, Ravenna, Italy, July 2007* (eds. Pierfrancesco Callieri and Luca Colliva), BAR International Series 2133, vol. 2, 122–131. Oxford: Archaeopress, 2010b.

Giunta, Roberta. "Gazni ii. Monuments and Inscriptions," in *Encyclopaedia Iranica*, online edition, [2000] 2012.

Giunta, Roberta. "Tombeaux et inscriptions funeraires de Ghazni (Afghanistan). Quelques documents inédits du XIe–XIIIe siècle." *Vicino Oriente* XXI (2017): 127–145.

Giunta, Roberta. "Les études sur la documentation archéologique et épigraphique de Ghazni: Résultats et nouvelles pistes de recherche," in *Texts and Contexts: Ongoing Researches on the Eastern Iranian World (Ninth–Fifteenth C.)* (eds. Viola Allegranzi and Valentina Laviola), 157–186. Rome: Istituto per l'Oriente C.A. Nallino, 2020.

Giunta, Roberta and Cécile Bresc. "Listes de la titulature des ghaznavides et des ghurides à travers les documents numismatiques et épigraphiques." *Eurasian Studies* III(1) (2004): 161–243.

Glatzer, Bernt. "The Madrasah of Shah-i Mashhad in Badgis." *Afghanistan* 25(4) (1973): 46–68.

Glatzer, Bernt. "Das Mausoleum und die Moschee des Ghoriden Ghiyat-ud-Din in Herat." *Afghanistan Journal* 7(1) (1980): 6–22.

Grenet, Frantz. "The Nomadic Element in the Kushan Empire (1st–3rd Century AD)." *Journal of Central Eurasian Studies* 3 (2012): 1–22.

Habibi, A. H. "The City of Ferozkoh: Where Was It?" *Afghanistan* 33(1) (1980): 34–44.

Hackin, Joseph and Johann Carl. *Nouvelles Recherches Archéologiques à Bamiyan, vol. III : Mémoires de la délégation archéologique française en Afghanistan*. Paris: Les Éditions G. Van Oest, 1933.

Haim, Ofir. "An Early Judeo-Persian Letter Sent from Ghazna to Bāmiyān (Ms. Heb. 4°8333.29)." *Bulletin of the Asia Institute* 26 (2012): 103–120.

Haim, Ofir. "What Is the 'Afghan Genizah'? A Short Guide to the Collection of the Afghan Manuscripts in the National Library of Israel, with the Edition of Two Documents." *Afghanistan* 2(1) (2019): 70–90.

Hammer, Emily, Rebecca Seifried, Kathryn Franklin, and Anthony Lauricella. "Remote Assessments of the Archaeological Heritage Situationin Afghanistan." *Journal of Cultural Heritage*, 2017, 20 pp.

Hansen, Erik, Abdul Wasay Najimi, and Claus Christensen. *The Ghurid Portal of the Friday Mosque of Herat, Afghanistan*. Aarhus: Aarhus University Press, 2015.

Helms, S. W. "Excavations at 'The City and the Famous Fortress of Kandahar, the Foremost Place in All of Asia.'" *Afghan Studies* 3/4 (1982): 1–24.

Helms, S. W. "Kandahar of the Arab Conquest." *World Archaeology* 14(3) (1983): 343–353.

Herberg, Werner. "Das Land Ghor in Afghanistan: auf der Suche nach einem verschollen Imperium." *Die Waage* 17(5) (1978): 216–220.

Herberg, Werner. "Die Wehrbauten von Ghor (Afghanistan): Zusammenfassende Dokumentation Der Bestandsaufnahmen von 1975, 1977 Und 1978." *Die Welt Des Islams* N.S. 22(1/4) (1982): 67–84.

Herberg, Werner and D. Davary. "Topographische Feldarbeiten in Ghor: Bericht über Forschungen zum Probleme Jam-Ferozkoh." *Afghanistan Journal* 3(2) (1976): 57–69.

Hillenbrand, Robert. "The Architecture of the Ghaznavids and Ghurids," in *The Sultan's Turret: Studies in Persian and Turkish Culture. Studies in Honor of Clifford Edmund Bosworth* (ed. Carole Hillenbrand), vol. 2, 124–206. Leiden: Brill, 2000.

Hillenbrand, Robert. "The Ghurid Tomb at Herat," in *Cairo to Kabul* (eds. Warwick Ball and Leonard Harrow), 123–143. London: Melisende, 2002.

Hunter, E. C. D. "Hebrew-Script Tombstones from Jam, Afghanistan." *Journal of Jewish Studies* 61(1) (2010): 72–87.

Inaba, Minoru. "Kandahar iii. Early Islamic Period," in *Encyclopaedia Iranica*, online edition, 2010.

Inaba, Minoru. "Chapter Two: Sedentary Rulers on the Move: The Travels of the Early Ghanzavid Sultans," in *Turko-Mongol Rulers, Cities and City Life* (ed. David Durand-Guédy), 75–98. Leiden: Brill, 2013.

Inaba, Minoru. "The Narratives on the Bāmiyān Buddhist Remains in the Islamic Period," in *Encountering Buddhism and Islam in Premodern Central and South Asia* (eds. B. Auer and I. Strauch), 75–96 (draft). Berlin: De Gruyter, 2019.

Jackson, Peter. "The Fall of the Ghurid Dynasty," in *The Sultan's Turret: Studies in Persian and Turkish Culture. Studies in Honor of Clifford Edmund Bosworth* (ed. Carole Hillenbrand), 2:208–235. Leiden: Brill, 2000.

Johnstone, T. M. "Ghaznawids." in *Encyclopaedia of Islam*, vol. II. Leiden: Brill, 1965.

Khan, M. S. "The Life and Works of Fakhr-i-Mudabbir." *Islamic Culture* LI (1977): 127–140.

Khazeni, Arash. "Fortressed: The Face of the Durrani Kingdom of Afghanistan, circa 1817," paper presented at Twelfth Biennial Iranian Studies Conference, University of California, Irvine, August 2018.

Klimburg-Salter, Deborah. *The Kingdom of Bamiyan: Buddhist Art and Culture of the Hindu Kush*, Series Maior, 5. Naples: Istituto universitario orientale, Dipartimento di studi asiatici, 1989.

Klimburg-Salter, Deborah. "Buddhist Painting in the Hindu Kush, ca. VIIth to Xth Centuries: Reflections on the Co-Existence of Pre-Islamic and Islamic Artistic Cultures during the Early Centuries of the Islamic Era," in *Islamisation de l'Asia Centrale* (ed. Étienne de la Vassière), 131–159. Paris: Association pour l'avancement des études iraniennes, 2008.

Kohzad, A. A. (Ahmed Ali). "Along the Koh-i Baba and Hari-Rud." *Afghanistan* 6(1) (1951a): 1–16.

Kohzad, A. A. "Along the Koh-i Baba and Hari-Rud. Part II." *Afghanistan* 6(2) (1951b): 1–21.

Kohzad, A. A. "Along the Koh-i Baba and Hari-Rud. Part III." *Afghanistan* 7(1) (1952): 50–55.

Kohzad, A. A. "Along the Koh-i Baba and Hari-Rud. Part IV." *Afghanistan* 8(4) (1953): 54–65.

Kohzad, A. A. "Along the Koh-i Baba and Hari Rud. Part V." *Afghanistan* 9(1) (1954a): 20–43.

Kohzad, A. A. "Along the Koh-i Baba and Hari-Rud. Part VI." *Afghanistan* 9(2) (1954b): 1–21.

Kohzad, A.A. "Afghanistan: Geographical and Historical Sketches of Some Localities." *East and West* 7(2) (1956): 128–137.

Kohzad, A. A. "Firoz Koh." *Afghanistan* 12(4) (1957): 31–34.

Kohzad, M. N. (Mohammed Nabi). "Tourist Sites of Afghanistan." *Afghanistan* 14(3) (1959): 1–7.

Kristy, Gwendolyn. "The Impact of Urban Sprawl on Cultural Heritage in Herat, Afghanistan: A GIS Analysis." *Digital Applications in Archaeology and Cultural Heritage* 10 (2018): 8 pp.

Kufi, Ali. *The Chachnamah, An Ancient History of Sind*, trans. Mirza Kalichbeg Fredunbeg. Delhi: Idarah-i Adabiyat-i Delli, 1900.

Laviola, Valentina. "Ziyarat of Ghazni: Three Case Studies about Marble Re-Employments." *Eurasian Studies* 13 (2015): 42–53.

Laviola, Valentina. "Starting the Analysis of Stucco Finds from Ghazni Royal Palace (11th–12th c.)," paper presented at Textes et Contextes: Rechèrches en cours sur le monde iranien oriental (IXe–XVe s.), Napoli, 18–19 September 2018.

Laviola, Valentina. *Islamic Metalwork from Afghanistan (9th–13th Century)*, Università degli Studi di Napoli l'Orientale, Dipartimento Asia, Africa e Mediterraneo, Series Maior 15. Rome: Unior Press, 2020.

Lawler, Andrew. "Satellites Trace Afghanistan's Lost Empires." *Science* 358(6369) (December 15, 2017): 1364–1365.

Le Berre, Marc. "Le monument de Danestama en Afghanistan." *Révue des Études Islamiques* 38 (1970): 43–53.

Le Berre, Marc, Henri Marchal, Jean-Claude Gardin, and Bertille Lyonnet. *Monuments Pré-Islamiques de l'Hindukush Central, vol. XXIV, Mémoires de La Délégation Archéologique Française en Afghanistan*. Paris: Éditions Recherche sur les Civilisations, 1987.

Lee, Jonathan. "Monuments of Bamiyan Province, Afghanistan." *Iran* 44 (2006): 229–252.

Leshnik, Lorenz. "Ghor, Firozkoh, and the Minar-i Jam." *Central Asiatic Journal* XII(1) (1968): 36–49.

Lintz, Ulrike-Christiane. "Persisch-hebräische Inschriften aus Afghanistan." *Judaica* 64(4) (2008): 333–358.

Lintz, Ulrike-Christiane. "Persisch-hebräische Inschriften aus Afghanistan (Teil II)." *Judaica* 65(1) (2009): 43–74.

Lintz, Ulrike-Christiane. "The Qur'anic Inscriptions of the Minaret of Jam in Afghanistan," in *Calligraphy and Architecture in the Muslim World* (eds. Mohammad Gharipour and Irvin Cemil Schick), 83–102. Edinburgh: Edinburgh University Press, 2013.

Litvinsky, Boris and Viktor Solov'ev. "The Architecture and Art of Kafyr Kala (Early Medieval Tokharistan)." *Bulletin of the Asia Institute*, Aspects of Iranian Culture, 4 (1990): 61–75.

Lohuizen-de Leeuw, J. E. van. "An Ancient Hindu Temple in Eastern Afghanistan." *Oriental Art* 5 (1959): 61–69.

Lorain, Thomas. "Chehel Dokhtaran et Shahr-e Gholgholah (Bamiyan): Nouvelles découvertes autour de l'architecture palatiale médiévale en Afghanistan," paper presented at Textes et Contextes: Recherches en cours sur le monde iranien oriental (IXe–XVe s.), Napoli, 18–19 September 2018.

Maitland, P. J. (Major). *Records of Intelligence Party, Afghan Boundary Commission. Diary of Major Maitland with Notes on the Population and Resources of Districts Visited, 1884 to 1887*, vol. II. Simla: Government Central Press, 1888.

Maitland, P. J. (Lieutenant-Colonel). "Chahar Aimak Tribes of Herat. No. III – Firozkohis," in *Records of the Intelligence Party, Afghan Boundary Commission. Reports on Tribes, Namely, Sarik Turkomans, Chahar Aimak Tribes, and Hazaras*, vol. IV, 112–141. Simla: Government Central Printing Office, 1891.

Malamud, Margaret. "The Politics of Heresy in Medieval Khurasan: The Karramiyya in Nishapur." *Iranian Studies* 27(1–4) (1994): 37–51.

Manhart, Christian. "UNESCO's Rehabilitation of Afghanistan's Cultural Heritage: Mandate and Recent Activities," in *Art and Archaeology of Afghanistan: Its Fall and Survival* (ed. Juliette van Krieken-Pieters), 49–60. Leiden: Brill, 2006.

Maricq, André and Gaston Wiet. *Le minaret de Djam: La découverte de la capitale des sultans ghorides (XIIe–XIIIe Siècles), vol. XVI: Mémoires de La Délégation Archéologique Française en Afghanistan.* Paris: Librairie C. Kinkcksieck, 1959.

Matthee, Rudi and Hiroyuki Mashita. "Kandahar Iv. From the Mongol Invasion through the Safavid Era," in *Encyclopaedia Iranica*, online edition, [2010] 2012.

Melikian-Chirvani, Assadullah Souren. "Remarques préliminaires sur un mausolée ghaznévide." *Arts Asiatiques* XVII (1968): 59–92.

Melikian-Chirvani, Assadullah Souren. "Le roman de Varque et Golšâh: essai sur les rapports de l'esthétique littéraire et de l'esthétique plastique dans l'Iran pré-mongol, suivi de la traduction du poème." École Française d'Extrême-Orient, 1970a.

Melikian-Chirvani, Assadullah Souren. "Eastern Iranian Architecture: Apropos of the Ghurid Parts of the Great Mosque of Harat." *BSOAS* XXXIII(2) (1970b): 322–327.

Melikian Chirvani, Assadullah Souren. *Islamic Metalwork from the Islamic World, 8th–18th Centuries*. London: Her Majesty's Stationery Office, 1982.

Melikian-Chirvani, Assadullah Souren. "The Buddhist Ritual in the Literature of Early Islamic Iran," in *South Asian Archaeology 1981*, 272–279. Cambridge: Cambridge University Press, 1984.

Melikian-Chirvani, Assadullah Souren. "Iran to Tibet," in *Islam and Tibet: Interactions along the Musk Routes* (eds. Anna Akasoy, Charles Burnett, and Ronit Yoeli-Tlalim), 89–115. Farnham: Ashgate, 2011.

Melikian-Chirvani, Assadullah Souren. "Buddhism ii. In Islamic Times," in *Encyclopaedia Iranica*, online edition, 2013.

Moline, Judi. "The Minaret of Gam." *Kunst Des Orients* 9(1/2) (1973/74): 131–148.

Morgenstierne, G. "AFGHANISTAN vi. Pašto," in *Encyclopaedia Iranica*, online edition, 1982.

Müller-Wiener, Martina. "Relief Ware: Of Moulds and Stamps," in *Herat through Time, vol. 3: Ancient Herat* (eds. Ute Franke and Martina Müller-Wiener), 184–229. Berlin: Staatliche Museen zu Berlin, 2016.

Najimi, Abdul Wasay. "The Ghurid Madrasa and Mausoleum of Shah-i Mashhad, Ghur, Afghanistan." *Iran* LIII (2015): 143–169.

Nicol, Norman D. "A Khwarizmian–Ghorid Hoard from the Time of the Mongol Invasion," in *Simoe Assemani Symposium on Islamic Coinage. The 2nd International Congress on Numismatic and Monetary History*, 151–190. Padua: Esedra, 2005.

Nizami, K. A. "The Ghurids," in *History of Civilizations of Central Asia, vol. IV: The Age of Achievement: AD 750 to the End of the Fifteenth Century* (eds. M. S. Asimov and C. E. Bosworth), 1st Indian edn., 77–190.. New Delhi: Motilal Banarsidass Publishers, 1999.

O'Kane, Bernard. "Salguq Minarets: Some New Data." *Annales Islamologiques* 20 (1984): 85–101.

O'Neal, Michael P. "The Ghurid Empire: Warfare, Kingship, and Political Legitimacy in Eastern Iran and Northern India," Tel Aviv University, 2013.

O'Neal, Michael P. "Mapping the Ghurid Empire: Numismatic Evidence and Narrative Sources." Hofstra University, Hempstead, New York, 2015.

O'Neal, Michael P. "Ghurids," in *Encyclopaedia of Islam* 3rd edn. (eds. Kate Fleet, Gudrun Krämer, Denis Matringe, John Nawas, and Everett Rowson). Leiden: Brill online, July 21, 2016a.

O'Neal, Michael P. "The Ghazna Coinage of the Ghūrid Sultan 'Alā' Al-Dīn Ḥusayn Jahān-Sūz." Hofstra University, Hempstead, New York, 2016b.

O'Neal, Michael P. "The Mongol Invasion of Afghanistan," paper presented at the Jordan Center for Persian Studies, University of California, Irvine, 2017.

O'Neal, Michael P. "Some New Numismatic Evidence for Ghurid History," in *Transactions of the State Hermitage Museum*, 199–221. St. Petersburg: State Hermitage Museum, 2020.

Pal, Pratapaditya. "Evidence of Jainism in Afghanistan and Kashmir in Ancient Times." *Bulletin of the Asia Institute* 21 ([2007] 2012): 25–34.

Paul, Jürgen. "The Histories of Herat." *Iranian Studies* 33(1/2) (2000): 93–115.

Paul, Jürgen. "Cities in Medieval Iran: A Review of Recent Publications." *Eurasian Studies* 16 (2018a): 5–20.

Paul, Jürgen. "Balkh, from the Seljuqs to the Mongol Invasion." *Eurasian Studies* 16 (2018b): 313–351.

Peacocke, Captain R. E., et al. *Records of Intelligence Party, Afghan Boundary Commission. Diary of Captain Peacocke, R.E. and Reports on Passes over the Range North of the Herat Valley*, vol. III. Simla: Government Central Press, 1887.

Pehrson, Robert N. *The Social Organization of the Marri Baluch* (ed. Frederik Barth), vol. 43, Viking Fund Publications in Anthropology. New York: Wenner-Gren Foundation for Anthropological Research, 1966.

Pinder-Wilson, Ralph. "Ghaznavid and Ghurid Minarets." *Iran* 39 (2001): 155–186.

Pugachenkova, G. A. "Little Known Monuments of the Balkh Area." *Art and Archaeology Research Papers* 13 (1978): 31–40.

Rao, Aparna. *Les Gorbat d'Afghanistan. Aspects économiques d'un groupe itinérant "Jat."* Paris: Editions Rechèrche sur les Civilisations, 1982.

Rasikh, Jawan Shir. "Early Islamic Ghur, 10th–12th Centuries CE: Rereading the Tabaqat-i Nasiri," unpublished PhD dissertation, University of Pennsylvania, 2019.

Rasikh, Jawan Shir. "The Many Lives of a Medieval Muslim Scholar: An Intoduction to the Life and Times of Minhaj Siraj al-Din Juzjani, 1193–1260 CE." *Afghanistan* 3(2) (2020): 111–134.

Rugiadi, Martina. "A Carved Wooden Door from Jam: Preliminary Remarks." *Iran* 44 (2006): 363–365.

Rugiadi, Martina. "Documenting Marbles of the Islamic Period from the Area of Ghazni: The Italian Contribution (1957–2007)," in *The IsIAO Italian Archaeological Mission in Afghanistan 1957–2007: Fifty Years of Research in the Heart of Eurasia. Proceedings of the Symposium Held in the Istituto Italiano per l'Africa e l'Oriente, Rome, 8 January 2008* (eds. Anna Filigenzi and Roberta Giunta), 21:105–115. Conferenze. Rome: Istituto Italiano per l'Africa e l'Oriente, 2009.

Rugiadi, Martina. "The Ghaznavid Marble Architectural Decoration: An Overview," 2010.

Scerrato, Umberto. "The First Two Excavation Campaigns at Ghazni, 1957–1958." *East and West* 10(1/2) (1959): 23–55.

Scerrato, Umberto. "Islamic Glazed Tiles with Moulded Decoration from Ghazni." *East and West* 13(2/3) (1962): 263–287.

Schlumberger, Daniel. "Le Palais Ghaznevide de Lashkari Bazar." *Syria* VI(12) (1952): 251–270.

Schlumberger, Daniel. *Lashkari Bazar: une résidence royale ghaznévide et ghoride, vol. IA: L'Architecture*, 2 vols. Paris: Diffusion de Boccard, 1978.

Schneider, Madeleine. "Remarques au sujet d'une inscription du mausolée dit de Baba Hatim." *Studia Iranica* 13(1) (1984): 165–167.

Shokoohy, Mehrdad. "The Shrine of Imam-i Kalan in Sar-i Pul, Afghanistan." *Bulletin of the School of Oriental and African Studies* 52(2) (1989): 306–314.

Sing, Hira. "Appendix to Firozkohi Report. Sub-Surveyor Hira Sing's Journey in the Firozkohi Cuntry," in *Records of the Intelligence Party, Afghan Boundary Commission. Reports on Tribes, Namely, Sarik Turkomans, Chahar Aimak Tribes, and Hazaras*, IV:142–204. Simla: Government Central Printing Office, 1891.

Sourdel, Dominique. *Inventaire des monnaies musulmanes anciennes du Musée de Caboul*. Damascus: Institut français de Damas, 1953.

Sourdel-Thomine, Janine. "Deux minarets d'époque seljoukide en Afghanistan." *Syria* 30 (1953): 108–136.

Sourdel-Thomine, Janine. "Stèles arabes de Bust (Afghanistan)." *Arabica* 3(3) (1956): 285–306.

Sourdel-Thomine, Janine. "L'art guride d'Afghanistan à propos d'un livre récent." *Arabica* 7 (1960): 273–280.

Sourdel-Thomine, Janine. "Le mausolée de Baba Hatim en Afghanistan." *Revue des Études Islamiques* 39 (1971): 290–320.

Sourdel-Thomine, Janine. *Lashkari Bazar: une résidence royale ghaznévide et ghoride, vol. IB: Le décor non-figuratif et les inscriptions*, 2 vols. Paris: Diffusion de Boccard, 1978.

Sourdel-Thomine, Janine. *Le minaret ghouride de Jam, un chef d'oevre du XIIe siècle*. Paris: Diffusion de Boccard, 2004.

Stark, S. *Archaeological Prospections in the Aktangi Valley System (Northern Tadjikistan) in 2005*. 2005, available at: http://www.orientarch.uni-halle.de/sfb586/c5/2005/index.htm.

Stark, S. *Archaeological Prospections in the Aktangi Valley System (Northern Tadjikistan) in 2006*. 2006a, available at: http://www.orientarch.uni-halle.de/sfb586/c5/2006/index.htm.

Stark, S. *Archaeological Prospections in the Aktangi Valley System (Northern Tadjikistan) in 2006*. 2006b, available at: http://www.orientarch.uni-halle.de/sfb586/c5/2006/2006b.htm.

Stewart, Rory. *The Places in Between*. Orlando: Harcourt, 2004.

Szabo, Albert and Thomas J. Barfield. *Afghanistan: An Atlas of Indigenous Domestic Architecture*. Austin: University of Texas Press, 1991.

Taddei, Maurizio. "Tapa Sardār. First Preliminary Report." *East and West* 18(1/2) (1968): 109–124.

Taddei, Maurizio. "A Note on the Barrow Cemetery at Kandahar," in *South Asian Archaeology 1977: Papers from the Fourth International Conference of the Association of South Asian Archaeologists in Western Europe, Held in the Istituto Universitario Orientale, Napoli* (ed. Maurizio Taddei), 2:909–916. Napoli: Istituto Universitario Orientale, 1979.

Taddei, Maurizio and Giovanni Verardi. "Tapa Sardār: Second Preliminary Report." *East and West* 28(1–4) (1978): 33–136.

Tarzi, Z. *L'architecture et le décor rupestre des grottes de Bamiyan*, 2 vols. Paris: Imprimerie Nationale, 1977.

Tarzi, Z. "Les fouilles de la mission archéologique française à Bamiyan sous la direction de Z. Tarzi," in *L'art d'Afghanistan de la préhistoire à nos jours: nouvelles données, actes d'une journée d'étude, UNESCO, 11 mars 2005*, 95–124. CEREDAF, 2007.

Tarzi, Z. "Bamian ii. History and Monuments," in *Encyclopaedia Iranica*, online edition, 1988.

Tate, George Passman. *Seistan: A Memoir on the History, Topography, Ruins, and People of the Country*. Quetta, Pakistan: Abid Bokhari, [1910] 1977.

Thomas, David. "The Ebb and Flow of Empires: Afghanistan and Neighboring Lands in the Twelfth–Thirteenth Centuries," in *Proceedings of the 5th International Congress on the Archaeology of the Ancient Near East*, 3:285–299. Madrid: UAM Ediciones, 2008.

Thomas, David. "Signifying the 'Ghurid Self': The Juxtaposition between Historical Labels and the Expression of Identity in Material Culture." *Journal of Historical and European Studies* 3 (2010): 71–88.

Thomas, David. "The Ebb and Flow of an Empire: The Ghurid Polity of Central Afghanistan in the Twelfth and Thirteenth Centuries," La Trobe University, 2011.

Thomas, David. "The Metamorphosis of the Minaret of Djam: From Ghurid 'Victory Tower' to Symbol of the New Afghanistan and Global Cultural Property." *Archaeological Review from Cambridge* 27(2) (2012): 139–159.

Thomas, David. *The Ebb and Flow of the Ghurid Empire*, Adapa Monographs. Sydney: Sydney University Press, 2018.

Thomas, David C. and Alison Gascoigne. "The Architectural Legacy of the Seasonally Nomadic Ghurids," in *Landscapes of the Islamic World: Archaeology, History, and Ethnography* (eds. Stephen McPhillips and Paul D. Wordsworth), 169–183. Philadelphia: University of Pennsylvania Press, 2016.

Thomas, D. C., K. Deckers, M. M. Hald, M. Holmes, and M. Madella. "Environmental Evidence from the Minaret of Jam Archaeological Project, Afghanistan." *Iran* 44 (2006): 253–276.

Thomas, David, Ustad Sayid 'Umar, Faisal Ahmad, and David Smith. "The Rediscovery of the 'Lost' Minaret of Qal'a-i Zārmurgh, Sāghar, Afghanistan." *Iran* LII (2014): 133–142.

Tissot, F. "Afghanistan ix. Pre-Islamic Art," in *Encyclopaedia Iranica*, online edition, [1983] 2011, available at: http://www.iranicaonline.org/articles/afghanistan-ix-preislamic-art.

Urban, Thomas. "Archaeological Research in Qal'a-e Ekhtyaruddin: Investigation of the Citadel Glacis – Trench 2," in *Excavations and Explorations in Herat City* (eds. Ute Franke and Thomas Urban), *Ancient Herat*, 3:321–331. Berlin: Staatliche Museen zu Berlin, 2017.

Utas, Bo. "Notes on Afghan Sufi Orders and Khanaqahs." *Afghanistan Journal* 7(1) (1980): 60–67.

Verardi, Giovanni and Elio Paparatti. *Buddhist Caves of Jāghūrī and Qarabāgh-e Ghaznī, Afghanistan*, Reports and Memoirs, New Series, 2. Rome: IsIAO, 2004.

Vercellin, Giorgio. "The Identification of Firuzkuh: A Conclusive Proof." *East and West* 26 (1976): 337–340.

Wannell, Bruce. "Echoes in Landscape: Western Afghanistan in 1989," in *Cairo to Kabul* (eds. Warwick Ball and Leonard Harrow), 236–247. London: Melisende, 2002.

Whitehouse, David. *The Barrow Cemetery at Kandahar*, vol. 36, Annali Dell'Istituto

Orientale Di Napoli, N.S. XXVI. Napoli: Istituto Orientale di Napoli, 1976.

Whitehouse, David. "Sites A and B: The Barrow Cemetery," in *Excavations at Kandahar 1974 and 1975* (eds. Anthony McNicoll and Warwick Ball), 1–18. Oxford: Tempus Reparatum, 1996.

Wordsworth, Paul. "The Hydrological Networks of the Balkh Oasis after the Arrival of Islam: A Landscape Archaeological Perspective." *Afghanistan* 1(1) (2018): 182–208.

Yate, C. E. "Notes on the City of Hirat." *Journal of the Asiatic Society of Bengal* 56 (1887): 84–106.

Works on Pakistan

Ahmad, Shamsuddin. *A Guide to Tattah and the Makli Hill*. Karachi: Manager of Publications, Government of Pakistan Press, 1952.

Ali, Taj. *Anonymous Tombs in the Gomal Valley and the Beginning of Tomb Architecture in Pakistan*, Memoirs of the Department of Archaeology, University of Peshawar No. 4. Peshawar: Department of Archaeology, University of Peshawar, 1988.

Ali, Taj. "Medieval Architectural Remains near Kabirwala, Khanewal District." *Ancient Pakistan* 8 (1993a): 125–131.

Ali, Taj. "Tomb of Shaikh Sadan Shahid, Its Decoration." *Ancient Pakistan* 8 (1993b): 133–139.

Andrews, Peter Alford. *Felt Tents and Pavilions: The Nomadic Tradition and Its Interaction with Princely Tentage*, 2 vols. London: Melisende, 1999.

Azeem, Rizwan. "Evolution of Sultanate Period Architecture in Multan," in *Sultanate Period Architecture in Pakistan. Proceedings of the Seminar Held in Lahore, November 1990* (eds. Siddiq Akbar, Abdul Rehman, and Muhammad Ali Tirmizi), Architectural Heritage of Pakistan II, 87–100. Lahore: Anjuman Mimaran, 1991.

Bagnera, Alessandra. "Preliminary Note on the Islamic Settlement of Udegram, Swat: The Islamic Graveyard (11th–13th Century A.D.)." *East and West* 56(1/3) (2006): 205–228.

Baloch, N. A. "The Kalmati Tombs in Sindh and Balochistan." *Pakistan Archaeology* 26 (1991): 243–256.

Bokhari, Hakim Ali Shah. "Chaukhandi Type Stone Tombs at Taung, History and Conservation." *Pakistan Archaeology* 27 (1992): 89–99.

Cousens, Henry. *The Antiquities of Sind with Historical Outline*, vol. 46, Archaeological Survey of India, Imperial Series. Calcutta: Government of India Central Publication Branch, 1929.

Dani, A. H., H. Humbach, and R. Gobl. "Tochi Valley Inscriptions in the Peshawar Museum." *Ancient Pakistan* 1 (1964): 125–135.

Dani, A. H. *Thatta: Islamic Architecture*. Islamabad: Institute of Islamic History, Culture and Civilization, 1982.

Edwards, Holly. "The Genesis of Islamic Architecture in the Indus Valley," PhD dissertation, New York University, 1990.

Edwards, Holly. "The Ribat of 'Ali B. Karmakh." *Iran* 29 (1991): 85–94.

Edwards, Holly. "Centralizing the Margins: Commemorative Architecture in the Indus Valley," in *The Architecture of the Indian Sultanates* (eds. Abha Narain Lambah and Alka Patel), 18–29. Mumbai: Marg Publications, 2006.

Edwards, Holly. *Of Brick and Myth: The Genesis of Islamic Architecture in the Indus Valley.* Karachi: Oxford University Press, 2015.

Farooq, Abdul Aziz. "Mosque or Khalid Walid's Tomb (A Ghorid Monument, Khanewal District)," n.d.

Flood, Finbarr B. "Ghurid Architecture in the Indus Valley: The Tomb of Shaykh Sadan Shahid." *Ars Orientals* 31 (2001): 129–166.

Friedmann, Y. and P. A. Andrews. "Multān," in *Encyclopaedia of Islam*, 2nd edn (eds. P. Bearman, Th. Bianquis, C. E. Bosworth, E. van Donzel, and W. P. Heinrichs). Leiden: Brill online, 2012.

Ghafur, M. A. "Two Lost Inscriptions Relation to the Arab Conquest of Kabul and the North West Region of West Pakistan." *Ancient Pakistan* 2 (1965/66): 4–12.

Haig, Malcolm Robert. *The Indus Delta Country: A Memoir, Chiefly on Its Ancient Geography and History, with Three Maps.* London and Karachi: Kegan Paul, Trench, Trubner and Indus Publications, 1894.

Hasan, Sheikh Khursid. "Pre-Mughal Tombs at Alore District Sukkur (Sindh)." *Journal of Central Asia* XIV(1) (1991): 123–129.

Hasan, Sheikh Khursid. *Chaukhandi Tombs in Pakistan.* Karachi: Royal Book Company, 1996.

Hassan, M. Usman (Brig. retd.). "Terracotta Plaque Decorated Tombs of Baluchistan," in *Sultanate Period Architecture in Pakistan. Proceedings of the Seminar Held in Lahore, November 1990* (eds. Siddiq Akbar, Abdul Rehman, and Muhammad Ali Tirmizi), Architectural Heritage of Pakistan II, 78–86. Lahore: Anjuman Mimaran, 1991.

Ibrahim, Asma and Kaleem Lashari. "Recent Archaeological Discoveries in the Lower Deltaic Area of Indus." *Journal of Pakistan Archaeologists Forum* 2(1/2) (1993): 1–44.

Kalhoro, Zulfiqar Ali. *Perspectives on the Art and Architecture of Sindh.* Karachi: Endowment Fund Trust for Preservation of the Heritage of Sindh, 2014.

Kevran, Monik. "The Fortress of Ratto Kot, at the Mouth of the Banbhore River (Indus Delta–Sindh–Pakistan." *Pakistan Archaeology* 27 (1992): 143–170.

Kevran, Monik. "Vanishing Medieval Cities of the Northwest Indus Delta." *Pakistan Archaeology* 28 (1993): 3–54.

Kevran, Monik. "Le Port Multiple des Bouches de l'Indus: Barbariké, Deb, Daybul, Lahori Bandar, Diul Sinde," in *Sites et Monuments Disparus D'après les Témoignages de Voyageurs* (ed. Rika Gyselen), 45–92, Res Orientales, 8. Bures-sur-Yvette: Groupe pour l'étude de la civilisation du Moyen-Orient, 1996a.

Kevran, Monik. "Entre l'Inde et l'Asie centrale: Les mausolées islamique du Sind et du Penjab." *Cahiers D'Asie Centrale* 1/2 (1996b): 133–171.

Kevran, Monik. "Caravanserails du delta de l'Indus: Réflexions sur l'origine du caravanserail islamique." *Archéologie Islamique* 8/9 (1999a): 143–176.

Kevran, Monik. "Multiple Ports at the Mouth of the River Indus: Barbarike, Deb, Daybul, Lahori Bandar, Diul Sinde," in *The Archeology of Seafaring:*

The Indian Ocean in the Ancient Period (ed. Himanshu Prabha Ray), 70–154. Delhi: Pragati Publications, 1999b.

Khan, Ahmad Nabi. *Multan: History and Architecture*. Islamabad: Institute of Islamic History, Culture & Civilization, Islamic University, 1983.

Khan, Ahmad Nabi. "A Group of Four Tombs in the Multan Style of Architecture at Lal Muhra Sharif (D. I. Khan)." *Journal of Central Asia* 7(1) (1984): 29–48.

Khan, Ahmad Nabi. "Naked Brick Architecture of Early Islamic Period of Pakistan." *Pakistan Archaeology* 23 (1988): 303–325.

Khan, Ahmad Nabi. *Islamic Architecture in South Asia, Pakistan–India–Bangladesh*. Oxford: Oxford University Press, 2003.

Khan, F. A. *Banbhore: A Preliminary Report on the Recent Archaeological Excavations at Banbhore*, 2nd edn. Pakistan: Department of Archaeology and Museums, 1963.

Khan, Gulzar Muhammad. "Pre-Mughal Mosques in Lahore," in *Sultanate Period Architecture in Pakistan. Proceedings of the Seminar Held in Lahore, November 1990* (eds. Siddiq Akbar, Abdul Rehman, and Muhammad Ali Tirmizi), Architectural Heritage of Pakistan II, 126–133. Lahore: Anjuman Mimaran, 1991.

Khan, Hasan Ali. *Constructing Islam on the Indus: The Material History of the Suhrawardi Sufi Order, 1200–1500 AD*. New York: Royal Asiatic Society of Great Britain and Ireland, Cambridge University Press, 2016.

Manna, Gabriella. "Some Observations on the Pottery from the Islamic Settlement of Udegram, Swat." *East and West* 56(1/3) (2006): 229–236.

Masson, Charles. *Narrative of a Journey to Kalât, Including an Account of the Insurrection at That Place in 1840; and a Memoir on Eastern Balochistan*. London: Richard Bentley, 1843.

Meister, Michael. "Temples along the Indus." *Expedition* 38(3) (1996): 41–54.

Meister, Michael. "Gandhara-Nagara Temples of the Salt Range and Indus." *Kala, The Journal of the Indian Art History Congress* 4 (1997/98): 45–52.

Meister, Michael. "Temples of the Salt Range," in *Religion, Ritual, and Royalty* (eds. N. R. Singhi and R. Joshi), 132–139. Jaipur: Rawat Publication, 1999.

Meister, Michael. "Pattan Munara : Minar or Mandir ?" in *Hari Smriti Studies on Art Archaeology and Indology* (ed. Banerji Arundhati), 113–121. New Delhi-110002: Kaveri Books, 2006.

Meister, Michael. "Exploring Kafirkot: When Is a Rose Apple Not a Rose." *Pakistan Heritage* 1 (2009): 109–128.

Meister, Michael. *Temples of the Indus: Studies in the Hindu Architecture of Ancient Pakistan*, Brill's Indological Library, vol. 35. Leiden: Brill, 2010.

Meister, Michael. "Continuities of Architectural Heritage in the Northwest," paper presented at American Council of Southern Asian Art Symposium XV, Minneapolis, MN, 2011.

Meister, Michael, Abdur Rehman, and Farid Khan. "Discovery of a New Temple on the Indus." *Expedition* 42(1) (2000): 37–46.

Mumtaz, Kamil Khan. *Architecture in Pakistan*. Singapore: Concept Media, 1985.

Pottinger, Henry. *Travels in Beloochistan and Sinde; Accompanied by a Geographical and Historical Account of Those Countries*. London: Longman, Hurst, Rees, Orme & Brown, 1816.

Rahman, Abdur. *The Last Two Dynasties of the Śahis: An Analysis of Their History, Archaeology, Coinage, and Palaeography*. Islamabad: Centre for the Study of the Civilizations of Central Asia, Quaid-i-Azam University, 1979.

Rahman, Abdur. "The Zalamkot Bilingual Inscription." *East and West* 48(3/4) (1998): 469–473.

Rahman, Abdur. "Arslan Jadhib, Governor of Tus: The First Muslim Conqueror of Swat." *Ancient Pakistan* 15 (2002a): 11–14.

Rahman, Abdur. "New Light on the Khingal, Turk and the Hindu Sahis." *Ancient Pakistan* 15 (2002b): 37–42.

Rehman, Abdul. "Sultanate Period Architecture in the Punjab (1000 A.D.– 1500 A.D.)," in *Sultanate Period Architecture in Pakistan. Proceedings of the Seminar Held in Lahore, November 1990* (eds. Siddiq Akbar, Abdul Rehman, and Muhammad Ali Tirmizi), Architectural Heritage of Pakistan II, 36–58. Lahore: Anjuman Mimaran, 1991.

Rehman, Abdul and Talib Hussain. "Expression of Paying Tribute to the Saint: Decorative Vocabulary on the Tomb of Ahmad Kabir." *Journal of Research in Architecture and Planning* 10(1) (2011): 59–75.

Scerrato, Umberto. "Research on the Archaeology and History of Islamic Art in Pakistan: Excavation of the Ghaznavid Mosque on Mt. Raja Gira, Swat." *East and West*, 35 (1985): 439–451.

Sharma, Sunil. *Persian Poetry at the Indian Frontier: Mas'ud Sa'd Salman of Lahore*, Permanent Black Monographs, Opus 1 Series. New Delhi: Permanent Black, 2000.

Stein, Aurel and Sten Konow. *An Archaeological Tour in Waziristān and Northern Balūchistān*, Memoirs of the Archaeological Survey of India, No. 37. Calcutta: Government of India Central Publication Office, 1929.

Stein, Aurel and Sten Konow. *An Archæological Tour in Upper Swāt and Adjacent Hill Tracts*, Memoirs of the Archaeological Survey of India, No. 42. Calcutta: Government of India Central Publication Branch, 1931.

Vogel, Jean Philippe. "Tombs at Hinidan in las Bela." *Annual Report* (1902–1903): 213–217.

Zajadacz-Hastenrath, Salome. *Chaukhandigr.ber: Studien sur Grabkunst in Sind u. Baluchistan*. Wiesbaden: Steiner, 1978.

Ziad, Waleed. "'Islamic Coins' from a Hindu Temple: Reconsidering Ghaznavid Interactions with Hindu Sacred Sites through New Numismatic Evidence from Gandhara." *Journal of the Economic and Social History of the Orient* 59 (2016): 618–659.

Anthropological Works

Amiri, Ghulam Rahman. *The Helmand Baluch: A Native Ethnography of the People of Southwest Afghanistan*, ed. William B. Trousdale, trans. James Gehlhar, Mhairi Gehlhar, and Babrak Amiri. New York: Berghahn Books, 2020.

Barfield, Thomas. *The Central Asian Arabs of Afghanistan: Pastoral Nomadism in Transition*. Austin: University of Texas Press, 1981.

Barfield, Thomas. *The Nomadic Alternative*. Englewood Cliffs, NJ: Prentice Hall, 1993.

Barfield, Thomas. "Conclusion," in *Nomadic Pathways in Social Evolution* (eds. N. N. Kradin and D. M. Bondarenko), English edn., 172–179, "Civilizational Dimension" Series. Moscow/Lac-Beauport: MEA Books, 2003.

Barth, Frederik. *Nomads of South Persia: The Basseri Tribe of the Khamseh Confederacy*, 2nd edn. Oslo and Boston: Oslo University Press and Little, Brown, 1961.

Beck, Lois. "Chapter 9: Iran and the Qashqai Confederacy," in *The Conflict of Tribe and State in Iran and Afghanistan* (ed. Richard Tapper), 284–313. London: Croom Helm, 1983.

Bronson, Bennet. "The Role of Barbarians in the Fall of States," in *The Collapse of Ancient States and Civilizations* (eds. Norman Yoffee and George L. Cowgill), 196–218. Tucson: University of Arizona Press, 1988.

Büssow, Johann, David Durand-Guédy, and Jürgen Paul (eds.). "Nomads in the Political Field." *Eurasian Studies* IX (2011): 1–9.

Cribb, Roger. *Nomads in Archaeology*. Cambridge: Cambridge University Press, 1991.

Elliott, Chris. "Understanding the Dialectic of Nomad and State." *Small Wars Journal*, December 2, 2013, available at: http://smallwarsjournal.com/jrnl/art/understanding-the-dialectic-of-nomad-and-state-0#_ednrefl.

Garthwaite, Gene. "Tribes, Confederation, and the State: An Historical Overview of the Bakhtiari and Iran," in *The Conflict of Tribe and State in Iran and Afghanistan* (ed. Richard Tapper), 314–336. London: Croom Helm, 1983.

Gellner, Ernest. "The Tribal Society and Its Enemies," in *The Conflict of Tribe and State in Iran and Afghanistan* (ed. Richard Tapper), 436–448. London: Croom Helm, 1983.

Glatzer, Bernt. "Political Organisation of Pashtun Nomads and the State," in *The Conflict of Tribe and State in Iran and Afghanistan* (ed. Richard Tapper), 212–232. London: Croom Helm, 1983.

Glatzer, Bernt and Michael Casimir. "Herds and Households among Pashtum Pastoral Nomads: Limits of Growth." *Ethnology* 22(4) (1983): 307–327.

Irons, William. "Cultural Capital, Livestock Raiding, and the Military Advantage of Traditional Pastoralists," in *Nomadic Pathways in Social Evolution* (eds. Nikolay N. Kradin, D. M. Bondarenko, and Thomas J. Barfield), English edn., 5:73–87, "Civilizational Dimension" Series. Moscow/Lac-Beauport: MEA Books, 2003.

Kradin, Nikolay N. "Nomadic Empires: Origins, Rise, Decline," in *Nomadic Pathways in Social Evolution* (eds. Nikolay N. Kradin, D. M. Bondarenko, and Thomas J. Barfield), English edn, 73–87, "Civilizational Dimension" Series. Moscow/Lac-Beauport: MEA Books, 2003.

Næss, Marius Warg. "Predatory or Prey – the Rise of Nomadic Empires." *Pastoralism, Climate Change and Policy* (blog), November 20, 2015, available at: https://pastoralism-climate-change-policy.com/2015/11/20/predatory-or-prey-the-rise-of-nomadic-empires.

Pijl, Kees van der. *Nomads, Empires, States*. London: Pluto Press, 2007.

Tapper, Richard (ed.). *The Conflict of Tribe and State in Iran and Afghanistan.* London and New York: Croom Helm and St Martin's Press, 1983.

Tapper, Richard. *Frontier Nomads of Iran: A Political and Social History of the Shahsevan*, Cambridge Middle East Studies, 7. Cambridge: Cambridge University Press, 1997.

Vasjutin, Sergey A. "Typology of Pre-States and Statehood Systems of Nomads," in *Nomadic Pathways in Social Evolution* (eds. N. N. Kradin and D. M. Bondarenko), 50–62, English edn, "Civilizational Dimension" Series. Moscow/Lac-Beauport: MEA Books, 2003.

Other Works

Akhmedov, A. "Chapter 7, Astronomy, Astrology, Observations and Calendars," in *History of Civilizations of Central Asia, vol. IV: The Age of Achievement: AD 750 to the End of the Fifteenth Century – Part Two: The Achievements* (eds. C. E. Bosworth and M. S. Asimov), 195–204. Paris: UNESCO Publishing, 2000.

Alam, Muzaffar. "The Culture and Politics of Persian in Precolonial Hindustan," in *Literary Cultures in History: Reconstructions from South Asia* (ed. Sheldon Pollock), 131–198. Berkeley: University of California Press, 2003.

Alam, Muzaffar. *The Languages of Political Islam in India, C.1200–1800.* Delhi: Permanent Black, 2004.

Ali, Daud. *Courtly Culture and Political Life in Early Medieval India. Cambridge Studies in Indian History and Society*, 10. Cambridge: Cambridge University Press, 2004.

Allegranzi, Viola. "Vers un réexamen des inscriptions historiques du monde iranien pré-mongol: Étude des cas des mausolées de Tim et de Termez en Ouzbékistan," in *Texts and Contexts: Ongoing Researches on the Eastern Iranian World (Ninth–Fifteenth C.)* (eds. Viola Allegranzi and Valentina Laviola), 103–134. Rome: Istituto per l'Oriente C. A. Nallino, 2020.

Amin, Shahid. "On Retelling the Muslim Conquest of North India," in *History and the Present* (eds. Partha Chatterjee and Anjan Ghosh), 24–43. New Delhi: Permanent Black, 2002.

Amin, Shahid. *Conquest and Community: The Afterlife of Warrior Saint Ghazi Miyan.* Chicago: University of Chicago Press, 2015.

Amitai, R. "Toward a Pre-History of the Islamization of the Turks: A Re-Reading of Ibn Fadlan's Rihla," in *Islamisation de l'Asia Centrale* (ed. Étienne de la Vassière), 277–296. Paris: Association pour l'avancement des études iraniennes, 2008.

Anawati, Claude. "Fakhr Al-Dīn al-Rāzī," in *Encyclopedia of Islam*, 2nd edn. (eds. P. Bearman, Th. Bianquis, C. E. Bosworth, E. van Donzel, and W. P. Heinrichs). Leiden: Brill online, 2012.

Anjum, Tanvir. *Chishti Sufis in the Sultanate of Delhi 1190–1400.* Karachi: Oxford University Press, 2011.

Anooshahr, Ali. "'Utbi and the Ghaznavids at the Foot of the Mountain." *Iranian Studies* 38(2) (June 2005): 271–291.

Anooshahr, Ali. "Mughal Historians and the Memory of the Islamic Conquest of India." *Indian Economic and Social History Review* 43(3) (2006): 275–300.

Anooshahr, Ali. *The Ghazi Sultans and the Frontiers of Islam*. Abingdon: Routledge, 2009.

Anooshahr, Ali. "The Shaykh and the Shah: On the Five Jewels of Muhammad Ghaws Gwaliori," in *India and Iran in the Longue Durée* (eds. Alka Patel and Touraj Daryaee), 91–102. Irvine, CA: Jordan Center for Persian Studies, 2017.

Anooshahr, Ali. "The Elephant and the Sovereign: India circa 1000 CE." *Journal of the Royal Asiatic Society* 28(4) (2018a): 615–644.

Anooshahr, Ali. *Turkestan and the Rise of Eurasian Empires: A Study of Politics and Invented Traditions*. Oxford: Oxford University Press, 2018b.

Ansari, A. S., Bazmee. "Gakkhaṛ," in *Encyclopaedia of Islam*, 2nd edn (eds. P. Bearman, Th. Bianquis, C. E. Bosworth, and W. P. Heinrichs). Leiden: Brill online, 2012.

Aquil, Raziuddin. *Sufism, Culture, and Politics: Afghans and Islam in Medieval North India*. New Delhi: Oxford University Press, 2007.

Asher, Catherine. *Delhi's Qutb Complex: The Minar, Mosque and Mehrauli*. Mumbai: Marg Publications, 2017.

Asif, Manan Ahmed. *A Book of Conquest: The Chachnama and Muslim Origins in South Asia*. Cambridge, MA: Harvard University Press, 2016.

Asif, Manan Ahmed. *The Loss of Hindustan: The Invention of India*. Cambridge, MA: Harvard University Press, 2020.

Auer, Blain H. *Symbols of Authority in Medieval Islam: History, Religion and Muslim Legitimacy in the Delhi Sultanate*, Library of South Asian History and Culture, 6. London: I. B. Tauris, 2012.

Auer, Blain H. "Chishtiyya," in *Encyclopaedia of Islam*, 3rd edn. (eds. Kate Fleet, Gudrun Krämer, Denis Matringe, John Nawas, and Everett Rowson), Leiden: Brill online, 2016.

Auer, Blain H. "Chapter 4. Persian Historiography in India," in *Literature from Outside Iran: The Indian Subcontinent, Anatolia, Central Asia, and in Judeo-Persian* (ed. John Perry), 94–139. London: I. B. Tauris, 2018.

Azarpay, Guitty. "The Islamic Tomb Tower: A Note on Its Genesis and Significance," in *Essays in Islamic Art and Architecture: In Honor of Katharina Otto-Dorn* (eds. Abbas Daneshvari and Katharina Otto-Dorn), 9–11. Islamic Art and Architecture, 1. Malibu, CA: Undena Publications, 1981.

Balasubramaniam, R. *The World Heritage Complex of the Qutub*. New Delhi: Aryan Books, 2005.

Barthold, W. *Turkestan down to the Mongol Invasion*, 3rd edn., vol. V, E. J. W. Gibb Memorial Series. London: Luzac, 1968.

Berggren, J. L. "Chapter 6, Mathematical Sciences; Part Two, the Mathematical Sciences," in *History of Civilizations of Central Asia, vol. IV: The Age of Achievement: AD 750 to the End of the Fifteenth Century – Part Two: The Achievements* (eds. C. E. Bosworth and M. S. Asimov), 182–193.. Paris: UNESCO Publishing, 2000.

Bhandare, Shailendra. "Transregional Connections: The 'Lion and Sun' Motif and Coinage between Anatolia and India," in *Turkish History and Culture in India* (eds. A. C. S. Peacock and Richard P. McClary), 203–247. Leiden: Brill, 2020.

Bhandarkar, D. R. "The Chahamanas of Marwar." *Epigraphia Indica* XI (1911/12): 26–79.

Biran, Michal. "True to Their Ways: Why the Qara Khitai Did Not Convert to Islam," in *Eurasian Nomads and the Sedentary World* (eds. Reuven Amitai and Michal Biran), 175–199. Leiden: E. J. Brill, 2004.

Biran, Michal. *The Empire of the Qara Khitai in Eurasian History: Between China and the Islamic World*, Cambridge Studies in Islamic Civilization. Cambridge: Cambridge University Press, 2005.

Biran, Michal. "Jovayni, Ṣāḥeb divan," in *Encyclopaedia Iranica*, online edition, [2009] 2012.

Blair, Sheila S. "The Madrasa at Zuzan: Islamic Architecture in Eastern Iran on the Eve of the Mongol Invasion." *Muqarnas* 3 (1985): 76–91.

Blair, Sheila S. *The Monumental Inscriptions from Early Islamic Iran and Transoxiana*. Leiden: Brill, 1992.

Blair, Sheila S. *Islamic Inscriptions*. Edinburgh: Edinburgh University Press, 1998.

Blayac, Johanna. "Sovereign Epigraphy in Location: Politics, Devotion and Legitimisation around the Qutb Minar, Delhi," in *Calligraphy and Architecture in the Muslim World* (eds. Mohammad Gharipour and Irvin Cemil Schick), 217–229. Edinburgh: Edinburgh University Press, 2013.

Bloom, Jonathan M. *Minaret: Symbol of Islam*, Oxford Studies in Islamic Art, vol. VII. Oxford: Oxford University Press, 1989.

Bopearachchi, Osmund. *The Pleasure Gardens of Sigiriya: A New Approach*. Colombo: Godage Book Emporium, 2006.

Bosworth, C.E. "The Political and Dynastic History of the Iranian World (AD 1000–1217)," in The Cambridge history of Iran. Volume V: the Saljuq and Mongol Periods.(ed. J.A. Boyle), 1–202. Cambridge: Cambridge University Press, 1968b.

Bosworth, Clifford Edmund. "The Heritage of Rulership in Early Islamic Iran and the Search for Dynastic Connections with the Past." *Iran* 11 (1973): 51–62.

Bosworth, C. E. and M. S. Asimov (eds.). *History of Civilizations of Central Asia, vol. IV: The Age of Achievement: AD 750 to the End of the Fifteenth Century – Part Two: The Achievements*, Indian edn. New Delhi: Motilal Banarsidass Publishers, 2000.

Boucharlat, Rémy. "Découvertes récentes de stucs en Iran sassanide et problèmes d'interprétation." *Syria* Supp. V (2019): 351–366.

Böwering, Gerhard. "ČEŠTĪYA," in *Encyclopaedia Iranica*, online edition, [1991] 2011.

Böwering, Gerhard and Matthew Melvin-Khoushki. "Khanaqah," in *Encyclopaedia Iranica*, online edition, [2010] 2012.

Bühler, G. "Eleven Land-Grants of the Chaulukyas of Anhilvad: A Contribution to the History of Gujarat." *Indian Antiquary* 6 (1877): 180–214.

Bulliet, Richard W. *The Patricians of Nishapur*. Cambridge, MA: Harvard University Press, 1972.

Bulliet, Richard W. "Local Politics in Eastern Iran under the Ghaznavids and Seljuks." *Iranian Studies* 11(1/4) (1978): 35–56.

Bulliet, Richard W. *Islam: The View from the Edge*. New York: Columbia University Press, 1994.

Burbank, Jane and Frederick Cooper. *Empires in World History: Power and the Politics of Difference*. Princeton, NJ: Princeton University Press, 2010.

Buswell, Robert and Donald Lopez. *The Princeton Dictionary of Buddhism*. Princeton, NJ: Princeton University Press, 2014.

Cahen, Claude, G. Deverdun, and P. M. Holt. "Ghuzz," in *Encyclopedia of Islam*, 2nd edn (eds. P. Bearman, Th. Bianquis, C. E. Bosworth, E. van Donzel, and W. P. Heinrichs), Leiden: Brill online, 2012.

Canepa, Mathew P. "Building a New Vision of the Past in the Sasanian Empire: The Sanctuaries of Kayansih and the Great Fires of Iran." *Journal of Persianate Studies* 6 (2013): 64–90.

Canepa, Mathew P. "Dynastic Sanctuaries and the Transformation of Iranian Kingship between Alexander and Islam," in *Persian Kingship and Architecture: Strategies of Power in Iran from the Achaemenids to the Pahlavis* (eds. Sussan Babaie and Talinn Grigor), 65–118. London: I. B. Tauris, 2015.

Chatterjee, Kumkum. "Scribal Elites in Sultanate and Mughal Bengal." *The Indian Economic and Social History Review* 47(4) (2010): 445–472.

Chattopadhyaya, B. D. *Representing the Other? Sanskrit Sources and the Muslims*. Delhi: Manohar, 1998.

Chattopadhyaya, B. D. *The Making of Early Medieval India*. Delhi: Oxford University Press, 1997.

Collinet, Annabelle. "Nouvelles rechèrches sur la céramique de Nishapur: la prospection du shahrestan," in *Greater Khorasan: History, Geography, Archaeology and Material Culture* (ed. Rocco Rante), 89–114. Berlin: De Gruyter, 2015.

Crossley, Pamela Kyle. *Hammer and Anvil: Nomad Rulers at the Forge of the Modern World*. Lanham, MD: Rowman & Littlefield, 2019.

Dähne, Burkart. "Recent Researches of the Uighur Capital Kharabalgasun (Ördu Balik) with Focus on the So-Called Temple – or Palace Area." *Drevnie Kul'tury Mongolii, Baikal'skoĭ Sibiri i Severnogo Kitaĭa: Materialy VII Mezhdunarodnoĭ Nauchnoĭ Konferentsii* 4 (2013): 21–28.

Dale, Stephen F. *Indian Merchants and Eurasian Trade, 1600–1750*, Cambridge Studies in Islamic Civilization. Cambridge: Cambridge University Press, 1994.

Dallapiccola, Anna Libera. "Vahanas," in *Brill's Encyclopedia of Hinduism* (eds. Knut A. Jacobsen, Helene Basu, Angelika Malinar, and Vasudha Narayanan). Leiden: Brill, 2019.

de Bruijn, J. T. P. *Of Piety and Poetry: The Interaction of Religion and Literature in the Life and Works of Hakīm Sanā'ī of Ghazna*, publication of the de Goeje Fund, No. 25. Leiden: Brill, 1983.

de Bruijn, J. T. P. "Sanā'i," in *Encyclopaedia Iranica*, online edition, 2012.

de Laugier de Beaureceuil, S. "'Abdallah Ansari," in *Encyclopaedia Iranica*, online edition, [1982] 2011.

Dani, Ahmad Hasan. "Part Two: Southern Central Asia," in *History of Civilizations of Central Asia, vol. IV: The Age of Achievement: AD 750 to the End of the Fifteenth Century – Part Two: The Achievements* (eds. C. E. Bosworth and M. S. Asimov), 557–584. Paris: UNESCO Publishing, 2000.

Daryaee, Touraj. "The Persian Gulf Trade in Late Antiquity." *Journal of World History* 14(1) (2003): 1–16.

Deloche, Jean. *Transport and Communications in India Prior to Steam Locomotion*, 2 vols, trans. James Walker, French Studies in South Asian Culture and Society, 7. Delhi: Oxford University Press, [1980] 1993/94.

Desai, Madhuri. "Interpreting an Architectural Past: Ram Raz and the Treatise in South Asia." *Journal of the Society of Architectural Historians* 72(4) (2012): 462–487.

Desai, Z. A. "Cultural Relations between Afghanistan and India during the Medieval Period." *Afghanistan* 28(3) (1975): 9–17.

Dhaky, M. A. "Kiradu and the Maru–Gurjara Style of Temple Architecture." *Bulletin of the American Academy of Benares* 1 (1967): 35–45.

Dhaky, M. A. "Maru-Gurjara Vastu-Sastraman Masjid-Nirmana-Vidhi." *Swadhyaya* 7(1) (1968): 64–79 (in Gujarati).

Dhaky, M. A. "The Genesis and Development of Maru-Gurjara Temple Architecture," in *Studies in Indian Temple Architecture* (ed.Pramod Chandra), 114–165. Varanasi: American Institute of Indian Studies, 1975.

Digby, Simon. "Early Pilgrimages to the Graves of Mu'in al-Din Sijzi and Other Indian Chishti Shaykhs," in *Islamic Society and Culture: Essays in Honour of Professor Aziz Ahmad* (eds. Milton Israel and N. K. Wagle), 95–100. New Delhi: Manohar, 1983.

Dodd, Erica Cruikshank, and Shereen Khairallah. *The Image of the Word: A Study of Quranic Verses in Islamic Architecture*, 2 vols. Beirut: American University of Beirut, 1981.

Durand-Guédy, David. *Iranian Elites and Turkish Rulers: A History of Isfahan in the Saljuq Period*, Routledge Studies in the History of Iran and Turkey. London: Routledge, 2010.

Durand-Guédy, David. "The Tents of the Saljuqs," in *Turko-Mongol Rulers, Cities and City Life* (ed. David Durand-Guédy), 149–189. Leiden: Brill, 2013a.

Durand-Guédy, David. "Ruling from the Outside: A New Perspective on Turkish Kingship in Iran," in *Every Inch a King: Comparative Studies on Kings and Kingship in the Ancient and Medieval Worlds* (eds. Lynette Mitchell and Charles Melville), 325–342. Leiden: Brill, 2013b.

Durand-Guédy, David. "Pre-Mongol Khurasan. A Historical Introduction," in *Greater Khorasan: History, Geography, Archaeology and Material Culture* (ed. Rocco Rante), 1–8. Berlin: De Gruyter, 2015.

Durand-Guédy, David. "Khargah and Other Terms for Tents in Firdawsi's Shah-Namah." *Iranian Studies* 51(6) (2018): 819–849.

Edwards, Holly. "Text, Context, Architext: The Qur'an as Architectural Inscription," in *Brocade of the Pen: The Art of Isalmic Writing* (ed. Carol Garret Fisher), 63–75. East Lansing, MI: Kresge Art Museum, 1991.

Ernst, Carl W. *Eternal Garden: Mysticism, History, and Politics at a South Asian Sufi Center*. Albany, NY: State University of New York Press, 1992.

Ernst, Carl W. and Bruce Lawrence. *Sufi Martyrs of Love: The Chishti Order in South Asia and Beyond*. New York: Palgrave Macmillan, 2002.

Ettinghausen, Richard. "Arabic Epigraphy: Communication or Symbolic Affirmation," in *Near Eastern Numismatics, Iconography, Epigraphy, and History Studies in Honor of George C. Miles*, 297–317. Beirut: American University of Beirut, 1974.

Falk, Harry. *Asokan Sites and Artefacts: A Source-Book with Bibliography.* Mainz am Rhein: Verlag Philipp von Zabern, 2006.

Ferrier, J. P. *Caravan Journeys and Wanderings in Persia, Afghanistan, Turkistan, and Beloochistan; with Historical Notices of the Countries Lying between Russia and India.* trans. Capt. William Jesse. Karachi: Oxford University Press, 1976.

Finster, Barbara. "The Saljuqs as Patrons," in *The Art of the Saljuqs in Iran and Anatolia* (ed. Robert Hillenbrand), 17–23. Costa Mesa, CA: Mazda, 1994.

Flood, Finbarr B. "Between Ghazna and Delhi: Lahore and Its Lost Manara," in *Cairo to Kabul* (eds. Warwick Ball and Leonard Harrow), 102–112. London: Melisende, 2002.

Flood, Finbarr B. "Refiguring Iconoclasm in the Early Indian Mosque," in *Negating the Image* (eds. Anne McClanan and Jeff Johnson), Burlington, VT: Ashgate, 2005.

Flood, Finbarr B. *Objects of Translation: Material Culture and Medieval "Hindu–Muslim" Encounter.* Princeton, NJ: Princeton University Press, 2009a.

Genito, Bruno. "Chapter 10. Landscape, Sources and Architecture at the Archaeological Remains of Achaemenid Sistān (East Irān): Dāhān-i Ghūlāmān," in *Excavating an Empire: Achaemenid Persia in Longue Durée* (eds. Touraj Daryaee, Ali Mousavi, and Khodadad Rezakhani), 163–178. Costa Mesa, CA: Mazda, 2014.

Ghanimati, Soroor. "New Perspectives on the Chronological and Functional Horizons of Kuh-e Khwaja in Sistan." *Iran* 38 (2000): 137–150.

Godard, André. "Khorasan." *Athar-i Iran* 4 (1949): 7–150.

Godard, André. "L'origine de la madrasa, de la mosquée et du caravansérail à quatre īwāns." *Ars Islamica* 15/16 (1951): 1–9.

Godard, Y. A. "Notice Épigraphique." *Athar-i Iran* I(2) (1936): 361–373.

Godard, Y. A. and Myron Bement Smith. "Material for a Corpus of Early Islamic Architecture: II. Manar and Masdjid, Barsian (Isfahan)." *Ars Islamica* 4 (1937): 6–41.

Golden, Peter. "Chapter One: Courts and Court Culture in the Proto-Urban and Urban Developments among the Pre-Chinggisid Turkic Peoples," in *Turko-Mongol Rulers, Cities and City Life* (ed. David Durand-Guédy), 21–73. Leiden: Brill, 2013.

Grabar, Oleg. "The Earliest Islamic Commemorative Structures, Notes and Documents." *Ars Orientals* 6 (1966): 7–46.

Green, Nile. *Making Space: Sufis and Settlers in Early Modern India.* New Delhi: Oxford University Press, 2012.

Green, Nile. "Introduction: The Frontiers of the Persianate World (c. 800–1900)," in *The Persianate World: The Frontiers of a Eurasian Lingua Franca* (ed. Nile Green), 1–71. Oakland, CA: University of California Press, 2019.

Grenet, Frantz. "The Nomadic Element in the Kushan Empire (1st–3rd Century AD)." *Journal of Central Eurasian Studies* 3 (2012): 1–22.

Habib, Irfan. "Formation of the Sultanate Ruling Class of the Thirteenth Century," in *Medieval India 1: Researches in the History of India 1200–1750* (ed. Irfan Habib), 1–21. Delhi: Oxford University Press, 1992.

Habib, Irfan. "Review of M. A. Asif, A Book of Conquest: The Chachnama and Muslim Origins in South Asia (Cambridge, MA: Harvard University Press), 2016." *Studies in People's History* 4(1) (2017): 105–117.

Haig, Malcolm Robert. *The Indus Delta Country: A Memoir, Chiefly on Its Ancient Geography and History, with Three Maps*. London and Karachi: Kegan Paul, Trench, Trubner and Indus Publications, 1894.

Hambly, Gavin. "Who Were the Chihilgānī, the Forty Slaves of Sulṭān Shams Al-Dīn Iltutmish of Delhi?" *Iran* 10 (1972): 57–62.

Hanifi, Shah Mahmud. "Kākaṛ," in *Encyclopaedia of Islam*, 2nd edn. (eds. P. Bearman, Th. Bianquis, C. E. Bosworth, E. van Donzel, and W. P. Heinrichs). Leiden: Brill online, 2012.

Haq, S. Moinul. "Shaykh Nizam Al-Din Awliya," in *Studies in Indian Culture: Dr. Ghulam Yazdani Commemoration Volume* (ed. A. K. Sherwani), 196–202. Hyderabad: Maulana Abul Kalam Oriental Research Institute, 1966.

Hardy, Adam. *Theory and Practice of Temple Architecture in Medieval India: Bhoja's Samaranganasutradhara and the Bhojpur Line Drawings*. New Delhi: Indira Gandhi National Centre for the Arts, 2015.

Hardy, Peter. *Historians of Medieval India: Studies in Indo-Muslim Historical Writing*. London: Luzac, 1960.

Hardy, Peter. "Growth of Authority over a Conquered Political Elite: Early Delhi Sultanate as a Possible Case Study," in *Kingship and Authority in South Asia*, 216–241. Delhi: Oxford University Press, 1998.

Hartmann, Angelika. "Al-Suhrawardi, Shihab al Din Abu Hafs Umar," in *Encyclopaedia of Islam*, 2nd edn. (eds. P. Bearman, Th. Bianquis, C. E. Bosworth, E. van Donzel, and W. P. Heinrichs). Leiden: Brill online, 2008.

Hegewald, Julia A. B. "The International Jaina Style? Maru–Gurjara Temples under the Solankis, throughout India and in the Diaspora." *Ars Orientalis* 45 (2015): 115–140.

Hillenbrand, Robert. *Islamic Architecture*. New York: Columbia University Press, 1994.

Hillenbrand, Robert. "The Seljuq Monuments of Turkmenistan," in *The Seljuqs: Politics, Society and Culture* (eds. Christian Lange and Songül Mecit), 277–308. Edinburgh: Edinburgh University Press, 2011.

Hillenbrand, Robert. "Islamic Monumental Inscriptions Contextualized: Location, Content, Legibility and Aesthetics." *Beiträge Zur Islamischen Kunst und Archäologie* 3 (2012): 13–38.

Hillenbrand, Robert. "Architecture and Politics: The North and South Dome Chambers of the Isfahan Jami'," in *The Age of the Seljuqs* (eds. Edmund Herzig and Sarah Stewart), *The Idea of Iran*, 6:148–173. London: I. B. Tauris, 2015.

Hodgson, Marshall G. S. *The Venture of Islam, Conscience and History in a World Civilization, vol. 2: The Expansion of Islam in the Middle Periods*. Chicago: University of Chicago Press, [1974] 1977.

Holdich, Thomas, Sir (Colonel). *The Gates of India, Being an Historical Narrative*. London: Macmillan, 1910.

Horn, Paul. "IX. – Muhammadan Inscriptions from the Suba of Dihli." *Epigraphia Indica* 3 (1894a): 130–159.

Horn, Paul. "Muhammadan Inscriptions from the Suba of Dihli No. II." *Epigraphia Indica* 3 (1894b): 424–437.

Horovitz, J. "The Inscriptions of Muhammad Ibn Sam, Qutbuddin Aibeg and Iltutmish." *Epigraphia Indo-Moslemica* 12 (1911): 12–34.

Hosain, Hidayet. "Hudjwīrī, Abu 'l-Ḥasan ʿAlī b. ʿUt̲h̲mān b. ʿAlī al-G̲h̲aznawī al-D̲julhlābī," in *Encyclopaedia of Islam*, 2nd edn. (eds. P. Bearman, Th. Bianquis, C. E. Bosworth, E. van Donzel, and W. P. Heinrichs). Leiden: Brill online, 2012.

Hua, T. "The Muslim Qarakhanids and Their Invented Ethnic Identity," in *Islamisation de l'Asia Centrale* (ed. Étienne de la Vassière), 339–350. Paris: Association pour l'avancement des études iraniennes, 2008.

Husain, Muhammad Ashraf. *A Record of All the Quranic and Non-Historical Epigraphs on the Protected Monuments in the Delhi Province*, Memoirs of the Archaeological Survey of India 47. Calcutta: Government of India Central Publication Branch, 1936.

Hüttel, Hans-Georg and Ulambayar Erdenebat. *Karabalgasun and Karakorum – Two Late Nomadic Urban Settlements in the Orkhon Valley. Archaeological Excavation and Research of the German Archaeological Institute (DAI) and the Mongolian Academy of Sciences 2000–2009*, trans. Vincent and Eva Chandler. Ulan Bator: Botschaft der Bundesrepublik Deutschland, 2010.

Inden, Ronald. "Hierarchies of Kings in Early Medieval India." *Contributions to Indian Sociology* 15(1/2) (1981): 99–125.

Inden, Ronald. "Introduction: From Philogical to Dialogical Texts," in *Querying the Medieval: Texts and the History of Practices in South Asia*, 3–28. Oxford: Oxford University Press, 2000.

Jackson, Peter. "Jala Al-Din, the Mongols, and the Khwarazmian Conquest of the Panjab and Sind." *Iran* 28 (1990): 45–54.

Jackson, Peter. "Jalāl Al-Dīn, the Mongols, and the Khwarazmian Conquest of the Panjāb and Sind." *Iran* 28 (1990): 45–54.

Jackson, Peter. *The Delhi Sultanate: A Political and Military History*. Cambridge: Cambridge University Press, 1999.

Jackson, Peter. *The Mongols and the Islamic World: From Conquest to Conversion*. New Haven, CT: Yale University Press, 2017.

Jackson, P. and P. A. Andrews. "Lāhawr," in *Encyclopaedia of Islam*, 2nd edn. (eds. P. Bearman, Th. Bianquis, C. E. Bosworth, E. van Donzel, and W. P. Heinrichs). Leiden: Brill online, 2012.

Jain-Neubauer, Jutta. *The Stepwells of Gujarat in Art-Historical Perspective*. New Delhi: Abhinav Publications, 1981.

Kalus, Ludwig. *Thesaurus d'Épigraphie Islamique*, online. Geneva: Fondation Max van Berchem, 2017, available at: http://epigraphie-islamique.org/epi/texte_acceuil.html.

Kaplony, A. "The Conversion of the Turks of Central Asia to Islam as Seen by Arabic and Persian Geography: A Comparative Perspective," in *Islamisation de l'Asia Centrale* (ed. Étienne de la Vassière), 277–296. Paris: Association pour l'avancement des études iraniennes, 2008.

Karamustafa, Ahmet T. *God's Unruly Friends: Dervish Groups in the Islamic Later Middle Period, 1200–1550*. Salt Lake City: University of Utah Press, 1994.

Karamustafa, Ahmet T. *God's Unruly Friends: Dervish Groups in the Islamic Middle Period 1200–1550*. Oxford: Oneworld, 2007.

Khazeni, Arash. *Tribes and Empire on the Margins of Nineteenth-century Iran*, Publications on the Near East, University of Washington. Seattle: University of Washington Press, 2009.

Khazeni, Arash. "Herat i. Geography," in *Encyclopaedia Iranica*, online edition, 2012a.

Khazeni, Arash. "Through an Ocean of Sand: Pastoralism and the Equestrian Culture of the Eurasian Steppe," in *Water on Sand: Environmental Histories of the Middle East and North Africa* (ed. Alan Mikhail), 133–158. New York: Oxford University Press, 2012b.

Khismatulin, Alexey. "Two Mirrors for Princes Fabricated at the Seljuq Court: Nizam al-Mulk's Siyar al-Muluk and al-Ghazali's Nasihat al-Muluk," in *The Age of the Seljuqs, vol. 6: The Idea of Iran* (eds. Edmund Herzig and Sarah Stewart), 94–130. London: I. B. Tauris, 2015.

Kielhorn, F. "The Chahamanas of Naddula." *Epigraphia Indica* IX (1907/8): 62–83.

Kimball, Fiske. "The Sasanian Building at Tepe Hissar," in *Excavations at Tepe Hissar, Damghan*, 347–350, figures 176, 177. Philadelphia, PA: University of Pennzylvania Press for the University Museum, 1937.

King, David A. "Astronomical Alignments in Medieval Islamic Religious Architecture," eds. Bill M. Boland, Justine Cullinan, and Noemi E. Varas. *Annals of the New York Academy of Sciences* 391 (1982): 303–312.

King, David A. *Astronomy in the Service of Islam*. Aldershot: Variorum, 1993.

King, David A. "The Orientation of Medieval Islamic Religious Architecture and Cities." *Journal for the History of Astronomy* 26 (1995): 253–274.

Knysh, Alexander. *Sufism: A New History of Islamic Mysticism*. Princeton, NJ: Princeton University Press, 2017.

Kröger, Jens. *Sasanidischer Stuckdekor, vol. 5: Baghdader Forschungen*. Mainz am Rhein: Verlag Philipp von Zabern, 1982.

Kröger, Jens. "Stucco Decoration," in *Encyclopaedia Iranica*, online edition, July 2005.

Kumar, Sunil. "The Value of Ādāb Al-Mulūk as a Historical Source: An Insight into the Ideals and Expectations of Islamic Society in the Middle Period (AD 945–1500)." *Indian Economic and Social History Review* 22(3) (1985): 307–327.

Kumar, Sunil. "Qutb and Modern Memory," in *The Partitions of Memory: The Afterlife of the Division of India* (ed. Suvir Kaul), 141–182. Bloomington: Indiana University Press, 2002.

Kumar, Sunil. *The Present in Delhi's Pasts*. Delhi: Permanent Black, 2002.

Kumar, Sunil. "Service, Status, and Military Slavery in the Delhi Sultanate: Thirteenth and Fourteenth Centuries," in *Slavery and South Asian History* (eds. Indrani Chatterjee and Richard Maxwell Eaton), 83–114. Bloomington: Indiana University Press, 2006.

Kumar, Sunil. *The Emergence of the Delhi Sultanate, 1192–1286*. New Delhi: Permanent Black, 2007.

Laleh, Haeedeh, Abolfazl Mokarramifar, and Zahra Lorzadeh. "Le paysage urbain de Nishapur," in *Greater Khorasan: History, Geography, Archaeology and Material Culture* (ed. Rocco Rante), 115–124. Berlin: De Gruyter, 2015.

Lambton, Ann K. S. *State and Government in Medieval Islam*, London Oriental Series, vol. 36. London: RoutledgeCurzon, [1981] 2006.

Lambton, Ann K. S. and Janine Sourdel-Thomine. "Isfahan," in *Historic Cities of the Islamic World* (ed. C. Edmund Bosworth). Leiden: Brill, 2008.

Le Strange, Guy. *The Lands of the Eastern Caliphate: Mesopotamia, Persia, and Central Asia from the Moslem Conquest to the Time of Timur*. Cambridge: Cambridge University Press, 1930.

Levi, Scott C. *The Indian Diaspora in Central Asia and Its Trade, 1550–1900*, Brill's Inner Asian Library. Leiden: Brill, 2002.

Lewis, Franklin. "Reading, Writing and Recitation: Sanā'i and the Origins of the Persian Ghazal," PhD dissertation, University of Chicago, 1995.

Litvinsky, Boris. "Ajina Tepe," in *Encyclopaedia Iranica*, online edition, [1984] 2011.

Litvinsky, Boris. "Buddhism iv. Buddhist Sites in Afghanistan and Central Asia," in *Encyclopaedia Iranica*, online edition, 2010.

Makdisi, George. "Madrasa and University in the Middle Ages." *Studia Islamica* 32 (1970): 255–264.

Makdisi, George. "Law and Traditionalism in the Institutions of Learning of Mediaeval Islam," in *Theology and Law in Islam* (ed. Gustave E. von Grunebaum), 75–88. Wiesbaden: O. Harrassowitz, 1971.

Makdisi, George. *The Rise of Colleges: Institutions of Learning in Islam and the West*. Edinburgh: Edinburgh University Press, 1981.

Malagaris, George. "Warfare and Environment in Medieval Eurasia: Turkic Frontiers at Dandanqan, Somnath and Manzikert," in *Turkish History and Culture in India* (eds. A. C. S. Peacock and Richard P. McClary), 25–55. Leiden: Brill, 2020.

Mani, B. R. *Delhi: Threshold of the Orient (Studies in Archaeological Excavations)*. New Delhi: Aryan Books International, 1997.

Meisami, Julie Scott. "The Past in Service of the Present: Two Views of History in Medieval Persia." *Poetics Today* 14(2) (1993): 247–275.

Meisami, Julie Scott. *Persian Historiography to the End of the Twelfth Century*. Edinburgh: Edinburgh University Press, 1999.

Meisami, Julie Scott. "Palaces and Paradises: Palace Description in Medieval Persian Poetry," in *Islamic Art and Literature* (eds. Oleg Grabar and Cynthia Robinson), 21–54. Princeton, NJ: Markus Wiener, 2001.

McClary, Richard P. *Medieval Monuments of Central Asia*, Edinburgh Studies in Islamic Art. Edinburgh: Edinburgh University Press, 2020.

Meister, Michael W. "Style and Idiom in the Art of Uparamala." *Muqarnas* 10 (1993): 344–354

Meister, Michael W. "Temples along the Indus." *Expedition* 38(3) (1996): 41–54.

Meister, Michael W. "Gandhara–Nagara Temples of the Salt Range and Indus." *Kala, The Journal of the Indian Art History Congress* 4 (1997/8): 45–52.

Meister, Michael W. "Temples of the Salt Range," in *Religion, Ritual, and Royalty*, 132–139. Jaipur: Rawat Publication, 1999.

Meister, Michael W. "Pattan Munara : Minar or Mandir ?" in *Hari Smriti Studies on Art Archaeology and Indology* (ed. Banerji Arundhati), 113–121. New Delhi-110002: Kaveri Books, 2006.

Meister, Michael W. "Exploring Kafirkot: When Is a Rose Apple Not a Rose." *Pakistan Heritage* 1 (2009): 109–128.

Meister, Michael, Abdur Rehman, and Farid Khan. "Discovery of a New Temple on the Indus." *Expedition* 42(1) (2000): 37–46.

Melchert, Christopher. "Sufis and Competing Movements in Nishapur." *Iran* 39 (2001): 237–247.

Melchert, Christopher. "Al-Bukhārī," in *Encyclopaedia of Islam*, 3rd end. (eds. Kate Fleet, Gudrun Krämer, Denis Matringe, John Nawas, and Everett Rowson), Leiden: Brill online, 2012.

Melikian-Chirvani, Assadullah Souren. "L'évocation littéraire du boudhisme dans l'Iran musulman," in *Le monde iranien et l'Islam, sociétés et cultures* (ed. Jean Aubin), II:59–92. Geneva: Librarie Droz, 1974.

Michailidis, Melanie. "In the Footsteps of the Sasanians: Funerary Architecture and Bavandid Legitimacy," in *Persian Kingship and Architecture: Strategies of Power in Iran from the Achaemenids to the Pahlavis* (eds. Sussan Babaie and Grigor Talinn), 135–174. London: I. B. Tauris, 2015.

Miles, George C. "Epigraphical Notice." *Ars Islamica* 6(1) (1939): 11–15.

Nazim, M. "The Pand-Namah of Subuktigan." *Journal of the Royal Asiatic Society of Great Britain & Ireland* (1933): 605–628.

Neelis, Jason. *Early Buddhist Transmission and Trade Networks: Mobility and Exchange within and beyond the Northwestern Borderlands of South Asia, vol. 2: Dynamics in the History of Religion.* Leiden: Brill, 2011.

Nizami, K. A. *Some Aspects of Religion and Politics in India during the Thirteenth Century.* Delhi: Mohammad Ahmad Idarah-i Adabiyat-i Delli, [1961] 1978 (reprint).

Nizami, K. A. *On History and Historians of Medieval India.* New Delhi: Munshiram Manoharlal, 1983.

Nizami, K. A. "Popular Movements, Religious Trends and Sufi Influence on the Masses in the Post-'Abbasid Period," in *The Age of Achievement: AD 750 to the End of the Fifteenth Century – Part One: The Historical, Social and Economic Setting, vol. 4: History of Civilizations of Central Asia* (eds. M. S. Asimov and C. E. Bosworth), 365–379. Paris: UNESCO Publishing, 1998.

Nizami, K. A. "Čishtī, Khwādja Mu'īn al-Dīn Ḥasan," in *Encyclopaedia of Islam*, 2nd edn. (eds. P. Bearman, Th. Bianquis, C. E. Bosworth, E. van Donzel, and W. P. Heinrichs). Leiden: Brill online, 2011a.

Nizami, K. A. "Čishtiyya," in *Encyclopaedia of Islam*, 2nd edn. (eds. P. Bearman, Th. Bianquis, C. E. Bosworth, E. van Donzel, and W. P. Heinrichs). Leiden: Brill online, 2011b.

O'Kane, Bernard. *The Appearance of Persian on Islamic Art*, vol. 4, Biennial Ehsan Yarshater Lecture Series. New York: Persian Heritage Foundation, 2009.

Patel, Alka. *Building Communities in Gujarāt: Architecture and Society during the Twelfth through Fourteenth Centuries*, Brill's Indological Library, vol. 22. Leiden: Brill, [2004] 2007.

Patel, Alka. "A Note on Mahmud Ghaznavi, Somanatha, and the Building of a Reputation," in *South Asian Archaeology 2001.* (ed. Vincent Lefèvre), 599–606. Paris: Editions Recherche sur les Civilisations, 2005.

Patel, Alka. "Revisiting the Term 'Sultanate'," in *The Architecture of the Indian Sultanates* (eds. Abha Narain Lambah and Alka Patel), 8–12. Mumbai: Marg Publications, 2006.

Patel, Alka. "Hind Wa Sind: Textual and Material Evidence of Muslim Communities in Seventh- and Eighth-Century South Asia," paper presented at the Association for Asian Studies, Philadelphia, PA, 2010.

Patel, Alka. "Architectural Cultures and Empire: The Ghurids in Northern India (c. 1192–1210)." *Bulletin of the Asia Institute* 21 ([2007] 2011): 35–60.

Patel, Alka. "The Rehmāṇa-Prāsāda Abroad: Masjid-i Sangī of Larwand (Farah Province, Afghanistan)," in *Prāsāda-Niddhī: Temple Architecture and Sculpture of South and Southeast Asia, Essays in Honour of Professor M. A. Dhaky* (eds. P. P. Dhar, Gerd Mevissen, and Devangana Desai), 84–99. New Delhi: Aryan Books, 2015.

Patel, Alka. "Text as Nationalist Object: Modern Persian-Language Historiography on the Ghurids (c. 1150–1215)," in *India and Iran in the Longue Durée* (eds. Alka Patel and Touraj Daryaee), 143–166. Irvine, CA: Jordan Center for Persian Studies, 2017.

Patel, Alka. "Periphery as Center: The Ghurids between the Persianate and Indic Worlds," in *The Idea of Iran: From Saljuq Collapse to Mongol Conquest* (eds. Sarah Stewart and Edmund Herzig), 29–53. London: I. B. Tauris, 2018.

Paul, J. "Islamizing Sufis in Pre-Mongol Central Asia," in *Islamisation de l'Asia Centrale* (ed. Étienne de la Vaissière), 297–318. Paris: Association pour l'avancement des études iraniennes, 2008.

Peacock, A. C. S. *Early Seljuq History: A New Interpretation*, Routledge Studies in the History of Iran and Turkey. New York: Routledge, 2010.

Peacock, A. C. S. *The Great Seljuk Empire*, Edinburgh History of the Islamic Empires. Edinburgh: Edinburgh University Press, 2015.

Peacock, A. C. S. "The Great Age of the Seljuks," in *Court and Cosmos: The Great Age of the Seljuqs* (eds. Sheila R. Canby, Deniz Beyazit, and Martina Rugiadi), 2–35. New York and New Haven: Metropolitan Museum of Art and Yale University Press, 2016.

Peacock, A. C. S. "Firdawsi's *Shahnama* in Its Ghaznavid Context." *Iran* 56(1) (2018): 2–12.

Pedersen, J., G. Makdisi, Munibur Rahman, and R. Hillenbrand. "Madrasa," in *Encyclopaedia of Islam*, 2nd edn. (eds. Th. Bianquis, C. E. Bosworth, E. van Donzel, W. P. Heinrichs, and P. Bearman). Leiden: Brill online, 2012.

Pons, Jessie. "Kushan Dynasty ix. Art of the Kushans," in *Encyclopaedia Iranica*, online edition, 2016.

Prasad, Pushpa. *Sanskrit Inscriptions of Delhi Sultanate, 1191–1526*. Delhi: Oxford University Press, 1990.

Rabbat, Nasser O. *The Citadel of Cairo: A New Interpretation of Royal Mamluk Architecture*. Islamic History and Civilization, vol. 14. Leiden: Brill, 1995.

Raikes, Captain Stanley Napier. *Memoir on the Thurr and Parkur Districts of Sind, 1856, vol. LIV: Selections from the Records of the Bombay Government*, New Series. Bombay: Education Society's Press, Byculla, 1859.

Rante, Rocco. "'Khorasan Proper' and 'Greater Khorasan' within a Politico-Cultural Framework," in *Greater Khorasan: History, Geography, Archaeology and Material Culture* (ed. Rocco Rante), 9–26. Berlin: De Gruyter, 2015.

Rante, Rocco and Annabelle Collinet. *Nishapur Revisited: Stratigraphy and Ceramics of the Qohandez.* Oxford: Oxbow Books, 2013.

Ray, H. C. *The Dynastic History of Northern India.* 2nd edn. 2 vols. Delhi: Munshiram Manoharlal Publishers, 1973.

Ray, Himanshu Prabha. "Maritime Archaeology of the Indian Ocean: An Overview," in *Tradition and Archaeology: Early Maritime Contacts in the Indian Ocean* (eds. Himanshu Prabha Ray and Jean-François Salles), 1998th edn., 1–10. Delhi: Manohar, 1996.

Ray, Himanshu Prabha. "The Beginnings: The Artisan and the Merchant in Early Gujarat, Sixth–Eleventh Centuries." *Ars Orientalis* 34 ([2004] 2007): 39–61.

Répertoire chronologique d'épigraphie arabe. Cairo, Egypt: Institut français d'archéologie orientale du Caire: vol. V (Tome cinquième)*, années 354 à 386 de l'Hégire,* 1934 ; vol. VI (Tome sixième)*, années 386 à 425 de l'Hégire,* 1935 ; vol. IX (Tome neuvième)*, années 550 à 601 de l'Hégire,* 1937.

Reu, Sāhityāchārya Pt. Bisheshwar Nath. "The Gāhaḍavālas of Kanauj from about V.S. 1125 (A.D. 1068) to about V.S. 1280 (A.D. 1223)." *Journal of the Royal Asiatic Society of Great Britain and Ireland* 1 (1932): 1–21.

Rezakhani, Khodadad. *ReOrienting the Sasanians: East Iran in Late Antiquity.* Edinburgh: Edinburgh University Press, 2017.

Rezakhani, Khodadad. "Pangul and Banji, Zhulad and Fulad: A Note on the Genealogy of the Shanasbid Amirs of Ghur," in *Dinars and Dirhams: Festschrift in Honor of Michael L. Bates* (eds. Touraj Daryaee, Judith Lerner, and Virginie Rey). Irvine, CA: Jordan Center for Persian Studies, 2020.

Rosenfield, John M. *Dynastic Arts of the Kushans,* 3rd edn. Berkeley: University of California Press, [1967] 1993.

Ross, E. Denison. "The Genealogies of Fakhruddin Mubarakshah," in *A Volume of Oriental Studies Presented to Edward G. Browne on His 60th Birthday (7 February 1922)* (eds. Thomas Walker Arnold and Reynold Alleyne Nicholson), 392–413. Cambridge: Cambridge University Press, 1922.

Ruthven, Malise and Azim Nanji. *Historical Atlas of Islam.* Cambridge, MA: Harvard University Press, 2004.

Sarkar, Jagadish Narayan. *History of History-Writing in Medieval India.* Calcutta: Ratna Prakashan, 1977.

Schmidt, Erich F. *Excavations at Tepe Hissar, Damghan.* Philadelphia, PA: University of Pennsylvania Press for the University Museum, 1937.

Schwarz, Florian. *Sylloge Numorum Arabicorum Tübingen. Balh und die Landschaften am oberen Oxus, XIV c Hurasan III.* Tübingen: Ernst Wasmuth Verlag, 2002.

Sen, Sudipta. "Historian as Witness: Ghulam Husain Tabatabai and the Dawning of British Rule in India," in *India and Iran in the Longue Durée* (eds. Alka Patel and Touraj Daryaee), 103–124. Irvine, CA: Jordan Center for Persian Studies, 2017.

Sevim, A. and C. E. Bosworth. "The Seljuqs and the Khwarazm Shahs," in *History of Civilizations of Central Asia, vol. IV: The Age of Achievement: AD 750 to the*

End of the Fifteenth Century – Part Two: The Achievements (eds. C. E. Bosworth and M. S. Asimov), 1st Indian edn., 145–176. New Delhi: Motilal Banarsidass Publishers, 1999.

Sharma, Sunil. *Persian Poetry at the Indian Frontier: Mas'ûd Sa'd Salmân of Lahore.* Permanent Black Monographs, Opus 1 Series. New Delhi: Permanent Black, 2000.

Shokoohy, Mehrdad and Natalie H. Shokoohy. "The Architecture of Baha Al-Din Tughrul in the Region of Bayana, Rajasthan." *Muqarnas* 4 (1987): 114–132.

Shokoohy, Mehrdad and Natalie H. Shokoohy. *Bhadreśvar: The Oldest Islamic Monuments in India,* Studies in Islamic Art and Architecture, 2. Leiden: Brill, 1988.

Siddiqui, Iqtidar Husain. *Authority and Kingship under the Sultans of Delhi (Thirteenth–Fourteenth Centuries).* Delhi: Manohar, 2006.

Siddiqui, Iqtidar Husain. *Indo-Persian Historiography up to the Thirteenth Century.* Delhi: Primus Books, 2010.

Smith, Frederick. "Trees and Plants," in *Brill's Encyclopedia of Hinduism* (eds. Knut A. Jacobsen, Helene Basu, Angelika Malinar, and Vasudha Narayanan). Leiden: Brill, 2019.

Smith, Myron Bement. "The Manars of Isfahan." *Athar-e Iran* I(2) (1936): 313–358.

Smith, Myron Bement. "Epigraphical Notice." *Ars Islamica* 6(1) (1939): 11–15.

Sobieroj, F. "Suhrawardiyya," in *Encyclopaedia of Islam,* 2nd edn. (eds. P. Bearman, Th. Bianquis, C. E. Bosworth, and W. P. Heinrichs). Leiden: Brill online, 2012.

Sourdel-Thomine, Janine. "Les décors de stuc dans l'est iranien à l'époque salgūqide." *Akten des vierundzwanzigsten international Orientalisten-Kongresses* 44 (1957): 342–344.

Sourdel-Thomine, Janine. "Réflexions sur la diffusion de la madrasa en orient du XIe au XIIIe siècle." *Révue des études islamiques* 44 (1976): 165–184.

Spooner, Brian. "Baluchistan i. Geography, History and Ethnography," in *Encyclopaedia Iranica,* online edition, [1988] 2010.

Spooner, Brian. "Epilogue: The Persianate Millennium," in *The Persianate World: The Frontiers of a Eurasian Lingua Franca* (ed. Nile Green), 301–316. Oakland, CA: University of California Press, 2019.

Subtelny, Maria Eva. "The Symbiosis of Turk and Tajik," in *Central Asia in Historical Perspective,* 45–61. Cambridge, MA and Boulder, CO: Harvard University Russian Research Center and Westview Press, 1994.

Tetley, G. E. *The Ghaznavid and Seljuq Turks: Poetry as a Source for Iranian History.* London: Routledge Taylor & Francis, 2009.

Thapar, Romila. *Somanatha: The Many Voices of a History.* New Delhi: Penguin/Viking, 2004.

Tor, D. G. "'Sovereign and Pious': The Religious Life of the Great Seljuq Sultans," in *The Seljuqs: Politics, Society and Culture* (eds. Christian Lange and Songül Mecit), 39–62. Edinburgh: Edinburgh University Press, 2011.

Trimingham, J. Spencer. *The Sufi Orders in Islam.* Oxford: Clarendon Press, 1971.

Tritton, A. S. *Materials on Muslim Education in the Middle Ages.* London: Luzac, 1957.

Trivedi, Harihar Vitthal. *Chaulukyan Inscriptions.* Madhya Pradesh: Commissioner of Archaeology, Archives and Museums, 1994.

Tye, Robert and Monica Tye. *Jitals: A Catalogue and Account of the Coin Denomination of Daily Use in Medieval Afghanistan and North West India*. Isle of South Uist: Robert Tye, 1995.

Van Renterghem, Vanessa. "Baghdad: A View from the Edge on the Seljuq Empire," in *The Age of the Seljuqs, vol. 6: The Idea of Iran* (eds. Edmund Herzig and Sarah Stewart), 74–93. London: I. B. Tauris, 2015.

Vàsàry, Istvàn. "Two Patterns of Acculturation to Islam: The Qarakhanids versus the Ghaznavids and Seljuqs," in *The Age of the Seljuqs, vol. 6: The Idea of Iran* (eds. Edmund Herzig and Sarah Stewart), 9–28. London: I. B. Tauris, 2015.

Welch, Anthony and H. Crane. "The Tughluqs: Master Builders of the Delhi Sultanate." *Muqarnas* I (1983): 123–166.

Wilkinson, Tony J. "Introduction," in *Landscapes of the Islamic World: Archaeology, History, and Ethnography* (eds Stephen McPhillips and Paul D. Wordsworth), 1–16. Philadelphia: University of Pennsylvania Press, 2016.

Wordsworth, Paul D. "Merv on Khorasanian Trade Routes from the 10th–13th Centuries," in *Greater Khorasan: History, Geography, Archaeology and Material Culture* (ed. Rocco Rante), 51–62. Berlin: De Gruyter, 2015.

Yusofi, Gholam-Hosayn. "Chahar Maqala," in *Encyclopaedia Iranica*, online edition, 1990.

Zysow, Aron. "Two Unrecognized Karrami Texts." *Journal of the American Oriental Society* 108(4) (1988): 577–587.

Zysow, Aron. "Karamiyya," in *Encyclopaedia Iranica*, online edition, [2011] 2012.

Index

Note: **bold** indicates illustrations

'Abbas ibn Shish, 90, 195, 238
Abi al-Fath ibn Muhammad, 48–9
Abu Ja'far Muhammad ibn 'Ali, 52
Abu Nasir Ahmad ibn Fadl, 48
Aditya temple, Multan, 282, 300
administrative structures, 48, 83, 116, 149, 150
Afshin, 194
agriculture, 18, 41, 61, 84, 87, 94–5, 154, 292–3
Ahangaran, 41, **81**, 84–7, **86**, **95**, 95
Ajmer, **9**, 135–6, 143, 146
'Ala' al-Din Husain, 62–5, 132–5, 154, 171, 173, 194–5, 208, 238, 241–2, 255–7, 262–3, 300–1, 322
'Ala' al-Din Muhammad, 65
Alana Valley, **92**
Ali, Taj, 278
'Ali ibn Abi Talib, 43
Allchin, F. Raymond, 150
Allen, Terry, 253
Alptigin, 16, 221
Ambh Sharif temple, Panjab, **290–1**
Amir Banji ibn Naharan, 43, 107, 108, 116
Anahilavada-pattana, 67
Anandapala, 285
Anatolia, 8, 59, 116, 292
Anooshahr, Ali, 42, 279
anthropomorphism, 198, 219
arabesque ornament, 50, **157**, 163, 244, 247, 259–60, 304, 323
arch motifs, 98, 103, **104–5**, 212–13, **216**
arches
    Bust monumental arch, **7**, **249**, 251–4, **252–3**, 264
    Chisht domed structures, **212**, 212–13, **215**
    Gandhara–Nagara school, 287, **288–90**

ribat of 'Ali ibn Karmakh, Multan, 304–5, **306–8**
Robat Sharaf, **57**
Sarkhushak, 160
tomb of Ahmad Kabir, Multan, 304, **316**
tomb of Sadan Shahid, Multan, 304, **313**
trefoil arches, 287, **288–90**, 303–5, **306–8**, **313**, **316**
architectural treatises, 298, 303, 306
Arhai Din-ka Jhonpra mosque, Ajmer, **9**
art-architectural historiography, 17–18, 81–2, 148, 241
artisans, 23, 27, 94–6, 108–9, 143–4, 191, 206, 221, 281, 296, 298, 302–3, 306, 327–8, 339
Asif, Manan Ahmed, 42, 79
Astarabad, 65
Audience Hall, Lashkari-Bazar, 259, 263, 265–7, **266–8**
Awbeh, 86
Azeem, Rizwan, 323
Azhd Zahhak, 42–3

Babur, 8
Bactria, 4–5, 148, 304
Badghis, 82, 86
Baghdad, 59, 107, 116
Baha' al-Din, 62, 64, 134, 135, 154–5, 194, 238
Baha' al-Din Tughril, 65
Bahram Shah, 62–3, 64, 109, 194, 208, 242
Bahram Shah *minar*, Ghazna, **58**, 109–11, **110**; *see also* minarets of Ghazni
Baihaqi, 41
baked brick, 25, 26, 50, 91, 100, 109, 139, 142–3, 250, 299, 305, 318
Baker, P. H. B., 150
Bakhtyari tribe, 240

Balasaghun region, 45–6
Balkh, 26, 52, 54, 61, 82, 109–11, 115, 133, 148, 153, 169, 190
Ball, Warwick, 57, 88, 90, 92
Baluchistan, 278, 283, 284, 289–98, **293**, 302, 323–4, 327
Bamiyan, 3, **5–6**, 54, 82–3, 86, 132–3, 139, **147**, 147–69, **149**, **151–3**, **156–68**, 173–5, 191–2, 238–40, 339
Bamiyan Shansabanis, 19, 26, 61–3, 82, 132, 154–5, 165–9, 171, 175, 190–2, 238, 267–8, 279, 281, 338, 339
Banbhore *see* Dibul-Banbhore
Bandian, 100
banditry, 41
Bara Gumbad mosque, Delhi, 310
barbarians, 18, 19–20, 21, 108
Barfak II, 156–9, **162–5**, 167
Barfield, Thomas, 341
Barsiyan mosque, 260
Basseri tribe, 240
bastions, 67, 90, 151–2, 157, 159, 160
Bhadreshvar, 295, **295–6**, **319**
Bhimadeva II, 67
Bhodesar temple, Nagarparkar, **297**
Bistam, 65
Blair, Sheila, 199, 214, 221, 254, 310
Bosworth, C. E., 41, 90, 114, 198
Brahmanical Hinduism, 56–7, 282, 285, 289, 304
Bronson, Bennet, 19
Buddha sculptures, **147**, 148
Buddhism, 1, 45–6, 56–9, 83, 109, 147–50, 157, 159, 167, 169–71, 239, 284–5, 287, 304
Buddhist monasteries, 56–9, **59**, 83, 148–50, 159, 169–71, **170**, 239, **284**, 284–5
building materials, 4, 23, 50, 90–1, 278, 287, 295, 299, 302, 305
al-Bukhari, 207
Bulliet, Richard, 217
Burbank, Jane, 10, 19
burial mounds, 3, **4**, 133, 171–2, **172**, 173; *see also* graves; tombs
burial practices, 171–2, 301
Bust galleried well, 249–51, **250–1**
Bust-Lashkari Bazar, 3, **7**, 23–5, 54, 63, 90, 133–4, 154, 164–5, 171–3, 192–3, 237–8, 241–2, 247–67, **248–61**, **265–70**, 281, 301, 308–9, 321

Bust monumental arch, **7**, **249**, 251–4, **252–3**, 264

Casimir, Michael, 200, 203, 240
cemeteries, 171–2, **172**, 320; *see also* burial mounds; graves; tombs
ceramics, 139, 155, 158, 162–3, 172, 242
ceremony, 54, 61, 106, 192, 206–7, 253, 265–7
Chach-nama (Kufi), 79
Chaghcharan, 84, 86, 134
Chagri, 48
Chahar Maqala (Nizami 'Aruzi), 154
Chaulukyas, 67, 296
Chehel Abdal, 84
Chehel Burj, **161**
Chhoti *masjid*, Bhadreshvar, **295**, **318**
Chihil Dukhtaran, Isfahan, 48–9, **50–2**
China, 10, 46
Chinggis Khan, 155
Chinggisids, 155
Chira, 320
Chisht, 81, 86, 133, 190–7, 210–17, **211–13**, **215–16**, 220, 221, 261, 309, 312
Chishtiyya, 215–17
Christianity, 45–6
cisterns, 139, **142**
citadels, **28**, **29**, **156**, **170**, 192, 248–54, **249**; *see also* fortifications; hilltop complexes
city walls, **7**, 248–9; *see also* fortifications
coinage, 44, 61, 62, 63–4, 65, 80, 263, 264, 340
commemoration, 67, 143, 146, 209–10, 218–19, 253–4, 282, 300–1, 316, 321, 322
commerce, 3, 42, 47, 51, 62–3, 107, 113–16, 133–9, 142, 148–50, 153–4, 169–75, 222, 239–40, 279, 282–5, 289–90, 294, 299–300, 329; *see also* trade
commercial architecture, 136, 139, 248, 294
communication routes, 51, 175, 195, 197, 220, 240, 279, 285, 323–4, 325
confederation, 5, 16, 40, 61–2, 116, 193, 240, 241, 338, 340
Congregational Mosques
    Herat, 4, **11**, **12**, 211
    Isfahan, 48, **49–50**
    Jam Jaskars Goth, **294**, 294–5
    Multan, 282, 283
Cooper, Frederick, 10, 19

corbeling, 161, 295, **296**
corridors, **66**, **153**, 161, 287–9, 304–5
cosmopolitanism, 23, 50, 59, 100, 103, 106, 108–13, 143–6, 175, 191, 221–2, 289–92, 323, 328
courts, 16, 21, 40, 42, 44–5, 60, 107, 146–7, 154–5, 192, 221, 222, 267–8, 341
courtyards
    Barfak II, 157, 158–9, **163**
    courtyard-*ivan* configuration, 51, 54, 157, 158–9, 163, 164
    Mas'ud III palace, Ghazna, **6**, 243–4, 262–3
    Robat Sharaf, 51, **56**
    Shahr-i Ghulghula, 163, 164
    South Palace, Lashkari Bazar, 255, 257, **258**, 263
Cousens, Henry, 295
Crossley, Patricia, 18
cruciform plans, 92, **94**, 164
cursive script, 194, 203, **209**, 209–11, **211–13**, 213–14

Da Qadi *minar*, 99–100, **100**, 108–12, 113, 143, 191, 281, 339
dadoes, **6**, **103**, 244, **246–7**, 247, 257, 259, 263
Damascus, 48
Dandanqan, battle of, 48, 61
Danestama *see* Barfak II
Darmashan, 84, 86
Daulatabad *minar*, 52, 99, **102**, 110–11
Daykundi 82
de Bruijn, Thomas, 8
decoration
    arabesque ornament, 50, **157**, 163, 244, 247, 259–60, 304, 323
    arch motifs, 98, 103, **104–5**, 212–13, **216**
    Baluchistan tombs, 292–3, **293**, 324, 327
    Bamiyan hilltop complexes, 156–7, **157**, **160**, **161**, **165**
    Bust monumental arch, 251–4, **252–3**
    ceramics, 162–3
    Chisht domed structures, 212–13, **216**
    Da Qadi *minar*, 99–100, **100**, 109–11
    epigraphic motifs, 247, 313, 315–16, 318, 327
    figural decoration, 292–3
    floral ornament, 50, 51, 98, **98–9**, 101, **102**, **104**, 111, 157, 244, 247, 259–60, 292, 304, 323

Gandhara–Nagara school, 287–9, **288–91**, 305–6, 309, 327
geometric ornament, 25, 50, 51, 99–100, 111, 144–5, **145**, 151–2, 156–7, **157**, 162, **165**, 247, 253, 255, 259, 292, 304, 315, 323
Ghur architectural remains, 90, 91, **96–9**, 96–103, **102**, **104**, 109
glazed tiles, 49, 50, **54**, 247, 278, 302, 320–4, **322**
Jam-Firuzkuh *minar*, 144–6, **145**, 322
Lal Mara Sharif tombs, 278, 302, 313, 320–4, **322**, 327–8
Mas'ud III palace, Ghazna, 242–7, **245–7**, 323
medallions, 25, 212–13
mural paintings, 152, 156, **161**, 267, **268**
overflowing pot motifs (*purnaghata*), 295, 305, **308**, **310**, 315–18, **318**
ribat of 'Ali ibn Karmakh, Multan, 302–3, 304–6, **306–8**, **310–11**
Robat Sharaf, 51, **57**
Saljuq architecture, 50, 98, 109
Sasanian architecture, 100–3, **103–5**
Shah-i Mashhad *madrasa*, 199, 202–3
South Palace, Lashkari Bazar, 255, 259–60, **260**, 263, 267, **267–8**
stucco decoration, 100–3, **102–4**, 111, 157, **165**, 212, **216**, 242–3, **245–6**, 251, 255, 259–60, **260**, **267**
Sukkhur tombs, 302, 313–18, **318**, 323, 327
terracotta decoration, 25, 242–7, 292–3, **293**, 324
Thamban Wari *masjid*, Jam Jaskars Goth, 295–6, 298
tomb of Ahmad Kabir, Multan, 277–8, 302–4, **314**, **316**
tomb of Muhammad ibn Harun, Lasbela, 324
tomb of Salar Khalil, Juzjan, 24–6, **25**
tomb of Sadan Shahid, Multan, 302–4, **313**
tomb of Shahzada Shaikh Husain, Bust, 24–5, **27**
vegetal ornament, 144–5, 157, 162, 295, 305
zoomorphic motifs, 247, 304, 323
see also epigraphy
defensive structures *see* fortifications

Délégation Archéologique Française en
    Afghanistan (DAFA), 161–2
Delhi, 44, 109, 282, 310–12
Delhi Sultanate, 15
Dhaky, M. A., 296
Dibul-Banbhore, 67, 289–90, **292**, 313
domes
    Chisht domed structures, 190–7, 210–17,
        211–13, **215–16**, 220, 221, 261
    Congregational Mosque, Isfahan, 48,
        49
    corbeled domes, 295, **296**
    domed cube tombs, 23–4, **24**, 213, 278,
        293, 302, 304, **314**, 315, **317**, **320**, 320,
        324, **326**
    Gandhara–Nagara temples, 287
    hilltop complexes, 152, 160
    Saljuq architecture, 50
    Sarkhushak, 160
    Umayyad Mosque, Damascus, 48
doxologies, 26, 209, 213, 220, 222, 243, 257,
        260, 261, 304, 307, 327
Dupree, Louis, 83
dwelling towers, **89**, 90–4, **91**, **92**

Edwards, Holly, 23, 278, 315, 320
enclosures *see* fortified enclosures; textile
    enclosures
endowments (*waqf*), 263, 281, 282, 283,
        327, 340
epigraphy
    Bara Gumbad mosque, Delhi, 310
    Barsiyan mosque, 260
    Bust monumental arch, 251–4, **252–3**,
        264
    Chihil Dukhtaran, Isfahan, **51**, **52**
    Chisht domed structures, 193, 194,
        210–14, **211–13**, **215–16**, 261, 309,
        312
    Congregational Mosque, Herat, 211
    cursive script, 194, 203, **209**, 209–11,
        211–13, 213–14
    and dating, 24, 26, 51, 109, 190, 194, 211,
        254–5, 262, 277
    Daulatabad *minar*, 52, **102**
    doxologies, 26, 209, 213, 220, 222, 243,
        257, 260, 261, 304, 327
    floriated Kufic script, 244
    foliated Kufic script, 211
    foundation inscriptions, 194–5, 203,
        203, 210, 277

funerary inscriptions, 204, 213–14
Gandhara–Nagara school, 305–6, 309,
        327
Hadith inscriptions, 193, 204, **206**, 207,
        222
historical inscriptions, **51**, 144–5, 204,
        304, 307
Jam-Firuzkuh *minar*, 143, 144–5, 190,
        193, 197, 217–20
Kufic script, 25, 26, 49, **102**, 111, 194,
        202–3, **203**, **205**, 209–11, 214, **215**,
        219, 244, 257, 304, 318, **319**
legibility, 145, 204–5, 219
Mas'ud III *minar*, Ghazna, **208–9**,
        208–10, 260
Mas'ud III palace, Ghazna, 243–7,
        257–9, 279
naskh script, **102**, 111, 201, 202, 204,
        206, 211, 244, 304
and patronage, 192, 204–8, 210, 219–20,
        262, 264, 307–13
Qasimabad *minar*, 53
Qur'anic inscriptions, 26, 144–5, 193,
        197, 203–4, 207–14, **212–13**, **215**,
        218–19, 222, 251–4, **252–3**, 259–62,
        260, 302–13, **313–14**, 327
Qutb mosque, Delhi, 311
ribat of 'Ali ibn Karmakh, Multan, 277,
        302–3, 304–6, **306–8**, 309
Robat Sharaf, 51
Saljuq architecture, 50, 254
Shah-i Mashhad *madrasa*, 193, 194–5,
        199, 201–10, **203–6**, 253, 260, 307–8,
        313, 339
Sharada script, 304
Shrine of Ibrahim, Bhadreshvar, **319**
Sin *minar*, 49
South Palace, Lashkari Bazar, 242,
        254–62, **257**, 263, 267, 308–9
thuluth script, 202, 203, **204**
tomb of Ahmad Kabir, Multan, 277,
        302–4, 309–10, **314**, **316**
tomb of Iltutmish, Delhi, 311–12
tomb of Mir Sayyid Bahram,
        Kirminiyya, 310
tomb of Sadan Shahid, Multan, 261,
        302–4, 309, **312**, **313**
tomb of Salar Khalil, Juzjan, 24,
        25–6
tomb of Shahzada Shaikh Husain, Bust,
        24

Fakhr al-Din Masʿud, 62, 63, 132, 134, 154, 238, 268

Fakhr-i Mudabbir, 282

Farah, 82, 87

Farah Rud, 87

Faryab, 82, 86

Fatimids, 282, 300

figural decoration, 292–3

fire damage, 241–2

Firozkohis, 94, 95

First Anglo-Afghan War, 29

Firuzkuh *see* Jam-Firuzkuh

Firuzkuh Shansabanis, 19, 26, 42, 61–8, 84, 132–47, 154–5, 167, 171–5, 190–7, 204, 210, 217–22, 238–41, 261–4, 279, 281, 313, 321, 338–9; *see also* Jam-Firuzkuh

Flood, F. B., 17–18, 20, 197, 219

flood damage, 137, 139

floral ornament, 50, 51, 98, **98–9**, 101, **102**, **104**, 111, 157, 244, 247, 259–60, 292, 304, 323

floriated Kufic script, 244

foliated Kufic script, 211

folk astronomy, 201, 214

fortifications, **5**, 41, 67, 81, 84, 87–98, **89**, **91–4**, **96**, 132–3, 136, 139, **140–1**, 142, 150–67, **151–3**, **156–68**, 191–5, 248–9, 294

fortified enclosures, 80, 90–2

foundation inscriptions, 194–5, 203, **203**, 210, 277

four-*ivan* plans, 164

Fuladi, 148

Funduqistan, 148

funerary inscriptions, 204, 213–14

Gandhara, 5, 283, **284**, 284–9, **286–91**, 304, 307

Gandhara–Nagara school, 285–9, **288–91**, 302, 303, 305–6, 309, 316, 319, 327

Ganga-Yamuna *duab*, 5, 67

Gar *minar*, 49

garm-sir encampments, 87, 105, 106, 139, 169, 194, 222, 237

Gellner, Ernest, 47

genealogies, **xviii**, 42–3

geometric ornament, 25, 50, 51, 99–100, 111, 144–5, **145**, 151–2, 156–7, **157**, 162, **165**, 247, 253, 255, 259, 292, 304, 315, 323

Gharjistan, 84, 133, 190–210, **196**, **200**, **202–6**, 220, 238

al-Ghazali, 154

Ghazna, 3, **6**, **28**, 53–68, **58**, 109–11, **110**, 132–4, 146, 154, 164–5, 171, 173–4, 192–3, **208–9**, 208–10, 219, 237–49, **243–7**, 254–5, 260, 262–7, 279–82, 301, 321–2, 338, 340

Ghazna Shansabanis, 19, 43, 61, 65, 174–5, 190–1, 217, 237–41, 262–70, 277–98, 301, 303, 313, 319–23, 325–8, 338, 340–1

Ghaznavids, 5, 8, 15–17, 26, 41, 44, 46–8, 53–68, 84, 98, 109, 113–16, 132, 144, 154, 163–5, 171, 173, 192–3, 195–8, 206–10, 218, 221, 237, 240–2, 248–54, 257, 262–9, 278–82, 285, 299–301, 307–8, 316, 321–2, 325–7, 339–41

Ghiyath al-Din, 4, 43, 62–7, 132, 135–7, 155, 173–4, 194–8, 210–11, 214, 238, 240, 254, 263, 322

*ghulam*s, 16, 53–4, 65, 79, 153–4, 221, 240, 311

Ghur, 1, 19–20, 27, 41–3, 46–7, 61, 80–117, **81**, **88–99**, **102**, **104**, 132, 135, 139, 150–4, 173, 174, 194, 198, 220–1, 238, 240, 248, 281, 283, 338

Glatzer, Bernt, 200, 203, 240

glazed brick, 139

glazed tiles, 49, 50, **54**, 247, 278, 302, 320–4, **322**

Godard, André, 51

Gol-Zarriun, battle of, 149

graves, 3, **4**, 133, 171–2, **172**, 173, 321; *see also* burial mounds; tombs

Greco-Roman architecture, 287

grottoes, 150, 157, 160

Gujarat, 67, 280, 289, 295, 296–8, 302, 303, 316

Hadiqat al-Haqiqa (Sanaʾi), 1

Hadith inscriptions, 193, 204, **206**, 207, 222

Halam ibn Shaiban, 282

Hanafi *madhhab*, 198, 199, 201, 214, 217, 219, 278–9

Hari Rud, 41, 84–7, **85**, **86**, 94, 115, 132, 139, 167, 195–7

Harun al-Rashid, 107

Helmand Province, **26**, 82, **248**

Helmand River, 248, 267, **269–70**

Hephthalites, 31, 81, 106, 149, 150, 153, 167

Herat, 4, **11–14**, **30**, 31, 52, 61, 63, 65, 81–2,
    86, 115, 133, 169, 173, 175, 190, 195,
    214–15, 220
Herberg, Werner, 88, 92, 97
hilltop complexes, 150–2, **151–3**, 155–7,
    156–68, 192
Hind, 237
Hindu Kush, 83, 155, 157
Hindu-Shahis, 285, 304
Hinduism, 56–7, 279, 282, 285–9, 304
historical inscriptions, **51**, 144–5, 204, 304,
    307
historiography
    art-architectural, 17–18, 81–2, 148, 241
    historiographic expectations, 44, 61,
        62
    Islamic, 15–16
    and nomadic groups, 20–1, 40–3, 174,
        205
    oral history, 40, 96, 205
    see also textual sources
Hodgson, Marshall, 44
House of Lusterware, Ghazna, 242, 247
Hsuan Tsang, 148
Hudud al-Alam, 41
Hurr Malika, 194
Husam al-Din 'Ali Abu al-Hasan, 154
Hussain, Talib, 277

Ibn al-Athir, 42, 43, 63
Ibn Karram, 198
Ibrahim ibn Ardashir, 194
iconography *see* decoration; epigraphy
'idgahs, 144, 145, 146
ilkhandids, **66**
Iltutmish, 282, 311–12
Indus region, 5, 14, 22, 27, 40, 46, 67,
        79, 190, 239, 262, 264, 277–328, 338,
        340–1
inheritance, 61, 174–5
inscriptions *see* epigraphy
interlocking Kufic script, 202, 209
Isfahan, 48–9, **49–52**, 51, 116, 237, 260
Islam, 8, 15–17, 43–8, 79–80, 108, 112–16,
        145–6, 171–2, 191–3, 197–9, 205–7,
        210, 214–22, 282–3, 290, 293,
        295–306, 309, 317, 338–9
Islamic historiography, 15–16
Islamization, 17, 43, 113–16, 192, 290, 339
Isma'ili Shi'ism, 217, 282–3, 300
Istiya, 134, 238

ivans, **12**, 51, 54, **56**, 157, 158–9, 163, 164,
    259
'Izz al-Din, 61, 62, 132, 134

Jalawar, 292
Jam-Firuzkuh, 2–3, **3**, 18, 62, 67–8, 80–1,
        84–7, **85**, 111, 115–16, 132–47, **138**,
        140–5, 163, 167, 173–5, 190–7, 217–22,
        218, 254, 267, 321, 322, 338–9; *see also*
        Firuzkuh Shansabanis
Jam-Firuzkuh *minar*, **3**, 18, 67–8, **85**, 87,
        111, 133, 137, 143–6, **144–5**, 190–3, 197,
        217–20, **218**, 221, 254, 321, 322, 339
Jam-Firuzkuh mosque, 87, 135, 137, **138**,
        142–3, 146, 221, 339
Jam Jaskars Goth, **294**, 294–8
Jam Rud, **85**, 115, 132, 137
Jauhar Malik, 194–5, 201, 210
Jayaprrcha, 298
Judaism, 43, 86, 107, 113, 115–16, 139, 142
Jurwas, 41
Juzjan Province, 23–7
Juzjani, Minhaj al-Din Siraj, 20, 42–4,
        61–7, 86–7, 90, 93, 100, 107–8, 112,
        115–16, 132, 134–40, 143, 146, 154–5,
        171, 193–4, 197, 237–8, 242, 279, 283,
        289

Kabul, 82, 83, 148, 149, 169, 239
Kachh coast, 295
Kakrak, 148
Kalar temple, Panjab, **288**
Kalat, 292, 323, 324
al-Kamil fi al-Tarikh (Ibn al-Athir), 42,
        43, 63
Karramiyya, 114, 146, 194, 197–9, 205–6,
        214, 217, 219–20, 339
Kashi, 63, 134, 154
Kashmir, 287, 304
Kevran, Monik, 278
Khamseh confederacy, 240
Khan, Ahmad Nabi, 278, 313
*khanaqah*s, 199, 215–17, 221–2, 300
Kharan, 292, 323
Khazars, 46, 113
Khirgai market, 84–6
Khusrau Shah, 64, 67, 263
Khwabin, 41
Khwaja Siyah Push, 109, **112**
Khwarazm-shahs, 26, 42, 45, 46, 65, 154
Khwash Rud, 87

Khyber-Pakhtunkhwa, **284**, 285, **286**, 316

Killigan, **160**

King, David, 200

kingship, 16–17, 21–2, 42, 44–60, 106, 115, 174, 191, 198, 221, 267–8, 338, 339, 341

Kirminiyya, 310

knowledge, 8–10, 83, 205, 221–2, 264, 298, 303

Kohzad, Ahmad Ali, 83, 84, 96

Kufi, 'Ali, 79

Kufic script, 25–6, 49, **102**, 111, 194, 202–3, **203**, **205**, 209–11, 214, **215**, 219, 244, 257, 304, 318, **319**

Kuh-i Khara, Jam-Firuzkuh, 139, **142**

Kukhars, 67

Kurraman, 65, 239

Kushanas, 4–5, 341

Kushkak, 115

Kushk-i Sultan, Jam-Firuzkuh, 135–6, 139–40, 146

labor, 13, 20, 22, 23, 113, 115, 136, 143–4, 167, 191, 195, 222, 264, 281, 302, 306, 339

Lahore, 26, 44, 65, 67, 79, 217, 237, 282, 283, 237

Lahore Fort, 282

Lahore *minar*, 282

Lahori Bandar, 290

Lal Mara Sharif, 278, 302, 313, **320**, 320–4, **322**, **325–6**, 327–8

language, 41, 47

Lasbela, 292, **293**

Lashkari-Bazar *see* Bust-Lashkari Bazar

Le Berre, Marc, 150, 157

legibility, 145, 204–5, 219

legitimacy, 18, 46, 106

literacy, 205–6, 219

literary production, 42, 53, 136, 154, 192, 221, 282

lusterware, 242

*madhhab*s, 114, 193, 197–201, 205–6, 207, 210, 214–17, 219–20, 278–9, 339

Madin, 134, 154

madrasa complexes

    Afshin, 194

    Chisht (possible *madrasa* complex), 190–7, 210–17, **211–13**, **215–16**, 220, 221

endowments, 282, 283

patronage, 2, 155, 194–5, 199, 210, 220

Shah-i Mashhad *madrasa*, **2**, 190–210, **196**, **200**, **202–6**, 220, 221, 253, 260, 307–8, 313, 339

Mahmud Ghaznavi, 16, 41, 53, 84, 114, 154, 198, 249, 278, 279–80, 282–3, 285

Mahmud, M. S. 41–2

Maimana, 82

Makran coast, 284, 289–98, 302, 303, 323–4

Male Alau *see* Muna Ala

Malik Shah, 48

Mandesh, 84, 86

marble, **6**, 242, 244, 247, 263

Mari Indus temple, Panjab, **289**

markets, 84–6, 221; *see also* commerce; trade

marriage alliances, 107, 175, 194

Maru–Gurjara style, 296–8, 302, 303, 306, 316–18, 327

Marv, 51, 65, 116

al-Marvarruzi, Fakhr al-Din Mubarak-shah, 43

masjid-i jami' *see* Congregational Mosques

Mas'ud I, 41, 48, 249, 279, 280, 282

Mas'ud III, 109, 164, 208–9, 243

Mas'ud III *minar*, Ghazna, **58**, 109–11, **110**, **208–9**, 208–10, 243, 260; *see also* minarets of Ghazni

Mas'ud III palace, Ghazna, **6**, **58**, 164, 242–7, **244–7**, 257–9, 262–3, 265, 279, 323

material culture, 20–1, 44, 61, 108, 139, 155, 158, 162–3, 172, 242

Maulana Siraj-i Minhaj, 136, 155

Mecca, 171, 201

medallions, 25, 212–13

Meister, Michael, 22, 285–9

Mele Hairam, 100

mercantilism *see* commerce; trade

metalwork, 21

migrations, 20, 47, 60, 86–7, 114, 116, 222, 269, 292, 323–4, 339; *see also* nomadism

*mihrab*s

    Barfak II, 157, **164–5**

    Chisht domed structures, 190, 212–13, 214, **216**

    Jam-Firuzkuh *minar*, *mihrab* motif, 144–6, **145**

    Lal Mara Sharif, 320

mihrabs (cont.)
   Mosque of the Forecourt, Lashkari
      Bazar, 255, 263
   Oratory F, Lashkari Bazar, 255, 260, **261**
   qibla orientation, 145–6, 199–201, 212,
      214, 278–9
   Rajagira mosque, Udegram, **287**
   ribaṭ of ʿAli ibn Karmakh, Multan,
      304–6, **306–8**, 309, **310–11**
   Sarkhushak, 160
   Sin mosque, **53**
   tomb of Muhammad ibn Harun,
      Lasbela, 293
minaʾi ware, 139
Minaret of Jam Archaeological Project
   (MJAP), 18, 136–9, 142–3
minarets of Ghazni, **28**, **58**, 109–11, **110**,
   208–9, 208–10, 243, 260
minars
   Chihil Dukhtaran, Isfahan, 48–9, **50–2**
   commemorative function, 67, 143, 146,
      209–10, 218–19, 254, 282, 322
   Da Qadi *minar*, 99–100, **100**, 108–12,
      113, 143, 191, 281, 339
   Daulatabad *minar*, 52, 99, **102**, 110–11
   Ghaznavid architecture, 54–9, 98, 109,
      218
   Gar *minar*, 49
   Jam-Firuzkuh *minar*, **3**, 18, 67–8, **85**, 87,
      111, 133, 137, 143–6, **144–5**, 190–3, 197,
      217–20, **218**, 221, 254, 321, 322, 339
   Lahore *minar*, 282
   Masʿud III *minar*, Ghazna, **58**, 109,
      208–9, 208–10, 243, 260
   minarets of Ghazni, **28**, **58**, 109–11, **110**,
      208–9, 208–10, 243, 260
   Qasimabad *minar*, 53, 99, **101**, 110–11
   Qutb *minar*, Delhi, 109
   Saghar *minar*, 80
   Saljuq architecture, 50, 98, 109, 218
   Sin, 49, **53–4**
   stellate construction, 56–9, 109, 110
mobility, 18, 23, 45, 51, 60, 112–13, 279, 338
Mongols, 10, 44, 82, 116, 137, 139, 155, 241,
   242, 278, 322
Mosque of the Forecourt, Lashkari Bazar,
   255, **258**, 263
mosques
   Arhai Din-ka Jhonpra mosque, Ajmer, **9**
   Bara Gumbad mosque, Delhi, 310
   Barsiyan mosque, 260

Chhoti *masjid*, Bhadreshvar, **295**, **318**
Congregational Mosque, Herat, 4, **11**,
   12, 211
Congregational Mosque, Isfahan, 48,
   49–50
Congregational Mosque, Jam Jaskars
   Goth, **294**, 294–5
Congregational Mosque, Multan, 282,
   283
constructed on temple sites, 282
Dibul-Banbhore, **292**
endowments, 282, 283
Jam-Firuzkuh mosque, 87, 135, 137, **138**,
   142–3, 146, 221, 339
Mosque of Kaman, Rajasthan, **10**
Mosque of the Forecourt, Lashkari
   Bazar, 255, **258**, 263
north Indian *duab*, 4, **9**, **10**
Qutb mosque, Delhi, 311
Rajagira mosque, Udegram, 285, **286**, **287**
Sarkhushak, 160–1
Shahr-i Ghulghula, 163
Sin mosque, 49, **53**
Thamban Wari *masjid*, Jam Jaskars
   Goth, **294**, 294–6, 298
Umayyad Mosque, Damascus, 48
Mughals, 15
Muhammad ibn Qasim, 282
Muhammad ibn Suri, 84
Muʿin al-Din Sijzi Chishti, 217
Muʿizz al-Din, 62–7, 79, 132, 135–7, 173,
   175, 219, 237–49, 254, 259–67, 278–85,
   289–92, 298–9, 313, 316, 325–7, 340
al-Muʿizz li-Din Allah, 282
Muʿjam al-buldan (Yaqut), 42
Mularaja II, 67
Multan, 64, 67, 79, 261, 277–8, 282–3, 289,
   300–13, **301**, **305–16**, 316, 321, 327, 328
Muna Ala, **91**, 98, **99**, **102**, 103, **104**
mural paintings, 152, 156, **161**, 267, **268**
Murghab River, 197, **200**

Nab, battle of, 63, 65
Najimi, A. W., 195, 201, 203–4
Nandana temple, Panjab, **291**
Nasir al-Din Muhammad, 134, 154
Nasir al-Din Qabacha, 79
naskhi script, **102**, 111, 201, 202, 204, **206**,
   211, 244, 304, **313–14**
Nigar, 148
Nimruz, 53

Nishapur, 51, 52, 65, 114, 194, 197, 198, 214–15, 220

Nizam al-Mulk, 48

Nizamabad, 101, **104**

Nizami 'Aruzi (al-Samarqandi), 42

nomad–urban continuum, 14, 18, 20, 27, 31, 47, 53, 86, 94–6, 106–8, 113, 167–8, 174, 195, 205, 221, 240, 269–70, 281, 338, 341

nomadic studies, 21, 108, 116, 240

nomadism, 18–21, 40–3, 60–1, 80, 83–7, 90, 94, 106–8, 113–17, 133, 136–47, 167–75, 191–3, 205–6, 221–2, 237, 240, 269–70, 280, 281, 292–3, 301, 321–4, 338–9, 341

north Indian *duab*, 4, 5–8, **7–10**, 14, 40, 59–60, 65–7, 79, 190, 218, 237, 250, 262, 277, 280, 282, 303, 325, 338, 340–1

North Palace, Lashkari Bazar, **270**

numismatics *see* coinage

Ögedey, 137

Oghüz, 51, 63, 64, 65, 132, 133, 167, 173, 195, 210, 219, 238–9, 241, 254, 263, 322

Old Qandahar *see* Tiginabad/Old Qandahar

Old Qandahar cemetery, 171–2, **172**

O'Neal, Michael P., 63

oral history, 40, 96, 205

oratories
    Robat Sharaf, 54, **56**
    South Palace, Lashkari Bazar, 255, **259–61**, 259–62, 263, 265, 309

Orientalism, 29

origin myths, 42–3, 107–8

ornament *see* decoration

overflowing pot motifs (*purnaghata*), 295, 305, **308**, **310**, 315–18, **318**

paganism, 113, 114

'Palace of Racquets', Lashkari Bazar, 255, 264–5, **265**

palaces
    Ghaznavid architecture, 163–5, 193
    Kushk-i Sultan, Jam-Firuzkuh, 135–6, 139–40, 146
    Mas'ud III palace, Ghazna, **6**, **58**, 164, 242–7, **244–7**, 257–9, 262–3, 265, 279, 323
    north Indian *duab*, 4, **7**, **8**

North Palace, Lashkari Bazar, **270**

patronage, 136, 155, 174, 191

Sarkhushak, **6**, 155, 160–1, **166–8**, 167, 192

Shahr-i Ghulghula, 163–4, 168, 339

Shahr-i Zuhak, **5**, 150, **151–3**, 155, 162, 192, 339

South Palace, Lashkari Bazar, 164, 242, 254–62, **255–61**, 263, 265–7, **266–9**, 308–9

symbolic function, 136, 140

textile palatial architecture, 139–42, 146

Panjab, 5, 64, 67, 79, 278, 282, 284, 285–7, **288–91**, 313, 316, **320**, 320–4, **322**, **325–6**, 327

Panjgur, 292

Parwan/Farwan, 62

patronage
    of artisans and labor, 21, 23, 27, 108, 136, 143, 191, 221, 281, 298, 302, 306, 328, 339
    cultural, literary and intellectual patronage, 22, 45, 47, 53, 154–5, 198, 221
    elite patronage, 22–4, 44, 45, 47–54, 106, 111–13, 136, 154–5, 174, 191–3, 219–22, 327
    and epigraphy, 192, 204–8, 210, 219–20, 262, 264, 307–13
    and kingship, 44, 45, 47–54, 106, 112–13, 154–5, 174, 198, 338
    of *madrasa* complexes, 2, 155, 194–5, 199, 207, 210, 220
    non-elite patronage, 23, 112, 299
    of palaces, 4, 136, 155, 167, 174, 191
    Saljuq patronage, 48–53, 109, 144, 199
    and sectarian affiliation, 193, 197–9, 210, 219–20, 339
    of temples, 285
    of tombs, 299, 301, 302, 306–13, 321–2, 327

paved floors, **6**, **138**, 142–3

Peshawar, 67, 283, 284–5

photographic documentation, 29–31, 88, 91, 109, 195

Pigeon House, Lashkari Bazar, **270**

pilasters, 305, **310**, 315, **318**

pilgrimage, 51, 62, 169, 239, 282, 285, 299–300

Pinder-Wilson, Ralph, 208–9

*pishtaq*s *see* portals

portals, 50, 143, 146, 203, **203**, **204**, 310
Powell, Josephine, 29, 88
prestige cultures, 8, 44–60, 112–13, 338
proselytism, 113, 114, 148, 198–9, 205–6,
    214, 300, 339

Qaitul Buddhist complex, 169–71, **170**
Qala'-yi Chahar Baradar, **98**, 98
Qala'-yi Gauhargin, **158**
Qala'-yi Zarmurgh, 99, 108, 113, 116, 143,
    281
Qandahar *see* Tiginabad/Old Qandahar
Qarakhanids, 26, 45–6
Qarakhitay, 26, 45–6, 167
Qashqai confederacy, 240
Qasimabad *minar*, 53, 99, **101**, 110–11
Qasr-i Zarafshan, Jam-Firuzkuh, 139,
    140–1
qibla orientation, 145–6, 199–201, 212, 214,
    278–9
Qunduz, 148, 150
Qur'an
    commentary (*tafsir*), 197
    illuminated texts, 197, 199
    Qur'anic inscriptions, 26, 144–5, 193,
        197, 203–4, 207–14, **212–13**, **215**,
        218–19, 222, 251–4, **252–3**, 259–62,
        260, 302–13, **313–14**, 327
    Surat al-Baqara (Q. II), 214, 251, 254,
        260
    Surat al-Fath (Q. XLVIII), 203, 204,
        208–10, 259–61, 307–9, 313
    Surat al-Fatiha (Q. I), 309
    Surat al-Hashr (Q. LIX), 203, 207, 210,
        214
    Surat al-Ikhlas (Q. CXII), 214, 260, 261,
        309, 312
    Surat al-Imran (Q. III), 214
    Surat al-Kauthar (Q.CVIII), 310, 312
    Surat Maryam (Q. XIX), 144–5, 146,
        197, 219
    Surat al-Rahman (Q. LV), 309–10
    Surat al-Saf (Q. LXI), 218
    Surat al-Shu'ura (Q. XLII), 310–12
    Surat al-Tauba (Q. IX), 309
    Throne verse, 214
Qutb al-Din Aibeg, 65, 311
Qutb al-Din Muhammad, 62, 132, 134–5,
    143, 194
Qutb *minar*, Delhi, 109
Qutb mosque, Delhi, 311

rahmana-prasada, 298, 306
Rajagira mosque, Udegram, 285, **286**,
    287
Rajasthan, **9–10**, 67, 296–8, 302, 316
Rayy, 51
al-Razi, Fakhr al-Din ibn 'Umar, 154
Rehman, Abdul, 277
re-inscription, 263–5, 280–4, 299, 321,
    325–8, 340
renovations, 3–4, 48, 51, 104, 210, 211, 237,
    242–7, 255–69, 303, 305, 308–9, 321,
    325
reoccupation, 155, 162, 165, 168, 174, 242,
    249, 263–4, 325
repurposing, 81, 96, 104, 106, 108, 133,
    155–60, 162, 165, 174, 192, 193, 263,
    281
residential architecture, 137–9, 248
revetments, 157–8, **165**, **247**, 255, **260**,
    262–3, **267**
ribat of 'Ali ibn Karmakh, Multan, 277,
    301, 302–3, 304–6, **304–11**, 309,
    327
Risala-yi Baha'iyya (al-Razi), 154
ritual, 106, 114, 150, 199, 287, 289, 296,
    303
Robat Sharaf, 51–2, 54, **55–7**
robber holes, 136, 139
Roman empire, 10
royal enclaves, 248–54
royal genealogies, **xviii**, 42–3
Rud-i Ghur, 87
al-Rukkhaj, 46, 105, 169, 171, 173–4, 300
Rutbils, 105–6, 149, 169, 239

Sabuktigin, 16, 53, 114, 153–4, 221, 248
Sadr al-Din 'Ali Haisam, Imam, 194
Safavids, 48
Saffarids, 105, 153
Saghar *minar*, 80
Sahih (al-Bukhari), 207
Saif al-Din, 61, 62, 64, 134, 195, 201, 207,
    238
Saljuq ibn Duqaq, 47
Saljuqs, 8, 19, 40, 42, 44–53, 59–64, 98,
    106, 109, 114–16, 139–42, 144, 154, 167,
    195, 197, 199, 218, 237, 290–2, 322–3,
    338
Samanids, 16, 53–4, 153–4, 221, 248
al-Samarqandi, Nizami 'Aruzi, 154
Sana'i, 1

Sanga, 134

Sanjar, 51, 63, 65

saraparda, 139–42

sard-sir encampments, 18, 68, 84, 87, 105, 116, 133, 136–7, 139, 143, 146, 190, 194, 217, 222, 237, 321, 339

Sar-i Pul, 82, 86

Sarkhushak, **6**, 155, 160–1, **166–8**, 167, 192

Sasanians, 31, 48, 53, 81, 100–6, 109, 149, 150, 153

Sceratto, Umberto, 322

Schlumberger, Daniel, 255, 265

Second Anglo-Afghan War, 29

sectarian affiliation, 193, 197–201, 204, 207, 210, 214–17, 219–20, 278–9, 339

sedentism, 18, 20, 60, 94, 108, 113, 146–7, 167–8, 191, 237, 267–70, 339, 341

Shafi'i *madhhab*, 197–8, 199, 201, 214, 217, 278, 339

Shahada, 198, 206, 213

Shah-i Mashhad *madrasa*, **2**, 190–210, **196**, **200**, **202–6**, 220, 221, 253, 260, 307–8, 313, 339

Shah-nama, 42

Shahr-i Ghulghula, **29**, 150–1, 155, **156–7**, 161–5, 192, 339

Shahr-i Zuhak, **5**, 150, **151–3**, 155, 162, 192, 339

Shaivite Hinduism, 285, 289

Shams al-Din *see* Ghiyath al-Din

Shams al-Din Nasri, 238, 267

Sharada script, 304

Sharaf al-Din Abu Tahir ibn Sa'd al-Din ibn 'Ali al-Qummi, 51

Shihab al-Din *see* Mu'izz al-Din

Shi'ism, 198, 204, 207, 217, 282–3, 300

Shish ibn Bahram, 107

Shishanis, 90, 107–8, 195

Shrine of Ibrahim, Bhadreshvar, **296**, **319**

Sialkot, 67

Sin *minar*, 49, **53–4**

Sin mosque, 49, **53**

Sindh, 67, 278, 282–4, 289–98, **292**, **294**, **297**, 302, 303, 313–18, **317–18**

Sistan, 52, 53, 56, 61, 65, 83, 87, 99, **101**, 104–6, 109–11, **111–12**, 114, 153, 238, 267

skilled labor *see* artisans

slavery, 42, 53

Somnath campaign, 280

Sourdel-Thomine, Janine, 22, 26, 144–5, 217–18, 219, 253, 254–9, 262

South Palace, Lashkari Bazar, 164, 242, 254–62, **255–61**, 263, 265–7, **266–9**, 308–9

squinches, 161, 287, 304, 315

stepwells, 250

stucco, 26, 50, 100–3, **102–4**, 111, 157, 212, **216**, 242–3, **245–6**, 251, 255, 259–60, **260**, **267**

*stupa*s, 58–9, **59**, 169, **170**

Sufism, 214–17, 220–1, 299–300, 339

Sukkhur, 278, 302, 313–18, **317–18**, 323, 327, 328

summer capitals *see sard-sir* encampments

Sunni Islam, 198, 207, 210, 219–20, 283

al-Surabadi, Abu Bakr 'Atiq ibn Muhammad, 197

Swat, 283, 284–5

Tabaqat-i nasiri (Juzjani) *see* Juzjani, Minhaj al-Din Siraj

Taimanis, 94

Taiwara, 87, **93**, **95**

Taj al-Din Yildiz, 65

Taj al-Mulk, 48

takbir of *tashriq*, 203, 204, 207

Takht-i Bahi Buddhist complex, **284**

Tapper, Richard, 21

Taq-i Bustan, 103, **105**

Tara'in, battle of, 311

Tarikh-i Sistan, 106

Tarzi, Z., 150

temples

    Aditya temple, Multan, 282, 300

    Ambh Sharif temple, Panjab, **290–1**

    Bhodesar temple, Nagarparkar, **297**

    Gandhara–Nagara school, 285–9, **288–91**, 302, 303, 305–6, 309, 327

    Kalar temple, Panjab, **288**

    Kashmiri, 287

    Mari Indus temple, Panjab, **289**

    Nandana temple, Panjab, **291**

    patronage, 285

    plunder and destruction, 279–80, 282

tents, 94–5, **95**, 139, 142, 222, 339, 340

Tepe Hissar, 100, 101, **103**

Tepe Sardar, 56–9, **59**

terracotta, 25, 242–7, 292–3, **293**, 324

textile enclosures, 139–42, 146

textiles, 21, 84–6, 139–42, 247

textual sources, 2, 17, 21, 40–4, 61, 80, 82, 84, 107–8, 134–7, 146–7, 174, 193–4, 199, 239, 242

Thamban Wari *masjid*, Jam Jaskars Goth, **294**, 294–6, 298

Thomas, David, 18, 109, 110, 136–7

thuluth script, 202, 203, **204**

Tiginabad/Old Qandahar, 3, **4**, **28**, 82, 132–3, 169–75, **170**, **172**, 191–2, 238–9, 242, 248, 300–1

Timurids, 8

tombs
　of Ahmad Kabir, Multan, 277–8, 301, 302–4, 309–10, **314–16**
　of 'Ala' al-Din Muhammad, Bistam, 65, **66**
　domed cube structures, 23–4, **24**, 213, 278, **293**, 302, 304, **314**, 315, **317**, **320**, 320, 324, **326**
　of Ghiyath al-Din Muhammad ibn Sam, Herat, 4, **13**, **14**
　of Iltutmish, Delhi, 311–12
　Indus region, 277–8, 299–324, **301**, **305–20**, **322**, **325–6**
　Lal Mara Sharif tombs, 278, 302, 313, **320**, 320–4, **322**, **325–6**, 327–8
　of Mir Sayyid Bahram, Kirminiyya, 310
　of Muhammad ibn Harun, Lasbela, 292–3, **293**, 324
　patronage, 299, 301, 302, 306–13, 321–2, 327
　ribaṭ of 'Ali ibn Karmakh, Multan, 277, 301, 302–3, 304–6, **304–11**, 309, 327
　of Sadan Shahid, Multan, 261, 277–8, 301, 302–4, 309, **311–13**
　of Salar Khalil, Juzjan, 23–7, **24**, **25**
　Sarkhushak, 160–1, **167**
　Shah-i Mashhad *madrasa* possible tomb, 190, 195, 201, **202**, 207
　of Shahzada Shaikh Husain, Bust, 23–5, **26**, **27**
　of Sheikh Yusuf Gardizi, Multan, **301**
　Shrine of Ibrahim, Bhadreshvar, **296**, **319**
　Sukkhur tombs, 278, 302, 313–18, **317–18**, 323, 327, 328
　see also burial mounds; graves

trade, 20, 21, 41–2, 84–6, 113–16, 142, 153, 169–73, 220, 239–40, 282–3, 289–90; *see also* commerce

trading routes, 19, 41, 51, 150, 153, 169–71, 173, 175, 239, 282, 289–90

transhumance *see* nomadism

Transoxiana, 46, 310

trefoil arches, 287, **288–90**, 303–5, **306–8**, **313**, **316**

tribute, 41, 61, 63

Tughril, 48

Tukharistan, 149, 154, 156, 167

Uchh, 67, 79

Udabhandapura, 285

Udegram, 285, **286**, **287**

Umayyad Mosque, Damascus, 48

Umayyads, 15, 104, 114, 169, 290

unbaked brick, 90–1, 93

UNESCO world heritage sites, 147–8

Uruzgan, 82

al-'Utbi, 41

vaulting, **12**, **66**, 152, **168**

vegetal ornament, 144–5, 157, 162, 295, 305

vernacular architecture, 23, 112, 328

victory commemoration, 67, 143, 146, 209–10, 218–19, 253–4, 282, 322

*vihara*s, 169

Wajiristan, 134

Warshada, 134

watch towers, **93**

wells, 249–51, **250–1**

Western Turks, 31, 47, 81, 106, 149–51, 153, 156, 157, 167

winter capitals *see garm-sir* encampments

Yakaulang, **158**, **160–1**

Yaman, **89**, 96, **96**

Yamini-Ghaznavids *see* Ghaznavids

Ya'qut, 42

yurts, 94–6, **95**

Zabulistan, 16, 43, 46, 105, 109, 149, 169, 221, 239–41, 243, 248, 264, 285, 325, 327, 340

Zamindawar, 16, 46, 63–4, 82–3, 87, 105–6, 114, 139, 154, 169–74, 194, 221, 239–43, 247–50, 255, 264, 282, 300, 325, 327, 340

Zaranj-Nad-i Ali, 53, 61, 109, **111**, 238

Ziad, Waleed, 279

zoomorphic motifs, 247, 304, 323